Turnaround Management and Bankruptcy

T0298462

Written by leading experts in the fields of business, finance, law, and economics, this edited volume brings together the latest thoughts and developments on turnaround management and business rescue from an academic, judiciary, and turnaround/insolvency practitioner perspective.

Turnaround Management and Bankruptcy presents different viewpoints on turnarounds and business rescue in Europe. The book presents a state-of-the-art review of failure research in finance such as on bankruptcy prediction, causes of decline, or distressed asset valuation. It also offers the latest insights from turnaround management research as well as a contemporary look into law debates on insolvency legislation reform, new theoretical perspectives on turnarounds in knowledge-intensive industries and in SMEs. Finally, the book provides two cases and a work-out game, extending turnaround management and business rescue research into the classroom and real-world practice.

In this way, the volume presents a modern, interdisciplinary, and scholarly overview of the latest insights, issues, and debates in turnaround management and business rescue, developing a European perspective in an attempt to redress the predominance of an American orientation in the academic literature. It aims at a wider audience interested in turnarounds and failure, such as faculty and students in the fields of law, business, economics, accountancy, finance, strategic management, and marketing, but also judges, insolvency practitioners, lawyers, accountants, and turnaround professionals, as well as the European Union (EU) and government officials, staffs of trade unions, and employers' associations.

Jan Adriaanse is Professor of Turnaround Management at Leiden University, the Netherlands.

Jean-Pierre van der Rest is Professor of Business Administration at Leiden University, the Netherlands.

Routledge Advances in Management and Business Studies

For a full list of titles in this series, please visit www.routledge.com

Turnaround Management and Bankruptcy

Edited by
Jan Adriaanse and
Jean-Pierre van der Rest

Routledge
Taylor & Francis Group

LONDON AND NEW YORK

First published 2017 by Routledge

2 Park Square, Milton Park, Abingdon, Oxfordshire OX14 4RN
52 Vanderbilt Avenue, New York, NY 10017

Routledge is an imprint of the Taylor & Francis Group, an informa business

First issued in paperback 2019

Library of Congress Cataloging-in-Publication Data
Names: Adriaanse, J. A. A., 1972– editor. | Van der Rest,
    Jean-Pierre, editor.
Title: Turnaround management and bankruptcy / edited by
    Jan Adriaanse and Jean-Pierre van der Rest.
Description: 1 Edition. | New York, NY : Routledge, 2017. |
    Series: Routledge advances in management and business studies ;
    69 | Includes bibliographical references and index.
Identifiers: LCCN 2016039425 | ISBN 9781138828742 (hardback :
    alk. paper) | ISBN 9781315738116 (ebook)
Subjects: LCSH: Corporate turnarounds. | Bankruptcy.
Classification: LCC HD58.8 .T78 2017 | DDC 658.15—dc23
LC record available at https://lccn.loc.gov/2016039425

ISBN: 978-1-138-82874-2 (hbk)
ISBN: 978-0-367-24287-9 (pbk)

Typeset in Sabon
by Apex CoVantage, LLC

Contents

Tables and Figures

Tables

Figures

Contributors

Rick Aalbers, PhD, is Associate Professor of Strategy and Innovation at the Institute for Management Research at Radboud University, the Netherlands. Founder of the Centre for Organization Restructuring and a former manager at Deloitte consulting, his research focuses on innovation and reorganization, with special interest in the evolution of organizations over time. He has published work in *Research Policy, MIT Sloan Management Review, Journal of Engineering and Technology Management, Journal of Product Innovation Management*, and the *British Journal of Management*, among others. His *MIT Sloan Management Review* contribution won the SMR Richard Beckhard Memorial Prize. He serves on the editorial board of the *Journal of Management Studies*.

Gianpaolo Abatecola, PhD, is an Associate Professor of Management at the Department of Management and Law of the University of Rome Tor Vergata, Italy, where he coordinates the PhD. Programme in Management. His research areas are organizational adaptation and evolution, managerial decision making, and turnaround management. On these topics, he has published journal articles and special issues in, among others, *Management Decision, European Management Journal, Futures, Corporate Governance*, and the *Journal of Management and Governance*. He currently serves the Annual Conference of the European Academy of Management as a cochair of the standing track about "Darwinism, organizational evolution, and survival."

Jan Adriaanse, PhD, is Professor of Turnaround Management and Head of the Department of Business Studies at Leiden University, the Netherlands. In addition, he is founder of BFI Global, a specialized business failure investigation firm. His research interests include business failure investigation and prevention, and decision making in a turnaround and bankruptcy context.

Yuval Bar-Or, PhD, is Assistant Professor of Finance at the Johns Hopkins Carey Business School, in Baltimore, United States. His areas of expertise include risk management, financial literacy, and corporate turnarounds. He received PhD and MA degrees from the Wharton School of the University of Pennsylvania and undergraduate degrees in engineering and economics from McMaster University. Over the course of his corporate career, he served in a variety of product management and strategy roles, including as a director at KMV and as managing director with Standard & Poor's Risk Solutions and Algorithmics. He is the author of seven books, including *Leveraging People for a Corporate Turnaround*, and has been quoted by publications such as the *Wall Street Journal, Forbes.com, BusinessWeek, USA Today,* and *US News & World Report.*

Vincent L. Barker III, PhD, is Professor of Strategic Management, Chair of the Management Area, and the Carl A. Scupin fellow at the School of Business at the University of Kansas in the United States. He has researched corporate turnarounds and distressed organizations for over two decades, and he has published more than a dozen refereed journal articles about corporate decline, turnaround, and downsizing. He serves on the editorial boards of the *Strategic Management Journal, Journal of Management Studies,* and the *Journal of Business Research.*

Donald Bibeault, PhD, JD (h.c.), is a well-known corporate turnaround executive and the first-ever recipient of the Lifetime Achievement Award for corporate turnarounds (Turnaround Management Association). During the course of his forty-seven-year career, he has been a chairman, board member, CEO, COO, and a turnaround advisor to numerous companies, including five multibillion dollar corporations. He is the author of the top-selling book *Corporate Turnaround: How Managers Turn Losers into Winners,* which he wrote based on his doctoral dissertation. The book has remained in print thirty-four years after its initial publication. He earned his BS in electrical engineering from the University of Rhode Island, an MBA from Columbia University, and a PhD from Golden Gate University, where he also received a Juris Doctor (honoris causa).

Gert-Jan Boon, LLM, MSc, is a Researcher at the Department of Business Studies at the University of Leiden, the Netherlands. His research focuses on the turnaround, rescue, and insolvency of financially distressed businesses, in particular, the international legal instruments for rescue and insolvency. He has participated in multiple international research projects including the European Law Institute's project on "Rescue of Business in Insolvency Law." He is a fellow of the European Law Institute and a member of the TRI Leiden research team. He regularly publishes in legal journals.

David Burdette, LLD, is a graduate of the University of South Africa (B Juris, LLB) and the University of Pretoria (LLD), South Africa. He was a Professor of Insolvency Law in the Faculty of Law at the University of Pretoria. In September 2007, he joined Nottingham Trent University in

Nottingham, England, where he was the director of the Centre for Business and Insolvency Law at Nottingham Law School until his departure from the University in October 2016. He is co-author of the leading insolvency textbook in South Africa, *Meskin, Insolvency Law and Its Operation in Winding-Up* (LexisNexis Butterworths, loose-leaf edition), and contributor to the first issue of *Henochsberg on the Companies Act 71 of 2008* in South Africa (LexisNexis Butterworths, loose-leaf edition). The proposals made in his LLD thesis have been included in draft legislation for the introduction of a unified Insolvency Act in South Africa. In 2007/2008, he was appointed to the King III Committee on Corporate Governance (South Africa) as convener of the subcommittee on corporate rescue. David is a senior consultant for the World Bank (Debt Resolution and Business Exit), and he was the INSOL Scholar for the Europe, Middle East, and Africa region for the 2006/2007 academic year. David holds appointments as Extraordinary Professor at the Faculty of Law at the University of Pretoria and at the University of the Free State in South Africa, as well as Visiting Professor at Radboud University in the Netherlands.

Mihaela Carpus Carcea, PhD, is a legislative officer in civil law matters at the Directorate General for Justice and Consumers of the European Commission. She holds a PhD in European Union law from the University of Birmingham (United Kingdom) and is a qualified attorney in Romania. She previously worked as an attorney in Romania, as a teaching assistant at the University of Birmingham, as a trainee in the Legal Service of the Council of the European Union, and as a researcher at the British Institute of International and Comparative Law in London.

Daria Ciriaci, PhD, is an economic advisor at the European Commission Representation in Italy. She holds a PhD in economics from the University La Sapienza in Rome. She previously worked as a senior consultant at the Inter-American Development Bank and in several think tanks, as an Adjunct Professor at the John Cabot University in Rome, and as a postdoc fellow at the Joint Research Centre of the European Commission in Sevilla (Spain) and at the Luiss University in Rome.

Carlos Cuerpo Caballero, MSc, has recently joined the Independent Authority for Fiscal Responsibility in Madrid, where he deals with macroeconomic projections and public debt sustainability analysis. He holds a master's degree in economic analysis from the London School of Economics (United Kingdom). He joined the Spanish Corp of State Economists in 2008 and worked for three years as an economic analyst in the Spanish Ministry of Economy and Competitiveness. From 2011 to 2014, he was a seconded national expert at the Directorate General for Economic and Financial Affairs of the European Commission, dealing with the implementation of the Macroeconomic Imbalances Procedure, notably the analysis of real estate markets and private sector balance sheets.

Nico Dewaelheyns, PhD, is Associate Professor of Corporate Finance in the Department of Financial Management at the KU Leuven, Belgium. His research interests include financial distress, bankruptcy reform, corporate governance, and business group finance. His has published work in journals such as *European Financial Management, Small Business Economics,* the *Journal of Business Research, and* the *Journal of Business Finance & Accounting.*

Sofie De Prijcker, PhD, is Assistant Professor of Corporate Finance in the Department of Financial Management at KU Leuven, Belgium. Her research interests focus on private equity, venture capital, small business finance, and bankruptcy. She has published in academic journals such as *International Business Review* and *Management Decision.*

Dave De ruysscher, PhD, is Associate Professor of Legal History at the Department of Interdisciplinary Legal Studies at the Vrije Universiteit Brussels. His research area is the history of commercial law, in particular maritime insurance, insolvency, and company law. He has published in, among others, the *Legal History Review* and the *Journal of Legal History.*

Simon Elo, BSc, is a member of the Parliament of Finland. He works on the Grand Committee handling affairs concerning the European Union and on the Constitutional Law Committee. He has a bachelor's degree in political science from the University of Turku.

Jörg Freiling, Dr. rer. oec., is Full Professor at the University of Bremen, Germany, Faculty for Business Studies and Economics, and the Head of the Chair in Small Business and Entrepreneurship. His research focuses on start-up management, internationalization of small businesses, governance of family firms, migration and diaspora entrepreneurship, and start-up ecosystems. He is currently editor of the *Journal of Competence-Based Strategic Management* and a member of the editorial board of the *Journal of Management, Entrepreneurship and Innovation.* He has published his research in *Organization Studies, International Small Business Journal, International Journal of Business and Information, Entrepreneurial Business and Economics Review, Service Industries Journal, International Journal of Technology Intelligence and Planning,* and *Management Revue,* among others.

Arnoud Griffioen, MSc, CA, is an independent turnaround and finance professional and a Lecturer at the international Hotelschool The Hague in the Netherlands. During his career at PwC, as interim manager and as a CFO of some hotel groups, he specialized in the area where finance and strategy meet in turnaround and insolvency situations, combining academic research with practical experience. He also works as a speaker and guest lecturer (among others at the Leiden University in the Netherlands and the World Bank Group), and uses simulation business gaming to increase the effectiveness of the learning experiences. Mr. Griffioen is a member of the Royal Netherlands Institute of Chartered Accountants.

Joost De Haas, MSc, MBA, is Adjunct Professor of Entrepreneurship & Family Enterprises at INSEAD, Fontainebleau, France. His academic areas of interest are turnaround management, distressed situations, and bankruptcy processes. Mr. De Haas currently is the CEO of the Roto Smeets Group, one of Europe's leading printing and multimedia companies.

Kathryn Rudie Harrigan, DBA, is the Henry R. Kravis Professor of Business Leadership at Columbia University, New York. She earned her doctorate from Harvard. As a former corporate director of three publicly traded NYSE firms, she teaches courses in strategic management and turnaround management. She is a specialist in corporate strategy, industry and competitor analysis, diversification strategy, joint ventures, mergers and acquisitions, turnarounds, industry restructurings, and competitive problems of mature- and declining-demand businesses. She is the author of several prize-winning books on strategy.

Lézelle Jacobs, LLD, is a Lecturer in Mercantile Law and Director of Research at the Faculty of Law, University of the Free State, South Africa. She was an attorney of the High Court of South Africa and specializes in company law, insolvency law, and corporate insolvency law. She has published several journal articles and is a contributor to the Close Corporations and Companies Service, LexisNexis. She received the National Research Foundation (South Africa) Thuthuka Bursary for her Doctoral studies. Her research is mainly focused on the fiduciary duties of Business Rescue Practitioners in South Africa and the development of a comprehensive code of conduct to be used by practitioners.

Alexandra Kastrinou, PhD, is a Senior Lecturer at Nottingham Trent University, Nottingham Law School, specializing in company and insolvency law for both the undergraduate law courses and the LLM. Dr. Kastrinou is also the house editor of the *Nottingham Insolvency and Business Law e-Journal.* She completed her PhD in 2009 under the supervision of Professor Parry at the University of Leicester, the focus of which was comparative insolvency law and, in particular, corporate rescue in France, Greece, and the United Kingdom. Her research interests are mainly in the area of comparative insolvency law and corporate rescue in particular. She is a winner of the Edwin Coe Prize for a paper given at the INSOL Europe Conference in Vienna in 2010 entitled "Cross-Border Insolvency of Corporate Groups and the Impact of the EC Insolvency Regulation."

Jukka Kilpi, PhD, F Fin, is Docent of Social and Moral Philosophy at the University of Helsinki and Docent of Business Ethics at the University of Turku, Finland. He is also CEO of the Finland-based corporate finance consulting company Kapai Oy and Fellow of the Financial Services Institute of Australia. Dr. Kilpi's book *The Ethics of Bankruptcy* is a part of Routledge's Professional Ethics series. He has published articles in books and journals including *Encyclopedia of Applied Ethics, Australasian Journal of Philosophy, Public Affairs Quarterly*, and *Journal of Business Ethics*.

Pieter Klapwijk, PhD, is involved in various consulting, academic, and entrepreneurial roles. He holds an MSc degree in physics and management science and a PhD degree in economics. He worked for the management consulting firm A. T. Kearney, where he played a leading role in supply chain management. He was a founding partner of Trimoteur, a management and investment firm that restructured companies such as Pharma Bio Research and created new companies such as Sandd, the second-largest national postal operator in the Netherlands. For over seventeen years, he has held a part-time full professorship at Nyenrode Business Universiteit. Since 2011, his primary research focus has been supply chain finance.

Dimitri Lorenzani, MSc, has been working as an economist at the Directorate General for Economic and Financial Affairs of the European Commission since 2011, first dealing with the assessment of the economic impact of structural reforms and then as a fiscal policy expert. He is currently in charge of the fiscal surveillance of Italy. He holds a master's degree in financial economics from the Sant'Anna School of Advanced Studies of Pisa (Italy). He previously worked as a teaching assistant of computational finance at the University of Florence (Italy).

Stephan Madaus, PhD, is Professor of Civil Law, Civil Procedure, and Insolvency Law at the Martin Luther University Halle-Wittenberg, Germany. His main interests lie in German and international insolvency law and civil procedure, and in particular the rescue of failing businesses. He acted as one of the co-reporters for the European Law Institute's project on Rescue of Business in Insolvency Law. He is a member of the International Insolvency Institute and the American Bankruptcy Institute's Advisory Committee on Comparative Law. He has published in prominent legal journals in Germany and beyond.

William McKinley, PhD, is Emeritus Professor of Management at Southern Illinois University at Carbondale and the University of Zurich. His research interests are organizational decline, organizational downsizing, entrepreneurship, and the history and sociology of organization science. He has published in a variety of scholarly outlets, including *Academy of Management Review, Academy of Management Journal, Administrative Science Quarterly, Journal of Management Studies, Organization Science, Organization Studies*, and other journals and edited books. He currently serves as senior editor for *Organization Studies*.

Hartmut Meyer, PhD, is a Lecturer at the Fachhochschule für Ökonomie und Management. His areas of expertise are turnaround management, business law and controlling, and family business management and entrepreneurship. Furthermore, he has specific research and lecturing interests in the areas of tourism industry and family-owned businesses. He is the author of different management books, has published a series of articles, and participated in various conferences by contributing papers. Aside from his lecturing and research interests, he is often engaged in various turnaround assignments as a consultant to small businesses through various public and private institutions in Germany.

Paul Omar, PhD, has worked in mainstream British academia for 20 years. He has had visiting appointments at the University of Pretoria, University College London, and Jersey Institute of Law, St. Helier. He has published over 200 articles. Paul's research interests include comparative and international insolvency law. He has served as a secretary of the INSOL Europe Academic Forum and as a member of the Steering Committee of the INSOL International Academic Group, the INSOL Europe Joint Academic-Practitioner Project on Cooperation and Communications, the Academic Advisory Group on the INSOL International Diploma Project, and the Course Committee of the INSOL International Global Insolvency Practice Course.

H. G. Parsa, PhD, is the Barron Hilton Professor of Lodging Management in the Fritz Knoebel School of Hospitality Management at Daniels College of Business, University of Denver, United States. His research interests include corporate social responsibility, behavioral pricing and revenue management, and restaurant failure. He is a recipient of the John Wiley & Sons Lifetime Research Achievement Award from the International Council on Hotel, Restaurant, and Institutional Education, and an associate editor for *Journal of Hospitality and Tourism Research*. His work has appeared in refereed journals such as *Cornell Hospitality Quarterly, Tourism Management, Journal of Services Research,* and *Journal of Business Research*. Previously, Dr. Parsa was editor-in-chief of the *Journal of Foodservice Business Research*.

Philippos Philippou, MSc, studied business administration at Radboud University. He is a member of the Centre for Organization Restructuring at the Institute for Management Research, Radboud University, the Netherlands. His prime research interest is downsizing and restructuring. He currently works at K. Treppides & Co (member of EuraAudit International) as a payroll officer.

Peter Pontuch, PhD, is an economist at the Directorate General for Economic and Financial Affairs of the European Commission, mainly dealing with housing markets and household and corporate indebtedness. He holds a PhD from the Paris-Dauphine University, where his research focused on the interactions between financing frictions and competition, and the effects of labor intensity on company performance. He previously worked as an economist and risk officer in the asset management sector and was a Visiting Scholar at the University of Maryland (USA).

Achim Schmitt, PhD, is Associate Professor of Strategic Management and Associate Dean, Graduate Programs at Ecole hôtelière de Lausanne, HES-SO // University of Applied Sciences Western Switzerland. After more than fifteen years in strategy consulting, he has gained academic experience at the University of Geneva (Switzerland), Columbia Business School (United States), and Audencia Business School (France). Achim holds visiting professorships at the University of Los Andes (Bogota, Colombia) and the University of Geneva (Switzerland). His research focuses on corporate decline, corporate turnarounds, and strategic management. He currently serves on the editorial board of *Long Range Planning*.

Vincenzo Uli, PhD, is a Postdoc Fellow in Management at the Department of Management and Law of the University of Rome Tor Vergata, Italy. His research areas are organizational adaptation and evolution, entrepreneurship, and turnaround management. On these topics, he has published journal articles and regularly presented papers in annual meetings such as the European Academy of Management, the Italian Academy of Business Administration and Management, and the International Forum of Knowledge Assets Dynamics. Before entering academia, Vincenzo developed a number of work experiences in turnaround consulting and investment firms.

Karen Van Den Heuvel, MSc, MSc, BA, is a PhD candidate and Researcher in the Department of Accountancy, Finance & Insurance at the KU Leuven, Belgium. Her research work focuses on bankruptcy reform and corporate reorganization procedures.

Jean-Pierre van der Rest, PhD, is Professor of Business Administration in the Department of Business Studies at the Leiden University, the Netherlands. His research area is price policy and law, revenue management, and turnaround management. He is the current associate editor of the International Journal of Revenue Management and has published in, among others, *European Journal of Operational Research, Journal of Strategic Marketing, Service Science, Cornell Hospitality Quarterly*, and *Tourism Management*.

Tim Verdoes, PhD, is Assistant Professor of Business Economics in the Department of Business Studies at the Leiden University, the Netherlands. His research interest focuses on the application of economic theory to the analysis of law, specifically the theory of the firm in the context of business rescue and failure. Recently, he contributed to Edward Elgar's *Research Handbook on Crisis Management in the Banking Sector*.

Jan Vis, PhD, is Adjunct Professor of Business Valuation and Value-Based Management in the Rotterdam School of Management at Erasmus University Rotterdam, the Netherlands. He earned his MSc in economics (cum laude) at Amsterdam University and his PhD (focused on the subjective nature of economic value) at Leiden University. He is cofounder of Talanton Valuation Services, Amsterdam, the Netherlands. He performed valuation engagements for M&A, disputes, court cases, and numerous other purposes and participates in arbitration proceedings. He is also chair of the 'Stichting Landelijk Register van Gerechtelijke Deskundigen' (Registered Court Experts) and chair of Platform Taxateurs-Accountants.

Foreword

A shiver is pulsing through the veins of restructuring and insolvency systems throughout the globe. The insolvency theater travels all over the world, with a leading role for restructuring. Countries such as Japan, Australia, India, and the United States (Ch. 11) have recently finalized or are contemplating renewal of their insolvency (bankruptcy) laws. In Europe in the last decade, Germany, Spain, Italy, and France have shifted their focus from traditional liquidation focused formal proceedings to out-of-court workouts to rescue financially distressed businesses. Even England is contemplating its restructuring mechanisms, which are already seen as shining examples of modern rescue tools with suggested improvements: a moratorium, cram-down, and protection for new finance. On top of these development are the European Union's proposals to harmonize member states' insolvency frameworks with mechanisms that one sees in practice or emerging over the globe. When a debtor is likely to go into financial difficulties, it should be in the position to negotiate a restructuring plan with its creditors; a stay should be available to halt creditors exercising their rights; the creditors should be put in voting classes; a certain majority should adopt the plan; a court should cram-down holdout creditors; specific new finance for the company should be protected; and the debtor in possession should be able to steer the whole process.

This worldwide gulf will roll out in the coming years. It will not so much shake, but surely stir business advisors, legislators, insolvency practitioners, and judges. It will require these advisor and turnaround managers to deepen their knowledge and skills to assist corporate management and the traditional legal industry in sketching out their future business models and helping implement new structures. Practitioners from whatever discipline will have to equip themselves to implement new rules according to their underlying policies. There truly is a need to develop a much broader insight and expertise in matters of insolvency law, company law, or general contract law and to develop know-how concerning such matters as financial restructuring, corporate finance, and organization of business and strategy.

The present book reviews these themes through different lenses, including the historic and economic background of turnaround management and bankruptcy, several scientific business studies and business prospects, legal issues on restructuring and insolvency and their economic justification, and ends with sector-specific issues and the unfolding of a case and a game. There are not many individual experts with this combination of knowledge and skills. Professors Jan Adriaanse and Jean-Pierre van der Rest, the editors, have managed to attract a large group of the best of these experts under one umbrella for the purpose of delivering this book.

A decade ago, none of us could have imagined just how much business and economic dimensions we would see in the restructuring and insolvency industry world of today. It may be bad news for the companies affected; however, we could not have imagined the creativity and dedication of scholars and practitioners in the field in presenting broader perspectives and legislation or the practice growing closer and converging. Where the world indeed grows smaller every day, legislations converge to common positions, at least on several key points. Against the backdrop of the recent financial crisis, the past years have witnessed developments of a stunning speed and sophistication in the attempt to find suitable responses to a widely endorsed policy of rescuing economically viable but financially distressed businesses. The obstacle facing anyone in producing a book on the economics and legal perspectives of restructuring and insolvency is the sheer pace of the developments. This book draws the ending punctuation mark in the second quarter of 2016. Although some developments will inevitably reach the stage of being out of date rather quickly, the value of the book is that it relates to the larger dimensions and questions of the underlying and novel approaches to companies in financial distress. The book, therefore, provides an important signpost on the way to improve methods of rescuing companies and supports the combined quest into the global turnaround and insolvency puzzle.

Bob Wessels
Professor Emeritus of International
Insolvency Law
Leiden University

Scientific Fellow at the Max Planck Institute
Luxembourg for International, European and
Regulatory Procedural Law

Part I
Historical Perspectives

1 The History of Corporate Turnaround Management

Personal Reflections

Donald Bibeault

First-ever recipient of the TMA Lifetime Achievement Award for corporate turnarounds

1.1 Introduction

Turnaround management is a process dedicated to corporate renewal. It uses analysis and planning to save troubled companies and returns them to solvency. It also identifies the reasons for failing performance in the market and rectifies them. The turnaround cycle is not truly complete unless the company returns to sustained revenue growth and profitability. Short of renewed growth, the process must be considered as restructuring rather than a turnaround. The confluence of three primary drivers preconditioned the rapid development of the turnaround profession in the latter part of the twentieth century:

1 The legal environment was reformed in a manner that recognized corporate resuscitation as beneficial to economic society.
2 The development of a professional body of knowledge allowed for the formal study required of a profession.
3 A more challenging business environment required new management skills beginning in the 1970s. The oil crises and rapid technological change drove the need for a different type of corporate leader.

1.2 The Legal Recognition of Resuscitation as Economically Beneficial

From its early beginnings, the profession of turnaround management has been highly influenced by national policy regarding the legal position of creditors versus debtors. In general, professional turnaround management practice developed more robustly in the United States because of the U.S. bankruptcy law emphasis on rehabilitation. In Ancient Greece, bankruptcy did not exist. If a man owed debt he could not pay, he and his wife, children, or servants were forced into 'debt slavery,' until the creditor recouped losses through their physical labor. Many city-states in Ancient Greece limited debt slavery to a period of five years; debt slaves had protection of life and limb, which regular slaves did not enjoy. However, the creditor could retain servants of the debtor beyond that deadline, and they were often forced to serve their new lord for a lifetime, usually under significantly harsher conditions. An exception to this rule was Athens, which by the laws of Solon forbade enslavement for debt; consequently, most Athenian slaves were foreigners (Greek or otherwise). There is also documentation of bankruptcy in East Asia. The Yassa of Genghis Khan contained a provision that mandated the death penalty for anyone who became bankrupt three times.

A failure of whole nations to meet bond repayments has been seen on many occasions. Philip II of Spain had to declare four state bankruptcies in 1557, 1560, 1575, and 1596. In medieval times, the plunder of victory staved off bankruptcy of the victors but often plunged the vanquished defeated nations into bankruptcy. Although the development of international capital markets was quite limited prior to 1800, there were, with some regularity, the defaults of France, Portugal, Prussia, Spain, and the early Italian city-states.

1.2.1   The History of United Kingdom Bankruptcy Law

The Statute of Bankrupts of 1542 was the first statute under English law dealing with bankruptcy or insolvency. During its long history, the United Kingdom's insolvency laws heavily favored banks' and other creditors' interests. The astonishing depravity of conditions in debtor prisons made insolvency law reform one of the most intensively debated issues in nineteenth-century England. The novelist Charles Dickens, whose father had been imprisoned while he was a child, pilloried injustice through his books, especially *David Copperfield* (1850) and *Hard Times* (1854). In spite of that, only one major reform bill was introduced to Parliament between 1831 and 1914.

The first minor reform step was the Joint Stock Companies Act of 1844. The law allowed the creation of companies by registration rather than royal charter. On top of this came the Limited Liability Act of 1855 which regulated that investors in companies had their liability limited to the amount of debt. The Debtors Act of 1869 finally abolished imprisonments for debt altogether. Among insolvent companies,' creditors' claims, secured claims, liquidators' expenses, and wages of workers were given statutory priority over other unsecured creditors. Up until recent times, the appointment of a liquidator for the benefit of creditors appeared to be absolute. In the infamous case of Laker Airways, and unlike U.S. carrier bankruptcies, the company's planes immediately stopped flying, never to be flown again under the Laker standard. It all came to an abrupt ending on the weekend of February 5, 1982. The appointed liquidator sold many of Laker's assets, including modern DC-10 and Airbus A 300 aircraft, at bargain basement prices within a few days' time.

After the "Cork Report" of 1982, the major new objective for UK insolvency law became creating a 'rescue culture' for business. Under Schedule B1, paragraph 3, the primary objective of the administrator is "rescuing the company as a going concern," but if that is not possible, then the administrator will usually sell the business. The administrator must oversea the realizing of the property distributed to creditors. Focus in the situation is with how, and by whom, ministries are appointed. The holders of a 'floating charge,' which is usually all of the company's creditors (typically the company bank), have an almost absolute right to select the administrator. The directors of the company may attempt to appoint an administrator out of court, but if the bank intervenes, it may install its own preferred candidate. The court has the power to refuse the bank's choice, but rarely exercises it. In practical situations, the bank has asked the company directors to appoint the administrator from the bank's own list.

In the UK Insolvency Act of 1986, any company could voluntarily ask the courts to reduce debt they owed in the hope that the company may survive. Importantly, secured preferential creditors' entitlements cannot be reduced without their consent. This differs markedly from Chapter 11 of the U.S. bankruptcy code where the so-called cram-down procedure allows the court to approve a plan over the wishes of creditors if they receive a value to what they were owed. The procedure takes place under the supervision of an insolvency practitioner, to whom the directors will submit a report on the company's finances in the proposal for reducing the debt. In practice, this procedure is infrequently used because a single creditor can veto the plan and seek to collect the debt.

1.2.2   United States Leadership in the Concept of Resuscitation

The history of bankruptcy in the United States has been a continual tug-of-war between various interests, mainly creditors versus debtors. The concept of resuscitation was not always dominant in the United States. The U.S. Constitution of 1789, Article 1, Section 8, gave Congress the power to establish uniform laws on the subject of bankruptcy throughout the United States. In 1800, Congress passed the first federal law relating to bankruptcy. The Bankruptcy Act of 1800 was very creditor oriented and only permitted involuntary bankruptcies of merchant debtors. diplomatist Edmund Roberts, President Andrew Jackson's envoy to the Far East, incorporated American concepts of bankruptcy protection into Article VI of the Roberts Treaty with Siam (Thailand) of 1833. Whereas the United States seemed committed to a balance between creditors' and debtors' rights, an objective review of the legislation at that time would indicate that creditors were in a superior position.

After the financial panic of 1837, Congress passed the Bankruptcy Act of 1841, which allowed voluntary bankruptcies to be filed by debtors, a truly modern evolution. The Bankruptcy Act of 1867 partially redressed what creditors felt was an imbalance in favor of debtors. The immense growth of the United States in the nineteenth century partially fueled the notion of rehabilitation. These early acts and the Bankruptcy Act of 1898, known as the Nelson Act, established the modern concepts of debtor-creditor relations. The Bankruptcy Act of 1898 was in effect until the Bankruptcy Reform Act of 1978.

Indeed, when the 1906 earthquake destroyed San Francisco, A. P. Giannini, then head of the Bank of Italy (shortly after the Bank of America) lent funds 'on account' to many merchants to rebuild the city. Additionally, because of careful reinvestment of the bank's earnings, Wells Fargo and Company not only prospered during the 1920s but was also in a good position to survive the Great Depression. Following the collapse of the banking system in 1933, Wells Fargo was able to extend immediate substantial help to its troubled correspondents. Ransom M. Cook, later chairman of Wells Fargo and an advisor on my landmark 1979 PhD dissertation, worked on many of those 'bank workouts' during the Great Depression and the postwar prosperity that followed. This excellent experience propelled him into the presidency of Wells Fargo in 1962 and subsequent chairmanship in 1964.

In most European Union member states, debt discharge is conditioned by a partial payment of the obligation and by a number of requirements concerning the debtor's behavior. In the United States, discharge from bankruptcy has fewer conditions as governed by the plan of reorganization. Within the European Union, there is a broad spectrum of approaches with the United Kingdom coming closest to the U.S. system. Other member states of the EU provide the option of a debt discharge. Spain, for example, passed a bankruptcy law in 2003 that provides for debt settlement plans that can result in a reduction of debt (the maximum of one-half of the amount) or an extension of the payment period for up to five years.

The principal focus of modern insolvency legislation and business debt restructuring no longer rests on the elimination of the insolvent entity. Most advanced countries in 2015 place an emphasis on the rehabilitation and continuation of the business entity.

1.3   Development of a Professional Body of Knowledge

In the case of professional turnaround management, the development of a meaningful and coherent body of knowledge poses a particularly unique problem. It is difficult, if not impossible, for those who teach but do not 'do' turnaround strategies to develop them in a purely academic setting. On the other hand, turnaround management is much more intensive than conservator management. The highly chaotic world of turnarounds is not conducive to the reflection necessary for practitioners to create a coherent body of knowledge. Up until the late 1970s, as turnaround management began to be carved out as a separate management specialty, there existed no coherent strategic framework to explain what was going on in the trenches.

The first glimmer of corporate turnaround tactics was based on the 'scientific management approach' first formulated by Frederick Wilson Taylor (1856–1915). Closer to the mark was the work of Henry Fayol (1841–1925). Indeed, Fayol was the earliest manager to examine his own personal experience systematically and try to extract from that a theory of management. A qualified mining engineer, he was made the manager of a coal mine at the early age of twenty-five. At thirty-one, he became general manager of a group of mines, and at forty-seven, he became the managing director the combined mines—a post that he held for thirty years.

Throughout his career, Fayol showed all the signs of a successful line manager. This became most obvious when he took over the top job of a steel combine, which was then almost bankrupt. By the time he retired, the business was more than twice its original size and one of the most successful steel combines in Europe. In 1916, he published the book *Administration Industrielle et Générale*, which was not available in English translation until 1929 (known as General and Industrial Management).

The works of Taylor and Fayol are complementary in a number of ways including those pertaining to processes, organizational rationality by the scientific technique, and the rules managers work with to encourage their workers. From a corporate turnaround perspective, I appreciate Fayol's contribution more because he dealt with the management of the organization as a whole, whereas Taylor stressed the management of the operations. Fayol directed his at the activities of all managers, whereas Taylor concerned himself with first-line managers and the scientific method. Fayol wrote from personal executive experience being the managing director of a large French mining firm.

In the 1950s and 1960s, there were occasional magazine articles and a paucity of academic treatises on the subject of turnaround management. There were a number of periodical articles dealing with a portion of the overall problem. Such titles as "Pruning the Product Line," "The Death and Burial of Sick Products," and "Phasing out Weak Products" were typical of the genre. None dealt with the fundamental strategic framework.

Beyond brief articles, the development of a body of knowledge progressed along two principal axes. First, there was the functional approach of functional turnaround actions as exemplified by the 1972 compendium assembled by Joseph Eisenberg. Eisenberg's approach was simple; it included individual chapters by experts in their functional areas. Only one of Eisenberg's twelve chapters discussed the essential role of the chief executive in the turnaround. Other chapters focused on marketing, production cash management, computer activity, and a supportive compensation program. Whereas commendable, this did not provide enlightenment on a comprehensive strategic framework.

In the mid-1970s, Dan Schendel moved away from the traditional case method by developing and testing mathematical performance models on strategy. Dan Schendel, Richard Patton, and James Rise wrote an interesting article entitled "Corporate Turnaround Strategies." This research work was the first to take the empirical direction in strategy analysis utilizing data analysis, although the sample size was small. Schendel's work was under the auspices of the Krannert Graduate School of Industrial Administration at Purdue University. Schendel and Patton closely followed the article with their own in August 1975 on the proceedings of the Academy of Management entitled "An Empirical Study of Corporate Stagnation and Turnaround." This article featured quantitative data on the difference between turnaround and nonturnaround companies. It also presented quantitative metrics that contrasted the decline and renewal stages of a turnaround.

The second axis was the contribution to our understanding of corporate decline. The management challenges posed by corporate growth were ably illustrated by the work of Larry E. L. Greiner, in "Evolution and Revolution as Organizations Grow." A meaningful contribution to the understanding of corporate decline was made by Michael J. Kami and Joel Ross in their book *Management Crisis: Why the Mighty Fall* (1973). John Argenti did an excellent job of explaining corporate collapse in his 1976 book *Corporate Collapse: The Causes and Symptoms*. The missing element in these academic approaches was the necessary input of experienced executive-level turnaround leadership to give nuance and realism to the description of the process. Nearly all the aforementioned contributions were descriptive in nature and not pre-scripted in nature. I've always felt that description is valuable but prescription is essential.

By the mid-1970s, I had been deeply involved in real-world turnarounds for a decade. I was perplexed that no fundamental strategic framework existed with meaningful insight. At the same time, I was pursuing a ten-year adult evening PhD program at Golden Gate University in San Francisco. I worked diligently for most of the 1970s filling the void that I felt existed in the body of knowledge of turnaround management. My doctoral committee advisors included two turnaround management pioneers, Mr. Frank Grisanti of the firm Grisanti & Galef and Mr. Ransom Cook, former chairman of Wells Fargo bank. In addition, I conducted taped interviews with nineteen other turnaround leaders. The transcripts of these taped interviews totaled more than 1,500 pages. Eighty-one other turnaround leaders kindly contributed to a detailed survey on their turnaround efforts. Altogether, my doctoral dissertation advisors, the executives interviewed, and those who responded to the questionnaire had turned around more than 300 companies during their careers. Many hundreds of articles and books were cited in a sixty-nine-page bibliography.

The result of this ten-year effort was a comprehensive thousand-page PhD dissertation entitled "Corporate Turnaround: Reasons for Decline; Challenges to Management: Strategies and Practices for Renewal" registered in May 1979. In my opinion, and that of numerous other experts, this 1979 dissertation is the breakthrough point in the creation of the body of knowledge for turnaround management. The very first time the strategic framework for corporate turnarounds was presented it included

- Types of turnarounds
  - The management process turnaround
  - The business cycle turnaround
  - Product breakthrough turnaround
- Stages in a turnaround cycle
  - The management change stage
  - The viability evaluation stage
  - The emergency stage
  - The stabilization stage
  - Return-to-normal growth stage
- Key factors (preconditions) and turnaround success
  - Decisive management leader
  - The viable core business
  - Adequate bridge financing and support of stakeholders
  - Improved motivation and morale
- Role of leadership and turnaround success
- Vital tactics for each stage of the turnaround
  - Evaluation stage tactics
  - Planning tactics in the turnaround
  - Emergency stage turnaround tactics
  - Stabilization stage turnaround tactics
  - Return to growth tactics

Although a registered PhD dissertation, few practitioners or academics knew of its existence in 1979 or 1980. In the 1980s, Kathryn Rudie Harrigan's (1980) book *Strategies for Declining Businesses* increased our knowledge of the strategies to be employed to maximize value in declining businesses. Although case heavy and descriptive, this well-researched book does not include prescriptive strategies for improvement that lead to substantially positive results.

In the summer of 1980, Charles W. Hoffer wrote an interesting article in the *Journal of Business Strategy* that laid out turnaround strategies in a generalized form. The article is logical and well laid out but does not have the specificity to be operationalized by business executives.

In October 1981, McGraw-Hill published the summary version of my dissertation in a professional management book entitled *Corporate Turnaround: How Managers Turn Losers into Winners*.[1] Corporate turnaround was the main selection of two popular book clubs in 1981. These were the Executive Book Club and the Fortune Book Club. Because of these and other book clubs, more than 25,000 copies of *Corporate Turnaround* went into distribution in the first few months of publication. The 1981–1982 recession created a demand in excess of the normal demand for a serious book of this nature. I'm gratified that many indicate today that *Corporate Turnaround* is a bible of the turnaround management industry.

In August 1985, the U.S. Academy of Management convened a symposium in San Diego California, where it examined the conceptual and practitioner issues of the turnaround profession. I was pleased to be invited to make a presentation at the symposium. Another presenter confirmed the breakthrough pivotal position of my 1979 PhD dissertation on the conceptual foundation of the corporate turnaround profession.

In my opinion, nothing of consequence beyond anecdotal case descriptions appeared in serious business journals until an outstanding article by John O. Whitney entitled "Turnaround Management Every Day" appeared in the *Harvard Business Review* in 1987. Whitney focused on the everyday executive task and leadership rather than strategy, but the advice was sound and based on actual leadership experience. Whitney's article was a precursor for any number of valuable books that deal more with day-to-day execution. Such books include John Whitney's "Taking Charge," Gary Sutton's "The Six Month Fix," and Amir Hartman's "Ruthless Execution." Even Mitt Romney's (2004) book on turning around the Olympic Games provides valuable management insights.

In late summer 1987, the Kenan Institute at the University of North Carolina assembled a group of well-known turnaround practitioners to review the professional state of the industry. Out of this meeting was the decision to form the Turnaround Management Association, which was incorporated in January 1988 in the state of North Carolina. I was fortunate to be one of the attendees at the formation meeting and a founding director of TMA. Like all organizations, it had its growing pains, but by 1993, it not only had chapters in thirteen states but also chapters in Montréal and Toronto, Canada.

In 1993, Professor Harlan Platt of Northeastern University was appointed the faculty dean to lead TMA's educational programs. A professional journal, the *Journal of Corporate Renewal*, was launched in 1998. International chapters were added in addition to the Canadian chapter: the United Kingdom chapter was established in 2000; Australia and France chapters in 2003; Africa and Taiwan in 2005; Finland and Germany in 2006; Czech Republic, Italy, the Netherlands, and Spain in 2007; and the Brazil and Sweden chapters were established in 2009.

In 1994—under the umbrella of the TMA—the Association of Certified Turnaround Professionals (ATCP) was formed to encourage the study of techniques for turnaround of financially troubled businesses, to set minimum standards for those individuals who seek certification as turnaround professionals, and to conduct examination processes to identify and certify turnaround professionals. To that end, the ACTP assembled an extensive body of knowledge comprising three areas: (a) "Management Body of Knowledge," (b) "Legal Body of Knowledge," and (c) "Insolvency Accounting Body of Knowledge."

I was gratified to be asked to write the preface to the "Management Body of Knowledge." In the end notes of each chapter, ACTP formally acknowledged that the "Management Body of Knowledge" is largely based on my 1979 PhD dissertation and my professional textbook "Corporate Turnaround: How Managers Turn Losers into Winners."

In the twenty-two years from 1995 to 2015, the promulgation of the TMA Professional Body of Knowledge has buttressed the recognition of turnaround management as a true profession.

1.4 Economic Turmoil Increased the Need for Decisive Turnaround Leaders

The Great Depression caused a very large increase in the business failure rate from 100 firms per 1,000 to 160 firms per 1,000 in 1932. This failure rate aided by a military buildup was about 60 per 1,000 on the brink of World War II. The percentage of firms with positive income declined from 61% in 1928 to only 18% in 1932. More than 25% of firms became distressed by 1938, where distress was defined as liquidation, filing for bankruptcy, undertaking court-ordered reorganization, undertaking a recapitalization on the stock, or the stock was listed as worthless or explicitly listed as financially distressed. Leverage (i.e., debt to total assets ratio) decreased during the Depression and increased slowly after economic conditions improved significantly in the 1940s.

From 1948 through 1973, real GNP (gross national product) growth in the United States averaged a robust 3.7%. Unemployment was relatively low. Inflation was considered high if it reached 5%, so interest rates were kept down. American business not only served a growing domestic market but also discovered Europe, Asia, and Latin America. Every year, America was a net exporter, piling up a surplus of $157 billion. Not surprisingly, the country developed a body of business practice and literature that suited this environment.

After the postwar prosperity of the 1940s, the United States prospered in the benevolent business environment of the 1950s and 1960s. The vertical organization with its short spans of control and powerful central staff made sense in a stable business climate. Executives made decisions deliberately with the concurrence of the organization's many layers. Long-term planning became a fetish. The number of dollars thrown off for reinvestment drove investment decisions. Long-term measures such as discounted cash flow were developed. Payback was scoffed at or ignored.

Companies rarely fired managers or employees—afraid to rock the richly laden boat. Management made concessions to unions not only in pay rates but also in work rules. Low interest rates and the stable environment encouraged the liberal use of debt. No one talked of negative leverage. In this amiable environment, turnarounds were rare. Certainly, some managers employed heroic measures to screw up a sure thing. Consumer product companies too firmly rooted in the past created the Studebaker, the Henry J, and the Edsel, but on balance, turnaround management was seldom necessary.

Then during the early 1970s, trouble appeared. Economists, political analysts, and social scientists debated the causes. The effects were palpable: the rate of environmental change accelerated and competition intensified. Turnarounds were no longer special cases but all-too-familiar parts of business life. In recent years, the corporate sick list has included names such as Continental Bank, Bank of America, International Harvester, Braniff, People Express, Commodore, Atari, Control Data, Storage Technology, and Fotomat. Chrysler, A&P, and Wickes seem to have recovered, and others on the list are on the road back. However, W. T. Grant and Polaroid have disappeared, and other ailing companies have experienced mergers, liquidations, or acquisitions. Even such blue chips as AT&T and IBM kept the lights burning late as they attempted to preserve long-cherished values while streamlining to compete.

We all remember what happened to oil prices after the Arab boycott in 1973. The prime rate was just as unstable. It reached 20% in 1981 and then fell to 8% in 1986. Real growth in GNP slowed way down, averaging only 2.3% from 1973 through 1985. In 1985, the U.S. net export deficit was $79 billion, equal to just half of the combined trade surpluses in the 1948–1973 period. America's once-corpulent overseas competitors had to become lean, and they had the temerity to invade U.S. markets. Competition from a variety of sources placed severe pressure on the affected U.S. industries.

As a result, when the prime rate soared, energy costs skyrocketed, and the Japanese, West Germans, and Koreans added their considerable skills to those of hungry domestic competitors, and many leaders of respected companies found they could no longer cope. Their legacies had failed them, and their ponderous organizations were not ready to adapt. They tried but could not mobilize to compete. Increased competition and technological change made companies 'more vulnerable' to poor performance, leading to a need for more turnarounds—and more people to mastermind them. The role of the professional turnaround manager was expanding. If a company was on the verge of bankruptcy, it needed a crisis manager, not just a good solid corporate manager.

The rate of technological change+ compounded these pressures. New items that substituted for once unassailable products had come to market. The film business of Kodak, for example, had been directly attacked by Fuji, Konica, and 3M and had been sideswiped by VCRs and video cameras that did not require film, which diverted money once spent on cameras. In addition, home computers, compact discs, audio component racks, and other toys diverted dollars previously available for photography.

1.5   Chronology of Turnaround Leadership

Accelerated change and intensified competition made the managers of the 1970s and 1980s look inept compared with their 1950s and 1960s counterparts. Yet these managers were better educated, better informed, and harder working than their predecessors. Their failures may be more clearly understood—if not exonerated—in the context of their legacies. Past practice and traditional business education prepared them, like generals, to fight the last war, not the present one—much less the next. Indeed, as Frank Grisanti so ably put it,

> A turnaround is a very difficult kind of task. It's all good to be done fast. It means, without a wealth of experience, without incredible insight, without the kind of personality that permits you to make bold decisive moves quickly without the ability to change your mind and reverse your feelings when you made a mistake you're not going to succeed. Timing is of a key importance because the company is bleeding millions of dollars per month, he can't afford the luxury of fact-finding junkets. Have to be able to make decisions based upon your experience.[2]

The economic turmoil beginning in the 1970s put a priority on the rapid decision style of turnaround leaders. Gradually management leaders attuned to the times emerged to help.

- The One-Off Turnaround Leader
- The Serial Turnaround Leader
- The Inside 'Troubleshooter'
- The Lone Ranger Model
- The Emergence of Boutique Turnaround Firms
- The Emergence of Large Firms

1.5.1   The 'One-Off' Turnaround Leader

General Motors was founded in 1908 by a flamboyant salesman named William Durant with the Buick Motor Company as its sole original holding. During a tumultuous eighteen-month period, Durant proceeded to acquire thirty other carmakers. These included Oldsmobile, Pontiac, and Cadillac. This rapid expansion through acquisition saddled General Motors with debt it could not repay. In 1912, GM's bankers gave Durant the boot. He was replaced by a stiff engineer, Alfred Sloan, whose business innovations nevertheless came to rival those of Henry Ford. Whereas Ford and his assembly line revolutionized the way cars were manufactured, Sloan, who ran General Motors until 1956, revolutionized the way they were marketed and sold.

Sloan's turnaround strategy enabled General Motors to gain market traction by segmenting the market and having a product strategy that tried to distinctively appeal to every segment. Under Sloan, GM strove to supply a car, as Sloan said, "For every purse and every purpose." In addition to segmentation, GM also produced many of the engineering innovations that came to define the modern automobile. Those innovations included power steering, power brakes, independent suspension, and the automatic transmission.

GM was the first auto company to change car features and styling almost at will—instilling Americans with the concept of replacing their cars every few years. GM factories turned out cars in virtually every price range, and sales soared under Alfred Sloan. By the 1950s, GM had produced more than half of the vehicles on America's roads. Eventually, the decentralized division approach led to Balkanization in the perverse effect of isolated management fiefdoms. This led to GM's bankruptcy in the early twenty-first century. Nonetheless, Alfred Sloan will go down as one of most successful corporate turnaround giants in history.

In 1979, the business world and most of the public were enthralled with the work of Lido Anthony 'Lee' Iacocca in his turnaround of Chrysler Corporation. Not only did Iacocca direct the strategic and tactical efforts of Chrysler, but he also became the very visible public spokesperson who garnered support for Chrysler. For example, Iacocca was able to acquire a U.S. government guaranteed loan. Because of reforms and clever marketing campaigns at Chrysler, he was able to repay the government loan seven years earlier than expected, thus guaranteeing his place in history as a turnaround hero.

At the same time as Chrysler's travails were ongoing, the second-largest problem company in the world was the Canadian-based Massey Ferguson. Although initially denied by management, total agricultural demand was in a decade-long sectoral decline. I had the privilege of advising Victor Rice, CEO, and Vincent Lorenzo, president, of Massey Ferguson in the early 1980s. Although my initial analysis was mostly out of the public eye, corporate spies purloined it, and the Canadian Parliament read the analysis. I assisted Mr. Rice in making very difficult decisions that led to the necessary downsizing of Massey's workforce. After stabilizing the company, Massey's management adroitly redeployed the company strategically away from the agricultural sector.

1.5.2   *The Serial Turnaround Leader Emerges*

Even by 1983, the number of corporate fixers was so limited that a word had not yet emerged to describe the trade that they plied. A few called it the 'Corporate R & R—repair and rebuild business.' Because crises come in many forms, the turnaround business emerged as a breed apart. This group thrived on turning around seemingly impossible situations. They were more akin to wartime generals or emergency room doctors than the button-down executives at banks and traditional American hierarchal companies. What catapulted them from one corporate cauldron to another unlike Alfred Sloan and Lee Iacocca? They thrived in the pressure-cooker climate that seemed characteristic of companies one step from bankruptcy. Along with the exhilaration that came from stress, they enjoyed high visibility, which, for most men who liked the work, was its own reward. It was obvious that they all had a common need to be number one.

In the early 1980s, the most visible corporate turnaround masters were Victor H. Palmieri, Stanley Hiller Jr., and Sanford C. Sigoloff in the United States and Bernard Arnault and Vincent Bollore in France. Victor Palmieri had a string of successful turnarounds culminating with the successful turnaround at Baldwin-United. His illustrious career was tarnished by a poor investment in the Crazy Eddie chain of retail electronic stores that was subject to a large inventory fraud. Sanford Sigoloff did an excellent turnaround of Republic Corporation's fortunes. When Republic started making money, Sigoloff received numerous phone calls for help from other troubled operations.

In 1975, Sigoloff became CEO of Daylin, the large West Coast retail chain. Daylin filed Chapter 11 in 1975 and emerged in 1977. By the time it emerged from bankruptcy, it was making a lot of money and was sold to W. R. Grace and Company. Sigoloff's largest challenge was the revitalization of Wickes Corporation, which in my opinion was only partially successful. One embarrassing episode was Sigoloff's decision to fire two executives from Wickes's Handy Dan subsidiary. Bernard Marcus and Arthur Blank then founded the Home Depot, which went on to enormous success in the home-improvement retail market. In sharp contrast, Handy Dan went out of business in May 1989.

Stanley Hiller was a businessman whose serial turnaround successes were unmatched in consistency and success. At the tender age of seventeen, the brilliant engineer sold his helicopter design to the U.S. military. After spending half a lifetime solving problems for his own companies, he decided to do it for others. From the Reed Tool company in the early 1970s to Key Tronic in the 1990s, Hiller never skipped a beat and successfully turned around companies. Along the way, he turned around such diverse companies as Baker International (now Baker Hughes) and York International.

Bernard Arnault became the richest man in France through his turnaround expertise. He began his ascent when he bought a struggling textile firm, Boussac, which happened to own the luxury brand Christian Dior. The principal reason behind his acquisition was to gain control of the Dior label and gain a foothold in the luxury market. His luxury market focus was enhanced by selling off the divisions of Boussac that had nothing to do with his luxury business goals. Much of the divestment money went to purchase a 24% stake in the large luxury company LVMH. Arnault continued to require luxury brands through the 1990s. He purchased such names as Givenchy, TAG Heuer, Sephora, and a number of well-known spirit labels.

Another one of the titans of the French business world, Vincent Bolloré ran the diversified holding company Bolloré Group, which had been in the Bolloré family since 1822. When Vincent assumed control in early 1981— not long after starting his career at Edmond de Rothschild bank—the family business that made paper for cigarettes and bibles was struggling. He overhauled it and turned it into one of the 500-largest companies in the world, with holdings in media, advertising, shipping, construction, logistics, and more. The renowned buyout artist held sizable stakes in telecom conglomerate Vivendi and advertising giant Havas. He was busy growing Blue Solutions, the manufacturer of electric car batteries that he took public in 2013.

Steve Miller is a contemporary example of a serial turnaround leader. He began his career at Ford Motor Company in 1968. Lee Iacocca recruited him to the Chrysler Corporation in 1979. While with Chrysler in the 1980s, he was the executive in charge of arranging the U.S. Government–insured program of loans with hundreds of banks that enabled Chrysler to avoid bankruptcy and to become an industrial powerhouse under the leadership of Iacocca. He became CEO of Delphi Corporation in July 2005. While at Delphi, he presided over a restructuring of the company while it was going through bankruptcy. American International Group named Miller their chairman in July 2010. Hawker Beechcraft named him CEO in February 2012 in an attempt to reverse the company's fortunes.

1.5.3   The Inside 'Troubleshooter'

Historic canal bankruptcies of the early nineteenth century and the later railroad bankruptcies of the same century involved relatively focused single-industry operations. One strategic result of the Great Depression was that companies decided to spread their risk among a number of industries rather than being vulnerable to the severe downturn of one industry. This created conglomerates with multidivisional structures facing a number of industries. One classic example the 1950s diversification was International Telephone & Telegraph, which bought such diverse companies as Sheraton Hotels, Continental Baking, Hartford Fire Insurance, and Avis Rent-a-Car. It was common to have at least twenty operating divisions in a Fortune 1000 company.

The corporate offices of a diversified company usually had an embedded brain trust at the top. The holding company did not have the skills or expertise to deal with problems in a particular industry for which they had no prior experience. They solved this dilemma by having internal company 'troubleshooters' who were dispatched to a losing division in order to effectuate an operational turnaround. According to the online *Merriam-Webster Dictionary*, the first known use of the word troubleshooter was in 1905. It means a person "skilled at solving anticipating problems or difficulties." One surprising thing discovered in my years of research during the 1970s was that the number of internal turnarounds within large corporation division structures exceeded single structure corporate turnarounds that garnered press coverage.

Typically, a company had a team of 'corporate troubleshooters' it dispatched to make dramatic changes in underperforming divisions. So pervasive was this corporate-troubleshooter approach that the BBC (British Broadcasting Company) aired a television series between 1965 and 1972 originally entitled *Moguls*. The show was renamed *The Troubleshooters* and featured younger dynamic field agents—the eponymous 'troubleshooters' who flew around the world to 'hotspots' to protect the company's interests. Troubleshooter organization was reputed to have been based on BP (British Petroleum), and there were many similarities and coincidences in terms of the international events.

Robin C. Wilson exemplifies the much-followed path from corporate troubleshooter to professional turnaround manager. Wilson was a long-term executive with General Electric and began his GE troubleshooting career in 1959 by turning around and reinvigorating the General Electric radio receiver department, which had been under pressure from Japanese manufacturers. With the cooperation of the union, he was able to increase GE's market share against the Japanese onslaught. By the time Wilson moved to the position of executive vice president at Rockwell International, his creative turnaround abilities were well recognized.

It was natural that when Rockwell's acquisition of Collins Radio began to flounder that the company appointed Wilson CEO of Collins. He engineered a remarkable turnaround, which reinvigorated Collins. Wilson's next challenge was the mission impossible turnaround of Memorex Corporation. Memorex became one of the most dramatic turnarounds in American corporate history. From a position of major losses, the company was most likely going bankrupt; Wilson restored the company to profitability and relisted it on the New York Stock Exchange. In 1981, Wilson established the turnaround advisory firm Wilson and Chambers, which continued for another fifteen years.

Marvin Davis became a corporate division troubleshooter at Pfizer. A chemical engineer with an MBA in finance, Davis was initially assigned to the controller's division. He was often selected to make presentations on divisional profit and loss before the management committee. These presentations led to Pfizer's president choosing him for specialty assignments to deal with particularly intractable problems. His first big assignment was how to separate out the contamination of an antibiotic line from another product line at the Brooklyn New York plant. His creative approach was to move the entire operation to Puerto Rico, which at that time offered huge tax incentives granted by Congress to jump-start its economy. This idea was so novel that it was controversial at the chairman's level. Davis convinced the chairman to support the move. He calculated that the payoff from the move, in spite of the substantial cost, would be take only nine months.

After that time, Davis was given assignment after assignment of the sensitive and controversial nature that required 'out-of-the-box' thinking and innovative approaches. Whereas he enjoyed the work immensely, his goal was to run a division of the company. When that path was blocked at Pfizer, he became open to new horizons. Through a mutual friend from graduate school, he was attracted to the boutique turnaround firm of Grisanti, Galef & Goldress, which he joined in 1983.

The building of the French company Dynaction by Christian Moretti and Henry Blanchet beginning in 1982 was a unique blend of turnaround management and private equity. With a socialist French government in power, many U.S. companies sold off their European holdings at bargain basement prices. Moretti and Blanchet bought their first acquisition, Cryodiffusion, for one Franc and convinced its U.S. group to recapitalize the company to cover its large debts. The two friends then streamlined the operations by getting rid of translators, U.S. lawyers, and transatlantic Concorde flights. They rehired the old management team, gave them access to equity at a favorable rate, and together brought the company back to profitability within six months. Dynaction set up a subsidiary called Dynaspring, which specialized in the takeover of companies with financial difficulties (the U.S. equivalent of Chapter 11). Altogether, Dynaspring took over fourteen troubled companies, of which twelve were successfully turned. In keeping with Dynaction's lean approach, the headquarters team consisted only of the two founders, a secretary, and an accountant. The biggest challenge was picking deals and management teams. Counterintuitively, their operational method did not include complex due diligence, and they were very quick in their decision making.

1.5.4   The 'Lone Ranger' Model

From the standpoint of organization models, the development of the turnaround management profession is akin to the establishment of law and order in the Western territories of the United States in the latter part of the nineteenth century. In the American West, law and order was first brought to town by lone U.S. Marshals. In less than two decades, the model changed to an elected sheriff backed up by several deputy sheriffs and an appointed part-time posse. Within another two decades, this model was replaced by large, and often bureaucratic, police departments.

Many early serial turnaround leaders operated on a one-on-one basis, much like the U.S. Marshals of the old West. In medium-size cases, an additional specialized and experienced operative was called in to assist. At the same time that the BBC was launching a quasi-fictional troubleshooter television series, I was living that experience in real life at a medium-sized financial conglomerate in California. The company was public but controlled by a wealthy Texas oil family. I had the title of 'vice president of corporate development' which allowed me to reign over the company's operations to tackle very difficult (and usually sensitive) operating issues. For example, I recommended that its 350 person sales force be cut in half, whereas the existing management requested an increase across the board. I initially lost that battle, but when the sales subsidiary lost more money, my drastic plan was adopted. Within two years, the subsidiary substantially increased revenues and became profitable.

1.5.5   The Emergence of Boutique Turnaround Firms

In the mid to late 1960s, small turnaround firms were established. For example, following a few years as a proprietorship, Grisanti & Galef, Inc. (currently GGG Partners, LLC) incorporated more than forty-eight years ago on Friday, May 31, 1968. In 1973, *Business Week* featured an article about the work of Grisanti & Galef entitled "They Do Repair Jobs on Small Companies." By the time I met Frank Grisanti in early 1978, the firm was well established and Frank had recently served as CEO of International House of Pancakes. To this day, GGG Partners has remained active as a boutique turnaround firm.

In September 1987, a summit meeting for the then well-known turnaround professionals was held at the Kenan Center of the University of North Carolina. The participants estimated that there were between 150 and 200 sole practitioners and small turnaround firms active in the United States. By 1993 when the U.S. publication *Turnarounds and Workouts* bestowed its prize for top turnaround firms, it had 220 workout firms in its database. In the mid-1990s, a consolidation movement began to appear. This culminated in the growth of very large turnaround firms such as Alvarez and Marcel, AlixPartners, Huron Consulting, and FTI.

1.5.6   The Emergence of Large Firms

Alvarez & Marsal, founded in 1983 by Tony Alvarez II and Bryan Marsal, helped pave the way for the growth of the large firm practice in the United States. During the 2000s, while continuing to specialize in turnaround work, and continuing to take executive and CRO (chief restructuring officer) roles, the firm expanded its practice into adjacent specialty areas. These areas included litigation support, forensic accounting, acquisition due diligence, and post-acquisition performance improvement. By 2015, Alvarez & Marsal had grown to approximately 2,500 personnel working from forty offices globally.

Jay Alix founded AlixPartners in 1981. From a base of three offices (in Detroit, New York, and Chicago), AlixPartners built a global reputation through work with many multinational clients. AlixPartners had been retained as a restructuring advisor and/or interim management in some of the largest Chapter 11 reorganizations, including General Growth Properties, General Motors, and Kodak. In 2012, CVC private equity announced a recapitalization by which funds affiliated with CVC purchased majority ownership of AlixPartners. Today, AlixPartners is a global firm of more than 1,500 professionals on four continents around the world.

Huron Consulting Group commenced operations in 2002 and is still in operation today. The company's initial employees came mainly from Arthur Anderson, including 25 partners and 250 other professionals. The company provides a balanced portfolio of services including turnaround and restructuring services. Its turnaround practice derived from its acquisition of midsize firms and remains a small portion of its total services. The company is largely grown through acquisitions of midsize firms in a number of areas of expertise.

FTI was founded as Forensic Technologies International Ltd. in 1982 and employs more than 4,500 staff members in twenty-six countries. In 2002, the company added over 1,000 employees to its forensic-in-litigation consulting division because of the passing of the 2002 Sarbanes-Oxley Act, which excluded auditors from providing consulting work to their public clients.

1.6   Contemporary Trends

What is common to large firms is that over time the turnaround consulting and restructuring practice has become a small percentage of firms' overall services. Whereas in the early days of the turnaround industry firms engaged principally in interim management, today's large firms are principally engaged in lucrative consulting activities and work within the legal framework of accredited committees in bankruptcy. It is a similar structure throughout the developed world with large firms working on megacases in concert with law firms. When large and midsize firms engage as interim management, it is usually in the capacity of CRO. This title does not carry with it the typical turnaround CEO responsibility to return the firm to its prior health and growth level.

The source of large cases usually comes from major bank groups. Often megalaw firms are involved in the selection of advisors, preferably those they trust to work in a skillful and 'compatible' manner. Compatible manner usually means mutual support for the huge fees charged in these cases. The Lehman Brother's bankruptcy proceeding in the United States has garnered attention because of the $3 billion in professional fees in the case. The Lehman case, whereas large and complex, nonetheless has drawn criticism for the myriad of attorneys and advisors garnering $1,000 per hour fees for years at a time. The large firms have 'gone down market' in their regional offices with mixed success.

Whereas large commercial banks formerly retained midsize and smaller credit problems for work by their internal bank 'workout/special assets' groups, this pattern has substantially changed. These banks have substantially reduced their internal groups. In today's fluid capital markets and with the existence of distressed private equity firms, the banks have the availability to liquefy their midsize positions as never before. Although content to sell their position at a discount rather than attempt resuscitation, they can on occasion even sell a position at par.

In the United States, as with many other countries, midsize firms that have not been acquired by larger firms have themselves merged to provide greater geographic coverage. Far from the multimillion-dollar or even multibillion-dollar cases are professionals throughout the world working in small and midsize companies. Individual practitioners and small firms in the United States continue to engage in a mix of interim management and consulting. The small company market in many respects remains a cottage industry. Regional banks are not entirely comfortable engaging the megafirms, whose fee structures are not economic in smaller cases. Most family-owned businesses tend to use local professionals.

Notes

1 Originally published in book form, New York: McGraw-Hill, (1981) ©1982; republished in paperback form, Washington, DC: Beard Books.
2 Frank Grisanti, President of Grisanti & Galef (Grisanti & Galef, now known as GGG partners is the earliest turnaround firm that has survived to this day).

References

Bibeault, D. B. (1981). *Corporate turnaround: How managers turn losers into winners*. New York: McGraw-Hill.

Eisenberg, J. (Ed.). (1972). *Turnaround management*. New York: McGraw-Hill.

Greiner, E. L. (1972). Evolution and revolution as organizations grow. *Harvard Business Review, 50*(July/August), 37–46.

Harrigan, K. R. (1980). *Strategies for declining businesses*. Lexington, MA: D.C. Heath.

Hartman, A. (2001). *Ruthless execution: What business leaders do when their companies hit the wall*. Upper Saddle River, NY: FT Prentice Hall.

Hoffer, C. W. (1980). Turnaround strategies. *Journal of Business Strategy, 1*(1), 19–31.

Kami, M. J., & Ross, J. (1973). *Why the mighty fall*. Englewood Cliffs, NJ: Prentice Hall.

Romney, M. (2004). *Turnaround: Crisis, leadership, and the Olympic Games*. Washington, DC: Regnery Publishing.

Schendel, D., & Patton, R. (1975). An empirical study of corporate stagnation and turnaround. *Proceedings of the Academy of Management*, 49–51.

Schendel, D., Patton, R., & Riggs, J. (1975). *Corporate Turnaround Strategies*. Paper No. 486, West Lafayette, IN: Krannert Graduate School of Industrial Administration.

Sutton, G. (2001). *The six month fix: Adventures in rescuing failing companies*. New York: Wiley.

Whitney, J. O. (1987). Turnaround management every day. *Harvard Business Review*, September/October, 65(5), 49–55.

Whitney, J. O. (1998). *Taking charge: Management guide to troubled companies and turnarounds*. Washington, DC: Beard Books.

2 Business Rescue, Turnaround Management, and the Legal Regime of Default and Insolvency in Western History (Late Middle Ages to Present Day)

Dave De ruysscher

2.1 Introduction

The legal concept of insolvency has changed tremendously over the past decades. Legal scholars and lawmakers have for a long time considered insolvency, in addition to the options provided for by legislation in case of permanent default, as a means of last resort. Inevitably, this concept has had an impact on the perception of the legal history of indebtedness and insolvency as well. Legal historians have for a long time addressed these themes as encompassing only fraud and expropriation of assets. Moreover, they have not usually been very interested in business history. This lack explains why intersections between the management of companies on the one hand and insolvency in legislation and court practice on the other have virtually not been analyzed from a legal-historical perspective.

As a consequence, the approaches mentioned regarding insolvency are outdated. Nowadays, reorganization and continuity of business are key paradigms in legislative reforms. Accordingly, the largely neglected legal history of corporate rescue can be revived. In the Middle Ages, examples can be found of legal regimes allowing for debt arrangements upon insolvency. This chapter will provide an overview of the gradual acceptance of compositions over long periods of time and across regions in continental Europe, in England, and in the United States. It sketches the slow emergence of a rescue culture in law. Furthermore, the chapter proposes some potential lines of research relating to turnaround management and its interactions with official approaches toward insolvency. One new area of research relates to the impact of legal modalities of debt recovery on turnaround management strategies. Especially in the late Middle Ages, changes were taking place in this regard. Moreover, the incrementally developing idea that companies could have separate capital and personhood is likely to have had consequences for turnaround management.

2.2 The Flexible Form of Firms and Repressive Insolvency Laws (Late Middle Ages)

In the 1200s, international commerce expanded. The Mediterranean was opened up for trade from Northwest Europe. The commercial boom resulted in the creative development of new credit instruments (bills of exchange, bills obligatory), of techniques for distributing risk (bottomry, maritime insurance), and of company contracts that allowed for shielding investments (e.g., the *commenda*) (Lopez, 1976). In spite of vibrant mercantile activity and the formulation of new contracts, which characterized the period until around 1400, how firms were constituted and how they operated demonstrate much uniformity throughout the ensuing centuries. The commercial revolution took place largely in Southern Europe, and the mentioned new developments were initiated above all from within the commercial cities on the Italian Peninsula. Innovations that came after originated mostly in England and Northwest Europe.

Over the course of the late nineteenth and twentieth centuries, scholars have analyzed the operations of many individual firms active in the late-medieval era (c.1250–c.1500) and in the sixteenth century. Early historical research focused on the links between entrepreneurs and the political elite (e.g., Ehrenberg, 1896); over the past decades, historians' attention has shifted toward family relations and merchant networks (e.g., Häberlein, 1998). The management of companies during the mentioned eras has often been examined from within these frameworks. Turnaround and shutdown management in these periods have not often been studied as such, or in detail, even though now and again major monograph studies have provided glimpses into the strategies that were deployed within companies under financial duress.

In the centuries that followed the commercial revolution of the thirteenth and fourteenth centuries, family firms still dominated the economic scene. Owners were typically family members or business relations within close-knit networks. These features were also characteristic for those companies concerned with international commodity trading and finance. Moreover, such firms did not usually specialize; merchant houses engaged in trading and financing, and although different activities were often confined to separate companies, they were closely intertwined. Studies have explored the management tactics of international banking firms, such as the Medici and Fugger holdings. Even when consortiums of partnerships were international, they depended on coordinated actions directed among owners; agent-managers could be given power of attorney, but they did not commonly have much leeway in assessing business opportunities. Company contracts generally provided restrictions in negotiating deals. Managers were salaried agents acting on instructions that were sent out by the general manager, who was the owner of the firm. Moreover, capital was drawn in the form of loans and shares but minor investors typically remained outside the decision-making processes (De Roover, 1966, pp. 90–107; Häberlein, 2012).

Family firms of this kind usually had the legal form of a general partnership. An important feature of general partnerships was that partners were held jointly and severally liable. Creditors could sue for the debts made on behalf of the company, against any of the partners and for the totality of the debts, even if those debts exceeded the investments made by the partners involved (Zimmermann, 1996, pp. 466–472). Another characteristic of partnership firms was that their capital was not entrenched. The notion of legal personhood was developed only slowly, albeit at a faster pace from the sixteenth century onward; still, it was acknowledged for private companies only haltingly over the course of the eighteenth and nineteenth centuries (Mehr, 2008). In the late Middle Ages and early modern period (c.1500–c.1800), general partnerships were joint ventures without a veil between private and company-related properties. Investments were not shielded from private creditors, thus exposing the firm to debt recovery actions by outsiders. Moreover, according to the law, partnerships were dissolved at the death of one of the partners, or when they resigned (Zimmermann, 1996, pp. 455–457).

The features of unlimited liability, lack of entrenched capital, and the risk of untimely ending have been described as weak in terms of investment protection and continuity (e.g., Hansmann, Kraakman, & Squire, 2006, pp. 1366–1372). These properties have often been linked to the fact that general partnership contracts were signed for specific short terms only. Usually, general partnerships were drafted for a period typically spanning between two to five years (De Roover, 1966, p. 241, pp. 247–248; Postan, 1973, p. 86). However, in spite of these deficiencies, limited liability companies were not very common throughout the periods mentioned earlier. They were used in naval trade, above all, and on a limited scale. Quite remarkably, the most prolific and successful firms of the late Middle Ages did not usually opt for this company type. Italian banking firms sometimes set up *commenda*-type daughter firms, but only if they ventured into a new market or with new partners. Even so, when investments were consolidated, general partnerships were preferred instead (De Roover, 1966, pp. 59–60, pp. 89–90, p. 237, p. 325).

There are a number of reasons that explain why general partnerships remained widespread. Flexibility is one of them. The structure of the company could easily be devised in the company contract. It could be provided that the partnership would continue, notwithstanding the death of a partner, for example. Furthermore, even though associates of a general partnership were held jointly and severally liable, there were important gray zones. A lack of information as to who the investors were meant that often only the visible actors were sued for debts. In many commercial hubs of Southern and Northwest Europe, company contracts were not made public. A lot of agreements remained informal as well: they were not written down, and the venture only materialized in books and letters, which were kept by the insiders. Some cities such as Florence provided that limited liability firms had to be registered. Yet even in that case, the main public information regarding which partners were accountable came via the name of the firm, which was used by its agents signing on behalf of the partners. Company names did not always mention all associates (they could have the form of '& Cie,' for example). As a result of these limited public sources, creditors relied on the information that they had received from their debtors, even if the latter were acting on behalf of a company. Moreover, directors of companies were the ones with whom creditors negotiated, and in case of default directors, they were the ones who answered for the debts. Creating separate partnerships for different activities thus signified a form of protection for non-active partners and investors (Goldthwaite, 2009, p. 77). Because personal and company-related assets were fenced only to a limited extent (Hansmann et al., 2006, pp. 1366–1372), in practice, liquidation of a company equaled the auctioning of the assets found with the 'administrator' (De ruysscher, 2015a).

An indirect explanation as to why in the late Middle Ages general partnerships were the most used legal form of business relates to late-medieval practices and law concerning debt enforcement. The custom of identifying companies with their agents, which served to protect outside investors, also followed on from legal regimes and mercantile practices that took persons rather than assets as preferential guarantees for debt. Most general partnerships had their business operations in cities. There and also at fairs, debt recovery was structured in such a way that expropriation of a defaulter's assets was not easy to obtain. At the thirteenth-century fairs in Champagne, and among fourteenth-century Flemish and German merchants, renewal of debts was the normal practice. If debts matured, debtor and creditor often matched claims and debts that were due within their credit networks (North, 1996, pp. 223–226). As a result, they avoided enforcement. This convention not only constituted mercantile practice, but it was also due to official rules that made expropriation dependent on proceedings. Generally speaking, only judgments were considered to be titles to organize an auction of debtors' assets, movable and immovable. Sometimes contracts provided for collateral, but this provision was in many instances not deemed sufficient for pre-judgment attachments or extrajudicial pursuit of properties (De ruysscher, 2015b). Moreover, debt execution proceedings were not swift. In late-medieval France, debts under seal were considered as entitled to fast-track proceedings of this kind, but even under those proceedings, the sequestration and auctioning of a defaulter's merchandise were far from automatic. Even when royal privileges granted procedural exemptions to traders, the public sale of the debtor's assets was subject to notification, delays, and judgments (e.g., Claustre, 2007, p. 158, p. 160, p. 299, pp. 300–308). Rules that were applied at fairs—for example, those of Champagne—were construed so as to avoid private seizures on debts and securities, and they hinged on control by officials (Edwards & Ogilvie, 2012, p. 135). The origins of these procedural bars are diverse. It is possible that they stem from earlier medieval periods, when property could be secured for debt by explicit agreement only (e.g., De Blécourt & Fischer, 1950, pp. 246–247). Another explanation is that incremental state formation during the twelfth and thirteenth centuries, which resulted in governmental control over the pursuit and punishment of criminal behavior, also meant that private enforcement of debt against assets, among other things, became restricted (e.g., Planitz, 1913, p. 52).

When considering such rules on debt enforcement, the imprisonment of debtors was a more efficient method of relief for creditors. Apprehension and incarceration put pressure on the defaulter to seek new credit or sureties. In most cities and regions of late-medieval Europe, coercive pre-judgment arrest and imprisonment for debt were relatively easy. In late-medieval France, since the later thirteenth century, incarceration of defaulters was a generalized practice (Claustre, 2007, pp. 105–106). Admittedly, citizens and residents were commonly granted protection against detention, and groups of merchants trading in a city usually applied for exemptions in this regard (Godding, 1987, p. 507). In practice, however, there are many examples of members of such privileged groups who were seized and imprisoned, even though they were given the opportunity to adduce and evidence the illegality of these measures in court. Merchants without fixed domicile could be locked away without reservations (e.g., for fifteenth-century Antwerp: De ruysscher, 2016, pp. 79–80).

These practices were largely directed against individuals, even when they were agents of firms. Moreover, they were detrimental for trade. Because merchants in financial difficulties faced the prospect of being incarcerated, which would ruin their reputations, they often fled the market, or they sought sanctuary in churches or religious institutions (Jones, 1979, p. 14; Kadens, 2010, pp. 1233–1234). In turn, municipal administrators responded by imposing severe penalties on debtors who absconded from their creditors. In thirteenth- and fourteenth-century Italy, ordinances of cities commonly proclaimed banishment for fled debtors, thus pushing them out of the mercantile community. After a while, more lenient penalties such as forfeiture of civil or political rights became common (Santarelli, 1998, pp. 74–78). Of course, even such softer measures did not increase the appeal of stepping forward when having financial difficulties. From the perspective of creditors as well, the effects of all these practices were disadvantageous. The repeated flights incited swift action on their behalf, out of fear that the debtor would abscond. As a result, debtors were often put in jail prematurely. Merchants having financial difficulties could then experience a ripple effect when one of their creditors had them imprisoned or started a lawsuit. Alarmed by the actions of their peers, other creditors then additionally executed on their debts (De ruysscher, 2013, p. 190).

The aforementioned bars on expropriation and pre-judgment attachment were lowered throughout Europe between the late thirteenth and sixteenth centuries. They disappeared fully only over the course of the early modern period, however. The speed at which these developments took place differed from region to region. This development had its roots in the idea of general collateral, which gained ground in many places and regions in Europe north of the Alps, from the later thirteenth century onward. The generalization of collateral meant that assets of a debtor were increasingly considered to be the common guarantee of his creditors and that they could be expropriated in case of default. General security interests and non-possessory pledges were accepted as lawful, for example (De Blécourt & Fischer, 1950, p. 252; Godding, 1987, pp. 217–218).

In terms of proceedings, however, introduction of swift seizure and expropriation of assets, pledged or otherwise, was long in the making. The aforementioned rules barring expeditious enforcement against assets remained problematic in this regard. As was the case before the end of the thirteenth century, in the 1300s, municipal ordinances commonly stressed that seizure of property of citizens and residents could only be granted following a proceeding in the town's courts (Godding, 1987, p. 507; Planitz, 1913, pp. 55–62). Even if a written contract had been drafted that waived this protection, judicial control was generally required. In fourteenth-century France and England, the acknowledgment of debts in court and cooperation of the debtor marked common features of rules of debt proceedings (Claustre, 2007, pp. 174–175; Cohen, 1982, pp. 154–155; Duffy, 1985, pp. 61–65). Slowly, however, in the course of the fifteenth and sixteenth centuries, municipal authorities as well as regional and central courts began to acknowledge that debt enforcement was directed first toward the assets of a defaulter and less toward his person (Claustre, 2007, pp. 267–271; Godding, 1987, pp. 510–511). This development unfolded in Antwerp between 1470 and 1540 (De ruysscher, 2013). The 1510 Parisian *coutumes* provided that pre-judgment *arrêt* of a debtor's assets upon his default was accepted if the debt was certain. All over the Continent, it became common that creditors were entitled to seizure before proceedings when they demonstrated that the debtor had signed or agreed on a debt (Verheul & Wade, 1992, p. 378). For such pre-judgment seizures, authorization from municipal administrators was often required. However, this was frequently a formality. Moreover, the increasingly widespread literacy among merchants made proof of debt easy. The plaintiff could substantiate his claim by submitting letters, books, or mercantile instruments such as bills obligatory.

As a result of all these developments, bankruptcy legislation came to concentrate more on pooling debtors' assets and on distributing their debts over many creditors. Because debt was more easily enforceable against a defaulter's estate, the problem of concurring claims had to be addressed. Late-medieval debt enforcement proceedings had commonly been devised for individual recovery only. The first municipal laws to break with this principle by imposing summons of all a defaulter's creditors were Italian (e.g., Amalfi 1274, Florence 1322) (Santarelli, 1998, p. 93). North of the Alps, this approach only slowly gained ground. In many regions of fourteenth- and fifteenth-century France, and also in the Low Countries of that time, it was still generally held that even when proceedings were collective, the first seizing claimant was given priority over those non-privileged creditors who laid attachment on the debtor's assets at a later stage (Brissaud, 1972; De ruysscher, 2008, p. 310). Early Northwest European examples of collective proceedings, in which proceeds of auctions among creditors were ratably distributed, existed in Hanseatic towns from the end of the thirteenth century in case the debtor had fled or died (Dalhuisen, 1968, p. 16; Fischer, 2013, p. 175). In Northwest Europe, such proceedings became more generalized in the three centuries that came after 1300. In 1510, the Parisian *coutume* provided that this 'first come, first serve' rule did not apply in case of *déconfiture*. *Déconfiture* consisted of a shortage of funds that was attested when more than one creditor sued for debt (Levinthal, 1918, p. 245). In the 1510s and 1520s, collective proceedings were imposed in Antwerp (1516), Freiburg im Breisgau (1520), and Augsburg (first mention in 1529) (De ruysscher, 2008; Fischer, 2013, pp. 176–177).

In the periods mentioned, these developments were happening within the jurisdictions of fairs and commercial towns in response to merchants' needs. The legislative actions of magistrates were also supported by a reception of views propagated within academic legal doctrine, which built further upon the solutions of Roman law. Some economic historians have claimed that bankruptcies might have been a new phenomenon in the fifteenth century, which became endemic in the second half of the sixteenth century (Safley, 2013, p. 3; Schulte-Beerbühl, 2016, p. 13). A full consideration of institutional configurations and mercantile practices, however, allows for the conclusion that collective insolvency proceedings were mainly due to incremental administrative innovation rather than economic developments.

Although this area has not been explored, it is quite likely that general collateral regimes meant that firm owners and general managers had to keep track of their loans and had to resort to retrenchment activities more often than before. Of course, partnership contracts were of limited duration, and they purported to assign liability to a few merchants only. Yet the new approach of addressing a defaulter's estate in an expedient fashion added to the dangers that these partnerships faced. Not only assets but also funds and claims could easily be seized upon default, which could hamper reputation and endanger the financial reliability of the firm. An earlier practice of renewing debts could continue, but now it hinged on the contacts with creditors and no longer on a lack of institutions supporting enforcement. There are several examples of bankruptcies that were caused by general economic and political conditions, but which were initiated through seizures laid by creditors. In the early sixteenth century in the commercial metropolis of Antwerp, this practice proved a common beginning to insolvency proceedings (De ruysscher, 2013, pp. 189–191).

2.3   Toward Voluntary Bankruptcy Proceedings (Early Modern Period)

Until the end of the Middle Ages, bankruptcies initiated by creditors (hence 'involuntary bankruptcy') were the most common. As mentioned earlier, debtors did not have much to look forward to when making their default public. Yet from the fifteenth century onward, in continental Europe, voluntary, collective, and outside-liquidation insolvency proceedings that involved a debtor applying for debt relief were slowly developed along three different tracks. One such approach, initially, unfolded in late-medieval Italy and encompassed a focus on post-bankruptcy negotiations in which decisions as to postponements and reductions were based on the insights of creditors. A second track, at first exceptionally pursued, both in Italy and Northwest Europe, involved the active mediation of authorities in seeking to draw up schemes of arrangement among creditors. A third line originated in government-granted temporary stays following petitions by debtors, which were common both south and north of the Alps. It was only in the eighteenth century that these three strands were more commonly blended together. In England, however, developments were different. In the early 1700s, bankruptcy proceedings were linked to a discharge of unpaid remainders of debt granted by the creditors. The concept of discharge remained largely unknown in continental Europe. Insolvency proceedings in early modern England remained mainly involuntary as well.

In the late Middle Ages, the aforementioned conception of insolvency as criminal behavior precluded a context in which continuity of business was preferred over liquidation. In most thirteenth-century Italian city-states, the denunciation of a defaulter as bankrupt was generally made by one or more creditors. It usually consisted of a declaration of the debtor's abscondence. From the late fourteenth century onward, municipal administrators of Italian cities reluctantly began to acknowledge debtor-creditor agreements (sometimes labeled *concordato*), which could be drawn up after the start of collective bankruptcy proceedings and the debtor's dispossession (Rocco, 1902, pp. 36–40). Fled defaulters could return and offer cooperation in inventorying their estate in exchange for extensions or reductions. It came to be acknowledged that in doing so debtors avoided criminal prosecution, were reinvested in their ownership rights, and protected from creditors' actions. The purpose of a *concordato*, then, was to grant a contractual moratorium (Rocco, 1902, p. 37).

In spite of the acknowledgment of post-bankruptcy deals, the legal configurations and mercantile practices in late-medieval Italy did not favor business rescue. A one-track approach toward insolvency in laws remained typical. Schemes of arrangement were drafted only following a declaration of bankruptcy. Many Italian municipal ordinances of the late Middle Ages provided that the debtor's flight or (publicly announced) insolvency was the first requirement to reach lawful debt adjustment or extension agreements. Moreover, negotiations could suspend collective expropriation proceedings and halt the public sale of the debtor's estate, but when they failed, liquidation was the only outcome. Creditors were summoned and involved in a collective proceeding that could easily switch from negotiations to a public sale when the legal conditions were not met (Rocco, 1902, p. 46; Santarelli, 1998, p. 103, pp. 106–107).

Such a change was not an unlikely scenario. Municipal laws commonly stipulated unwieldy majority requirements. They provided that creditors representing a quorum of claims had to agree in order to impose the contents of the agreement on dissenting and absent creditors. Such rules marked exceptions to the general principle, upheld in legal scholarship of the era, that no one could be bound under a contract who had not been present at its drafting. The majority requirements were necessary for ensuring that a contractually negotiated stay on claims and threats was effective. Non-consenting creditors had to be blocked out in order to avoid their actions jeopardizing the moratorium. As a result of the derogation from principles of contract law, in fifteenth- and sixteenth-century legal academic writings of municipal laws regarding imposed debt arrangements, in particular those encompassing reductions, were received only reluctantly (Dalhuisen, 1968, pp. 19–24; Migliorino, 1998, pp. 131–138, pp. 164–194; Santarelli, 1998, p. 104).

Majority requirements as established in Italian city ordinances of the fifteenth and sixteenth centuries were often strict, thus marking a high bar for achieving a legally enforceable agreement. In Genoa, for example, for involuntary bankruptcies, a majority rate of seven-eighths (in claims) applied (Rocco, 1902, pp. 41–42, n. 21). Other impediments made late-medieval Italian debt schemes on bankruptcy a flawed measure for rescuing a business. Legislative provisions limited the duration of such arrangements (Rocco, 1902, p. 43), and short periods of time were imposed during which they had to be negotiated (Rocco, 1902, p. 40). Most municipal laws concerning insolvency allowed for the full resuscitation of creditors' rights upon the slightest breach of the agreement (Rocco, 1902, p. 44). Moreover, the moratorium features of debt schemes implied that the debtor was still held to repay his creditors when he came to acquire new means, even in cases where they had conceded reductions (Rocco, 1902, p. 45).

In spite of a general administrative approach that did not promote lasting continuity of insolvents' business activities, there were exceptions as well. One of them was Venice, where the government's administrators actively sought to craft debtor-creditor agreements. Already in 1395, the Venetian Great Council had provided that absconded debtors who returned and deposited their account books and a survey of their property were exempted from criminal prosecution. When cooperating, they were deemed of good intent. Within a certain period of time, protection against debt enforcement served to initiate negotiations with the creditors. Their consent was required for any debt adjustment scheme, but municipal officials mediated in order to assure that a deal was struck. In most cases, this practice resulted in arrangements that were accepted by all creditors (Ressel, 2016, p. 123; Santarelli, 1998, pp. 105–106, pp. 107–108). However, the normal start of this proceeding remained denunciation of flight, as elsewhere in late-medieval Italy. Voluntary debt negotiation proceedings that were started outside of bankruptcy were very rare (Rocco, 1902, pp. 45–46).

Because legal scholarly texts had a European-wide readership, ordinances allowing for a 'cram-down' of post-bankruptcy negotiated deals on unwilling creditors appeared relatively late outside of Italy. In Nuremburg, majority compositions of this kind were held lawful for the first time in 1564; Augsburg copied the arrangement in 1574 (Birnbaum, 2014, pp. 50–53; Dalhuisen, 1968, p. 21, n. 99). In Antwerp, majority debt schemes were acknowledged only in 1608, long after that city's heyday. Frankfurt followed suit in 1611. The 1673 French *Ordonnance sur le commerce* labeled majority arrangements as lawful provided they were supported by creditors representing three-quarters of claims (Dupouy, 1960, pp. 153–154). Furthermore, academic doctrine provided another obstacle for proceedings of composition, which concerned the position of creditors with pledges and hypothecs. According to Roman law, compositions involving reductions could be rejected by secured creditors (Dalhuisen, 1968, p. 11, p. 24, p. 27). As a result, imposing majority debt schemes on dissenting secured creditors had proved the exception in most Italian city-states (Rocco, 1902, p. 43). It remained a conundrum into the sixteenth and seventeenth centuries as well. The 1673 French *Ordonnance sur le commerce*, for example, provided that creditors with hypothecs could not be affected if they did not consent to a plan for debt relief (Dupouy, 1960, p. 154).

In early modern England, debt adjustment agreements were discouraged. In the sixteenth and early seventeenth centuries, the Privy Council still mediated among creditors following petitions for delays or reductions. In addition, in those periods, the High Court of Chancery handed out bills of conformity, binding the minority of dissenting creditors to comply with a scheme accepted by the majority. Yet by the 1640s, these measures were abolished and compositions were discarded (Dalhuisen, 1968, p. 32; Treiman, 1938, pp. 511–521). Therefore, the differences between continental Europe and England with regard to debt adjustment agreements upon insolvency are striking. In seventeenth- and eighteenth-century France, for example, it was relatively easy for a debtor to invite creditors to negotiate on postponement of payment, even outside bankruptcy proceedings (Sgard, 2013). By contrast, in England, negotiations on debtor-creditor arrangements were easily categorized as 'acts of bankruptcy.' Such acts triggered the start of a liquidation proceeding that was for a large part organized by the creditors (Jones, 1979, p. 25). This convention meant that the only insolvency proceeding in English law for a long time was liquidation. In the English approach, collective proceedings initiated by creditors were considered the only option for safeguarding the interests of all creditors. As a result, according to English law for most of the seventeenth century, a moratorium did not exist; only upon the start of insolvency proceedings did an automatic stay apply, but it was exclusively devised so as to maintain the debtor's estate and thus protect the interests of the creditors. All the while, the debtor was not left in possession of his effects (Sgard, 2013).

In many early modern jurisdictions on the Continent, municipal administrators, princely courts, and other administrations had powers to grant protection from seizure and arrest. Their injunction orders were most commonly intended to impose a cooling down period, during which negotiations on reductions or extensions were begun. Some Italian cities of the late Middle Ages had well-known remedies of this kind (*salvocondotto, inducia*) (Santarelli, 1998, p. 106). In the sixteenth and seventeenth centuries, these approaches spread across larger areas. A government-imposed moratorium to allow for negotiations on compositions was opted for in the 1603 Hamburg *Stadtrecht* as well as in the 1643 insolvency ordinance of the city of Amsterdam. In some regions, the stay was more or less automatic. In that case, creditors were not invited to support a debt scheme, but at the same time, they could only contest the validity of the applicant's statements. Particularly in France, this practice seems to have been the case. The disparate jurisdictions in matters of insolvency offered French merchant debtors several options. They could apply for *Lettres de Répit* and other comparable measures, which stipulated a period of protection. These letters had to be registered with civil courts, which were required to audit the debtor's statements. In practice, however, this supervision was minimal. Petitions for letters more or less imposed a moratorium on the creditors, who could not easily contest their contents (Deshusses, 2008, pp. 28–30; Dupouy, 1960, pp. 138–145; Sgard, 2013, p. 227). *Lettres de répit* and the like (e.g., *lettres de saufconduite*) were commonly granted in the Low Countries as well by provincial princely courts. Yet in contrast to France, and at least since the late 1520s, they were considered mere remedies, meant to initiate negotiations. The princely injunctions did not extend so far as to impose delays upon and reductions to the creditors (De ruysscher, 2016, pp. 83–86). Even so, all the mentioned instruments did allow for pressure to the advantage of debtors; they constituted a stick for incentivizing creditors to accept or negotiate debt relief. The voluntary nature of these measures, which were requested by debtors, meant that the defaulter stayed out of liquidation proceedings. Yet again, the widely held principle that all creditors had to consent to agreements meant that enforcing the initiation of talks was not a guarantee of success (e.g., De ruysscher, 2016, pp. 90–93).

For most of the sixteenth century, in many cities and regions on the European continent, other acknowledged voluntary proceedings concerned the debtor's surrender of his entire estate to his creditors. This practice was generally called *cession*, after the arrangement of *cessio bonorum* from Roman law. This proceeding was generally adopted earlier than a compulsory negotiations regime directed at compositions. Although *cession* was not intended to grant the debtor a fresh start, its procedural characteristics often marked the patterns for voluntary negotiation proceedings outside bankruptcy that came after. *Cession* entailed the forfeiture of all assets in exchange for liberation from prison. *Cession* was commonly defamatory: the act of ceding one's property in order to be liberated from prison was public, and rituals and ceremonies were organized in order to destroy the applicant's reputation (Whitman, 1996, pp. 1871–1883). With the reception of Roman law, which in continental Northwest Europe became stronger over the course of the 1400s, came a transformation of this earlier practice. *Cession* came to offer temporary protection against seizure and arrest instead. Additionally, typical for the Romanized *cession* was that debts were not discharged. If the transferred assets were not sufficient to compensate all debts, then creditors could pursue their debtor for the remainder afterward. Even though they had to give the debtor time, the latter had to swear an oath that he had not hidden assets from his creditors and pledge to repay debts when he later acquired sufficient funds to do so (Pakter, 1988, pp. 495–496). An important building block of negotiation proceedings that were implemented after *cession* concerned the voluntary nature of the arrangement. The permeation of Roman law meant that proposals of forfeitures could not be refused by the creditors (Zambrana Moral, 2001, pp. 81–84, pp. 146–147). Because it was often considered too easy a way out, some commercial cities did not allow *cessions*: they were not applied in Bruges and Genoa, for example (Birnbaum, 2014, p. 32; De ruysscher, 2015b).

Voluntary bankruptcy proceedings focusing on negotiation among all creditors developed from these beginnings. An important turn was the growing awareness that insolvency did not equal fraudulent behavior in all cases. The latter had been a general paradigm in the High Middle Ages (c.1000–c.1250), subsumed in the maxim '*decoctor ergo fraudator.*' In this period, flight, recourse to sanctuary, or the subtracting of assets were considered the events that launched insolvency proceedings. From the fourteenth century onward, Italian municipal governments incrementally started using the criterion of insolvency. Absent debtors were indicted to appear before the town's authorities. If they responded, they were deemed insolvent and not *fugitivus*. This categorization allowed for their exemption from criminal prosecution. Moreover, city laws provided that those who 'stopped' payments were subjected to insolvency proceedings (Santarelli, 1998, pp. 71–74). In practice, all these conditions marked a (modest) incentive for debtors to return and negotiate with creditors.

In continental Europe north of the Alps, starting from the later fifteenth century onward, the ideas regarding bona fide and treacherous bankrupts slowly trickled down into the legal systems. For most of the fifteenth century, insolvency legislation of commercial cities in those regions only stipulated public auctions of a bankrupt's effects, and laws did not generally distinguish between unfortunate insolvents and criminal bankrupts. In the course of the sixteenth century, this situation changed. Beginning in the 1510s in the Low Countries, princely authorities started to impose, as requirement for princely injunctions, that the debtor had acknowledged the interests of all creditors and had not plotted his insolvency (De ruysscher, 2016, pp. 83–84). In the Holy Roman Empire, the 1548 *Reichspolizeiordnung* provided for strict punishments of 'bankrupts,' meaning fraudulent insolvents, which incited municipal lawmakers to adjust their rules. In 1564, the Augsburg 1447 *Gantordnung* and the Nuremberg *Reformation* of 1479 were replaced with *Faillitenordnungen*, based on insolvency as the criterion (Fischer, 2013, p. 179). In many areas, this approach changed an earlier idea of equaling 'impending flight' or 'fear of flight' with factual abscondence (Spann, 2004, pp. 183–184). Benvenuto Stracca's treatise *De conturbatoribus sive decoctoribus*, which was published in 1553, contributed to a growing awareness: this author distinguished between accidental insolvents and those that had become insolvent due to their own actions (De ruysscher, 2008, pp. 319–320).

In some areas, petitions for princely moratoriums were transformed into voluntary collective negotiation proceedings. The three aforementioned strands were in that case blended together in a proceeding outside bankruptcy in which local administrators engaged in pressuring dissenting creditors into accepting a composition. Such was the case in Antwerp, for example. From the later 1520s onward, every petition for a measure from princely courts and councils was sent over to the municipal administrators. They appointed commissioners who invited the creditors and, as had been the case in late-medieval Venice and in the sixteenth-century English Privy Council, they attempted to seek an agreement among all of them. When a deal on debt adjustment was made, which was often the case, it was confirmed by the court or council that had transferred the case (De ruysscher, 2016, pp. 86–93).

The Antwerp and Venice examples were followed elsewhere only later. In Hamburg, government-directed negotiations upon a debtor's petition emerged in the eighteenth century. In 1753, the Hamburg *Faillitenordnung* provided that an innocent insolvent had to be granted the option of reaching an agreement on debt adjustment. According to the law, majority rules applied, but in practice, the municipal commissioners supervising the negotiations actively brokered consensus among all creditors (Misler & Misler, 1781, p. 3, pp. 30–31). It was also deemed possible that three-quarters of creditors allowed the debtor to remain in possession of his estate during the proceedings (Misler & Misler, 1781, p. 20). Comparable approaches were imposed in Amsterdam in 1777 in a new insolvency ordinance. The insolvent was granted a temporary stay in order to negotiate with his creditors.

The ordinance provided explicitly that the commissioners of the Insolvency Chamber, which was the subordinate municipal court competent for bankruptcy litigation, had to persuade minority creditors to accept negotiated deals (Roestoff, 2005, p. 83). It was also in the eighteenth century that secured creditors, with the exception of owners, were more frequently required to support debt schemes. The Hamburg 1753 law stipulated that secured creditors were to receive a higher percentage from compositions than unsecured creditors. A distinction was made between prior and recently secured creditors as well (Misler & Misler, 1781, pp. 25–27). As a result of this pooling of secured and unsecured debt, pre-packaged deals became feasible. Negotiations could then take place before any government intervention (Misler & Misler, 1781, p. 31).

In the tradition on the Continent, discharge had been uncommon before the middle of the eighteenth century. When in late-medieval Italy a *concordato* was drafted, acquittals lasting beyond the contractual moratorium were not usual. The voluntary forfeiture of assets by imprisoned debtors (*cessio bonorum*) also failed to bring about a fresh start. In England, however, at the beginning of the eighteenth century, discharge became important. Because bankruptcy proceedings had always been oriented toward the auctioning of the debtor's assets, this discharge came after the public sale. It was conceived of as a method of ensuring cooperation from the debtor in guaranteeing a modest rehabilitation. Continuity of his business was thus not intended. In 1706, a royal statute provided that bona fide debtors were discharged for the parts of their debt that had not been compensated with the proceeds from their auctioned effects. In 1707, however, a new statute stated that this discharge could only be granted by the creditors, at a high majority rate (four-fifths in claims and persons) (Kadens, 2010, pp. 1262–1270). Probably following the English model, continental municipal laws started providing for majority discharges as well. The aforementioned 1753 Hamburg law stated that an unfortunate insolvent who transferred his properties to his creditors, and who signed a composition for repayment of a certain portion of the remaining debts, was considered discharged for the remainder (Misler & Misler, 1781, pp. 50–52).

2.4   Corporate Rescue: A Further Perfection of Preventive Compositions, Two-Track Proceedings, Administration and Government Control (Nineteenth to Twenty-First Century)

In spite of the development of voluntary collective proceedings that were centered on creditor-debtor negotiations between the sixteenth and eighteenth centuries, by the beginning of the nineteenth century, a true rescue culture was still lacking in Europe. The aim of preserving distressed companies as going concerns developed in interactions between England, continental Europe, and the United States. It came together with further legal acknowledgment of preventive composition proceedings and with a mounting entrenchment of company capital in the form of legal personhood. Furthermore, throughout Europe, but foremost on the Continent, the role of governments and judges had grown more considerable. Increased legislative efforts to impose accountability upon firms meant that official authority to detect indebtedness and to prevent insolvencies increased. However, throughout the nineteenth and twentieth centuries, as was the case in the centuries before, path dependence and hesitance regarding the best methods for safeguarding the balance of interests meant that solutions remained different across regions. This is still the case today, notwithstanding attempts toward harmonization (in the EU, for example) (Madaus, 2015).

On the European continent, the age of codifications brought about a relapse into older models of insolvency laws. In particular, the Napoleonic *Code de commerce* of 1807 marked a break with the practices and laws of Old Regime France. Preventive and pre-pack compositions were replaced with court-controlled majority arrangements on bankruptcy. These compositions (*concordats*) could entail debt adjustment and extensions. However, the debtor was not rehabilitated until the full repayment of his debts. Proceedings were involuntary and the *Code* imposed imprisonment or confinement of the insolvent during the course of the proceedings. A one-track approach was imposed. Liquidation was the default proceeding; it was the only outcome of bankruptcy proceedings if negotiations failed or if the required majority of consenting creditors (three-fourths in claims and persons) was not achieved. Secured creditors were not required to comply. Moreover, the *Code de commerce* did not consider the interests of maintaining a business as a going concern. The duties of court-appointed trustees were mainly to preserve the assets for the public sale (Szramkiewicz & Descamps, 2013, pp. 384–394). The *Code de commerce* was introduced across wide areas of continental Europe, and for many European countries, it determined insolvency policies well into the second half of the nineteenth century. The Belgian law of 1851, the Prussian *Konkursordnung* of 1855, and the Italian commercial code of 1865 were all heavily influenced by the French code.

In England, preventive compositions were slowly reintegrated into official insolvency proceedings after their demise in the seventeenth century. In 1793, majority compositions concerning the aftermath of the liquidation were officially allowed. Preventive debt arrangements for merchants were considered lawful after 1849. The Bankruptcy Law Consolidation Act of that year provided that debtors could initiate bankruptcy proceedings and avoid liquidation if three-fifths of the creditors (in persons and claims) agreed on extensions, a partial sale, or reductions (Dalhuisen, 1968, p. 33). However, the one-gateway approach still prevailed, which put the applicant in jeopardy of losing his business if the requirements for a composition were not met. The new Bankruptcy Acts of 1861 and 1869 allowed for compositions but, again, they were dependent on creditors' votes and thus factually were initiated only following the formal declaration of the debtor's bankruptcy (Dalhuisen, 1968, pp. 33–34).

It was only near the end of the nineteenth century that two-gateway approaches emerged. The 1883 Belgian law was the first nineteenth-century law to allow for preventive majority compositions outside bankruptcy (*concordat préventif*). It remained possible to turn such a proceeding into bankruptcy proceedings, but formally the two were separate. For a *concordat préventif*, it was sufficient that the debtor was 'unfortunate,' and it was not required that he had 'stopped payments' (*cessation de paiements*), which triggered the bankruptcy proceedings. However, the approaches of the *Code de commerce* still loomed in the background, as was evident in high majority requirements (two-thirds of claims), the exclusion of secured creditors, and a relatively easy switch to bankruptcy proceedings (Dalhuisen, 1968, pp. 50–53; Dunscombe, 1893, pp. 128–132). In 1883, in addition, England started promoting pre-packaged majority compositions ('deeds of arrangement'). Other countries maintained preventive compositions within the framework of bankruptcy proceedings (Germany, *Reichskonkursordnung* 1877, Italy 1903), or offered compositions as a possible outcome of liquidation proceedings outside bankruptcy (France 1889) (Hautcœur & di Martino, 2013). As a result, over large areas, and even in spite of the aforementioned innovative Belgian and English reforms, liquidation was still a normal outcome of insolvency proceedings. Near the end of the nineteenth century, everywhere in, Europe majority requirements remained high and secured creditors were not obliged to conform to the wishes of creditors having unsecured debts.

The approach of considering a business as a going concern was rooted in the English practice of deeds of arrangements. These extrajudicial agreements involved all creditors or—after 1883—a majority, which could leave the debtor in possession of his effects in combination with discharge. In the French commercial code, a *concordat* had been devised as a means to grant temporary relief to the debtor. As had been the case in the Italian tradition, a *concordat* was not considered an instrument to allow the debtor to be rehabilitated. Only upon full repayment of his debts could the debtor deploy new commercial activities and be reintegrated in the market. The English concept of discharge—which had gained some acceptance in eighteenth-century continental Europe as well, but disappeared afterward—marked the veritable start of a paradigm of business rescue. As was mentioned, in the early eighteenth century, discharge had been crafted as a compensation for liquidation. Over the course of the nineteenth century, however, when compositions left the debtor in possession of his estate, contractually agreed definitive reductions marked a veritable basis for business rescue.

The effects of these legal changes on management strategies have not often been analyzed. One can presume that the context of corporate finance was a major factor for how owners and managers dealt with financial distress, even with several available options for maintaining the firm's activities. When ownership of companies was dispersed, an exit forced by creditors was a likely scenario. This situation is what happened near the end of the nineteenth century in the United States. Railroad companies were not often wound up but, rather, continued to exist even in the face of financial difficulties. The management of the company set up a public sale of parts of the firm and distributed the proceeds to bondholders who agreed with the operation. Shareholders and dissenting creditors were given small portions on their debts (Skeel, 2001, pp. 48–70). This practice of *receivership* had a corollary in England, where one creditor (typically a financial institution) could expropriate a firm when he had been granted a 'floating charge.' Therefore, insolvency could result in the lender taking over the firm. Even before floating charge became accepted in the third quarter of the nineteenth century, 'deeds of inspectorship' allowed English creditors to supersede the managers-owners of firms (Duffy, 1985, pp. 336–340; Hoppit, 1987, p. 29).

A context of family firms with majority block owners—which remained more common in France than in the United States, for example—also prevented legal approaches that kept a lender perspective from being fully embraced. The early twentieth-century divorce of ownership from control, which took place above all in the United States, meant that managers could easily be replaced, within or outside a context of insolvency (Morck, 2005). Differences among countries explain why administration proceedings, which involve the sale or reorganization of the firm by an administrator, working under court control but with wide discretion, have only very recently been introduced in continental Europe (e.g., Germany 1999). The typical solution on the Continent is for a trustee to act as agent of the court rather than as an independent administrator (Westbrook, 2010, pp. 135–136).

Over the course of the twentieth century, even in continental Europe, the replacement of managers was made possible because of the combined separation of ownership from control along with the development of legal personhood for firms. The early nineteenth-century codifications had devised the corporation with shareholders as the only legal entity among a number of company types. This designation changed in the second half of the nineteenth century. Government control over corporations was reduced (the preliminary authorization was abolished in France in 1867, in Belgium in 1873). Legal personhood was extended to other company types as well (e.g., limited partnerships). Even though more research is needed in this regard, these developments most probably facilitated a conception of firms as pools of assets rather than personal ventures, and they may have incited or facilitated administration proceedings and repositioning strategies.

Until the last decades of the twentieth century, the threshold for obtaining a formal rescue arrangement was often so high that official proceedings equaled liquidation. Under the influence of American legislation (Chandler Act of 1938, Bankruptcy Act of 1978), continental European countries slowly started reducing majority requirements. The inclusion of secured creditors, rules on fresh money ('superpriorities'), and division of stakeholders into classes were American elements that trickled down into European bankruptcy reforms. The Belgian reform of 1997 and the German

Insolvenzordnung (1999) included secured creditors in majority compositions, for example. A German reform of 2012 allowed for priority for fresh loans. In a concurring development—which is still ongoing, and again following on from the American example—judges were given powers to 'cram-down' viable reorganization schemes on classes of stakeholders in which the required majority was not reached (e.g., Germany 1999, Spain 2014). This new approach blended in with an older European tradition of temporary government-imposed stays upon simple request of the debtor (*salvocondotto, répit*). In the second half of the twentieth century, especially France but also Spain had gone far in enforcing the powers of courts to preserve businesses with the debtor being left in possession (Dalhuisen, 1968, pp. 62–65). This approach is still evident in proceedings before bankruptcy, combining a temporary court-ordered stay with mediation with creditors or preparation of negotiations on composition (e.g., the French *sauvegarde*) (Madaus, 2015).

Since the late nineteenth century, furthermore, governments have obliged companies to submit financial reports, and their contents were used over the course of the twentieth century in insolvency proceedings. Already in the late 1800s, laws commonly provided recourse to shareholder meetings when the company capital dropped under critical levels. Nowadays, many European countries require that courts are informed when companies face financial difficulties. The competence of courts to declare debtors bankrupt *ex officio*, even when no request has been made, has been acknowledged by law in continental European countries since the early nineteenth century (*Code de commerce* of 1807) (Bariatti & van Galen, 2014, p. 29). Today it serves as a means to screen financial reports in order to detect indebtedness and to prevent the untimely initiation of insolvency proceedings (e.g., Belgium since 1997).

References

Bariatti, S., & Van Galen, R. (2014). *Study on the new approach to business failure and insolvency: Comparative legal analysis of the member states' relevant provisions and practices*. European Commission Report.

Birnbaum, S. (2014). *Konkursrecht der frühen Augsburger Neuzeit mit seinen gemeinrechtlichen Einflüssen*. Berlin: Hopf.

Brissaud, J. (1972). *Le créancier 'premier saississant' dans l'ancien droit français*. Paris: Presses universitaires de France.

Claustre, J. (2007). *Dans les geôles du roi. L'emprisonnement pour dettes à Paris à la fin du Moyen Âge*. Paris: Publications de la Sorbonne.

Cohen, J. (1982). The history of imprisonment for debt and its relation to the development of discharge in bankruptcy. *The Journal of Legal History*, 3, 153–171.

Dalhuisen, J. H. (1968). *Compositions in bankruptcy: A comparative study of the laws of the E.E.C. countries, England and the U.S.A.* Leiden: Sijthoff.

De Blécourt, A. S., & Fischer, H. F. W. D. (1950). *Kort begrip van het oud-vaderlands burgerlijk recht*. Groningen: Wolters.

De Roover, R. (1966). *The rise and decline of the Medici bank, 1397–1494.* New York: Norton.

De ruysscher, D. (2008). Designing the limits of creditworthiness. Insolvency in Antwerp bankruptcy legislation and practice (16th–17th centuries). *The Legal History Review (Tijdschrift voor Rechtsgeschiedenis), 76,* 307–327.

De ruysscher, D. (2013). Bankruptcy, insolvency and debt collection among merchants in Antwerp (c1490 to c1540). In Th. M. Safley (Ed.), *The history of bankruptcy: Economic, social and cultural implications in early modern Europe* (pp. 185–199). London: Routledge.

De ruysscher, D. (2015a). A business trust for partnerships? Early conceptions of company-related assets in legal literature, and Antwerp forensic and commercial practice (later sixteenth-early seventeenth century). In B. Van Hofstraeten & W. Decock (Eds.), *Companies and company law in late-medieval and early modern Europe* (pp. 9–27). Leuven: Peeters.

De ruysscher, D. (2015b). *Debt recovery and debt adjustment: Assessing institutional change in Antwerp (ca. 1490-ca. 1560)* (Working Paper No. 2015–3). Retrieved from http://www.vub.ac.be/CORE/wp.

De ruysscher, D. (2016). The struggle for voluntary bankruptcy and debt adjustment in Antwerp (c. 1520–c. 1550). In A. Cordes & M. Schulte-Beerbühl (Eds.), *Dealing with economic failures: Extrajudicial and judicial conflict regulations* (pp. 77–95). Frankfurt: Peter Lang.

Deshusses, F. (2008). Mesurer l'insolvabilité? Usages statistiques des dossiers de faillite. *Histoire & Mesure, 23*(1), 19–41.

Duffy, I. P. (1985). *Bankrupty and insolvency in London during the industrial revolution.* New York: Garland.

Dunscombe, S. W. (1893). *Bankruptcy: A study in comparative legislation.* New York: Columbia College.

Dupouy, C. L. (1960). *Le droit des faillites en France avant le Code de commerce.* Paris: Librairie générale de droit et de jurisprudence.

Edwards, J., & Ogilvie, S. (2012). What lessons for economic development can we draw from the Champagne fairs? *Explorations in Economic History, 49,* 131–148.

Ehrenberg, R. (1896). *Das Zeitalter der Fugger. Geldkapital und Creditverkehr im sixteen. Jahrhundert* (2 Vols). Jena: Fischer.

Fischer, P. (2013). Bankruptcy in early modern German territories. In Th. M. Safley (Ed.), *The history of bankruptcy: Economic, social and cultural implications in early modern Europe* (pp. 173–184). London: Routledge.

Godding, P. H. (1987). *Le droit privé dans les Pays-Bas méridionaux 12e-18e siècles.* Brussels: Royal Academy.

Goldthwaite, R. A. (2009). *The economy of Renaissance Florence.* Baltimore: John Hopkins University Press.

Häberlein, M. (1998). *Brüder, freunde und betrüger. Soziale Beziehungen, Normen und konflikte in der Augsburger Kaufmannschaft um die mitte des sixteen. jahrhunderts.* Berlin: Akademie Verlag.

Häberlein, M. (2012). *The Fugger of Augsburg: Pursuing wealth and honor in Renaissance Germany.* Charlottesville, VA: University of Virginia Press.

Hansmann, H., Kraakman, R., & Squire, R. (2006). Law and the rise of the firm. *Harvard Law Review, 119,* 1333–1403.

Hautcœur, P. C., & Di Martino, P. (2013). The functioning of bankruptcy law and practices in European perspective (ca.1880–1913). *Enterprise & Society, 14*(3), 579–605.

Hoppit, J. (1987). *Risk and failure in English business, 1700–1800.* Cambridge: CUP.

Jones, W. S. (1979). *The foundation of English bankruptcy: Statutes and commissions in the early modern period.* Transactions of the American Philosophical Society, *69*(3), 1–63.

Kadens, E. (2010). The last bankrupt hanged: Capital punishment for bankruptcy in 18th century England. *Duke Law Journal, 59,* 1229–1319.

Levinthal, L. (1918). The early history of bankruptcy law. *University of Pennsylvania Law Review, 66,* 223–250.

Lopez, R. S. (1976). *The commercial revolution of the middle ages, 950–1350.* Cambridge: CUP.

Madaus, S. (2015, June 10). Vorinsolvenzliche sanierungsverfahren—Perspektiven einer europäisch geprägten Rechtsentwicklung. *Kölner Schriften zum Wirtschaftsrecht,* 183–190.

Mehr, R. (2008). *Societas und universitas. Römischrechtliche institute im unternehmensgesellschaftsrecht vor 1800.* Cologne: Böhlau.

Migliorino, F. (1998). *Mysteria concursus. Itinerari premoderni del diritto commerciale.* Milan: Giuffrè.

Misler, J. N., & Misler, J. G. (1781). *Essai sur le droit de Hambourg touchant les faillites.* Geneva: Froullé.

Morck, R. K. (Ed.). (2005). *A history of corporate governance around the world: Family business groups to professional managers.* Chicago: The University of Chicago Press.

North, M. (1996). Von den warenmessen zu den wechselmessen. Grundlagen des europäischen zahlungsverkehr in spätmittelalter und früher neuzeit. In P. Johanek (Ed.), *Europäische messen und märktesysteme im mittelalter und neuzeit* (pp. 223–238). Cologne: Böhlau.

Pakter, W. (1988). The origins of bankruptcy in medieval canon and Roman law. In P. Linehan (Ed.), *Proceedings of the seventh international congress of medieval canon law* (pp. 485–506). Vatican City: Bibliotheca Apostolica Vaticana.

Planitz, H. (1913). Studien zur Geschichte des deutschen Arrestprozesses. *Zeitschrift der Savigny-Stiftung für Rechtsgeschichte / Germanistische Abteilung, 34,* 49–140.

Postan, M. M. (1973). Partnership in medieval English commerce. In *Medieval trade and finance* (pp. 65–91). Cambridge: CUP.

Ressel, M. (2016). Norms and practice of handling complex and international insolvencies in early modern Venice. In A. Cordes & M. Schulte-Beerbühl (Eds.), *Dealing with economic failures: Extrajudicial and judicial conflict regulations* (pp. 115–138). Online: H-Net.

Rocco, A. (1902). *Il concordato nel fallimento e prima del fallimento. Trattato teorico-pratico.* Turin: Bocca.

Roestoff, M. (2004–05). Skuldverligtingsmaatreëls vir individue in die Suid-Afrikaanse Insolvensiereg: 'n historiese ondersoek. *Fundamina, 10,* 113–136 and *11,* 78–111.

Safley, Th. M. (2013). Introduction. In Th. M. Safley (Ed.), *The history of bankruptcy: Economic, social and cultural implications in early modern Europe* (pp. 1–16). London: Routledge.

Santarelli, U. (1998). *Mercanti e società tra mercanti*. Turin: Giappichelli.

Schulte-Beerbühl, M. (2016). Introduction. In A. Cordes & M. Schulte-Beerbühl (Eds.), *Dealing with economic failures: Extrajudicial and judicial conflict regulations* (pp. 9–25). Frankfurt: Peter Lang.

Sgard, J. (2013). Bankruptcy, fresh start and debt renegotiation in England and France (seventeenth to eighteenth centuries). In Th. M. Safley (Ed.), *The history of bankruptcy: Economic, social and cultural implications in early modern Europe* (pp. 223–235). London: Routledge.

Skeel, D. A. (2001). *Debt's dominion: A history of bankruptcy law in America*. Princeton: Princeton University Press.

Spann, M. (2004). *Der Haftungszugriff auf den Schuldner zwischen Personal- und Vermögensvollstreckung. Eine exemplarische Untersuchung der geschichtlichen Rechtsquellen ausgehend vom Römischen Recht bis ins twenty-one. Jh. unter besonderer Berücksichtigung bayerischer Quellen*. Münster: Lit.

Szramkiewicz, R., & Descamps, O. (2013). *Histoire du droit des affaires*. Paris: LGDJ.

Treiman, I. (1938). Majority control in compositions: Its historical origins and development. *Virginia Law Review*, 24, 507–527.

Verheul, J. J., & Wade, J. P. (1992). Prejudgment attachment of movables in French, Dutch and English law. *Netherlands International Law Review*, 39, 377–390.

Westbrook, J. L. (Ed.). (2010). *A global view of business insolvency systems*. Leiden: Martinus Nijhoff.

Whitman, J. Q. (1996). The moral menace of Roman law and the making of commerce: Some Dutch evidence. *Yale Law Review*, *105*, 1841–1889.

Zambrana Moral, P. (2001). *Derecho concursal histórico I. Trabajos de investigación*. Barcelona: Cometa

Zimmermann, R. (1996). *The law of obligations: Roman foundations of the civilian tradition*. Oxford: OUP.

Part II

Business Failure

3 Some Causes of Organizational Decline

William McKinley

3.1 Introduction

Since Whetten's (1980a) call for a research program on organizational decline, a considerable body of academic work has accumulated on this topic. Most of this research has focused on the consequences of organizational decline rather than its causes. For example, one stream of literature (e.g., Cullen, Anderson, & Baker, 1986; Ford, 1980; Freeman & Hannan, 1975; McKinley, 1992) has examined the effects of organizational decline on organizational structure. A major issue in this research is whether organizational decline reverses the increase in structural complexity and formalization that typically takes place during organizational growth (Blau, 1970; Cullen et al., 1986). Whereas intuition would lead one to answer 'yes,' researchers have identified asymmetries in the magnitude (Freeman & Hannan, 1975; Hannan & Freeman, 1978) and direction (Cullen et al., 1986) of structural change during organizational decline. In the former case, structural complexity and formalization decrease during decline, but at a slower rate than they expand during growth. In the latter case, these structural variables, as well as the size of the administrative component, actually increase during organizational decline. This counterintuitive asymmetry may be due to control needs that arise during decline such as the need to discover new product niches or the need to administer a bureaucratic apparatus to conduct layoffs (McKinley, 1992).

A second important topic in the literature dealing with the consequences of organizational decline is the effect of decline on innovation. Staw, Sandelands, and Dutton (1981) argued that threat in organizations reduces managerial information processing and leads to centralization of decision making and an emphasis on conserving resources. The result of these changes is organizational rigidity. Because rigidity is an obstacle to innovation, and organizational decline is likely to constitute a threat for managers, the implication of Staw et al.'s (1981) framework is that decline will inhibit innovation. Considerable evidence for this position has accumulated from empirical research on declining organizations (see, for example, Bozeman & Slusher, 1979; Cameron, 1983; Cameron, Whetten, & Kim, 1987; Whetten, 1981).

On the other hand, prospect theory (Kahneman & Tversky, 1979) suggests that decision makers operating in the domain of losses will be risk-seeking, and this perspective provides the foundation for an alternate view on the effect of organizational decline on innovation. If decline involves losses for an organization, managers may become more risk-seeking after an episode of organizational decline in an effort to recoup those losses. If risk-seeking is conducive to innovation, organizational decline will encourage innovation. Evidence that supports a positive decline-innovation link is also present in the literature (e.g., Bowman, 1980, 1982, 1984; McKinley, 1984; Wiseman & Bromiley, 1996).

These two contrasting positions have been termed the 'necessity is the mother of rigidity' position and the 'necessity is the mother of invention' position (McKinley, 1993; McKinley, Latham, & Braun, 2014). Efforts have been made to reconcile these two perspectives by specifying the contingency variables that determine whether organizational decline will be a stimulus or an inhibitor of innovation (McKinley et al., 2014; Mone, McKinley, & Barker, 1998). To date, this effort has yielded some interesting theoretical insights, but no definitive empirical test.

By comparison with the consequences of organizational decline, much less attention has been devoted to its causes. The purpose of this chapter is to rectify this imbalance by identifying several important causal drivers of organizational decline. Some of these causes have been discussed previously in the organizational decline literature (see, for example, Greenhalgh, 1983; Miles & Cameron, 1982), but there has been no effort, to my knowledge, to incorporate them into an integrated theory. This chapter makes a start at developing such a theory.

I begin by reviewing the various conceptualizations of organizational decline that have appeared in the literature and then provide a definition of organizational decline for use in this chapter. Next, I turn my attention to three external causes of organizational decline: competition, technological change, and regulatory shifts. Whereas these causes certainly do not exhaust all the external drivers of organizational decline, I consider them among the most important. Next I focus on two internal causes of organizational decline: organizational rigidity (Staw et al., 1981) and inflexible innovation (McKinley et al., 2014). I describe the effects of each of the five variables on organizational decline and specify the conditions under which these effects are expected to be strongest. Finally, I draw on the literature on self-serving attributions (Bettman & Weitz, 1983; Salancik & Meindl, 1984; Staw, McKechnie, & Puffer, 1983) to discuss 'native' theories of organizational decline—theories developed by non-scholarly parties. Work on the self-serving attribution suggests that executives will formulate native theories of decline that are biased toward external causes. Other observers, such as Wall Street security analysts and business news reporters, will be more likely to invoke internal causes to explain the same phenomenon. Thus the composition of a native theory depends on who originates it and particularly on whether or not that person has responsibility for organizational performance outcomes. And depending on whose native theory becomes dominant in public discourse about a particular case of decline, the public will have different views of that decline episode.

Because an important objective of this chapter is building testable theory, I state propositions to capture the causal relationships discussed. In order to encourage empirical testing of these propositions, I also describe the data required to assess them and the operationalization of the relevant constructs. My hope is that empirical research designed to test these propositions will stimulate a body of work that clarifies the ways in which organizational decline is initiated and propagated. In this way, I seek to begin moving the decline literature beyond its limited focus on consequences. This is important for scholarly understanding, but it also has potential value for practitioners, because they cannot avoid organizational decline unless they understand its causes. I also wish to clarify how the cognitive biases of managers, and their need to save face, can lead to native theories about decline that highlight external causes and downplay internal ones. Understanding how this managerial sense making (Weick, 1995) works, and can influence the schemas of constituents, leads to interesting insights about the formation of popular wisdom about organizational decline.

3.2 The Phenomenon of Organizational Decline

Organizational decline has been conceptualized in a variety of ways in the literature, and these conceptualizations form a rough historical sequence. Early in the development of the literature, decline was conceived as a life-cycle stage, drawing on the popularity of the life-cycle model of organizational change (Cameron, Kim & Whetten, 1987; Kimberly & Miles, 1980; Whetten, 1980b). In the organizational life-cycle model, decline was considered a predictable event that all organizations pass through, although the timing of this stage could differ for different organizations. Champions of the life-cycle model were implicitly adopting the metaphor of old age and decline in the human life cycle to guide their theorizing. Whether this metaphor is applicable to change in organizations has been the subject of some controversy (see, for example, Cameron et al, 1987), and it is not clear whether all organizations inevitably experience organizational decline.

In the mid-1980s, Zammuto and Cameron (1982, 1985) introduced a second approach for conceptualizing decline. They argued that decline was best defined at the environmental level of analysis and developed a four-cell model of environmental decline, in which different types of decline resulted from different kinds of change in an organization's environmental niche. According to Zammuto and Cameron (1985), niches can change in size (level of demand) or shape (nature of demand), and this change can be either continuous (predictable) or discontinuous (unpredictable). Continuous decline in the size of an organization's environmental niche is termed erosion, whereas discontinuous decline in niche size is labeled contraction. Continuous decline in niche shape is called dissolution, whereas discontinuous decline in niche shape is termed collapse. Zammuto and Cameron (1985) predicted different managerial behaviors and organizational responses for each of these four types of environmental decline. These responses ranged from reactive to proactive and also involved different kinds of change in the organization's domain.

In the late 1980s, Weitzel and Jonsson (1989) introduced yet another conceptualization of organizational decline, returning to the idea of stages that was the distinguishing feature of the life-cycle model. Weitzel and Jonsson (1989) maintained that decline begins long before its symptoms are manifest in financial difficulties—in fact, the first stage of decline occurs when managers become blinded to problems that can threaten the effectiveness of the organization. Subsequent stages of decline include inaction, faulty action, crisis, and dissolution. Weitzel and Jonsson's (1989) model was not deterministic in the sense that the life-cycle models were, because at each stage of decline, management has a chance to reverse the decline through prompt action, correct action, or effective reorganization. In other words, Weitzel and Jonsson's framework envisioned the possibility of organizational turnaround, connecting the organizational decline literature with the burgeoning stream of research on turnaround (Barker & Mone, 1994; Bibeault, 1982; Hambrick & Schecter, 1983; Robbins & Pearce, 1992; Trahms, Ndofor, & Sirmon, 2013).

Contemporary conceptualizations of organizational decline have moved away from the idea of stages and typically define decline as an organization-level episode in which there is a decrease in the resource base of an organization. Such episodes are not necessarily inevitable, may be interspersed with periods of growth, and may occur repeatedly over the life history of an organization. For example, Cameron et al. (1987, p. 224) defined organizational decline as "a condition in which a substantial, absolute decrease in an organization's resource base occurs over a specified period of time." McKinley et al. (2014, p. 90) refined this definition by stating that organizational decline is "a successive year-after-year decrease in an organization's resource base that lasts for at least two years." The latter definition is the one I will follow in this chapter, although I make no claim that this definition is the only possible one.

Note that the latter-day conceptualizations of organizational decline distinguish decline from downsizing, a phenomenon that has become increasingly common in corporations and public-sector organizations (Cameron, Freeman, & Mishra, 1991; McKinley, Sanchez, & Schick, 1995; McKinley, Zhao, & Rust, 2000). Today, organizational decline is understood as an involuntary decrease in resources that happens to an organization, whereas downsizing is a voluntary, planned workforce reduction program (Freeman & Cameron, 1993). Organizational downsizing may be a consequence of organizational decline, but today many downsizing programs occur even when the financial condition of an organization is robust.

3.3   External Causes of Organizational Decline

3.3.1   *Competition*

In considering external causes of organizational decline, I first focus on competition. Whereas competition has been an important construct in strategic management (e.g., Porter, 1980, 1985), it has been less salient in organization theory. However, one important organization theory paradigm that has explicitly modeled the effects of competition on organizations is the population ecology paradigm. In their density dependence theory, Hannan and Carroll (1992) argued that increasing population density increases the level of competition, which in turn results in higher organizational death rates and lower birth rates. Hannan and Carroll (1992; see also Hannan & Freeman, 1977) conceived of competition as a rivalry for resources that does not necessarily involve direct interaction between competitors. Because competition increases the difficulty of acquiring and keeping resources, Hannan and Carroll's (1992) theory is consistent with the position that competition can trigger organizational decline. However, as a population-level framework, the theory expresses the results of competition as an abstract 'rate,' rather than an outcome at the organizational level of analysis.

Porter (1980, 1985) also discussed the competitive forces that restrict firm profitability in an industry and described the ways that firms can cope with these forces to gain a sustainable, competitive advantage. Porter (1980, 1985) identified three generic strategies used by firms to position themselves in an industry. Porter (1991) also developed the concept of the value chain and emphasized that specific activities along this chain are the underlying sources of a firm's competitive advantage.

In this chapter, I adopt Hannan and Carroll's (1992) definition of competition as a rivalry for resources that does not necessarily involve direct interaction between rivals. I argue that competition can cause decline in a focal firm in at least two ways. First, if competing firms offer customers of a focal firm a better value proposition (the same product at a cheaper price or a product that is differentiated in some unique value-adding manner), the focal firm will experience customer defection. Over time, this defection will lead to a decline in revenues. Second, if the focal organization recognizes the competitive moves of its rivals, it may be forced into spending money to combat them by enhancing its own value proposition. This can be done by increasing the efficiency of production, which results in lower per-unit costs and permits lower pricing, or by initiating product differentiation that attracts customers. If the costs of these efforts are not compensated by higher revenues, an episode of decline in profitability will be initiated. Either way, competition is a potent causal variable that can trigger organizational decline, although its effect will vary with the strength of customer ties to the focal organization.

An excellent example of the role of competition in the decline of organizations is the case of the online retailer Amazon. By creating a value proposition that challenged that of brick-and-mortar bookstores, Amazon caused declines in the customer bases of many of these stores. Amazon offered more convenience to book buyers, and in many cases lower prices, so customers defected to Amazon. This reduced the revenues of the brick-and-mortar bookstore chains and helps explain the decline and eventual death of chains such as Borders. Initially, it was believed that customers would not buy books unless they were able to look them over before purchase, but Amazon found ways to replicate the experience of leafing through a book at a bookstore with its 'Look Inside' feature. Amazon has now expanded into the retailing of many other products besides books, but its value proposition remains the same: convenience at an equal or lower price. Whereas brick-and-mortar stores such as Barnes & Noble, Walmart, and many others have started their own online divisions, Amazon is further down the experience curve (Amit, 1986; Day & Montgomery, 1983) than these competitors. It is difficult to know how much impact Amazon has had in any particular case of organizational decline, but it seems clear that the decline of many retail chains is at least partly attributable to competition from Amazon.

Whereas the case of Amazon makes the role played by competition in organizational decline more concrete, it was noted earlier that the effects of competition on decline will vary depending on how closely customers are tied to a focal organization. In particular, if customers have high switching costs (Klemperer, 1987), a compelling value proposition from a competitor may not be enough to make them abandon the focal organization. Switching costs are the costs customers incur by moving from one rival's product to another, and they have been classified into transaction costs, learning costs, and costs imposed by organizational strategy (Klemperer, 1987). For example, customers may experience transaction costs while changing their checking accounts from one bank to a rival. Airlines intentionally create switching costs for customers by the use of frequent-flyer programs, which have become an important part of their competitive strategies. To the extent that an organization is protected by customer switching costs, the ability of competitors to attract its customers with a better value proposition will be restricted. In contrast, organizations unprotected by switching costs (like many brick-and-mortar bookstores) will be more likely to experience customer defection as a result of the competitive moves of their rivals. This logic can be summarized as an empirically testable proposition:

Proposition 1: The fewer the switching costs experienced by customers of a focal organization, the greater the probability that competition will trigger decline in that organization.

3.3.2 Technological Change

The second external cause of organizational decline that I analyze in this chapter is technological change. Whereas many theories of technological change have been developed in economics and management studies (e.g., Chandler, 1977; Marx, 1904; Schumpeter, 1934), one of the most useful for my purposes is the framework presented by Tushman and Anderson (1986; see also Anderson & Tushman, 1990). These authors argued that technological change evolves through periods of incremental innovation that are interrupted by major technological discontinuities. A technological discontinuity is a product or process innovation that results in a dramatic performance and/or quality improvement (Anderson & Tushman, 1990; Tushman & Anderson, 1986). An example of a technological discontinuity is the development of integrated circuits for computers, or the invention of automatic machinery for plate and container glass production, which replaced human glass blowers (Anderson & Tushman, 1990; Tushman & Anderson, 1986). According to Tushman and Anderson, technological discontinuities can be classified as either competence enhancing or competence destroying. The former build on the existing competences of established firms in an industry, whereas the latter (such as quartz watches or integrated circuits) make the competences of incumbent firms obsolete.

Based on studies of the airline, plate glass, container glass, cement, and minicomputer industries, Tushman and Anderson (1986; see also Anderson & Tushman, 1990) concluded that technological discontinuities are followed by an 'era of ferment' in which competing product or process designs vie for supremacy. This period is marked by high customer uncertainty and intense rivalry between firms promoting alternative designs. In most cases, a dominant design eventually emerges that accounts for a majority of the sales in the industry. Examples of dominant designs include the DC3 aircraft and the IBM personal computer (Anderson & Tushman, 1990). Dominant designs are not necessarily the best-performing product or process configuration in the industry, as Anderson and Tushman (1990) emphasize. Instead, dominant designs often lag the technical frontier in an industry, suggesting that their emergence is not entirely a matter of technical rationality, but also reflects social and political forces.

Because a dominant design cannot be known in advance (Tushman & Anderson, 1986), firms choosing to invest in a particular product or process configuration in an era of ferment are taking a considerable risk. If the configuration they are championing does not turn out to be the dominant design, they stand to lose customers and experience a decline in their revenues. These dynamics are illustrated by the early automobile industry, in which a rivalry between competing engine designs followed the technological discontinuity represented by the first introduction of automobiles to the market. Automobiles were produced with engines powered by steam, batteries, and gasoline (Anderson & Tushman, 1990). It took some time before a dominant design emerged in the form of the internal combustion engine fueled by gasoline. Firms manufacturing cars with other engine designs lost customers once the internal combustion design had become established and eventually declined to the point of extinction.

One puzzle raised by this account is why firms promoting rival designs do not just switch to the dominant design once market preferences become clear and the dominant design begins to emerge. Why, for example, did not firms manufacturing automobiles with steam or battery-powered engines simply start producing cars with internal combustion engines once this engine design evolved into the industry standard? If rival power-plant designs championed by competing firms had closely resembled the internal combustion engine in product architecture (Henderson & Clark, 1990), this might have been possible. But to the extent that competing power-plant designs used a different product architecture, with different components that were configured in different ways, a transition to the internal combustion design would be more difficult. New design and production competences would need to be acquired, and relations with new suppliers would have to be formed. This takes time and effort, and may require considerable investment, so the capacity of a firm to adapt to a dominant design with different components and a different architecture is limited. This increases the risk of decline as the firm struggles to conform to a product or process configuration that is foreign to it.

Generalizing from this example, I offer the following proposition about the role of technological change in triggering organizational decline:

> *Proposition 2: The more a given firm's product or process design diverges from the dominant design that is emerging during an era of ferment, the greater the probability that that firm will experience organizational decline.*

3.3.3   Regulatory Change

I now consider regulatory shifts as a third external cause of organizational decline. Whereas regulation has been an important topic in law and economics (e.g., Christainsen & Haveman, 1981; Pegrum, 1949; Shapiro, 2003), it has not been a major focus of attention in organization theory (for an exception, see Sanchez & McKinley, 1995). I define 'regulation' as any set of rules originating with legislatures or government agencies that are designed to control the production, marketing, or internal operations of business organizations. Regulations are as diverse as the legislatures and agencies that generate them, and they include rules governing the safety of workers; the development, testing, and production of pharmaceutical products; the disposal of industrial waste; and many other business activities.

Here I argue that regulatory shifts, like competition, can cause organizational decline in two distinct ways. First, changes in regulation can restrict the domain in which a firm's product or services can be used. By 'domain,' I mean either geographical locations, demographic segments of a population, or temporal domains (as in the regulation of hours in which alcohol can be served in a bar). If a change in regulation narrows any of these dimensions of a firm's domain, the firm can be expected to lose customers and experience declines in its resource base. The firm may respond by finding new markets in which the use of its product or service is not limited (Miles & Cameron, 1982), but this effort is not always successful.

Perhaps the most obvious recent example of the role that regulation-mandated domain restriction has played in organizational decline is the tobacco industry (Miles & Cameron, 1982). In the past four decades, an increasingly restrictive set of regulations has evolved governing the physical locations in which smoking of tobacco products can occur. Smoking tobacco is now restricted in the United States and many European countries to outdoor spaces and the smoker's personal living space. Tobacco consumption is also limited to certain demographic groups, in particular those classified as adults. New regulations governing the packaging of tobacco require graphic warnings about the health effects of the product, and these regulations are intended to further limit the market for tobacco. All these regulatory changes have been an important cause of the steady decline of smokers in industrialized countries (Miles & Cameron, 1982), and they have resulted in declines in revenues for the major tobacco firms. Although the tobacco firms have explored new markets in which regulations are not as strict (Miles & Cameron, 1982) and recently began selling substitute products such as e-cigarettes, these strategic initiatives have not compensated for the declines in their core customer base.

Regulatory change can also contribute to organizational decline by increasing the cost of doing business. If, for example, new regulations require improved safety equipment for workers, more elaborate reporting of financial transactions, or expanded audits of a company's accounts by external audit firms, the company must incur costs in order to comply with these regulations. These costs will restrict the cash flow of the business and narrow or perhaps even eliminate profit margins. This is a particular problem for small firms, which cannot amortize the costs of regulatory compliance over a large volume of business transactions. Unless the costs of regulatory compliance are offset by higher revenues, a firm can find itself in a difficult position. Based on the argument outlined in the earlier paragraphs, I offer a third proposition:

Proposition 3: Regulatory changes that restrict the domain in which a firm's product or service can be used, or that increase the firm's costs, will increase the probability of organizational decline.

3.4   Internal Causes of Organizational Decline

3.4.1   *Organizational Rigidity*

Moving on from the external causes discussed in the previous section, I now focus on two causes of organizational decline that are internal to the organization. The first of these is organizational rigidity. In presenting their theory of threat-rigidity (see earlier discussion), Staw et al. (1981) discussed the feedback effects of threat-induced rigidity on the future level of threat. Staw et al. (1981) argued that under conditions of incremental environmental change, rigidity might reduce the degree of future threat, but that under conditions of radical environmental change, the effects of rigidity would be the reverse. That is, rigidity would increase the future level of threat by inhibiting the adaptations that are necessary to avoid threat under radical environmental change. This suggests that in some circumstances, rigidity may be an important internal driver of organizational decline. Greenhalgh (1983) also emphasized the effects of rigidity on future organizational decline, and Marcus (1988) noted that rule-bound behavior in the responses of power plants to regulatory shifts perpetuated their declining performance.

Following McKinley et al. (2014), I define rigidity as an organization-wide condition in which routines previously selected by the organization are perpetuated and variation from those routines is suppressed. Under circumstances of market instability, such as those brought about by competition, technological discontinuities, or regulatory shifts, rigidity can inhibit changes to internal organization structure and processes that are necessary to respond to the instability and avoid organizational decline. For example, when competition threatens an organization, rigidity can prevent modifications in strategy and procedure that would allow the organization to create innovative switching costs or explore new domains that are less affected by rivalry. When a technological discontinuity sets an era of ferment in motion and gives rise to competing product or process designs, rigidity can interfere with the creation of environmental surveillance units and new engineering competences that would help organizations detect and adopt evolving dominant designs. And when regulatory shifts narrow the domain of an organization, rigidity can inhibit the domain defense, domain offense, and domain creation strategies that tobacco companies and other corporations have used to combat organizational decline (Miles & Cameron, 1982). In addition, rigidity is likely to limit an organization's 'absorptive capacity' (Cohen & Levinthal, 1990; Zahra & George, 2002), or ability to learn, and this can be an important internal driver of organizational decline when environments are unstable and learning is at a premium. Drawing on this logic, a fourth proposition can be stated:

> *Proposition 4: The greater the environmental instability, the more likely organizational rigidity will trigger organizational decline.*

3.4.2 Inflexible Innovation

In most organizational research, innovation is seen as a remedy for poor organizational performance. For example, a number of empirical researchers (e.g., Jimenez-Jimenez, Sanz Valle, & Hernandez-Espallardo, 2008; Rosenbusch, Brinckmann, & Bausch, 2011; Verhees & Meulenberg, 2004) have reported positive relationships between innovation and performance in a variety of firms of different sizes and nationalities. If innovation is successful at increasing performance, then innovation should be a means of reversing organizational decline, particularly if it allows the firm to tap new markets. Yet population ecology researchers have urged caution about the salutary effects of innovation and change on organizational performance. Hannan and Freeman (1984) argued that reorganization increases the risk of organizational death, and Barnett and Carroll (1995) noted that the process of change can be precarious, even when the outcome of change is beneficial. Barnett and Freeman (2001) showed that multiple product introductions increase the hazard of organizational death, suggesting that such innovation events may create disruptions that put an organization at risk. In summary, based on current organizational theory and research, there is considerable uncertainty about whether innovation increases or reduces organizational performance, and therefore whether it is a solution or a stimulus for organizational decline.

Here I argue that it depends on the nature of the innovation. In pursuing this argument, I draw on the distinction between flexible and inflexible innovations made by McKinley et al. (2014). These authors defined flexible innovations as new products or manufacturing processes that are easy to change after introduction to the market. Inflexible innovations, on the other hand, are new products or processes that are less easy to modify after market introduction. More precisely, in flexible innovations, there are a wide range of feasible post-introduction design configurations, and it is possible to move between those configurations rapidly. On the other hand, an inflexible innovation, while a novel departure from existing routines, has a narrow range of possible post-introduction configurations, and transition between those configurations is slow (McKinley et al., 2014). A good example of a flexible innovation is a new video game, because it is easy to change the game software after product introduction, introducing new characters and story lines rapidly. The multiple versions of the video game Grand Theft Auto bear witness to the post-introduction flexibility of this kind of innovation. In contrast, an example of an inflexible innovation would be a new software platform for managing a supply chain. Once the software has been adopted by customers, it is difficult to modify it quickly because of the complexity of supply chains and the interdependence between suppliers and buyers in such chains. If there are bugs in the platform or customers are unhappy with its performance, there is a limited range of feasible post-introduction changes, and introducing them is likely to be slow.

Because it is difficult to predict the exact nature of customer demand before the introduction of a new product, inflexible innovations can create problems for organizations, particularly in unstable markets. If the configuration of product attributes is not exactly what customers want, the difficulty of changing those attributes may trap the organization into a product configuration that does not generate adequate revenue to offset its costs. Lynn, Morone, and Paulson's (1996) studies of GE's introduction of CT scanners, Motorola's development of cell phones, and Corning's design of optical cables demonstrate the post-introduction tinkering that is often necessary to find a product configuration that adds value for customers. If an inflexible innovation binds the organization to a product architecture that is inconsistent with changing customer demand and revenues fall, escalating commitment to a failing course of action (Brockner, 1992; Staw, 1976) may compound the problem, making it even more difficult to change the product architecture. In extreme cases, executives may blame the customers for their intransigence in failing to embrace a clearly superior product, rather than modifying the product to fit customer demand. Based on this logic, we can offer a second proposition about internal causes of organizational decline:

Proposition 5: The greater the environmental instability, the more likely inflexible innovations will trigger organizational decline.

It should be noted that innovation inflexibility is not the same thing as organizational rigidity, because organizational rigidity is a condition that characterizes the entire organization, whereas innovation inflexibility is an attribute of a single product or process innovation.

3.5   Native Theories of Organizational Decline

Up to this point in the chapter, I have presented a scholarly theory of organizational decline, singling out some external and internal causes of decline. But scholars are not the only people who produce theories of decline—executives faced with the need to explain their organizations' decline episodes and non-scholarly observers charged with analyzing organizations (e.g., Wall Street security analysts) also do so. As a supplement to the scholarly theorizing offered earlier, it is interesting to examine the dynamics that influence the production of 'native' theories and to speculate about how they might differ depending on the person producing them. Native theories of decline are important because the general public is more exposed to them than to scholarly theories published in journals, and therefore they have more potential to influence public perceptions of decline.

Executives in charge of a declining organization will experience pressure to explain the decline to internal and external audiences, such as investors, customers, suppliers, and employees. These executives are not impartial observers, but individuals whose reputations and self-esteem are closely tied to the performance of their organizations. The literature on self-serving attributions (e.g., Bettman & Weitz, 1983; Salancik & Meindl, 1984; Staw, McKechnie, & Puffer, 1983) suggests that executives tend to attribute negative outcomes to external causes, and positive outcomes to internal causes. Assuming that a decline in an organization's resource base is seen by managers as a negative outcome, we can predict that they will have a bias toward explaining that outcome by reference to external causes. The native theories of decline articulated by executives, and distributed through such media as letters to shareholders, interviews, and speeches, are likely to highlight external causes and downplay internal ones. Internal causes will tend to be 'masked' in the accounts of decline presented by these executives.

In contrast, external, non-scholarly observers of declining organizations will not be prone to the self-serving attribution, because they are not expected to control organizational outcomes, and will have little need to save face by attributing decline to external causes. Their native theories of organizational decline will be more likely to emphasize internal causes. For example, instead of explaining an episode of decline by reference to external competition, an external observer, such as a security analyst or business news reporter, would more likely stress the combination of strong competition and internal rigidity. Whereas an executive might explain organizational decline through reference to technological discontinuities, an external observer would be more likely to argue that lack of engineering competence and the presence of internal rigidity made it difficult for the organization to adapt to the discontinuity. In sum, the native theories of managers of declining organizations will be biased toward external causes, whereas the native theories of external observers will be more likely to stress the interaction of external and internal causes. Executives, as the consummate insiders, will look outward to account for organizational decline, whereas outsiders will look inward to help account for the same phenomenon. This reasoning suggests the following proposition:

> *Proposition 6: The ratio of external to internal causes invoked in executives' accounts of their organizations' decline will be higher than the ratio of external to internal causes in observers' accounts of the same decline episodes.*

3.6   Testing the Propositions

In this section of the chapter, I discuss the data and measures that would be necessary to test each of the six propositions specified earlier. This discussion is intended to facilitate future empirical research based on the theory developed in this chapter.

In order to test Proposition 1, a researcher could select a random sample of corporations, each of which is subject to high levels of competition from rivals. The researcher could then measure the variance in customer switching costs across those organizations, with the expectation that those corporations with lower customer switching costs would be more likely to experience organizational decline. Competition could be measured by the density of rivals in a focal corporation's niche (Hannan & Carroll, 1992), or by the average number of competitive moves (e.g., advertising campaigns) introduced by those rivals in a given period of time. Switching costs could be operationalized through customer perceptions (Burnham, Freis, & Mahajan, 2003), or by more objective measures such as the average time required for a customer to change from one rival's product to another. Organizational growth/decline could be measured by the change in an organization's resource base over the two-year period after data on switching costs is gathered. A continuous variable could be used, ranging from high growth to high decline (McKinley, 1987). Given adequate controls for confounding factors, a significant negative relationship between customer switching costs and the level of organizational decline in these high-competition contexts would provide support for Proposition 1.

Testing Proposition 2 would require the researcher to evaluate the characteristics of competing product designs during an era of ferment and to assess the degree to which each product design diverges from the dominant design (or industry standard). Such research would be easiest to conduct retrospectively, after the dominant design is known, using secondary sources to evaluate product design attributes in past eras of ferment. Differences between each firm's product design and the dominant design could be assessed along multiple dimensions such as number of components and complexity of component configuration. A summary measure of divergence between each firm's product design and the dominant design could be computed, and a positive association between this index and the degree of organizational decline on the index described earlier would provide support for Proposition 2.

An assessment of Proposition 3 could be performed by randomly selecting a sample of organizations from different industries, each of which has recently been subject to a shift in regulation. The characteristics of the regulatory shift affecting each industry could be analyzed and each shift could be scored on the extent to which it restricts the product domain of the firms in the industry, as well as the extent to which it raises their operating costs. Each organization in the sample would be assigned the appropriate values for these variables, depending on its industry. Under controls for confounds, a positive relationship between these scores and the level of organizational decline would furnish support for Proposition 3.

Proposition 4 asserts that in unstable environments, organizational rigidity has a positive effect on the likelihood of organizational decline. In order to test this proposition, one would need a sample of organizations whose task environments vary in instability. To obtain such a sample, one could use the measure of environmental instability employed by Keats and Hitt (1988; see also Dess & Beard, 1984). Organizational rigidity could be operationalized by the restriction in information processing, constriction of control, and conservation of resources dimensions described by Staw et al. (1981). A cross-product term capturing the interaction between environmental instability and organizational rigidity could be computed, and the effects of that interaction on the level of organizational decline could be assessed. Analysis of interactions is best conducted through graphing (Cohen, Cohen, West, & Aiken, 2003; McKinley, 1987), and if graphs showed positive slopes for the rigidity-decline relationship under conditions of high environmental instability, the results would be consistent with Proposition 4.

In order to test Proposition 5, one could use the same sample employed in evaluating Proposition 4. Each firm could be examined to identify recent product or process innovations, and the flexibility of those innovations could be rated by using McKinley et al.'s (2014) two-dimensional scheme. If an innovation exhibited a wide range of possible post-introduction configurations and a rapid transition between them, it would qualify as flexible. On the other hand, if an innovation had a narrow range of possible post-introduction configurations and the transition between them required considerable time, the innovation would be rated as inflexible. A summary measure of flexibility/inflexibility could be computed for each firm by averaging across all its recent innovations, and the level of organizational decline could be regressed on a cross-product term between that index and the degree of environmental instability, controlling for confounding factors. The results could be graphed, and if they showed higher positive slopes for the innovation inflexibility-decline relationship under conditions of high environmental instability, there would be support for Proposition 5.

Proposition 6 is different from the others because it is concerned with native theories of organizational decline, rather than scholarly theories. This proposition is important because it provides a window into the different ways that various organizational constituencies explain organizational decline. The logic of Proposition 6 is that managers of declining organizations will be more likely to attribute decline to external causes than will external observers. To test this proposition, one could assemble reports about organizational decline originating with executives of the declining organizations such as those in letters to shareholders or executive speeches. One could compare the reports with accounts generated by external observers of the same organizations—e.g., Wall Street security analysts and business reporters. The causal attributions for decline in each document could be identified and then classified as to locus of causality (internal or external). Examples of such coding can be found in Bettman and Weitz (1983), Salancik and Meindl (1984), and Staw et al. (1983). The ratio of external to internal attributions could be computed for each document, and an average could be calculated for the documents produced by executives of a declining organization and the documents produced by external observers of that same organization. If the documents generated by executives showed a higher average ratio of external to internal attributions than the documents produced by observers, and this finding generalized across a number of declining organizations, Proposition 6 would be supported.

3.7   Discussion and Conclusion

The testing of the propositions contained this chapter could enhance our knowledge of the causes of organizational decline and also our understanding of how various constituencies attribute causality in their native theories of decline. In addition, such research could provide valuable insight about the factors that protect organizations from decline in competitive environments. The implications of the logic used to derive Proposition 1 is that switching costs are one such factor, providing a prophylactic against customer defection when rivals are enhancing their value propositions. Future research might focus on other 'decline prophylactics' that could shelter organizations from decline in competitive contexts. This kind of research would have important implications for practice, because it would suggest methods that executives could use to forestall decline in highly competitive environments.

Second, this chapter also draws attention to the importance of technological change as an instigator of organizational decline. Research stimulated by Proposition 2 could reveal the ways that product design characteristics, and their degree of conformity to an evolving dominant design, influence the chances that an organization will prosper or founder. The problem for managers is that a dominant design cannot be known in advance, so it is partly a matter of luck if a firm succeeds in originating or matching that design. However, firms sometimes pursue strategic initiatives to entrench their own product design as dominant (Anderson & Tushman, 1990), and this is an arena in which large firms are likely to have an advantage. A study of the techniques used by large corporations to establish their product configurations as dominant designs in an era of ferment, and thus force decline on their rivals, would be an interesting addition to the organizational decline literature.

Third, this chapter suggests that a research initiative directed at studying the effects of regulation on organizational decline would bear important fruit. Real-time studies could examine the manner in which **declining** organizations respond to regulation that limits their domains or increases their costs. Large organizations that are in a period of decline may use their power and political clout to forestall or roll back such regulations, through techniques such as lobbying and political campaign contributions. The example of tobacco companies' domain defense strategies (Miles & Cameron, 1982) provides an illustration of how decline-inducing regulation can be forestalled, delayed, or watered down. Large corporations are not generally passive in the face of regulatory threat, and organizational decline researchers could benefit from studying how corporations actively attempt to manipulate regulation in order to reduce its capacity to induce their organizations' decline.

Fourth, the logic behind Propositions 4 and 5 suggests that factors internal to the organization are sometimes as important as external competition, technological change, or regulation in explaining organizational decline. In fact, these factors, particularly the degree of organizational rigidity, compound the effects of external variables by inhibiting adaptation to them. For example, high organizational rigidity reduces the likelihood that organizations will find innovative switching costs to buffer themselves from competition, or put in place surveillance mechanisms that can enhance the detection of a dominant design as it evolves. In other words, there is an interaction between internal and external causes that increases the probability of decline, while magnifying the complexity of the organizational decline phenomenon. Future organizational research based on the propositions in this chapter might 'unpack' this complexity to a greater extent than has been done thus far.

Fifth, this chapter's theorizing on native theories of organizational decline suggests that explanations of organizational decline may vary markedly depending on who is doing the explaining. Organizational decline theories articulated by scholars may be interesting, but they are unlikely to have much influence on the general public, because the general public is not exposed to the academic journals in which such theories appear. Theories articulated by non-scholarly observers of decline or by executives of declining organizations are likely to be much more influential, because the public can more easily gain access to them through shareholder reports, business news articles, television news, and so on. Thus influential native theories of decline can lead to self-fulfilling prophecies (Edwards, McKinley, & Moon, 2002; Merton, 1948) in which predictions of decline lead customers of an organization to avoid its products, or suppliers to tighten credit terms, and therefore bring about the very decline that they fear. Further study of native theories of organizational decline, and the self-fulfilling effects they sometimes have on organizations, would add valuable knowledge about the dynamics through which decline is propagated.

In conclusion, this chapter has attempted to rectify the imbalance in current organizational decline literature between theories about the consequences of organizational decline and theories about its causes. Sometimes, of course, consequences can also be causes, as in the downward spiral scenarios described by McKinley et al. (2014). Nevertheless, I believe that at this juncture in the development of the decline literature, there is value in prioritizing research on exogenous causes of organizational decline. This chapter represents a step in this direction, but much additional work remains to be done.

References

Amit, R. (1986). Cost leadership strategy and experience curves. *Strategic Management Journal, 7*(3), 281–292.

Anderson, P., & Tushman, M. L. (1990). Technological discontinuities and dominant designs: A cyclical model of technological change. *Administrative Science Quarterly*, 35(4), 604–633.

Barker, V. L. III., & Mone, M. A. (1994). Retrenchment: Cause of turnaround or consequence of decline? *Strategic Management Journal*, 15(5), 395–405.

Barnett, W. P., & Carroll, G. R. (1995). Modeling internal organizational change. *Annual Review of Sociology*, 21, 217–236.

Barnett, W. P., & Freeman, J. (2001). Too much of a good thing? Product proliferation and organizational failure. *Organization Science*, 12(5), 539–558.

Bettman, J. R., & Weitz, B. A. (1983). Attributions in the board room: Causal reasoning in corporate annual reports. *Administrative Science Quarterly*, 28(2), 165–183.

Bibeault, D. B. (1982). *Corporate turnaround*. New York: McGraw-Hill.

Blau, P. M. (1970). A formal theory of differentiation in organizations. *American Sociological Review*, 35(2), 201–218.

Bowman, E. H. (1980). A risk/return paradox for strategic management. *Sloan Management Review*, 21(3), 17–31.

Bowman, E. H. (1982). Risk-seeking by troubled firms. *Sloan Management Review*, 23(4), 33–42.

Bowman, E. H. (1984). Content analysis of annual reports for corporate strategy and risk. *Interfaces*, 14(1), 61–71.

Bozeman, B., & Slusher, E. A. (1979). Scarcity and environmental stress in public organizations: A conjectural essay. *Administration and Society*, 11(3), 335–355.

Brockner, J. (1992). The escalation of commitment to a failing course of action: Toward theoretical progress. *Academy of Management Review*, 17(1), 39–61.

Burnham, T. A., Freis, J. K., & Mahajan, V. (2003). Consumer switching costs: A typology, antecedents, and consequences. *Journal of the Academy of Marketing Science*, 31(2), 109–126.

Cameron, K. S. (1983). Strategic responses to conditions of decline: Higher education and the private sector. *Journal of Higher Education*, 54(4), 359–380.

Cameron, K. S., Freeman, S. J., & Mishra, A. K. (1991). Best practices in white-collar downsizing: Managing contradictions. *Academy of Management Executive*, 5(3), 57–73.

Cameron, K. S., Kim, M. U., & Whetten, D. A. (1987). Organizational effects of decline and turbulence. *Administrative Science Quarterly*, 32(2), 222–240.

Cameron, K. S., Whetten, D. A., & Kim, M. U. (1987). Organizational dysfunctions of decline. *Academy of Management Journal*, 30(1), 126–138.

Chandler, A. D. (1977). *The visible hand: The managerial revolution in American business*. Cambridge, MA: Harvard University Press.

Christainsen, G. B., & Haveman, R. H. (1981). The contribution of environmental regulations to the slowdown of productivity growth. *Journal of Environmental Economics and Management*, 8(4), 381–390.

Cohen, J., Cohen, P., West, S. G., & Aiken, L. S. (2003). *Applied multiple regression/correlation analysis for the behavioral sciences*. Mahwah, NJ: Lawrence Erlbaum.

Cohen, W. M., & Levinthal, D. A. (1990). Absorptive capacity: A new perspective on learning and innovation. *Administrative Science Quarterly*, 35(1), 128–152.

Cullen, J. B., Anderson, K. S., & Baker, D. D. (1986). Blau's theory of structural differentiation revisited: A theory of structural change or scale? *Academy of Management Journal*, 29(2), 203–229.

Day, G. S., & Montgomery, D. B. (1983). Diagnosing the experience curve. *Journal of Marketing, 47*(2), 44–58.

Dess, G. G., & Beard, D. W. (1984). Dimensions of organizational task environments. *Administrative Science Quarterly, 29*(1), 52–73.

Edwards, J. C., McKinley, W., & Moon, G. (2002). The enactment of organizational decline: The self-fulfilling prophecy. *International Journal of Organizational Analysis, 10*(1), 55–75.

Ford, J. D. (1980). The occurrence of structural hysteresis in declining organizations. *Academy of Management Review, 5*(4), 589–598.

Freeman, J., & Hannan, M. T. (1975). Growth and decline processes in organizations. *American Sociological Review, 40*(2), 215–228.

Freeman, S. J., & Cameron, K. S. (1993). Organizational downsizing: A convergence and reorientation framework. *Organization Science, 4*(1), 10–29.

Greenhalgh, L. (1983). Organizational decline. In S. B. Bacharach (Ed.), *Research in the sociology of organizations* (Vol. 2, pp. 231–276). Greenwich, CT: JAI Press.

Hambrick, D. C., & Schecter, S. M. (1983). Turnaround strategies for mature industrial product businesses. *Academy of Management Journal, 26*(2), 231–248.

Hannan, M. T., & Carroll, G. R. (1992). *Dynamics of organizational populations: Density, legitimation, and competition.* New York: Oxford University Press.

Hannan, M. T., & Freeman, J. (1977). The population ecology of organizations. *American Journal of Sociology, 82*(5), 929–964.

Hannan, M. T., & Freeman, J. (1984). Structural inertia and organizational change. *American Sociological Review, 49*(2), 149–164.

Hannan, M. T., & Freeman, J. H. (1978). Internal politics of growth and decline. In M. W. Meyer & Associates (Eds.), *Environments and organizations* (pp. 177–199). San Francisco: Jossey-Bass.

Henderson, R. M., & Clark, K. B. (1990). Architectural innovation: The reconfiguration of existing product technologies and the failure of established firms. *Administrative Science Quarterly, 35*(1), 9–30.

Jimenez-Jimenez, D., Sanz Valle, R., & Hernandez-Espallardo, M. (2008). Fostering innovation: The role of market orientation and organizational learning. *European Journal of Innovation Management, 11*(3), 389–412.

Kahneman, D., & Tversky, A. (1979). Prospect theory: An analysis of decision under risk. *Econometrica, 47*(2), 263–292.

Keats, B. W., & Hitt, M. A. (1988). A causal model of linkages among environmental dimensions, macro organizational characteristics, and performance. *Academy of Management Journal, 31*(3), 570–598.

Kimberly, J. R., & Miles, R. H. (Eds.). (1980). *The organizational life cycle: Issues in the creation, transformation, and decline of organizations.* San Francisco: Jossey-Bass.

Klemperer, P. (1987). Markets with consumer switching costs. *The Quarterly Journal of Economics, 102*(2), 375–394.

Lynn, G. S., Morone, J. G., & Paulson, A. S. (1996). Marketing and discontinuous innovation: The probe and learn process. *California Management Review, 38*(3), 8–37.

Marcus, A. (1988). Responses to externally induced innovation: Their effects on organizational performance. *Strategic Management Journal, 9*(4), 387–402.

Marx, K. (1904). *A contribution to the critique of political economy.* Chicago: Charles H. Kerr.

McKinley, W. (1984). Organizational decline and innovation in manufacturing. In B. Bozeman, M. Crow & A. Link (Eds.), *Strategic management of industrial R&D* (pp. 147–159). Lexington, MA: Lexington Books.

McKinley, W. (1987). Complexity and administrative intensity: The case of declining organizations. *Administrative Science Quarterly, 32*(1), 87–105.

McKinley, W. (1992). Decreasing organizational size: To untangle or not to untangle. *Academy of Management Review, 17*(1), 112–123.

McKinley, W. (1993). Organizational decline and adaptation: Theoretical controversies. *Organization Science, 4*(1), 1–9.

McKinley, W., Latham, S., & Braun, M. (2014). Organizational decline and innovation: Turnarounds and downward spirals. *Academy of Management Review, 39*(1), 88–110.

McKinley, W., Sanchez, C. M., & Schick, A. G. (1995). Organizational downsizing: Constraining, cloning, learning. *Academy of Management Perspectives, 9*(3), 32–42.

McKinley, W., Zhao, J., & Rust, K. G. (2000). A sociocognitive interpretation of organizational downsizing. *Academy of Management Review, 25*(1), 227–243.

Merton, R. K. (1948). The self-fulfilling prophecy. *The Antioch Review, 8*(2), 193–210.

Miles, R. H., & Cameron, K. S. (1982). *Coffin nails and corporate strategies*. Englewood Cliffs, NJ: Prentice Hall.

Mone, M. A., McKinley, W., & Barker, V. L. III. (1998). Organizational decline and innovation: A contingency framework. *Academy of Management Review, 23*(1), 115–132.

Pegrum, D. F. (1949). *The regulation of industry*. New York: R.D. Irwin.

Porter, M. E. (1980). *Competitive strategy: Techniques for analyzing industries and competitors*. New York: The Free Press.

Porter, M. E. (1985). *Competitive advantage: Creating and sustaining superior performance*. New York: The Free Press.

Porter, M. E. (1991). Toward a dynamic theory of strategy. *Strategic Management Journal, 12*, 95–117.

Robbins, D. K., & Pearce, J. A., II. (1992). Turnaround: Retrenchment and recovery. *Strategic Management Journal, 13*(4), 287–309.

Rosenbusch, N., Brinckmann, J., & Bausch, A. (2011). Is innovation always beneficial? A meta-analysis of the relationship between innovation and performance in SMEs. *Journal of Business Venturing, 26*(4), 441–457.

Salancik, G. R., & Meindl, J. R. (1984). Corporate attributions as strategic illusions of management control. *Administrative Science Quarterly, 29*(2), 238–254.

Sanchez, C. M., & McKinley, W. (1995). The effect of product regulation on business global competitiveness: A contingency approach. *Management International Review, 35*(4), 293–305.

Schumpeter, J. A. (1934). *The theory of economic development*. Boston: Harvard University Press.

Shapiro, S. A. (2003). Outsourcing government regulation. *Duke Law Journal, 53*(2), 389–434.

Staw, B. M. (1976). Knee-deep in the Big Muddy: A study of escalating commitment to a chosen course of action. *Organizational Behavior and Human Performance, 16*(1), 27–44.

Staw, B. M., McKechnie, P. I., & Puffer, S. M. (1983). The justification of organizational performance. *Administrative Science Quarterly, 28*(4), 582–600.

Staw, B. M., Sandelands, L. E., & Dutton, J. E. (1981). Threat-rigidity effects in organizational behavior: A multilevel analysis. *Administrative Science Quarterly, 26*(4), 501–524.

Trahms, C. A., Ndofor, H. A., & Sirmon, D. G. (2013). Organizational decline and turnaround: A review and agenda for future research. *Journal of Management, 39*(5), 1277–1307.

Tushman, M. L., & Anderson, P. (1986). Technological discontinuities and organizational environments. *Administrative Science Quarterly, 31*(3), 439–465.

Verhees, F., & Meulenberg, M. T. (2004). Market orientation, innovativeness, product innovation, and performance in small firms. *Journal of Small Business Management, 42*(2), 134–154.

Weick, K. E. (1995). *Sensemaking in organizations*. Thousand Oaks, CA: Sage Publications.

Weitzel, W., & Jonsson, E. (1989). Decline in organizations: A literature integration and extension. *Administrative Science Quarterly, 34*(1), 91–109.

Whetten, D. A. (1980a). Organizational decline: A neglected topic in organizational science. *Academy of Management Review, 5*(4), 577–588.

Whetten, D. A. (1980b). Sources, responses, and effects of organizational decline. In J. R. Kimberly & R. H. Miles (Eds.), *The organizational life cycle: Issues in the creation, transformation, and decline of organizations* (pp. 342–374). San Francisco: Jossey-Bass.

Whetten, D. A. (1981). Organizational responses to scarcity: Exploring the obstacles to innovative approaches to retrenchment in education. *Educational Administration Quarterly, 17*(3), 80–97.

Wiseman, R. M., & Bromiley, P. (1996). Toward a model of risk in declining organizations: An empirical examination of risk, performance and decline. *Organization Science, 7*(5), 524–543.

Zahra, S. A., & George, G. (2002). Absorptive capacity: A review, reconceptualization, and extension. *Academy of Management Review, 27*(2), 185–203.

Zammuto, R. F., & Cameron, K. S. (1982). Environmental decline and organizational response. *Academy of Management Proceedings, 8*, 250–254.

Zammuto, R. F., & Cameron, K. S. (1985). Environmental decline and organizational response. In L. L. Cummings & B. M. Staw (Eds.), *Research in organizational behavior* (Vol. 7, pp. 223–262). Greenwich, CT: JAI Press.

4 Predicting Business Failure

Nico Dewaelheyns, Sofie De Prijcker, and Karen Van Den Heuvel

4.1 Introduction

Being able to make an objective assessment of a firm's probability of getting into distress and eventually failing is of great importance to a large number of economic agents. The best-known example is the case of a financial institution that needs to make a credit decision, but there are many potential applications outside of banking as well. For instance, suppliers will need failure assessments to decide which customers can safely receive trade credit; investors want to carefully trade off failure risk against the potential gains of investing in shares of distressed companies; in mergers and acquisition deals, firms and management consultants want to measure the financial health of the target company and of the new merged company after the deal in order to determine the maximum amount of leverage that can be used; in collective wage negotiations, trade unions need externally validated financial health measures to determine their bargaining strategy vis-à-vis firm management or sectoral organizations; government agencies can use failure probability scores in order to target subsidies at companies with an appropriate level of financial strength.

Because of its importance to this wide array of practitioners, it is not surprising that business failure or bankruptcy prediction is one the most extensively researched topics in the corporate finance and financial accounting literature. Although some earlier examples of academic studies and practical applications exist, the modern era of failure prediction is generally considered to have started in the 1960s, with relatively straightforward analyses of bankruptcy likelihood for small samples of stock exchange quoted companies in the United States. Ever since, researchers have attempted to improve the performance and the validity of prediction models in various ways. One important source of improvement has been the application of more sophisticated statistical methods, from univariate tests and discriminant analysis in the 1960s and 1970s, over logit and probit regressions in the 1980s and 1990s, to the more recent hazard models and artificial intelligence techniques. Moreover, a better understanding of the potential causes of distress and failure has led to the inclusion of many new predictors, ranging from more complex accounting ratios and market variables to macroeconomic and industry-related measures and non-financial information (e.g., company ownership or managerial characteristics). Finally, due to ever-better data availability, many studies have also widened the scope of prediction in terms of the type of companies that are studied (e.g., models for private companies or SMEs), in terms of geography (in both developed and emerging markets), and in terms of the definition of failure (i.e., not only formal bankruptcy but also reorganization procedures, voluntary liquidations, and company sales).

The continuous search for improvement has led to a vast and rich literature consisting of hundreds of published prediction studies. It goes without saying that this chapter can never hope to give a complete discussion of this body of work, which means that it should be read as a primer to the main insights and developments in the field and as a starting point in exploring the literature. We predominantly include studies that have been highly influential and papers published in high-quality business and economics journals. Our discussion is non-technical in nature, meaning that we focus on the intuition behind the different methodologies and approaches and refer to the original sources for the mathematical and statistical details.

The remainder of this chapter is organized as follows. First, we briefly introduce the foundational models that set the standard for most of the subsequent research. Next, we discuss a number of methodological improvements and the inclusion of additional predictor types, followed by an overview of studies that widen the scope of prediction. We conclude by identifying potential avenues for further research.

4.2   The Foundational Models

Bankruptcy prediction research dates back to the first half of the previous century. Initial studies were rather descriptive in nature and stressed the heterogeneity between failing and non-failing businesses in terms of their financial ratios. One of the breakthroughs in bankruptcy prediction research is the pioneering work of Beaver (1966), who was among the first to adopt a statistical approach. His univariate discriminant model served as an important tool to describe how financial ratios differ between failing and non-failing businesses. Additionally, in exploring the predictive value of thirty financial ratios, he showed that only a small minority (e.g., net income/total debt, cash flow/total assets, and cash flow/total debt) are well able to capture the likelihood of corporate bankruptcy. However, being aware of the limitations of a univariate approach, Beaver (1966) opened the call for more complex techniques such as multivariate discriminant analysis (MDA). As such, his research paved the way for one of the most well- known prediction measures, which is the Z-score, developed by Altman through an MDA approach and published in the *Journal of Finance* in 1968. This Z-score derives from a linear combination of five measures that reflect corporate performance in addition to the financial health of the balance sheet. The value of the Z-score lies in its high predictive ability, especially one year prior to failure, but also in its high practical and theoretical applicability. This explains why it became one of the most widely used predictors of corporate bankruptcy with over 1,700 academic citations today. Altman's Z-score also marked the beginning of a fruitful era of contributions using MDA as the standard approach to predict bankruptcy. Two notable examples in this research stream are Deakin (1972), who applied MDA to predict bankruptcy within a sample of listed companies and Edmister (1972), who focused on bankruptcy prediction of small businesses. Edmister (1972) also contributed to the development of MDA studies by integrating three years of accounting data rather than just one cross section of annual accounts. Finally, Altman, Haldeman, and Narayanan (1977) updated the initial Z-score model to develop a ZETA model, triggered by the increasing size of failing businesses and adjustments to the financial reporting standards. This ZETA-score outperforms the original Z-score model for up to five years prior to failure.

The use of MDA in bankruptcy prediction research is not without controversy, however. Eisenbeis (1977) and Ohlson (1980) highlighted the violation of assumptions of MDA (e.g., equal covariance matrices for failing and non-failing companies). Others questioned the intuitive interpretation of the results, because no benchmark score for failure versus going concern was provided. Finally, the selection of individual predictors in MDA is based on prior studies and driven by empirical and statistical considerations, because there is no theory indicating which variables are the best predictors (Altman et al., 1977; Balcaen & Ooghe, 2006). To overcome these issues, conditional probability models such as logit (LA) and probit models (PA) were introduced in the bankruptcy literature by Ohlson (1980) and Zmijewski (1984). Due to its low computational effort, LA became the most popular conditional probability model and has dominated the bankruptcy literature since the beginning of the 1980s (Balcaen & Ooghe, 2006). Nevertheless, there is a broad consensus that MDA and LA lead to comparable classification and prediction accuracy levels (Wilson & Sharda, 1994).

4.3   A Continuous Search for Improved Prediction Methods

Next to the methods discussed in the previous section, various techniques of artificial intelligence (AI) have been applied to the problem of failure prediction from the 1980s onward. It is a field of study that aims to develop computer systems that are capable of performing tasks that normally require human intelligence such as visual perception, language processing, and decision making. In contrast to traditional statistical methods, AI techniques do not require the a priori specification of a functional form or the adoption of restrictive assumptions with respect to the distribution of predictors

(Beynon & Peel, 2001). These advantages triggered academics to use AI techniques for the classification of failed versus non-failed firms, with the sole purpose of finding a method that outperforms existing techniques in terms of classification accuracy. The use of these models is thus not based on theoretical assumptions, but is highly application driven (Kirkos, 2012). For an overview of the most widely employed techniques, their main features, advantages, and drawbacks, we refer to Table 4.1.

In general, two types of AI bankruptcy studies can be distinguished—i.e., single classifier and hybrid classifier studies. Studies that adopt a single classification method aim to present an improved version of the technique and compare its performance with benchmark techniques such as MDA or LA. The most commonly applied techniques in these studies are neural networks (NN), followed by rough sets approaches (RSA) and case-based forecasting systems (CBFS). Whereas single classifier studies dominated the bankruptcy research in the 1990s, today, many studies propose hybrid classifiers that combine well-established AI techniques such as NN with, for example, evolutionary algorithms. As their overall performance is better than individual AI and statistical techniques, some academics believe that the integration of various methods should be the focus of future research (Kumar & Ravi, 2007).

Kirkos (2012), however, argues that future AI studies should not solely focus on performance advantages, but also address issues of model interpretation and knowledge extraction, which is so far highly understudied and has created a gap between academics and practitioners. Whereas NN models, for example, are very popular among academics because of their impressive accuracy rates, practitioners pay little attention to these models as they cannot readily interpret their output. Nevertheless, some AI methods such as RSA and recursively partitioned decision trees (RPDT) do offer a set of meaningful condition-action decision rules. The few studies that employ these user-friendly AI techniques, however, present very divergent results, hence there is still considerable room for improvements in this area (Kirkos, 2012).

Although AI methods have dominated a large part of the bankruptcy prediction research over the last twenty-five years, their lack of interpretability has renewed the interest in the more intuitive and user-friendly statistical models and resulted in updated and more sophisticated versions of existing models. Shumway (2001), for example, addresses the fact that the majority of statistical models only use one cross section of data, even though a firm's bankruptcy risk is not constant over time. He proposes a hazard model that incorporates time-varying covariates and finds that his model significantly outperforms cross-sectional methods, especially when both accounting and market-based data are used. With an extended data set, Chava and Jarrow (2004) confirm the superiority of Shumway's model over Altman's Z-score model and Zmijewski's probit specification. In addition, they show that the use of monthly time intervals significantly improves the model's forecasting

Table 4.1 Overview of Artificial Intelligence Techniques

Technology	Basic Idea	Advantages	Disadvantages	Seminal Studies
Expert systems (with inductive learning) (ES)	ES are computer systems that use both quantitative and qualitative information to emulate the decision-making process of a human expert. This process is often simulated by inductive learning techniques.	• user-friendly: the output is a set of condition-action rules • outperforms MDA	• acquisition of the expert's knowledge about the problem can be time and effort consuming • fit inferior to other AI techniques	Shaw and Gentry (1988), Messier and Hansen (1988)
Recursively partitioned decision trees (RPDT)	RPDT creates a binary classification tree by recursively splitting the sample based on the principle of minimizing the expected cost of misclassification errors.	• user-friendly: the output is a set of condition-action rules • outperforms MDA	• problems of overfitting. • requires a large amount of data	Frydman, Altman, and Kao (1985)
Neural networks (NN)	A NN model consists of a network in which a number of homogeneous processing units are interconnected. Each unit in the system functions as a computation device that applies mathematical functions to aggregate input signals from other units and to generate an output signal.	• very strong classification and forecasting performance • outperforms MDA, LA, CBFS	• requires a lot of training data and training cycles • difficulties when the number of predictors is large • problems of overfitting • the output is not readily interpretable • performance strongly depends on configuration choices	Odom and Sharda (1990), Tam (1991), Wilson and Sharda (1994), Jo and Han (1996)

Technique	Description	Advantages	Disadvantages	References
Support vector machines (SVM)	SVM perform a non-linear mapping of input vectors into a high-dimensional feature space. In this space, an optimal separating hyperplane is constructed that maximizes the distance from the hyperplane to the data points.	• excellent generalization ability, less susceptible to problems of overfitting • outperforms MDA, LA • superior to NN when training set is small	• algorithms are complex • requires a lot of memory • performance strongly depends on configuration choices	Min and Lee (2005), Shin, Lee, and Kim (2005)
Case-based forecasting systems (CBFS)	CBFS is based on the fundamental ability of humans to understand and solve current problems by linking them to old ones and predicting the current outcome based on analogical inferences.	• works well for small data sets	• poor generalization ability • underperforms LA	Bryant (1997), Jo and Han (1996)
Rough sets approach (RSA)	RSA deals with the classification of a set of indiscernible objects by approximating the set through a subset that includes objects that unquestionably belong to the set and another subset that contains all objects that possibly belong to the set. Through the help of an expert, RSA can induce decision rules.	• user-friendly: the output is a set of condition-action rules • outperforms MDA and LA	• problems of overfitting • discretization of variables by experts is subjective and implies a loss of information	Slowinski and Zopounidis (1995), Beynon and Peel (2001)
Hybrid models	The combination of different techniques (e.g. NN, genetic algorithms).	• minimizes the disadvantages of individual techniques while maximizing their advantages • generally performs better than individual prediction techniques		Jo and Han (1996), Min, Lee, and Han (2006)

ability. Jones and Hensher (2007) finally propose a mixed-ordered logit model to relax some of the restrictive assumptions inherent to LA and also find a high forecasting accuracy.

4.4   Bankruptcy Signals: The Predictive Value of Corporate Information

Whereas numerous studies explore different techniques to predict bankruptcy more accurately, improvements in predictive ability have been equally achieved by changing or adding information in existing bankruptcy models. In the following paragraph, we give an overview of this progress, starting with a discussion of financial variables in bankruptcy prediction models. Thereafter, we describe the integration of non-financial indicators of distress in bankruptcy prediction models.

Initially, failure prediction relied solely on accounting information and incorporated four categories of ratios: activity, profitability, solvency, and liquidity ratios (Pompe & Bilderbeek, 2005). Ratios were chosen rather arbitrarily based on empirical considerations or on their predictive ability in prior studies but not on theoretical foundations.[1] Due to these arbitrary selection methods, the selection of ratios as well as the predictive ability of these measures varied substantially (Balcaen & Ooghe, 2006). In essence, this is not surprising because virtually all ratios have *some* predictive power. There is also no fixed order in which activity, profitability, solvency, and liquidity ratios become predictive (Pompe & Bilderbeek, 2005). Nevertheless, there is some consensus on the importance of solvency measures and more specifically on the effect of cash flow over total debt as a key predictor of bankruptcy (e.g., Beaver, 1966; Blum, 1974).

Another debate in the context of financial accounting information is the predictive value of accrual-based accounting measures versus cash flow ratios. A large set of researchers advocate the use of cash flow measures. Blum (1974), for example, describes a company as a reservoir of financial resources, implying that the flow of financial resources toward the company determines the probability of failure. Similarly, Gentry, Newbold, and Whitford (1985) report that adding cash flow variables significantly increases the explanatory power of bankruptcy prediction models. Aziz, Emanuel, and Lawson (1988) even introduce a model that is solely based on cash flow and market data, and show that this model outperforms the ZETA model in providing an early signal of failure. However, the findings described earlier are in contrast to a large set of studies that argue that cash flow predictors have no incremental power over standard accrual-based ratios (e.g., Casey & Bartczak, 1985; Gombola, Haskins, Ketz, & Williams, 1987). In the end, accounting-based ratios dominate cash flow data in business failure research and remain the main source of information.

In the early 2000s, scholars began to question the value of accounting data in general and accrual-based measures in particular, as they reflect past performance. As such, they may not be informative in predicting future events. In addition, accounting numbers can be manipulated by the management, making them less reliable (Agarwal & Taffler, 2008; Hillegeist, Keating, Cram, & Lundstedt, 2004). To counter these criticisms, the use of market-based data was suggested, as they are unlikely to be manipulated and reflect expectations about future cash flows. Moreover, under the condition of market efficiency, financial markets fully capture all sources of publicly available information, making financial statement information redundant. A notable example of market-based models is the BSM-Prob measure, developed by Hillegeist et al. (2004) on the basis of the Black-Scholes-Merton option-pricing model. This measure is a valuable bankruptcy predictor but inconsistent with the efficient market hypothesis; accounting-based bankruptcy predictors still add incremental information to the BSM-Prob score (Hillegeist et al., 2004). Another well-known market-based model is Moody's KMV[2] credit model, which relates the failure probability to the difference between the asset value and the face value of debt (the so-called distance to default). This model is widely used by practitioners, although academic research documents that it does not adequately capture bankruptcy risk (Campbell, Hilscher, & Szilagyi, 2008; Hillegeist et al., 2004).

In general, market models have sound theoretical underpinnings, but they tend to perform rather poorly in practice, as they are prone to model misspecifications and measurement errors (Agarwal & Taffler, 2008). In addition, market-based models have a limited scope, as market-based data is solely available for listed firms that are generally less exposed to bankruptcy risk. As a result, the value of market models lies primarily in the combination with traditional accounting ratios. They are seldom the only relevant predictor of bankruptcy (Campbell et al., 2008; Shumway, 2001).

In addition to financial predictors of bankruptcy, a great number of studies consider the inclusion of non-financial measures such as size, age, and group structure in bankruptcy prediction models. These firm characteristics might provide insights in the company's risk profile and hence improve the prediction of bankruptcy. This is certainly valid for small and medium-sized enterprises (SMEs) that are not listed on the stock market and whose statements may suffer from incompleteness and unreliability by creative accounting practices (Keasey & Watson, 1987; Lee & Yeh, 2004). First, size increases the likelihood of survival, as larger firms, for example, have access to a wide range of financing sources and possess more flexibility to rearrange their assets (Back, 2005). The marginal benefits of increased size diminish, however, as firms become larger (Cefis & Marsili, 2012). Second, numerous studies (e.g., Madrid-Guijarro, García-Pérez-de Lema, & Van Auken, 2011) highlight the impact of age on corporate bankruptcy, meaning that failure rates decrease substantially with age. The question remains whether failure rates monotonically decrease during the first years of existence—which would be in line with the liability of the newness argument. In contrast, some scholars support the liability of the adolescence argument, indicating that newly established firms are able to survive for a short time, as they can still rely on their initial stock of assets and the support of their stakeholders. Consistent with this liability of the adolescence argument, they show that mortality rates shoot up two to three years after founding (Altman, Sabato, & Wilson, 2010; Everett & Watson, 1998). Finally, a firm characteristic that is often overlooked in bankruptcy prediction studies is the group structure of companies. However, Dewaelheyns and Van Hulle (2006) suggest to incorporate group-level data in bankruptcy models because subsidiaries have an additional buffer against financial problems, especially when the surrounding group itself is sound (Altman et al., 2010). However, subsidiaries of larger groups may suffer from increased levels of bureaucracy that reduce flexibility toward environmental changes, thereby reducing survival rates under conditions of environmental jolts (Bradley, Aldrich, Shepherd, & Wiklund, 2011).

A subsequent category of non-financial variables that are included in bankruptcy prediction models are symptoms of distress. Altman et al. (2010) and Back (2005), for example, control for payment disturbances and find a significant positive relationship between the number of publicly registered payment disturbances, or non-payments, and the likelihood of failure. The probability of failure also increases for companies with reporting lags and/or qualified audit opinions, implying that these factors reflect bad news or deteriorating financial conditions (Altman et al., 2010; Keasey & Watson, 1987; Peel, Peel, & Pope, 1986). Despite its predictive ability, however, Lennox (1999) points out that an audit-opinion dummy doesn't provide incremental information once the bankruptcy model also controls for size, industry, and the economic cycle.

Third, a large number of bankruptcy studies incorporate predictors that reflect the causes rather than the symptoms of bankruptcy. Poor management, for example, is often cited as one of the main causes of failure (Argenti, 1976; Carter & Auken, 2006; Ooghe & De Prijcker, 2008; Xu & Wang, 2009). Several managerial characteristics, such as the age, experience, and tenure of CEOs have, therefore, been incorporated in bankruptcy prediction models (Carter & Auken, 2006; Darrat, Gray, Park, & Wu, 2014; Platt & Platt, 2012). In addition, it is often argued that bankruptcy becomes more likely when the CEO chairs the company's board. However, empirical evidence on this so-called CEO-chairman duality is inconclusive so far (Daily & Dalton, 1995; Elloumi & Gueyie, 2001; Platt & Platt, 2012). Further, some studies examine the characteristics of the top management team and the board of directors rather than solely focusing on the CEO. The inclusion of factors such as the size, composition, expertise, education, tenure, and compensation of these groups significantly improves the explanatory power of prediction models (Daily & Dalton, 1995; Greening & Johnson, 1996; Hambrick & D'Aveni, 1992; Platt & Platt, 2012). In this respect, lower levels of independent and outside directors are strong predictors of default (Daily & Dalton, 1995; Elloumi & Gueyie, 2001). Although empirical findings generally suggest that corporate governance features exhibit strong explanatory power beyond the traditional accounting ratios, Darrat et al. (2014) point at two important caveats. First, corporate governance variables only provide early signals of bankruptcy. Their explanatory power reduces once bankruptcy approaches. Second, the effectiveness of corporate governance depends on the characteristics of the firms as well as the environment in which they operate. As a result, one should be careful with making general inferences on how certain governance features might affect failure or bankruptcy.[3]

Besides poor management and governance, an extensive list of internal and external factors have been examined in the context of failure prediction. For example, the likelihood of failure increases by poor strategic planning and a limited use of professional advisors (Carter & Auken, 2006; Lussier, 1995). Other notable bankruptcy predictors are corporate diversification, technological complexity, limited investment opportunities and low levels of efficiency that increase the likelihood of bankruptcy (e.g., Becchetti & Sierra, 2003; Lyandres & Zhdanov, 2013; Xu & Wang, 2009). External factors such as the competition, adverse founding conditions, interest, and unemployment rate are also significantly related to the likelihood of failure (Baum & Mezias, 1992; Everett & Watson, 1998; Richardson, Kane, & Lobingier, 1998; Swaminathan, 1996). A broader discussion of the effect of external factors on bankruptcy falls, however, outside the scope of this literature review.

4.5   Widening the Scope of Prediction

4.5.1   *An Increasing Focus on Entrepreneurial Companies*

Early studies on failure prediction almost exclusively focus on large and publicly listed companies. Due to limitations in terms of data availability, entrepreneurial companies, such as SMEs, family firms, or growth-oriented firms were limitedly examined, although they represent the lion's share of all companies, account for the majority of employment, and have higher failure rates. One of the first SME bankruptcy prediction models was developed by Edmister (1972). His attempt to predict SME failure was, however, solely based on financial statement data. Later on, many scholars highlighted the incremental explanatory power of non-financial variables. As such, the classification and prediction results significantly improve when both financial and non-financial variables are included in SME failure prediction models (Altman et al., 2010; Back, 2005; Carter & Auken, 2006; Keasey & Watson, 1987). Among non-financial variables, audit reports and qualifications, submission and reporting lags, the number of directors and payment delays are significant predictors of SME failure. Regarding financial predictors, the company's cash position, retained earnings, current indebtedness, profitability, and interest expenses appear to have good predictive ability (Altman & Sabato, 2007; Altman et al., 2010). Gupta, Gregoriou, and Healy (2014), however, note that the three latter financial variables become insignificant when failure is predicted for a sample of microfirms. As the survival of these firms depends mainly on internal sources of finance, such as cash and retained earnings, the authors argue that microfirms should be considered separately from SMEs for the purpose of bankruptcy prediction.

Whereas several studies highlight the importance of examining failure of small firms, only a few look into the high mortality rates among young or newly founded firms (Laitinen, 1992). According to Audretsch (1991), the survival chances of new firms are shaped by the company's start-up size and the industry's growth and technological regime. Specifically, companies that enter innovative and growing industries with a large start-up size face a lower likelihood of failure. Evidence on this third factor is, however, inconclusive, as Laitinen (1992) finds that failure risk is higher for large start-ups. Other external factors that predict bankruptcy among young firms are high entry and unemployment rates and a high concentration in the industry (Audretsch & Mahmood, 1995). Laitinen (1992) and Lussier (1995) further show that high indebtedness, insufficient revenue financing, and the absence of planning, professional advisors, and education all increase failure risk among young firms. In general, although the causes of bankruptcy might be different for young firms compared to mature ones, they tend to have very similar predictors of bankruptcy. Nevertheless, as young firms do not gradually slide toward bankruptcy but often face this event in an abrupt and unexpected way, the prediction of bankruptcy for this type of firm is more difficult (Pompe & Bilderbeek, 2005).

4.5.2   The Impact of Industry

A promising area in the context of bankruptcy prediction is exploiting the effect of industry. After all, industries might differ strongly in terms of competition, accounting conventions, etc., resulting in heterogeneous bankruptcy risks for similar firms operating in different industries (Chava & Jarrow, 2004). As a result, models developed for a single industry, such as retailing, may perform better than those developed in mixed industry samples (McGurr & DeVaney, 1998). Some scholars have already developed models for a particular industry such as broker-dealers (Altman & Loris, 1976) and hospital software (Singh, 1997). Most of the single-industry failure prediction models focus on the banking industry, however, because of its importance for the economy as a whole. Good discriminators for bank failure are the asset composition, loan characteristics, capital adequacy, sources and uses of revenue, efficiency, and profitability (Santomero & Vinso, 1977; Sinkey, 1975).

4.5.3   Bankruptcy Prediction in Emerging Regions

Since the 1980s, several attempts have been made to extend bankruptcy research, which so far mainly focused on U.S. companies, to emerging countries. Alareeni and Branson (2012), Rashid and Abbas (2011), and Wang and Campbell (2010), for example, test traditional bankruptcy models on samples of, respectively, Jordanian, Chinese, and Pakistani companies. Sandin and Porporato (2008) and Ugurlu and Aksoy (2006), on the other hand, start from scratch and develop new bankruptcy prediction models based on data of, respectively, Argentinian firms and Turkish banks. Whereas the former study focuses on a period of economic stability, the latter examines bankruptcy in a period of economic turbulence. Sung, Chang, and Lee (1999) consider both normal and crisis conditions by comparing firm failure during and after the Korean crisis of 1997–1998. They find that under crisis conditions, cash flow is a better predictor when scaled by total liabilities instead of total assets, reflecting the more volatile nature of liabilities compared to total assets. Similarly, Richardson et al. (1998) find that leverage plays a more important role when bankruptcy is predicted for firms in crisis periods. In addition, they show that the importance of predictors changes not only when failure takes place during a crisis but also when annual accounts are prepared in a period of crisis.

4.5.4 A Wider Definition of Failure

In the previous sections, we interchangeably used the terms failure and bankruptcy, as most failure prediction models focus exclusively on bankruptcy. Although this definition is objective and thus practical to use, the concept of failure is much broader than just bankruptcy because failing businesses often try to avoid bankruptcy and opt for alternative exit paths such as a merger or acquisition (M&A), a voluntary liquidation, or a private reorganization (Balcaen, Manigart, Buyze, & Ooghe, 2012). In a similar vein, bankruptcy might also occur for strategic reasons rather than failure. Hence the use of this definition can lead to biased estimates and erroneous conclusions (Balcaen et al., 2012; Everett & Watson, 1998). Various attempts have, therefore, been made to model a wider range of distress-related exit types. Already in 1989, Peel and Wilson modeled the acquisition of a distressed firm as an alternative to bankruptcy, thereby reducing the number of misclassifications. Åstebro and Winter (2012), in addition, use a multinomial model of firms in distress in order to separate non-exited businesses from those that exit through bankruptcy and those that exit through acquisition. They find that this approach is superior to models that combine the alternatives to bankruptcy. However, these models (e.g., Åstebro & Winter, 2012; Cefis & Marsili, 2012) do not yet fully encompass the whole spectrum of exit possibilities (Balcaen et al., 2012). For this reason, more recent studies model the process and resolution of distress in multiple consecutive steps instead of one multinomial choice (Balcaen et al., 2012; Jacobs, Karagozoglu, & Layish, 2012). The underlying logic of these models is that, in the event of a distress-related exit, companies first move towards a private (i.e., out-of-court) or a public (i.e., court-driven) resolution. In a second step, the final exit is modeled within the subgroup of private or public exit strategies. Regarding the selection between in-court and out-of-court exits, findings show that the avoidance of court-driven exits is positively related to resource slack, liquidity, operating cash flows, and the level of intangible assets (Balcaen et al., 2012; Jacobs et al., 2012). Further, leverage decreases the likelihood of a public exit, but the positive effect of leverage largely depends on the type of debt, with a preference for bank over public debt in addition to a preference for unsecured over secured debt or a mixture of debt classes. (Hotchkiss, John, Thorburn, & Mooradian, 2008; Jacobs et al., 2012). Firm size, on the other hand, reduces the likelihood of an out-of-court exit. (Jacobs et al., 2012). In addition, if it comes to a court-driven exit after the first step, the probability of a formal reorganization over a liquidation increases with firm size, leverage, and the level of intangible assets, whereas it is negatively related to the level of liquidity and secured debt (Bergström, Eisenberg, & Sundgren, 2002; White, 1981). The same variables are finally also used to model whether such a court-driven reorganization process is successful, meaning that the firm emerges as a going concern (Hotchkiss et al., 2008).

A research stream that is inspired and somewhat related to the aforementioned topic of distress-related exit paths focuses on all exits, thereby combining harvest (i.e., successful) exits with distress-related exits. Moreover, what characterizes both research streams is the role of legal institutions as the main contingency factor for the availability and the preference for a particular exit type (Wennberg, Wiklund, DeTienne, & Cardon, 2010). Insolvency systems can, for example, differ in terms of judicial efficiency in addition to the debtor versus creditor orientation and are shown to influence the path companies choose to resolve their distress (Wang, 2012). In addition, some countries such as Sweden do not offer a formal reorganization procedure, but instead have an auction code that involves the public sale of the company's assets. Insolvency systems can thus strongly differ among countries, which might affect the performance of prediction models and limit the generalizability of empirical findings.

4.6   Conclusions and Future Research

This chapter aims to provide a concise overview of the research on corporate failure prediction. In the first section, we briefly present the seminal papers that established the foundational bankruptcy prediction models. In the next two sections, we focus on the continuous search in the bankruptcy literature for improved performance through the use of alternative models and the inclusion of different types of corporate information. In the final section, we elaborate on how the scope of failure prediction can been widened, either by focusing on specific types of companies and regions or by taking a broader view on the concept of failure.

Over the last fifty years, the prediction of bankruptcy has evolved from simple ratio analysis to a widely covered topic in both the domains of corporate finance and intelligence systems. Despite the topic's maturity, there is still substantial disagreement on the most suitable methodology to predict bankruptcy. Whereas AI methods generally show slightly higher predictive accuracy rates, several academics question their fixation on model performance and prefer more intuitive statistical models. Nevertheless, as both classes of techniques manage to predict failure with accuracy rates of up to 80% or 90%, future studies might look into the synergies of combining them in hybrid systems instead of just comparing them. These efforts to improve performance should, however, also be balanced with the needs of practitioners such as managers, analysts, and lending institutions. With some older exceptions—for instance, Altman's straightforward Z-score—practitioners thus far make relatively little use of state-of-the-art academic bankruptcy prediction models because they are too complex, which limits their interpretability and usefulness in practice. Along the same lines, although the prediction of bankruptcy becomes more accurate when traditional accounting ratios are complemented with market-based data and firm-specific characteristics, including a large number of predictors from different data sources—of which some need be carefully validated before use—might be too time consuming or unfeasible from a practitioner's point of view.

Whereas the contribution of studies that focus on performance improvements has become rather marginal, substantial improvements are currently being achieved by considering a wider definition of failure. After all, failure entails more than just bankruptcy and can be followed by alternative solutions such as M&As, voluntary liquidations, or reorganizations. Studies that model this wider range of failure outcomes not only better capture the reality but are also more relevant for policy makers, as alternative exit routes possibly imply lower welfare losses. We, therefore, believe that this can be a fruitful focus for future research. Another interesting area for future studies is the time dimension of failure, which is often neglected in the literature. Although several authors have emphasized that a one- or three-year observation period is insufficient to fully grasp the dynamics of failure, so far, only a few studies have investigated this time dimension.

Notes

1 See Balcaen and Ooghe (2006) for a discussion of variable selection methods.
2 KMV stands for Kealhofer, McQuown, and Vasicek, the founders of the firm that was a leading provider of quantitative credit analysis tools. The firm was acquired by Moody's in 2002.
3 A comprehensive discussion on the role of managerial and governance characteristics in the context of bankruptcy prediction can be found in, for example, Daily and Dalton (1995), Darrat et al. (2014), Elloumi and Gueyie (2001), Peel et al. (1986), and Platt and Platt (2012).

References

Agarwal, V., & Taffler, R. (2008). Comparing the performance of market-based and accounting-based bankruptcy prediction models. *Journal of Banking & Finance*, *32*(8), 1541–1551.

Alareeni, B. A., & Branson, J. (2012). Predicting listed companies' failure in Jordan using Altman models: A case study. *International Journal of Business and Management*, *8*(1), 113–126.

Altman, E. I. (1968). Financial ratios, discriminant analysis and the prediction of corporate bankruptcy. *The Journal of Finance*, *23*(4), 589–609.

Altman, E. I., Haldeman, R. G., & Narayanan, P. (1977). ZETA TM analysis a new model to identify bankruptcy risk of corporations. *Journal of Banking & Finance*, *1*(1), 29–54.

Altman, E. I., & Loris, B. (1976). A financial early warning system for over-the-counter broker-dealers. *The Journal of Finance*, *31*(4), 1201–1217.

Altman, E. I., & Sabato, G. (2007). Modelling credit risk for SMEs: Evidence from the US market. *Abacus*, *43*(3), 332–357.

Altman, E. I., Sabato, G., & Wilson, N. (2010). The value of non-financial information in small and medium-sized enterprise risk management. *The Journal of Credit Risk*, *6*(2), 1–33.

Argenti, J. (1976). Corporate planning and corporate collapse. *Long Range Planning*, *9*(6), 12–17.

Astebro, T., & Winter, J. K. (2012). More than a dummy: The probability of failure, survival and acquisition of firms in financial distress. *European Management Review*, *9*(1), 1–17.

Audretsch, D. B. (1991). New-firm survival and the technological regime. *The Review of Economics and Statistics*, *37*(3), 441–450.

Audretsch, D. B., & Mahmood, T. (1995). New firm survival: New results using a hazard function. *The Review of Economics and Statistics*, *77*(1), 97–103.

Aziz, A., Emanuel, D. C., & Lawson, G. H. (1988). Bankruptcy prediction-an investigation of cash flow based models [1]. *Journal of Management Studies*, *25*(5), 419–437.

Back, P. (2005). Explaining financial difficulties based on previous payment behavior, management background variables and financial ratios. *European Accounting Review*, *14*(4), 839–868.

Balcaen, S., Manigart, S., Buyze, J., & Ooghe, H. (2012). Firm exit after distress: Differentiating between bankruptcy, voluntary liquidation and M&A. *Small Business Economics*, *39*(4), 949–975.

Balcaen, S., & Ooghe, H. (2006). 35 years of studies on business failure: An overview of the classic statistical methodologies and their related problems. *The British Accounting Review*, *38*(1), 63–93.

Baum, J. A., & Mezias, S. J. (1992). Localized competition and organizational failure in the Manhattan hotel industry, 1898–1990. *Administrative Science Quarterly*, *37*(4), 580–604.

Beaver, W. H. (1966). Financial ratios as predictors of failure. *Journal of Accounting Research*, *4*, 71–111.

Becchetti, L., & Sierra, J. (2003). Bankruptcy risk and productive efficiency in manufacturing firms. *Journal of Banking & Finance*, *27*(11), 2099–2120.

Bergström, C., Eisenberg, T., & Sundgren, S. (2002). Secured debt and the likelihood of reorganization. *International Review of Law and Economics*, 21(4), 359–372.

Beynon, M. J., & Peel, M. J. (2001). Variable precision rough set theory and data discretization: An application to corporate failure prediction. *Omega*, 29(6), 561–576.

Blum, M. (1974). Failing company discriminant analysis. *Journal of Accounting Research*, 12(1), 1–25.

Bradley, S. W., Aldrich, H., Shepherd, D. A., & Wiklund, J. (2011). Resources, environmental change, and survival: Asymmetric paths of young independent and subsidiary organizations. *Strategic Management Journal*, 32(5), 486–509.

Bryant, S. M. (1997). A case-based reasoning approach to bankruptcy prediction modelling. *Intelligent Systems in Accounting, Finance and Management*, 6(3), 195–214.

Campbell, J. Y., Hilscher, J., & Szilagyi, J. (2008). In search of distress risk. *The Journal of Finance*, 63(6), 2899–2939.

Carter, R., & Auken, H. V. (2006). Small firm bankruptcy. *Journal of Small Business Management*, 44(4), 493–512.

Casey, C., & Bartczak, N. (1985). Using operating cash flow data to predict financial distress: Some extensions. *Journal of Accounting Research*, 23(1), 384–401.

Cefis, E., & Marsili, O. (2012). Going, going, gone. Exit forms and the innovative capabilities of firms. *Research Policy*, 41(5), 795–807.

Chava, S., & Jarrow, R. A. (2004). Bankruptcy prediction with industry effects. *Review of Finance*, 8(4), 537–569.

Daily, C. M., & Dalton, D. R. (1995). CEO and director turnover in failing firms: An illusion of change? *Strategic Management Journal*, 16(5), 393–400.

Darrat, A. F., Gray, S., Park, J. C., & Wu, Y. (2014). Corporate governance and bankruptcy risk. *Journal of Accounting, Auditing & Finance*. Retrieved from http://dx.doi.org/10.2139/ssrn.1710412.

Deakin, E. B. (1972). A discriminant analysis of predictors of business failure. *Journal of Accounting Research*, 10(1), 167–179.

Dewaelheyns, N., & Van Hulle, C. (2006). Corporate failure prediction modelling: Distorted by business groups' internal capital markets? *Journal of Business Finance & Accounting*, 33(5–6), 909–931.

Edmister, R. O. (1972). An empirical test of financial ratio analysis for small business failure prediction. *Journal of Financial and Quantitative Analysis*, 7(2), 1477–1493.

Eisenbeis, R. A. (1977). Pitfalls in the application of discriminant analysis in business, finance, and economics. *The Journal of Finance*, 32(3), 875–900.

Elloumi, F., & Gueyie, J.-P. (2001). Financial distress and corporate governance: An empirical analysis. *Corporate Governance: The International Journal of Business in Society*, 1(1), 15–23.

Everett, J., & Watson, J. (1998). Small business failure and external risk factors. *Small Business Economics*, 11(4), 371–390.

Frydman, H., Altman, E. I., & Kao, D.-L. (1985). Introducing recursive partitioning for financial classification: The case of financial distress. *The Journal of Finance*, 40(1), 269–291.

Gentry, J. A., Newbold, P., & Whitford, D. T. (1985). Predicting bankruptcy: If cash flow's not the bottom line, what is? *Financial Analysts Journal*, 41(5), 47–56.

Gombola, M. J., Haskins, M. E., Ketz, J. E., & Williams, D. D. (1987). Cash flow in bankruptcy prediction. *Financial Management, 16*(4), 55–65.

Greening, D. W., & Johnson, R. A. (1996). Do managers and strategies matter? A study in crisis. *Journal of Management Studies, 33*(1), 25–51.

Gupta, J., Gregoriou, A., & Healy, J. (2014). Forecasting bankruptcy for SMEs using hazard function: To what extent does size matter? *Review of Quantitative Finance and Accounting, 45*(4), 1–25.

Hambrick, D. C., & D'Aveni, R. A. (1992). Top team deterioration as part of the downward spiral of large corporate bankruptcies. *Management Science, 38*(10), 1445–1466.

Hillegeist, S. A., Keating, E. K., Cram, D. P., & Lundstedt, K. G. (2004). Assessing the probability of bankruptcy. *Review of Accounting Studies, 9*(1), 5–34.

Hotchkiss, E. S., John, K., Thorburn, K. S., & Mooradian, R. M. (2008). *Bankruptcy and the Resolution of Financial Distress.* Retrieved from http://dx.doi.org/10.2139/ssrn.1086942

Jacobs Jr, M., Karagozoglu, A. K., & Layish, D. N. (2012). Resolution of corporate financial distress: An empirical analysis of processes and outcomes. *The Journal of Portfolio Management, 38*(2), 117–135.

Jo, H., & Han, I. (1996). Integration of case-based forecasting, neural network, and discriminant analysis for bankruptcy prediction. *Expert Systems with Applications, 11*(4), 415–422.

Jones, S., & Hensher, D.A. (2007). Evaluating the behavioural performance of alternative logit models: An application to corporate takeovers research. *Journal of Business Finance and Accounting, 34*(7), 1193–1220.

Keasey, K., & Watson, R. (1987). Non-financial symptoms and the prediction of small company failure: A test of Argenti's hypotheses. *Journal of Business Finance & Accounting, 14*(3), 335–354.

Kirkos, E. (2012). Assessing methodologies for intelligent bankruptcy prediction. *Artificial Intelligence Review, 43*(1), 1–41.

Kumar, P. R., & Ravi, V. (2007). Bankruptcy prediction in banks and firms via statistical and intelligent techniques—A review. *European Journal of Operational Research, 180*(1), 1–28.

Laitinen, E. K. (1992). Prediction of failure of a newly founded firm. *Journal of Business Venturing, 7*(4), 323–340.

Lee, T.-S., & Yeh, Y. H. (2004). Corporate governance and financial distress: Evidence from Taiwan. *Corporate Governance: An International Review, 12*(3), 378–388.

Lennox, C. S. (1999). The accuracy and incremental information content of audit reports in predicting bankruptcy. *Journal of Business Finance & Accounting, 26*(5–6), 757–778.

Lussier, R. N. (1995). A nonfinancial business success versus failure prediction model for young firms. *Journal of Small Business Management, 33*(1), 8–20.

Lyandres, E., & Zhdanov, A. (2013). Investment opportunities and bankruptcy prediction. *Journal of Financial Markets, 16*(3), 439–476.

Madrid-Guijarro, A., García-Pérez-de Lema, D., & van Auken, H. (2011). An analysis of non-financial factors associated with financial distress. *Entrepreneurship and Regional Development, 23*(3–4), 159–186.

McGurr, P., & DeVaney, S. (1998). Predicting business failure of retail firms: An analysis using mixed industry models. *Journal of Business Research, 43*(3), 169–176.

Messier, W. F., & Hansen, J. V. (1988). Inducing rules for expert system development: An example using default and bankruptcy data. *Management Science, 34*(12), 1403–1415.

Min, J. H., & Lee, Y.-C. (2005). Bankruptcy prediction using support vector machine with optimal choice of kernel function parameters. *Expert Systems with Applications, 28*(4), 603–614.

Min, S.-H., Lee, J., & Han, I. (2006). Hybrid genetic algorithms and support vector machines for bankruptcy prediction. *Expert Systems with Applications, 31*(3), 652–660.

Odom, M. D., & Sharda, R. (1990). *A neural network model for bankruptcy prediction.* Retrieved from http://dx.doi.org/10.1109/IJCNN.1990.137710

Ohlson, J. A. (1980). Financial ratios and the probabilistic prediction of bankruptcy. *Journal of Accounting Research, 18*(1), 109–131.

Ooghe, H., & De Prijcker, S. (2008). Failure processes and causes of company bankruptcy: A typology. *Management Decision, 46*(2), 223–242.

Peel, M., Peel, D., & Pope, P. (1986). Predicting corporate failure—Some results for the UK corporate sector. *Omega, 14*(1), 5–12.

Peel, M., & Wilson, N. (1989). The liquidation/merger alternative some results for the UK corporate sector. *Managerial and Decision Economics, 10*(3), 209–220.

Platt, H., & Platt, M. (2012). Corporate board attributes and bankruptcy. *Journal of Business Research, 65*(8), 1139–1143.

Pompe, P. P., & Bilderbeek, J. (2005). The prediction of bankruptcy of small-and medium-sized industrial firms. *Journal of Business Venturing, 20*(6), 847–868.

Rashid, A., & Abbas, Q. (2011). Predicting bankruptcy in Pakistan. *Theoretical and Applied Economics, 9*(9), 103–128.

Richardson, F. M., Kane, G. D., & Lobingier, P. (1998). The impact of recession on the prediction of corporate failure. *Journal of Business Finance & Accounting, 25*(1–2), 167–186.

Sandin, A. R., & Porporato, M. (2008). Corporate bankruptcy prediction models applied to emerging economies: Evidence from Argentina in the years 1991–1998. *International Journal of Commerce and Management, 17*(4), 295–311.

Santomero, A. M., & Vinso, J. D. (1977). Estimating the probability of failure for commercial banks and the banking system. *Journal of Banking & Finance, 1*(2), 185–205.

Shaw, M. J., & Gentry, J. A. (1988). Using an expert system with inductive learning to evaluate business loans. *Financial Management, 17*(3), 45–56.

Shin, K.-S., Lee, T. S., & Kim, H.-J. (2005). An application of support vector machines in bankruptcy prediction model. *Expert Systems with Applications, 28*(1), 127–135.

Shumway, T. (2001). Forecasting bankruptcy more accurately: A simple hazard model. *The Journal of Business, 74*(1), 101–124.

Singh, K. (1997). The impact of technological complexity and interfirm cooperation on business survival. *Academy of Management Journal, 40*(2), 339–367.

Sinkey, J. F. (1975). A multivariate statistical analysis of the characteristics of problem banks. *The Journal of Finance, 30*(1), 21–36.

Slowinski, R., & Zopounidis, C. (1995). Application of the rough set approach to evaluation of bankruptcy risk. *Intelligent Systems in Accounting, Finance and Management, 4*(1), 27–41.

Sung, T. K., Chang, N., & Lee, G. (1999). Dynamics of modelling in data mining: Interpretive approach to bankruptcy prediction. *Journal of Management Information Systems, 16*(1), 63–85.

Swaminathan, A. (1996). Environmental conditions at founding and organizational mortality: A trial-by-fire model. *Academy of Management Journal, 39*(5), 1350–1377.

Tam, K. Y. (1991). Neural network models and the prediction of bank bankruptcy. *Omega, 19*(5), 429–445.

Ugurlu, M., & Aksoy, H. (2006). Prediction of corporate financial distress in an emerging market: The case of Turkey. *Cross Cultural Management: An International Journal, 13*(4), 277–295.

Wang, C. A. (2012). Determinants of the choice of formal bankruptcy procedure: An international comparison of reorganization and liquidation. *Emerging Markets Finance and Trade, 48*(2), 4–28.

Wang, Y., & Campbell, M. (2010). Do bankruptcy models really have predictive ability? evidence using China publicly listed companies. *International Management Review, 6*(2), 77–82.

Wennberg, K., Wiklund, J., DeTienne, D. R., & Cardon, M. S. (2010). Reconceptualizing entrepreneurial exit: Divergent exit routes and their drivers. *Journal of Business Venturing, 25*(4), 361–375.

White, M. J. (1981). *Economics of bankruptcy: Liquidation and reorganization.* New York: Salomon Bros. Center for the Study of Financial Institutions, Graduate School of Business Administration, New York University.

Wilson, R. L., & Sharda, R. (1994). Bankruptcy prediction using neural networks. *Decision Support Systems, 11*(5), 545–557.

Xu, X., & Wang, Y. (2009). Financial failure prediction using efficiency as a predictor. *Expert Systems with Applications, 36*(1), 366–373.

Zmijewski, M. E. (1984). Methodological issues related to the estimation of financial distress prediction models. *Journal of Accounting Research, 22*, 59–82.

5   A Theoretical Framework for Restructuring

Joost de Haas and Pieter Klapwijk

5.1   Introduction

Companies create value by investing the capital they attract in projects that generate excess returns, which means generating future cash flows at higher rates of return than the cost of capital (Koller, Goedhart, & Wessels, 2015). In reality, companies do not always deliver excess returns on all projects; on the contrary, companies end up in financial distress for a variety of reasons and in different degrees of severity, ranging from 'plain loss' of shareholder value to liquidity crisis and (eventually) bankruptcy. Management and/or turnaround managers—at any point on the path of decline—try to avoid further deterioration of financial distress and subsequently regenerate value for old and new stakeholders by turning the business around and restoring its cash-generating capacity. We define a turnaround process as

> *a set of coherent actions undertaken to reverse a (significant) decline in enterprise value through restructuring the cash-generating processes and rebalancing the operational and financial structure of the firm.*

The turnaround process can be divided into three types of actions:

1   **Operational restructuring**: Redesigning business processes and (re)allocating assets in order to achieve maximal cash generation
2   **Asset restructuring**: 'Cleaning up the balance sheet' by liquidating non-operating assets and excess operating assets[1]
3   **Financial restructuring**: Restructuring of liabilities in order to rebalance (cash generation) assets and liabilities

In this chapter, we will focus on turnaround processes including all of the aforementioned types of actions. This means we disregard turnarounds of companies not requiring asset and/or financial restructuring.

We aim to increase the understanding of the mechanics of financial distress and of the subsequent financial and operational restructuring by answering three basic questions: (1) what triggers a restructuring, (2) which outcomes can a restructuring process have, and (3) how is a turnaround process executed? Before doing so, however, we will provide a framework for putting these questions in an appropriate context.

5.2   Framework for Restructuring[2]

In a stable situation, the value of the company is the value of the future expected cash flows discounted at the weighted average cost of capital (WACC). As long as companies generate excess rates of return, no (apparent) conflicts of interest arise between providers of capital and other holders of claims on the company. Plainly speaking, 'The pie is large enough to serve everybody at the table.' However, when cash flows significantly fall behind their projected patterns and/or the risk profile of those cash flows changes negatively (i.e., they become more unpredictable), the company value deteriorates and conflicts of interest over control of the firm and its cash flows arise. In such situations, these conflicts of interest can stand in the way of a solution going forward and of continuation of the company. 'The pie is no longer large enough!'

In order to understand how conflicts of interest arise, who controls a turnaround situation, and how a turnaround is executed, we need to understand what happens to the value of a company and the value of the various claims on that value when a company slides into decline.

Therefore, we propose a framework that looks at company value and its distribution over claim holders on a more detailed level than customary in traditional company valuations, where totalized (company) cash flows are discounted with a weighted average cost of capital.[3]

5.2.1   Unbundling Cash Flows

Under the discounted cash flow (DCF) method, the sum of totalized value of the free cash flows discounted at the WACC, plus the value of non-operating assets is called the enterprise value.[4] Stakeholders who have provided the company with funds have a claim on the enterprise value, meaning they have a recognized title on the free cash flows generated in order to get their investment back (with a return). Generally speaking, there are two types of claims: fixed claims and residual claims, alternatively called 'hard' and 'soft' contracts' (Hotchkiss, John, Mooradian, & Thorburn, 2008). Several financial instruments may further differentiate claims within these categories and change the ranking and order in which these claims are repaid. The order in which claims are settled in the case of default or bankruptcy is called the 'liquidity preference'. As long as the fixed claims are completely satisfied and the residual claims have a satisfactory chance of (eventually) getting repaid their risk-adjusted return, the liquidity preference is not relevant. It is when the enterprise value (significantly) declines that conflicts between claim holders may arise. Depending on the level of financial distress, claim holders will set off their claim against the alternatives (a sale of the assets or [eventually] liquidation of the company) depending on the security rights they have. In other words, when the pie is not as large as was expected, all parties will reevaluate their claim and try to get control over the distribution of the remaining pie.

We start developing our framework by redefining the free cash flows generated by the company. Under the DCF method, the enterprise value is the sum of the free cash flows generated by the individual projects the company exploits, discounted at the appropriate (project) discount rate. Even if the company is a pure project-driven (and project-financed) business, the financiers of the company will rather look at the overall free cash flows generated than those of the underlying projects. If the total free cash flows are not sufficient anymore to satisfy the fixed and residual claims, the value of the underlying securities becomes relevant. We define the free cash flows along these lines and split the enterprise value in three components:

1 **Liquidation value of the assets.** In a (forced) liquidation scenario of a company (i.e., 'dead'), its assets have a market value, usually the proceeds from a bankruptcy auction or other distressed asset sales process. The minimum value of a company is, therefore, the present value of this liquidation value (minus the liquidation cost) in case of demise.
2 **Excess value of the assets.** In order to have economic logic, companies obviously must create more cash with the assets under management than their liquidation value. The excess value is calculated as the discounted value of the cash-generating value of the assets minus the liquidation value. The assets have a higher value 'alive' than 'dead.'
3 **Growth premium.** On top of the former two components, companies that can grow the cash-generating capacity of their enterprise have a growth premium ('thrive'). This is the present value of future cash-generating opportunities through, for example, competitive advantages, autonomous growth, new business opportunities, or acquisitions (or being taken over).

The sum of the excess value of the assets plus the liquidation value is referred to as the going-concern value of a company in a steady state (i.e., no growth/ no opportunity) situation.

5.2.2 *Defining the Capital Structure*

Given their asset and cash-flow-generating structure, companies should find an optimal capital structure. Finance theory does not offer us a simple solution: "There is no universal theory of capital structure, and no reason to expect one" (Myers, 2003, p. 217). Myers (2003) offers four conditional theories of capital structure, ranging from irrelevance of capital structure (i.e., 'Modigliani-Miller') to information- and agency-cost-based theories.

His conclusion is that we need 'new foundations' for corporate finance, requiring a deeper understanding of the motives and behavior of management and employees of the firm.

We propose researching a deeper understanding of *all* stakeholders and start with trying to explain the behavior of the claim holders of the company—i.e., the financiers and other financially dependent actors of the company. As a start, we 'slice up' the right-hand (liability) side of the balance sheet.

In return for their investments, financiers get a claim on any cash generated by the company. Black and Scholes (1973) show that shareholders have the equivalent of an option on the company's assets. Their premise is that "the bondholders own the company's assets, but they have given options to the stockholders to buy the assets back."

We make two adjustments to their proposition:

1   'Bondholders' here should be viewed as *all* creditors of the company, even if they don't have a formalized or a not-yet recognized claim on the company's assets. Shareholders will only own all the company's assets if they fulfill *all* the company's debts, including those that are not formalized through claim contracts (such as redundancy schemes for employees).
2   The position of all (classes of) claim holders can be viewed as an option on claims with a higher priority in the liquidity preference. Executing the option(s) will not 'buy the assets back,' but will transfer the claim on the cash flows of the company from one claim holder to the other. Viewing all claims as options is an essential assumption to the mechanics of our framework.

For our framework, we differentiate between the following types of claim holders.[5]

1   **Secured claim holders (SCH)** have a collateral on specific assets such as a mortgage on real estate or a lien on machinery. In case of liquidation or bankruptcy, they are first in line to receive cash returns produced by a sale of the specific assets securing their claim.
2   **Priority claim holders (PCH)** do not have collateral but they have a claim on the company's assets or cash flows only in the case of bankruptcy. Depending on the jurisdiction this could, for instance, be tax authorities, the bankruptcy administrator, or employees. Usually these claims have priority over unsecured claims.
3   **Unsecured claim holders (UCH)**—creditors with no specific collateral—are next in line. They can be distinguished as 'formal' financiers, such as bondholders, and 'informal' financiers (i.e., without formalized financing agreements), such as trade creditors who agree on payment at a

later date. We also include the part of secured claims over and above the liquidation value of the corresponding asset(s) here.[6]

4 **Shareholders** are, at first instance, the residual claim holders and are last in line in terms of payouts.[7] Residual claim holders get paid when all other claim holders with a higher order claim are satisfied. Of course, shareholders require a higher (ex ante) return for the additional risk they run.

5.2.3 Balancing the Operational and Financial Structure

Companies must make a decision about how to find a balance between their operational structure (i.e., their cash-generating capacity) and their financial structure (i.e., the amount and structure of the hard and soft financing contracts). Obviously, increasing the relative amount of debt in the capital structure leads to lower taxes (if interest on debt is tax-deductible) and raises the (potential) return to shareholders. The downside is—debt being a hard contract—the risk of default when free cash flows are not sufficient to repay the hard contracts. To avoid or minimize the risk of financial distress, companies try to finance their cash-generating capacity with financial instruments that match the maturity (i.e., length of the contract and payment scheme) and risk profile of the underlying free cash flows.

This concludes the introduction of our framework, a graphical presentation of which is shown in Figure 5.1.

We will now proceed by answering the questions we raised in our introduction.

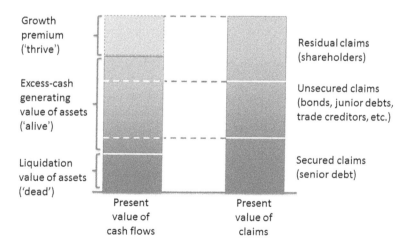

Figure 5.1 A Theoretical Framework for Restructuring

Note: Priority Claim Holders are not shown as they only materialize in the case of bankruptcy.

5.3   Triggers for Restructuring

Financial distress arises when a company is not able to meet its current and/ or future financial obligations. Some authors limit this to the immediate inability to fulfill short-term financial obligations: "A firm is in financial distress at a given point in time when the liquid assets of the firm are not sufficient to meet the current requirements of its hard contracts" (Hotchkiss et al., 2008, p. 238). In this case, 'hard contracts' are defined as contracts with a defined payment scheme, whereby violation of the contract opens the route to seek legal recourse to enforce the contract. Examples of hard contracts are obligations to bondholders, suppliers, and employees. 'Soft contracts,' on the other hand, carry expectations of payouts but are not (legally) enforceable. Soft contracts are only satisfied after the company has obliged the terms of its hard contracts. For companies in distress, soft contracts become the residual claims on the cash flow of the firm (instead of the shareholders).

Claim holders—whether they have hard or soft contracts—protect the value of their claims by incorporating covenants into the terms of the contract. Covenants strive to alleviate agency issues between the specific claim holder and other claim holders, but also between claim holders and management.

Besides conflicts of interest between management (in a broad sense) and claim holders, agency problems between (categories of) claim holders may exist. One obvious conflict is between bondholders and shareholders, or, in a broader sense, holders of hard contracts and of residual claim contracts. When a company is underperforming and the residual claim holders see their claim getting 'out of the money,' they may have incentives to take measures that are not in the interest of other claim holders. Holders of hard contracts mitigate their risk by imposing covenants on management actions that favor holders of soft contracts, such as dividend payouts, investments/ divestments, and new debt contracts.

Clearly, financial distress is an immediate trigger for restructuring, but even long before distress occurs, reasons for restructuring may arise. As industries mature or become more competitive and companies do not adjust accordingly, the growth premium dissolves. Shareholders are not expected to earn their anticipated (risk-adjusted) returns; declining shareholder value is the result. If the enterprise value of the company deteriorates further—by decreasing cash flows and/or increasing risk—other claim holders face the risk of not having their claims satisfied. In other words, the value of each claim holder's option declines as soon as the enterprise value declines. For more senior claim holders (i.e., with a high liquidity preference), the decline may not be very large (at first), but for every class of claims, there is a point when the value of their claim declines significantly. The aforementioned dynamics are graphically presented in Figure 5.2.

An interesting—and, as of yet, unanswered—question is of course what the 'pain point' for each individual claim holder is to trigger restructuring.

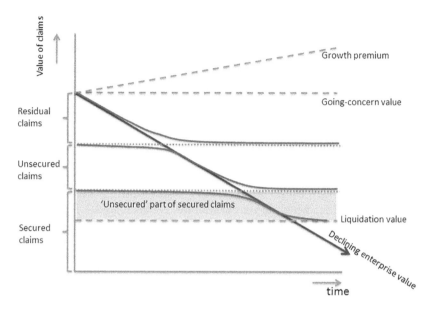

Figure 5.2 Value of Claims Over Time

In other words, how much of the claim's value should be lost before a claim holder forces a restructuring. The answer cannot be expressed in one simple equation (unfortunately), but depends on three factors:

1 The value of the alternative
2 The certainty of the information
3 The ability to exercise control

The combination of these factors will determine whether and when a claim holder will exercise his or her rights, take control, and force all other (to him or her subordinated) claim holders into restructuring.

The discussion about restructuring and the decision of whether, and when, to take measures is driven to a large extent by agency theory. Managers are, in most cases, the prime cause of the decline (Adriaanse, 2005). Management (acting as agents) may have a conflict of interest with claim holders (as principals). They may be in denial or at least not willing to concede that their strategy is not delivering promised results, and as a result, they are not only losing their jobs but also not finding new jobs.[8] Claim holders (of all categories) will trigger restructuring if the following three conditions are met:

- A: Claims are 'out of the money.' As we have seen, claims can be seen as options to fulfill the claims of more senior claims. As enterprise value declines, all claims lose value. When claim holders will trigger restructuring depends on the threshold they have in the loss of value of their claim.

- B: Incumbent 'top structure' of the company (management, directors, supervisory board, etc.) has lost credibility to restore value to original levels.
- C: Covenants or legal rules allow claim holder(s) to take control. For instance, in the United Kingdom, breaching covenants is a sufficient bankruptcy trigger, whereas in France, only the cessation of payments constitutes such a trigger (Davydenko & Franks, 2008).

If these conditions are fulfilled, a restructuring process can be triggered. We will now show which different outcomes a restructuring process can have and what determines which of the possibilities is effectuated.

5.4 Possible Outcomes of a Restructuring Process

Restructuring is a process to come to a restructured business where the (renewed) enterprise value is higher than the liquidation value and the business continues. In other words, it makes more sense for claim holders to continue the business than to break it up. The alternative to a restructured business is a liquidation of all of the company's assets and [partial] repayment of the claims against the proceeds from the sale. The outcome and the path toward the outcome are determined by a set of sequential questions.

Whether a business is restructured or liquidated depends on a simple first question: "Is it worth it?" In terms of our framework, it means answering the question if the residual enterprise value (REV) is positive, where REV equals the enterprise value (EV) minus the liquidation value (LV). The EV should be substantially larger than LV to result in sufficient value to be distributed to the various claim holders and to pay for the cost of the restructuring process; otherwise, liquidation makes more sense. If REV is negative (or not significantly positive to offset the risk of restructuring), liquidation will follow.

The second question is more subtle and requires some introduction. Both restructuring and liquidation can be resolved in or out of court (i.e., on a voluntary basis). "Bankruptcy is a legal mechanism *allowing* creditors to take over when a firm defaults" (Brealey et al., 2011). Bankruptcy provides the legal framework for creditors to exercise their property rights, but they have a choice. Distress can also be resolved without intervention of the court; creditors can *decide* to restructure out of court. In-court restructuring poses the risk of losing control over the process (by handing it over to—depending on the jurisdiction—a court, an administrator, or a creditor's committee), it takes time (during which enterprise value may decline), and it leads to considerable cost.[9]

In absolute terms, direct bankruptcy costs go from relatively small to billions of dollars as in the cases of Enron and Lehmann Brothers. Indirect costs of bankruptcy are harder to measure. Indirect costs can be, for instance, loss of customers, unfavorable payment terms, or key employees leaving the company. Loss of management attention is also often quoted as an indirect cost.

There is one element of bankruptcy costs that is generally ignored in research, but which is relevant to claim holders in their trade off between in- or out-of-court restructuring: the existence of priority claim holders (PCH). PCH have a recognized claim only in the case of bankruptcy and have priority over unsecured claim holders. PCH 'jump the queue' and get paid out of the bankruptcy proceeds before unsecured claim holders do.[10] Outstanding salaries, payment during the termination period, and other claims are usually taken over by the government (or a designated agency), for which that party receives a claim on the estate. Tax authorities could be another PCH for the amount that the company has deducted VAT from its VAT bill for its invoiced (but now left unpaid) supplies.

We have not found evidence of the amount of priority claims and their influence on decision making by residual claim holders but postulate the amount can (dependent on the jurisdiction) be significant and is relevant in the choice between in- and out-of-court restructuring. We call the sum of direct bankruptcy costs, indirect bankruptcy costs, and PCH total bankruptcy costs (TBC).

For the alternative-out-of-court restructuring, consensus between all claim holders is needed. This process provides the creditors with control, but it also takes time and leads to costs. Claim holders will have different interests, different perspectives on the situation, and different ideas about their influence. Based on claim holders' desire to continue the business, their risk assessment, and their willingness and ability to exercise power, they will (at least) demand a premium over their estimated proceeds from liquidation. Every claim holder, secured or not, has the power to hold out and obstruct an agreement and thereby create the possibility to demand a part of the REV. The premium over LV, as well as whatever part of the REV that has to be promised in order to get all claim holders on board, is called the cost of consensus (COC).

Now we are ready to formulate our second question. "Is TBC larger or smaller than COC?." If TBC is larger than COC, claim holders have an incentive to reach consensus and to come to an out-of-court solution (whether it is liquidation or continuing the restructured business). If TBC is smaller than COC, an in-court solution will be the outcome. Taking the restructuring process to court effectively fixates (and lowers) the COC by means of the bankruptcy rules installed by the court.

Based on the two questions we have discussed, there are four possible paths for a restructuring process that either lead to a restructured business or liquidated assets (Figure 5.3):

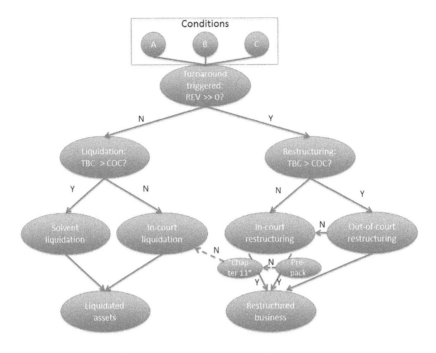

Figure 5.3 Four Possible Paths for a Restructuring Process

1 **Solvent liquidation.** If claim holders agree on taking control of the company and realize that the LV is larger than the (potential) EV, the company will be liquidated. If the anticipated TBC is relatively large, the 'in control' claim holders may have an incentive to look into the possibility for the company to be wound down under 'solvent liquidation.' Solvent liquidation means selling the company's assets in whole or in parts and distributing all proceeds to stakeholders as agreed (beforehand). Stakeholders need to include non-claim holders (such as employees), and 'beforehand' agreement among all parties is required for this option to succeed. The COC must be less than the TBC.

2 **In-court liquidation.** When REV is not positive and no 'beforehand' agreement can be reached—i.e., COC is larger than the TBC—in-court liquidation is the only option. A court (or court-appointed administrator) will oversee a wind down of the company and the distribution of the proceeds of the estate.

3 **Out-of-court restructuring.** An out-of-court restructuring (or 'informal reorganization') is "a reorganization route which takes place outside the statutory framework with the objective of restoring the health of a company in financial difficulties within the same legal entity" (Adriaanse, 2005). 'Outside the statutory framework' means that out-of-court

restructuring is only possible on a voluntary basis and with the consent of all parties involved that hold some sort of control over the decision to restructure. The latter implies a positive COC; on the other hand, the TBC are saved. So the simple logic seems to be that if COC < TBC, 'out-of-court restructuring' is the preferred option. There is, however, something subtle about the aforementioned COC/TBC comparison. Both COC and TBC are costs *as perceived* by the party that assumes the responsibility for the restructuring—i.e., claim holders who (collectively) have obtained sufficient control. The COC, however, are in fact *benefits* for 'the remaining stakeholders.' For all stakeholders taken together, the COC is, therefore, *not* a cost, whereas the TBC *is* (at least to a large extent).[11]

4 **In-court restructuring.** Information asymmetry, holdout problems, complex creditor structures, or just the lack of time to reach an agreement, often stand in the way of an out-of-court restructuring. Claim holders may not agree on the COC (and the TBC), even though, objectively (or theoretically), there may be an optimal solution. Most jurisdictions have a mechanism in the bankruptcy code to see if creditors can come to terms (under court supervision), or—if not—they are forced to accept a court decision on the distribution of the residual claims when the business continues.[12] Most of those mechanism (such as Chapter 11 in the United States) include an 'automatic stay,' which freezes all claims and at the same time gives the company some breathing space to formulate a restructuring proposal. The essence of trying to restructure in court is that information is made symmetric for all creditors and an impartial third party aims to raise the maximum proceeds for the estate. This process requires openness and pre-defined rules and procedures, thereby giving a result that is equally 'fair' to all parties. The downside is that such Chapter 11–type procedures take time and may destroy asset value by its very openness. To increase speed in coming to a resolution (a group of), claim holders or new investors may prepare a 'pre-pack' solution and then bid for the assets of the company. The bidder(s) will try to create a situation where a trustee or the court cannot refuse the offer. Having cash in hand, controlling specific assets (lease contracts, intellectual property, etc.) as a secured claim holder, or exploiting a time-critical situation may provide 'an offer that cannot be refused' by the administrator. The bidder obviously takes the risk that the administrator will rather take time to look for a higher offer. 'Official' (i.e., court-administered) pre-packs are gaining in popularity in quite a few jurisdictions. The U.S. Bankruptcy Code has provided the possibility of pre-pack sales since 1978; the United Kingdom revamped its Insolvency Act in 2002 to allow an administrator to assist in preparing the pre-pack before his or her appointment.[13]

If 'in-court restructuring' fails for any reason, 'in-court liquidation' follows automatically.

5.5   Executing Turnaround Processes

Once the conditions for a restructuring are met, the company needs to develop a restructuring plan and realign its operational and financial structure. We distinguish five phases in executing an out-of-court restructuring (Figure 5.4).

5.5.1   *Take Control*

Within our framework, the party/parties with options (i.e., claims), not completely out of money, and with sufficient loss of value will act and take control of the restructuring. Claim holders are, generally speaking, not willing to take direct control themselves. Besides lacking the necessary skills and/or resources, taking (statutory) control poses a risk for claim holders. Banks, for instance, may hold all the cards to obtain control in restructuring (by controlling most of the collateral), but they may be reluctant to have direct influence as to avoid management liability in case the turnaround does not succeed.

Incumbent management rarely is the designated party to retain control in an out-of-court restructuring. Incumbent management are, after all, 'the ones who got us here in the first place.' Boards may resort to simply replacing the CEO. But changing CEO's is in itself not always enough: success depends on the incumbent's degree of misfit and the successor's degree of fit

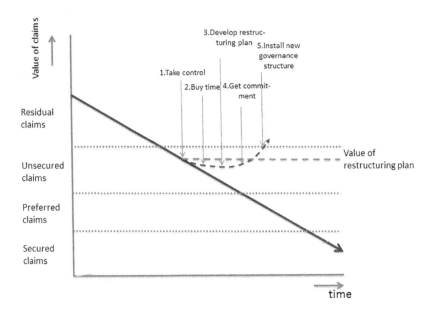

Figure 5.4 Five Phases in Executing an Out-of-Court Restructuring

(Chen & Hambrick, 2012). Furthermore, turnaround management requires skills and experiences most 'regular' managers do not possess. Pretorius and Holtzhauzen (2008) identify six 'liabilities' (i.e., situational deficiencies inherited from previous decision making) turnaround managers most overcome. They define no less than twenty-three required skills that turnaround managers most possess in order to overcome those liabilities.

Specialized turnaround managers or turnaround firms are better suited to execute a restructuring. They may take on a statutory position, act as chief restructuring officers, or act as advisors to incumbent management, depending on the severity of the situation and the power of claim holders. Control has to be formalized and communicated, both internally and externally.

Once formalized, control has to be taken up immediately. In general, the old saying stands: "Sit on the incoming mail and the outgoing cash." Quick changes in the authority to make payments are needed, which could be as simple as notifying the relevant bank(s) of the changes.

5.5.2 Buy Time

Essential in a turnaround situation is buying time to develop a restructuring plan and at the same time keep the company operating (and thus preserve value). Claim holders, at this stage, are usually uncertain about the prospects of the company, of the (residual) value of their claim, and of the positions of other claim holders. Turnaround managers take three types of actions to buy time:

1   **Manage short-term cash.** Because restructuring usually takes place in situations where companies are on a steep slope of decline and may be cash negative, generating cash in order to survive in the short term may be necessary. Reduction of the working-capital requirement (e.g., selling off surplus inventories at discounts, collecting accounts receivable sooner) or reducing the asset base (e.g., selling non-operating and/or obsolete equipment) may give temporary relief. Under the uncertainty of the value of their claim and the timing of (any) return, claim holders are generally not willing to increase their exposure. The fear that other claim holders may be moved into preferential positions makes it necessary to guarantee equal treatment of all claim holders and not to increase exposure. Paying cash on delivery and committing to withhold any payouts to other claim holders are common measures taken.

2   **Make information symmetric.** The level of information between (classes of) claim holders can vary widely. Whereas secured claim holders and large unsecured claim holders (e.g., large suppliers) usually have covenants in place guaranteeing sufficient and timely information, smaller or less-influential claims holders may be in the blind. In order to establish trust, turnaround managers practice transparency to all parties on an equal basis.

3   **Make a draft restructuring plan.** In order to able to choose between in- or out-of-court restructuring, a global analysis of the business potential and the asset value in liquidation should be made, essentially estimating REV.

5.5.3   Develop a Restructuring Plan

A final restructuring plan should give the company a new prospect at recovery of (part of) the enterprise value and determine the way the proceeds are distributed. A restructuring plan has three elements:

1   **New business plan and asset analysis.** In general, turnaround managers work on the cost structure of the firm first under the premise 'costs are determined by us, revenues are determined by somebody else.' Cost reductions are quicker to realize and require less cash than growth of revenues.
2   **Liability analysis.** In an efficient and perfect market, all contracts would be perfect. All claim holders would have—in any state of nature—an undisputable, irrevocable property right. In reality, imperfect contracts are abound and numerous. Assets may have been collateralized more than once; assets may be in less valuable shape (or not present at all); claims may not have been documented or registered properly. Claim holders may have a different view on the value of their claims. The value of claims should, therefore, be determined (or estimated) and agreed upon with claim holders.
3   **Aligned operational and financial structure.** Various ways exist to restructure the financial structure, but in general, they comprise two broad categories: lowering liquidity preference or increasing maturity. Debt-for-equity swaps are a prime example of lowering liquidity preference. (Un)secured creditors with a 'hard' contract trade their claim for a 'soft' contract with a lower liquidity preference and a higher risk profile. Increasing maturity can be another instrument to adjust the financial structure. Creditors may agree to deferred payment of their claims (such as interest waivers, delayed payment terms, or prolonged redemption terms of loans). Whatever instruments are used, turnaround managers must balance the future obligations of the financial structure with the cash-generating capacity of the business in order to prevent financial distress from recurring.

5.5.4   Get Commitment

In order to create a new equilibrium situation, all stakeholders must commit to the restructuring plan and the choice between in- or out-of-court restructuring. All (renewed) claims of all stakeholders relevant to the restructuring plan must be in the money, there must be trust in the new governance structure, rules to take control must be in place (i.e., new covenants), and there must be consensus among claim holders.

5.5.5 *Install New Governance Structure*

Even if evidence suggests that management mostly causes financial distress, this does not mean that in all cases management is replaced. Gilson (1989) finds that 'only' 52% of the sampled firms in financial distress experience management turnover. More recent studies, such as (Nini, Smith, & Sufi, 2012), find a significant increase in CEO turnover when covenants are violated. When 'vulture investors' are involved, boards tend to change as well and take active control in management after the turnaround (Hotchkiss & Mooradian, 1997).

5.6   Conclusion and Further Research

We present a framework that explains the mechanics of restructuring and predicts who takes control and when, which methods of restructuring exist, and how restructuring is executed. The basis of our framework is the premise that all claims against the cash flows of the company can be seen as options, irrespective of being equity or debt. When the enterprise value of the company declines (and thereby the chance that *all* claim holders will be satisfied fully), the value of all claims declines, whether they are (completely) in the money or not. There is a point for each claim holder when he or she will exercise his or her rights and force the other claim holders to restructure the operations and (possibly) the financial structure.

An as-of-yet unanswered question is what the 'pain point' is for (categories of) claim holders—i.e., how much of the value of their option should be lost before they trigger a restructuring. An analysis of covenants may give an (ex ante) indication of the room claim holders are willing to give before they (formally) react.

Notes

1 Non-operating assets are all assets not directly related to generation of operational cash flows of the company, such as unused equipment or unused real estate. Assets that are used for operations but are on the balance sheet at a too high level are 'excess operating assets,' such as excess inventories.
2 The authors wish to thank Paul Vervoort for his comments on a previous version of this framework.
3 The discounted cash flow method assumes a stable risk profile and unchanged capital structure over the valuation period. In distressed situations, these assumptions do not necessarily hold any longer.
4 Other DCF-based valuation methods exist; see Koller et al. (2010) for an overview. The essential assumptions behind these various models do not differ greatly. Therefore, we compare our framework only to the standard DCF method.

5 Claim holders come in many shapes and forms. We simplify by reducing the types of claims to these four categories. Any further differentiation does not influence our framework or its propositions.

6 Secured claim holders retain their claim on the estate in case of bankruptcy for the part that is not returned as an unsecured claim.

7 Claim holders with lower liquidity preference essentially finance any payout to shareholders, such as dividends. The company could have paid off more secured creditors instead of paying a dividend to the shareholders.

8 Gilson (1989) finds that managers incur significant personal cost when their firms become financially distressed. A majority of senior management is fired and do not find similar occupations for at least three years after their departure.

9 Academic research usually distinguishes between direct and indirect costs of bankruptcy. Direct cost can directly be attributed to the bankruptcy event such as legal and professional fees. The amount of direct bankruptcy costs can vary widely, both in relative and absolute terms. Findings range from 3% (Weiss, 1990) to 40% of the proceeds from liquidation (Franks & Sussman, 2005). According to Worldbank (2007), Japan ranks first out of 178 economies in efficiency of its bankruptcy process, which takes 0.6 years on average with a 92.6% recovery rate at 4% cost of the estate. In Venezuela, on the other hand, it takes four years to go through bankruptcy with a recovery rate of only 6.6% and at 38% cost of the estate.

10 The restructuring of the automotive and banking sectors of the recent past saw governments stepping in to rescue companies, but in return getting a priority claim on future cash flows.

11 Only about half of the restructuring situations end with a restructured and continued business (Gilson, John, & Lang, 1990; Ivashina, Iverson, & Smith, 2016). Apparently, reaching consensus among claim holders is not that easy, although overall it is beneficial for claim holders as a group. Gilson et al. (1990) find that claim holders have an incentive to restructure out of court: the stock returns are significantly higher when debt is restructured privately (i.e., out of court). Furthermore, restructuring has a higher chance of success when companies have more intangible assets—relatively more debt is owed to banks and less classes of debt (more general, a lesser number of claim holders with different interests).

12 Corporate bankruptcy codes across jurisdictions provide a variety of measures "to mitigate bargaining frictions in financial distress" (Smith & Strömberg, 2003). In general, bankruptcy codes are meant to resolve agency problems between claim holders and non-claim holders as well as among claim holders, to bring clarity to imperfect contracts, and to buy time to create a solution.

13 The United Kingdom now has around one hundred pre-pack sales a month (Crouch & Amirbeaggi, 2011).

References

Adriaanse, J. A. A. (2005). *Restructuring in the shadow of the law: Informal reorganisation in the Netherlands*. Deventer: Kluwer.

Black, F., & Scholes, M. (1973). The pricing of options and corporate liabilities. *Journal of Political Economy, 81*, 637–654.

Brealey, R., Myers, S., & Allen, F. (2011). *Principles of corporate finance*. New York: McGraw-Hill/Irwin.

Chen, G., & Hambrick, D. (2012). CEO replacement in turnaround situations: Executive (mis)fit and its performance implications. *Organization Science, 23*(1), 225–243.

Crouch, N., & Amirbeaggi, S. (2011). Pre-packs: A legitimate means to phoenix an insolvent company. *Recovery, Summer 2011.*

Davydenko, S., & Franks, J. (2008). Do bankruptcy codes matter? A study of defaults in France, Germany and the UK. *The Journal of Finance, LXIII*(2), 565–608.

Franks, J., & Sussman, O. (2005). Financial distress and bank restructuring of small to medium size UK companies. *Review of Finance, 9*, 65–96.

Gilson, S. (1989). Management turnover and financial distress. *Journal of Financial Economics, 25*, 241–262.

Gilson, S., John, K., & Lang, L. (1990). Troubled debt restructurings: An empirical study of private reorganization of firms in default. *Journal of Financial Economics, 27*, 315–353.

Hotchkiss, E., John, K., Mooradian, R., & Thorburn, K. (2008). Bankruptcy and financial distress. In B. E. Eckbo (Ed.), *Handbook of corporate finance: Empirical corporate finance* (Vol. 1, Handbooks in Finance Series) (pp. 235–287). Amsterdam: Elsevier/North-Holland.

Hotchkiss, E., & Mooradian, R. (1997). Vulture investors and the market control for distressed firms. *Journal of Financial Economics, 43*, 401–432.

Ivashina, V., Iverson, B., & Smith, D. (2016). The ownership and trading of debt claims in chapter 11 restructurings. *Journal of Financial Economics, 119*, 316–335.

Koller, T., Goedhart, M., & Wessels, D. (2015). *Valuation, measuring and managing the value of companies.* New York: John Wiley & Sons.

Myers, S. (2003). Financing of corporations. In G. Constantinides, M. Harris & R. Stulz (Eds.), *Handbook of the economics of finance* (pp. 215–253). Amsterdam: Elsevier.

Nini, G., Smith, D., & Sufi, A. (2012). Creditor control rights, corporate governance, and firm value. *Review of Financial Studies, 25*, 1713–1761.

Pretorius, M., & Holtzhauzen, G. (2008). Critical variables of venture turnarounds: A liabilities approach. *South African Business Review, 12*(8), 87–107.

Smith, D., & Strömberg, P. (2003). *Maximizing the value of distressed assets: bankruptcy law and the efficient reorganization of firms* (Working Paper). Retrieved from http://www1.worldbank.org/finance/assets/images/Smith-Stromberg_Maximizing.pdf

Weiss, L. (1990). Bankruptcy resolution: Direct costs and violation of priority of claims. *Journal of Financial Economics, 27*, 285–314.

Worldbank. (2007). *Doing business 2008: Comparing regulation in 178 economies.* Retrieved from http://www.doingbusiness.org/~/media/GIAWB/Doing%20Business/Documents/Annual-Reports/English/DB08-FullReport.pdf

6 Valuation in Good Times and Bad

Jan Vis

This chapter focuses attention on the role of the concept 'economic value' in decision making. Although the mathematical method required for valuation has been known for many centuries, it was only in the early twentieth century that a wider interest in this phenomenon began to develop within economics (e.g., Irving Fisher). Since 1951, the mathematical method has been included in the standard literature on decision making with regard to both investment in companies and the investments made by companies. However, the fact that a good approach exists does not mean that it will actually be followed. Even today, much use is still made in practice of methods and 'rules of thumb' that, from the theoretical standpoint, are not properly substantiated. Accounting approaches and 'market multiples' remain popular among certain groups of users. This is not without its dangers.

Technically speaking, the valuation of thriving businesses is not very different from the valuation of businesses with problems. However, the context in which the valuation takes place is naturally completely different. This aspect is often largely overlooked in practice. Valuation experts are quite frequently afflicted with 'excelleritis' (i.e., the compulsion to open Excel files), and then give insufficient attention to the quality of the variables involved. Even more than in the valuation of thriving businesses, in the case of problem businesses, it is essential to take human factors into account. The relationship between performance and human behavior has the character of two-way traffic. Behavior can influence performance, and the performance in turn influences the behavior. Many turnaround managers have discovered that simply flipping the cultural switch does not mean that anything actually changes in reality. Good mathematical exercises are useful and necessary but not sufficient!

Because the technical aspects of calculating economic value are not familiar to everyone, the first part of this chapter will discuss the principles that are important for determining economic value. First, attention will be given to the concept of economic value; followed by the question, "Profit or money?"; and then a reflection on the role played by the past and the future. The next element, cost of capital, is the subject of an impressive quantity of literature; in this chapter, 'opportunity cost' is assumed to be the most important consideration in investment decision making. Given that people can only make decisions in a situation of uncertainty, it is helpful to point out the difference between uncertainty and risk; in practice, this distinction is often not given the attention it deserves. The theoretical discussion concludes in a section that explicates the subjective nature of the concept of economic value.

The second part of this chapter will explain, on the basis of a case study, how a simple assessment of an investment plan can work out in practice. All the lights appear to be green, but unforeseen circumstances cause an imminent bankruptcy. The question of whether the company should be liquidated or continued is elucidated and answered using the concept of economic value.

6.1   The Concept of Economic Value

Much is said and written about value; the entire science of economics revolves around the concept of value. People act to improve their position and situation in the expectation that the envisaged action will add value. Economic action usually takes the form of an exchange: acquiring a certain object by sacrificing another object. This action is economically sensible if the sacrificed object, the price, is worth less—in the eyes of the actor—than the acquired object. The concept of economic value is by definition subjective; it is a mental construction and cannot be observed directly by others. The price, on the other hand, is often observable, which perhaps explains why much economic research focuses purely on prices and price formation. The fact that prices are observable does not mean, however, that they have an objective character. Prices are exchange ratios that arise on the basis of individual valuations. Value and price are both subjective. The price is the final agreement of a negotiating process. At the moment when agreement is reached, the parties agree about the price and, by definition, disagree about the value. Our society is based on voluntary division of labor and therefore has a high degree of specialization. The development of a generally accepted means of exchange, money, enables exchange actions to take place efficiently. Money is not only important as a means of exchange; the fact that money exists also allows us to use a currency unit that explicates the process of decision making. Economic value arises mathematically by converting ('discounting') expected cash flows to the present: the moment of decision making. Within the quantity of information available to the decision maker, a distinction is drawn between decision making information and accountability information.

In everyday life, many people are careless in their use of the concept of value. For instance, accountants often use the concept of book value. In most cases, however, this is the price that was once paid for an object minus any depreciations. Annual financial statements frequently contain the concept of market value, which means the price that can be obtained, or must be paid, for the object concerned at the end of the financial year. This price derived from an anonymous market is clearly not the same as the object's economic value. The fact that assets appearing on the balance sheet have not yet been sold entails that the value, the expected revenue, will be higher than the price that can be obtained at the present moment. The term 'fair market value' is also used in the literature; the addition of 'fair' suggests much, but from the economic perspective, it is meaningless. All these concepts of value have minimal importance for economic decision making. Within the available quantity of information, they are classed under the term 'accountability information.'

The main focus in this chapter will be the concept of economic value, which can be defined as the present value of expected cash flows.

6.2   Profit or Money?

The concept of profit has, in most cases, an accounting nature, and is therefore at the mercy of regulators who prescribe how profit must be calculated. Accounting is based on conventions, and these are one reason why revenues and costs are not the same as income and expenditure. Thus, for instance, some of the sales will not yet have been paid for at the time when the annual financial statements are produced. Yet the earnings statement will show the total turnover, with these unpaid-for sales reported under the heading 'accounts receivable' on the balance sheet. If a loss is expected in the future, it is standard practice to create a provision as soon as this becomes apparent. The provision immediately reduces the result, although the actual expenditure will take place later. Tangible fixed assets, such as buildings and machinery, are depreciated according to accounting principles over a certain period of time. However, the purchase price is paid at the time of supply. When rules are changed in the area of depreciation, for instance, this can affect the annual result without any change occurring in the cash flow. In this connection, some attention must be given to the corporate income tax that may be payable, because it is possible that the concept of taxable profit will differ from the concept of accounting profit. In such cases, the item 'deferred taxes' will probably appear in the annual financial statements.

The determination of economic value should be based on the expected cash flow and not on expected profit. Profit is a number in the accounts, whereas people actually operate with ready money. From the standpoint of economics, money represents a certain good; money is—as it were—a claim on the productivity of others. Given that people prefer to arrive at their desired better position and situation sooner rather than later, which is known in economics as 'time preference,' present and immediately available goods have more value than corresponding future goods. This time preference is an important factor in calculating the present value of expected cash flows. Because profit is not the same as money, it is methodologically incorrect to calculate the present value of expected profits; in practice, however, this erroneous approach still occurs.

6.3 Future Cash Flow

People act in order to achieve an expected improvement in their position and situation. This is why the concept of economic value has a prospective character. The past has no economic value; the past shows how we have arrived at our present position and situation, but this does not say what our next step must be. Plans relate to the future. It is impossible to undo an action once it has been done: at most, something can be done about the consequence of the action. A crucial factor is the quality of the decision-making information that is used. The envisaged consequences of human action cannot be known in advance, but this does not mean that the decision maker must resort to guesswork. Economic phenomena are the consequence, desired or otherwise, of human action. The desired consequences of an intended action are charted using explicit expectations. Expectations are based on causal relationships, and so we draw a distinction between 'hoping for' and 'expecting.' A good plan will, therefore, emphasize causality. Entrepreneurs observe that consumers are interested in a certain good. The question of whether the entrepreneur should actually produce that good can only be answered if estimates are made about the expected demand and the prices that will be established. The income deriving from this must outweigh the expenditure needed to bring the product to market. Entrepreneurs 'see' more clearly than others how paying present prices can lead to the addition of economic value.

Example I

Suppose that an entrepreneur detects that consumers in the market are interested in good M. At the moment, 'M' is not yet offered. To produce it, the entrepreneur needs a machine. This costs €900 and it will function for three years; the residual value is set at zero. In addition, labor and raw materials are needed, and these will require a sum of €200 per year. The machine can generate turnover of €633.33. The applicable rate of corporate income tax is 25%. On the basis of the example, the expected result (in €) is calculated.

Turnover	633.33
Costs	200.00
Depreciation	300.00
Profit before tax	133.33
Corporate income tax	33.33
Net profit	100.00

The question now is whether the annual net profit is high enough to justify buying the machine. Accountants often use the concept of average accounting rate of return (also known as return on investment (ROI)), which involves dividing the average net profit by the amount of the average investment. The return in this case is 22.22% (= 100/450). This sounds attractive, but caution is advised.

The reason for caution is that the investment requires expenditure of €900, and this money must be supplied by a capital provider. If the capital provider wants an annual return of 10%, this must be taken into account. Moreover, on the basis of time preference, money that is received later has less value than money that becomes available sooner. Instead of ROI, it is, therefore, better to work with 'net present value.' The reasoning is as follows. If the aforementioned expectation materializes, a cash flow per year of €400 (= net profit plus depreciation) can be expected. The present value of this cash flow at T_0 (time of valuation) is $\sum_{t=1}^{3} \frac{cash\,flow}{(1+c)^t}$.

In this case, $$\frac{400}{(1+0.10)^1} + \frac{400}{(1+0.10)^2} + \frac{400}{(1+0.10)^3} = 994.74.$$

If the amount required for the investment (= €900) is deducted from the present value, the remainder is the net present value (= €94.74). The positive net present value indicates that the investment is economically sensible, on the basis of the assumptions used.

6.4   Cost of Capital

Capital goods are an essential requirement for generating future cash flows. From the perspective of economics, anything that can produce a cash flow can be called a capital good; not only buildings and machinery but also patents, processes, and ideas. Even a practicable business plan qualifies as a capital good. Within economics, a distinction is made between consumer goods and capital goods. Consumer goods are bought because they provide the buyer with (marginal) utility for a short or longer time; they satisfy needs. Capital goods are bought because they produce consumer goods or other capital goods. Therefore, the production of capital goods requires a partial renunciation of consumption. This diversion is profitable when it yields a greater return than if immediate consumption had taken place. In order to invest, and to transform capital into capital goods, it is necessary to temporarily refrain from consumption. Immediate gratification is sacrificed for deferred gratification. The loss of immediate gratification is known by the term 'opportunity cost.' The consequence is that the capital providers want a payment for supplying that capital. The return wanted by the capital providers, investing their money in companies, constitutes an expense for the user of that capital: the cost of capital. In this connection, it is important to point out that in fact there are two kinds of capital. The shareholders supply the 'equity capital' for the company. This is also known as 'share capital,' and it remains permanently invested in the company; there is no formal obligation to repay the equity capital. Such a repayment obligation does, however, exist for the company's 'debt capital,' which is provided on a temporary, short- or longer-term basis. There are also 'hybrid' forms of capital, such as convertible bonds, but these will not be further discussed here. In general, debt capital providers supply that capital on pre-determined conditions, and collateral is demanded. The outcome is that a lower return is associated with debt capital than with equity capital. The shareholders expect the investment that they make in the company to yield a certain return, consisting of a dividend and, if possible, share price gain. No collateral is provided; therefore, equity capital demands a higher return than debt capital. In addition, it should be pointed out that the remuneration paid by the company for the use of debt capital is treated differently by tax authorities than the remuneration given to the shareholders. In many countries, interest paid on debt—unlike distributed dividend—is treated as a tax-deductible expense. This gives rise to a tax effect, also known as a 'tax shield,' by which a company that is partially financed with debt capital has a higher economic value than an analogous company that is financed only with equity capital.

Example II

Debt Capital and the Tax Shield

Suppose that in a certain year, a company makes a profit before tax of €1,000. If the rate of corporate income tax is 25%, then €250 must be paid in tax. Until this time, the company has only been financed with equity capital.

Now suppose that the company decides to substitute some of the equity capital—say €5,000—with debt capital. The bank is willing to loan this amount at interest of 6% per year, and the tax authorities treat interest paid on debt as a tax-deductible expense. The substitution of equity capital by debt capital naturally has no impact on the achieved operating result. The profit before interest and taxes is, therefore, still €1,000. Now, however, the profit before taxes is lower, because €300 of interest must be paid. The taxable profit is then €700 (= 1,000 – 300) and the corporate income tax payable on this is €175 (= 0.25 × 700). The company now has a tax advantage of €75 (= 250 – 175). This so-called tax shield consists of rate of corporate income tax x interest x debt capital sum (0.25 × 0.06 × 5,000).

Cost of capital is a prominent factor in economic decision making. If capital providers do not receive their desired return, they will not supply any (more) capital, and the company will consequently lose its right to exist. The level of the cost of capital can be estimated from the behavior of the capital providers, in which the following elements play a part. Time preference gives rise to a payment known as 'interest'; another factor is the expected risk, and account must also be taken of possible changes in the purchasing power of money. Because the provision of capital precedes the materialization of expected results, the quality of the expectations is particularly important. Capital providers not only use differing expectations, they also have differing possibilities and act from differing positions. The group of capital providers is far from homogeneous. Cost of capital can never be objectively determined; in everyday life there is no such thing as a standard capital provider and no such thing as a standard company. Nonetheless, it might be wise to look at what other capital providers are currently demanding for other, analogous, investment facilities. These observations will, however, only serve as illustration material and cannot be used as an objective requirement. That would only be possible in a world consisting of efficient markets, and a world of this kind can only be found on school blackboards. The capital provider is autonomous in determining its own return requirement, although it will naturally be in competition with all other capital providers.

6.5   Uncertainty and Risk

The assessment of investments and furnishing of capital to companies inevitably involves the concepts of uncertainty and risk. The concept of uncertainty means that people cannot know the future, so we can only make decisions in a situation of uncertainty. In a world of certainty, there is no need to make decisions; it is simply clear what must be done. The passage of time can cause some uncertainties to disappear, but at the same time, other ones will appear. In our world, it is impossible to eliminate uncertainty. Uncertainty is a quality, a property, that is inherent to human life. The existence of uncertainty allows economic profit to be achieved. In a world of certainty, that is not possible. In that world, although all factors of production are remunerated, 'profit' does not exist. Economic profit is the reward that can accrue for people who operate under uncertain circumstances.

However, some uncertainties occur frequently and quite regularly, which sometimes makes it possible to quantify them. A probability distribution can be developed from the observation of events and, if it is plausible to use history as a predictor, it becomes possible to make a judgment about expected risks. This does, however, lead us into a minefield. In the literature, we often see the concept of standard deviation mentioned in this connection. It makes sense to work with the deviation from a mean if there is an almost normal distribution. However, most economic phenomena do not display a normal distribution. Economists study human behavior, and there is a temptation here to make use of methods that are more appropriate for studying phenomena of physics. Laws of economics, however, are of a different character than the laws of physics. In this case too, observers can naturally use their own judgment as a guideline, but then the risk premium is established on a subjective basis.

6.6   Economic Value Is Subjective

Economic value can be visualized mathematically by means of a fraction. The numerator contains the expected cash flows and the denominator consists of the discount rate, the so-called hurdle rate, that is used by the decision maker. It is clear from the aforementioned that both the numerator and the denominator have a subjective character. Different observers come to different value judgments. This makes it sensible to negotiate, and from this a price can arise. The parties apparently agree about the price, but this also means that they disagree about the economic value. The concept of economic value has an ordinal ranking character. In the example given earlier (I), an economic value of more than €994 arises. This value says that in this case, assuming the expectations actually materialize, it is beneficial for the decision maker to invest the necessary €900 in the project if the calculation involves a discount rate of 10%. Another observer can assume a different expected cash flow and a different discount rate. The ordinal character of the concept of economic value precludes the summation of values. Thus it is only possible to speak metaphorically about the economic value of 'the Netherlands plc': the actual calculation cannot be performed. The concept of economic value is a construct located only in the decision maker's head. It is not directly observable by others; we can only deduce from people's behavior what value motivates their actions.

Example III

The following example shows how the economic value of a company is determined in practice. The valuation is based on the following assumptions:

- The expected cash flow for the years T_1 to T_4 is €50, €75, €110, and €140.
- The expected cash flow for the years T_5 and onward is €150.
- The cost of equity capital (unlevered) is 10%.
- The cost of debt capital is 6%.
- The rate of corporate income tax is 25%.
- Interest paid is classed as a tax-deductible expense.
- The debt capital at T_0 is €100, at T_1 to T_4 it is €200, and from T_5 the company will be financed with debt capital of €750.

Calculation

The expected free cash flow can be divided into two parts. The years for which the amounts vary are called the 'explicit forecast period,' and the subsequent years are called the 'residual period.' The two periods are discounted to present value separately and then added together. For the explicit forecast period, this comes to $\sum_{n=1}^{4} \frac{FCF}{(1+0.10)^n} = €285.70$. The residual value then comes to $\frac{150}{0.10} / (1+0.10)^4 = €1,024.52$. The total operating economic value at T_0 is, therefore, €1310.22 (= €285.70 + €1024.52). To calculate the tax shield, we use the same approach. For the explicit forecast period, the years T_1 to T_4, this comes to €8.14 $\left(= \sum_{n=1}^{4} \frac{TS}{(1+0.10)^n}\right)$, and for the residual

period, €71.71 $\left[= \frac{11.25}{0.10} / (1 + 0.10)^4\right]$, therefore in total €79.86. The eco-

nomic value of the company at T_0 is therefore €1,390.08 (= €1,310.22 + €79.86).

6.7   How a Good Expectation Can Still Lead to Disappointing Results

Case Study: Res Manufacturing & Development Ltd.—Liquidate or Continue?

The controller of Res is scrutinizing a recently submitted investment pro-posal. On the basis of a plan formulated by the head of development, it seems to be a valid proposal. The duration of the investment is set at four years; the rate of return in the first year is expected to be 11.25%, and the average rate of return 22.5%. The calculation is based on the following assumptions. To manufacture the product, Dorsum, the company will need a machine that requires an investment of €1,000. The machine will be depreciated in equal amounts over the duration. It is expected that the machine will be able to produce one hundred units per year and that it will be possible to actually sell these units. The selling price per unit is set at €9. The unit cost (materials and labor) is €5 per unit, according to the production planning department. It is stipulated by Res management that investment proposals must be based on a 'hurdle rate' of 10%. According to the marketing department, the expected market size is estimated to be 600 units per year. The marketers also agree with the proposed selling price of €9 per unit. The corporate income tax depends on how much accounting profit is made, and the rate is 25%.

On the basis of the explanation in the proposal, the aforemnetioned fig-ures for the rate of return were determined as follows. If one hundred units are sold, the profit before tax is €150 (= €900–€500–€250). After deduc-tion of the corporate income tax, there remains €112.50. In relation to the investment of €1000, the accounting rate of return for the first year comes to 11.25%. After two years, the book value of the machine has fallen to €500 and, if the profit stays the same, the accounting rate of return is then 22.5%. The controller has his doubts; it often turns out in practice that expectations are over-optimistic. Nonetheless, the management board takes the view that a certain amount of risk is not out of place with this expected rate of return and gives its approval. Implementation is started expeditiously. However, it is decided that a new company will be set up for bringing Dorsum to the market. In view of the market size, the management board wants to quickly bring the production up to speed, and is, therefore, intending to obtain debt capital. In the past, the management board has taken the view that invest-ment in expansion must be financed from the profits. In this case, however, this would mean that a second machine can only be bought during the third year. By obtaining debt capital, it is possible to buy a new machine every year. For the sake of caution, the expansion will initially only take place once 'zero net investment' has been reached—i.e., when the annual investment is equal to the total of the depreciations. The management board also wants to have a buffer of at least €95 (balance sheet position at financial year-end). It is agreed with the bank that at T_1 it will provide a loan of €750 and that at T_2 the amount of the loan will be increased for two years to €1,050. After this, €400 will be repaid at both T_4 and T_5. The remainder, €250, can be repaid one year later. The interest on an annual basis is 7%. In making this decision, the management board was strongly guided by a comment made by the controller. He said that, if the expectations materialize, the economic value of the new company when it is established can be set at €2,700 if zero net investment is assumed. In that case, the free cash flow (in €) will develop as follows (Table 6.1):

Table 6.1 Development of Free Cash Flow (FCF)

	T1	T2	T3	T4→∞		
PbIT	150.0	300.0	450.0	600.0		
CIT 0.25	37.5	75.0	112.5	150.0		
NOPAT	112.5	225.0	337.5	450.0		
Depreciation	250.0	500.0	750.0	1,000.0		
Investment	−1,000.0	−1,000.0	−1,000.0	−1,000.0		
FCF	−637.5	−275.0	87.5	450.0		
	T1	T2	T3	T4	T5	T6
Debt Capital	750.000	1,050.000	1,050.000	650.000	250.000	0.000
Interest Rate 0.07	0.000	52.500	73.500	73.500	45.500	17.5000
Tax Shield	0.000	13.125	18.375	18.375	11.375	4.375

On the basis of the aforementioned information, the economic value of the operating activities during the explicit forecast period (T_1 to T_6) comes to €99.70 (time of valuation T_0). The economic value of the residual period at this time of valuation is €2,540.13. Therefore, the total operating economic value at T_0 is €2,639.83. If the aforementioned capital structure is applicable, the economic value of the tax shield for years T_1 to T_6 can be calculated to be €46.73, if the unlevered cost of equity capital (C_{eu}) is used as the discount rate. This brings the total economic value to €2,686.57 (= €99.70 + €46.73 + €2540.13), which rounds up to €2,700. The cash flow shown in Table 6.1 is discounted to present value on the basis of a 'hurdle rate' of 10%.

After three years, mild panic develops in the management board, and they call in an advisor. On his first visit, the management board tells the advisor that the project started off according to plan, but the realized results are very different from what the company expected. The management board presents the following summary (Table 6.2):

Table 6.2 Results for the Years T$_1$ to T$_3$

	T1 – r	T2 – r	T3 – r	T3 – e
Turnover	350	1,200	1,800	2,700
Costs	650	1,100	1,650	1,500
Depreciation	250	500	750	750
Profit Before Interest and Tax	-550	-400	-600	450
Interest	0	112	210	73.5
Profit Before Tax	-550	-512	-810	376.5

Table 6.2 shows the realized (r) results for the years T$_1$ to T$_3$. For comparison, the expected (e) result for T$_3$ is added.

Further analysis reveals the following points. Because of start-up problems, the turnover in the first year was lower than expected. The decision was also made to offer a discount to the first buyers. During the first year, fifty units were sold at €7 per unit. The start-up problems also resulted in higher costs. In addition, it appears that very little attention was given to the accounts receivable policy. At the end of T$_1$, the accounts receivable balance is €200 and at the end of T$_2$ there is an accounts receivable item of €500 on the balance sheet. Due to the unexpected difficulties, the bank had to provide additional debt capital. At the end of the first year, the bank supplied an additional credit of €850; at T$_2$, the total bank debt amounted to €3,000. The intended investments had actually been made.

At the end of the third year, the bank refused to give more credit. If the policy remains unchanged, the balance sheet at T$_3$ is expected to display the picture shown in Table 6.3.

If the planned investment goes ahead, the item 'tangible fixed assets' will consist of four machines, which represent a combined book value of €2,500. However, the planned investment of €1,000 at T$_3$ will not be possible if the bank refuses to increase the credit. If this is not done, the book value will be €1,500. The proceeds for the oldest machine will probably now be zero, and the total net proceeds for the other two are estimated at €450.

The controller has estimated the amount that can become available in the event of liquidation. The estimate is that they can actually collect 80%

Table 6.3 Balance Sheet at T$_3$

Machinery	2,500	Equity Capital	-872
Accounts Receivable	250	Debt Capital	3,000
Cash	-622		
Total Debit	2,128	Total Credit	2,128

of the accounts receivable balance. The cost of liquidation, which is esti-mated to be €250, is also taken into account. This means the company can expect an income of €650 (= €450 + €200), which leaves no more than €400 (= €650 – €250) for the debt capital provider. The bank is willing to have further investigation carried out into the possibilities of continu-ing the production and sales of Dorsum. On the basis of a sound business plan, the bank could grant additional credit—the amount under consid-eration is €650—although in that case the interest would be increased to 8% (annual basis).

Further analysis offers the following points. The technicians concerned say that the production problems can be resolved within one year, and from T_5, production can take place with four machines. The marketing depart-ment is still just as positive about Dorsum's possibilities. According to the credit managers, the accounts receivable balance—which is €250 at the end of T_3—can also be maintained in the future. The controller's view is that the incurred loss can be offset for tax purposes; therefore, no corporate income tax will be payable over the next few years. On the basis of these assump-tions, the expectation shown in Table 6.4 (in €) is derived.

These expected accounting profits result in the following cash flow shown in Table 6.5.

Table 6.4 Expected Accounting Profits

	T4	T5	T6	T7
Turnover	3,150	3,600	3,600	3,600
Costs	1,750	2,000	2,000	2,000
Depreciation	1,000	1,000	1,000	1,000
Profit Before Interest and Tax	400	600	600	600
Interest	292	292	264	240
Profit Before Tax	108	308	336	360
Corporate Income Tax	0	0	0	0
Net Profit	108	308	336	360

Table 6.5 Expected Cash Flow

	T4	T5	T6	T7
Profit Before Interest and Tax	400	600	600	600
Corporate Income Tax	0	0	12.5	150
Net Operating Profit After Tax	400	600	587.5	450
Depreciation	1,000	1,000	1,000	1,000
Investment	–1,000	–1,000	–1,000	–1,000
Change in Net Working Capital	0	0	0	0
Free Cash Flow	400	600	587.5	450

In making a decision about whether to allow extra credit, the economic value to be determined on the basis of the aforementioned free cash flow can be helpful. Before proceeding to do this, however, it is wise to first reflect on what caused the disappointing results. It is not necessarily sensible to simply provide more capital to a company in difficulties. The creditors will perhaps regard it as a sympathetic gesture, but more than this is needed to ensure viability. The additional capital that is provided must make it possible for the company to generate additional free cash flow. The economic value of the company does not depend on the capital position but on the possibilities of creating free cash flow.

6.7.1   What Went Wrong?

Unreliable Performance Indicator

The assessment of investment plans requires more than a simple calculation of the rate of return. The fact that the original plan shows the expected rate of return for the first year, 11.25%, increasing to an average of 22.5% gives cause for thought. After all, the expected results are identical for all years. In reality, the result does not increase at all; the rising rate of return is purely the consequence of depreciations. On the first day, the book value of the machine—the price paid minus depreciations—is €1,000; on the last day, the machine has been fully depreciated. However, depreciation does not produce any money. This shows that (net) profit is a dangerous performance indicator. In most cases, it is better to use money as the basis. In this case, a clearer picture would be obtained by using the concept of cash flow. According to the original plan, the annual accounting cash flow is €362.50 (= net profit plus depreciation); when this is compared with the investment, it can be said that the cash yield of the proposed investment is 36.25% per year (= €362.50/1,000). The plan states that the machine will generate the same yield each year. No rising percentages are involved. Yet this approach too is not without its dangers. The accounting cash flow is not the same as the 'free cash flow.' For most companies, goods are bought and sold on account, and also, in many cases, a stock position will arise. In addition, the expected growth—the increase in the number of machines—also needs to be financed. For the implementation year, see Table 6.2, this means that the accounting cash flow changes from minus €300 (= −€550 + €250) into a negative free cash flow of €1,500. Not only is a new machine purchased (= −€1000), but account must also be taken of the net working capital. The item 'accounts receivable' at the end of the first year is €200. It is clear that additional credit must be obtained at the end of the first year. The expectations for the first year were over-optimistic. Start-up problems, lower production, and higher costs per unit had a very negative impact on the result. Moreover, the first buyers could take advantage of a discount, and this too had a negative impact on the result. Presented in Table 6.6 is the comparison for the first year between what was expected and the ultimate realization (in €):

Table 6.6 Comparison of Expected Accounting Profit and Realization

	T1 – e	T1 – r
Turnover	900	350
Costs	500	650
Depreciation	250	250
Profit before Interest and Tax	150	–550
Interest	0	0
Profit before Tax	150	–550

Not only the accounting profit but also the free cash flow (in €) in the first year diverges significantly from the expectations (Table 6.7):

Table 6.7 Comparison of Expected Cash Flow and Realization

	T1 – e	T1 – r
Profit Before Interest and Tax	150.00	–550.00
Corporate Income Tax	37.50	0.00
NOPAT	112.50	–550.00
Depreciation	250.00	250.00
Investment	–1,000.00	–1,000.00
Change in Net Working Capital	0.00	–200.00
Free Cash Flow	–637.50	–1,500.00

The disappointing result is made worse by the unforeseen item 'net working capital.' The failure of the expected free cash flow to materialize means that the envisaged amount of debt capital (= €750) is insufficient if the planned investment is actually implemented. At the end of the first year, additional debt capital (= €850) will then have to be obtained. It is naturally up to the debt capital provider to make a decision about this. In practice, a contribution will perhaps also be expected from the equity capital providers.

This example shows that the assessment of investment plans must make use of expected cash flows and not of accounting performance indicators. The example also shows where the problems lie in this case. Making plans on paper is rather different from the implementation of plans. It is found in practice that when investment plans are formulated, insufficient information is requested from other involved parties. Why were the expected sales not realized? Was it really necessary to give introductory discounts? Why was the planned production level not achieved? What caused the amount of net working capital? In this case, it is possible that timely consultation of marketers, technicians, and credit managers would have led to better results. The assessment of investment plans is more than a mathematical exercise.

6.7.2   What Should Be Done Now?

It is clear that liquidation, also in this case, does not yield very much. It is sensible to continue if, at the time of valuation (= T_3), a positive economic value is found. This can only arise if the company and the debt capital provider are convinced of the possibility that the results will show a strong improvement as from T_4. If the marketers still have a positive view of the sales potential, and if the technicians can solve the problems in the production process, the worst is over. If this is indeed the case, the following expectation (Table 6.8) arises with regard to free cash flow (in €):

Table 6.8 Expected Free Cash Flow

	T4	T5	T6	T7 → ∞
Profit Before Interest and Tax	400	600	600	600
Corporate Income Tax	0	0	12.5	150
Net Operating Profit After Tax	400	600	587.5	450
Depreciation	1,000	1,000	1,000	1,000
Investment	−1,000	−1,000	−1,000	−1,000
Change in Net Working Capital	0	0	0	0
Free Cash Flow	400	600	587.5	450

The economic value at T_3 (= time of valuation) then comes out at €4682. The calculation proceeds as follows:

$$\sum_{n=4}^{6} \frac{FCFn}{(1+Ceu)^n} + \sum_{n=7}^{\infty} \frac{FCFn}{(1+Ceu)^n}.$$

Mathematically, this is

$$\frac{400}{(1+0.10)} + \frac{600}{(1+0.10)^2} + \frac{587.5}{(1+0.10)^3} + \frac{\dfrac{450}{0.10}}{(1+0.10)^3} = €4681.82.$$

In addition, there is a tax shield. If the debt capital provider agrees to the new business plan, additional debt capital will be made available. The interest will also be increased by one percentage point. The development of the debt capital (in €) is shown in Table 6.9.

Table 6.9 Development of Debt Capital

	T3	T4	T5	T6	T7	T8	T9	T10	T11	T12	T13	T14
Debt Capital	3,650	3,650	3,300	3,000	2,600	2,200	1,800	1,500	1,100	750	350	0
Interest		292	292	264	240	208	176	144	120	88	60	28
Tax Shield		0	0	12.5	150	150	136	36	30	22	15	7

Because the first years are characterized by loss-making operation, an off-settable loss arises. At T_3, the amount of this loss is €1,872 (see Table 6.10). Assuming that all the loss can be offset against future profits, the following forecast (in €) can be formulated:

The earlier summary shows that the accumulated profits (before tax) for the years T_4 to T_9 amount to €1,928 and the accumulated loss amounts to €1,872, which means that for T_9 it will be necessary to pay corporate income tax on €56 (= €1,928 – €1,872). At a rate of 25%, this comes to an amount of €14. The corporate income tax is calculated on the profit after taking the interest into account. However, determination of the economic value is based on the expected net operating cash flow. The cumulative loss of €1,872 includes an amount of interest of €322 (= €112 + €210). This means that the operating loss is €1550 (= €1872 – €322). This loss is offset against future operating profits. Table 6.10 shows that tax will be paid on the operating result from T_6. It is now easy to determine the tax shield. Tax should actually be paid on the operating result from the sixth year. In fact, however, it follows from the earnings statement that as yet, no corporate income tax is paid, because there is still an outstanding offsettable loss. The difference is used to offset the interest part of the offsettable loss.

Table 6.10 presents the totality of the tax shields. If these are discounted to present value using the cost of equity capital (C_{eu}), an additional economic value arises of €331.79. The total economic value then comes to €5,013.60. This value must be divided between the equity capital providers and the debt capital providers. In this case, it is assumed that at T_3, the debt capital provider supplies an amount of €3,650. There then remains €1,363.40 for the equity capital.

It is now also possible to determine, on the basis of the supplied information, how the economic value will change over the lifespan of the company (Table 6.11).

The following points can be derived from Table 6.11. At the time of valuation (T_3), the economic value is €5,013.604. The fourth year, therefore, starts with that total capital. The debt capital is €3,650 and the rate of interest payable on this is 8%; the €292 is paid on the last day of the fourth year from the free cash flow of €400. The ratio Interest/FCF (= 292/400) of 0.73 is high; in many cases, the debt capital provider will not want to go much higher than a ratio of 0.25–0.30.

Table 6.12 shows the development of the balance sheet (in €), which reveals that up to and including T_6 there is negative (accounting) equity capital.

At T_3, there is negative accounting equity capital of €872. At that point in time, the total economic value is €5,014. There then remains €1,364 (= €5,014 – €3,650) for the equity capital. The accounting equity capital reflects the past and is therefore not important in economic decision making.

Table 6.10 Forecast

	T1	T2	T3	T4	T5	T6	T7	T8	T9	T10	T11	T12	T13	T14
Turnover	350	1,200	1,800	3,150	3,600	3,600	3,600	3,600	3,600	3,600	3,600	3,600	3,600	3,600
Cost	650	1,100	1,650	1,750	2,000	2,000	2,000	2,000	2,000	2,000	2,000	2,000	2,000	2,000
Depr	250	500	750	1,000	1,000	1,000	1,000	1,000	1,000	1,000	1,000	1,000	1,000	1,000
PbIT	-550	-400	-600	400	600	600	600	600	600	600	600	600	600	600
Interest	0	112	210	292	292	264	240	208	176	144	120	88	60	28
PbT	-550	-512	-810	108	308	336	360	392	424	456	480	512	540	572
CIT	0	0	0	0	0	0	0	0	14	114	120	128	135	143
Net Profit	-550	-512	-810	108	308	336	360	392	410	342	360	384	405	429
PbIT	-550	-400	-600	400	600	600	600	600	600	600	600	600	600	600
CIT	0	0	0	0	0	12.5	150	150	150	150	150	150	150	150
Oper Profit	-550	-400	-600	400	600	587.5	450	450	450	450	450	450	450	450
Depr	250	500	750	1,000	1,000	1,000	1,000	1,000	1,000	1,000	1,000	1,000	1,000	1,000
N.Invest	-1,000	-1,000	-1,000	-1,000	-1,000	-1,000	-1,000	-1,000	-1,000	-1,000	-1,000	-1,000	-1,000	-1,000
NWK	-200	-300	250	0	0	0	0	0	0	0	0	0	0	0
FCF	-1,500	-1,200	-600	400	600	587.5	450	450	450	450	450	450	450	450
TS	0	0	0	0	0	12.5	150	150	136	36	30	22	15	7

Table 6.11 Economic Value Over the Lifespan of the Company

V3	5,013.604	1,363.604	0.153535	209.3604		
CC4	501.3604	3,650	0.08	292	0	0.1
	5,514.964					
FCF4	400					
V4	5,114.964	1,464.964	0.149831	219.4964		
CC5	511.4964	3,650	0.08	292	0	0.1
	5,626.461					
FCF5	600					
V5	5,026.461	1,726.461	0.138228	238.6461		
CC6	490.1461	3,300	0.08	264	12.5	0.097513
	5,516.607					
FCF6	587.5					
V6	4,929.107	1,929.107	0.131102	252.9107		
CC7	342.9107	3,000	0.08	240	150	0.069569
	5,272.018					
FCF7	450					
V7	4,822.018	2,222.018	0.123402	274.2018		
CC8	332.2018	2,600	0.08	208	150	0.068893
	5,154.219					
FCF8	450					
V8	4,704.219	2,504.219	0.11757	294.4219		
CC9	334.4219	2,200	0.08	176	136	0.07109
	5,038.641					
FCF9	450					
V9	4,588.641	2,788.641	0.11291	314.8641		
CC10	422.8641	1,800	0.08	144	36	0.092155
	5,011.505					
FCF10	450					
V10	4,561.505	3,061.505	0.109799	336.1505		

Table 6.12 Development of the Balance Sheet

	T0	T1	T2	T3	T4	T5	T6	T7	T8
Mach	1,000	1,750	2,250	2,500	2,500	2,500	2,500	2,500	2,500
Debit	0	200	500	250	250	250	250	250	250
Cash	0	100	188	28	136	94	130	90	82
Tot Dt	1,000	2,050	2,938	2,778	2,886	2,844	2,880	2,840	2,832
Equity	1,000	450	-62	-872	-764	-456	-120	240	632
Debt	0	1,600	3,000	3,650	3,650	3,300	3,000	2,600	2,200
Tot Cr	1,000	2,050	2,938	2,778	2,886	2,844	2,880	2,840	2,832

If the expectations materialize, it is possible to implement the business plan. The answer to the question, "What should be done now?", is, therefore, "Continue."

6.7.3   What Price Can Be Expected If the Company Is Sold?

Now suppose that a buyer is interested in this company. The basic principle here is that the expected cash flow should be presented realistically, also in the eyes of potential buyers. When calculating the economic value, the buyer naturally uses the cost of capital that is applicable for the buyer. In view of the company's difficult situation, in this case, the buyer bases the calculation on a cost of equity capital of 12%. The buyer can obtain debt capital at an interest rate of 6%. The (current) debt capital provider informs the buyer that the loan is eligible for penalty-free early repayment from T_6; for the years T_4 and T_5, the previously agreed interest of 8% will have to be paid. The buyer assumes that after the early repayment at T_6, the company can be financed on the basis of the financing ratio desired by the buyer. For the buyer, the future picture (in €) is as follows in Table 6.13:

Table 6.13   Outlook

	T3	T4	T5	T6	T7	T8	T9	T10→∞
FCF		300	450	450	450	450	450	450
Debt C	3,650	3,650	3,300	2,500	2,000	1,000	0	0
Interest		292	292	264	150	120	60	0
TS		73	73	66	37.5	30	15	0
Interest		292	292	264				
Repayment		0	350	3,300				
Total		292	642	3,564				
Ec. Value	3,839	3,777	3,362					

At T_6, some of the debt capital will be repaid; at T_7 and T_8, further repayments will follow, and from T_9 there is no longer any debt capital. Because the old capital structure applies for the years T_4 and T_5, a disadvantage arises for the buyer. Instead of financing at 6%, the rate to be paid is 8%. In consequence of this, the economic value of the debt capital is higher than the book value. When calculating the economic value of the equity capital, the buyer will take this into account. The economic value of the debt capital at T_3 is €3,839. The calculation proceeds as follows:

$$\frac{292}{(1+0.06)} + \frac{642}{(1+0.06)^2} + \frac{3564}{(1+0.06)^3} = €3839.25.$$ The future 'debt service,'

interest and repayment, is discounted to the present using the current interest rate applicable for the buyer. The economic value of the debt capital naturally changes, because interest payments and repayments change and because time passes. One year later, the economic value of the debt capital is €3,777.61, and at T_5, the economic value of the debt capital is €3,362.26 (= €3,564/1.06).

For the buyer, the following picture now arises: at T_3, the economic value of the free cash flow is $\sum_{n=4}^{9} \frac{FCFn}{(1+Ceu)^n} + \sum_{n=10}^{\infty} \frac{FCFn}{(1+Ceu)^n}$. The present value of the cash flow for the years T_4 to T_9 is €1,716.20. The present value of the

residual period is calculated to be $\dfrac{\dfrac{450}{0.12}}{(1+0.12)^6} = \dfrac{3750}{(1+0.12)^6} = €1,899.86.$ The

economic value of the operating activities, therefore, comes to €3,616.07. The fact that interest is paid gives an advantage if the tax authorities allow the interest to be treated as a tax-deductible expense. This gives rise to a lower corporate income tax assessment, and this advantage accrues to the equity capital providers. In this case, the present value of the tax shield is €218.80. This brings the economic value of the company to €3,834.87. It was already established that the economic value of the debt capital (at T_3) is €3,839.25. Now the economic value of the equity capital can be calculated to be (minus) €4.37. Because there is no formal 'additional payment' obligation for the equity capital, the economic value can never be lower than zero. If the buyer wants to add value by means of the transaction, he will have to persuade the seller to inject an additional amount. The seller might be able to do this because he will perhaps have been released from all his obligations at the time of the transaction. In practice, it is indeed observed that buyers of badly performing companies receive a 'money payment.' In many cases, another important factor is the danger of damage to the reputation. By selling a company, the seller can be relieved of a troublesome burden. For the debt capital provider, the world looks a better place. Interest and repayments can be paid according to plan.

Yet this is not the end of the story. The fact that the company being sold has a tax offsettable loss deserves further attention. The negative value calculated earlier arises if the buyer must immediately start paying corporate income tax on the profit that is expected from T_4. In certain cases, however, it is possible that the loss accrued by the seller during the first three years can be offset by the buyer. This gives a different economic value, because now no corporate income tax is payable for the first few years. If the buyer continues the company and is permitted to make use of the offsettable loss, the picture in Table 6.14 (in €) arises:

Table 6.14 Economic Value

	T4	T5	T6	T7	T8	T9	T10
PbIT	400	600	600	600	600	600	600
Interest	292	292	264	150	120	60	0
PbT	108	308	336	450	480	540	600
CIT	0	0	0	0	0	87.5	150
NP	108	308	336	450	480	452.5	450
PbIT	400	600	600	600	600	600	600
CIT	0	0	0	82	150	150	150
NOPAT = FCF	400	600	600	518	450	450	450
TS	0	0	0	82	150	62.5	0

The economic value of the company now comes to €4,143.80. The difference occurs because, in this case, no corporate income tax needs to be paid for the years T₄ to T₈. If the free cash flows are compared, the difference (in €) can be seen in Table 6.15:

Table 6.15 Difference in Cash Flow

	T1	T2	T3	T4	T5→∞
FCF without offset	300	450	450	450	450
FCF with offset	400	600	600	518	450
FCF difference	100	150	150	68	0

The present value of this difference is €358.84. Because the losses can be offset, the tax shield also acquires a different value. Without offset, the value is €218.80 and with offset the economic value is €168.89, a negative difference of €49.91. The net addition to the economic value is therefore €308.93. The negative economic value of €4.37 changes into a positive value of €304.55. Here, too, the buyer will want to add value by means of the transaction. The price to be paid will then be lower than the calculated value. The situation could turn out even more favorably for the buyer if the company being bought can be combined in terms of taxable results with existing profitable units. If the taxable profit permits, it might be possible to offset the entire tax offsettable loss in the first year after the company is bought. In such a case, the value of the offsettable loss is calculated to be €468 (= 0.25 x €1872). In this theoretical discourse, the author can bend the world to his will. In practice, however, a part is played by the tax rules applicable at the time of sale. It is, therefore, important that the due diligence investigation prior to the sale is conducted thoroughly. The world does not have uniform tax laws, and governments can make frequent changes to the laws and rules.

6.8   Conclusion

The valuation of a company in difficulties is mathematically no different from the valuation of thriving businesses. However, those calculation rules are applied within a completely different playing field. In the considerations that must lead to a decision, the most important question is 'why.' Why has the company run into a difficult situation? It makes a big difference whether, as in this case, the company is having problems because the investment decision was not made carefully, or whether it is because the potential size of the market was wrongly estimated. Can technical problems be resolved in a short time? What is the quality of the management and the employees of the company being acquired? In some cases, all the employees must be included in the acquisition of a company. Is that desirable? The buyer must also have sufficient financial strength. Companies in difficulties are often financed both too heavily and too expensively. It is extremely important that the buyer should have a thorough due diligence investigation conducted. Especially for companies with problems, it is not enough to ask for a standard type of investigation. The primary requirement that must be imposed is will the buyer actually obtain what he wants and the reasons why the company is being acquired? The motives can vary widely: greater spread of customers, size of the market, or utilization of offsettable loss. The analysis must mainly focus on answering that question. Above all, it is essential that the buyer views the entire analysis in light of the possibility of adding economic value.

Part III

Turnaround Management

7 Turnaround Planning

Insights From Evolutionary Approaches to the Theory of the Firm

Gianpaolo Abatecola and Vincenzo Uli

7.1 Introduction

Why, in this new century, did the Lehman Brothers fail? Why, conversely, was the turnaround of the Fiat Group successful? To a certain extent, why, to date, has the Italian government decided to save some banks from bankruptcy?

Over time, turnaround scholars have devoted considerable attention not only to understanding the possible antecedents of corporate decline and failure but also to the development of pioneering conceptual models aimed at implementing effective and efficient strategies of business rescue (e.g., Barker III & Mone, 1994; Bibeault, 1982; Harrigan, 1980). In this regard, for example, Barmash seminally stated that "corporations are managed by men; and men, never forget, manage organizations to suit themselves. Thus corporate calamities are calamities created by men" (1973, p. 299).

On this premise, it is a matter of fact that, to date, crises and failures continue to occur at both macro and microeconomic levels, and they can be presently considered as physiological components of our society. Some turnarounds are successful, whereas some others fail. This is why, in general, strategists currently conceive the research and practice about turnaround planning and management as a constantly progressing discipline (e.g., Adriaanse, Van der Rest, & Verdoes, 2015; McKinley, Latham, & Braun, 2014; Parsa, Van der Rest, Smith, Parsa, & Bujisic, 2015; Raisch, 2013; Tangpong, Abebe, & Li, 2015; Trahms, Ndofor, & Sirmon, 2013). This is also why, in particular, we have developed this chapter to discuss how the progress of this discipline might specifically gain useful insights from those approaches to the theory of the firm labeled as *evolutionary* over time.

Organizational evolutionists have provided much debate on what common features and differences exist in how organisms and organizations behave. At the same time, these scholars continue to devote important commitment to elaborating on whether important phenomena associated with the current practice of business can be conscientiously explained through the partial (or general) adoption of Charles Darwin's thoughts in social sciences (e.g., Abatecola, Belussi, Breslin, & Filatotchev, 2016; Cafferata,

2014; Hodgson, 2013; Price, 2014; Stoelhorst, 2014). Examples include the studying of global issues such as the current financial crisis; the different rates of organizational birth and infant death worldwide; the competition or integration between social systems, national and international communities; the diverse adoption of technological innovation; and even the way through which culture, beliefs, values, and norms diffuse.

With this taken into account, the remainder of this chapter is composed as follows: first, we provide our readers with a brief explanation of the distinctive features regarding the evolutionary approaches to the theory of the firm. Second, we discuss how the deterministic and voluntarist approaches to organizational evolution conjecture about the possible antecedents of corporate decline, crisis, and, eventually, failure. Third, with this constituting the core idea of the chapter, we elaborate on the implications of these conjectures for the prospective research and practice about appropriate turnaround planning. In particular, through a number of case narratives from the practice of business, we explain how, if properly managed, some building blocks from the evolutionary approaches can constitute an important element for all those scholars, practitioners, and students interested in understanding how substantive actions of business rescue can be timely set.

7.2   The Evolutionary Approaches to the Theory of the Firm

At least since the second half of the twentieth century, the evolutionary approaches to the theory of the firm have been continuously flourishing in the management, organization theory, and economics literature. In general, those management or economics scholars who have developed evolutionary approaches to organizational/economic change have been committed to studying the competitive relationship between organizations and their environment (e.g., McCarthy, Lawrence, Wixted, & Gordon, 2010). However, we can argue that what makes their approach distinctive is the application of biological comparisons (in some cases even analogies) to the understanding of this relationship.

Over time, the evolutionary approaches to the theory of the firm have taken different, although connected, lines of inquiry about organizational behavior. Some evolutionists have dedicated effort to generally explain what environmentally driven or firm-specific factors shape organizational evolution (e.g., Van de Ven & Sun, 2011). Some others, at the same time, have been more specifically committed to studying the survival challenges of start-ups (e.g., Aldrich, 2011) and the associated environmental fit (or failure) of organizations during their life cycles (e.g., Mellahi & Wilkinson, 2010). Some others, to date, have increasingly started to draw on the foundations of biological *exaptation* (Gould & Vrba, 1982) for providing an understanding of what processes can boost major technological or organizational changes, as well as radical product and process innovations (e.g., Andriani & Carignani, 2014). Finally, some other organizational evolutionists are even focusing on the notion of adaptation without any change on behalf of a firm. In this regard, Milne's seminal ideas (1961) about competition among animals have offered thought-provoking insights that the struggle against the environment (rather than predators or competition) is a legitimate focus of any firm struggle. Thus how can organizational adaptation be explained when firms do nothing but become better adapted as a result of environmental change driven by their competitors or other unrelated factors?

As we have introduced, to date, evolutionary approaches can be considered as all those attempting to explain important phenomena associated with the current practice of business through the partial (or general) adoption of Charles Darwin's seminal principles of biological evolution (e.g., Abatecola, 2014a; Cafferata, 2016). In fact, it is a matter of fact that, although controversial, *The Origin of Species* (1859) has also inspired the inception and constant development of evolutionary metatheories in other research domains, such as social sciences in general, and management and organization theory in particular. In this regard, a pioneering catalyst has been the seminal work by Richard Nelson and Sidney Winter (1982). More specifically, in their book entitled *An Evolutionary Theory of Economic Change*, these two scholars proposed the analogy between the construct of routines in management and that of genes in biology.

With this taken into account, some schools of thought have attempted to develop formal theories of organizational evolution (Dosi & Marengo, 2007; Sammut-Bonnici & Wensley, 2002). In this regard, for example, *population ecologists* (Hannan & Freeman, 1977) have applied the Darwinian mechanism of *variation* (of the *genotype*), *selection* (of the associated *phenotype*), and *retention* (of the underlying *genotype*) to organizational populations, conventionally defined as sets of organizations with the same organizational features within the same environment. Although also associated with non-Darwinian assumptions, the attempts of population ecologists have been aimed at understanding, over the long term, a possible explanation for the evolution, in terms of birth and death rates, of such populations.

To date, generalized Darwinists (e.g., Hodgson & Knudsen, 2010; Stoelhorst, 2008) have tried to import, in its full form, the Darwinian biological metaphor into the organization science domain. These scholars maintain that, if we assume some degree of abstraction, the Darwinian general principles of evolution in the natural sciences can be used to explain evolution not only in biology but also in disciplines such as management and organization science (Breslin, 2011). In particular, generalized Darwinists have attempted to adapt the notions of *genotype* and *phenotype* (pertaining to the biological domain) into the social constructs of *replicator* and *interactor* (Hodgson & Knudsen, 2004). In particular, Hull (1988, p. 488) defined the replicator as something of which copies are made and the interactor as 'an entity that directly interacts as a cohesive whole with its environment in such a way that this interaction causes replication to be differential.'

Evolutionary economists (e.g., Gowdy, Dollimore, Wilson, & Witt, 2013; Witt, 2008), instead, adopt a partially different perspective on evolution. In fact, these scholars aim at explaining change through focusing on industrial or cross-country structural dynamics, thus untangling evolutionary complexity mostly at the macroeconomic level. Whereas clearly stemming from the Darwinian biological analogy, evolutionary economists also heavily rely on Joseph Schumpeter's *creative destruction*. According to the famous Austrian economist, the "gale of creative destruction describes the process of industrial mutation that incessantly revolutionizes the economic structure from within, incessantly destroying the old one, incessantly creating a new one" (1942, pp. 82–83).

As far as the attempts to develop formal theories of organizational evolution are concerned, we should finally consider also the numerous models of organizational life cycle developed over the years (Phelps, Adams, & Bessant, 2007). Although differences exist among them, their common denominator is that most of these models have conceptualized the evolutionary path of organizations in *quasi*-biological terms—i.e., birth, growth, maturity, decline, and death. For example, this is the case with Steinmetz's model (1969) regarding the problems of monoproduct enterprises, Parks's model (1977) regarding the *hurdle races* along the evolutionary paths of organizations, the model by Dewhurst and Burns (1983) about the relationship between economic and financial equilibrium in the organizational life cycle, and Pettigrew's model (1979) about organizational *dramas*.

Finally, some of the life-cycle models (e.g., Andriani & McKelvey, 2009) have even attempted to test the suggestive *punctuated equilibrium* theory seminally proposed by the paleontologists Eldredge and Gould (1972). The main hypothesis behind this theory conflicts with Darwin's gradual and slow evolutionary mechanism; these two paleontologists, in fact, observed that, for most of their geological life cycle, a number of fossils are substantially featured by the absence of evolutionary change. At the same time, when evolution occurs in these fossils, it is usually associated with a radical and rapid change, rather than a slow and gradual evolution, as proposed by Darwin.

7.3   Determinism and Voluntarism in Organizational Adaptation and Evolution

Charles Darwin (1859) seminally used the term *adaptation* to define the process by which organisms search for their most appropriate fit within the external environment. This fit eventually happens because organisms possess or acquire the resources/capabilities required; adapted organisms then reproduce themselves and, thus, evolution takes place.

Since Darwin's pivotal observations on natural selection and survival, the *deterministic view* has been assumed, more than once, as the predominant theoretical perspective to explain phenomena associated with adaptation in the natural sciences. In the management and organization theory literature, many schools of thought have substantially adhered to this deterministic view in characterizing the competing relationship between organizations and their external environment. For example, in terms of strong deterministic arguments, we can add contingency theory (e.g., Lawrence & Lorsch, 1967) and neo-institutionalism (Di Maggio & Powell, 1983) to the mentioned population ecology. The common denominator for all these diverse theoretical grounds is that, basically, they consider organizational adaptation as the organizational reaction (sometimes even inaction) to environmental pressures.

Determinists maintain that the environment, defined as a sum of completely rational organizations whose strategic behavior is mainly shaped by macroeconomic forces, is the main driver behind organizational adaptation. In this regard, some management scholars (e.g., Cafferata, 1984) have asserted that works by classical writers, such as Follett, Barnard, and Homans, inspired the perspectives of subsequent deterministic approaches such as contingency theory, in that these classical works already embraced embryonic contingent views on organizational adaptation.

Indeed, over the past fifty years, much of the growing debate on organizational adaptation and evolution has also witnessed the juxtaposition of determinism and voluntarism. In the words by Hrebiniak and Joyce, "The term organizational adaptation has been employed in a number of ways, ranging simply from change, including both pro-active and reactive behavior, to a more specific denotation of reaction to environmental forces or demands" (1985, p. 387). In sum, we should acknowledge that the developing literature about organizational adaptation and evolution has also counted numerous schools of thought distant from the deterministic view. In this regard, we refer to all those approaches that have stressed, albeit in different manners, the role of strategic intentionality and strategic choice in defining organizational behavior. In particular, the behavioral theory of the firm (Cyert & March, 1963) has constituted the seminal contribution around which all the other theoretical perspectives found fertile ground to discuss organizational adaptation in terms of strategic and managerial voluntarism. Thus, in this vein, also the strategic choice theory (Child, 1972), resource-based view of the firm (e.g., Hamel & Prahalad, 1990), organizational learning approach (e.g., Zollo & Winter, 2002), and upper echelons theory (Hambrick & Mason, 1984) could be considered as *voluntarist* approaches.

Voluntarists concur that organizations may exert their own force on the external environment through the appropriate combination of internal resources and capabilities. Voluntarists have thus maintained that organizational adaptation is proactively driven by the internal forces within organizations, with their beliefs about evolution much more oriented toward subjectivity, bounded rationality (Simon, 1947), and proactivity. Indeed, in promoting the role of strategic intentionality, voluntarists have moved far beyond the strictly Darwinian (i.e., deterministic) interpretation of organizational evolution presented earlier. Assuming a voluntarist view implies that organizations also can be (or become) substantially independent from their external environment. Still, including voluntarism within the evolutionary approaches to the theory of the firm can provide both scholars and practitioners with the most exhaustive picture on organizational evolution to date.

Indeed, until the 1980s, the dichotomy between determinism and voluntarism appeared as much stronger than it is to date, as confirmed by the most recent reviews on the topic (e.g., Abatecola, 2012a). In this regard, the reason for its continuous (although gradual) convergence has to be retrieved in the emergence and development of a number of contributions, both theoretical and empirical, which have looked at organizational adaptation through more moderated lenses based on the *dialectical* perspective (Benson, 1977). Weick's *sense-making* approach (1969) greatly inspired the dialectical construct in that he substantially contrasted the idea that reality has to be considered something that is objective. Conversely, he maintained that reality is *enacted* by human decision makers on the basis of their experience and cognitive mechanisms. Once enacted, reality retrospectively influences individuals' behavior, thus creating a *circular* relationship with them.

Taking this into account, those works expressing moderated views on organizational adaptation have been specifically labeled as *co-evolutionary* (e.g., Lewin & Volberda, 2011; Murmann, 2013) and have considered adaptation as the joint outcome between environmental determinism and strategic voluntarism. The driving idea behind co-evolutionary interpretations is that adaptation has to be considered as a dynamic outcome over the entire life cycle of organizations within their external environment. This outcome, in other words, itself possesses an evolving nature, because of the dynamic configurations existing between environmental determinism and managerial voluntarism during the entire firm life cycle.

Among the different kinds of multilevel analysis, co-evolutionary scholars to date have attempted to link the organizational routines theory and the dynamic capabilities framework. The academic debate has defined organizational capabilities as routines of different order. In particular, whereas the routines in a steady state have been defined as *operational routines*, routines that contribute to organizational change are considered the building blocks of dynamic capabilities (Teece, Pisano, & Shuen, 1997). Thus co-evolutionary scholars argue that multilevel models, indeed, can be developed to investigate relevant routine dynamics such as formation, inertia (endogenous stability), endogenous change, and learning (e.g., Pentland, Feldman, Becker, & Liu, 2012).

The routine-as-entity view assumes that knowledge is a static bundle of rules contained within organizational boundaries. Considering knowledge as a separate entity from individuals or groups may hinder the understanding of important social interrelationships useful in opening the routines' black box. The routines-as-practice view, on the other hand, hypothesizes that all individuals and groups can influence the evolution of an organization over time by effectively changing corporate routines. The practice-based view assumption implies that macrolevel phenomena both influence and are influenced by microlevel behaviors. In other words, evolution occurs within the practice as individuals *learn to evolve* (Breslin, 2016).

7.4   How Evolutionary Approaches Conjecture About Organizational Decline and Failure

To date, those evolutionists who adhere to the deterministic view of organizational adaptation concur that corporate crises can be better explained through environmental factors rather than through organizational issues. For example, the population ecology research stream moves from two core assumptions. First, it assumes that the external environment may exert specific forces on organizations that may hinder their degree of strategic intentionality. Second, it assumes that the majority of companies operating in a certain industry, or within a certain segment of it, pursue similar competitive strategies. Accordingly, population ecologists have developed a set of concepts and statistical techniques to examine the causes of survival or failure of populations of firms. In this regard, the *density* of the population and the *size* and *age* of companies within the same population are the most predominant factors in determining corporate crises.

Measured as the number of organizations in a certain population at a given time, population density shows a non-monotonic pattern about birth and death rates within the population. In other words, population density increases until reaching the maximum level in a given historical moment, and then starts to decrease. When the birth rate of businesses tends to be high, the population, consequently, increases, whereas the mortality rate, symmetrically, remains slow. This trend continues up to a maximum, after which the mortality rate begins to exceed the birth rate; from that moment on, population density starts to decrease. Therefore, population density can be graphically exemplified by an inverted U-shaped curve. In this regard, it is worth noting that when there is an already high population density, new venture creation further increases the mortality rate of a population. For this reason, according to the population ecology perspective, start-ups may face survival issues because of the lack of resources, which are jeopardized by industry incumbents.

Regarding the relationship between population density and mortality rates, the strategic positioning of a company within a certain technological niche plays a major role in estimating the probability of crises. Some contributions, in particular, demonstrate that an increase in the market concentration causes a higher mortality rate for organizations located in the center of the niche, than for those located on the periphery (e.g., Dobrev, Kim, & Carroll, 2002).

Regarding the relationship between size and death rates, a number of studies seem to favor the theory that there is an inverse relationship between the two, with the probability of failure being higher when the size of the organization is relatively smaller (e.g., Dobson, Breslin, Suckley, Barton, & Rodriguez, 2013; Gordini, 2014). In particular, the hypothesis is that small firms normally underperform compared to larger companies, because of difficulties in raising capital, attracting skilled workers, and in finding a legitimization toward external stakeholders.

Regarding the relationship between age and death rate, empirical evidence has shown interesting results. In fact, most of the studies show that the mortality rate is higher in younger firms than in mature companies. This phenomenon has been labeled the *liability of newness* (Stinchcombe, 1965). Because of consolidated organizational structures and processes, mature companies possess a significant competitive advantage compared to younger ventures, hence shifting a substantial risk of death on them. On this side, a construct partially integrating the liability of newness is called *liability of adolescence* (Fichman & Levinthal, 1991). The idea here is that firms can survive quite easily during the most vivid beginning of the start-up period because of a stock of (generally locked-in) initial assets, such as venture capital funds or bank loans. This view, therefore, implies that businesses face higher mortality rates only after some months following the start-up phase.

The relationship between radical changes (Pettigrew, 1979), either in corporate strategy or structure, and corporate crises is somehow also linked to the liability of newness construct, even if, also in this regard, the academic debate does not converge to conclusive interpretations. Some scholars, in particular, argue that a radical change, by destroying consolidated corporate structures and processes, brings a firm to the same condition of a new venture, with a higher mortality rate due to the aforementioned liability of newness phenomenon. Conversely, other contributions on the topic maintain that organizational change does not increase the failure risk, but rather, in some cases, can produce a significant positive impact on performances. For example, this has been observed when companies try to reduce the degree of environmental determinism by enacting the appropriate structural changes needed to find the right fit with their environment (e.g., Haveman, 1992).

Finally, it is important to mention how the relationship between size, age, and mortality rate has been analyzed with reference to the industry life cycle (e.g., Agarwal, Sarkar, & Echambadi, 2002). In particular, as for the age-mortality relationship, it has been observed that the early selection probability for newborn enterprises is higher during the maturity stage than during the growth phase of the industry life cycle. With reference to size, whereas during the maturity phase of an industry the mortality rate is high for all companies regardless of the specific size, in the growth phase of an industry, this rate seems to be higher for small firms.

This explains the deterministic view of organizational crises, whereas the voluntarist view is rather contrasting. In fact, we have written that, according to voluntarists, corporate top decision makers play a major role in defining and shaping the relationship between the organization and its own environment. Therefore, according to these scholars, the possible causes of corporate crises and failures have to be found within the organizational boundaries, rather than outside in the competitive environment. The voluntarist perspective, in sum, implies that corporate crises are primarily caused by the corporate top decision makers during the planning and/or management of the adaptation process of the firm to its environment. According to this view, managerial actions are largely influenced by the cognitive mental models that managers inherently possess. Therefore, the misperception of the firm-environment relationship because of the top managers' biased decision-making process constitutes the origin of a corporate crisis (e.g., Abatecola, 2012b; Mellahi & Wilkinson, 2004).

Taking this into account, the relationship between corporate crises and the firm's governance, especially in terms of composition and tenure of its board members, merits particular attention here. In this regard, upper echelons theory has more than once evidenced that, especially in turbulent environments, a heterogeneous composition of the distressed firm's board is more effective in reacting to corporate crises than a homogeneous one. Empirical evidence from the same research stream has also highlighted how, during corporate crises, boards with a higher tenure often tend to explain the crisis through external factors, thus underestimating internal determinants (e.g., Abatecola, Farina, & Gordini, 2014).

With regard to board's composition, exploring the relationship between the historical performance of a firm and the crisis situation it may face at a given time also seems to be particularly interesting. In fact, a number of scholars have highlighted the risk that, especially after significant competitive success, top decision makers can sometimes develop a certain presumption of invincibility. Given the important role of such decision makers in the strategic decision-making process, this presumption can thus assume an important role in the inception of a corporate crisis. In this regard, Roberto Cafferata has introduced the relevant concept of *strategic dormancy* (2014, p. 293). In particular, he refers this expression to the simultaneous occurrence of two intertwined elements: first, the organization has acquired, over time, a dominant competitive positioning within a particular industry; second, the industry exerts only a modest competitive pressure on the organization. In this market structure configuration, typically, the monopoly the organization succeeds in keeping its dominant position, despite the modest degree of strategic choice exerted on its environment. Nevertheless, according to Cafferata, this can have potentially negative effects on firms' survival, if the low level of environmental determinism unexpectedly increases.

From what we have written about voluntarism, the idea that psychological determinants also matter in determining corporate crises seems to emerge as pivotal (e.g., Abatecola, 2014b; Hammond, Keeney, & Raiffa,

1998). In this regard, for example, the academic literature has introduced the concept of *denial* (Brown & Starkey, 2000) to indicate the possible refusal of decision makers to recognize potentially critical situations that their company may face in a given period. The denial may sometimes be due to cognitive misperceptions; sometimes, instead, it might depend on the managers' intentional desire to avoid personal responsibility for strategic decisions undertaken in the past, which turned out to be ineffective. In the latter case, denial can have negative implications of different degrees and intensity (Mellahi, Jackson, & Sparks, 2002).

In sum, the voluntarist perspective argues that the analysis of a corporate crisis must start from the identification of the managerial decisions responsible for the crisis itself. Although firms' competitive behavior depends not only upon managers, it is undeniable that the success or decline of a firm is influenced by the contribution of those individuals who have a relatively high decision-making power within the organizational structure, such as skilled workers, researchers, and financial or marketing experts. Thus these individuals should be taken into account when analyzing the causes of a corporate crisis. In this regard, Donaldson (1994) maintains that, in order to be effective, a restructuring process does not need to be imported from the outside of a firm's boundaries; rather, it can also be promoted internally. His arguments are based on the analysis of twelve major U.S. firms that, despite their strong competitive advantage during the '60s and '70s, suffered a profound corporate crisis during the '80s. In particular, adopting a multiple case study methodology, Donaldson shows how these companies have been able to implement radical and effective restructuring processes, redefining and reformulating strategic paths, without drawing necessarily on outside intervention.

Hence Donaldson defends the thesis that a voluntary restructuring process can work just as effectively as one triggered, for example, by a hostile takeover, which, because of its own nature, interrupts the business continuity. According to him, although longer than an external intervention, a voluntary restructuring process has a higher probability of success. In conclusion, Donaldson's position seems not far from the voluntarist perspective, which, as already noted, stresses the importance of entrepreneurial and managerial decision-making deficiencies as the most prominent explanation for corporate crises, especially when the enterprise-environment relationship is intense.

7.5 Implications for the Research and Practice of Turnaround Planning

In this section, we draw from a series of historical narratives from the practice of business to discuss how the evolutionary elements explained in the preceding pages can constitute useful building blocks when planning appropriate turnaround strategies for distressed firms.

7.5.1   *Innovation and Technological Niche*

Anecdotal evidence from Fiat's crisis in the second half of the 1990s can be useful for explaining this issue. In 1993, the performance of the famous Italian automobile group registered a huge loss, with a proportional reduction of its automobiles' market shares in Italy. Thus the group decided to implement a series of structural investments and introduced some new car models, with some of them, such as the Punto, being particularly successful from the very beginning. In general, the product innovations caused a temporary increase in the group's performance between 1994 and 1997.

In 1998, however, Fiat's performance started to deteriorate once again; as a result, in 2002, the group publicly acknowledged its crisis and announced a turnaround plan. Thus in the subsequent years a number of strategic actions defined Fiat's corporate restructuring. In particular, the firm strongly refocused on the automobile core business and sold some non-core subsidiaries to improve its financial position. Also, Fiat launched new car models, such as the restyling of the Punto, Panda, and 500 vehicles, which immediately met with customer satisfaction. As a result, the firm's performance saw a major upturn between 2003 and 2007.

In the narrative provided, one of the main crisis drivers seems to rely on the relationship between population density and Fiat's technological position in its market niche (Abatecola, 2009). In particular, in the previous section, we explained that, if population density decreases, crises might be positively associated with firms on the periphery of the niche. The automotive market concentration in Italy registered a major downturn from 72% in 1997 to 57% in 2007; on this basis, the analysis of Fiat's data for the period of 1997–2007 highlights that its financial performance systematically decreased within the period of 1997–2002, with the sole exception of the fiscal year 2000. Therefore, according to the extant literature, Fiat should have appeared to be one of the firms furthest from the center of the niche. In this regard, findings reveal that four of the biggest car manufacturers—i.e., Fiat, General Motors, BMW, and Ford—were, among all the industry players; they were the firms closest to the niche center. More importantly, the findings also reveal that Fiat was about twenty-five times more distant from the center than another 'generalist player,' such as Toyota, which did not suffer any performance decline during the '90s. Conversely, in the same period, General Motors registered a performance deterioration that was even deeper than the one that occurred at Fiat (Adriaanse, 2011), with the estimated distance from the niche center three times higher than that of Fiat itself. Thus, consistent with the literature, Fiat's technological position in the niche seems to have counted as a determinant of its crisis in that period. As further support, during the corporate turnaround, Fiat's distance from the niche center constantly decreased between 2004 and 2007, until reaching its lowest value; at the same time, during those years, its performance significantly improved.

7.5.2   Age

We have written that, according to Stinchcombe's liability of newness (1965), newborn enterprises have a lower survival rate compared to that of more established firms. In particular, Stinchcombe seminally argued that the main determinants behind early selection are the start-ups' lack of experience and legitimization toward external stakeholders, because structure, processes, and trust require time to be nurtured. To date, data show that organizational infant mortality continues to derive from a number of factors similar to those initially hypothesized by Stinchcombe, such as the lack of market demand, cash shortage, and inappropriate founding team features. In this regard, the narratives of both Critica and Orat.io, two American social media companies, can provide interesting food for thought.

Critica was an American start-up that developed a browser extension that allowed people to annotate every website. In particular, users would have been able to select any section of a web page and start a conversation on that. Unfortunately, the company went bankrupt in March 2015. Consistent with the data cited earlier, addressing users' needs in the correct manner is the main explanation for a firm's early selection. As a matter of fact, Critica spent months of work in building many complex features for a product that did not have a user base. The entrepreneurial approach was 'build it and they will come.' Another important explanatory factor for the start-up's failure was the founding team's corporate culture. In fact, since its inception, the commitment of the company, in terms of working hours, was extreme, but this did not translate into corporate performance. Critica received the so-called Zombie Award, a special prize from Boost, the venture capital firm that invested in the company at the beginning: on this, Jason Huertas, CEO of the company, commented: "It was a stark reminder that the more hours you work, do not necessarily correlate to a successful outcome."

As already stated, another good example of infant failure primarily caused by the lack of market demand is provided by Orat.io, another U.S.-based start-up founded in the summer of 2013. This start-up was conceived as a widget to help bloggers and publishers integrate people's discussions on their websites. The start-up failed for a number of reasons. First, it made important mistakes during the market segmentation phase; in fact, the revenue streams of Orat.io were revealed to come, in large part, from corporations and media houses, rather than from bloggers themselves. Second, the wrong market positioning of the company also led to cash shortage issues because of inevitable upfront costs. In the words of the start-up's CEO:

> We offered a 30 day free trial for our service. Whereas most individual customers required 1-month acquisition time, most corporations needed about 1–2 months to evaluate the outcome and then ask their manager for budgets. This ended up in 3–4 months' acquisition time, which is too much for a start-up with only 25k in funding and a 6-month runtime.

Third, again according to the start-up's CEO, the technological features were of secondary importance compared to the customer base, and this is also consistent with the earlier considerations concerning Critica:

> You can build the best and most performant software ever, still no one bats an eye. The only thing which is important is your product, not your codebase. You can have the worst codebase on earth, if people love your product, it's ok.

7.5.3 Radical Changes

Consistent with the academic findings according to which radical changes can, in some cases, produce a significant positive impact on corporate performance, the case of Luxottica is impressive.

Luxottica is an Italian company originally founded in 1961 as a contract manufacturer of eyewear parts with fourteen employees. In 1967, the company started manufacturing eyewear under its own brand, thus producing its products, while also continuing to produce semi-finished items for clients. Since 1974, Leonardo Del Vecchio, the company's founder, promoted a vertical integration strategy aimed at directly controlling the distribution channels. During the '80s, Luxottica entered international markets either through opening flagship stores or through acquiring local distribution companies. In 1988, the firm started a key strategic partnership with Giorgio Armani, thus entering the luxury and fashion segment, with other important licensing agreements following in subsequent years. In 1995, Luxottica concluded one of the most important deals of its history, acquiring the United States Shoe Corporation, which is the largest optical service firm in the North America. As a result, Luxottica became the first producer of eyewear operating in the retailing business. In 2003, the group acquired OPSM, which is the greatest retailer in the Asian market, whereas in 2007, it acquired Oakley, the California-based leading sport optical brand.

Over the decades, Luxottica was able to succeed in spite of facing several threats such as globalization, sustainability, and cooperation in the fast-moving eyewear business. These extraordinary adaptation capabilities descended substantially from the radical innovations enacted by the company in its logistics processes. In particular, as explained earlier, over the years, the distribution network of Luxottica grew mainly through M&A operations; thus, its main problem was the downstream integration of different entities, an issue that could have led to the firm's crisis and, in the worst case, its extinction. In fact, recent empirical studies show that, in the last decade, only a small amount of M&A operations have been successful. Considering that, because of its radically innovative centralized distribution system, Luxottica succeeded in integrating the European market together with its American and Chinese counterparts.

Over time, the effectiveness of the logistics process has been improved through implementing the SAP system in all the Luxottica's distribution centers and, in doing so, through substantially increasing the managerial control over the manufacturing and distribution functions. Since 2010, the company has developed and applied a software called RAISE (Reserve Assignment and Integrated Shipping Environment), which is aimed at optimizing the logistics flow of orders and existing stock. In particular, RAISE decides whether products need to be brought inside a certain warehouse or have to be delivered directly to the client. Moreover, this software helps in the stock's segmentation process by prioritizing a certain quantity for a specific market or client. Thus the entire distribution activity is arranged and scheduled for the subsequent thirty weeks. In order to ensure the highest level of efficiency, the data warehouse collection and linking of all the company's branches is kept online on Luxottica's global server facilities.

Reflecting the Schumpeterian seminal conceptualization of the entrepreneur as innovator, Del Vecchio highlighted the importance of the distribution structure by introducing vertical integration from the very beginning. He then had the intuition of overcoming the weaknesses naturally related to the wholesale business model through the acquisition of several American retailers, which led to Luxottica also becoming a leader in the retail market.

7.5.4   Board Composition

This narrative refers to American Airlines, which is one of the biggest players in the U.S. airline industry. In 2012, its revenues were equal to around $25 billion, with a fleet composed of 620 elements serving more than 270 destinations all over the world. The company is the result of an eighty-year story beginning in the '30s, when more than eighty small carriers decided to cooperate with the purpose of reinforcing their competitive position. The brand 'American Airlines' was introduced in 1934, when the conglomerate was purchased by Errett L. Cord and gathered into a single legal entity. The company's expansion began in the postwar period, thanks to a series of acquisitions aimed at engaging in new routes toward Mexico, South America, and Europe.

In the '80s, American Airlines introduced the hub system and entered a number of alliances, networks, and agreements that represented one of the key elements of the outstanding growth of the firm. During the '90s, the airline business began its deregulation process, and American Airlines took advantage of the market momentum by expanding its boundaries through the acquisition of bankrupted carriers. The situation dramatically changed in 2001 after the September 11 terroristic attack, in which two American Airlines' planes were destroyed. A tough period followed for the overall aviation industry, which witnessed a sharp fall in profits—American Airlines was no exception—and the exit of several players from the industry. After struggling for a decade in an attempt to recover a sustainable competitive position, American Airlines formally went bankrupt in November 2011. At the same time, the company announced a massive restructuring plan culminating in the merger with U.S. Airways and its formal exit from the bankruptcy procedure in November 2013.

On this basis, we can draw from upper echelons theory to discuss the eventual influence of board composition on the American Airlines' performance deterioration. In particular, the two years characterized by the highest board tenure—namely, 2008 and 2011—are those in which the company reported the largest losses. These data seem to be consistent with the extant theoretical suggestions about a positive correlation between board tenure and the likelihood of a corporate crisis. Moreover, the second observation pertains to the firm's CEO turnover dynamics, with a double CEO replacement in the new century: In 2002, Donald Carty left in favor of Gerard Arpey, who was then replaced by Tom Horton in 2011. Both of these turnovers seemed to be considerably important for the American Airlines' business: The former turnover coincides with the huge loss following the Twin Towers attack; as for the latter, 2011 was a turning point for the American Airlines' history in that it marked the formal beginning of the bankruptcy procedures. Although the literature seems not to converge on a clear relationship between CEO turnover and corporate crisis, we believe that the governance changes in this narrative are more likely to be considered as an outcome, rather than antecedents, of the crisis.

7.5.5 *Misperceptions and Strategic Dormancy*

Anecdotal evidence from the most recent Fiat's crisis can also be useful in this regard. In fact, we have written that one of the key determinants of this crisis was the lack of product innovation in the automobile core business, which was the consequence of the firm's decision to reduce Fiat's R&D expenditures in car vehicles in the '90s. One of the possible interpretations of this reduction might come if Fiat's positive past performance in the first half of that decade is considered. In particular, how did *strategic dormancy* affect Fiat in the 1990s? In this regard, Giovanni Agnelli, one of the most important historical leaders of the firm, argued that, in the automobile industry, the firm's performance has often fluctuated between decline and growth. This means that firms have moved from vicious to virtuous circles, in which the effective competitive action has empowered the commitment of both managers and employees. As a result, further successful initiatives might have been implemented. In this vein, several crises and corporate turnarounds also characterized Fiat's history in the twentieth century.

In searching for past evidence throughout the firm's evolution, Agnelli argued that the situations of crisis preceding that of the 1990s had been overcome by the firm through the launch of very successful automobile milestones, such as the 127 model in 1971, Panda in 1980, Uno in 1985, and Punto in 1993. In this regard, experts have argued that, between 1997 and 2002, Fiat was not able to repeat Punto's success because it did not launch an equally successful car model. One reason for this can be the possible strategic dormancy of the high-tenured board in charge of the firm, which was unable to react effectively to the changes affecting the national and international competition within the automobile industry. In fact, matters have only started to improve effectively since 2004, when a series of new and successful vehicles were introduced by the new (and lower-tenured) board.

Thought-provoking counterfactual evidence about strategic dormancy can be represented by the evolution of the music industry and of its main players—i.e., the majors' recording labels. In particular, recent studies (Uli, 2015) show that, despite a first displacement effect because of the illegal download phenomenon that exploded in the period of 1999–2003, the players who survived in the music business have exerted, although with their own peculiarities, a high degree of strategic choice on their environment, especially after the piracy explosion during the period 2004–2008. The most widespread strategic option among the industry players was an aggressive differentiation strategy promoted through innovation in technological infrastructures. Moreover, every major label promoted a different strategy, consistent with its own resources and capabilities.

Being the market leader, with a market share equal to about 29%, Universal pursued a growth strategy through M&A operations, which led to the acquisition of BMG Music Publishing in 2007. In 2004, Sony and BMG created Sony BMG Music Entertainment, a joint venture that includes the recording businesses of the two majors. The resulting entity registered the highest degree of differentiation in the industry; however, because of irreconcilable issues related to the integration of the two businesses, in 2008, Sony acquired the remaining 50% stake from BMG, thus becoming the sole owner of the BMG artists' portfolio and renaming the company Sony Music Entertainment. Warner exerted a degree of differentiation through innovation lower than the industry average; nevertheless, its market share increased from 11% in 2004 to 14% in 2008, thanks to effective marketing efforts on artists' portfolios. Finally, in 2007, EMI was acquired by the private equity fund Terra Firma, and its market share decreased from around 13% in 2004 to around 10% in 2008.

7.6 Conclusion

In his outstanding work *Origin of Species* (1859), Charles Darwin seminally conjectured that natural selection among living organisms never stops: "Multiply, vary, let the strongest live and the weakest die" (reprint 2008, p. 241). On this basis, and conscious of the physiological differences between the evolution of living organisms and those of entrepreneurial organizations (Cafferata, 2016), we thus intended this chapter to be for all those scholars, practitioners, and students interested in understanding how to plan appropriate turnaround strategies in the case of distressed firms. To this end, we have explained how the *art and science* of turnaround planning can gain insights from the evolutionary approaches to the theory of the firm. In particular, through our final series of case narratives from the practice of business, we have specifically put forward some ideas regarding why some organizations last over time, whereas others perish.

References

Abatecola, G. (2009). Bridging adaptation perspectives to explore corporate crisis determinants. Evidence from Fiat. *International Journal of Business & Economics, 8*(1), 163–184.

Abatecola, G. (2012a). Organizational adaptation. An update. *International Journal of Organizational Analysis, 20*(3), 274–293.

Abatecola, G. (2012b). Interpreting corporate crises: Towards a co-evolutionary approach. *Futures, 44*(10), 860–869.

Abatecola, G. (2014a). Research in organizational evolution. What comes next? *European Management Journal, 32*(3), 434–443.

Abatecola, G. (2014b). Untangling self-reinforcing processes in managerial decision making. Co-evolving heuristics? *Management Decision, 52*(2), 934–949.

Abatecola, G., Belussi, F., Breslin, D., & Filatotchev, I. (2016). Darwinism, organizational evolution and survival: Key challenges for future research. *Journal of Management and Governance, 20*(1), 1–17.

Abatecola, G., Farina, V., & Gordini, N. (2014). Board effectiveness in corporate crises. Lessons from the evolving empirical research. *Corporate Governance: The International Journal of Business in Society, 14*(4), 531–542.

Adriaanse, J. A. A. (2011). *Back to the future—The General Motors restructuring plan.* Global Insolvency Practice Course, The Hague, The Netherlands.

Adriaanse, J. A. A., Van der Rest, J. I., & Verdoes, T. L. M. (2015). Recovery and resolution plans in banking: A theoretical turnaround management perspective. In M. Haentjens & B. Wessels (Eds.), *Research handbook on crisis management in the banking sector* (pp. 236–260). Cheltenham, UK: Edward Elgar.

Agarwal, R., Sarkar, M. B., & Echambadi, R. (2002). The conditioning effect of time on firm survival: An industry life cycle approach. *Academy of Management Journal, 45*(5), 971–994.

Aldrich, H. E. (Ed.). (2011). *An evolutionary approach to entrepreneurship: Selected essays by Howard E. Aldrich.* Cheltenham, UK: Edward Elgar.

Andriani, P., & Carignani, G. (2014). Modular exaptation: A missing link in the synthesis of artificial form. *Research Policy, 43*(9), 1608–1620.

Andriani, P., & McKelvey, B. (2009). From Gaussian to Paretian thinking: Causes and implications of power laws in organizations. *Organization Science, 20*(6), 1053–1071.

Barker, V. L. III, & Mone, M. A. (1994). Retrenchment: Cause of turnaround or consequence of decline? *Strategic Management Journal, 15*(5), 395–405.

Barmash, I. (1973). *Great business disasters.* New York, NY: Ballantine Books.

Benson, J. K. (1977). Organizations: A dialectical view. *Administrative Science Quarterly, 22*, 1–21.

Bibeault, D. B. (1982). *Corporate turnaround: How managers turn losers into winners.* New York: McGraw-Hill.

Breslin, D. (2011). Reviewing a generalized Darwinist approach to studying socio-economic change. *International Journal of Management Reviews*, *13*, 218–235.

Breslin, D. (2016). What evolves in organizational co-evolution? *Journal of Management and Governance*, *20*(1), 45–67.

Brown, A. D., & Starkey, K. (2000). Organizational identity and organizational learning: A psychodynamic perspective. *Academy of Management Review*, *25*(1), 102–120.

Cafferata, R. (1984). *Teoria dell'organizzazione. Un approccio non contingente*. Milan: Franco Angeli.

Cafferata, R. (2014). *Management in adattamento. Tra razionalità economica, evoluzione e imperfezione dei sistemi*. Bologna: Il Mulino.

Cafferata, R. (2016). Darwinist connections between the systemness of social organizations and their evolution. *Journal of Management and Governance*, *20*(1), 19–44.

Child, J. (1972). Organizational structure, environment and performance: The role of strategic choice. *Sociology*, *6*(1), 1–22.

Cyert, R. M., & March, J. G. (1963). *A behavioural theory of the firm*. Englewood Cliffs, NJ: Prentice Hall.

Darwin, C. R. (1859). *On the origin of species by means of natural selection or the preservation of favoured races in the struggle for life*. London, UK: John Murray.

Dewhurst, J., & Burns, P. (1983). *Small business: Finance and control*. London, UK: Macmillan.

Di Maggio, P. J., & Powell, W. W. (1983). The iron cage revisited: Institutional isomorphism and collective rationality in organizational fields. *American Sociological Review*, *48*(2), 147–160.

Dobrev, S. D., Kim, T. Y., & Carroll, G. R. (2002). The evolution of organizational niches: U.S. automobile manufacturers, 1885–1981. *Administrative Science Quarterly*, *47*(2), 233–264.

Dobson, S., Breslin, D., Suckley, L., Barton, R., & Rodriguez, L. (2013). Small firm survival and innovation: An evolutionary approach. *International Journal of Entrepreneurship & Innovation*, *14*(2), 69–80.

Donaldson, G. (1994). *Corporate restructuring: Managing the process from within*. Boston, MA: Harvard Business School Press.

Dosi, G., & Marengo, L. (2007). On the evolutionary and behavioral theories of organizations: A tentative roadmap. *Organization Science*, *18*(3), 491–502.

Eldredge, N., & Gould, S. J. (1972). Punctuated equilibria: An alternative to phylethic gradualism. In T. J. M. Schopf (Ed.), *Models in paleobiology* (pp. 82–115). San Francisco, CA: Freeman, Cooper & Company.

Fichman, M., & Levinthal, D. A. (1991). Honeymoons and the liability of adolescence: A new perspective on duration dependence in social and organizational relationships. *Academy of Management Review*, *16*(2), 442–468.

Gordini, N. (2014). A genetic algorithm approach for SMEs bankruptcy prediction: Empirical evidence from Italy. *Expert Systems with Applications*, *41*(14), 6433–6445.

Gould, S. J., & Vrba, E. S. (1982). Exaptation. A missing term in the science of form. *Paleobiology*, *8*(3), 4–15.

Gowdy, J. E., Dollimore, D. E., Wilson, D. S., & Witt, U. (2013). Economic cosmology and the evolutionary challenge. *Journal of Economic Behaviour and Organization*, *90*, S11–S20.

Hambrick, D. C., & Mason, P. A. (1984). Upper echelons: The organization as a reflection of its top managers. *Academy of Management Review*, *9*(2), 193–206.

Hamel, G., & Prahalad, C. K. (1990). The core competence of the corporation. *Harvard Business Review, 68*(3), 79–91.

Hammond, J. S. III, Keeney, R. L., & Raiffa, H. (1998). The hidden traps of decision making. *Harvard Business Review, 76*(5), 47–58.

Hannan, M. T., & Freeman, J. H. (1977). The population ecology of organizations. *American Journal of Sociology, 82*(5), 929–964.

Harrigan, K. R. (1980). *Strategies for declining businesses*. Lexington, MA: Lexington Press.

Haveman, H. A. (1992). Between a rock and a hard place: Organizational change and performance under conditions of fundamental environmental transformation. *Administrative Science Quarterly, 37*(1), 48–75.

Hodgson, G. M. (2013). Understanding organizational evolution: Toward a research agenda using generalized Darwinism. *Organization Studies, 34*, 973–992.

Hodgson, G. M., & Knudsen, T. (2004). The firm as an interactor: Firms as vehicles for habits and routines. *Journal of Evolutionary Economics, 14*, 281–307.

Hodgson, G. M., & Knudsen, T. (2010). *Darwin's conjecture: The search for general principles of social and economic evolution*. Chicago, IL: University of Chicago Press.

Hrebiniak, L. G., & Joyce, W. M. (1985). Organizational adaptation: Strategic choice and environmental determinism. *Administrative Science Quarterly, 30*, 336–349.

Hull, D. L. (1988). *Science as a process*. Chicago, IL: University of Chicago Press.

Lawrence, P. R., & Lorsch, J. W. (1967). *Organization and environment: Managing differentiation and integration*. Boston, MA: Harvard University Press.

Lewin, A. Y., & Volberda, H. K. (2011). Co-evolution of global sourcing: The need to understand the underlying mechanisms of firm-decisions to offshore. *International Business Review, 20*, 241–251.

McCarthy, I. P., Lawrence, T. B., Wixted, B., & Gordon, B. (2010). A multidimensional conceptualization of environmental velocity. *Academy of Management Review, 35*, 604–626.

McKinley, W., Latham, S., & Braun, M. (2014). Organizational decline and innovation: Turnarounds and downward spirals. *Academy of Management Review, 39*(1), 88–110.

Mellahi, K., Jackson, P., & Sparks, L. (2002). An exploratory study into failure in successful organizations: The case of Marks and Spencer. *British Journal of Management, 13*(1), 15–29.

Mellahi, K., & Wilkinson, A. (2004). Organizational failure: A critique of recent research and a proposed integrative framework. *International Journal of Management Reviews, 5–6*(1), 21–41.

Mellahi, K., & Wilkinson, A. (2010). Managing and coping with organizational failures: Introduction to the special issue. *Group & Organization Management, 35*(5), 531–541.

Milne, A. (1961). Definition of competition among animals. In F. L. Milnethorpe (Ed.), *Mechanisms in biological competition* (pp. 40–61). Cambridge: Cambridge University Press.

Murmann, J. P. (2013). The co-evolution of industries and important features of their environments. *Organization Science, 24*(1), 58–78.

Nelson, R. R., & Winter, S. G. (1982). *An evolutionary theory of economic change*. Cambridge, MA: Harvard University Press.

Parks, G. M. (1977). How to climb a growth curve: Eleven hurdles for the entrepreneur-manager. *Journal of Small Business Management, 15*(1), 25–29.

Parsa, H. G., Van der Rest, J. I., Smith, S. R., Parsa, R. A., & Bujisic, M. (2015). Why restaurants fail? Part IV. The relationship between restaurant failures and demographic factors. *Cornell Hospitality Quarterly, 56*(1), 80–90.

Pentland, B. T., Feldman, M. S., Becker, M. C., & Liu, P. (2012). Dynamics of organizational routines: A generative model. *Journal of Management Studies, 49*(8), 1484–1508.

Pettigrew, A. M. (1979). On studying organizational cultures. *Administrative Science Quarterly, 24*(4), 570–581.

Phelps, R., Adams, R., & Bessant, J. (2007). Life cycles of growing organizations: A review with implications for knowledge and learning. *International Journal of Management Reviews, 9*(1), 1–30.

Price, I. (2014). *Organizational Darwinism and research methodology.* Paper presented at the EURAM Conference, Valencia, Spain.

Raisch, S. (2013). Corporate turnarounds: The duality of retrenchment and recovery. *Journal of Management Studies, 50*(7), 1216–1244.

Sammut-Bonnici, T., & Wensley, R. (2002). Darwinism, probability and complexity: Market-based organizational transformation and change explained through the theories of organizational evolution. *International Journal of Management Reviews, 4*(3), 291–315.

Schumpeter, J. A. (1942). *Capitalism, socialism and democracy.* New York, NY: Harper & Row.

Simon, H. A. (1947). *Administrative behaviour.* New York, NY: Macmillan.

Steinmetz, L. L. (1969). Critical stages of small business growth: When they occur and how to survive them. *Business Horizons, 12*(1), 29–36.

Stinchcombe, A. L. (1965). Social structure and organizations. In J. March (Ed.), *Handbook of organizations* (pp. 142–193). Chicago, IL: Rand McNally.

Stoelhorst, J. W. (2008). The explanatory logic and ontological commitment of generalized Darwinism. *Journal of Economic Methodology, 15*(4), 343–363.

Stoelhorst, J. W. (2014). The future of evolutionary economics is in a vision from the past. *Journal of Institutional Economics, 10*(4), 665–682.

Tangpong, C., Abebe, M., & Li, Z. (2015). A temporal approach to retrenchment and successful turnaround in declining firms. *Journal of Management Studies, 52*(5), 647–677.

Teece, D. J., Pisano, G., & Shuen, A. (1997). Dynamic capabilities and strategic management. *Strategic Management Journal, 18*(7), 509–533.

Trahms, C. A., Ndofor, H. A., & Sirmon, D. G. (2013). Organizational decline and turnaround: A review and agenda for future research. *Journal of Management, 39*(5), 1277–1307.

Uli, V. (2015). Innovazione tecnologica e co-evoluzione nell'industria musicale. *L'industria, 36*(2), 277–308.

Van de Ven, A. H., & Sun, K. (2011). Breakdowns in implementing models of organizational change. *Academy of Management Perspectives, 25*(3), 58–74.

Weick, K. E. (1969). *The social psychology of organizing.* Reading, MA: Addison-Wesley.

Witt, U. (2008). What is specific in evolutionary economics? *Journal of Evolutionary Economics, 18*(5), 547–575.

Zollo, M., & Winter, S. G. (2002). Deliberate learning and the evolution of dynamic capabilities. *Organization Science, 13*(3), 339–351.

8 Turnaround Strategies

Practical Insights From a 47-Year Career

Donald Bibeault

8.1 Introduction

Two fundamental questions are starting points for the selection of appropriate turnaround strategies. First, should the entity be turned around? Second, can the company be turnaround? It may seem trivial to ask whether the company should be turned around because nearly everyone would say— 'definitely.' But this is not a trivial question in the sense that in the economic landscape, some economic entities are more important than others. For example, the turnaround of General Motors was deemed necessary from a societal point of view because of its impact on the economy and employment. It thus occupied a bandwidth with individuals of the highest levels of the federal government of the United States. Yet there are also many smaller entities for which a turnaround could be deemed trivial; their disappearance would in fact enhance the competitive nature of the industry. This chapter, therefore, will focus on strategies to turn around the company (i.e. not strategies in declining industries were liquidation is the best alternative).

Whether a company can be turned around is an important question. Just as turnaround strategies differ markedly from those utilized in stable and growing firms, nuanced turnaround strategies have substantial differentiation depending on three important factors:

1 external market conditions, especially industry demand trends;
2 the criticality of the company situation with special regard to its cash flow and how far away it is from its breakeven point; and
3 the resources available to come into play during the turnaround effort: internally with regard to company's balance sheet and externally with regard to the support of all stakeholders including creditors and suppliers.

8.2 The Impact of External Market Conditions on Turnaround Strategies

My experience, and that of hundreds of other turnaround professionals, indicates that most company problems are internally generated by management deficiencies. That said, it cannot be denied that external economic and industry conditions substantially affect the probability of a successful turnaround and the strategies utilized. Severe external conditions decrease the probability of a successful turnaround unless turnaround leaders possess excellent business skills and a high degree of creativity. Market redeployment activities require innovation and creativity not always found in turnaround leaders. For example, Lee Iacocca's introduction of the 'K-car' was a brilliant stroke by matching consumer demand for smaller automobiles and the limited resources of Chrysler Corporation at that time. The simplest analogy I have for this is that a declining industry or economy is similar to a serious storm at sea. The good captain is constantly monitoring conditions and takes two significant actions to minimize or completely avoid the detrimental results. First, he (she) does not unduly burden the ship with excessive cargo (debt) so that the margin of error in a storm is greatly attenuated. Second, by properly monitoring storm conditions, the good captain plots a course around the storm or through its least lethal aspects. Wells Fargo Bank made prudent investments and was able to weather the storm of the Great Depression with alacrity compared to many failed U.S. banks.

I once was appointed CEO of a very large plumbing wholesaler that had been a leveraged buyout and was already losing money under benign market conditions. To compound my challenge, the real estate market in the United States for new housing starts was under severe pressure. This resulted in an expected decline of 60% in the markets we served at the time of my arrival. By repositioning the company in the repair-and-remodeling portion of the market, we were able to partially ameliorate the severe decline in the demand of our served markets. Similarly, I ran a large steel supply company that principally provided steel products for the oil drilling industry. Our customer base consisted of small independents and tax-sheltered drillers, many of whom went out of business. The company was saved only by our adroit ability to gain substantially more business from major blue-chip oil companies that still had substantial drilling programs.

8.3 Criticality of the Company Situation

I approach the determination of turnaround strategies by utilizing a triage concept as a starting point. In the first few hours of my turnaround tenure, I want to know where the organization is on the turnaround continuum. Are we talking about an underperforming tune-up, or is the company in dire threat of liquidation? From the most general perspective, I triage companies as follows: (1) mild trouble, (2) moderate losses and liquidity issues, and (3) severe losses and viability issues. The criticality of the company situation thus affects the turnaround strategy.

8.3.1 *Mild Trouble*

Underperforming companies can be on an unsatisfactory trajectory but not at the point where their very existence is questionable. Their 'independent' existence, however, may be in question.

Situation overview: Underperforming companies with mild trouble have a declining market position and mild losses, but still have a strong balance sheet. The company is typically losing market leadership both from a distribution and product standpoint, leading to a declining market share. Usually the declining market share is accompanied by declining operational margins. The company may still have a positive return on equity, but the return is at the low end of the industry.

Management considerations: Existing management is still in control, but the board of directors is usually unhappy and possibly sullen but not yet rebellious. The board has begun to doubt management and feels it is not listening to input from its members or ideas from substantial shareholders.

Critical needs: The company sorely needs fresh management thinking, even as basic as the introduction of sound practices across the board. Most of the time a streamlining strategy is required that usually includes every aspect of the company's marketing elements. The company should streamline its product line by relying on its strong market segments.

8.3.2   *Moderate Losses and Liquidity Issues*

Moderate loss companies are akin to a stage II burn victim. Usually, a clear losing trajectory has been established because of more than one year of losses. If losses continue at their going rate, the exhaustion of the balance sheet as a buffer is calculable.

Situation overview. Moderate loss companies begin with at least one year of loss and the prospect for continuing losses. These losses are almost always accompanied by declining revenues. The balance sheets of these companies are noticeably deteriorating and cannot provide a buffer indefinitely at the level of losses being incurred. Nearly always there are noticeable margin decreases, and margins are now at an unsatisfactory level. Declining revenue levels cause the company to have unused capacity.

Management considerations. Generally, management is losing credibility in the board room and with the company's external credit sources. The board usually becomes less insular and listens to outside parties including shareholder activists. Lenders put the company on a watch list and are nervous about further deterioration.

Critical needs. It becomes obvious to most parties and stakeholders that a change of management is required. The company has to undertake more substantial pruning and redeployment activities.

8.3.3   *Severe Losses and Viability Issues*

Severe loss companies are akin to stage III burn victims. Companies in this condition have continuingly amassed losses of a magnitude that threatens it's very existence. These are companies with severe operating losses, substantial negative cash flow, and viability issues, whose survival is both at stake and at hand.

Situation overview. A liquidity crisis is at hand with payables piling up and creditors threatening to cut off supplies or credit lines. At this point, the shareholder equity in the company is usually nearly exhausted. Concurrently, both short- and long-term debt has piled up. The balance sheet is a mess and cannot provide liquidity in the short term. In its most severe cases, the creditor position is such that they could force involuntary bankruptcy. All these factors are weighing heavily on the employee and management morale at the company.

Management considerations: Creditors want a management change and a route to liquidating their positions. Usually, the bank or creditor loan covenants have been breached, which frequently gives creditors preferential rights above the company's board of directors and shareholders. Usually, the board is forced to acquiesce to creditor pressure.

Critical need: Cash flow has become the major survival issue with trade creditor and long-term creditor pressure becoming acute. Drastic cost reductions, severe product pruning, and redeployment efforts must be undertaken to stem the tide of negative cash flow.

8.4   The Resources Available to Come Into Play During the Turnaround Effort

Available company resources that come into play during a turnaround are a combination of intenral sources from the company's own balance sheet and external sources from the support of all stakeholders including trade creditors and suppliers. Great turnaround strategies executed in a hostile external environment and without certain necessary attributes of the company itself are akin to throwing good seed on bad soil. The preconditions for the high probability of a successful turnaround include the following:

- a viable core business to shrink back to
- a transformational management team to affect astute/rapid change in company strategies
- availability of a financial bridge to get the company a sustainable positive cash flow
- a change of the company's culture into a positive winning culture

1   A Viable Core Business to Shrink Back To

This core business must be both economically and competitively viable and of the magnitude to support the level of debt existing after the turnaround effort. The most commonplace trajectory is companies get into trouble strategically by moving into areas away from their core business and attempt to diversify beyond their management competence and financial resources. Normally, the fix for this is to shrink back to the original core business. To be viable, the core must possess a revenue umbrella and gross margins sufficient to support operations and debt service. In order to achieve that, it must have a strategy congruent with its core competencies that provide its customers with competitive products and services. The company must have a group of profitable customers in a set of attractive markets.

Personally, I've had a number of cases where the original core itself was not viable and had to be made viable. This took a very high level of turnaround expertise and the adroit repositioning of the company toward more lucrative markets. In my first turnaround, the company had a large mutual fund complex that had a severe redemption problem. Due to the need of many of the company's clients for security, we were able to redirect what normally would have been mutual fund redemptions to single premium annuities issued by one of its insurance companies. This proved to be a very lucrative redeployment.

2   A Transformational Management Team *Must Be Present*

The team must be led by an astute turnaround leader put in place to affect rapid change in the company strategies. At the top must be a hardworking CEO who can create and sell a realistic turnaround plan that energizes the company's executives and it's rank and file. Even in midsize companies, the transformational job often is too big for one person to realize, so successful turnaround leaders need to attract a strong senior management team. Usually, there are a few key management executives from a prior team who can play an important role in the turnaround of the company.

3   *There Must Be the Ability to Assemble a Financial Bridge*

The financial bridge must be of a sufficient magnitude to get the company to a sustainable positive cash flow position. Sick companies generally do not see any way to help themselves, but in most cases, a good portion of the financial bridge can be wrung out of existing assets from the company itself. Very few external lenders will come to the table unless they see the company has a realistic plan to liquefy internal assets. Astute negotiations must be entered into with trade creditors so they can be assured that they will not be putting good money into a continuing bad situation. In difficult situations that have a viable plan, some creditors will be asked to convert debt to an equity position. With the advent of distressed equity funds, external equity capital is rarely provided without a change of control.

4   *The Company's Culture Must Be Changed Into a Positive Winning Culture*

Just as General George Patton was able to energize and re-invigorate his troops in North Africa, a good turnaround leader must gain trust and enhance efforts at all levels of the organization. The best way to achieve this is to have a turnaround plan with realistic, achievable turnaround strategies.

Most company employees will rally around a well-thought-out plan that is believable.

8.5   Stages of the Turnaround That Are an Important Determinant of Strategy

Most turnarounds include the following stages:

1   The Management Change Stage
2   Evaluation or Viability Assessment Stage
3   Emergency Action Stage
4   The Stabilization and Redeployment Stage
5   The Rejuvenation and Return to Growth Stage

Not all turnaround efforts require strategies for each stage, because not all turnarounds go through all five stages. For example, whereas there is a change of management in more than 80% of level III crisis companies, only about 25% of managements are changed in level I rejuvenation situations. Generally, mildly underperforming companies require a strategic rejuvenation plan, but seldom require an emergency action plan. Moderate-loss companies may not require an absolute viability analysis, but certainly do require detailed plans for returning to positive cash flow and profitability.

8.4.1   *The Management Change Stage*

Management change can mean bringing in new leaders, or it can mean that management changes its approach. The former case is the most common, because very few managements can really change their stripes. A serious threat to the company's existence may spur them to a flurry of inadequate or poorly timed activity, because usually these managers view the problems through rose-colored glasses.

There are three principal strategies with regard to the management change stage:

1   Must the CEO be changed?
2   Should the new CEO be an outsider or an insider?
3   What personal characteristics seem to best describe the successful turn-around leader?

8.4.2   *Must the CEO Be Changed?*

Sometimes the board decides to ride with current management, but usually there is a specific underlying reason for this. If the principal problems of a company are external—that is, beyond management control—a board may decide that a CEO change is inappropriate. In other instances, management may control board membership loyalties through stock holdings.

Unfortunately, it is pretty easy for smart management to 'snow' a board of directors right up to the time that profits start to cave in. As much as they think otherwise, most boards have inadequate access to the true inside information of the company. For example, how can the board tell whether the company's marketing practices will start losing ground to a more aggressive competitor in a period of two or three years?

Most studies find that boards of directors do not do an effective job in evaluating, appraising, and measuring the company CEO. They wait until financial and other results are so dismal that some remedial action is forced upon them. CEOs instinct is to attribute poor results to factors over which he (or she) has no control. The inclination is for friendly directors to go along with these apparently plausible explanations. Boards generally act only in cases where the financial results demand some real action on the board's part.

8.4.3 Should the New CEO Be an Outsider or an Insider?

In seven out of ten cases where a turnaround is required, the board appoints a new CEO. Surprisingly, in 60% of those cases, the CEO is an outsider rather than an insider (these figures do not include the turnarounds of divisions within companies). Where the problems are mostly internal, a new CEO is brought in 80% of the time. Where problems are deemed to be external only, new CEOs are brought in only 13% of time (personal source: survey of eighty-one turnaround company chief executives). In almost all cases where the problems are deemed to be external only, insiders are used to replace the CEO. For the heavy lifting required in the serious turnaround, the advantage of a management insider is that he (she) knows where the bodies are buried or how to find out where they're buried. If they can move with detachment and unchallenged authority, they will probably make fewer mistakes than an outsider would.

Even when forced to go outside, the board may have trouble offering the challenge and rewards that would attract a CEO with a good track record. Surprisingly, eight out of ten turnarounds are led by outsider chief executives who were not turnaround specialists. The most popular outsider type is growth-oriented executives followed by those who had an entrepreneurial reputation. Few conservator-style managers are ever selected for the heavy lifting necessary in a turnaround. In a critical turnaround situation, where very tough decisions are necessary, insiders are at a disadvantage. It is difficult for people who have grown up in the business to shrink it back to the viable core base from which they can again move forward.

8.4.4 What Personal Characteristics Seem to Best Describe the Successful Turnaround Leader?

Generally, people who clean up companies are constructive negative thinkers, as opposed to the optimistic positive thinkers who may have gotten the company into trouble. Constructive negative thinkers break the business down into small segments where value judgments can be made. They then perform the surgery of divesting companies of those segments of the business that are not performing. In some cases, even reasonably performing segments must be converted to cash that the company can use to survive to fight another day.

There are three very important aspects of leadership in a turnaround situation:

- The turnaround leader must be the architect of a realistic turnaround plan.
- The turnaround leader must be able to successfully execute the difficult undertakings that the plan usually encompasses.
- The tone and personal style of the turnaround leader must engender trust and confidence to rebuild employee morale under stressful conditions.

1   The Turnaround Leader Must Be the Architect of a Realistic Turnaround Plan

In order to be the architect of a realistic turnaround plan, a turnaround leader typically must possess broad business experience, analytical abilities, entrepreneurial skill creativity, and self-awareness. In my personal opinion, the most important ability in putting together a realistic plan is the ability to cut through the fog and haze created by self-serving interests within the company. A leader who does not have the ability to cut through this can be blinded by the realities necessary to create a realistic turnaround plan. Turnaround leaders must have a lot of self-discipline. They must not be afraid to make decisions or to live with the consequences of their decisions. More than anything else, true leadership is not deterred by opinion leader makers. He (she) should have many of the characteristics of an entrepreneur, especially the ability to grasp an opportunity and to move aggressively to affect change.

In the mid-'80s, I became CEO of a medium-size supply company that had once been much larger. It was, as one new-move newspaper described it, "amongst the walking dead." In spite of it's dire situation, certain hubris had remained in the company. The company's customer base was decimated by a severe oil patch decline. The company had been unsuccessful in getting business from the large major oil companies. Survival was not possible unless we were able to transform our served customer group to the better-financed large oil companies that continued substantial drilling activities.

America's largest bank at the time had completely cut off the ability of the company to order steel throughout the world with huge back-to-back letters of credit. One day I walked into the head of purchasing's office and noticed he was slicing open and throwing letters into the wastebasket. Curiously, I asked why he threw those thick envelopes into the wastebasket without even taking a look. He said, "Those are surplus oil country tubular pipe offerings from trucker yards that we never do business with." He added,

"The OCTG pipe was offered at distressed prices and was OK if accompanied by the right certified test documents."

I was amazed that we would throw this information away, given that we were cut off from our usual source of supplies, rather than compiling it into an effective database. I immediately ordered that the practice be stopped and a computer database of those supplies be constructed. Within one month, we were able to provide business to a major oil company with an impossible demand for oil drilling pipe on short notice and at twice the normal industry margins. In addition, the oil company paid us before we owed money to the supplier. This very simple break from arrogant hubris allowed the company to crack into a highly profitable customer base. Being able to reposition from a weak set of customers to a strong set of blue-chip customers was the key to this successful turnaround.

2 The Turnaround Leader Must Be Able to Successfully Execute the Difficult Undertakings That the Plan Usually Encompasses

As the implementer of strategy, the turnaround leader must be effective at promoting and defending the turnaround plan. The leader must be able to integrate conflicting interests, which necessarily derive around a plan for radical change. In order to effectively do this, the turnaround leader should possess good interviewing skills and high standards of evaluation. The organization's essential needs must be met, and a turnaround leader must judge results. Requirements for this role are tough mindedness, objective orientation, and solid self-confidence. Good negotiating skills are also important as well as some impatience to get something done. Successful turnaround leaders seem to be able to sense the task with the highest priority, seize the initiative, and devote enormous energy to driving the organization to critical task completion. They are usually very dogged in the pursuit of objectives and the accomplishment of goals while maintaining the flexibility to change goals as the situation develops. The role of the turnaround leader is to look at the whole corporate body, to diagnose the problems. What are the business' strong and weak segments? They must determine which segments should be cut away, including the peeling off of individuals. Done properly, it will quickly move to reinforce the remaining corporate body, which scaled back becomes a solid core business platform.

This takes a special kind of constructive negative thinking that most managers are not used to dealing with. The behavioral patterns observed of turnaround leaders generally center on objectives rather than methods. The turnaround leader must be able to command and if necessary to spread a little blood and guts around the organization. Turnaround leaders command with the understanding that they are doing the greater good over the long pull rather than being possessed by the shorter-term massacre that may be necessary. Not everybody is capable of taking these nerve-racking actions. In fact, most executives are not cut out for radical surgery.

3   *The Tone and Personal Style of the Turnaround Leader*
    Must Engender Trust and Confidence to Rebuild
    Employee Morale Under Stressful Conditions

Whatever his (her) temperament, the turnaround leader's individual personality leaves a vivid impression on company affairs. Without an image of confidence, the survival of a troubled company would be in doubt. Turnaround leaders are not required to have a given personality style. The effort to correlate personality traits to executive effectiveness was abandoned long ago. Successful business leaders generally are likely to be characterized by substantial drive, intellectual ability, intuition, creativeness, flexibility, and social ability. These qualities, however, can exist amid a fairly wide range of styles, so long as they are dynamic and energetic. What is important is that the personal traits inspire confidence in the ultimate survival and renewal of a troubled company. It is insufficient for the turnaround leader to be self-confident; they must project a positive outlook and stimulate that self-confidence throughout the organization.

If the company really is a good company with a messed-up balance sheet, the new turnaround leader may be more of a financial type out of Wall Street (with a lot of sophistication on the banking side). If a financial restructuring is needed in an otherwise good company, the board would thus likely bring in a financial type. Typically, if it is a management operation type of turnaround, the successful turnaround leader should come out of the multidivisional operation of a company where there were internal turnaround people—troubleshooters. Troubleshooting is usually where they have learned how to identify corporate sore spots. Many of these operations' troubleshooters have engineering backgrounds.

In many cases, turnaround leaders are not attractive people from a social standpoint and are not so much people oriented. They are people users. Some are known simply as blood-and-guts people. They are the George Patton's of the business world and generally there's a lot of loner in them. They like to make decisions and are very decisive. This comes from both a natural feel and lots of prior experience. The average leader avoids prescribing corporate euthanasia for a limping company. Not because they cannot read the numbers, but because they came up through a system that excessively rewards the ability to get along other people.

In the battle for the resurrection of an underperforming company, the first necessity is to be able to stave off disaster. Possession of this ability by turnaround leaders does not guarantee success, but the lack of it guarantees failure. There must be hunger for achievement; most times a leader with that kind of hungry personality will carry others with them. They are action oriented. You cannot turn a business around without a hands-on style of management

Today, a general business belief is that the best managers are those whose people are happy and that happiness comes from encouragement and praise. Consistent demand for better performance is viewed as bad for morale. With this conventional wisdom often comes the simultaneous toleration of ineffective subordinates. Successful turnaround leaders do not tolerate ineffectiveness. They have the courage to 'act on people' and clearly differentiate between outstanding and mediocre performance in their reward systems. They promptly terminate or move aside nonperformers and counterproductive politicians.

8.4.5   Evaluation or Viability Assessment Stage— The Turnaround Plan

In a turnaround situation, too often the urge to begin doing something is so compelling that we fail to define completely just what it is that we are about to do. Action-oriented turnaround leaders thrive on immediate tangible satisfaction—results! Turnaround leaders have a natural inclination to 'get on with it.' Planning is an inglorious task, especially when relegated to a 'staff' function. Is ridiculously easy to make on-the-spot decisions if you have previously thought out and evaluated all of the feasible alternatives. If your strategy is wrong, the operational implementation is going to be many degrees more difficult than if you have the right strategy. Even in a crisis business environment, the best and most effective change is orderly change.

The turnaround company needs more than the 'back-of-an-envelope' type plan, but more than any other type of company, it must avoid the basic planning errors that make planning just lip service. The plan must be simple, realistic, involve line management, and concentrate on segmenting the business into its strong and weak elements. Turnaround companies do not need two-hundred-page plans. Another insidious trap management falls into using the more-is-better approach is to increase their planning horizon beyond a reasonable time.

If anyone still suffers from the delusion that we are able to forecast beyond a very short time span, let them look at the headlines in yesterday's paper and ask which of them they could possibly have predicted a decade ago. I have yet to meet anyone who has a reliable crystal ball that tells what the future holds. Yet there are thousands of planning departments throughout the world that claim to be able to plan on a five-to-ten-year basis. Even then, long-range plans are usually a fool's trap. At the least, long planning horizons are not appropriate for turnaround situations.

The ponderous approach to turnaround plans usually creates a reality gap. These plans are often written by business school types with little real product or customer knowledge in the particular market involved. Line management must be involved; otherwise, there will be a serious reality gap. In order to be meaningful, planning must get down to the line management level and pay attention to the concerns of the people actually running the business. This requires a push by the company's CEO. Plans that concentrate on hundreds of accounting spreadsheets usually lead to uncritical forecasting, not to a strategic plan. The usual fundamental weakness in most corporate plans is that they do not lead to the right major decisions that must be made currently to ensure the success of the enterprise in the future.

There are four important guidelines to test whether the turnaround plan has a chance for being effective:

1   Are the strategies consistent with the external competitive environment? This consistency goes beyond today's situation and applies to the competitive environment as it appears to be changing.
2   Is a strategy internally consistent? Internal consistency refers to the cumulative impact of individual strategies on overall corporate goals. For example, are product expansion plans consistent with critical cash flow needs?
3   Does the strategy have an appropriate view of available resources? There must not be a gap between the plan strategy and the company's three critical resources: money, human competence, and physical facilities/technological capabilities.
4   Does the strategy involve an acceptable degree of risk? Strategic goals and resources taken together determine the degree of risk that the company is undertaking. Particularly in fragile turnaround situations, these can be corporate life-or-death decisions.

Many companies undertake strategies that if accomplished would truly be game changers. Unfortunately, and particularly in fragile turnaround situations, the company often runs out of money before it can accomplish anything meaningful with regard to the opportunity. This is not to say the strategy was bad, but it was in the unacceptably high-risk strategy and a prelude to disaster

There Are Usually Three Distinctly Different Plans During a Turnaround Cycle

The first is the 'emergency plan,' which usually is formulated from fifteen to ninety days after the turnaround leader arrives. The objective is to get the company to positive cash flow and to ensure its survival. A high degree of hands-on management on a daily basis is required to assure the outcome of the plan. Cash is managed on a daily and weekly basis. I usually implement detailed weekly operating reviews of key indicators reported in by the major divisions of the company. The strategies include the shutdown of unprofitable divisions, product-line elimination, severe headcount reductions, and asset liquidation, all of which must be done in a hard-nosed fashion. Every company has a few sacred 'sacred cows.' Get rid of them.

Once a high probability of survival is achieved, a second or 'stabilization plan' is formulated that usually takes a company from the point of positive cash flow through the second year of the turnaround. The stabilization plan objective is enough profit improvement to reach positive net income along with consistent profitable cash flow. By the end of the stabilization stage, an acceptable return on investment (ROI) should be achieved. The division plan would typically include divestments rather than closures. The product mix should be improved in a more nuanced fashion than wholesale product-line elimination. This is achieved by adding managerial accounting capabilities that provide insights into individual customer and product profitability.

The third plan is the 'return to growth plan' which should be implemented in less than two years after the turnaround begins. This plan emphasizes redevelopment efforts that grow revenues, enhance margins, and increase profitability. Normal growth is typically defined as growth that is equal to or exceeds the industry's growth. Modest market-share-growth goals should be implemented along with increased market penetration for new products, new markets, and joint ventures. A limited acquisition program is usually undertaken. In addition to market element profitability, weekly operating reviews will be simplified, but highly detailed quarterly business reviews will be implemented.

8.6   The Performance Gap

I have found a simple concept useful to better understand a troubled company's situation. By definition, a troubled company has a sizable performance gap between what the board of directors and shareholders expect compared to its actual performance trajectory. It is useful to break this performance down further into two distinct components:

The first is strategic. A troubled company often is in businesses (products and services) where it does not belong, and it may be subject to overdiversification, overexpansion, excessive leverage, or perhaps all of those problems altogether. These are the root causes of a troubled company's poor (strategic) performance. The root cause of the strategic performance gap is the inexperience or inability of a company's management team to operate that type of business because of a lack of management or financial resources. Strategic gaps can occur from being in the wrong businesses as well as not being in the right business. In the initial stages of a turnaround, errors of commission (being in the wrong business) are usually identified rather than those of omission (not being in the right businesses).

The second is operational. A troubled company usually has a second type of performance gap—the operational performance gap. Whereas management is legitimately capable of running certain core businesses, they are not running them very efficiently. They are not operating their core business(es) up to their potential. The operational performance gap is the difference between the actual and potential performance of existing businesses that should be retained.

I'm often asked what performance gap is most critical. In my mind, the strategic performance gap is more critical in most cases than the operational performance gap. A business can tolerate a truly enormous number of operational shortcomings if its strategic direction is relevant and correct. No organization has ever done or will ever do anything of significance in the most efficient way possible. All operational actions must inevitably be relatively inefficient. It is only when the inefficiency level becomes intolerable that effectiveness, too, begins to suffer. The inefficiency tolerance level of business is surprisingly high. The profit margins for a product line may be only 31% compared to the planned 40%, but the firm will survive even at such a level of mediocrity.

8.5.1   *The Strategic Gap*

A successful corporate strategy starts with a core purpose that defines the organization. The business units in total can share competencies and resources to achieve greater performance as a result of being part of an organization. In short, make the total greater than the sum of its parts. To this end, the strategic mission (core purpose) of the corporation must articulate the special formula by which these synergies are achieved. It seems almost biblical. Companies grow through diversification to the point of being a conglomerate, but become too complex and diverse to manage. They then go about dismantling most of their diverse acquisitions that were supposed to be a panacea for growth, which rather turned out to be an albatross around their neck.

One of the most common strategic problems of business is caused by managers' overreaching. In order to grow, they readily accept a strategic fit that is tenuous. The required technologies, customers, and channels are not always congruent, or even parallel with the existing business(es), and so cannot be integrated readily, which dims growth prospects. Boards of directors most often fall for the argument presented by management that the acquisitions are a growth initiative that will reduce overhead as a percentage of revenues. In reality, however, there are very few truly lean management companies that make acquisitions. One is a Swiss conglomerate, ABB Ostia Brown, which successfully reduced overhead in spite of making substantial acquisitions.

Bain and Company estimated that 75% of the biggest business blunders really were caused or made worse by growth strategies going awry. One of the most common mistakes occur when a company looks too far away from its natural adjacencies to its core business. It assembles a patchwork of businesses that seem related but don't provide any real synergies. Later, the company is often forced to sell off its new purchases, usually at a steep discount. For example, Bausch & Lomb, with a great core business of personal optics, diversified into hearing aids and other medical equipment. While it did so, its position in its core market, contact lenses, slipped from first to fourth. Aluminum maker Alcoa Inc. took a charge of $845 million before selling its consumer packaging and automotive-related businesses as part of an effort to return its focus to basic metal making.

Another classic example is Quaker Oats' acquisition of Snapple. It was a predictably bad deal on the very day it was made. Some industry analysts estimated that the $1.7 billion purchase price was as much as $1 billion too much. The stock price of both companies declined on the day the deal was announced. Problems with implementation plus a downturn in the market for new age drinks quickly led to severe performance problems. Just twenty-eight months after the acquisition, Quaker sold Snapple to Triarc Companies for less than 20% of what it had paid. Quaker Oats' and Triarc's stock prices went up the day the deal was announced.

8.5.2 Strategies to Close the Strategic Gap

The key to closing the strategic gap is strategic focus. Strategic focus is the antithesis of growth for growth's sake. A focused strategy includes the reduction of complexity and the concentration of resources on the disproportionately profitable elements of the business. It is thus important to consider alternatives that might be available to divest subsidiaries or divisions that are not core to the future of the company. Some level of asset reduction can be applied almost immediately, because situations in trouble are normally fat and begging for correction. The basic concept is to offload nonperforming and nonessential strategic assets to provide a bridge for financing to get the positive cash flow.

Divestment is commonly, but not always, the consequence of a prior growth strategy, often driven by a desire to diversify. Much of the corporate downsizing of the 1990s was the result of acquisitions and takeovers that were the rage in the 1970s and early '80s. One should always realize that time and money should not be poured into marginal operations when that same capital could be yielding higher returns in more positive operations. Robert Murdoch, head of the News Corporation of Australia, amassed excessive debt through acquisition. His first move was to dramatically improve his debt-to-equity ratio by unloading non-core subsidiaries.

Firms often acquire other businesses with operations in areas with which the acquiring firm has little experience. After trying for a number of years to integrate the new activities into the existing organization, many firms elect to divest themselves of portions of the business in order to concentrate on those activities in which they have a competitive advantage. Atradius, a diversified credit insurance company in Germany, decided on a new strategy to increase and secure profits, create sustainable growth in revenues, and decrease volatility of both revenues and earnings. This strategy included the shedding of businesses and markets where the company lacked potential to achieve critical mass or profitability. Atradius decided to shed itself of its consumer credit and outsourced credit management subsidiaries.

An interesting study in strategic contrast is that of the storied battle between Nike and Reebok. Way back in 1990, the companies had almost identical financials. Nike's revenues were $2.3 billion; Reeboks were $2.2 billion. Nike's operating income was $481 million compared to Reeboks $300 million. At that time, both companies were almost entirely focused on athletic shoes. Nike focused more on the performance and athletes, whereas Reeboks focus was more diffuse and in the recreational athlete area. Both had very well-known brands. However, at the same time, Nike's core shoe business was under severe attack.

By the end of the next ten years, Nike's fortunes were quite different from Reebok's. Nike's market capitalization had increased by almost 400%. Reeboks had shrunk in half. Nike had a focused strategy that it utilized in a repeatable fashion and refined over the decade to increase its share one product after another. In contrast, Reebok moved far afield in a number ways, referring to itself as a sports performance company. It made many unrelated investments, with a classic being the purchase of the Boston Whaler boat manufacturer.

Many studies have confirmed the anecdotal evidence, and I have my own experience about better returns from a focused strategy. My favorite is a study conducted by EVA Dimensions, which utilized economic value added (EVA) as a metric. What I like about this study is that it featured sustainable EVA over at least a ten-year period. Seventy-eight percent of companies with one core and a leadership position were able to sustain an EVA of greater than 5% over a ten-year period or more. In spite of leadership in their market, only 17% of corporations with multiple cores were able to do so. Even worse, those in other situations (lack of leadership, highly diversified, etc.) had a 95% chance of failure to meet EVA sustainability.

The natural temptation is to blur strategy and diffuse concentration. Focus involves deliberately limiting potential sales volume to enhance profitability. Lack of focus can cause managers to lose sight of the reasons for their success and compromise the company's focus strategy of 'growth for growth's sake.' The strategic gap is closed by harnessing the power of focus:

1 Without focus, over time companies find their way into all sorts of efforts and initiatives. Each seems to make perfect sense at the time, but after a while, focus is lost and unsuccessful projects pile up.

2 Focus is most often brought back by returning a company to what got it successful in the first place. This often revives corporate vitality.

3 Believe it or not, your problem can be someone else's success, framed in cash for your balance sheet to invest in your particular better performers.

4   It is important to analyze the cash-producing characteristics of each line of business in order to preserve overall capital.

8.5.3   *The Operational Gap*

Sloughing off yesterday is an even more important element in companies going through a turnaround than more stable companies. Sloughing off yesterday has both a strategic and operational component. The reasons for product elimination and divestment vary by the stage of the turnaround cycle. I find this a common phenomenon in dealing with companies that underperform. When the core market seems to be under attack or in trouble, management reflexively takes resources away from its core business and often foolishly invests it in other areas. In most cases, they are better served by digging deeper into the reasons for the sluggishness of the core business and by redeploying to more profitable areas within the core or to more adjacent areas to complement a core.

It is thus key to first clearly identify the core business strengths and weaknesses and to identify any product, service, investment, or market that is not aligned with the core business. Consider alternatives that might be available to divest product lines that are not key to the future of the company. Look at each part of the organization that supports and strengthens core capabilities. Identify any department, asset, or investment that does not support or strengthen core capabilities and get rid of it. Go out and visit customers and ask them what they think of your company, products, deliveries, and customer support.

A classic example of a successful operational turnaround strategy is Steve Jobs' turnaround of Apple in 1996, which began by shrinking the firm to a scale and scope appropriate for the niche producer it was at that time (4% of the total market). Jobs got Microsoft to invest $150 million in Apple and developed new Microsoft Office software for Apple to deflect Gates' worries over antitrust prosecution. Jobs also cut the number of desktop models (too confusing) from fifteen to one and the number of portable and handhelds to one; he cut out all printers and other peripherals, cut development engineers and software development, made a cut in distributors and five of its six national retailers (part of the rationale for too many models), moved manufacturing to Taiwan, began selling direct via the web, and waited for 'the next big thing.' Two years later, the iPod came, then online music, and later the iPhone (actually, except for waiting for 'the next big thing,' the previous list consisted of 'actions,' not strategy).

Many companies fail to properly manage the weak areas of their business, even among their customers, which must be cut versus the stronger areas that should be preserved and enhanced. By focusing the operating strategy, the resource deployment can be limited to highly profitable customer groups in an attempt to meet their needs exceptionally well. Resource alignment thus is key. What does your targeted customer group value? Do you need to have low costs because they are so price sensitive, or can you be so customer responsive that they are willing to pay average or above prices for your products or services?

If you're losing money, cut the losses quickly, even if it means selling off a division, abandoning a venture, or severely cutting back. Successful executives have often been the quickest to cut their losses and as a result saved money on new efforts or product lines that had fallen short of expectation. Larger corporations, in recent years, have started behaving in the same way. Focus has become critical to compete and to preserve capital.

8.5.4   *Closing the Operational Gap With Emergency Stage Strategies*

Emergency strategies usually call for shrinking back to a viable core business or businesses. The following is an overview of strategies typically undertaken in key areas during the emergency stage of the turnaround:

- *The basic thrust* of emergency stage strategies is to assure the survival of the enterprise, which normally requires defensive rather than offensive steps.
- *Product-line strategies*. It is absolutely necessary to develop product-line profitability analysis and to eliminate unprofitable product lines.
- *Cost-reduction strategies*. Costs have to be reduced dramatically, preferably by surgical cuts but by 'meat ax' cuts if necessary.
- *Capacity strategies*. Human capacity is reduced through headcount reductions, the closure of plants, and the consolidation of operations, which are carried out on the compressed-time schedule.
- *Financial strategies*. Drastic actions are necessary to move the company from negative to positive cash flow, even at the expense of short-term profitability.
- *Dividend strategy*. The dividend must be eliminated.

The emergency plan assumes cost avoidance and cost prevention are in effect and centers on cost elimination and cost reduction. At the same time, if possible, terminating people must be avoided during the first sixty days, as a piecemeal approach to headcount reduction has a devastating effect on morale throughout the business. It is more effective to start with cost *elimination*. It is amazing how much energy is wasted on trying to reduce costs and functions of products that should have been eliminated in the first place.

There are cases where a situation is so severe that the 'meat-ax' approach is required, and if that is the situation, then use the meat ax. Generally, although it takes a little more study, the selective surgical approach to cost reduction works best. The surgical cut approach is based on an assessment of what functions are absolutely necessary to run the business versus those expenses that are being incurred and have a future payoff. Cost reduction usually starts with headcount reduction, and there is always a great reluctance to reduce headcount. The turnaround leader would not like headcount reduction any more than anyone else but realizes that it is necessary. The troubled company is like an overloaded lifeboat: either every third person has to get off or the boat will sink.

Seldom are attrition and hiring freezes enough to accomplish most staff-reduction requirements in an emergency turnaround situation. Cost-reduction programs focused on methods improvements, etc., sound nice, but take too long; they seldom meet expectations and are usually not part of an emergency plan. Selective surgery is the best bet if an emergency plan requires a reduction of 20% (plan for 25%, as there will always be some slippage because of some plausible reasons or just plain timidity). Surgical cost reduction generally does not imply cutting across the board in departments. Some departments may be eliminated altogether, their headcounts can be drastically reduced, or they can be merged with other departments.

In one case, I made surgical cuts to reduce headquarters staff from 571 to 356 in year one. Headquarters staff were further reduced to 247 personnel by the end of year two. Four years after the first cuts, total company revenues were two-and-a-half times what they were on the day I walked in the door. Some departments such as 'OR (operations research)' were eliminated altogether. IT was cut back 65%. The legal department was cut back by two-thirds. Even direct sales were reduced to proven producers and then later rebuilt. A colleague of mine reduced headquarters staff from 250 people to just 17. Whereas 40% of the drastic change was staff reduction, 60% of the people were placed in operating departments where they would be more productive.

Marketing is often called the whipping boy of the turnaround. Marketing often suffers the most retrenchment. There must be differentiation between marketing staff reductions and direct sales activity. Generally, I reduce marketing staff but not always sales. It depends on a study of the situation. In one case, because of the highly differentiated performance of sales reps, a sales force was initially reduced by 50%. Revenues doubled over the next three-year period. This was accomplished because the 50% of the retained sales personnel were responsible for 86% of sales revenues and had far greater growth potential. The laggards in the sales force had been dragging the rest of the sales force down.

8.5.5 Stabilization Stage Strategies

Positive cash flow must be restored before the emergency phase is complete. The objective of the stabilization stage of the turnaround is to create a stable platform for future growth. Stabilization strategies concentrate on improving profits from that stable platform. The company must substantially improve its profitability and earn an acceptable return on investment by the end of the stabilization phase. The strategies used in stabilization contrast substantially with those in the emergency stage. The following is an overview of strategies typically undertaken in key areas during the stabilization stage:

- *The basic thrust* is the careful enhancement of all elements of the business to become more competitive and to create a stable base from which normal growth can proceed.
- *Products strategy.* Normally, bold product-line pruning has occurred during the emergency stage. There may be some additional cleanup in that regard, but the concentration focuses on individual product contribution.
- *Profitability strategies* are now focused on margin improvement rather than meat-ax cost reductions: nuanced cost reductions and other profitability initiatives to improve margins and retain businesses.
- *Capacity strategies.* The company's human resources may still require some reduction as well as consolidation initiatives on physical capacity. Wholesale closings have typically ended.
- *Financial strategies.* Operations concentrate on sustained and enhanced profitability. It is balance-sheet cleanup time and the time to normalize and strengthen bank relationships.
- *Dividend strategy.* The reinstatement of the dividend may be considered, but is usually rejected until sustained profitability is assured.

Improving profitability in the stabilization stage focuses on two fundamental tactics. First, making nuanced retention/divestment decisions. Second, reducing cost through productivity improvement and increasing prices to achieve higher margins. The retention/divestment decision differs markedly from the emergency stage. In the emergency stage, if necessary for cash flow and under extreme time pressure, certain operations may be liquidated as opposed to divested. In extreme situations, the company may be forced to sell one of its clear winners—a course of action seldom taken once a company has been stabilized.

Surprisingly, but which most turnaround leaders agree, underperforming companies often do a terrible job in pricing. This underpricing may amount a material portion of the firm's operating losses. Moreover, product proliferation is both a huge problem and a huge operating opportunity. Product proliferation stems from trying to be all things to all people. My survey of 100 turnaround leaders (who turned around over 300 companies) found that they eliminated an average of 17% of their products. This is far from a drastic approach. I know of one company that went from 250 different models to just 33 and had a substantial increase in sales within eighteen months. During the stabilization stage, the company is not necessarily striving for improved volume as much as improved margins. Total volume may even decline in the short term as unprofitable volume is eliminated. The combination of cost elimination, cost discipline, more effective pricing, and elimination of losing products will usually lead to substantial margin improvement.

Companies with insufficient information to provide for effective decision making should ramp-up their IT capability during the stabilization stage. There should be the necessary time available for management to take a fresh and detailed look at every facet of the operation. After a company has completed its planned withdrawal from unprofitable products and market segments, it must look toward business areas that are more attractive from the standpoint of future profitability and growth. Before full-scale development programs can be launched, the balance sheet must be cleaned up to provide a suitable financial platform for growth. By the end of the stabilization stage, the company should have a better-organized balance sheet both in terms of its debt structure and how its wares major assets are deployed.

Turnaround strategies are directed to new development areas on a modest basis. It is almost a natural order of things that assets tend to gravitate to those segments of the company that have the greatest mass (gross revenues), because revenues have a high attraction power. Over time, other areas will suffer from shortages of assets, and these are likely to become the less-developed segments of the company. These very segments may be the ones that have the greatest profit potential. For example, in the soft goods area, the primary profit leverage comes most often from the marketing area, with manufacturing returns low in comparison. Many companies have, therefore, subcontracted a large part of their integral manufacturing, which they formally performed themselves. This has liberated assets that could be more effectively used in the retail segment.

8.5.6   *Strategies in the Return to Growth Stage*

A company that has successfully implemented the stabilization of its core business may be running out of profit-improvement potential in its existing businesses. The balance between emphasis on existing businesses and the effort directed toward the development of new products and services is a delicate one. The turnaround company has of necessity been forced by the severity of its problems to be internally oriented and will place less emphasis on change in the world around it. However, excessive emphasis on existing product lines will result in the eventual stagnation and decline of the company. The company must, therefore, tilt the balance more in a direction of new market elements. The following is an overview of strategies typically undertaken in key areas during the return to growth stage:

- *The basic thrust* of return to growth turnaround strategies is to initiate high-probability development opportunities.
- *Product strategies* revolve around the extension and improvement of the product line rather than product pruning. New product moves are usually limited to 'adjacent' tactics.

- *Cost improvement strategies* are focused on investing in productivity through automation and information technology improvements.
- *Capacity strategies*, particularly human capacity, focus on marketing and sales initiatives to build volume and, if appropriate, to rebuild share.
- *Financial strategies* include the normalization of credit covenants and obtaining a modest amount of external funding.
- *Dividend strategy*, assuming a public company. A prudent level of dividend reinstatement should be accomplished.

During the emergency stage, most underperforming companies have both severe strategic and operational performance gaps. Strategic gaps should be closed in the emergency stage. During the stabilization stage, after the misfit businesses have been divested, operational gaps prevail. By the end of the stabilization effort, the company will have run out of most of its low-hanging operating profit improvement potential (from its existing businesses and products). In the return to the growth stage, the turnaround company usually starts out by initiating internal development efforts and later may emphasize its external acquisition efforts.

Of utmost importance is a realization that the sum total of growth strategies should not be able to sink the company financially. Financial resources still must be carefully appraised. It is wise for the turnaround company to direct its external growth initiatives to adjacency strategies as opposed to diversification strategies. This means sticking close to existing technologies, products, and markets. Product improvement should come before product replacement and new geographic markets with the same customer typology comes before new customer typologies. Taking on new technologies in new markets with new customer typologies is generally excessively risky. The company is not out of the woods yet.

Peter Drucker (1973) neatly defined the boundary condition risk of overdiversification when he explained that overdiversification takes place when the management of the company cannot test quantitative and qualitative information coming from a subsidiary against its own concrete experience. If they cannot, then judgment becomes abstract and action or improper decisions are likely to follow.

Reference

Drucker, P. F. (1973). *Management: Tasks, responsibilities, practices*. New York: Harper & Row.

9 Why Must Companies Reorganize, and Why Do They Wait So Long?

Insights From Practice[1]

Kathryn Rudie Harrigan

9.1 Introduction

Many companies would benefit from confronting the marketplace realities that a turnaround process necessitates. Too many firms are lagging in performance, and owners are restive about successive quarters of reported losses. Operating cash is becoming scarce for them, and financing options are becoming limited because management cannot deliver anything more than breakeven financial results.

Even when a firm is *not* on the precipice of filing for court protection in bankruptcy restructuring, viable organizations often need dramatic changes in operations to keep abreast of changing business conditions. Unfortunately, the people within organizations do not like to change—unless driven to do so by strong leadership or response to a crisis. Tolerating resistance to change results in hidebound practices that can make a firm's products less attractive to new generations of customers, whereas its practices become less appealing to new generations of clever employees. Worst, resistance to making prophylactic changes to operations can drive a firm into crisis vis-à-vis its creditors at the very time when access to funding becomes critical in order for the firm to make the competitive changes that are needed to respond to significant exogenous industry changes.

9.2 Why Companies Must Use Turnarounds to Change

Companies typically undertake the turnaround process because they (a) must repay their creditors, (b) must retain their customers' patronage, and (c) hope to preserve some fraction of their workers' jobs when the firm is in trouble. Even when an enterprise is not facing an obvious crisis, it is important for its managers to act with a sense of urgency in bringing about changes (to avert their firm's impending demise). Instead, too many managers will not make changes to their firm's operations in a timely fashion—perhaps because they are afraid to face the inevitable bloodletting that accompanies reorganization during the turnaround process when some customers, employees, and suppliers are inconvenienced (or perhaps they loathe confronting what turnaround analysis will suggest about the nature of their current business arrangements).

Making operations become net cash positive may mean denying credit to the firm's long-term customers who have become slow to pay the firm's invoices. Perhaps they pay late because the firm has not enforced its credit terms, but maybe slow-to-pay customers are themselves becoming insolvent. It is difficult to extricate the firm from sickness when its customers become ill financially, but failure to enforce established credit terms and limits risks letting sick clients drag down their supplier as well. Firms should be imposing practices to accelerate cash collection long before competition within their industry grows more intense (in order to ascertain whether their product quality commands customer loyalty or whether they have been buying sales volumes instead).

Reducing working-capital costs may require inventory reductions that infuriate sales people (who want their firm to make available a prolific variety of products—just in case their customer should request to purchase a unit of two of esoteric merchandise). Information obtained while performing inventory triage analysis may reveal that some customers are unprofitable to serve (or that sales personnel are not maximizing the profitability potential of their selling efforts). Necessary price increases (associated with the higher costs of serving less-profitable customer accounts) may reduce overall sales volumes and create a crisis in utilizing fixed assets profitably. Variable costs that could be adjusted to accommodate lower sales volumes may prove to be difficult to alter.

Stretching accounts payable to conserve the firm's cash could set off a domino effect of crises among its suppliers who may also be on the precipice of insolvency because of mismanagement. Few firms actively inquire into the solvency of their suppliers and do not take precautions to prevent suppliers from becoming overly dependent on their patronage, until it is too late to make prophylactic changes in their purchasing policies.

It is management's responsibility to move quickly to reorganize symptoms of failing operations and to restructure the firm's financial structure (if necessary) by providing good stewardship for the use of the firm's assets, which have been entrusted to them, and selling them for cash if it becomes necessary to do so. Swift and deliberate action is needed during the turnaround process to obtain the highest salvage values on any merchandise and assets that must be jettisoned; incompetent managers delay in restructuring their companies until the timing advantage available from acting quickly has been lost, because the higher prices that might have been enjoyed by selling off underperforming assets in a timely fashion typically plunge when it becomes widely recognized that an industry is troubled and several competitors may be bailing out of distressed situations. Worse, inaction erodes the value of a troubled company's assets, which must be maintained (and value of its customer list, which must be preserved) in case it becomes necessary to sell off all (or parts) of the firm's assets to another owner.

9.2.1 Using Creditors' Money

When the firm's performance becomes distressed, management is obliged to perform a corporate triage to recover as much value as is salvageable to service debt (or repay creditors). If the firm's operations cannot be returned to a state that generates positive net cash flows, the liquidation process should begin immediately, because funds are draining out of a company even while management is pondering how to proceed against its performance problems. Improvement of cash flows is always the starting point in bringing a sick firm back to life, and cash conservation is the main reason why the turnaround professionals should immediately be called in to help (if needed) with assessing the firm's viability as an ongoing concern—i.e., one that is worth more alive than dead. If debts are not serviced and creditors doubt that their loans will be repaid, future credit availability for turnarounds will dry up, and derelict managers will poison the well for obtaining future funding of all other would-be turnarounds if their firm's restructuring does not happen in a timely fashion. Reorganizing sooner rather than later is consistent with maximizing the time value of money—other parties' money.

If the troubled firm must reorganize by changing its financial structure—e.g., swapping debt for equity or otherwise modifying the distressed firm's governance structure—management will have more discretion to lead the change-making events if the reorganization process is initiated earlier than they might be allowed to enjoy if the troubled company were forced into a court-supervised restructuring by disgruntled creditors. Delays always produce adverse results (and increase risks that the firm's operations will fail) when necessary decisions are procrastinated. As shareholders forfeit their voice to the firm's creditors by condoning management inaction, they also sacrifice the potential value of their equity ownership by delaying demands for a reorganization that should be occurring.

9.2.2 Keeping Customers

When a firm enters the turnaround process, there is a high risk that customers will stop buying its products and services if they become disappointed by low quality, lack of supporting service, or miss other attributes that they consider to be necessities (but which cost-cutting managers typically stop funding in their efforts to stop the cash from hemorrhaging). Competitors have learned to attack the clientele list of wounded firms—correctly expecting that firms in distress cannot afford to fight back in the battle to maintain their customers' loyalty. Firms in need of a turnaround are easy prey to better-funded rivals. With so many vendors clamoring for customers' patronage as part of the normal competitive process (and with so few incentives for past customers to remain loyal to a seller who is underserving their needs), customer accounts are lost and buyers will shop elsewhere if a distressed company skimps on normal marketing and servicing outlays (often lost customers do not return; it is frequently more difficult to regain a past customer who has been mistreated or underserved by a sickly vendor than it is for that firm to enter a new market and garner new customers from scratch).

9.2.3　Preserving Jobs

A third reason to reorganize troubled operations in a timely fashion (assuming that a company continues to have some viable line of business that is net-cash-flow positive) is to save jobs for some portion of the firm's employees. Headcount reductions are an important part of the turnaround process, and it is not fair that some people will lose their jobs (because the workers did not mismanage the company into distress), but the outcome of many restructurings will often be a downsized labor force (or operations that will close completely). Preserving a portion of the former corporate entity to operate as a going concern with a reduced body count may be better than facing a total liquidation of operations and abolishment of all jobs.

Managers have an obligation to preserve the morale of the firm's remaining workers, even as jobs are disappearing. Workers are the principal means that management has of implementing their envisioned turnaround. Employees must believe that timely actions are being taken in order to maintain their productivity and serve customers effectively as the turnaround process unfolds; otherwise, shoddy product quality and defecting customers will turn the need for a turnaround process into a moot topic.

9.3　Why Managers Procrastinate

Firms fail because they have been mismanaged. Managerial errors have been made in the distressed firm, and the impact of those problems is being compounded by failing to take corrective actions fast enough. On a spectrum that ranges from ignorance to incompetence, procrastination can be remedied with varying degrees of success, depending on how long the firm's performance has lagged and the dire the consequences of managerial neglect. Change is driven by fear and necessity.

9.3.1　Ignorant Managers

Laggard performers may lose money because their firm's managers do not realize that the firm is underperforming relative to what competitors can accomplish. Competitive benchmarking should always be a dimension of how management (and owners) keep score of the firm's performance over time. Intervention in operating autonomy is the responsibility of top management (and the corporate board). Impatience in demanding reform is a virtue when the period by which a firm underperforms its rivals is allowed to drag on too long.

More serious than managerial ignorance concerning the troubled firm's relative competitive performance is managerial ignorance concerning what must be done to remedy the firm's troubled operations. Mid-level managers are unlikely to draw attention to conditions that could result in their own termination, so they are unlikely to request consulting investigations that showcase their own ineptitude; they are often unwilling to ask for help in solving their firm's problems. Perhaps these managers do not want to 'King Lear' themselves out of a job by diminishing the scope of their firm's range of operations (by suggesting facility shutdowns or other downsizing steps); the conspiracy of silence where action is required may extend to top management if owners' representatives are passive in the face of poor performance.

Because ignorant managers do not know how to confront creditors, customers, suppliers, and owners (among others) with necessary requests for changes that are needed to save their companies, managers may delude themselves into believing that business conditions within their distressed companies are less dreadful than they truly are and will recover on their own, given enough time. In this manner, ignorant managers allow themselves to procrastinate.

9.3.2 Conflict-Averse Managers

Beyond the category of managers who are simply ignorant of what needs to be done is the group of managers who understand what needs to be done to restore their firms to profitability, but do not want to take the necessary actions. Some managers do not like to take the mandatory, draconian actions needed to get their firms out of trouble, because it is unpleasant to shut down operations and fire redundant workers. Many people do not want the reputational damage that comes from eliminating product lines (or lines of business) to occur while they are leading troubled operations. If they have invested in the social fabric of the communities where their firms operate, socially entrenched managers do not want to be seen by their neighbors to be taking take harsh actions; such managers do not want to face the families of employees whose jobs have been eliminated (some conflict-averse managers will even seek employment elsewhere rather than take the mandatory triage steps to perform a needed turnaround).

In performing the triage process (to decide what can be saved), management must look realistically at the scope of the firm's operations to assess their firm's ability to serve their different groups of customers competitively. Managers must decide which of their firm's lines of business are core to the realization of its strategy and should ponder whether the remaining assets might be sold outright or leased back for continuing operations. Briefly, a non-core portion of their firm's lines of business may need to be sold (to find fast cash in order to handle emergencies during the transition period as the turnaround process is being implemented); in essence, a 'crown jewel' product line may have to be sold to keep other parts of the corporate family alive, and some managers do not want to the carry the stigma of being the leader who sold off the company's cash cow business.

9.3.3   *Conceptually Flawed Strategy*

Lenders do not give sweetened credit prices or terms for conceptually flawed strategies, and some conflict-averse managers may fear that scrutiny under court-protected restructuring (or otherwise) will reveal that unjustified diversification has occurred under their leadership; managers who perpetrated the acquisitions that created such flawed diversifications may be unwilling to confront how bustable their firm's corporate strategy really is. The same conflict-averse managers who are unwilling to take the necessary actions to avert losses may be unwilling to acknowledge that their corporate strategy is flawed. If it is discovered that the pieces of their diversified firm do not create synergy when they operate together, managers should begin the process of selling off attractive (but ill-fitting) lines of business for cash, while liquidating unattractive assets that may have been consuming cash.

Paralysis in unraveling a flawed diversification of businesses does not help anybody (except creditors and rapacious vultures who wish to take control of mismanaged firms), because it is difficult to carry a bundle of ill-fitting businesses through the bankruptcy process intact. Most likely, inappropriate pieces of the firm must be sold off to fund the rest of the enterprise's survival, and creditors will take pragmatic actions (if management cannot do so) to salvage valuable pieces of business while liquidating the rest. Conflict-averse managers who are reticent to enter a reorganization process without being forced to do so will discover to their chagrin that creditors demand sweeter terms when strategic concessions were not made earlier in the restructuring process, and underperforming assets are worth less when a firm is troubled.

In assessing how much working capital will be needed to complete a turnaround process, managers may be reluctant to ask for court protection in their restructuring process because doing so places the claims of the creditors over those of shareholders (which typically include managers who have been awarded stock and stock options as part of their compensation). Moreover, when creditors drive a restructuring process, turnaround plans that generate fast cash (but may cut into the muscle of the firm's former strategy) will be more acceptable to irate creditors than those who try to preserve assets and strategic position in a corporate strategy that ultimately has proven not to be viable. If managers believe in their corporate vision, they need to protect it by taking timely actions to ensure its ultimate implementation.

9.3.4   *Ineffective Implementation*

Even managers who know what steps to take in turning around a distressed company may fail in implementation if their systems are wrong; inappropriate performance metrics, wrong milestones, and frequency of providing feedback to employees, or other incentive (or communication) flaws should be corrected long before the firm's organizational structure, management systems, and decision-making processes are stressed when doing a turn-around. Managerial ranks should be well staffed with an ingenious team of experienced and flexible leaders who can spearhead the firm's turnaround process (or else such managers must be seconded from specialized turn-around consulting firms at premium prices). Top management should be charged with recruiting, rewarding, and retaining the type of entrepreneur-ial managers who can motivate their teams to nurse old assets and jerry-rig machines into running longer, if needed. The turnaround team should build a spirit of camaraderie that allows useful ideas to percolate upward from the factory floor (or customers' worksite) long before it becomes necessary for employees to accept the need to make severe changes to preserve as much as is salvageable from distressed operations.

To obtain such results, supervisors should be given freer rein to change working policies and empower hourly employees to trim excessive fat to engage in cost-effective activities before an operating crisis occurs. Dedicated cadres in each functional area who believe they will benefit from working smarter should be encouraged to talk with their counterparts in related oper-ations and other functional areas in order to avoid stupid mistakes—such as making expenditures for excessive advertising campaigns at times when inventories are low (and cannot easily be built up). Responding successfully to pressures from owners to improve operations requires the unleashing of a leadership style that can motivate heroic actions during turnaround processes. But managers must be mindful that employee cooperation dur-ing a time of difficulty represents a two-edged sword; employees must be equitably rewarded if they have excelled in making sacrifices during the turnaround process, and their suggestions should be solicited when devis-ing a plan to meet necessary objectives. In one crisis where employees sug-gested ways to eliminate redundant operations and cease production of low-volume products, headcount reductions were accomplished by down-sizing through retirements, while cross-training extant workers to become their replacements. Gain-sharing of productivity gains was used in another situation to reward employees for accepting stringent terms during the crisis period. In one creative gesture for recognizing especially productive work-ers, a firm leased lakefront property in a wooded area, subdivided it into campsites (including boat-docking facilities), and rented out the sites to their best-performing, hourly employees for a token amount—e.g., $10 per year. The outcome in behavior was similar to that obtained by rewarding exceptional performance with gym memberships or other socially bonding activities; high-performing employees (and their weekend guests) discussed ways to further improve their firm's performance while fishing or hunting together—even when they were not on the clock at work. The firm's turn-around process began sooner and was less arduous than many other firms experienced because the firm's workforce led the charge to bring about nec-essary changes in a timely fashion, and their supervisors trusted the employ-ees' suggestions. Tasks that had formerly been subcontracted to outsiders were brought back in house to allow for retention of experienced workers' problem-solving skills during the difficult period.

9.4 Slash-and-Burn Managers

If a distressed firm's management systems are so flawed and its leaders are so imperfect that a successful turnaround process cannot be undertaken, outside help may be needed. Indeed, when creditors drive a turnaround, they typically rent the services of an artist who motivates cooperation from surviving workers through the sight of their former colleagues' empty desks. Because their charge is to manage for cash, such turnaround managers do not invest in developing smart and flexible employees; the slash-and-burn manager may release cash that was trapped in underperforming assets and lackadaisical management practices, but their short-term activities may sap worker morale and disrupt the fragile trust that should exist between leaders and those whom they lead. A major drawback to resorting to shock therapies to remedy poor performance is the danger that employees will become cynical when they see that a business is being drained of necessary cash instead of reinvesting cash to build long-term competitive viability.

My remarks have been offered with the assumption that a firm needing turnaround has the potential to survive competitively if timely changes can be made to its operations; the inevitable fate of firms that cannot make necessary changes quickly enough is reorganization (if court protection under bankruptcy is an option) or liquidation. The challenges of changing activities inside distressed companies is similar to the need to confront the implications of industry-wide declining demand for a firm's products and to take action before competitors can do so more effectively. In both cases, too many managers resist making changes to their firms' operations until it is too late to do so effectively. As Harrigan (1980) reported, the likelihood of a successful outcome to a firm's endgame strategy exceeded 90% if appropriate actions were taken early (instead of waiting).

Note

1 This chapter draws upon examples contained in Harrigan, K. R. (1988). Matching Management Systems to Maturity. In K.R. Harrigan (Ed.), *Managing Maturing Businesses: Restructuring Declining Industries and Revitalizing Troubled Operations*. Lexington, MA: Lexington Books.

References

Harrigan, K. R. (1980). Strategies for declining businesses. *Journal of Business Strategy, 1*(2), 20–34.

Harrigan, K. R. (1988). Matching management systems to maturity. In K. R. Harrigan (Ed.), *Managing maturing businesses: Restructuring declining industries and revitalizing troubled operations* (pp. 73–92). Lexington, MA: Lexington Books.

10 Human Considerations in Turnaround Management

A Practitioner's View

Yuval Bar-Or

10.1 Introduction

A common refrain from CEOs is that "People are our greatest asset." And yet when an organization is in distress, people are suddenly viewed as liabilities—as targets of blame and finger-pointing and as costs to be slashed through firings or 'rightsizing' (the politically savvy word for 'firing').

Yes, in some cases, employees and managers may be part of the problem that is hurting the organization. But in any turnaround situation, people are also necessarily part of the solution.

When embarking on a turnaround, staff may be demoralized, disillusioned, and scared, and they likely no longer trust management. They may be found clustered around the watercooler fearfully exchanging gossip, or sneaking out back to share an anxious cigarette, or meeting after hours to drown their concerns in a nearby pub. But make no mistake, this shaken and demoralized group represents your best chance for success—if they can be united in a common cause.

As a turnaround manager, your greatest human challenges are to rebuild trust, re-establish communication, and initiate collaboration. Of course, a turnaround manager must focus on improving short-term cash flows, achieving stability, selling assets, revamping product lines, etc. But he or she must simultaneously and consistently consider the human needs of all stakeholders. The list of stakeholders extends beyond employees to: suppliers, clients, strategic partners, and owners. Each of these groups presents its own challenges and may require the manager to address concerns, to clear the air, and to build a constructive momentum.

Thus, at its very core, a turnaround manager's success requires an understanding of the key drivers of human behavior in the workplace. This will be the starting point in this chapter. We will then proceed with a review of the emotional effects of distress on employees, including assessing existing human capital, improving human capital, empowering people, taking decisive action, celebrating the small wins, and having an awareness of all relevant stakeholders. The ultimate aim is to establish that acknowledging the humanity of others is a sign of strength, not weakness.

10.2   Understanding the Key Drivers of Human Behavior

The key drivers of human behavior are, unsurprisingly, quite obvious. We all need to feel that (1) we are fairly compensated, (2) we have a reasonable opportunity at promotion and upward mobility, (3) management is articulating a clear sense of corporate direction, (4) our job provides us with satisfaction, (5) we have personal dignity and respect from others, and (6) we have control over our professional lives.

For example, in 2011, I was involved with an Adult Day Health Care Center in California. The company's founders had a bright, fresh vision, calling for a modern, stimulating, multi-disciplinary approach to serving disabled adults. In the early stages, there was a palpable sense of excitement. Employees deeply believed in the mission, and everyone had a sense that their key drivers were being addressed. As a result of this high motivation, a remarkable amount of work was completed as the staff happily committed their time and ingenuity. In a short amount of time, a large retail space was transformed into a facility offering a wonderland of activities, including a huge fireplace; waterfall; fish pond; modern kitchen, dining, exercise, and therapy areas; nurse's station; game rooms, etc.

When people are properly motivated and believe in a cause, the stage is set for over-achievement (subsequently, the company's circumstances were reversed, and all this goodwill quickly evaporated. We will revisit this example later).

10.3   The Emotional Effects of Distress

To make constructive decisions, a turnaround leader must understand the dynamics of a typical firm's decline and the emotional stresses experienced by employees.

10.3.1   *Typical Decline Dynamic for a Firm*

The emotional roller coasters for stakeholders in turnaround situations are varied and complex. But there are often commonalities that are useful for a manager to keep in mind. Kanter (2003) describes a company's cycle of decline, as follows:

> After an initial blow to the company's fortunes, people begin pointing fingers and deriding colleagues in other parts of the business. The resulting tensions curtail collaboration and degenerate quickly into turf protection. Increasing levels of isolation throughout the company then engender secrecy … people find themselves less able to effect change, and eventually many come to believe they are helpless. Passivity sets in. Finally, the ultimate pathology of troubled companies takes hold: Collective denial.
>
> (Kanter, 2003, p. 62)

This sequence can turn into a downward spiral. As competitors, partners, employees, and clients see this decline, they take actions that harm the company even further, plunging it ever deeper into distress, which leads to more staff departures, more canceled contracts, more defecting clients, more suspicion, more isolation, etc.

As this decline plays out, stakeholders experience waves of fear, grief, shock, disappointment, lack of control, and general anxiety. Some employees respond with loitering and reduced productivity, as well as indifference, disengagement, and passivity. Others may respond with a mixture of concern and hope that change will bring favorable outcomes. Yet others respond with active resistance to proposed changes. The latter often become targets for management, who view them as boat rockers and non-team players.

Management teams sometimes think they can hide the firm's true (declining state) from employees. This is never the case. There is always leakage of information, and hiding the truth only serves to undermine management's credibility.

10.3.2 Emotional Dynamics for Employees During Corporate Distress

To understand the turnaround manager's challenge fully, let's review the emotional dynamics a typical employee may undergo during a corporate decline and subsequent turnaround effort. With each negative news item, the employee must appraise the new circumstances and deal with any emotions that are elicited in an effort to cope and continue to perform. Here's a sample sequence of shocks and related anxieties:

> *An employee becomes aware of his firm's declining performance. He worries about the size of his bonus (e.g., concerns about compensation). He expresses his immediate concerns to a supervisor, who tells him to relax—all is well.*
>
> *Within a few months, it becomes clear that not all is well; problems at the firm are more systematic, leading to concerns about his career trajectory (e.g., will his promotion be delayed). In time it becomes clear that the firm is really struggling, and some senior people leave or are fired (e.g., concerns about corporate direction). There are more conflicts at work as people's anxieties play out. The formerly collegial atmosphere becomes one of turf battles, blame games, and suspicion (e.g., erosion of respect; personal dignity comes under assault). The employee begins to worry about keeping his job and is concerned about supporting his family. He also fears the humiliation of being fired and of being judged and found wanting by people whose opinions are valued (e.g., peers, family, and friends).*
>
> *A turnaround is formally announced, and the employee now worries about whether the new management will like and approve of his*

performance. He is constantly anxious about the feeling of performing under a microscope. Another announcement comes a few weeks later, stating that the turnaround phase and associated austerity measures will take longer than originally expected.

Two weeks later, several talented colleagues leave the firm, but there is no budget to hire replacements, so the remaining employees' workload increases. This leads to fatigue combined with guilt over increased absence from family.

Eventually, there is some improvement at the firm, and the situation seems to be stabilizing, but now the employee begins to suspect that the new management doesn't like him and plans to fire him once the firm's circumstances are fully stabilized.

Imagine this process playing out over a year or more. Each appraisal, emotion, and coping response in the sequence is shaped and influenced by prior emotions, all of which blend into a swirling mass of complex anxiety. Recognition that this turmoil is taking place in each employee's mind helps to make one thing clear: turnaround managers cannot treat people as robots or automatons. This is especially inadvisable during times of change and turnarounds, in particular, which are fraught with fear and stress for everyone.

Clearly, employees are subjected to a series of interrelated stresses, anxieties, and emotions. And yet, per Klarner et al. (2011), many studies of employee emotions during organizational change oversimplify reality. It is often assumed that employees are subject to one emotion. Or that the change in question is a single event. Reality is far more complicated.

A direct implication is that a turnaround manager needs to be sensitive to the emotional complexities and must take actions that build trust, alleviate concerns, and set people on a constructive path. This is not an overnight process. One cannot order people to stop being concerned. Active steps must be taken that address the concerns. Before taking decisive, remedial action, a turnaround manager must first assess the existing employee base.

10.4   Assessing Existing Human Capital

There are many ways to assess existing employees. The bottom line is that a process is needed that allows the classification of people in one of three categories: value creators, value destroyers, and spectators. Value creators, as the name implies, are those who do good work, get along well with others, are proactive, and find creative ways to contribute. Value destroyers underperform, waste time, drag morale down for everyone around them, and, at the extreme, engage in illegal behavior including fraud or embezzlement. Spectators are just that—they seem to hang around without making much of a contribution. They are watching instead of doing.

It is imperative that a turnaround manager correctly classifies all employees. Whereas time is of the essence in a distress situation, misclassification serves the company poorly. So it is important to take as much time as is needed to assess all personnel at all levels. Here's a common example:

> *Two of your direct reports are at each other's throats—each accusing the other of being the 'problem' (i.e., of being a value destroyer). How do you resolve this? Resist making a judgment too quickly. You don't want to jump to a conclusion, only to discover that the person you supported, who happened to be more eloquent, politically savvy, and deceitful, was really the problem. Avoid the temptation to address organizational structure and firing decisions during the assessment phase. Ideally, give yourself an opportunity to understand the individual roles and how they fit into the big picture first.*

As seen in the aforementioned example, the turnaround manager should solicit information (without expressing judgment) from the direct reports and from their peers. The wider the net is cast, the more well-rounded the perspective will be. Often, the value destroyers among senior ranks are well known to the junior staff. But those junior employees are powerless to initiate change. Reaching out to them directly gives them an opportunity to be heard. Yes, a turnaround manager may be reluctant to break the chain of command when he or she arrives on the scene. After all, one does not want to undermine middle managers, but it is appropriate (even necessary) to break the chain of command when the corporation's fate is at stake.

10.4.1   Recognize the Owner as Destroyer

Sometimes the destroyer is an owner (or owners), creating a challenging dynamic, which requires a deft touch from the turnaround manager. Inconsistent, irresponsible, inept, and even dishonest owners may be the ones causing the firm's decline and the emotional difficulties of employees.

A bad owner may carelessly confuse, undermine, and offend the personal dignity of employees.

Voluntary agreement from an owner to step aside (effectively an admission of culpability) may not be easy to obtain. It may not be possible to entirely remove bad owners from the firm, but a turnaround manager must strive to remove them from direct managerial responsibilities. Sometimes the best option is to place oneself as a buffer between the owner and employees.

More will be said about the owner-as-destroyer situation later in this chapter.

10.4.2   Prioritize

A turnaround manager may not have the time to meet everyone and assess everyone. He or she must prioritize—a common refrain during a turnaround. The rule of thumb for distressed organizations is that *cash is king*, because without generating cash immediately, the company will not survive. The implication is that one must prioritize meeting with, and make decisions about, those people who are in the direct cash path. This begins with those who are most directly responsible for revenue generation and expenses. That is, those in sales, accounts receivable management, as well as those purchasing supplies, equipment, services, etc. A turnaround manager needs the best people generating revenue, collecting receivables, and slashing expenditures wherever possible.

10.4.3   *Identify Efficiency Seekers*

During a long-drawn-out decline, inefficiencies often creep into an organization. Some supplies are more expensive than they need to be. They may be brand-name products rather than available generics. Some delivery volumes may be unnecessarily high or subject to minimum payments that are excessive given actual usage. Some materials may be sourced far away, with higher shipping fees than would apply to alternatives found in closer geographic proximity. Unnecessary costs may persist because of an organizational inertia and passivity on the part of employees who have lost the will to care.

Because of this lethargy and inability to think sharply, some employees may assure you that all inefficiencies have been wrung out of their domains. But a turnaround manager must dig deeper and identify other like-minded employees who are motivated to stamp out inefficiencies. Unearthing inefficiencies can help to jar the complacent employees out of a state of malaise and into a much higher state of alertness.

Look for people who respond favorably to the challenge of raised performance standards. Who rises to that challenge? Who shies away? Empower those who exhibit enthusiasm. Turnaround managers need their grassroots support. They will help you to win over the more skeptical employees. They will help to convert fellow employees to your desired path. And this all helps to build the correct momentum, fueled by hope and a belief that the organization's fortunes are finally changing for the better.

10.5   Improving Human Capital in the Organization

Improving the human capital in the organization is a crucial imperative. Once people are assessed and a turnaround strategy is formulated, it is time to ensure that the value creators have all the skills required for success, that they are motivated by high expectations, and that the value destroyers have been reformed or let go. In the latter case, it is important to have replacements lined up in advance to ensure continuity.

10.5.1   *Do the Current Employees Have the Required Skills?*

Do current employees have the skills to accomplish the desired strategy? Great care must be taken to truly understand each job description, its impact on strategy, and the person occupying that role. It may be necessary to provide additional training. In some cases, it may make sense to transfer people to different roles, where their skills can be put to better use. Turnaround managers will likely find that some job descriptions must be amended or discarded.

10.5.2   Ensuring That All Employees Share a Lofty, Ambitious Mind-Set

During periods of decline, a common occurrence is that managers set low performance bars. *Why is that?* Because less ambitious goals are more likely to be met successfully.

Generally, meeting goals makes a manager's position more secure within an organization and increases his or her influence within the management team. During turnarounds, managers tend to get very defensive. When a manager whose department fails to meet its goals attempts to criticize a peer whose unit meets its goals, the former may be dismissed as petty and unprofessional. This may be the case even when the former manager has set far more ambitious goals.

But why aren't managers given credit for setting or accepting more ambitious goals? Because during times of decline, the overall shift is toward risk aversion. Managers do not want to take risks. They do not want to give their peers any ammunition for the 'blame game.' So conservatism reigns supreme, and those who stand out from the crowd by demanding more may find themselves criticized and blamed.

Thus a turnaround manager must shatter this *status quo* of mediocrity. This very attitude has brought the organization to its knees. Instead, the organization must refocus on excellence.

I once let go a senior manager who complained to me in front of his staff members that he just wanted to eke out survival for his unit. I wanted them to be great—not to be content with hanging on by their fingernails. But he was giving them an excuse to be mediocre. Why perpetuate an unfavorable, hopeless situation? It should be replaced with lofty goals that build pride and a sense of purpose and in turn restore dignity and self-respect. People want to be inspired. They want to see light at the end of a long and arduous and painful tunnel. They want better things and are usually happy to work hard to achieve such ends. Give them a common direction and instill a winning attitude. People want to be part of something special.

It is often hard to achieve renewal when a company is doing well because it's easy for people to ignore exhortations for improvement. But when there are existential threats at the doorstep, suddenly you have people's attention and cooperation. Thus a turnaround scenario can be a powerful vehicle for change and renewal. Take advantage of that dynamic and set a high bar.

10.5.3   Identifying and Hiring Good People

Firms that have been in decline for an extended period usually lose at least some of their most capable employees. This is simply because the more capable employees are the ones who have the most external opportunities. Competitors recognize their skills and actively seek to poach them. Even the most loyal workers eventually realize that forces outside their control are making it impossible for them to succeed in the distressed organization.

So one of the turnaround manager's key tasks is to identify and hire good people—value creators!

An advantage with the new hires is that they will not be encumbered by the emotional baggage and lack of confidence that may characterize those employees who suffered through the extended period of decline, finger-pointing, suspicions, etc.

There is often a tendency during the turnaround doldrums to hire anyone who will accept a job offer. Thus a selection bias works against the organization. The only people applying to a firm that is known to be troubled are those who cannot get jobs anywhere else. Desperate to fill positions, the turnaround organization hires those subpar employees—spectators and value destroyers. This merely propagates poor performance and creates an even greater disadvantage for the firm with respect to its competitors. This is part of the vicious cycle of decline. You must break that counterproductive cycle.

Qualified people will be naturally reluctant to join a firm with a bad reputation. A turnaround manager's charisma and influencing skills are crucially important in attracting talent and infusing in them a genuine sense of excitement.

The rule of thumb when examining prospective new employees should be: is this new hire going to make us more or less capable of defeating our competitors? Or, alternatively, does each hire improve or hurt our relative situation?

A useful analogy may be found in a professional football team. When contemplating the addition of a new player, the key questions asked by the team's managers are the following: will this new player make us a better team? Will this new player help us to defeat our arch rival?

The more senior the new hire, the greater her potential impact on the firm's fortunes. This applies to both positive and negative contributions. A highly capable and committed senior leader can make a huge positive difference. But she can also cause great damage if she is the wrong person for the job. One example may be found in Hammermesh (2012), which discusses the heavy damage caused by an inept leadership team to a business with initially favorable prospects. Under the incapable leadership team, the business, Explo Leisure Products (a golf ball recycler), deteriorates from being somewhat financially challenged, to a much deeper level of distress.

10.5.4   Retaining the Value Creators

As a newly arrived turnaround manager, it can initially be very difficult to distinguish the value creators from the destroyers. Lots of people will be happy to express their critical opinions of others, but everyone also has a personal agenda. This is not necessarily motivated by a nefarious motive; it is simply natural.

At the aforementioned Adult Day Health Care Center, several factors contributed to revenues stalling and to the onset of financial difficulties. As the problems mounted, so did the finger-pointing. The patient care coordinators blamed the drivers for forgetting or refusing to pick patients up; the drivers accused the care coordinators of doing a poor job explaining pickup rules and general eligibility to prospective participants. From there, the accusations deteriorated to questioning peers' motives and skills.

Instead of seeking the root causes and dealing with them together, there was assignment of blame, sometimes in full view of patients and their families.

Managers should have taken the time to listen and document the opinions expressed by employees. They should have separated the antagonists and dug deeper for answers. Why were the drivers not picking certain people up? Because some patients were more significantly disabled than others. Some of the drivers did not feel safe picking up wheelchair-bound participants and carrying them onto the vans. Others didn't feel they could leave the vans to help pick up other patients for fear that the patients on the van suffering from dementia may wander away. So the drivers felt that some participants should have been denied admission, or their families should have been made to understand their responsibility in helping to load patients on vehicles.

The drivers, whose pay was connected to completing their routes in a timely fashion, felt compelled to leave patients behind without explanation. In response, irate family members complained to the care coordinators.

More constructive responses could have included deciding which levels of disability could be handled and explaining this clearly and unambiguously to families, as well as assigning a junior staff member to each van to help with loading/unloading and monitoring patients with a tendency to wander. There may well have been other options, including optimizing drivers' routes for greater efficiency, training drivers in handling a wider spectrum of disabilities, etc. But none of these constructive solutions could be pursued in the absence of trust.

The value creators were those who understood that there was a middle ground and whose opinions and actions were focused on reaching it. They were the ones who resisted finger-pointing and instead tried to figure out how to communicate better. But they were in the minority and became overwhelmed without more senior support.

A turnaround manager must identify those who are willing to explore the middle ground—those who seek to build bridges and trust. These are the people you want around. These are the team players. These are the ones who work to create rather than to destroy value.

10.5.5   *Letting the Value Destroyers Go*

Identifying and removing value destroyers is crucial to setting the organization on a more productive path and clearing the air from the poison that is left in their wake. Nevertheless, a turnaround manager may find him or herself procrastinating when it comes to implementing firings. There are several reasons, including (1) knowing the employee has a family and feeling guilty about causing the family financial distress, (2) being intimidated by the prospect of having to look someone in the eye and fire him or her—this is especially difficult for those who know that person well and even more so when it is a friend—(3) worrying that the affected employee will make a scene, or (4) being concerned that the affected employee may initiate legal action.

There may, of course, be other reasons for the reluctance to fire someone. But any manager, and in particular a turnaround manager, must have the conviction and courage to make these decisions.

As noted earlier, a turnaround manager should not jump to conclusions and fire people prematurely, before fully understanding their skill gaps, attitude deficiencies, or other circumstances. But once it is recognized that someone must be let go, there is an obligation to all other stakeholders to make that transition as quickly as possible. *Value destroyers damage the organization.* And the longer they remain in their positions of influence, the more damage they will cause and the more value they will destroy. This in turn imperils everyone else. It makes the organization less competitive, thereby increasing the probability of complete failure. If the turnaround fails, *all* stakeholders will suffer. *All* employees will lose their jobs. *All* suppliers will lose their contracts. *All* clients will lose their product maintenance plans. *All* owners will lose their equity in the firm. As the leader, the turnaround manager owes it to all of these stakeholders to make the right decision. This is his or her mandate. A turnaround manager is hired to make these tough decisions.

My most difficult task when charged with turning around an ailing division was to fire a twenty-year veteran of the firm. The person had ridden the incumbent CEO's coattails for two decades, thanks to a close friendship. He was not capable of the duties assigned to him and was being paid a very large amount for what was a minor contribution. To highlight the extent of the skill mismatch, I was able to replace him with a young person who was two levels lower on the organizational chart, at about one-third of the salary!

The employee in question was pleasant and friendly. He was simply incapable. This wasn't his fault. The fault was that of senior managers who, over the years, instead of telling him the truth and giving him an opportunity to develop appropriate skills, simply promoted him to please his CEO friend. They didn't do him any favors.

And so there I was, forced to let him go. And I did it with a heavy heart. But I knew I had to because it was the right move for the firm. We simply could not justify keeping him on in that role. It was hurting our competitiveness at a time when we could least afford such a disadvantage.

Many managers agree that firing employees is their hardest task. Draw your conviction and courage from the knowledge that it must be done to save the organization.

10.5.6   *Having Replacements Lined Up in Advance of Firing*

Prior to letting anyone go, a turnaround manager should be sure of who will take on those duties. The replacement may be from inside or outside the organization. The key is not to be left with a vacuum. To a great extent, this is because any vacuum may have to be filled by the turnaround manager. One should avoid this and continue to focus on the big picture.

10.6   Empower People to Implement the Changes Necessary for a Successful Turnaround

Kanter (2003, p. 62) has made an impassioned plea:

> The only way a CEO can reverse a corporate decline is to change the momentum and empower people anew, replacing secrecy and denial with dialogue, blame and scorn with respect, avoidance and turf protection with collaboration, and passivity and helplessness with initiative.

In the spirit of this quote, here are some actions that empower people to make a turnaround successful:

- Improve communications. Make it clear that communication must be open and transparent. Open communication leads to familiarity, relationship building, and trust.
- Put everything on the table, abolish private lobbying, and be transparent. A transparency example at Gillette, discussed in Kanter (2003), was to create quarterly report cards for senior management. These were posted for the entire management team to see. Subsequently, senior managers openly presented their priorities for the next quarter and "Secrecy and denial were relegated to the trash bin" (Kanter, 2003, p. 62). Another way to enhance transparency is to hold town hall meetings during which everyone hears the same information and questions are answered honestly and openly.
- Restructure to remove unnecessary layers of management or silos that stifle communication. Add cross-reporting structures that force people

to communicate (in many cases, for the first time in a long time). Communication is a necessary condition for collaboration.

- Don't allow people to get caught up in formality and ceremony. Get to the substance and get things done. Management teams that insist on stroking their own egos are wasting time and corporate resources. They are sorely in need of some grounding and humility. People have to want the enterprise to succeed more than they want to prove their own superiority. They must put the organization first. Otherwise, they must be removed.

- Don't allow so-called facts to go unchallenged or sacred cows to go unexamined. Demand real information and don't settle for anything less than receiving the best information the company has. Often, there are people in the company who can tell you what is not working well and what the barriers are to success. The problem, of course, is that others are spewing noise that obscures meaningful information. Factions may take opposing sides, and facts may be withheld in an effort to stymie your efforts. This obstructionism is initiated by individuals who have something to lose. The key is to recognize that the necessary knowledge is most likely already in the company and to find ways to give it voice.

- Everyone represents the firm. Demand a professional commercial orientation from everyone. Remind all employees that they are, at all times, ambassadors of the firm and that their words and actions can either contribute to the brand or damage it. This should get everyone focused and give them a sense of pride in their institution. Where there is a sense of belonging (and no second-class citizens), there is personal dignity. Everyone's value and contribution should be appreciated. People want to be part of something meaningful or special, regardless of their educational background or job description. (Being an ambassador of the firm doesn't mean that everyone is allowed to make formal statements to the media, but it does create a sense of unity and common purpose).

- Put an end to the blame game. Finger-pointing and blame are very common in struggling organizations, and they must be stopped. People's energy should be redirected to solving problems rather than wasting time allocating blame. Clamping down on the blame game reduces everyone's anxiety and sense of unfair victimization, allowing people to get back to work.

- Offer opportunities for upward mobility. Establish credibly that there are real and attainable opportunities for upward mobility and career moves within the organization. It is often necessary to prove this to cynics and skeptics. Do so by rewarding early contributions and celebrating even small successes. As Brenner (2008) points out, even small wins help to neutralize naysayers.

- Don't hang the 'boat rockers.' According to Ford, Ford, and D'Amelio (2008), it is quite common to treat employees who resist change as troublemakers and 'bad guys' who must be overcome and overwhelmed. Indeed, in some cases, resistance (by value destroyers) is mindless and disruptive to others and must be dealt with firmly. But in many other cases, those providing opposition are doing so for honorable reasons. They care. And they have the courage to speak up when many others do not. Furthermore, shutting them down without due process sends a signal to everyone else that speaking up is 'bad,' and this undermines the overall goals of improved communication and broad participation. Instead of silencing or ridiculing a boat rocker, use the opportunity to honestly face real issues. Give people an opportunity to vent, to be heard.

10.7   Taking Decisive Action

Taking decisive action sends the message that someone is in charge and making things happen. This reduces the need for individual employees to struggle for control because there is already a corporate or organizational sense of control. One example of decisive action is to fire the value destroyers. Another is in reducing costs wherever possible, as soon as possible.

From a personnel perspective (the focal point of this chapter), some of the most important decisive actions revolve around putting the right people with the right skills in the right jobs within the right teams and under the right supervision.

Some decisions are fairly obvious, but they do not take place because of dysfunction within the organization. When a turnaround manager finally takes the (obvious) action, a large fraction of the employees will likely breathe a collective sigh of relief.

As the situation at the California Adult Day Health Care Center worsened, there was significant dysfunction that stymied decisions. The major stockholders fractured into two factions, forcing staff to choose sides. It became nearly impossible for decisions to be made collectively because one faction almost instinctively put a stop to any initiative put forward by the other faction.

As an example, one side put forward an idea to alleviate cash shortages by renting the Center and its new state-of-the-art commercial kitchen after hours for private functions (weddings, corporate functions, etc.). In principle this seemed acceptable to both groups, but one side wanted to allow renters to use the kitchen themselves, whereas the other side (which included all kitchen staff) insisted that the kitchen was too valuable to take a chance on its being damaged by a third party and refused to allow any clients access to the kitchen. Instead, clients would have to use a catering team provided by the Center.

Most prospective clients wanted to control their menus and have free access to the kitchen facility. So instead of collaborating on the use of the kitchen to keep the Center alive, this conflict denied access to a potential source of much-needed cash. But it also had another insidious effect—the cost of distraction. Every minute the factions spent arguing was a minute that was not spent on making decisions to resolve other outstanding challenges.

10.7.1 *Don't Wait for Perfect Solutions*

A common error for first-time turnaround managers is to hold off on decision making while waiting for a perfect solution to materialize. There are no perfect solutions in turnaround situations! It is far more effective to be decisive and implement an imperfect plan with a sense of urgency. One does not have the luxury of time in a turnaround situation.

A decent decision that addresses even just one issue is a move in the right direction. Taking action, even if it addresses something seemingly small, also has other benefits. It provides (often much-needed) clarity and a path forward for all employees. It may also do the same for other stakeholders such as suppliers and clients.

If the accepted solution is a creative one, the turnaround manager also gets the benefit of signaling to staff that creativity and courage are applauded and supported.

Because there are no perfect solutions, one must also accept that some decisions will not be successful. Do not respond by (proverbially) causing heads to roll when an imperfect solution leads to a setback. Such harsh action will reinforce for everyone at the firm that showing initiative is a bad idea. This is the opposite of what a turnaround manager wants. Broad participation is needed. The energy, ideas, and courage of all employees needs to be harnessed.

This means a turnaround manager must live with the understanding that there are no perfect answers and, therefore, that there will occasionally be setbacks and reversals. But decisions still need to be made and in a timely fashion.

10.8 Celebrating Small Wins and Building Positive Momentum

When one is weighted down by serious concerns, it is easy to ignore small positive signs. After all, a serious mistake on a turnaround manager's part may push the firm into bankruptcy or even worse, liquidation. But even under the weight of that grim reality, a turnaround manager should take the time to acknowledge, nurture, and celebrate small wins.

Imagine that you are stranded on a deserted island and after great effort finally manage to light a small fire. Your survival depends on maintaining that flame. In our context, the momentum you need to succeed in your turnaround is analogous to that flame.

In much the same way that you will desperately want to nurture that small fire, you must nurture your turnaround momentum. Even a marginal strengthening of positive momentum is very meaningful, especially when starting from next to nothing. In a turnaround situation, all wins affect momentum favorably. People create wins. You can create some yourself to gain credibility and feed the momentum flame, or you can empower others to create wins and build momentum further. Give credit to others and congratulate them publicly on their successes. This motivates everyone to do more in the hope of receiving praise as well. Celebrations allow recognition of individuals and teams, and show respect for, and appreciation of, staff.

Examples of small but meaningful wins are signing a new client, negotiating new payment terms with a supplier, making positive progress in building a relationship with a source of referrals, completing redesign of marketing material, etc. As a turnaround manager publicly commends those responsible, a sense of pride in their achievements is given, and everyone else will be imbued with inspiration to match their colleagues' successes. All employees get something even more important—a sense of hope. There is light at the end of the tunnel. Expect employees to show up the next morning with a bit more energy, a bit more confidence, and a new attitude reflecting the realization that success is within reach.

10.9   Being Aware of All Stakeholders

Remember that all stakeholders require attention. They may be owners, creditors, customers, suppliers, employees, or government agencies. They are all likely to have their own agendas and priorities.

A firm's survival depends on building trust and maintaining constructive relationships with all stakeholders. A turnaround manager (a) needs owners (equity holders) who give leeway to make key decisions, (b) suppliers to deliver much-needed equipment and materials, (c) clients to keep buying, and (d) creditors to extend a lifeline. Each stakeholder is a person, or a corporate entity representing people, who wants to be heard, respected, and appreciated.

So before accepting a turnaround leadership role, speak with as many stakeholders as possible. Ask yourself, are these people I can do business with? Will they support or hinder my efforts? The relationships with owner(s) will be among the most pivotal and will likely dictate ultimate success or failure.

10.9.1   Owner as Destroyer, Revisited

Let's return now to the issue of owner (or board member) as value destroyer. Destruction of value may come in the form of poor decision making by an owner who holds a leadership or management position at the firm. It may also come in the form of obstructionism. That is, the owner may not have formal managerial duties, but actively interferes with your efforts. A common example is that a turnaround manager concludes that someone in the organization must be fired, but that someone happens to be a family member or special friend of the owner. Efforts to have the underperforming employee removed are thwarted by nepotism. The only thing worse than getting into an argument with an owner over a nepotism-based appointment is having the decision to fire the person in question reversed by the owner. This makes a turnaround manager appear weak in the eyes of all other employees, and it only serves to reinforce to them that the situation is hopeless.

A turnaround manager's negotiating leverage is often highest just before accepting the turnaround job. Management/ownership teams are usually desperate to solve turnaround situations, and that desperation means they are more likely to agree to harsh measures as a condition of taking the job. Once a turnaround manager is on the job, usually with mixed success early on, he or she will gain enemies, and they will undermine the turnaround manager, thus decreasing his or her power. So the more one knows about the organization ahead of time, the better. One of the main benefits is that one can insist that value destroyers (whether owners themselves or those protected by nepotism) be removed from the scene before agreeing to take the job.

10.9.2   *Do Not Make Promises That Cannot Be Kept*

Turnaround managers should not make promises they cannot keep. In fact, it may be wise to avoid making promises entirely early on. For example, one may be inclined to assure employees that the most recent round of layoffs will be the last, or to assure suppliers that the company is still committed to using their services, or to assure clients that the company will continue to support their favorite product line. If a position has to be reversed later, credibility will be undermined, and it will be much harder to retain or regain the future support of affected stakeholders. It can be tempting to give employees, suppliers, or clients assurances. It is human nature to do so, and making promises helps in the short term to obtain the cooperation of others. But one must avoid providing such assurances because it is almost a given that one will regret it.

Why am I so firm in this conviction? Two reasons: (1) personal experience and (2) because the reality of turnarounds is almost always worse than you think, which will force you to take even harsher measures after your initial efforts come up short. More specifically, once a turnaround job is accepted and one begins to poke around in the firm's finances or operations, things always turn out to be worse in some ways than one has originally been led to understand. Why are initial expectations often more optimistic than reality? Because the incentives of owners is to get the turnaround manager to save them by taking the job. They will be concerned that telling the whole truth will scare a turnaround manager off. So they have every incentive to fudge and mislead.

10.9.3 *Being Professional and Courteous at All Times*

Do turnaround managers need to be courteous with a supplier they have determined has been overcharging? Isn't it a turnaround manager's duty in a market economy to fire the supplier and to do so with some flair and drama that will encourage the supplier to mend its ways? Here are some immediate personal observations: (1) it's not your task to expend energy on saving the market economy and capitalism as we know it—it's your job to save your firm; (2) that supplier may be expensive, but you may need it as a Plan B in the event that your preferred solution falls through; and (3) what if you're wrong? What if you erroneously concluded that the supplier was overcharging you, possibly based on information provided by someone in your organization who turns out to be less than credible? That someone may be trying to steer you to embrace his preferred supplier (possibly to an in-law or a deal with an under-the-table kickback).

Any of this could happen. Just ask Rivka Belzer, who took over the task of turning around the St. Louis Lyric Dinner Theatre (Hammermesh & Sharpe, 2013). After a few weeks on the job, she terminated the agreement with the existing caterer, only to realize later that the replacement chef she hired lacked the required managerial experience to do the job. The original caterer was alerted and came in to effectively save the day. Had she irreparably destroyed that relationship at the outset, she would have been in even bigger trouble.

10.10 Acknowledging that Humanity Is a Sign of Strength, Not Weakness

Some people believe that acknowledging the humanity of others in the workplace is a sign of weakness in a leader. There are those who believe that a turnaround should be an emotionless exercise in logic. Both viewpoints (discussed in the following sections) are wrong. The best long-term outcomes are achieved by leaders who place humanity at the center of the turnaround effort.

10.10.1 *Saying Good-bye to the Great Man Theory*

Not coincidentally, those who view humane leaders as weak tend to adhere to some version of the outdated Great Man Theory. The Great Man Theory holds that some men (always men) are born to greatness and therefore have a natural claim to leadership positions. Also predictably, such a birthright is viewed by adherents as the sole preserve of aristocratic families.

This was the dominant theory throughout centuries of monarchic and tyrannical rule. The spread of democracy and advances in science have helped to debunk this theory and establish that leaders are made—not born. And those leaders who consider business with humanity in mind hold the moral-and-performance high ground.

10.10.2   *Aren't Turnarounds Simply Exercises in Logic?*

There are also those who view turnaround decision making as an exercise of pure logic. Many newly installed CEOs present logically compelling plans to their new coworkers. They anticipate that all stakeholders will respond rationally by immediately recognizing the plan's logical soundness and will quickly commit to executing the plan efficiently.

According to Brenner (2008), statistical evidence shows that such logical/rational responses are rarely the case. He goes on to explain that a successful turnaround is based much more on psychological/emotional factors than on cognition (logic):

> Examples of the critical success factors include trust, motivation, commitment, character, self-discipline and patience. One does not have to be a behavioral strategist to realize that a CEO's lack of attention to the role these psychological responses play will negatively affect his or her ability to grab the hearts and minds of the organization's leaders and workforce.
>
> (Brenner, 2008, p. 132)

The main message for the turnaround leader is that hearts and minds matter, and if one cannot win those over, it does not matter how logical or rational the approach is.

10.10.3   *Running the Organization With a Firm but Fair Hand*

A turnaround manager can be a leader who respects humanity and still runs a tight ship with a firm hand. People can be challenged to perform; discipline, focus, and commitment can still be demanded. The difference is that a good turnaround manager recognizes people's need for emotional support, treats them with dignity and respect, compensates them fairly, and provides merit-based opportunities for upward mobility.

A turnaround manager typically pores over financial statements in search of inefficiencies. He or she draws red lines through budget items, signaling intent to reduce expenditures. Assets are listed to be sold. A need for stability is declared. But none of these decisions are implemented by decree. These changes only take place by empowering other humans to take real actions. People can and must be a turnaround manager's greatest asset in a turnaround situation. But only if they are embraced and supported as human beings.

References

Brenner, M. (2008). It's all about people: Change management's greatest lever. *Business Strategy Series*, 9(3), 132–137.

Ford, J. D., Ford, L. W., & D'Amelio, A. (2008). Resistance to change: The rest of the story. *Academy of Management Review*, 33(2), 362–377.

Hammermesh, R. G. (2012). Explo leisure products. *Harvard Business School Publishing.* Case Study 9–399–053.

Hammermesh, R. G., & Sharpe, J. M. (2013). Lyric dinner theater (A). *Harvard Business School Publishing.* Case Study 9–813–043.

Kanter, R. M. (2003). Leadership and the psychology of turnarounds. *Harvard Business Review*, June, 58–67.

Klarner, P., By, R. T., & Diefenbach, T. (2011). Employee emotions during organizational change—Toward a new research agenda. *Scandinavian Journal of Management*, 27(3), 332–340.

Whitney, J. O. (1987). Turnaround management every day. *Harvard Business Review*, September-October, 65(5), 49–55.

11 The Executioner's Dilemma

Explaining Role Stress by Ethical Conflict Among Those Who Carry Out a Downsizing Event

Rick Aalbers and Philippos Philippou

11.1 Introduction

Workforce downsizing, "the intentional reduction in the number of people of an organization accomplished through managerial actions such as hiring freezes, normal or induced attrition, and layoffs" (Brauer & Laamanen, 2014, p. 3), has been a widely used practice among organizations during the last thirty years, primarily aiming at cost cutting and improved organizational performance (Cascio, 2005; Trevor & Nyberg, 2008). Downsizing is the more narrow term compared with reorganization. Reorganizing is the planned set of policies and practices to realign the workforce with the goal of improving organization performance and, hence, does not include reduction of the workforce per se (Aalbers & Dolfsma, 2015).

Scholars have been chiefly focused on the impact of downsizing on organizational performance on the one hand—with different findings regarding short-term and long-term performance (Guthrie & Datta, 2008; Love & Nohria, 2005)—and on the other hand on the perceptions of the employees directly affected—namely, downsizing victims and survivors. These prior works, typically, find support for the moderating effects of human resource practices and justice in decision making (Paterson & Cary, 2002; Trevor & Nyberg, 2008). Prior empirical work conclusively shows reorganizations to deeply affect employees as well as the operational routines central to the functioning of the organization as key individuals involved leave (Aalbers et al., 2014; Brauer & Laamanen, 2014). Given this context, labor force downsizing forms a disruptive instrument available to management to achieve organizational recovery. Whereas downsizing has attracted ample scholarly attention in the downsizing and the strategic HRM literature, it remains unclear why some organizations recover successfully and others do not (Datta, Guthrie, Basuil, & Pandey, 2010). Yet inability to recover inflicts direct costs upon society, as resulting bankruptcies escalate social security expenses (Aalbers & Dolfsma, 2014).

Like most strategic initiatives, the impact of downsizing is significantly influenced by the way it is implemented (Aalbers & Dolfsma, 2014; Mellahi & Wilkinson, 2010). Cameron (1994) posits various means of downsizing and subsequently positions *workforce reduction* strategies as the most radical form, focused primarily on reducing headcount and often implemented fast and top-down. Our study is dedicated to this most disruptive form of managerial intervention. Speed, size, and motives of downsizing activities each have been extensively studied as influencing factors by many researchers (e.g., Feldman, 1995; Mellahi & Wilkinson, 2008, 2010).

Given the suddenness by which organizations may find themselves in a downsizing situation, outcome downsizing trajectory can become an event that has been consciously or unconsciously delayed by management as being a very last resort to realign strategy with the organization. As a consequence, frequently, management has been found to communicate poorly regarding downsizing objectives and approach, which has been found to result in a low perceived distributive fairness among the surviving employees (Brockner et al., 1988). For instance, Greenhalgh & Rosenblatt (1984) report that as a result of abrupt downsizing procedure, downsizing negatively affects employees in terms of stress and uncertainty.

11.1.1   The Downsizing Executioner: What's in a Name?

Whereas downsizing survivors have received scant scholarly attention, executioners of a downsizing strategy have been quite shy of conceptual empirical exploration. Literature refers to those individuals responsible for implementing downsizing as downsizers (Burke, 1998), downsizing agents (Clair & Dufresne, 2004), layoff agents (Parker & McKinley, 2008), or downsizing executioners (Gandolfi, 2009b). Following the definition of Gandolfi (2009b), this study labels such agents of radical change as executioners of downsizing. According to Gandolfi (2009b, p. 186), these executioners are "individuals entrusted with responsibilities in regard to the planning, execution, and evaluation of downsizing-related activities." This definition is deliberately broad so that it is applicable to any individual in an organization that has formal responsibilities to carry out a downsizing process. The executioners' role may include a variety of activities, from planning the events during a layoff, to deciding which employees should be fired, to breaking the news to those unlucky individuals (Parker & McKinley, 2008). Our research focuses on the consequences of downsizing on executioners because of their important and dual roles in the process, as both receivers and agents of the change (Dewitt et al. as cited in Clair & Dufresne, 2004).

To implement a downsizing, both internals and externals can take up the (joint) role of agents of change. Internals, much like internal consultants, here are a derivation of the staff concept of management, in which specialist managers assist the board of directors of the restructuring organization by identifying and studying problems and opportunities related to the downsizing task, preparing recommendations, and assisting in their implementation (Johri, Cooper, & Prokopenko, 1998; Wright, 2009). In the context of downsizing, however, external human capital is often—additionally—called in to assist (Appelbaum & Steed, 2005). Hence those involved in the execution of downsizing and as such fulfilling a dual role as receivers and agents of change may be both internally or externally employed (Dewitt et al. as cited in Clair & Dufresne, 2004). For a variety of tasks, and in comparison to internally employed employees, external advisors have been found to be emotionally 'detached' from the organization in which they are deployed, for instance (Drucker, 1981). What some have referred to as "the divorce between command and accountability in organizations" (Sennett, 2006, p. 70), has been shy of scholarly attention, leaving the way in which such 'social distance' affects organization reforms, their nature and progress, ill understood, resulting in calls for further research on the subject (Sturdy, 2011).

Whereas downsizing provides a setting in which the emotional divide between internal and external employees may be expected to come to the fore in particular, research on the implications of downsizing on both categories has been scarcely researched (Datta et al., 2010). Scholarly research has largely ignored the distinction between either forms of executioner. Yet downsizing practice provides ample example of external advisors hired to fulfill a role of downsizing agent, commonly alongside a selected team of internal change agents. Executioners (Gandolfi, 2009a) are not only responsible for the planning and implementation of the downsizing process, but they may also affect how employees perceive the decisions and how they react to them. The few academic studies available that do distinct between both executioner *modes* are either conceptual or of a qualitative nature (Clair & Dufresne, 2004; Gandolfi, 2009a; Parker & McKinley, 2008), modeling downsizing agents' reactions to carrying out downsizing by incorporating the impact of their proximity to the emotional aspects of the event, or their previous experience with downsizing and their relationship ties with downsizing victims on how the agents experience their role.

This chapter, addressing the role of role stress and ethical conflict as perceived by those who are responsible for the operational execution of a downsizing event, contributes to the ongoing debate on the impact of downsizing on organizations and their members. The consequences of downsizing are commonly assumed to occur via effects on employees' social capital, but scholars fail to measure and examine these individual-level constructs and outcomes (Datta et al., 2010). In addition to highlighting the role of ethical conflict on role stress as perceived by the downsizing executioner, we introduce a scenario-based scale that allows future research to capture the main ethical aspects of a downsizing event. We present our findings by quantitatively testing how expressed ethical conflict of both types of executioners being internally or externally associated affects role stress, leading to new directions for further research about the effects of workforce downsizing.

11.2 Theoretical Background and Hypotheses

11.2.1 *The Human Consequences of Downsizing*

Despite the popularity of downsizing as a managerial initiative to pursue strategic goals, prior research on downsizing has not yet succeeded in showing consistent results that downsizing indeed yields these intended outcomes (Brauer & Laamanen, 2014; Gandolfi, 2008). In fact, the effectiveness of downsizing has been seriously challenged because of the many negative and sometimes contradictory results that can be found in the existing literature (Gandolfi, 2008). In a sense, downsizing always leaves scars among those involved (Mishra, Mishra, & Spreitzer, 2009). With respect to the consequences (or results) downsizing activities can produce, Gandolfi (2009a) distinguishes three categories: financial consequences, organizational consequences, and human consequences. Whereas the first two categories have received ample attention, researchers remain undecided on performance outcomes. The third category, human consequences, has primarily focused on employees who remain in the organization after the downsizing is implemented; they are commonly referred to as the survivors (e.g., Appelbaum & Donia, 2001; Devine et al., 2003; Trevor & Nyberg, 2008). The importance of analyzing downsizing's impact on survivors lies in the responsibility these very employees bear to make the organization operate effectively and to succeed after human resources have been reduced (Aalbers, 2012; Allen et al., 2001; Brauer & Laamanen, 2014).

Survivors, for instance, were found to experience work overload, which leads to reduced job and life satisfaction because of reduced work-life balance (Virick et al., 2007). A study by Maertz et al. that zoomed in on downsizing, offshoring, and outsourcing survivors showed that employees who survive such events are associated with higher levels of turnover intentions and were less likely to express high organizational performance and job security (Maertz et al., 2010). Experiencing workforce downsizing proved to impact survivor's perception of organizational justice, creating a feeling of job insecurity (Hopkins & Weathington, 2006). Paulsen et al. found that job insecurity among downsizing survivors is associated with greater levels of emotional exhaustion and lower levels of job satisfaction (Paulsen et al., 2005).

Executioners, those managerially and operationally responsible for the carrying out of a downsizing event, have to cope with a double burden, because they experience both their own emotional reactions as well as those of the survivors who are faced with the consequences of their instrumental actions. Executioners have to deal with a major change and at the same time experience it themselves as managerially, positions are made redundant in the process (Kets de Vries & Balazs, 1997; Wright & Barling, 1998). Downsizing executioners, as operationalized in this study, are directly involved in the planning phase of the downsizing process, making decisions for the employees to be laid off, while at the same time they are entrusted with communicating these decisions to the employees. Downsizing executioners are hence at the same time agents of the directors of the organizations when they have to communicate the change plans and receivers of the perceptions and reactions of the employees, either victims or survivors, which have to be communicated to the management in order to improve the process.

An important distinction regarding downsizing executioners needs to be made. The executioners, as mentioned earlier, can either be internally employed by the organization (internal executioners) or externally hired to help during the downsizing process (external executioners). The importance of this distinction lies in the differences between the two categories of executioners regarding their perceptions of their roles and duties within the organization and in relation to the organization's employees, either survivors or victims.

11.2.2   The Relation Between Executioner Type and Role Stress

The process of downsizing is typically perceived as a stressful event for those involved (Aalbers et al., 2015; Devine et al., 2003; Trevor & Nyberg, 2008). Role stress is defined as the employee's perception of a situation as being potentially or actually threatening (Gilboa et al., 2008). According to Brief et al. (1979), role stress is the result of role ambiguity and role conflict. The two constructs have been studied extensively in both organizational and stress research streams and were found to be related with outcomes such as reduced job satisfaction and commitment (Villanueva & Djurkovic, 2009), intention to leave (Glazer & Kruse, 2008), justice perceptions (Chipunza & Samuel, 2012), and reduced performance (Fried et al., 2003). Role ambiguity is defined by House and Rizzo (1972) as "the lack of clarity and predictability of the outcomes of one's behavior." Using role ambiguity as a construct of role stress is in line with previous downsizing research where the lack of clarity and predictability resulted in higher levels of stress among downsizing executioners (Clair & Dufresne, 2004). Role conflict is "the degree of incongruity or incompatibility of expectations associated with the role" (House & Rizzo, 1972). According to Wong et al. (2007), role conflict is more likely to emerge among employees when they have to satisfy conflicting requirements from different individuals or groups of people. Similarly, downsizing executioners receive demands from the organization, which can take the form of downsizing plans or managerial decisions and simultaneously receive demands from employees, either survivors or victims, about how they perceive the downsizing process.

Based on the distinction made regarding downsizing executioner 'types,' whether internal or external to the organization, such differentiation is expected to affect how downsizing executioners, first, perceive their role and, second, whether their role becomes emotionally taxed. According to Wright (2009), internal consultants are more prone to structural ambiguity and are often faced with the struggle of gaining organizational acceptance because of their role between the employees and the management of the organization. On the other hand, as external advisors have been found to be more easily 'detached' from the organization in which they are deployed, in contrast to those who hold an internal association (Drucker, 1981), one might expect a difference in perceived levels of occupational stress when comparing this category to internal executioners. Internal executioners are socially embedded within the organization that experiences a downsizing event, and hence they are more likely to express higher levels of role stress as a result of increased ambiguity and conflicting demands within the organization (House & Rizzo, 1972). Clair and Dufresne (2004), Gandolfi (2009a), and Grunberg et al. (2006) found that whether the role of the executioner becomes emotionally taxing depends on the proximity of executioners' duties with the emotional aspects of the downsizing process. Executioners who are entrusted with communicating downsizing decisions are more emotionally taxed than executioners who are only involved in the planning and decision-making process. Clair and Dufresne (2004) and Gandolfi (2009a) extended their studies to also include the previous experience of the executioner with downsizing events and found that it affects the degree to which executioners will get emotionally taxed, with more experienced executioners perceiving lower levels of such emotions and at the same time experiencing emotional numbing, which in turn leads to reduction of stress and more objectivity.

Hence we pose the following:

Hypothesis 1: *Internal executioners are associated with higher levels of perceived role stress than external executioners during a downsizing event.*

11.2.3   The Relation Between Executioner Type and Ethical Conflict

In a context of employee downsizing, employee's perception of compatibility between their own ethical values and priorities and the values and priorities of the organization they are a part of has remained rather understudied over the years. Yet employees are confronted with expectations from different parts of the organization regarding the ethical aspects of their duties and operations (Schwepker et al., 1997), also when these involve the downsizing of the organization. During downsizing, executioners may face conflicting ethical demands either when selecting the employees to be laid off or communicating the decisions to the victims (Clair & Dufresne, 2004). Ethical conflict may rise when downsizing executioners perceive their own ethical values to be incompatible with the ethical values of the top management of the organization or with the overall event of downsizing (Thorne, 2010). In addition, Ulrich and Soeken's work (2005) suggested that ethical conflict can be predicted largely by the ethical environment of the organization and also by the ethical concern of the employee and the government regulations.

In general, business ethics research suggests that ethical conflict may rise because of environmental factors such as the ethical and regulatory environment but also because of personal factors such as the level of one's ethical concern and perceptions of compatibility with the organization's ethics (Mulki Jaramillo, & Locanader, 2009; Schwepker et al., 1997). Ethical conflict perceived by downsizing executioners is studied in relation to role stress, and it is expected that executioners who express higher levels of ethical conflict will be associated with higher levels of the perceived role stress construct. This leads to the following hypothesis:

Hypothesis 2: *Ethical conflict of executioners will positively affect perceived role stress during a downsizing event.*

Similar to role stress, whether an executioner is internally employed or externally hired by the organization is also expected to affect the impact of their perceived ethical conflict on their levels of perceived role stress. As already discussed, external executioners are more easily detached from the organization (Drucker, 1981) and thus they are expected to express lower levels or perceived role stress compared to internal executioners with the same levels of ethical conflict. Additionally, they are expected to be able to normalize the consequences of the event, in contrast to their internality employed counterparts who have higher levels of relational proximity with the victims and the survivors of the downsizing event.

Thus we hypothesize the following:

Hypothesis 3: *Type of executioner will moderate the impact of ethical conflict on perceived role stress among executioners during a downsizing event.*

11.3   Research Method

The empirical analysis underlying this chapter tests the dependence of perceived role stress among downsizing executioners on their levels of perceived ethical conflict and on whether they are internal or external agents of change, meaning if they are employed or hired on a temporary basis by the downsized organization or are associated internally instead. In this section, we explain our research method as designed for this purpose in detail.

11.3.1   Sample and Data Collection

Data is collected for both internal and external downsizing executioners from organizations that downsized at a percentage of at least 5% of their workforce and consulting organizations that provided downsizing services to such companies. These data were collected from organizations operating in Cyprus in light of the recent financial recession. A survey design rendered forty-three responses, with 24% or 55.8% of the participants representing internal employees of the downsized organization, whereas the remaining 19% or 44.2% were turnaround management consultants hired on a temporary basis. The survey resulted in a response rate of 17.2% of a total of 250 persons initially contacted. Regarding gender, male participants accounted for 46.5% (20) of the sample and female for 53.5% (23). In the sample, 46.5% (20) of the downsized organizations operate within the services field, whereas 20.9% (9), 16.3% (7), and 9.3% (4) are in the construction, retail, and import/export industries. The remaining 7% (3) operate in other fields—namely, manufacturing (2) and various (1). Participants were also asked to indicate their age, yielding the following results: 37.2% (16) fall within the age group of 26–34 years old, 39.5% (17) within the group of 35–54 years old and the remaining 23.3% (10) are between 55 and 64 years old. Finally, 51.2% (22) of the participants said that they had experience with implementing and/or designing downsizing events, whereas the remaining 48.8% (21) did not.

11.3.2 Measures

Perceived Role Stress

In order to measure perceived role stress, the fourteen-item scale introduced by Rizzo et al. (1970) is used. The goal is to measure role ambiguity and role conflict caused by the disruption in organizational routines and ethical conflict and specifically its impact on how executioners perceive their responsibilities, authority, and organizational expectations. The scale is used and found to be reliable in previous studies within the organizational stress and performance context (Acker, 2004; Koustelios et al., 2004; Tubre & Collins, 2000). The scale is also used by Kalbers and Cenker (2008) to measure role ambiguity in relation to job experience, job autonomy, and job performance, and they found it to be reliable. In this study, the scale of Rizzo et al. (1970) is also used because of the similarity of research design.

The participants were asked to answer on a Likert-type, seven-point scale, ranging from very false to very true to statements such as "I feel certain about how much authority I have" and "I receive incompatible requests from two or more people."

Positively formed questions were reversed so that greater numbers in the responses would represent higher levels or perceived role stress. A composite variable (i.e., Role_Stress) is created using the mean of values of the responses. Similar to other studies (e.g., Acker, 2004; Koustelios et al., 2004; Tubre & Collins, 2000), the scale is found to be reliable with a Cronbach's alpha coefficient of 0.944. The mean value for the scale is 3.2508. The explanatory variables used for this research are type of executioner (Type_Executioner) and ethical conflict (Ethical_Conflict).

Type of Executioner

The type of executioner is captured by checking whether the executioner is employed within the organization (i.e., internally associated), or a consultant hired by the organization on a temporary basis (i.e., externally associated). The mean for the original variable is 1.44 with values of 1 and 2 representing internal and external executioners, respectively, and the mean values for the respective dummy variable were 0.56 and 0.44.

Ethical Conflict

To measure ethical conflict, a scenario-based scale similar to the one used by Schwepker et al. (1997) is adjusted to the context of this research using scenarios that capture ethical aspects of downsizing events as proposed by Watson et al. (1999). Downsizing organizations can employ various policies, and the ones used by the authors include the use of temporary employees, consideration of seniority, consultation with the community, employee retraining, and employee participation in decision making. Respondents were asked to reflect on five different scenarios, one for each of the aspects, using the six-item scale of Schwepker et al. (1997) to indicate the similarity between themselves and the top management of the downsizing organization for each of the six statements regarding the scenario, using a seven-point scale ranging from 'very similar' to 'very dissimilar.' In each of the scenarios, the organization's name and location are changed to avoid biased responses, while in all of the scenarios, the organization is planning a substantial workforce downsizing. The scores for each scenario were then summed to measure ethical conflict with lower scores indicating lower levels of the variable. The composite variable constructed using the mean value of responses to each of the questions has a mean value of 3.9589 whereas using the same value range as the original items. This scale is also tested regarding its internal consistency and is found to be reliable with a Cronbach's alpha value of 0.982, whereas none of the items are found to improve the scale if deleted. The complete scale, including all the scenarios and the questions to which the participants were asked to respond, can be found in the appendix.

An interaction variable is created using the centered variables of Internal_Executioner and Ethical_Conflict in order to test Hypothesis 3. Centered variables, instead of normal variables, are used in order to reduce multicollinearity.

Control Variables

Apart from the main variables, four control variables are included in the analysis (experience, age, gender, and industry). In this section, the control variables are discussed, including the reasoning of their inclusion and their descriptive statistics.

The relationship between prior experience of the executioner and their perceived levels of role stress has been studied in recent downsizing literature about downsizing executioners (Clair & Dufresne, 2004; Gandolfi, 2009a). Previous experience of the executioner with downsizing events affects the degree to which executioners will get emotionally taxed and subsequently experience higher levels of occupational stress because it acts as a numbing mechanism for executioners, leading to reduction of stress and increased objectivity (Gandolfi, 2009a), and moderating the relationship between stress and distancing reactions of the executioner (Clair & Dufresne, 2004).

Drawing on the relationship between the type of executioner and experience, a control variable capturing the executioner's past experience with downsizing is included in order to control for the effect of experience on perceived role stress. The mean for the original variable is 1.49 with values of 1 and 2 representing experienced and inexperienced executioners, respectively, and the mean values for the respective dummy variable were 0.49 and 0.51.

Finally, three variables controlling for the effect of age, gender, and industry were included in the analysis with mean values of 2.86, 1.53, and 2.09, respectively. The frequencies, score range, and values for these variables were discussed earlier. Dummy variables were created for the categorical variables of gender and industry. None of the variables was found to statistically differ from normal distribution.

11.4 Results

The mean values and correlations for the main variables included in the analysis are presented in Table 11.1 and Table 11.2, respectively. Table 11.3 reports the results of the regression analysis, including four models where the first (basic) model includes all the control variables and subsequently the remaining models are created by adding Internal_Executioners, Ethical_Conflict, and the interaction term between the two variables.

Table 11.1 Descriptive Statistics

	Mean	*Min*	*Max*	*Std. Deviation*
Perceived Role Stress	3.2508	1.29	5.43	1.08208
Ethical Conflict	3.9589	1	6.70	1.25247
Type of Executioner	1.44	1	2	0.502
Experience	1.49	1	2	0.506
Age	2.86	2	4	0.774
Gender	1.53	1	2	0.505
Industry	2.09	1	5	1.288

Table 11.2 Correlations

	Perceived Role Stress	Ethical Conflict	Type of Executioner	Experience	Age	Gender
Ethical Conflict	0.625**					
Type of Executioner	0.606**	−0.293				
Experience	0.228	0.220	−0.214			
Age	0.150	0.053	−0.083	0.300		
Gender	0.166	0.160	−0.391**	0.165	0.196	
Industry	−0.133	0.009	0.229	0.145	−0.058	0.068

Table 11.3 Regression Models

	Dependent Variable: Perceived Role Stress			
Variable	Model 1	Model 2	Model 3	Model 4
Age	0.070	0.104	0.118	0.0109
Experience	−0.112	−0.059	0.014	−0.012
Industry (Services)	0.102	−0.016	−0.031	−0.050
Gender (Male)	−0.146	0.110	0.137	0.115
Type of Executioner (Internal)		0.634**	0.512**	0.514**
Ethical Conflict (Centered)			0.497**	0.532**
Interaction (Type of Executioner and Eth. Conflict)				−0.081
Adjusted R^2	0.030	0.307	0.544	0.535
Change in R^2		0.322**	0.219**	0.003
F	0.693	4.723**	9.346**	7.901**

Notes: N = 43. Standardized regression coefficients are reported.

* $p < 0.05$, ** $p < 0.01$ (two-tailed tests)

Model 1 shows that none of the control variables significantly affects perceived role stress among downsizingexecutioners. The finding was partially expected as age, gender, and industry were not found to be related with perceived role stress in previous studies regarding downsizing executioners and thus no theoretical framework has been developed that supports such relationships. Whereas experienced executioners are suggested to express lower levels of role stress (b= −0.112), the coefficient is not statistically significant, and the model does not explain a sufficient amount of variance included in the dependent variable (R Square = 0.068).

In Model 2 the dummy variable Internal_Executioners, is included. The variable contributes a significant value change to the explanatory power of the model (R Square change = 0.322), which is also statistically significant

(Sig. F Change = 0.000). The finding suggests that internal executioners are associated with higher levels of perceived role stress (b = 0.634) compared to external executioners (p < = .001), thus providing support for the first hypothesis (Hypothesis 1) which stated that "Internal executioners are associated with higher levels of perceived role stress." The variable's coefficient at the final model (b = 0.514) is also significant (p < = .001). The model has a statistically significant explanatory power (p = 0.002) with an adjusted R Square of 0.307.

As mentioned before, in Model 3, Ethical_Conflict_Centered is included, yielding to a coefficient value of 0.497 with a significance value of p < 0.001. Similarly, in Model 4, ethical conflict's effect on perceived role stress (b = 0.532) remains significant (p < = .001), which provides strong support to Hypothesis 2. The variable also contributes a significant improvement to the model's explanatory power (R Square change = 0.175), thus increasing adjusted R square to 0.544.

In the final model, (i.e., Model 4), the interaction term of Ethical_Conflict_Centered and the dummy variable for the type of executioner (i.e., Internal_Executioner) is included in order to test Hypothesis 3, which states that ethical conflict moderates the impact of the type of executioner on perceived role stress. The effect of the interaction term (b = –0.081) is not statistically significant (p = 0.583), and the inclusion of the variable decreases adjusted R square to 0.535, whereas the model's R Square increases slightly to 0.612 (p = 0.003).

These results suggest that the interaction term does not significantly affect perceived role stress, and thus Hypothesis 3 is rejected. At this stage, the variables were also tested for multicollinearity. Looking at the variance inflator factors (VIF) in the coefficients table, all values are lower than the highest acceptable value of ten. In addition, tolerance values are relatively high and close to 1.0. Both the values of VIF and tolerance indicate that multicollinearity is not present in the analysis, and thus the results are statistically powerful and generalizable.

11.4.1   Interpretation of Results

Drawing on the theories of role stress, ethical conflict, and social embeddedness, it was hypothesized and found that the downsizing events negatively affect downsizing executioners through perceived role stress caused by ethical conflict and violation of social contract. Based on previous qualitative research on the impact of downsizing on executioners (Gandolfi, 2009b), the present study analyzed the results of employee layoffs and concluded that such events can cause higher levels of role stress among the managers who plan and implement them, leading to negative outcomes for the organization in general.

The main findings of the study suggest that internal executioners are more likely to express higher levels of perceived role stress compared to external executioners, such as management consultants and change agents, because of their embeddedness in the organization's routines and structures. External managers, on the other hand, are less likely to express high levels of perceived role stress, as they are not embedded in the organization and are not affected in the same way by the employee layoffs and the reorganization.

Furthermore, ethical conflict is found to positively affect the levels of perceived role stress among executioners in a way that higher levels of ethical conflict result in higher levels of perceived role stress as a result of the perception of violation of the social contract between the organization and the laid-off employees.

The hypothesized interaction effect of perceived ethical conflict on the relationship between the type of executioner and perceived role stress among executioners was not supported, leading to the conclusion that the effect of ethical conflict does not depend on the embeddedness of the executioner. This means that when downsizing executioners, as a consequence of their role during the reorganization process, perceive their task and duties to be unethical, either because the organization's management violates the social contract with employees or because their personal ethical values do not comply with the emotional aspects of layoffs, not being a part of the organization does not moderate the negative effects of the event on them.

Summarizing the main findings of the research, it is shown that downsizing executioners are negatively affected by employee layoffs because of their embeddedness in the organization and the conflicting ethical demands that are laid upon them from their own ethical values and the ethical values formed by the social contract between employees and organizations.

11.5   Discussion

Ongoing restructuring has become a common denominator of many growth-aspiring organizations (Guthrie & Datta, 2008). This may be to quickly free up financial resources or for the sole purpose of short-term survival. Whereas restructuring by means of downsizing was originally thought of as a last resort for struggling organizations, nowadays, it seems to represent good management practice (Chadwick, Hunter, & Walston, 2004; Datta et al., 2010; Gandolfi, 2009; Love & Nohria, 2005). The human side to downsizing makes it a potentially stressful event, surely for those enduring it, but also for those executing it. This study shows that the levels of perceived role stress among executioners are affected by two main factors—namely, the type of executioner and the levels of perceived ethical conflict. Drawing on these findings, it is concluded that downsizing executioners are affected by organizational and personal/individual factors. Organizational factors refer to whether the executioners are employed by the downsized organization or are consultants hired on a temporary basis.

As it was shown, internal executioners are more likely to express higher levels of perceived role stress than external executioners.

Personal/individual factors refer to the levels of perceived ethical conflict among executioners. As discussed before, downsizing executioners with lower levels of ethical conflict are less likely to express higher levels of perceived role stress.

Our findings contribute to organizational research on workforce downsizing by quantitatively analyzing the impact of downsizing events on the employees who are entrusted to plan and implement them. By creating a theoretical framework based on past research on workforce downsizing, downsizing survivors, and downsizing executioners, the present study tested proposed relationships and effects by drawing on the two main theories—i.e., organizational routine perspective and social exchange theory. Furthermore, this study highlighted the importance of ethical conflict among downsizing executioners.

The results of this research quantitatively proved that complex relationships exist among those constructs that affect how downsizing executioners perceive their role and at what levels they are negatively affected by downsizing events and layoffs.

In addition, this study adds to the discussion around workforce downsizing by enforcing the focus on internal and external executioners and their differences regarding their levels of perceived role stress following downsizing events. This addition can extend the available knowledge regarding workforce downsizing events and create new ways of looking at the subject.

Summarizing, the main contribution of the present study to academic knowledge for workforce downsizing is the analysis of ethical conflict and type of executioners as predicting constructs for the impact of layoffs on downsizing executioners.

11.5.1 Managerial Implications

This study has a number of managerial implications. The results of the study showed that downsizing events can cause negative effects on the managers who implement them. Thus it is important for organizations to find ways to reduce and minimize this impact, because, first, internal downsizing executioners remain in the organization after the downsizing process is completed and are required to adapt to the changes and manage the organization while having to suffer the negative consequences.

Second, based on the findings regarding the impact of the type of executioner—i.e., if he or she is an internal manager or a consultant hired on a temporary basis—organizations seeking minimum negative impact after a downsizing may have to hire external consultants to help them plan and implement the change process. External managers' expertise and experience can help organizations initiate the downsizing event while avoiding negative outcomes such as role stress among the organization's managers.

Of course, internal guidance is also important regarding issues of organizational routines and structures that are found to be vital for the organization's future.

Third, our results suggest that managers need to realize the role of ethical conflict that may come with the execution of downsizing within the organization. To minimize the ethical conflict perceived from downsizing, executioners can help to diminish conflicting demands. Having to undergo a downsizing process will inevitably cause ethical conflicts in the managers who have to decide which employees are going to leave the organization, especially when they interact with them regularly and maintain social ties. Normalizing of the event and its consequences, but also emotional numbing, can help executioners in their attempts to effectively perform their duties during the downsizing event and to promote the organization's efficiency, thus leading to a successful implementation of the reorganization.

11.5.2   Research Limitations and Future Research

Our quantitative analysis was based on a sample of organizations operating specifically in Cyprus. This could be the reason for the findings to be region specific and thus should be interpreted and generalized with caution. Therefore, the generalizability of our findings, for example, with regard to the individual perception of role conflict, but also regarding the degree of engaging external executioners in the restructuring procedure, should be explored in future studies. Given that the social context in small and medium-sized companies—as those we studied for the purpose of this research—might be very different because of organization size, alternative outcomes are feasible. In the same vein, the study of downsizing in family organizations might be a worthwhile avenue for future research, as these types of organizations have been claimed to provide a special social context that may amplify negative affect and thus lead to different implications. Moreover, because of the financial crisis currently going on in the country, the findings could also be time specific. According to Folger and Skarlicki (1998), managers' reactions to layoffs depend on their perception of the reason that led to the downsizing decision. Managers who perceive poor organizational performance as a result of mismanagement are more likely to react using distancing behaviors and rationalizing the layoff decisions compared to managers who perceived performance decline as a result of external conditions.

The present study intended to set the quantitative basis for the organizational research regarding downsizing events and their impact on executioners. Future research could also examine the impact of workforce downsizing on executioners by looking at the different constructs of role stress, such as role ambiguity and role conflict, independently and not combined as done in the present study. Downsizing's impact on executioners could also be tested based on executioners' performance during and following the events, in order to gain additional knowledge regarding the practical consequences of increased role stress as a result of employee layoffs.

Finally, future research could be extended to include different environmental contexts where the incentives of organizations for undergoing downsizing events is not only the economic downturn but also the provisional adjustment of the organization's size and flexibility. Studying the effect of the incentives behind the decision for workforce downsizing can contribute to understanding executioners' and employees' reactions to the events and the organizational consequences following employee layoffs.

References

Aalbers, H.L., & Dolfsma, W.A. (2015). *Innovation networks: Managing the networked organization*, Routledge, London, New York.

Aalbers, H.L., and Dolfsma, W. (2014). Sociale reorganisatie en bedrijfsresultaat. *Maandblad voor Accountancy en Bedrijfseconomie, 88*(4). pp. 157–162.

Aalbers, H. L., Dolfsma, W., & Blinde-Leerentveld, R. (2014). Firm reorganization: Social control or social contract? *Journal of Economic Issues, 48*(2), 451–460

Acker, G. M. (2004). The effect of organizational conditions (role conflict, role ambiguity, opportunities for professional development, and social support) on job satisfaction and intention to leave among social workers in mental health care. *Community Mental Health Journal, 40*(1), 65–73.

Allen, T. D., Freeman, D. M., Russell, J. E., Reizenstein, R. C., & Rentz, J. O. (2001). Survivor reactions to organizational downsizing: Does time ease the pain? *Journal of Occupational and Organizational Psychology, 74*(2), 145–164.

Appelbaum, S. H., & Donia, M. (2001). The realistic downsizing preview: A multiple case study, part I: The methodology and results of data collection. *Career Development International, 6*(3), 128–150.

Appelbaum, S. H., & Steed, A. J. (2005). The critical success factors in the client-consulting relationship. *Journal of Management Development, 24*(1), 68–93.

Brauer, M., & Laamanen, T. (2014). Workforce downsizing and firm performance: An organizational routine perspective. *Journal of Management Studies, 51*(8), 1311–1333.

Brockner, J., Grover, S. L., & Blonder, M. D. (1988). Predictors of survivors' job involvement following layoffs: A field study. *Journal of Applied Psychology, 73*(3), 436–442.

Burke, R. J. (1998). Downsizing and restructuring in organizations: Research findings and lessons learned-introduction. *Revue Canadienne des Sciences de l'Administration, 15*(4), 297–299.

Cameron, K. S. (1994). Strategies for successful organizational downsizing. *Human Resource Management-New York, 33*(2), 189–212.

Cascio, W. F. (2005). Strategies for responsible restructuring. *The Academy of Management Executive, 19*(4), 39–50.

Chipunza, C., & Samuel, M. O. (2012). Effect of role clarity and work overload on perceptions of justice and job insecurity after downsizing. *Journal of Social Science, 32*(3), 243–253.

Clair, J. A., & Dufresne, R. L. (2004). Playing the grim reaper: How employees experience carrying out a downsizing. *Human Relations, 57*(12), 1597–1625.

Datta, D. K., Guthrie, J. P., Basuil, D. & Pandey, A. (2010). Causes and effects of employee downsizing: A review and synthesis. *Journal of Management, 36,* 281–348.

Devine, K., Reay, T., Stainton, L., & Collins-Nakai, R. (2003). Downsizing outcomes: Better a victim than a survivor? *Human Resource Management, 42*(2), 109–124.

De Vries, M. F. K., & Balazs, K. (1997). The downside of downsizing. *Human Relations, 50*(1), 11–50.

Drucker, P. F. (1981). *Managing in turbulent times.* London: Pan Business Management.

Dubinsky, A. J., & Ingram, T. N. (1984). Correlates of salespeople's ethical conflict: An exploratory investigation. *Journal of Business Ethics, 3*(4), 343–353.

Feldman, D. C. (1995). The impact of downsizing on organizational career development activities and employee career development opportunities. *Human Resource Management Review, 5*(3), 189–221.

Folger, R., & Skarlicki, D. P. (1998). When tough times make tough bosses: Managerial distancing as a function of layoff blame. *Academy of Management Journal, 41*(1), 79–87.

Fried, Y., Slowik, L. H., Shperling, Z., Franz, C., Ben-David, H. A., Avital, N., & Yeverechyahu, U. (2003). The moderating effect of job security on the relation between role clarity and job performance: A longitudinal field study. *Human Relations, 56*(7), 787–805.

Gandolfi, F. (2008). Reflecting on downsizing: What have managers learned? *SAM Advanced Management Journal, 73*(2), 46–56.

Gandolfi, F. (2009a). Executing downsizing: The experience of executioners. *Contemporary Management Research, 5*(2), 185–200.

Gandolfi, F. (2009b). Unravelling downsizing–What do we know about the phenomenon? *Review of International Comparative Management, 10*(3), 414–426.

Gilboa, S., Shirom, A., Fried, Y., & Cooper, C. (2008). A meta-analysis of work demand stressors and job performance: Examining main and moderating effects. *Personnel Psychology, 61*(2), 227–271.

Glazer, S., & Kruse, B. (2008). The role of organizational commitment in occupational stress models. *International Journal of Stress Management, 15*(4), 329–344.

Greenhalgh, L., & Rosenblatt, Z. (1984). Job insecurity: Toward conceptual clarity. *Academy of Management Review, 9*(3), 438–448.

Grunberg, L., Moore, S., & Greenberg, E. S. (2006). Managers' reactions to implementing layoffs: Relationship to health problems and withdrawal behaviors. *Human Resource Management, 45*(2), 159–178.

Guthrie, J. P., & Datta, D. K. (2008). Dumb and dumber: The impact of downsizing on performance as moderated by industry conditions. *Organization Science, 19*(1), 108–123.

Hopkins, S. M., & Weathington, B. L. (2006). The relationships between justice perceptions, trust, and employee attitudes in a downsized organization. *The Journal of Psychology, 140*(5), 477–498.

House, R. J., & Rizzo, J. R. (1972). Role conflict and ambiguity as critical variables in a model of organizational behavior. *Organizational Behavior and Human Performance, 7*(3), 467–505.

Johri, H. P., Cooper, J. C., & Prokopenko, J. (1998). Managing internal consulting organizations: A new paradigm. *SAM Advanced Management Journal, 63*(4), 4–10.

Kalbers, L. P., & Cenker, W. J. (2008). The impact of exercised responsibility, experience, autonomy, and role ambiguity on job performance in public accounting. *Journal of Managerial Issues, 20*(3), 327–347.

Koustelios, A., Theodorakis, N., & Goulimaris, D. (2004). Role ambiguity, role conflict and job satisfaction among physical education teachers in Greece. *International Journal of Educational Management, 18*(2), 87–92.

Love, E. G., & Nohria, N. (2005). Reducing slack: The performance consequences of downsizing by large industrial firms, 1977–93. *Strategic Management Journal, 26*(12), 1087–1108.

Maertz, C. P., Wiley, J. W., LeRouge, C., & Campion, M. A. (2010). Downsizing effects on survivors: Layoffs, offshoring, and outsourcing. *Industrial Relations, 49*(2), 275–285.

Mellahi, K., & Wilkinson, A. (2008). A study of the association between downsizing and innovation determinants. *International Journal of Innovation Management, 12*(4), 677–698.

Mellahi, K., & Wilkinson, A. (2010). A study of the association between level of slack reduction following downsizing and innovation output. *Journal of Management Studies, 47*(3), 483–508.

Mishra, A.K., Mishra, K.E., & Spreitzer, G.M. (2009). How to downsize your company without downsizing morale. *MIT Sloan Management Review, 50*(3): 39–44.

Mulki, J.P., Jaramillo, J.F., & Locander, W. B. (2009). Critical role of leadership on ethical climate and salespersons behaviors. *Journal of Business Ethics, 86*(2), 125–141.

Parker, T., & McKinley, W. (2008). Layoff agency a theoretical framework. *Journal of Leadership & Organizational Studies, 15*(1), 46–58.

Paterson, J. M., & Cary, J. (2002). Organizational justice, change anxiety, and acceptance of downsizing: Preliminary tests of an AET-based model. *Motivation and Emotion, 26*(1), 83–103.

Paulsen, N., Callan, V. J., Grice, T. A., Rooney, D., Gallois, C., Jones, E., & Bordia, P. (2005). Job uncertainty and personal control during downsizing: A comparison of survivors and victims. *Human Relations, 58*(4), 463–496.

Rizzo, J. R., House, R. J., & Lirtzman, S. I. (1970). Role conflict and ambiguity in complex organizations. *Administrative Science Quarterly, 15*(2), 150–163.

Schwepker Jr, C. H. (1999). Research note: The relationship between ethical conflict, organizational commitment and turnover intentions in the salesforce. *Journal of Personal Selling & Sales Management, 19*(1), 43–49.

Schwepker, C. H., Ferrell, O. C., & Ingram, T. N. (1997). The influence of ethical climate and ethical conflict on role stress in the sales force. *Journal of the Academy of Marketing Science, 25*(2), 99–108.

Sennett, R. (2006). *The culture of the new capitalism.* New Haven, CT: Yale University Press.

Sturdy, A. (2011). Consultancy's consequences? A critical assessment of management consultancy's impact on management. *British Journal of Management, 22*(3), 517–530.

Thomas, C. H., & Lankau, M. J. (2009). Preventing burnout: The effects of LMX and mentoring on socialization, role stress, and burnout. *Human Resource Management, 48*(3), 417–432.

Thorne, L. (2010). The association between ethical conflict and adverse outcomes. *Journal of Business Ethics, 92*(2), 269–276.

Trevor, C. O., & Nyberg, A. J. (2008). Keeping your headcount when all about you is losing theirs: Downsizing, voluntary turnover rates, and the moderating role of hr practices. *Academy of Management Journal*, 51(2), 259–276.

Tubre, T. C., & Collins, J. M. (2000). Jackson and Schuler (1985) revisited: A meta-analysis of the relationships between role ambiguity, role conflict, and job performance. *Journal of Management*, 26(1), 155–169.

Ulrich, C. M., & Soeken, K. L. (2005). A path analytic model of ethical conflict in practice and autonomy in a sample of nurse practitioners. *Nursing Ethics*, 12(3), 305–316.

Villanueva, D., & Djurkovic, N. (2009). Occupational stress and intention to leave among employees in small and medium enterprises. *International Journal of Stress Management*, 16(2), 124–137.

Virick, M., Lilly, J. D., & Casper, W. J. (2007). Doing more with less: An analysis of work life balance among layoff survivors. *Career Development International*, 12(5), 463–480.

Watson, G. W., Shepard, J. M., & Stephens, C. U. (1999). Fairness and ideology an empirical test of social contracts theory. *Business & Society*, 38(1), 83–108.

Wilkinson, A. (2005). Downsizing, rightsizing or dumbsizing? Quality, human resources and the management of sustainability. *Total Quality Management and Business Excellence*, 16(8–9), 1079–1088.

Wong, S. S., DeSanctis, G., & Staudenmayer, N. (2007). The relationship between task interdependency and role stress: A revisit of the job demands–control model. *Journal of Management Studies*, 44(2), 284–303.

Wright, B., & Barling, J. (1998). 'The executioners' song': Listening to downsizers reflect on their experiences. *Canadian Journal of Administrative Sciences*, 15, 339–355.

Wright, C. (2009). Inside out? Organizational membership, ambiguity and the ambivalent identity of the internal consultant. *British Journal of Management*, 20(3), 309–322.

Appendix

Ethical Conflict Scenarios

Scenario 1

In an effort to increase profits, Senace Inc. announced plans to undergo a substantial layoff at their Limassol location. Senace plans to replace the laid-off employees with temporary employees in order to minimize costs and improve profitability.

Scenario 2

Because of poor financial performance, Noceries Ltd. has announced a downsizing plan for their organization aimed at reducing employees of their business in Nicosia. The employees of the company will not participate in the decision making regarding the layoffs, either as part of employee focus groups or advisory committees.

Scenario 3

Following a large decrease in their yearly revenues, Topside Inc.'s management decided to proceed with a considerable decrease of their employees' number later this year. The company announced that the decision making for the layoffs will not be based on the seniority of employees.

Scenario 4

As a part of their general reorganization process, Nyacon Ltd announced plans for layoffs accounting for more than 5% of their human resources. When asked, Nyacon officials said they are not planning to retrain any of the employees selected for layoff to fill positions that are currently vacant.

Scenario 5

In an effort to increase profits, OMP Co. is currently designing a downsizing plan aimed at reducing its labor costs by dismissing a significant number of employees. OMP Co. has operated in Larnaca for over ten years and is considered an important part of the community. Community officials were surprised by the announcement, as OMP Co. did not coordinate with the Larnaca planning commission when making layoff plans.

Scale							
Fair/Unfair	1	2	3	4	5	6	7
Just/Unjust	1	2	3	4	5	6	7
Culturally Acceptable/Unacceptable	1	2	3	4	5	6	7
Traditionally Acceptable/Unacceptable	1	2	3	4	5	6	7
Morally Right/Wrong	1	2	3	4	5	6	7
Acceptable/Unacceptable to Family	1	2	3	4	5	6	7

Table 11.4 Literature Review on Ethical Conflict

Study	Tested Relationship	Findings
Dubinsky & Ingram (1984)	Role conflict, role ambiguity, length in present position, length in sales, level of education, major source of income, intensity of market competition (all constructs were tested in relation to ethical conflict for salespersons)	**All of the proposed** relationships were found to be not **significant**.
Dubinsky & Ingram (1984)	Role conflict, role ambiguity, length in present position, length in sales, level of education, major source of income, intensity of market competition (all constructs were tested in relation to ethical conflict for salespersons)	**All** of the proposed relationships were found to be not **significant**.
Schwepker et al. (1997)	Ethical conflict (with sales managers and top management) to role conflict	Ethical conflict (with sales manager) to role conflict—**significant positive**. Ethical conflict (with top management) to role conflict—**not significant**.
Schwepker (1999)	Ethical conflict in relation to organizational commitment and turnover intentions	Ethical conflict to organizational commitment—**significant positive**. Ethical conflict to turnover intentions—**not significant**.

Study	Tested Relationship	Findings
Schwepker (1999)	Ethical conflict in relation to job performance of salespersons	Ethical conflict negatively affects only one of the performance elements, meeting objectives. No significant relationship is found between ethical conflict and use of knowledge, providing information, controlling expenses, or making effective presentations.
Thorne (2010)	Effect of ethical conflict on stress, org. commitment, turnover intention, and absenteeism	Positively related to stress, turnover intention, and absenteeism, and negatively related to org. commitment.
Ulrich and Soeken (2005)	Ethical concern, income, practice setting, ethical environment, unionization, and government regulation (all constructs were tested in relation to ethical conflict) Ethical conflict with perceived autonomy	Ethical environment was the **strongest predictor** (43% of variance); ethical concern and government regulation were **significant**. Autonomy and ethical conflict negatively related with each other.
Schwepker (1999)	Ethical conflict in relation to job performance of salespersons	Ethical conflict negatively affects only one of the performance elements, meeting objectives. No significant relationship is found between ethical conflict and use of knowledge, providing information, controlling expenses, or making effective presentations.
Thorne (2010)	Effect of ethical conflict on stress, org. commitment, turnover intention, and absenteeism	Positively related to stress, turnover intention and absenteeism, and negatively related to org. commitment.

Part IV

Legal Issues and Ethics

12 Why Rescue?

A Critical Analysis of the Current Approach to Corporate Rescue

David Burdette and Paul Omar

This chapter presents a number of different ideas. First, how has rescue come to evolve to its current state? Based on the medieval creditors' bargain and the focus on liquidation in corporate legislation, imported from its analogue (dissolution of the estate) in bankruptcy, the authors will attempt to show that insolvency frameworks (as such) begin with flawed parentage and origins that do not serve it well as a basis for the development of a rescue culture. Second, how the 'invention' of rescue in the twentieth century and consequent competition between jurisdictions to improve rescue has brought about views as to what should be the ideals of rescue: some of which may simply be urban myths and which do not have a sustained basis in economic terms. Third, a number of developments: a paradigm shift in focus to out-of-court rescues, upstream procedures, and 'secret' (pre-pack style) rescues contributing to a redefinition of rescue and the denaturing of formal processes and rendering them of less value to reorganizations and only of limited use in operational restructurings. Pressure from these alternative procedures may also be contributing to the perceived evolution of rescue in the formal context from a focus on entity or business rescue to the sale of assets, as reality has bitten as to the achievable outcomes of rescue and the utility of such procedures the closer to insolvency they get. Curiously, the changes in the financial sector to insolvency frameworks may have turned this tide and rendered some formalism of benefit, but for select debtors only (quid: how to identify the lucky ones?). Concomitantly, the definition itself of what is to be insolvent has changed, making the artificial divide between formal and informal processes of less use than hitherto. Nonetheless, for those formal processes that exist and in those jurisdictions where it may still matter, identifying the ideal intervention moment is still an issue. Finally, based on the aforementioned, the authors will suggest why current approaches to insolvency do not wholly or really work and will attempt to provide a taxonomy of what rescue may change to encompass—i.e., determining issues such as when to intervene, for whom rescue may still be useful, and what rescue itself might mean in the future.

12.1   Rescue From the Middle Ages to the Dawn of the Limited Liability Company

In the Middle Ages, when bankruptcy was in its infancy, options for debtors were limited. Once creditors had worked out a multidimensional zero-sum game analysis that more was to be gained by cooperation than competition and piecemeal dismemberment of the debtor's property, the embryo of what was to be an insolvency procedure for traders was formed, called the *fallimento* or *faillite*. This process might in part have been inspired by the *cessio bonorum* (transfer of goods) procedure in Roman law, which was reputed to have been introduced by the Emperor Augustus (27 BCE–14 CE), in stark contrast to the penal procedures of earlier Roman law, which could see the debtor sold into slavery or even put to death as a warning to other would-be defaulters. Such cession-type procedures, which came to be used mostly for non-traders, still exist in a number of civilian law systems, buried in the detail of the civil codes of these jurisdictions, where they serve as a mechanism for the transfer of property from indebted party to creditors in satisfaction of their claims, albeit a process that does not always regulate issues such as discharge, the effect of stays, or whether rehabilitation ensues at procedure's end, although these tended to be used in the application of the procedure to non-traders. For example, in Jersey, a mixed jurisdiction, where the medieval French law still applies in the domestic procedure also called *cession de biens*, a discharge was only introduced by Article 10 of the Law of 1832 (*loi sur les décrets*), but remains unavailable in the case of an uncooperative debtor (*Birbeck v. Midland Bank* 1981 JJ 121) (Omar, 2013, p 128). An alternative view of where the medieval procedure *fallimento* originated, although there is scant evidence for this, may be in the commercial customs of the trade fairs (such as the *Foires de Champagne*), where rules that later coalesced into the *lex mercatoria* evolved as need arose, dealing with matters as diverse as short weight in sales, degradation of goods, loss of property, warranties, etc., and perhaps also the consequences of the insolvency of trading debtors.

In any event, irrespective of the origins of the *fallimento* procedures, the result was that, where initiated, such procedures commonly saw debtors put their goods in creditors' hands to be dealt with as the latter saw fit. The process would normally see creditors agreeing to a mutual suspension of pursuit of claims (the modern 'standstill' or 'stay'), the placing of a trusted party (perhaps fellow trader or other notable of the marketplace) in charge of gathering and turning assets into value notionally available for the settlement of claims and the costs of the process, paying dividends on the basis of proven claims, and administering the estate with the assistance or under the supervision of a creditors' committee. Eventually, courts would get involved in the creation of principles and rules, developing these creditor-led procedures further and also dealing with the fallout from such procedures, particularly whether there were bars to the debtor resuming trade or whether any discharge was available from any debts left unpaid. In many systems, there was no discharge, and trading debtors remained liable to settle all outstanding debts following the essentially liquidative process. Once legislatures became interested in formalizing rules, this early structure would inform the way in which later insolvency procedures developed, from bankruptcy for individuals to liquidation for incorporated bodies. Even modern informal workout regimes owe some of their framework to the principles developed in this early environment. However, legislatures tended also to emphasize their views on the phenomenon, importing notions of fault (hence the name of the procedures; *fallimento* or *faillite*, which derives from the same root as in the English 'failure') in holding debtors liable for the consequences of their indebtedness and instituting penalties for default that ranged from civil to criminal in nature. One of the reasons may well have been to underline the sanctity of the contract, as expressed in the principle of *pacta sunt servanda*. The term 'bankruptcy' itself is said to derive from the practice of breaking the trader's bench in the marketplace (*banca rotta* = broken bench) to prevent further risk of the debtor continuing in trade and further defaulting (once a bankrupt, always a bankrupt). Interestingly, though, in the United States, bankruptcy as a term now embraces individual and corporate insolvency and is the universal expression for insolvency-related processes. An echo of this medieval mind-set exists in the definition of *banqueroute* in French law, where, as a result of legislation in the sixteenth century embodying prevailing views as to penal policy, it carries overtones of criminal behavior and fraud (Sgard, 2013, p. 227). Also of note in this regard is that some of the earliest expressions of international insolvency law, the Treaties of 1204 (Verona and Trent) and 1306 (Verona and Venice) (Wood, 1995, p. 291) deal with issues such as the return of absconding debtors and the recovery of assets they may have concealed or taken with them, reinforcing the penal elements of the process, whereas it is possible that the writ *ne exeat regno* (do not leave the kingdom), a Plantagenet creation in England, might also have evolved to deal with this phenomenon, which still remains an issue today.

It must be remembered, however, that the principal orientation of the medieval paradigm was toward the liquidation of assets and satisfaction of creditors. Rescue was not an option, unless creditors concurred in viewing the debtor's problems as temporary in nature. They could then choose to alleviate these by a waiver or postponement of debt recovery in which all creditors would collectively participate, subject to mutually negotiated terms. It might be said that, no matter how sophisticated the terms of such deals or plans may be in modern law, all such 'rescues' amount, in the case of financial restructurings, to no more than alleviation/waiver of claims (the 'haircut') or postponement of recovery to aid the debtor's rehabilitation with a little gloss to deal with, *inter alia*, issues such as security, guarantors, and subordination. The advantage in medieval times, just as in the modern day, would be seen in the satisfaction of more debt than could be achieved in the short-term through a liquidation-oriented procedure and avoidance of the 'fire sale,' but instances of creditors agreeing that are thought to be rare. Nonetheless, the institution of the *concordato* was known to have developed, through which creditors could allow the debtor to recover some assets for the purpose of continuing trading and even vote to 'cram-down' dissenting creditors, with a view to the eventual settlement of a good proportion of debt. Needless to say, such 'rescues' could only exist with a high level of trust or the presence of a guarantor as to future conduct and/or liabilities. Furthermore, whereas the decision lay mostly in the hands of the creditors, sanction or support by judicial authority seemed to be required to support such a *concordato* (Sgard, 2013, p. 224). This model of the settlement agreement allowing for some trading to continue is known in a number of jurisdictions that adopted the Italian model directly or indirectly, and its descendants still exist today (e.g., the *concordato preventivo* of Italian law or the composition in bankruptcy). Arguably, the scheme of arrangements adopted in the United Kingdom in 1870 also forms part of this family of procedures inasmuch as it enables compositions or arrangements in the case of financial and/or capital restructurings, as does its insolvency analogy, the company voluntary arrangement.

In the case of traders, the civil law also developed a system of *Lettres de Répit* (letters of respite), which went further than the *concordato*, by which fortunate individuals obtained the protection of the sovereign (and, later, of the courts) to postpone for a period the claims of creditors, allowing for a suspensory procedure that might improve the debtor's prospects of recovery and creditor repayment, such as seen in the French Ordinance of 1673, which put under judicial control the former sovereign practice of granting *Lettres de Répit* (Saint Alary-Houin, 2006, para. 11). In Jersey, where the procedure still survives, called *remise de biens* (surrender of assets), echoes of its focus on debtors are found in the fact it can only be initiated by the debtor, subject to a precondition of having immoveable property and only such property as is necessary need be realized by the court-appointed *jurats* for the discharge of the secured creditors (plus a dividend for the unsecured) within the currency of the procedure (six to twelve months) (Omar, 2013, pp. 128–129). One feature of this procedure, the idea of the stay on creditor claims for a period to enable their discharge through a court-supervised process, is arguably the more proximate ancestor of the moratorium or stay known in most modern insolvency laws.

The insolvency regimes that emerged from the Middle Ages did not largely change in emphasis, stigmatizing failure and penalizing debtors with imprisonment for their inability to pay. Nevertheless, insolvency has since undergone a number of revolutions, many of which have depended on the impetus and drive from novelties arising from the growth in the diversity of company forms and the rise in the volume of trade. Chief among these changes is said to be the quantum leap in Western capitalist societies seen in the creation of the company and the subsequent introduction of limited liability (Davies, 1997, pp. 36–46). The first institution, although it had its counterparts in antiquity (the *societas* or *commenda*), was a revolution in enabling the conjunction of capital and labor to produce results that the use of one or the other could not have achieved alone. This enabled the separation of enterprise from investment and from labor. A person who had the means to invest but not the skill to see the investment into profit could confide the management of the investment to an entrepreneur. Similarly, an employee whose labor was limited by physical constraints to a certain daily rate could combine his energies with the energies of others to the production of goods from raw materials, paid for by investors, thus avoiding the limitations of a lack of capital that prevented individual advancement. In essence, the company combined the interests of three very different groups in a constructive manner, thus fulfilling the concept of the civil society, being that society in which the needs of individuals and those of groups could only be satisfied through cooperation with others. This has led directly to the creation of a managerial class, whose success is not dependent on having capital or contributing labor, but the skills to manage both. Limited liability for companies was a consequence of the divorce of investment and entrepreneurship and the transfer of the risks of management to the entrepreneur. Capital investors felt sufficiently rewarded by the payment of an adequate rate of return on their investment, in essence equating their investment to a loan, although made through the subscription of shares and a participation in the deliberative institutions of the company. Limited liability offered protection for the investor against the risks of bad management and the failure of the company to prosper. It also offered a limit to the maximum investment that could theoretically be wagered and thus put a price on the investment, thus enabling individuals to assess the risks for their personal economies and their investment strategies.

As a result, however, the development of limited liability has shifted the burden to creditors, only partially palliated by their ability to use their bargaining power to obtain further information through diligence processes or to dictate the terms of the contract. Information asymmetry remains a problem in this relationship that is only partly alleviated by duties such as that in section 214 of the Insolvency Act 1986 (United Kingdom) obliging directors to have regard to the interests of creditors and to prevent further harm to them by notably avoiding wrongful (or insolvent) trading. A by-product of concern for the creditor's position has been the orientation in many jurisdictions toward involving creditors in the conduct of the insolvency process, from committee structures supervising the officeholder (further echoes of medieval developments) to rights to initiate procedures (e.g., the out-of-court appointment of an administrator in the United Kingdom). It could be said that the framework for asset security and the availability of enforcement rights in the insolvency context, including whether or not creditors are entitled to 'separation' of secured assets from the general insolvency pool, as well as priorities, privileges, and preferential status, all arise from this general concern.

The beginnings of the process of depenalization/decriminalization of insolvency may also have resulted from the gradual acceptance of limited liability as the standard and the realization that insolvency was an unavoidable risk of trade. The fact that insolvency became an inevitable corollary to commercial life may have done much to lessen the stigma attached to it, as one can witness progressive attempts to lighten penalties seen as early as the Bankruptcy Acts 1883 and 1914 (United Kingdom). It remains the case, however, that even today, insolvency law has not fully shaken off the associations of stigma and fault, as revealed in the September 2003 report of the *Best Project on Restructuring, Bankruptcy and a Fresh Start: Final Report of the Experts' Group*, commissioned by the European Community (now Union).

It may also be possible that early attempts at cooperation between insolvency courts, known as early as 1849, stem from the need to deal with the consequences of the expansion of commercial activity as imperial ambitions grew. Nonetheless, one feature of note here is the influence of the bankruptcy legislation and frameworks when it came to designing a procedure for the termination of corporate activity. In fact, in the United Kingdom, the earliest examples of corporate liquidation simply applied the bankruptcy framework *mutatis mutandis*, leaving the courts to administer the process by interpreting bankruptcy law in light of the specific nature of the company (Markham Lester, 1995, pp. 222–223). Only when changes to bankruptcy law itself came into effect in 1883, instituting a novel method of dealing with the estate, did there arise a need to craft specific legislation for companies, which again simply took the principles of bankruptcy law and tailored provisions based on them to companies (Markham Lester, 1995, pp. 227–228). An echo of this 'one-size-fits-all' process can be seen in the way the Jersey law of *désastre*, which coincidentally was a curial creation to deal with the then 'novel' phenomenon of trading insolvencies in the late eighteenth century, is also predicated on its application to all types of debtor, although the law (the Bankruptcy (*Désastre*) (Jersey) Law 1990) does contain a Part 10 dealing with the specifics of artificially created debtors (companies and certain partnerships) (Omar, 2013, p. 130).

Thus the insolvency regimes for corporate entities that emerged in the mid-nineteenth century concentrated proceedings on the liquidation of companies and realization and distribution of assets, thus retaining the aspect of a penalty by depriving the failed entrepreneurs of their commercial vehicle, in itself an effective sanction for that particular failed venture. Legislation that disenfranchised bankrupts and those involved in wrongful or fraudulent trading from being involved in the management of companies was designed to weed out the managerial class of those judged unfit, leading usually to their disqualification or other measures preventing access to the market (e.g., the Company Directors' Disqualification Act 1986 (United Kingdom)). In some jurisdictions, such as France, debtors faced civil death, an infamous procedure reducing the emancipated adult to the status of a non-person by deprivation of civic entitlements to stand for office, cast votes, and dispose of property.

The essential liquidation focus of developments in the nineteenth century can be said to have led to a culture of enabling exits from the market in the least painful way. Nevertheless, this culture, and the procedures based on the essential philosophy of an orderly quietus for companies, was not designed to take into account the effects on the economy from cyclical decline in manufacturing capacity and large-scale insolvencies across the board, largely a result of the increasing dependence of all economies on international trade and the rise of global tides of economic depression. The effect of mass waves of insolvency may thus have quickly led to the reappraisal of the role of insolvency legislation and two very important developments. First, there began the search for alternatives to the pure liquidation of companies, as it was realized liquidation could no longer be seen as the only desirable result for a company, despite the high likelihood that this might be the result of the process. Second, there began a search for solutions to the problem of insolvencies with an international effect and the beginnings of cooperation between jurisdictions over the affairs of insolvent companies with an international dimension. Only the first of these issues will be treated in the next section.

12.2   The 'Invention' of Rescue in the Modern Age

In the economic environment, there gradually occurred a realization that what mattered was the preservation of the economic benefits of a continued existence for the company. Why this should have captured the imagination of corporate lawyers and academics has long been a subject of debate. In part, this might be because of the pointers offered by procedures, such as the *concordato*, scheme, or composition, which suggested that liquidation was not the only option, albeit it is still likely today to constitute the majority of procedures initiated in any jurisdiction, with the only concern of legislators being how to achieve a balance between rescue and liquidation as well as how to promote rescue as a desirable option for those best placed to take advantage of it. Fletcher also offers the suggestion that recognition of the loss of confidence likely in a system that delayed creditors' recovery till formal insolvency had an 'enlightened' effect in generating the need for timely intervention in failing businesses. The goals and likely effect of this timely intervention were felt to be the restoration of the equilibrium of the company and prudence in its governance, measures that ultimately would avoid the disaster of real insolvency (Fletcher, 1999, p. 4). Ultimately, whatever the truth, it is notable that it is only in the twentieth century that the notion of rescue becomes a reality, perhaps in light of the many waves of corporate insolvency that accompanied fluctuations in economic cycles in that period and since. There is a debate about when rescue first appeared; contenders put forward a 1906 Qin Dynasty law in China, the South African judicial management procedure in the Companies Act 46 of 1926, and French *règle-ment judiciaire* (judicial settlement), which first appeared in the Decree of May 20, 1955. All of these are championed as possible first attempts at a rescue law, although it might be said that rescue as a concept did not achieve great prominence until the advent of Chapter 11 of the U.S. Bankruptcy Code in 1978.

This and other rescue-focused texts were the result of the development, which began in earnest in the 1960s, of preservation measures and external controls on the liquidation process to try and halt an irreversible decline. The introduction of a 'rescue culture' was seen as expressing the need for more control by economic entities of their destiny. The legislative expression of this culture would also allow governments to create effective and efficient legal systems for the management of insolvency, an economically sensitive subject for many states, while not compromising essential philosophical views on the nature of entrepreneurship and employment. Part of the search for the ideal rescue procedure has also led to the introduction of early inter-ventionist measures before the formal moment of insolvency, to attempt to resolve the problem by the use of such 'insolvency-avoidance' techniques before the problem presents itself in a further unfavorable aspect. This twin-track approach has virtually shaped the economic thinking of today, albeit the duality reflected in this approach can also be used to describe the contrast, not only between insolvency and pre-insolvency procedures but also between formal and informal procedures. Insolvency proceedings are no longer thought of as a final measure but, in their rescue form, can occur throughout the life of the company, often as a type of reconsolidation or 'reorganization' (a term often encountered in the United States). The use of informal as well as formal measures is regarded as being part of the range of tools for use by business for its betterment. In relation to companies, the term that has arisen to preservation measures applied to these entities is of course 'corporate rescue,' which is also said to have first seen light in developments taking place with regard to businesses in general in the United States, where the major distinction in types of rescue regimes rested on whether the bankrupt entity was consumer or commercial. As the term 'corporate rescue' suggests, the rescue of companies is at the heart of the institution and is firmly rooted in its ethos, although there gradually arose a distinction reflected in later texts between 'entity rescues' (or corporate rescue pure and simple) and 'business rescues' (the saving of the business in the ownership of that entity).

Seized upon as the inspiration for many other laws then and since (e.g., administration in the United Kingdom and *sauvegarde* in France), Chapter 11 also introduced a novelty into insolvency law, the idea being that the debtor in possession could initiate and direct the path of proceedings, albeit with a view to producing a plan that had to meet with the creditors' approval. Much of the world since has been divided between debtor- and practitioner-in-possession models, with mixed models only recently appearing (such as in the French procedure of *sauvegarde*, where the presumption is that, for businesses below a certain threshold, the directors remain in charge). Interestingly, in common with many rescue precursors, such as the scheme, Chapter 11 embraced the concept of entity rescue, because it (and many of the other procedures it inspired) was aimed at attracting the debtor entity to preserve its future prospects by undergoing a process of financial reconstruction and economic rehabilitation. Much at the same time, an alternative conception of business rescue, usually interpreted as the saving of the business as a 'going concern,' also began to appear in a number of systems, with some including both entity and business rescue as options (e.g., France, where *redressement judiciaire* (judicial restructuring) allows for the option of continuation plans, sales plans, and 'hybrid' plans), whereas practice developments in others tended to opt for one variety over the other, such as in the United Kingdom, where the rescue purpose in the old section 8 of the Insolvency Act 1986 (administration) was usually achieved by a hive down and sale of the business as a going concern, even though administration could be used as an entity rescue procedure.

Rescue procedures are known in many developed jurisdictions. Initial adopters included major trading jurisdictions, such as Australia (introduced by the Corporate Law Reform Act 1992, now in the Corporations Act 2001), Canada (Companies Creditors Arrangement Act 1985; Bankruptcy and Insolvency Act 1992), France (Book VI of the Commercial Code, replacing two Laws of 1984 and 1985), and, of course, the United Kingdom, where two procedures, both rescue focused (company voluntary arrangements and administration) were introduced by the Insolvency Act 1986 following recommendations made in the "Cork Report," or the *Report of the Review Committee on Insolvency Law and Practice* (1982). Depending on the date of introduction of the various procedures, there can be seen a gradual change in emphasis from the requirement that the undertaking pay all debts in full for the benefit of creditors to a more holistic approach requiring the debtor and creditors to cooperate in the recovery of the business concerned, necessitating sacrifices on the part of both sets of stakeholders.

There remain differences over the precise nature of rescue, apart from any conceptual differences between entity and business rescue, and definitions abound. For Brown, it is said to connote the "removal of danger, perhaps an imminent one" (Brown, 1996, p. 1). For Belcher, "if rescue is defined simply as the avoidance of distress and failure, all management activity can be thought of as constant and repeated rescue attempts" (Belcher, 1997, p. 12). Nevertheless, rescue in its legal and now accepted sense as the availability of procedural recourse for businesses in financial difficulties has been rapidly transplanted to the rest of the world, including, inter alia, Singapore (Companies Act 1967, amended in 1987) and South Africa (Chapter 6 of the Companies Act 71 of 2008). Many jurisdictions now feature as part of the arsenal of tools to deal with insolvency one or more specifically rescue-oriented measures, albeit coverage is not universal and, in too many places still, rescue is a relatively unknown term. By way of encouraging rescue-focused reforms, UNCITRAL have taken the concept on board by placing it at the heart of their 2004 Legislative Guide, which contains a ready-made template for those embarking on insolvency law reform, whether in the developed, developing, or emerging worlds. Many benchmarks and guidelines produced by international bodies active in the insolvency law field reflect rescue, not just as a useful tool, but as a desirable goal in the quest to develop mature insolvency regimes. Even the *Doing Business Report*, published annually by the World Bank, uses, as one of its eight indicia, the presence of a workable insolvency regime, including rescue and liquidation options, in jurisdictions worldwide. Such is the pressure to have workable rescue regimes that practitioners in those jurisdictions that have not embarked on reforms (or are not likely to) have been known to press alternative procedures into use, such as the scheme, which has undergone a renaissance in the Caribbean (Kawaley, 2011, pp. 209–210), or the just and equitable winding up in Jersey as a pre-pack substitute (Omar, 2014 (*in extenso*)).

In its present incarnation, corporate rescue is now associated with what is termed the revival of companies on the brink of economic collapse and the salvage of economically viable units to restore production capacity and employment, as well as the continued rewarding of capital and investment. What has become clear is that preservation of a company has acquired a status as a desirable end for the insolvency process, either as a reconsolidation of the company's economic health and well-being or as a restructuring, with the excision of unviable elements. Nevertheless, one of the key topics of debate in corporate rescue remains the ultimate benefit of rescuing a company. There are many interests competing in the arena of corporate rescue, which must all be considered in the approach to the salvaging of companies. There are the very diverse interests of the investors, the entrepreneurs, the employees, creditors and debtors, and society at large, normally represented by the state, which may itself have an interest through its representative organs. Certain of these 'stakeholder' interests are more palpable than others. Employees and their dependent's benefit from continued employment being offered, which may also have indirect benefits in terms of skill acquisition and social mobility. Investors have an expectation of continued reward, and in these days of continued democratization of share-ownership, the definition of investors may encompass both employees and a wider section of the public. Creditors and debtors are encouraged by business and have most to gain from continuation of trading. There are differences in the status of creditors and their importance to the continued activity of the business—a fact reflected in their organization into discrete categories dependent on their enjoyment of security and privileges recognized by law. Entrepreneurs, of course, owe their *raison d'être* to the continued existence of these vehicles of commerce. These interests may be reflected in the design of the insolvency systems in questions, such as in

France, where the priorities in Article 3 of the Law of 1985 were set as being the consolidation of the business, preservation of employment, and satisfaction of creditors. Preservation of the business, but not necessarily of its corporate structure, was also an aim mentioned in the "Cork Report," whereas the orientation of administration, as first introduced in the United Kingdom in 1986, took an outcomes-based approach in the old section 8 of the Insolvency Act 1986.

These interests are, however, not the only ones at stake. Beyond them lie the intangible elements of benefit. It is true to say that insolvency law has traditionally had a strong interest for the state. This has often been described as flowing naturally from the close interest the state has in the creation of companies, which encompasses their dissolution. There is still a strong element of national interest that has its expression in periodic revisions of legislation in this field. The interests of the state may be said to be both active and passive. The active elements come from the obligations individuals may have toward the state to pay necessary taxes, customs duties, and other revenues, whether this is as a result of direct business activity or through the payment of taxes on income and spending, derived indirectly from the company and its constituent elements. The passive element is the interest the state has in maintaining general conditions of access to the market, from which all companies have the capacity to benefit or not, as the case may be. It is the sum of all these benefits, its aggregate, which has shaped the reappraisal of insolvency and its transformation into corporate rescue. It is also perhaps true that because of the intimate interest of the state in insolvency that it has been one of the areas in which international cooperation has been slowest in developing.

The establishment of corporate rescue as the prevailing ethos of business brings in its wake considerations of ethics, particularly where there is conflict between the interests alluded to earlier. In this situation, there is the added ambiguity of the role of the state, given its active role, as beneficiary of business, and its passive situation as guarantor of economic freedom, not to mention the ambiguity of state institutions participating in the insolvency process as creditors. It is arguable that corporate rescue cannot exist as a separate concept and an end in itself. As a result, it must reflect contemporary and prevailing views of what constitutes corporate rescue, which definition must, of necessity, differ from country to country. However, 'corporate rescue' is increasingly viewed as being that gradual tendency toward the saving of more businesses than was the case in systems traditionally preferring liquidation as the ultimate outcome for business failure. It is in considering what interests are to be protected and which are to be preferred that the state, in its role as legislator, intervenes the most. For this reason, insolvency and corporate rescue are continually evolving subjects. From the standpoint of the legal commentator, a law cannot be isolated from its context. It is precisely this view of the flux in which corporate rescue finds itself—the shifts in procedures between the various competing interests, the intervention of the state, whether administrative or judicial, the views of participants in the process—that makes this subject one worthy of close examination.

Pausing a moment, one might conclude from the aforementioned, while a definition may be difficult to pin down and although there has not been universal adoption of rescue as an option in all jurisdictions, that rescue is alive and well and set to stay. This may be not least because of the support of the international institutions active in the field of insolvency law reform. That would be partially correct, insofar as the concept of rescue is concerned. In this context, two things have changed: where in time rescue is to be attempted and, concomitantly, what type of rescue is now associated with the more formal procedures. These are the subject of the next section.

12.3   The Stresses on Rescue: The Times Are a Changing

12.3.1   *Moving Back in Time: Upstreaming Insolvency*

More recently, rescue has taken on new overtones in a number of jurisdictions, signifying that the concept of rescue there has been evolving. Pre-insolvency and 'secret' procedures appear to be the way forward. The concept of upstream rescue entered the vocabulary of the insolvency practitioner sometime in the 1980s. The simple idea is that rescue of the entity or its business should occur at a point much earlier than the moment in time it becomes susceptible to the formal procedures of insolvency, for which it would normally qualify by entering into a state of insolvency. This would tend to occur when the debtor ceased to be able to make payments to its creditors and meet those liabilities, which, once contingent and possibly unquantified, were now certain and had fallen due. This is true in France, where the concept of *cessation de paiements* (cessation of payments) governs access to the procedures of *redressement judiciaire* (judicial rescue) and *liquidation judiciaire* (judicial liquidation), but not in the United Kingdom, where only entry to winding up is associated with formal insolvency being demonstrated; it is possible to qualify both company voluntary arrangements and administration as pre-insolvency procedures based on the absence of a strict requirement to demonstrate actual insolvency. The former approach is more usually found in European insolvency laws, where both '(actual) insolvency' and 'imminent insolvency' tests are seen. In the period since the millennium, however, pre-insolvency procedures have become more common. In some respects, their use may be described as having become 'institutionalized' in the laws of many of the European Union's member states, just as formal rescue was from the 1980s onward. In a similar way, debtor-in-possession type procedures, of which Chapter 11 is a prime example, have become more popular and, although not widespread in practice, have even been adopted in some national laws—for example, the French *sauvegarde* procedure. A further change in some countries has seen the introduction of the practice of the 'pre-pack,' with the idea being to enable the combination of business or asset sales with the desirable effects of upstream rescue by confining formal processes to the end point of negotiations taking place *sub rosa*, principally to avoid reputational damage and potential loss of value and trading partners. Although not yet universally available, the pre-pack was adopted in France in 2010 as the *sauvegarde financière accélérée* (accelerated financial preservation) procedure, whereas, in the United Kingdom, its use, as a variant of the administration procedure, is sanctioned by Statement of Insolvency Practice No. 16. Jurisdictions such as the Netherlands are in the process of adopting analogous procedures.

The cumulative impact of the presence of these procedures on the insolvency map, including also recourse to out-of-court workouts and other turnaround techniques, is to expand the definition of what constitutes rescue to encompass not just formal, but informal, pre-insolvency and, in some cases, non-insolvency procedures. An example of the latter being the use in the United Kingdom of the scheme, despite the presence of formal insolvency procedures, for the financial restructurings of European companies, because of the non-application of the center of main interests test is usually found to allocate jurisdiction in insolvency (Seelinger & Daehnert, 2012 (*in extenso*)). An unintended by-product of this expansion of what rescue covers is the rather tortuous definition in Article 1(1) of the Recast European Insolvency Regulation (Regulation No. 2015/848), which treads a cautious line by providing three separate definitions of proceedings to be included within the scope of the text so as to carefully demarcate between the 'sheep' and the 'goats,' with the avowed intention being to exclude 'secret' and non-insolvency procedures from those procedures eligible to benefit from the framework, including the automatic recognition facility and cooperation provisions it contains. This also avoids the need to draw the boundary by using a formal insolvency test, thus drawing both upstream and downstream procedures together within an overall definition of rescue for the purposes of the text. That said, the wider definition of rescue and concentration on its upstream variants may in the end be more propitious for certain types of rescue, including entity and business rescue, as early intervention undoubtedly allows for more to be undertaken, including both financial and operational restructurings, with greater possibility of successful outcomes. In fact, the European Union issued a 2014 Recommendation on a New European Approach to Business Failure and Insolvency, encouraging the adoption by member states of what is termed a 'preventive restructuring framework.' An unintended result, perhaps, of this change in emphasis, has been to also shift the focus of the more formal procedures, where it is felt that fewer options remain because of the comparative lateness of the point at which these procedures can be engaged.

12.3.2   *The Evolution of Rescue in Formal Insolvency*

Perhaps as a result of the way in which upstream and other procedures have occupied the 'rescue space,' formal procedures have seen their role change to enable rescue in the form of asset sales. The example may be given of the way in which Chapter 11 is increasingly used to effect what is called a '[section] 363 sale' as the preferred option for disposal of the business or of substantial assets with a 'stalking horse' used to benchmark the value to be achieved through the auction process. In the United Kingdom, the 'enhanced liquidation' function of administration, present from the very beginning in the law (old section 8(d) of the Insolvency Act 1986), has been seen more and more in use, just as in Canada, there is the modern phenomenon of the 'liquidating CCAAs,' which use a statute designed for reorganization (and not liquidation!) to carry out a sales plan (of the business or of a group of assets) that has the same effect as a liquidation (Girgis, 2011, pp. 108–109). However, one area in which formalism still seems to allow a wider range of options is in the financial insolvency arena, where bank resolution regimes, allowing for rescue and liquidation options require entry through formally instituted structures, mainly because of concern over systemic integrity. Paradoxically, the London Approach, which is the paradigm for consensual or out-of-court workouts, was first developed to deal with situations where large corporate debtors were financed by more than one bank. Its practice-developed framework, largely led by the Bank of England, set the 'rules' that all the banks were expected to adhere to, given that finance was largely provided by the clearing banks at that time. It also involved spreading the burden and risk by getting more than one lender to provide financing going forward. Although the London Approach was not initially aimed at dealing with insolvent banks, its principles have served to govern workouts in relation to large entities and have been on occasion encountered in the banking sector. However, today's preference in the banking sector seems to be more for predictable structures and certain frameworks (Moffatt, 2015, pp. 493–494).

12.4   Rescue: The Brave New World?

Whither rescue then in this brave new world? As entity rescue gives way to business rescue, which in turn is superseded by sales and enhanced liquidation options, is there cause to revisit what is meant by rescue? Belcher's observation (quoted earlier) may have had echoes in the past, given its emphasis on the rescue of the firm and the assets it was using. Whereas this may be the basis on which entity rescue is predicated, what then is the rationale for business rescue or enhanced liquidation? Although entity rescue is firmly associated with the preservation of employment, continued benefit to society, and other desirable by-products of rescue, the modern literature has begun to question whether value is best achieved by retaining assets within the firm or, rather, whether assets should be returned to economic productivity by allowing creditors to 'recycle' them, or others, better placed to maximize the use-value of those assets, to acquire them through an asset or business sale (Girgis, 2011, fns. 1 and 24).

In a forward-looking paper on the role of the law of corporate distress in the twenty-first century, Paterson proposes a new taxonomy where 'the law of corporate distress' (the umbrella term used by Paterson to describe both the liquidation and rescue of companies) consists of two distinct parts—namely, insolvency law and restructuring law (Paterson, 2014, *in extenso*). Paterson argues that the central tenet of insolvency law as proposed by Jackson (that the role of bankruptcy law is to reduce the incentive for individual enforcement against the assets of a distressed debtor) remains appropriate for part of that taxonomy, but then draws a distinction between its constituent parts. Paterson's paper reframes the unifying aim of the law of corporate distress as "the facilitation of the reallocation of resource in the economy to best use" and draws a distinction between the role of insolvency law in reducing the incentive for individual enforcement and the role of restructuring law in providing a deadlock resolution procedure. This is all done with reference to an Anglo-American comparison and highlights the fact that not only the law but also the markets and the participants in those markets dictate the success or not of the various procedures in these two jurisdictions. Whereas the conclusions reached by Paterson are no doubt accurate in the context of developed economies such as the United States and the United Kingdom, it does beg the question as to whether this would also ring true in developing economies where the need to balance liquidation and rescue is not predicated on the same types of issues, but are nonetheless important in the context of ensuring that these jurisdictions comply with international best practice.

As domestic laws continue to be amended and replaced at great speed across the world, every change further embodying perceived desirable canons of rescue, the question may be fairly asked whether rescue has reached the point where it is protean in form, given that it now is capable of very different meanings and has even crossed the traditional divide between so-called rescue and liquidation. This raises difficult issues for proponents of rescue, particularly those engaged in law reform having to justify recommendations for the adoption of rescue in developing jurisdictions. In the last analysis, what rescue is may ultimately depend on the imagination of the rescuer. If certain predictions may be offered, these are they:

- **Tweaks and variations:** As rescue mechanisms fail to deliver on the very purpose they were designed for, more and more pressure will be placed on lawmakers to make changes that will allow these mechanisms to work more effectively.
- **Variations on a theme:** Having a single, central, and formal rescue mechanism is no longer sufficient in many jurisdictions; some are more

effective than others, and some are only effective in relation to the type or size of the entity concerned. It is anticipated that more variations on rescue mechanisms will be introduced over time in order to try and facilitate the rescue of specific types of debtor. This can already be seen with the World Bank and UNCITRAL Working Group V conducting research on a rescue mechanism for micro, small, and medium enterprises, which are particularly prevalent in developing economies.

- **Earlier intervention**: It is widely accepted that the earlier the intervention, the more likely the rescue mechanism will succeed. As already pointed out, waiting until the point of insolvency has already been reached before intervening is probably one of the main causes of rescue failures in practice. The point at which a rescue mechanism should intervene has been the subject of much debate, and this debate promises to continue. This trend can already be seen in the European Union where member states have been encouraged to introduce pre-insolvency mechanisms and are likely to continue.
- **Less court intervention**: Rescue proceedings involving the courts have always been expensive and drawn out, leading to a return in many jurisdictions to informal creditor workouts that can be accomplished outside the formal court structures. In many countries, especially those in the developing world, the courts are ill equipped to deal with the complex problems that can be thrown up by companies in financial distress, and so more and more requests are made to design a rescue mechanism that can operate effectively without a great deal of intervention by the courts. More developing countries are adopting principles for informal creditor workouts based on the principles espoused by INSOL International.
- **The role of employees**: Many rescue mechanisms, especially in the developing world, obtain the political will to implement them on the back of a promise that the mechanism will save jobs. Whereas this is a very useful tool in order to get lawmakers to introduce these mechanisms, there is a growing realization that in many cases, the employee protective clauses can be counterproductive in a rescue scenario.

References

Belcher, A. (1997). *Corporate rescue*. London: Sweet & Maxwell.

Brown, D. (1996). *Corporate insolvency law in practice*. Chichester: Wiley.

Davies, P. (1997). *Gower's principles of company law* (6th ed.). London: Sweet & Maxwell.

Fletcher, I. (1999). *Insolvency in private international law* (1st ed.). Oxford: Clarendon Press.

Girgis, J. (2011). Corporate reorganisation and the economic theory of the firm. In B. Wessels & P. Omar (Eds.), *Insolvency and groups of companies* (pp. 89–110). Nottingham: INSOL Europe.

Kawaley, I. (2011). Cross-border insolvency in the British Atlantic and Caribbean world: Challenges and opportunities. In B. Wessels & P. Omar (Eds.), *Insolvency and groups of companies* (pp. 169–216). Nottingham: INSOL Europe.

Markham Lester, V. (1995). *Victorian insolvency*. Oxford: Clarendon Press.

Moffatt, P. (2015). The European Union special resolution mechanism: A necessary fix? *Nottingham Insolvency and Business Law e-Journal, 3*(2), 493–515.

Omar, P. (2013). UK cross-border cooperation: Extending rescue to the Jersey Debtor on a 'Passporting' basis. *International Insolvency Review, 22*(2), 119–143.

Omar, P. (2014). Rescue by any other name. *Jersey and Guernsey Law Review, 18*(3), 200–214.

Paterson, S. (2014). *Rethinking the role of the law of corporate distress in the twenty-first century* (LSE Law, Society and Economy Working Paper No. 27/2014). Retrieved from https://www.lse.ac.uk/collections/law/wps/WPS2014–27_Paterson.pdf

Saint-Alary-Houin, C. (2006). *Droit des entreprises en difficulté* (5th ed.). Paris: Montchrestien.

Seelinger, J., & Daehnert, A. (2012). International jurisdiction for schemes of arrangement. *International Corporate Rescue, 9*(4), 243–252.

Sgard, J. (2013). Bankruptcy, fresh start and debt renegotiation in England and France (seventeenth to eighteenth century). In T. Safley (Ed.), *The history of bankruptcy* (pp. 223–235). London: Routledge.

Wood, P. (1995). *Principles of international insolvency*. London: Sweet & Maxwell.

13 Toward a European Business Rescue Culture

Gert-Jan Boon and Stephan Madaus

13.1 Introduction

Business failure is a phenomenon of all ages. Yet, the times of economic downturn have shown to be a true catalyst for reform of insolvency regimes. A strong rise in the number of financially distressed businesses during the financial (and economic) crisis following 2008 made insolvency law a global prompting issue on the legislative and political agendas. It (re-)opened discussions on the objectives of insolvency law and especially at balancing the interests that are involved, including not only creditors but also the debtor and employees. In recent years, many reform initiatives have been taken around the world—both at a national and supranational level—to further insolvency law, where, more than before, the object was to facilitate the rescue instead of piecemeal liquidation of economically viable but financially distressed businesses.

Over the past two decades, a paradigm shift has become apparent in legislative reforms by moving away "[...] from the sacrosanct 'pay what you owe' to the balanced promotion of the continuity of companies in distress [...]" (Wessels, 2014a). This development has not gone unnoticed. The European Commission observed[1] that various Member States[2] have introduced (some kind of) a pre-insolvency framework. They also stated that such legislation was neither guided by a common approach nor driven by a shared European framework to promote the development to rescue businesses in financial distress. With regard to a broader view on the interests at stake, the European Union has taken a leading role in promoting rescue options to be introduced and strengthened in national insolvency regimes. Insolvency proceedings shall allow for efficient piecemeal liquidations for non-viable businesses and also feature (in)formal restructuring proceedings for viable businesses, including out-of-court solutions, in order to maximize the value for creditors, ensure continuation of the business, and preserve jobs.

This chapter portrays, in particular, how the European Union has been working to develop a European business rescue culture.[3] Part one of this chapter will elaborate on the efforts of the European Parliament and European Commission to develop a shared perspective on rescuing distressed businesses. Subsequently, part two will discuss the role of current research in this field. The authors discuss a research project of the European Law Institute on 'Rescue of Business in Insolvency Law.' In part three, some observations will be made with regard to the recent developments in the EU, including a discussion on several barriers that need to be overcome to successfully achieve a European business rescue culture.

13.2   Driving Factors of European Legislative Action

At the European level, 2011 was the starting point for a series of impulses to enhance insolvency legislation in Europe, with the aim of facilitating the rescue of economically viable but financially distressed business. Ever since, the European Union seems restless to bring further harmonization of national insolvency laws. The European Parliament initiated discussions with a Resolution in November 2011. Subsequently, the European Commission presented two Communications in 2012 and also the Entrepreneurship 2020 Action Plan. This was followed by a Recommendation of the Commission on a new approach to business failure and insolvency in March 2014. At about the same time, efforts were made in drafting the revised European Insolvency Regulation ('EIR (recast)'), which further stimulated discussions on developing a shared European approach to business insolvency, in particular tailored for the opening of procedures on rescuing distressed businesses. With the initiative for a Capital Markets Union, the Commission also published a legislative proposal on substantive harmonization of insolvency law.

13.2.1   Paving the Way for Harmonization

In November 2011, the European Parliament took the initiative for harmonization of national insolvency laws by presenting a "Resolution [...] with recommendations to the Commission on insolvency proceedings in the context of EU company law" (hereinafter: 'Resolution').[4] The European Parliament requested the European Commission to submit legislative proposals on a selected number of topics relating to "insolvency proceedings in the context of EU company law." The Parliament observed a paradigm shift where, besides liquidation, corporate rescue has also become an alternative. In the annex to the Resolution, the European Parliament laid down a detailed legislative agenda with recommendations for harmonization of, among others, (i) opening of insolvency proceedings, (ii) filing of claims, (iii) avoidance actions, (iv) role of insolvency practitioners, (v) restructuring plans, and (vi) groups of companies.[5] This should take place against the background that "insolvency law should be a tool for the rescue of companies at Union level," and also, that "a legal framework should be established that better suits cases of companies which are temporarily insolvent."[6] Furthermore, the Resolution defines that the benefits of a rescue should be addressed to the debtor, creditors, and employees. Besides that, the Resolution remains somewhat vague. For example, it does not elaborate on the meaning and content of constructs such as 'rescue,' 'tool,' or 'temporal insolvency.'[7]

The 2011 Resolution can be considered a stepping stone in the development of a European approach to rescue of distressed businesses. It reopened a discussion on substantive harmonization of insolvency laws across Europe, which was considered impossible for many years (Wessels, 2011). It is for this very belief that the European Insolvency Regulation (hereinafter: 'EIR') adopted in 2000 promoted procedural harmonization (coordination and recognition of insolvency proceedings for cross-border insolvency proceedings in Europe), whereas it basically does not provide for substantive harmonization of national insolvency laws.[8]

The European Commission responded in 2012 to the Resolution of the European Parliament by publishing two Communications. In October 2012, the Commission presented a Communication on "Single Market Act II, Together for New Growth" which contained a list of twelve key actions for an improved single market. Under key action 7 it is stated: "Modernise EU insolvency rules to facilitate the survival of businesses and present a second chance for entrepreneurs."[9] It was announced that a subsequent communication would further elaborate on this key action.

Only two months later, the Commission's Communication on "A New European Approach to Business Failure and Insolvency" (hereinafter: 'Communication') was published. The Commission supports the idea that an effective approach to rescue of distressed businesses requires approximation of national insolvency laws. Facing the economic downturn of 2008–2012 with increasing rates of insolvencies across Europe and their detrimental effects on the economic activity in the EU, the Commission stated, "[t]he European response should be to create an efficient system to restore and reorganise business so that they can survive the financial crises, operate more efficiently and when necessary, make a fresh start."[10] The disparity of national insolvency laws, with regard to such a rescue framework, hindered an immediate and efficient European response.[11]

In its Communication, the Commission calls for a "new approach to insolvency" which should lead to the development of a "rescue and recovery culture across the Member States." In this regard, the Commission pointed out specific areas where approximation (the Commission does not apply the word 'harmonization' in this respect) of national insolvency laws may be most beneficial, including (i) providing a second chance for entrepreneurs, (ii) opening of insolvency proceedings, (iii) filing and verification of creditor's claims, (iv) restructuring plans, and (v) special needs of small and medium-sized enterprises ('SMEs').[12]

The Commission, at about the same time, published the "Entrepreneurship 2020 Action Plan: Reigniting the Entrepreneurial Spirit in Europe."[13] This Action Plan also touches upon companies in financial distress and invites

Member States to limit discharge periods for honest entrepreneurs to a maximum of three years after a bankruptcy, provide advisory services to bankrupt entrepreneurs, and to "[o]ffer support services to businesses for early restructuring, advice to prevent bankruptcies and support for SMEs to restructure and re-launch."[14]

By the end of 2012, major EU institutions had expressed their determination for a harmonization of substantive national insolvency laws and laid down specific areas to start with. The general theme of this modernization of insolvency laws across Europe was to "facilitate the survival of businesses,"[15] and it has been this theme that has carried subsequent EU legislative efforts.

13.2.2   *A New Approach to Business Failure and Insolvency*

Public consultations and intense legislative efforts in 2013 resulted (only) in the publication of the Commission's "Recommendation on a New Approach to Business Failure and Insolvency" (hereinafter: 'Recommendation') on March 12, 2014.[16] The task of harmonizing substantive insolvency law proved difficult to achieve in a short term. The directive that the Commission aimed at initially in 2013 was turned into a (non-binding) recommendation in 2014. At the same time, the Recommendation does not include all topics referred to by the Resolution of the European Parliament or the Commission's Communication on a new approach to business failure and insolvency (Madaus, 2014). For example, there are no recommendations on filing and verification of creditors' claims, avoidance actions, and the role of insolvency practitioners. Instead, the Recommendation focuses on two—maybe less controversial—topics.

The Recommendation's objective is twofold: (i) "to ensure that viable enterprises in financial difficulties, (...) have access to national insolvency frameworks which enable them to restructure at an early stage with a view to preventing their insolvency, and therefore maximise the total value to creditors, employees, owners and the economy as a whole" and (ii) to give "honest bankrupt entrepreneurs a second chance across the Union."[17] According to the Commission, the differences between national insolvency frameworks are significant and lead to additional costs and uncertainty for involved parties, which hamper the rescue of viable enterprises in financial difficulties, as well as a second chance for honest entrepreneurs. 'Greater coherence,' as the Commission calls it, would facilitate more effective and cost-efficient insolvency frameworks and at the same time maximize value for creditors. This should promote entrepreneurship, (cross-border) investment, and employment, as well as smooth functioning of the internal market.[18] Therefore, the interests involved are, similar to the 2011 Resolution of the European Parliament, not only creditors but also the debtor and employees, and the economy as a whole.

The Commission provides numerous recommendations of minimum standards that should be implemented in national insolvency frameworks.[19] These should facilitate the debtor to:

1   **Restructure at an early stage.**[20] The Commission promotes out-of-court solutions for debtors where there is (only) a likelihood of insolvency. It relates to the idea that restructuring at an early stage is to prevent the debtor from becoming insolvent and to ensure business continuation, which is for the benefit of creditors, employees, the debtor, and the economy as a whole.
2   **Keep control over day-to-day operation of its business.**[21] To facilitate that debtors seek early recourse, they should be left in control of their day-to-day operation of the business. Only where necessary should a mediator or a supervisor be appointed.
3   **Request a temporary stay of individual enforcement actions.**[22] This stay, to be applied in light of negotiations on a restructuring plan, should relate to all creditors, including secured and preferential creditors. The court should grant only a temporal stay, which can take initially no more than four months and, including renewal, should not exceed twelve months. Furthermore, the stay should be lifted when it is no longer necessary.
4   **Adopt a restructuring plan, also on dissenting creditors.**[23] Adoption of a restructuring plan should be possible by the creditors that are affected by the plan, including both secured and unsecured creditors. To this end, different classes of creditors should be distinguished, at least for secured and unsecured creditors. Distance voting by creditors should be possible too. Court confirmation of restructuring plans is necessary when the plan affects the rights of dissenting creditors, or when the plan includes new financing.
5   **Accept new financing for the implementation of a restructuring plan.**[24] When a restructuring plan providing for new financing is confirmed by the court, it should not be declared void, voidable, or unenforceable. Also, the providers of this new financing should, except in case of fraud, be exempted from civil and criminal liability relating to the restructuring process.
6   **Resolve financial distress by employing out-of-court procedures.**[25] In its aim to prevent insolvency and to promote restructuring of businesses at an early stage, the Recommendation provides for minimum court involvement. Parties should be able to negotiate a restructuring plan themselves, out-of-court, which can be submitted to the court for confirmation. However, the Commission recommends, when necessary, the appointment of a mediator for negotiating a restructuring plan, or a supervisor to ensure that the interests of creditors and interested parties are safeguarded.

Although the Recommendation is non-binding, the Commission requested Member States to report in twelve months' time on its implementation in national laws.[26] These reports allowed the Commission to evaluate the impact of the Recommendation. In the evaluation, published on September 30, 2015, the Commission found that only "a few Member States have undertaken reforms which, in some cases, resulted in legislation implementing the Commission's Recommendation," whereas legislative initiatives in some Member States were and still are pending—for example, in the Netherlands and Lithuania. Also, the Commission noted that "the main elements of the Recommendation are implemented in different ways in the Member States", which leads the Commission to conclude that the Recommendation has not yet had the desired impact.[27]

13.2.3   *The European Insolvency Regulation (Recast)*

The push for a harmonized European restructuring framework described earlier was accompanied by the efforts and discussions on the decennial revision of the EIR.[28] The EIR of 2000 achieved procedural harmonization of cross-border insolvency proceedings across the EU by harmonizing provisions of international civil procedure and international private law (especially on jurisdiction, recognition, and the applicable insolvency law to ensure coordination of measures taken regarding an insolvent debtor's assets), which was a major accomplishment at the time. Following two extensive studies on the working of the EIR[29] and public consultations, various draft texts of a revised and improved regulation were discussed (Wessels & Boon, 2015), leading to the adoption of the European Insolvency Regulation (recast) (hereinafter: 'EIR (recast)') on May 20, 2015.[30]

Although the respective aims of the EIR (recast) and the Commission's Recommendation are different, the Commission did not consider the work on both instruments autonomous. Instead, it is stated in the Recommendation that:

> "[t]he Commission proposal for the amendment of that Regulation [EIR] should extend the scope of the Regulation to preventive procedures which promote the rescue of an economically viable debtor and give a second chance to entrepreneurs. However, the proposed amendment does not tackle the discrepancies between those procedures in national law".[31]

The main elements of a preventive restructuring framework, as described in the Recommendation, are brought within the scope of the EIR (recast), as is stated in recital 10 of the EIR (recast):[32]

> "The scope of this Regulation [EIR (recast)] should extend to proceedings which promote the rescue of economically viable but distressed businesses and which give a second chance to entrepreneurs. It should, in particular, extend to proceedings which provide for restructuring of

a debtor at a stage where there is only a likelihood of insolvency, and to proceedings which leave the debtor fully or partially in control of its assets and affairs. [...] Because such proceedings do not necessarily entail the appointment of an insolvency practitioner, they should be covered by this Regulation if they take place under the control or supervision of a court. In this context, the term "control" should include situations where the court only intervenes on appeal by a creditor or other interested parties".

Also, as one of the reasons to amend the EIR, the Commission pointed out that "the Regulation does not sufficiently reflect current EU priorities and national practices in insolvency law, in particular in promoting the rescue of enterprises in difficulties." In this respect, it is noted that the EIR does not include various hybrid and pre-insolvency proceedings, which should be brought within its scope, in particular as various member states have introduced such proceedings with regard to rescuing financially distressed businesses.[33] Therefore, in addition to the EIR (which concerns "collective insolvency proceedings which entail the partial or total divestment of a debtor and the appointment of a liquidator"),[34] the EIR (recast), explicitly states that it relates to proceedings that:[35]

- "promote the rescue of economically viable but distressed businesses and which give a second chance to entrepreneurs".
- "provide for restructuring of a debtor at a stage where there is only a likelihood of insolvency".
- "leave the debtor fully or partially in control of its assets and affairs".
- "grant a temporary stay on enforcement actions brought by individual creditors where such actions could adversely affect negotiations and hamper the prospects of a restructuring of the debtor's business".
- "are opened and conducted for a certain period of time on an interim or provisional basis before a court issues an order confirming the continuation of the proceedings on a non-interim basis".
- "are triggered by situations in which the debtor faces non-financial difficulties, provided that such difficulties give rise to a real and serious threat to the debtor's actual or future ability to pay its debts as they fall due".

Furthermore, the EIR (recast) mentions that rescue proceedings do not necessarily need to be collective proceedings aimed at all creditors. It is required, however, that all affected creditors are involved in the proceedings.[36]

The aforementioned amendments to the EIR show that the Commission has followed an integrated approach that includes both substantive and procedural matters in order to extend the focus of EU insolvency law. With the EIR (recast) entering into force on June 26, 2017,[37] the procedural harmonization will be in place to facilitate cross-border treatment of restructuring proceedings besides liquidation proceedings.

13.2.4 Building a European Capital Markets Union

With the Recommendation evaluated and the EIR (recast) adopted, the task to further harmonize European insolvency law has been reallocated to a different context: a European Capital Markets Union (hereinafter: 'CMU').

It was in February 2015 when the European Commission announced a new ambitious project on the development of a CMU that aims at building a single capital market that furthers the free flow of capital within the EU.[38] In the long run, such a capital market should function as a sound complementary source of finance for European businesses to the, in Europe, more common bank financing. In this respect, the CMU aims to promote diversification of funding, and, therewith, addresses the investment needs of all sorts of companies, including SMEs.

Following a public consultation, the Commission adopted an 'Action Plan on Building a Capital Markets Union' (hereinafter: 'Action Plan') in September 2015, which sets out the prime focus of the CMU.[39] The Action Plan strives, in particular, to (i) unlock more investment from the EU and the rest of the world, (ii) better connect financing to investment projects across the EU, (iii) make the financial system more stable, and (iv) deepen financial integration and increase competition. To this end, the Action Plan states twenty key actions by which the Commission intends to establish the CMU. Insolvency matters are discussed as well in the context of facilitating cross-border investments by minimizing costs of cross-border risk assessments. The Commission finds that differences between the national laws of Member States inhibit cross-border investments and risk sharing within the EU; this relates in particular to differences in property, insolvency, and securities laws. Here the Commission deems it necessary to promote the further convergence of insolvency and restructuring proceedings.[40] This should bring more legal certainty and promote timely opening of restructuring proceedings. Overall, the Commission has decided to "consult on the key insolvency barriers and take forward a legislative initiative on business insolvency, addressing the most important barriers to the free flow of capital and building on national regimes that work well."[41] The Action Plan also states:

> "[t]he Commission will propose a legislative initiative on business insolvency, including early restructuring and second chance, drawing on the experience of the Recommendation. The initiative will seek to address the most important barriers to the free flow of capital, building on national regimes that work well".[42]

The Commission's statements in the context of the CMU started a legislative process. On November 22, 2016 a legislative proposal for a directive on preventive restructuring frameworks, second chance and measures to increase the efficiency of restructuring, insolvency and discharge procedures (hereinafter: Restructuring Directive) was presented.[43] The proposal relates, in particular, to (i) common principles to promote early restructuring frameworks, (ii) provisions to allow honest entrepreneurs to benefit from a second chance, and (iii) targeted measures to increase the efficiency of insolvency, restructuring and discharge regimes.[44]

13.2.5   Some Observations

Developments on the European level have been driven by the political need to overcome a staggering economic crisis that is characterized by unbearable levels of public and private debt. Lifting this debt burden is essential for a recovery and the prosperous business activity of many companies across Europe. An efficient restructuring framework could work well in this context, as it offers over-indebted businesses a remedy to address their financial situation without the stigma of insolvency and the possibility of an involuntary liquidation once they disclose their balance sheets. The efforts of the European legislator to promote a European business rescue culture reflect this policy goal. At the same time it also explains why legislative initiatives started only in 2011 and have focused on the issue of a preventive framework to rescue distressed businesses (and a quick fresh start for honest entrepreneurs).

The new initiative toward a European Capital Markets Union, however, has the capacity to broaden the scope of the discussion about whether to harmonize substantial insolvency laws. A unified capital market not only calls for harmonized (pre-insolvency) restructuring frameworks but also for a harmonized approach on how to handle a defaulting debtor in general. Also, any facilitated risk assessment not only checks restructuring risks but also—and first of all—the investor's position in insolvency (liquidation) proceedings overall. The broader policy objective that underlies the CMU initiative would, therefore, require and justify legislative action far beyond the scope of the 2014 Recommendation.

It remains to be seen whether such an ambitious 'top-down approach' to harmonization of insolvency law will find sufficient political support. The very careful use of vocabulary that EU institutions have applied since 2011 might indicate an awareness of the many political obstacles that are already connected to the ongoing process of harmonization. In official publications, the term 'harmonization' has often been avoided and replaced by terms such as 'convergence,' 'coherence,' 'approximation,' and 'unification,' as they may appear less intrusive.

Irrespective of the political process, the academic discussion about common principles and best practices in (pre-)insolvency proceedings across Europe must continue and intensify.[45] It is time to assess where national insolvency laws in the books and in practice stand in every Member State, and, starting from there and based on unveiled common standards, at least for specific topics, fundamentals of a European insolvency law could be discussed and developed. In addition, the regulatory competition between member states that initiated the introduction of business rescue provisions on a number of local insolvency laws may bring further approximation of insolvency laws.[46] Where differences between national insolvency laws has resulted in a practice of forum shopping in a common (insolvency law) market, national legislators feel the urgency to ensure they have a competitive insolvency regime (e.g., the German law reform of 2012 was an explicit attempt to stop the migration of troubled major companies to the United Kingdom for restructurings). It is fair to say that regulatory competition (in connection with numerous soft law principles[47]) has established a bottom-up approach to harmonization that might even be more effective and efficient than any top-down approach from Brussels.

13.3   Where Does Europe Stand?

The first step in a discussion about the convergence or harmonization of national insolvency law is to map the status quo. We need to investigate the widely diverging national laws and determine the areas for possible harmonization. To that end, several projects have been initiated over the past years, of which the European Law Institute's Project on Rescue of Business in Insolvency Law will be discussed here.[48]

13.3.1   *Rescue of Business in Insolvency Law*

In September 2013, the European Law Institute (hereinafter: 'ELI')[49] initiated a project called 'Rescue of Business in Insolvency Law' (hereinafter: 'Business Rescue Project'). Against the rise of insolvencies following the economic downturn starting in 2008,[50] the ELI decided to conduct an extensive study in the field of business failure and insolvency law. The Business Rescue Project aims to design (elements of) an appropriate legal-enabling framework that will enable the further development of coherent and functional rules for business rescue in Europe. This should facilitate a better coordinated approach to business rescue (comprising reorganization and restructuring), and will include certain statutory procedures that could better enable parties to negotiate solutions where a business becomes financially distressed. Such a framework would include rules to determine in which procedures and under which conditions an enforceable solution can also be imposed upon dissenting creditors and other stakeholders.

13.3.2   *Structure and Outcomes of the Business Rescue Project*

For this project, Professors Bob Wessels (University of Leiden, the Netherlands) and Stephan Madaus (Martin-Luther-Universität Halle-Wittenberg, Germany) act as project reporters. They are leading this two-phase project, which consists of (i) an in-depth analysis of national laws and of international recommendations from standard-setting organizations, which will be prepared by insolvency experts from across Europe, and, subsequently, this will form the basis of (ii) a report from the reporters comprising (elements of) a legal enabling framework on business rescue. Final reports are expected in 2017.

The project involves twenty-six national correspondents from thirteen EU jurisdictions who prepared extensive national inventory reports and normative reports, and one correspondent (Gert-Jan Boon) for the inventory report on international recommendations from standard-setting organizations. National reports have been prepared for the following jurisdictions: Austria, Belgium, England and Wales, France, Germany, Greece, Hungary, Italy, Latvia, the Netherlands, Poland, Spain, and Sweden.

There are fourteen members of the Advisory Committee who have been selected as outstanding experts in Europe and beyond in the field of insolvency and related areas (such as security law, company law, contract law, labor law, insolvency law practice, turnaround management, accountancy rules). The European Commission acts as an observer and holds a specific interest in the developments of the project and its outcomes. In addition, there is a so-called Members Consultative Committee comprising ELI members who take an interest in the Business Rescue Project. This committee is chaired by Professor Tatjana Josipović (University of Zagreb, Croatia).

13.3.3　Scope of the Business Rescue Project

The project is centered on ten topics on business rescue. These have been derived from publications of the EU[51] and a related project that took place in the United States, where an extensive study was conducted on the reform of Chapter 11 U.S. Bankruptcy Code (on business reorganizations).[52] The resulting ten topics relate very well with the content of the Commission's Recommendation of 2014.[53] The following ten topics are central to the Business Rescue Project:

1　**Governance and supervision of a rescue in court and 'out of court.'** This first topic is an umbrella that covers four subtopics. (i) Conditions for opening out-of-court workouts and (pre-)insolvency proceedings: this relates to who can request the opening of (pre-)insolvency proceedings, the insolvency test, and publicity rules related to the opening of (pre-)insolvency proceedings. (ii) The role of courts, supervisory judges, and other government agencies: this relates to who is supervising the (pre-)insolvency proceedings and the scope of this supervising role. (iii) The role of insolvency practitioners: this concerns the qualifications that are required to be appointed as insolvency practitioner, the procedure for appointment, and powers and duties of insolvency practitioners, as well as their remuneration. Furthermore, it relates to the possibilities for a debtor to remain in possession and overcome appointment of an insolvency practitioner. (iv) The circumstances and conditions for a conversion of unsuccessful reorganizations.

2　**Financing a rescue and the stay.** Whereas a business in financial distress faces an acute shortage of financial means, financing is an obvious and critical aspect to facilitate a successful rescue. The study seeks ways to ensure that third parties are willing to provide financing during this phase of a business in order to assure that the company can keep running its business. This relates, in particular, to the extension of security to the providers of rescue finance. With regard to the stay, the Business Rescue Project considers the conditions under which a stay is provided (automatically/ex officio), the duration, and the impact of the stay on, for example, secured creditors, pending lawsuits, and petitions for liquidation.

3 **Executory contracts.** Similar to rescue finance, discontinuity of the businesses may result quickly when suppliers start to withdraw their services from the debtor. The issue is who has the power to terminate, modify, or transfer executory contracts after commencement of (pre-) insolvency proceedings.

4 **Ranking of creditor claims and governance role of creditors.** Ranking of creditor claims is a much debated topic. It concerns, among others, the ranking of pre-commencement creditors, possible preferential or subordination statuses, and verification of claims. Another topic is the modes that are available for governance of (pre-)insolvency proceedings by creditors—for example, involvement of a creditor's committee or a general meeting of creditors.

5 **Labor, benefit, and pension issues.** Although there is EU legislation on the position of employees in the transfer of businesses, this has been left optional for liquidation proceedings.[54] As there is no harmonization in this respect, the Business Rescue Project considers how national regimes treat employees when the employer is in distress and in particular how their pensions are treated.

6 **Avoidance powers.** This relates to the possibility of avoiding transactions entered into by the debtor in out-of-court workouts and pre-insolvency and insolvency proceedings, as well as how such legal actions are funded.

7 **Sales of substantially all of the debtor's assets, including going-concern sales.** Negotiating a going-concern sale may be an appropriate way to ensure continuation of the debtor's business, but who can negotiate such a sale, and under what conditions? Furthermore, can such a sale be achieved via a pre-packaged deal?

8 **Rescue plan issues.** Rescue plans are a major topic in the attempt to rescue distressed businesses.[55] This regards the scope of a rescue plan, the parties that should be involved (including the secured and unsecured creditors, as well as other stakeholders), and the contents of the plan itself. It also relates to the process of negotiating the rescue plan and manner of voting on the rescue plan, in addition to the possibility to cram-down dissenting stakeholders. Finally, it concerns whether court confirmation is required, and if so, what the conditions are under which this confirmation is received.

9   **Multiple enterprise cases/issues.** Treatment of insolvent multiple enterprise cases poses specific questions on insolvency regimes, but do insolvency laws provide for specific rules? If so, do they provide for procedural consolidation or a substantive consolidation of proceedings of the involved entities?

10   **Special arrangements for small and medium-sized enterprises ('SMEs').** The limited resources available to SMEs also limit the options they have to rescue the business when it faces financial distress. Therefore, the manner in which insolvency regimes could accommodate the specific needs of SMEs and/or whether separate provisions for SMEs would be feasible is studied.

The project on Rescue of Business in Insolvency Law has a broad scope, not only with regard to the various topics that are included in the study but also because it extends to frameworks that can be used by (non-financial) businesses out of court and in a pre-insolvency and insolvency context. With the reports of the national correspondents and the comparative analysis of the project's reporters presented in 2017, the project not only aims at influencing the academic discussion on possible methods for harmonization but also intends to assist ongoing legislative processes in Brussels and across Europe.

13.4   Barriers to a Successful European Business Rescue Culture

The EU faces various barriers when trying to make progress in the quest for harmonizing insolvency laws. These barriers include, among others, (i) the great differences between insolvency laws of Member States, (ii) the embeddedness of insolvency law in other fields of law, and (iii) the interrelatedness of European insolvency law with other EU law and international norms.

13.4.1   *Diverging Insolvency Laws of Member States*

First, the fact that national rules on insolvency proceedings and legal positions of stakeholders in insolvency proceedings vary to a great extent across Member States is common knowledge. It was already in the recitals to the EIR (and repeated in the EIR (recast)) that "as a result of the widely differing substantive laws it is not practical to introduce insolvency proceedings with universal scope in the entire Community."[56] The divergence of national insolvency laws has also been recognized by the European Parliament in its 2011 Resolution, where it stated that there is "progressive divergence in the national insolvency laws". The Parliament concludes, however, that "even if the creation of the body of substantive insolvency law at EU level is not possible, there are certain areas of insolvency law where harmonisation is worthwhile and achievable".[57] And, the Commission's Recommendation of 2014 noted as well that the national insolvency regimes differ to a great extent when stating that "[n]ational insolvency rules vary greatly in respect of the range of the procedures available to debtors facing financial difficulties in order to restructure their business".[58] Furthermore, even in the Explanatory Memorandum to the Restructuring Directive, the Commission reiterates that the diverging national insolvency law are a primary reason for this proposal, but also limit its scope. Harmonising core aspects of insolvency law is, due to the differences, still unfeasible.[59]

The EU institutions are certainly right when they start their endeavors in the field of insolvency law by acknowledging a status quo that marks any attempt to harmonize substantive insolvency law in Europe to be challenging. The Commission, in the EIR and EIR (recast), observed that any such developments regarding insolvency proceedings should not be providing for new proceedings. Instead, harmonization in this area should be about bringing convergence of national insolvency laws. At the same time, it might be easier to start harmonization by a European legislation providing for new proceedings in (relatively) novel areas, such as a pre-insolvency restructuring framework or group coordination proceedings in the EIR (recast). Such first steps create a first common ground to start from. A substantive harmonization of insolvency rules that have existed in jurisdictions for decades or even centuries are a far more difficult task, because these rules are derived from local experiences, culture, and beliefs that need to be investigated and, if well founded, respected.

13.4.2   *Insolvency Law as an Embedded Law*

Second, insolvency law can be considered an embedded law, as it is closely intertwined with various fields of law, including company law, contract law, employment law, tax law, and security law.[60] This brings additional complexity to harmonization of insolvency-related issues in Europe. Therefore, harmonization might be realized most easily for those topics that are especially (and exclusively) dealt with under insolvency law (Laukemann, 2013). Again, the Commission selected such topics in 2014 when they recommended the introduction of a preventive insolvency framework that is new to most Member States, including a limited discharge period. For a CMU, such efforts would fall short. In that context, we will see proposals that address topics that are at the cross-roads of various fields of law, which will, of course, bring additional complexity to the harmonization efforts.

13.4.3   *Interrelatedness With EU Law and International Norms*

Third, a coherent and consistent EU-wide approach to business failure and insolvency not only requires that respective national laws are brought in line (a horizontal perspective), but also requires consistency with the body of EU law and with international norms in which insolvency regimes function (a vertical perspective).[61] The body of EU law includes especially EU legislative measures (and jurisprudence) that relate to both insolvency and related areas of law.[62] In particular, this includes the EIR (recast), which has already been aligned with the Commission's Recommendation by extending its scope to (pre-)insolvency proceedings aimed at restructuring where there is only a likelihood of insolvency.[63]

Besides, there is an extensive body of international norms that have been developed by international standard-setting organizations such as UNCITRAL, the World Bank, American Bankruptcy Institute, INSOL Europe, etc. These so-called formulating agencies or standard-setting organizations have a good repute for their expertise and/or experience. They develop comprehensive sets of recommendations, usually of a non-binding nature, which can be of assistance to legislators, practitioners, judges, professional organizations, and policymakers in their respective activities (Wessels, 2015). Consistency with international norms can assist in ensuring a uniform application of harmonized insolvency law across Europe.

13.4.4   Some Observations

With regard to widely diverging national insolvency laws, strongly embedded in various fields of law, which are functioning within a broader body of EU law and international norms, harmonization efforts seem to require a holistic rather than an isolated approach. In this regard, incremental improvements may be more feasible than a radical or revolutionary adjustment of national regimes.[64] EU legislators are well aware of this fact, and it comes as no surprise that a step-by-step approach to the harmonizing national insolvency regimes has been reflected in the legislative initiatives of EU institutions since 2011. After they shared their perspectives on how to deal with financially distressed businesses by publishing the Resolution of the European Parliament and two Communications of the European Commission, the Commission's Recommendation addressed national legislators directly by providing guidance for specific legislative reform on two particular topics: a pre-insolvency restructuring framework and a quick discharge. Overall, we see a very cautious activity. First, a non-binding recommendation is a modest instrument (Madaus, 2014). Second, whereas the recommended reform asked for the implementation of a very specific procedure, the Recommendation used terms that left a considerable amount of discretion to Member States on how to design their restructuring framework. Maybe the Recommendation was too cautious here, because many Member States ceased the opportunity and interpreted their existing national law as compliant with the Recommendation. Third, the Commission's proposal for a Restructuring Directive takes it to the next level and proposes, where feasible, binding minimum standards, in particular for preventive restructuring frameworks and a discharge for honest entrepreneurs.

Overall, the legislative process moves at a moderate pace, which allows all stakeholders to adjust to the idea that insolvency laws are an essential part of a common market and a Capital Markets Union. In between, ideas, common principles, and best practices may be discovered, highlighted, and distributed, which could lead to a slow convergence of the legal systems by way of regulatory competition and stakeholders' demand. The widespread development of some type of pre-insolvency proceedings could be seen as an example of such convergence. The first experience from our comparative analysis also highlights the importance of functioning key role players (court, insolvency practitioners, advisors) who need to apply a well-intended new rule, or demonstrate the need for legal reform in the first place. An upside of the current pace of law reform and harmonization efforts is that it allows for engagement with stakeholders and an in-depth analysis of national laws, related EU law, and international norms, as done by the ELI Business Rescue Project, which seems essential to further support and shape any legislative efforts.

13.5   The Next Step

If we begin to understand that the task of harmonizing European insolvency and rescue law is a long-term project, a marathon rather than a legislative jump, the focus of our attention should be both at the development of common principles and the legislative reforms. The journey has just begun. If new developed rescue frameworks prove to be beneficial for European businesses, they will form a best practice and help to develop a European business rescue culture. Some might argue the current results are not very convincing yet, however, the picket poles have been set and await subsequent and more substantive advancement by both European and national legislators.

   In preparation of the legislative proposal that was announced in the CMU Action Plan, the European Commission appointed a group of European experts on restructuring and insolvency law with the task to "[a]ssist the Commission in the preparation of legislation or in policy definition".[65] The Commission is dedicated to take the development of a European business rescue culture to the next level. The 2014 Recommendation only works as a base to start from. Currently, the Commission uses the assistance of a group of experts to investigate a wider range of topics, including:

- Common definitions
- Common principles and rules in the area of preventive restructuring procedures as well as formal insolvency procedures and insolvency of natural persons with a view to giving honest debtors a second chance
- Common principles and rules in connected areas, such as the qualifications of insolvency practitioners and the duties, liabilities, and disqualifications of directors in the vicinity of insolvency
- Coordination between the European Insolvency Regulation (recast) and the Restructuring Directive
- Special rules for SMEs' (both as debtors and as creditors)
- Any other measures aiming at reducing the costs and length of insolvency proceedings

The Commission published its proposal for a Restructuring Directive on November 22, 2016. However a Directive may look eventually, it will only constitute another step on a long march. A harmonized European rescue or even insolvency law will not be developed over a few years, and it will not be set by European legislators alone. It will develop over time and result from a convergence of best practices in a European single market that will be driven by the regulatory competition between member states in a common (insolvency) market—a competition that has always been initiated by the needs of market participants (failing companies and their advisors, but also creditors and shareholders) and evaluated by the expertise of capable and trustworthy institutions (courts, IP associations, etc.). Hence a European business rescue culture is becoming a reality, step by step.

Notes

1 Recital 2 of the European Commission's Recommendation of 12.3.2014 on a new approach to business failure and insolvency.

2 Member States is used throughout this chapter to refer to those states that are a member of the European Union.

3 This chapter states the developments as per December 1, 2016.

4 European Parliament resolution of November 15, 2011, with recommendations to the Commission on insolvency proceedings in the context of EU company law (2011/2006(INI)).

5 The Resolution follows two studies that were commissioned by the European Parliament: European Parliament, "Harmonisation of Insolvency Law at EU Level, Note," European Parliament 2010, PE419.633, and European Parliament, "Harmonisation of Insolvency Law at EU Level With Respect to Opening of Proceedings, Claims Filing and Verification and Reorganisation Plans, Note,' 2011, PE 432.766. These studies proposed the following areas for harmonisation: (i) opening of insolvency proceedings, (ii) filing and verification of claims, (iii) reorganisation plans, (iv) avoidance actions, (v) termination of contracts, (vi) directors,' shareholders' and lenders' liability, and (vii) groups of companies. This relates to insolvency proceedings that fall within the scope of article 2(a) European Insolvency Regulation.

6 European Parliament resolution of November 15, 2011, with recommendations to the Commission on insolvency proceedings in the context of EU company law (2011/2006(INI)), recital J and L.

7 See also Fletcher and Wessels (2012).

8 Council Regulation (EC) no 1346/2000 of May 29, 2000, on insolvency proceedings. In 2015, the revised regulation was adopted. Regulation (EU) 2015/848 of the European Parliament and the Council of May 20, 2015, on insolvency proceedings (recast).

9 Communication from the Commission to the European Parliament, the Council, the European Economic and Social Committee and the Committee of the Regions, Single Market Act II, Together for New Growth, 3.10.2012, COM(2012) 573 final, at 11.

10 Communication from the Commission to the European Parliament, the Council and the European Economic and Social Committee, A New European Approach to Business Failure and Insolvency, 12.12.2012, COM(2012) 742 final, at 2.

11 This was also observed in Recital 11 EIR as well as the European Parliament resolution of November 15, 2011, with recommendations to the Commission on insolvency proceedings in the context of EU company law (2011/2006(INI)), recital A.

12 Communication from the Commission to the European Parliament, the Council, and the European Economic and Social Committee, A New European Approach to Business Failure and Insolvency, 12.12.2012, COM(2012) 742 final, p. 3, 5–8.

13 Communication from the Commission to the European Parliament, the Council, the European Economic and Social Committee and the Committee of the Regions, Entrepreneurship 2020 Action Plan: Reigniting the Entrepreneurial Spirit in Europe, 9.1.2013, COM(2012) 795 final.

14 Ibid at 18.

15 Ibid at 2.

16 Commission Recommendation on a New Approach to Business Failure and Insolvency, March 12, 2014, C(2014) 1500 final.

17 Recital 1 of the Recommendation.

18 Recommendation 1.

19 See also Van Zwieten (2014).

20 Recitals 1, 11 and 16 of the Recommendation and Recommendation 6(a).

21 Recital 17 of the Recommendation and Recommendations 6(b), 8 and 9.

22 Recitals 18 and 19 of the Recommendation and Recommendations 6(c), 10–14.

23 Recommendations 6(d), 15–26.

24 Recommendations 6(e), 27–29.

25 Recitals 2 and 17 of the Recommendation and Recommendations 7–9.

26 Recommendations 34–36.

27 Directorate-General Justice & Consumers of the European Commission, "Evaluation of the Implementation of the Commission Recommendation of 12.3.2014 on a New Approach to Business Failure and Insolvency," 30 September 2015 at 2 and 5. This conclusion was reiterated in the Communication from the Commission to the European Parliament, the Council, the European Economic and Social Committee and the Committee of the Regions, Action Plan on Building a Capital Markets Union, 30.09.2015, COM(2015) 468 final, p. 25.

28 Council Regulation (EG) No 1346/2000 of 29 May 2000 on insolvency proceedings (OJ L 160/1, June 30, 2000). This revision was prescribed in Article 46 EIR.

29 See Report from the Commission to the European Parliament, the Council, and the European Economic and Social Committee on the Application of the Council Regulation (EC) No. 1346/2000 of May 29, 2000 on insolvency proceedings, COM(2012) 743 final, at p. 3. For the comparative legal study see Burkhard Hess, Paul Oberhammer, and Thomas Pfeiffer, European Insolvency Law, The Heidelberg-Luxemburg-Vienna Report on the Application of Regulation (EC) No. 1346/2000/EC on Insolvency Proceedings (External Evaluation JUST/2011/JCIV/PR/0049/A4), 2014.

30 Regulation (EU) 2015/848 of the European Parliament and of the Council of 20 May 2015 on insolvency proceedings (recast) (OJ L 141/19, 5 June 2015).

31 Commission Recommendation on a new approach to business failure and insolvency, 12 March 2014, C(2014) 1500 final, Recital 5.

32 For a more critical comparison of the Recommendation and the EIR (recast), see Eidenmüller and Van Zwieten (2015), para. III.

33 See Proposal for a Regulation of the European Parliament and of the Council amending Council Regulation (EC) No 1346/2000 on insolvency proceedings, 12.12.2012, COM(2012) 744 final, Explanatory Memorandum, p. 2, 5, and 6. In the European Commission's report on the evaluation of the application EIR, the Commission lists various pre-insolvency and hybrid procedures that have been introduced by member states, but which fall outside the scope of the EIR. See the Report from the Commission to the European Parliament, the Council and the European Economic and Social Committee on the application of the Council Regulation (EC) No 1346/2000 of 29 May 200 on insolvency proceedings, p. 5 and 6.

34 Article 1(1) EIR.

35 Recitals 10–17 EIR (recast) and Article 1 EIR (recast).

36 Recital 14 EIR (recast).

37 Article 92 EIR (recast), an exception to this date has been made for a few provisions of the EIR (recast).

38 Communication from the Commission to the European Parliament, the Council, the European Economic and Social Committee and the Committee of the Regions, Action Plan on Building a Capital Markets Union, 30.09.2015, COM(2015) 468 final, p. 3.

39 Communication from the Commission to the European Parliament, the Council, the European Economic, and Social Committee and the Committee of the Regions, Action Plan on Building a Capital Markets Union, 30.09.2015, COM(2015) 468 final.

40 Ibid at p. 24 and 30. Related to the CMU is, among others, the Proposal for a Regulation of the European Parliament and of the Council Laying Down Common Rules on Securitisation and Creating a European Framework for Simple, Transparent and Standardised Securitisation and Amending Directives 2009/65/EC, 2009/138/EC, 2011/61/EU and Regulations (EC) No 1060/2009 and (EU) No 648/2012, COM(2015) 472 final.

41 Ibid at p. 6.

42 Ibid at p. 26 and 30.

43 Proposal for a Directive of the European Union and the Council on preventive restructuring frameworks, second chance and measures to increase the efficiency of restructuring, insolvency and discharge procedures and amending Directive 2012/30/EU of November 22, 2016, COM(2016) 723 final.

44 Recitals 1 and 2 Restructuring Directive.

45 A starting point for this could be International Working Group on European Insolvency Law, Principles of European Insolvency Law, 2003, available at: www.iiiglobal.org/sites/default/files/21-_PEILABIjournal_appended.pdf.

46 See also: Eidenmüller and Van Zwieten (2015), paras I and IV(1).

47 See, for example, common codes of conduct for restructuring negotiations initiated by central banks or other institutions in Austria, United Kingdom, Greece, or Italy, but also INSOL International Statement of Principles for a Global Approach to Multi-Creditor Workouts (2000), EBRD Core Principles for an Insolvency Law Regime (2004), World Bank Principles for Effective Insolvency and Creditor/Debtor Regimes (2015), EU Cross-Border Insolvency Court-to-Court Cooperation Principles (2014), or UNCITRAL Legislative Guide on Insolvency Law (2004).

48 Another project that should be mentioned is the study on substantive insolvency law that the Commission contracted to the University of Leeds. It is an EU-wide study of national insolvency regimes on selected topics, including (i) directors' liability and disqualifications, (ii) insolvency practitioners, (iii) ranking of claims and order of priorities, (iv) avoidance and adjustment actions, and (v) procedural aspects. See also www.law.leeds.ac.uk/research/projects/study-on-substantive-insolvency-law.

49 The European Law Institute is an independent non-profit organisation established to initiate, conduct and facilitate research, make recommendations, and provide practical guidance in the field of European legal development. For more information visit www.europeanlawinstitute.eu.

50 For a more extensive overview of the background of the project, see Wessels, B. (2014b).

51 A primary source was the Communication from the Commission to the European Parliament, the Council and the European Economic and Social Committee, A New European Approach to Business Failure and Insolvency, 12.12.2012, COM(2012) 742 final and the subsequent public consultation.

52 This projected was conducted by the American Bankruptcy Institute (ABI), for which Professor Michelle Harner acted as reporter. The final report (comprising over 400 pages and containing 241 recommendations) is available here: http://commission.abi.org/full-report.

53 The majority of topics covered by the Recommendation are studied by the reporters of the ELI project on Rescue of Business in Insolvency Law, although the scope of the projects is much larger (in addition to the Recommendation, the project comprises, among others, executory contracts, labor issues, avoidance powers, going-concern sales, treatment of multiple enterprise groups, and treatment of SME's). With its focus on business rescue, the ELI project does not include consumer bankruptcies.

54 Council Directive 2001/23/EC of 12 March 2001 on the approximation of the laws of the member states to the safeguarding of employees' rights in the event of transfers of undertakings, businesses or parts of undertakings, or businesses, O.J. L 82/16.

55 This is also reflected in, for example, the Commission Recommendation on a new approach to business failure and insolvency, March 12, 2014, C(2014) 1500 final.

56 Recital 11 EIR and Recital 22 EIR (recast).

57 European Parliament resolution of November 15, 2011, with recommendations to the Commission on insolvency proceedings in the context of EU company law (2011/2006(INI)), para. A, C, and D.

58 Recital 4 of the Recommendation. This is contrary to the Resolution of the European Parliament of November 15, 2011, with recommendations to the Commission on insolvency proceedings in the context of EU company law (2011/2006(INI)), where the Parliament only observes that "there is a progressive convergence in the national insolvency laws of the Member States."

59 Explanatory Memorandum to Restructuring Directive, p. 6 and Recitals 1, 3, 6, 7 and 11 Restructuring Directive.

60 See, for example, European Parliament, "Harmonisation of Insolvency Law at EU Level, Note," European Parliament 2010, PE419.633, p. 27, and Bob Wessels, "Harmonisation of Requirements for Insolvency Holders on a European Level," in: *Festschrift für Bruno M. Kübler zum 70. Geburtstag*, München: Verlag C.H. Beck oHG 2015, p. 760.

61 See also Fletcher and Wessels (2012), Laukemann (2013) and Wessels (2014a).
62 The body of EU insolvency law comprises several directives related to financial institutions, according to Advocate General R.-J. Colomer's opinion in the Saigon/Deko Marty Case. See Opinion of October 16, 2008, in Case C-339/07, ECLI:EU:C:2008:575 (Saigon/Deko Marty), para. 59, and footnote 47.
63 Recital 10 and Article 1(1) EIR (recast).
64 See also Wessels, B. (2014a), para. 31, where he advocates a similar approach that he describes as follows: "A balanced development of decision making, with time for consultation, study, constructive criticism and debate, with strong involvement of all players in the market."
65 European Commission, 2015, http://ec.europa.eu/transparency/regexpert/index.cfm?do=groupDetail.groupDetail&groupID=3362. The group consists of twenty-two experts (comprising academics, judges, and practitioners) and two international organizations. At the aforementioned website, the Commission will publish minutes on the discussions with the group of experts.

References

Eidenmüller, H., & Van Zwieten, K. (2015). Restructuring the European business enterprise: The EU commission recommendation on a new approach to business failure and insolvency. *European Corporate Governance Institute (ECGI)—Law Working Paper No. 301/2015 — Oxford Legal Studies Research Paper No. 52/2015*, para. III.

Fletcher, I., & Wessels, B. (2012). *Harmonisation of insolvency law in Europe.* Reports presented to the Nederlandse Vereniging voor Burgerlijk Recht (Netherlands Association of Civil Law). Deventer: Kluwer.

Laukemann, B. (2013). Structural aspects of harmonization in European insolvency law. In J. F. Vandrooghenbroeck (Ed.), *Hommage au Professeur Gilberte Closset-Marchal, Louvain-la-Neuve* (pp. 383–394). Brussels: Bruylant.

Madaus, S. (2014). The EU recommendation on business rescue—Only another statement or a cause of legislative action across Europe? *Insolvency Intelligence*, 27(6), 81–85.

Van Zwieten, K. (2014). *Restructuring law: Recommendations from the European Commission.* Retrieved from http://www.ebrd.com/downloads/research/law/lit114e.pdf

Wessels, B. (2011). Harmonization of insolvency law in Europe. *European Company Law*, 8(1), 27–37.

Wessels, B. (2014a). On the future of European insolvency law. In R. Parry (Ed.), *European insolvency law: Prospects for reform* (pp. 131–158). Nottingham: INSOL Europe.

Wessels, B. (2014b). *Business rescue in insolvency Law—Setting the scene.* Retrieved from www.europeanlawinstitute.eu/fileadmin/user_upload/p_cli/General_Assembly/2014/Business_Rescue_in_Insolvency_Law___Setting_the_Scene.pdf

Wessels, B. (2015). *International insolvency law.* Deventer: Kluwer.

Wessels, B., & Boon, J. M. G. J. (2015). *Cross-border insolvency law: International instruments and commentary.* Alphen aan den Rijn: Kluwer Law International.

14 Effectiveness of Preventive Insolvency Frameworks in the EU[1]

Mihaela Carpus Carcea, Daria Ciriaci, Carlos Cuerpo Caballero, Dimitri Lorenzani, and Peter Pontuch

14.1 Introduction

Many EU member states are at present dealing with the legacy of high private sector debt. In this context, efficient national insolvency frameworks—meant as including both preventive insolvency (sometimes referred to as 'pre-insolvency' or 'preventive restructuring') instruments as well as proper insolvency proceedings—can play a crucial role in two respects: (i) fostering a culture of early restructuring and second chance that encourages economic agents to be entrepreneurial and take sound economic risk and (ii) speeding up deleveraging processes and easing their economic adjustment costs for both households and firms. By the same token, inefficiencies in national pre-insolvency and insolvency frameworks may slow down deleveraging, delay loss recognition, and impede the flow of credit to solvent corporations and individuals.

An efficient insolvency framework should, therefore, enable early and cost-effective rescue of viable businesses in order to avoid subsequent liquidation (Djankov et al., 2008). Moreover, it could limit the economic and social consequences of bankruptcy for entrepreneurs, provided that business failure occurred in good faith (European Commission, 2011; Fan & White, 2003). Less adverse legal consequences of personal insolvency can in fact promote entrepreneurship by providing entrepreneurs with partial insurance against the consequences of failure (Adler, Polak, & Schwartz, 2000; Jackson, 1985; Lee et al., 2007). Efficient insolvency regimes could also foster better ex ante assessment of the risks involved in lending and borrowing decisions by creditors and debtors, leading to an overall healthier development of credit markets (Djankov et al., 2007). Moreover, because several EU member states are currently experiencing a challenging situation of private-sector debt overhang[2] (Cuerpo et al., 2015), insolvency frameworks are crucial to smooth the adjustment and minimize its economic and social costs (IMF, 2013b).

Notwithstanding several EU initiatives aimed at ensuring harmonization and better coordination of insolvency proceedings among member states, insolvency remains an area where uniformity of approach is limited even in the presence of similar legal origin (Djankov et al., 2008). To further address some of these inefficiencies, the European Commission issued, in March 2014, a Recommendation setting out a series of common principles for national insolvency frameworks, whose aim was to encourage the restructuring of viable businesses at an early stage of financial distress as opposed to their insolvency and liquidation, as well as to give a second chance to entrepreneurs (European Commission, 2014a).[3] This study, as part of the analytical work underlying this Recommendation, delves into the crucial role played by efficient preventive insolvency regimes within national economies. It does so by investigating the extent by which cross-country differences in efficiency of these frameworks could explain different levels of entrepreneurship and contribute to better functioning of credit markets, including during deleveraging episodes.

To this end, we study twelve features of efficiency of preventive restructuring frameworks for all EU member states, based on a comparison of the legal provisions encompassed by their pre-insolvency frameworks. The information provided by these indicators is then summarized in four composite indicators proxying (i) the ease of access to preventive restructuring proceedings; (ii) the existence of direct and indirect costs, such as reputational costs or red tape related to courts involvement; (iii) facilitations to continuation for the debtor's operations; and (iv) the chances of effective debt restructuring. These composite indicators are then used to analyze the overall economic impact of the quantified efficiency of preventive restructuring frameworks on entrepreneurship and deleveraging processes, respectively. The analysis suggests that efficient preventive restructuring frameworks are positively associated with levels of entrepreneurship across member states and, at the same time, could lead to less adverse outcomes of deleveraging episodes in terms of financial stability and economic activity.

The chapter is organized as follows. Section 2 outlines the range of available insolvency proceedings, reviews the relevant dimensions of early restructuring mechanisms, and presents the construction of the four composite indicators of efficiency. Section 3 uses these indicators to analyze the economic impact of the efficiency of preventive restructuring frameworks on entrepreneurship and deleveraging processes, respectively. Section 4 discusses the results and concludes.

14.2   Methodology: Measuring the Efficiency of Early Restructuring Frameworks

14.2.1   The Range of Restructuring and Insolvency Procedures

In general, the procedures through which firms can address their financial difficulties through debt restructuring fall into three main categories: (i) out-of-court procedures, (ii) formal in-court proceedings, and (iii) hybrid procedures combining the benefits of judicial supervision with the easiness

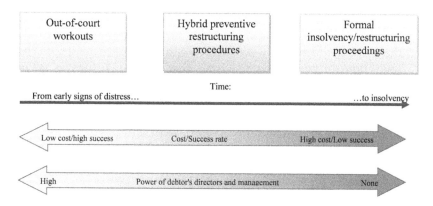

Figure 14.1 Restructuring Possibilities in Time

and low cost of informal procedures. Whereas almost all member states had formal in-court restructuring proceedings as of October 2013,[4] the options of informal and/or hybrid restructuring were limited in many cases. Scarce availability of less formal procedures is a problem, particularly for smaller companies, given that the costs of legal proceedings are to some extent fixed and, in many cases, not affordable. This incomplete legal framework pushes some solvent firms in financial difficulties, actual or foreseen, into formal insolvency proceedings, and, ultimately, into premature liquidation. This leads in turn to the closure of potentially viable firms, creating financial and non-financial losses (including avoidable job destruction) borne by firms' creditors, shareholders, employees, and public authorities across the EU.

Debtors should be able to address their financial difficulties at different moments in time and by different means that respond to their particular needs and those of their creditors. Figure 14.1 illustrates the existence of different options that may be used at different moments in time, depending on the situation, or that may be used as alternatives at a given moment, and which imply an increasing degree of judicial intervention and formality in general. As a general observation, the later a business initiates restructuring proceedings, the higher the costs of restructuring and the lower the management powers as well as the success rate. Therefore, the existence of an option of early intervention increases the chances of survival of an ailing company and minimizes the costs of the restructuring for the economy as a whole. Some of the main features of the different restructuring options can be summarized as follows:

- **Out-of-court workouts:** Debtors facing financial difficulties always have the option of renegotiating with their creditors over the terms and conditions of their contracts without formal intervention by the courts. This may result, for example, in the rescheduling of payments, reduction of interest rates, or total/partial write-off of the debt or of new loan facilities. These are purely contractual transactions based on the individual consent of affected creditors, whereas no specific legal restrictions or criteria are required. This means that there is no possibility in purely out-of-court agreements of imposing a restructuring plan on dissenting creditors who do not sign up for the agreement. For this reason, out-of-court restructuring usually involves the debtor and a small number of creditors (often one or two).

- **Hybrid preventive restructuring procedures:** These combine the advantages of both informal agreements (e.g., ease of negotiation, debtor remaining in possession) and formal insolvency proceedings (e.g., stay on enforcement actions, binding effects of a restructuring plan on a dissenting minority of creditors). The economic function of these hybrid procedures is to reduce the risk that a minority of creditors could stop the restructuring process without the need to incur the costs associated with formal insolvency proceedings. Binding the minority of creditors is a necessary condition for the success of restructuring so as to avoid the company being forced into a formal insolvency process. In order to balance this sort of 'expropriation of the individual consent' outside formal insolvency proceedings, legal systems lay down certain safeguards (e.g., approval by a majority of creditors and confirmation by a court).

- **Formal insolvency/restructuring proceedings:** These are collective proceedings (involving all creditors) subject to the control or supervision of a court and/or an insolvency administrator, which means that the debtors can lose control of their assets or are greatly restricted in their actions. This procedure implies an automatic moratorium (stay of individual enforcement actions) and can result in either restructuring (where this is possible) or, more often, liquidation. The restructuring plan is binding on all creditors, whether they are in favor of it or not.

14.3   Dimensions of Pre-Insolvency Efficiency

The estimation of the impact of preventive restructuring regimes hinges upon the construction of a quantitative indicator reflecting the efficiency of the existing regulations across EU member states. Several attempts to quantify or compare the efficiency of different insolvency frameworks exist in the literature. A number of previous studies rely, for instance, on the construction of a score from legal provisions of bankruptcy acts (index of secured creditors' rights by La Porta et al., 1997, later enhanced and used by Djankov et al., 2007), the calculation of an index based on a survey of insolvency practitioners regarding the expected outcome of a fictitious insolvency case (Djankov et al., 2008), or the assessment of cross-country samples of insolvency cases (such as the study of insolvency outcomes by Davydenko & Franks, 2008). Somewhat similar to the first approach, we construct indicators of efficiency of preventive restructuring frameworks in EU countries based on the comparison of the legal provisions in their insolvency frameworks.

In principle, a preventive restructuring procedure should contain certain features to be effective. In the following, we compare member states according to twelve major pre-insolvency legislative framework dimensions (see Table 14.1). These have been identified on the basis of international best practices, lessons drawn from a comparative study of member states systems, the analysis of reforms of restructuring laws in the member states, and from the conclusions of the Commission Expert Group on Insolvency, the results of the Public Consultation on the Commission Recommendation "A New Approach to Business Failure and Insolvency"[5] (July-October 2013), and dedicated evaluations.

The twelve identified dimensions are (a) existence of early restructuring possibilities, (b) conditions for initiating the early restructuring process, (c) existence of alternative preventive procedures, (d) debtor remaining in possession of its assets in preventive procedures, (e) possibility of a moratorium (i.e., stay of individual enforcement actions by the creditors against the debtor), (f) length of the moratorium, (g) majority decision on plan approval as opposed to the requirement of full consensus among creditors (also called 'cram-down'), (h) possibility to obtain new financing in preventive procedures; (i) limited court involvement,[6] (j) confidentiality of the agreement, (k) existence of early warning procedures of insolvency (particularly useful for SMEs), and (l) debt discharge possibilities following an entrepreneur's bankruptcy.[6]

We converted the qualitative information on the selected twelve dimensions into ordinal variables—i.e., variables whose increasing value reflects increasing efficiency of the preventive restructuring frameworks in the member states under scrutiny, using legal expert judgment.[7] The third column of Table 14.1 presents for each indicator the categories and their corresponding qualitative meaning.

A quick look at the individual data presented in the annex (Figure 14.9) reveals significant heterogeneity among member states along the twelve dimensions, which were assessed on the basis of the legislation applicable as of October 2013. Some countries tend to rank high in most of them, pointing to a generally high efficiency of their pre-insolvency frameworks (e.g., the United Kingdom), whereas others seem to be ranking systematically low (the most striking example being Bulgaria).

For most dimensions, member states are distributed rather equally over the range of indicator values. By contrast, the distribution is more concentrated in the lower scores for the 'possibility of stay' and 'court involvement,' where the number of high-ranking cases is more limited.

Table 14.1 Indicators Characterizing Relevant Dimensions of Preventive Restructuring Frameworks

Indicators	Objective	Effectiveness Features from Low (0) to High (4)
Early possibility of restructuring	*Needed to ensure that restructuring avoids the insolvency of the debtor*	0 - no possibility of early restructuring 1 - late possibility inside insolvency procedures 2 - somewhat earlier possibility, when firm is in imminent insolvency 3 - early possibility, when debtor is in financial difficulty
Conditions for initiating the procedure	*Provide incentives to debtors and creditors to enter process; screens for viable companies*	0 - debtor must be insolvent 1 - insolvency must be imminent, evidenced by a certificate or other expert evidence 2 - insolvency must be imminent, but no expert evidence required 3 - debtor must be in financial difficulty 4 - no test required
Existence of alternative preventive procedures	*More alternative procedures cater better to the different needs and situations*	0 - no preventive restructuring procedure 1 - 1 such procedure 2 - 2 or 3 such procedures 3 - more than 3 such procedures
Debtor in possession	*Debtor's control of assets is needed to facilitate the continuation of its operations*	0 - debtor may be divested of the day-to-day operation of business and an insolvency practitioner is appointed by court 1 - an insolvency practitioner is appointed by the court, but he does not take over the administration of business, or the court itself supervises the procedure 2 - an insolvency practitioner can be appointed outside court (e.g. elected by the committee of creditors) 3 - no obligation to appoint an insolvency practitioner
Moratorium (stay of enforcement actions)	*Protection from individual enforcement is needed to allow time for negotiations with creditors and address the holdout problem*	0 - no possibility of stay 1 - stay is general and automatic 2 - stay is general but on request 3 - stay is targeted and on request
Length of the moratorium	*Ensures balance between the interests of debtors and of creditors*	0 - no possibility of stay 1 - possibility of stay for longer than four months or for an indefinite period 2 - possibility of stay for less than two months 3 - possibility of stay between two and four months

Indicators	Objective	Effectiveness Features from Low (0) to High (4)
Majority decision on plan approval	*Needed to avoid jeopardizing the restructuring effort and the unanimity problem*	0 - no possibility of majority decision or no possibility of affecting the rights of creditors 1 - possibility of majority decision, but certain creditors excluded(tax authorities, employees, secured creditors, commercial creditors) 2 - possibility of majority decision involving all types of creditors and all creditors, whether affected or not 3 - possibility of majority decision involving all types of creditors and possibility to involve only those who would be affected by the plan
Possibility of new financing	*Needed to increase the success of restructuring plans*	0 - new financing not allowed 1 - new financing not forbidden, but on the risk of debtor 2 - new financing can have super-priority status 3 - new financing is exempted from avoidance actions
Limited court involvement	*Needed to ensure the legality of acts having legal effects on third parties and reduce costs*	0 - full court involvement, from launch of the procedure to end, including appointing an insolvency practitioner and voting by creditors in court 1 - court involvement from launch, but negotiations and voting outside court 2 - limited court involvement, only for appointing the insolvency practitioner or the confirmation of plan
Confidentiality	*Needed to ensure the successful conclusion of negotiations*	0 - publicity from day one by opening court procedures 1 - confidentiality up to the moment of granting a stay 2 - confidentiality up to the moment of plan confirmation 3 - confidentially throughout
Existence of early warning tools	*Needed to provide SMEs with tools to identify financial distress*	0 - no tools 1 - 1 or 2 tools 2 - 3 or 4 tools 3 - 5 tools or more
Discharge possibilities for bankrupt entrepreneurs	*Needed to free entrepreneurs of debts a reasonable period of time after their bankruptcy and enable them to have a fresh start*	0 - no discharge possibility 1 - indefinite discharge period or discretion for the judge or discharge period of more than three years 2 - discharge period of three years but conditional on certain factors—e.g., payment of a percentage of debt 3 - discharge period of three years or less with no repayment threshold

14.4   Construction of Composite Indicators of Pre-Insolvency Efficiency

The collected information on the efficiency of all twenty-eight member states' pre-insolvency frameworks has been summarized through the use of principal component analysis and composite indicator techniques. The principal component analysis led to the identification of four component factors explaining most of the variability in the original data set. By looking at the dominant dimensions in each of these components reported in Figure 14.2, the four composite indicators/dimensions of efficiency have been labeled accordingly as follows: (i) easiness/availability of preventive measures, (ii) facilitations to continuation of the debtors' operations, (iii) direct and indirect costs of the measures, and (iv) debt sustainability.

The factor loadings are used as intermediate weights for the individual original variables in the construction of a composite indicator for each common component, according to the proportion of the total variance of the indicator explained by the specific factors (see OECD, 2008). The indicators are designed so that higher efficiency along the four dimensions is reflected by higher values of the corresponding indicators.

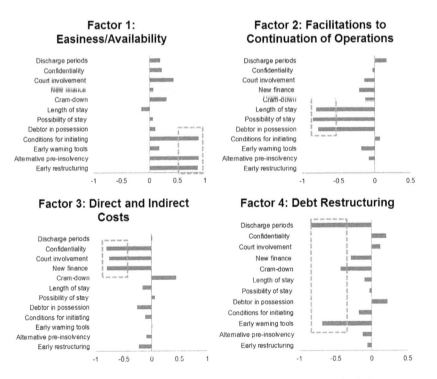

Figure 14.2 Factor Loadings of Individual Questions Using Principal Component Analysis

The first indicator reflects the availability of early restructuring possibilities, the conditions for initiating the procedure, and the existence of alternative preventive procedures. It can therefore be interpreted as representing the easiness and availability of engaging in preventive proceedings. The second indicator reflects the absence of short-term constraints on operations during a pre-insolvency procedure, such as the debtor remaining in possession of the assets and the possibility of stay-of-enforcement actions by individual creditors. The third indicator represents the direct costs (financing flexibility or administrative burden) and indirect costs (e.g., reputational) associated with preventive restructuring procedures. The fourth indicator could be interpreted as reflecting the chances to restructure debt to sustainable levels (ex ante, with early warning procedures, during the procedure with better majority decision possibilities, and ex post with easier and faster debt discharge possibilities). Finally, an index of overall efficiency of national pre-insolvency frameworks has been constructed on the basis of all four component indicators.

The results are presented in Figures 14.3 and 14.4 for the overall efficiency indicator and for each of the four dimensions of efficiency, respectively.[8] For all these indicators, higher values of the indicator score denotes higher efficiency along a given dimension of the national pre-insolvency framework. As shown in Figure 14.3, among the EU pre-insolvency frameworks the overall efficiency is the lowest in Bulgaria, whereas the highest value is obtained for the United Kingdom. The poor performance of Bulgaria is mainly due to very low availability of restructuring tools, leading to limited chances to bring debt back to sustainable levels as well as the lack of incentives for debtors to

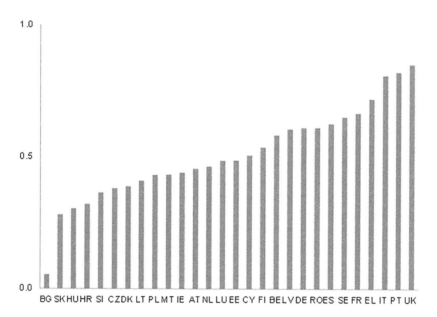

Figure 14.3 Overall Efficiency of the EU Pre-Insolvency Frameworks, 2013

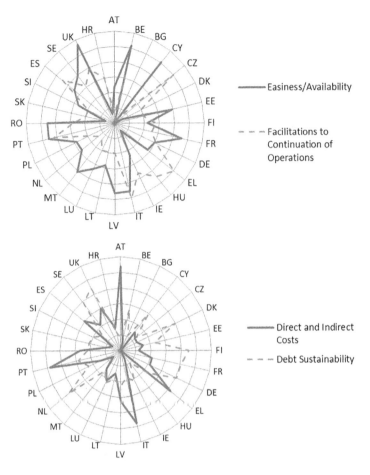

Figure 14.4 The Four Dimensions of Pre-Insolvency Efficiency, 2013

enter a pre-insolvency procedure, as denoted by null values of three out of four composite indicators in Figure 14.4. High levels of efficiency are found in Portugal and Italy, also as a result of their recent reforms, which position them close to the performance of the United Kingdom. On the other hand, lower levels of efficiency can be found in Slovakia, Hungary, and Croatia, especially because of the relatively low easiness and availability of engaging in preventive proceedings and high direct and indirect costs of preventive restructuring procedures, as observable in Figure 14.4.

As a *caveat*, one should bear in mind that the constructed scores do not reflect efficient implementation of national pre-insolvency frameworks, but only their ex ante efficiency from a legal viewpoint. The efficiency of the outcomes of these procedures could thus still face bottlenecks related, for example, to inefficiencies of the justice system or lack of the required expertise among legal practitioners.

Moreover, the information conveyed by the constructed indicators describes the situation of the analyzed member states as of October 2013. Insolvency legislation is, nevertheless, an active policy area, where regulatory changes have recently been enacted in a number of member states. These include Germany, Italy, Latvia, Portugal, and Spain during the years 2011 and 2012;[9] Ireland, Spain, and Slovenia in 2013; and Croatia in 2015. In order to use the composite indicators to estimate the economic impact of pre-insolvency legislation throughout the crisis, an adjustment is made for five countries that experienced a change in the relevant legislation—namely, by computing the corresponding pre-reform values for Germany, Italy, Latvia, Portuga, and Spain (the indicator for Ireland already reflects the pre-reform conditions). Figure 14.5 reports the pre- and post-reform values along the four dimensions, yielding some insights on the main effects of the regulatory changes.

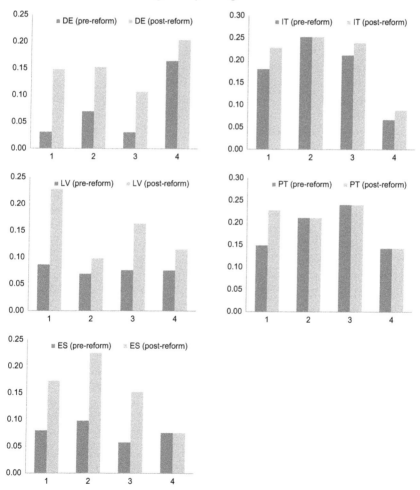

Figure 14.5 Impact of Recent Reforms of Preventive Restructuring on the Four Efficiency Dimensions

14.5   Economic Impact of an Efficient Preventive Restructuring Framework in the EU

14.5.1   *Economic Impact of Preventive Restructuring Framework on Entrepreneurship*

There is a well-established link in the literature between legislative and institutional features affecting the entry/exit of firms (including the insolvency framework) and entrepreneurship, which in turn affects economic growth. The link between entrepreneurship and growth is not direct, yet it operates through the main channels of innovation (intended as product, process, and organizational innovation) and competition. This is why legislation aimed at facilitating entrepreneurship and business dynamics could, through the channels of increased competition and innovation, enhance in turn productivity, employment, and, ultimately, economic growth.

A number of legal and institutional variables have been shown to affect entrepreneurship, including taxation (Fölster, 2000; Gompers & Lerner, 1998; Parker & Robson, 2003; Poterba, 1989; Poutziouris et al., 2000),[10] property rights protection across countries (see Bigus, 2006; Claessens & Laeven, 2003; Lerner, 2002), and labor market regulation (Parker & Robson, 2003).

Notwithstanding the theoretical and intuitive link between insolvency legislation and entrepreneurship, the extant empirical evidence on it is still relatively limited. Among the few examples of previous analyses, Armour and Cumming (2008) investigated the relationship between bankruptcy laws and entrepreneurship using data on self-employment and compiling a series of indices reflecting how 'forgiving' personal bankruptcy laws are in the analyzed countries. Their findings suggest that bankruptcy law has a statistically and economically significant effect on self-employment rates, providing partial insurance against the consequences of a failure and thereby stimulating at the margin the entry of entrepreneurs who would otherwise be too risk averse (see Adler et al., 2000; Jackson, 1985; Lee et al., 2007). Previous empirical evidence has also shown that a forgiving bankruptcy law, above all when offering a fresh start from pre-bankruptcy debts, allows entrepreneurs to reenter the economy rapidly after a business failure (Ayotte, 2007; Georgakopoulos, 2002; Landier, 2004). According to Baird and Morrison (2005) and Stam et al. (2006), such repeat entrepreneurship is common in jurisdictions in which a fresh start is allowed.

Taking stock of the mentioned studies, we analyze the impact of the efficiency of national pre-insolvency frameworks in the EU on the proportion of self-employed population, which can be regarded as a good proxy for entrepreneurship and has been previously used to this aim in the literature (among others, Armour & Cumming, 2008). The tested hypothesis is that, everything else being equal, more efficient pre-insolvency frameworks tend to stimulate entrepreneurship.

In our model, the logarithm of the self-employment rate, drawn from Eurostat Structural Business Statistics, is regressed on the constructed indicators of preventive restructuring efficiency along the four relevant dimensions as well as the overall efficiency measure. The random effect pooled panel estimation of the model covers the period 2003–2010 for twenty-four EU member states[11] using the following specification:

$$selfempl_{it} = \alpha + \beta\ insol_i + \gamma\ gdppercap_{it} + \theta EPL_{it} + \nu_t + \eta_i + \varepsilon_{it},$$

where the *insol* variable is either one of the four composite indicators (along the four common factors) or the overall indicator of efficiency. As control variables, the model includes real GDP per capita (to control for country-specific factors such as the level of economic development or the general economic situation); the Organisation for Economic Co-operation and Development (OECD) indicator of employment protection legislation, measuring the procedures and costs involved in dismissing individuals or groups of workers and in hiring workers on fixed-term or temporary work agency contracts;[12] and time-fixed effects controlling for common cyclical shocks. The estimation results are presented in Table 14.2. Different versions of the model were estimated including the four relevant composite indicators both separately (versions 1 to 4) and jointly (version 5). As in the previous section, caveats to take into due account relate to both data availability and methodological choices. First, the main shortcoming is represented by the lack of more than one point in time for the efficiency index, except for a few cases where both pre-reform and post-reform values are available. If the sample contained more pre- and post-reform observations, a natural extension of this analysis would be to consider a control and a treatment group, the latter including member states where reforms affecting the efficiency of their pre-insolvency system have taken place. Moreover, the explanatory power of the estimated models finds a natural upper bound in the explanatory power of the single-efficiency factors and, even more, of their aggregation obtained through the principal component analysis.

The estimation results reported in Table 14.2 suggest that pre-insolvency efficiency has a positive impact on self-employment rates and, in particular, that an increase by one percentage point in the efficiency of the national preventive restructuring systems (measured by the constructed aggregate index) is associated with a higher self-employment rate by some 0.75 % on average.[13] This overall impact is in line with the economic expectation that a more efficient preventive restructuring framework should foster entrepreneurship. Moreover, once the model is estimated using the four separate factors as explanatory variables (see versions 1 to 4), the 'continuation' dimension appears to be the most important to explain the overall positive impact of the aggregate index, as it is the only one to present a statistically significant positive coefficient, whereas the other factors do not have a statistically significant impact when taken separately.

A visual inspection of the self-employment levels against the distribution of EU member states across the different efficiency indicators, reported in Figure 14.6, appears to confirm the results obtained in Table 14.2

Table 14.2 Estimation Results for the Self-Employment Model

	Dependent Variable: Log (Self-Employment Rate)					
	Baseline	*Version 1*	*Version 2*	*Version 3*	*Version 4*	*Version 5*
GDP per capita	−0.000 (−2.09)	0.000 (−0.56)	0.000 (−1.55)	−0.000 (−1.50)	−0.000 (−0.94)	−0.000 (−1.40)
EPL	0.0935** (0.043)	0.0923** (0.043)	0.0923** (0.42)	0.0848** (0.043)	0.0856*** (0.043)	0.0832*** (0.043)
Overall efficiency	0.747* (0.406)					
Availability dimension		0.411 (0.946)				0.055 (0.995)
Continuation dimension			3.148*** (0.876)			2.812*** (0.914)
Cost dimension				1.592* (0.821)		0.946 (0.858)
Restructuring dimension					−1.625 (1.112)	−1.051 (1.148)
Constant	−2.681*** (0.198)	−2.399*** (0.169)	−2.606*** (0.164)	−2.438 (0.149)	−2.144*** (0.219)	−2.638*** (0.235)
Time fixed effects	Yes	Yes	Yes	Yes	Yes	Yes

t statistics in parentheses

* $p < 0.1$, ** $p < 0.05$, *** $p < 0.01$

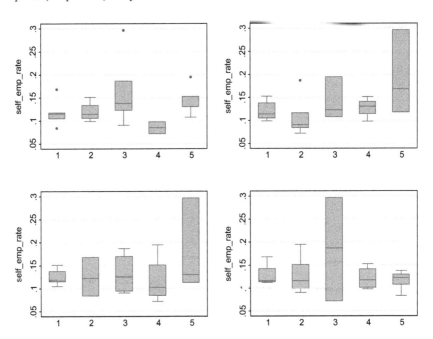

Figure 14.6 Box-and-Whisker Plot of Self-Employment Against Each Pre-Insolvency Dimension: 'Easiness,' 'Continuation,' 'Costs,' and 'Restructuring'

(versions 1 to 4)—i.e., the existence of a positive and significant relationship between self-employment levels and pre-insolvency efficiency alongside the 'continuation' dimension. The 'costs' dimension also shows some signs of an increasing pattern, whereas no clear one is apparent along the two remaining dimensions.

14.6 Economic Impact of Preventive Restructuring Framework on Corporate Deleveraging and Financial Stability

This section focuses on the impact of national preventing restructuring frameworks on corporate deleveraging, in particular in terms of financial stability and economic activity. The analysis is based on the period following the recent financial and economic crisis, and is performed in two steps: (i) first, inspecting how preventive restructuring frameworks shaped the dynamics of the aggregate nonperforming loans' rate of national banking sectors,and (ii) second, looking into the outcomes of corporate deleveraging on overall economic activity, as measured by GDP growth.

14.6.1 Impact of Preventing Restructuring Frameworks on NPL Dynamics

The share of nonperforming loans (NPL) in the banking sector is a commonly used measure of financial sector soundness and is a factor affecting credit supply (Becker & Ivashina, 2014). During deleveraging episodes in the non-financial private sector, the NPL rate usually rises as an increasing share of debtors become incapable of servicing or paying pay back their debt in an orderly manner. Rising NPL rates are often observed at the onset of a banking crisis (Kaminsky & Reinhart, 1999). Deteriorating loan portfolios and increasing losses force banks to curtail their credit supply, further increasing pressures on the non-financial sector to deleverage. The dynamics of NPLs, therefore, play a central role in the intensity of the feedback loop between the non-financial and financial private sectors (Nkusu, 2011).

Slow recognition of bad loans leading to several years of upward-drifting NPL rates usually deteriorates the outcomes of deleveraging episodes, as it generates macroeconomic uncertainty, impairs the intermediation function of banks, and leads to protracted periods of tight credit for the whole economy, including its viable parts. A desirable property of NPL dynamics would, therefore, be their swift reaction to adverse macroeconomic shocks, followed by a gradual normalization.

As an illustration, Figure 14.7 shows the different profiles of NPL rates for the United States and Spain in the years around the onset of the financial crisis. In the former case, the reaction of the NPL rate to the financial stress was quick, with the peak of the NPL rate observed as early as 2009. In the case of Spain, the rate started drifting upward in 2008 and continued doing so in the following years.

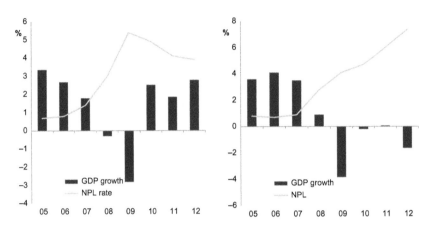

Figure 14.7 Nonperforming Loans Rate and Economic Activity in the United States
Versus Spain

The analysis is based on NPL data from the IMF Financial Soundness
Indicators, covering twenty-seven EU member states and the period from
2007 to 2012. The overall NPL rate covering firms and households is
used due to data availability reasons. We propose two models of adjustment of the NPL rate to macroeconomic shocks, where the adjustment
coefficient is interacted with a dummy variable indicating the terciles of
all preventive restructuring indexes variables. The use of tercile dummies
is useful, as it allows us to directly test the difference between the groups
of countries with medium or high efficiency on a given dimension of
the preventing restructuring framework, relative to those with relatively
lower efficiency.[14] At the same time, this specification is useful, as it does
not impose a linear relationship between the efficiency indicators and the
adjustment speed.

The first model is based on a simple partial adjustment equation in
which the change of the NPL rate is regressed on the current GDP growth
rate, the previous period's level of corporate debt to gross operating surplus, and the previous period's level of the NPL rate, whose coefficient γ
captures the adjustment speed:

$$\Delta \, npl_{it} = \alpha + \beta_1 \, gdpgr_{it} + \beta_2 \, debt_{it-1} + \\ \gamma + \gamma_1 tercile2_i + \gamma_2 tercile3_i \, npl_{it-1} + \varepsilon_{it} \, ,$$

where the lagged *npl* term is then interacted with two dummy variables, representing the middle and upper tercile of the efficiency indexes, respectively.

However, because panel tests of stationarity of the NPL rate seem to
signal possible non-stationarity, at least in our relatively short sample, a

second specification proposes an error-correction model, capturing the relationships among variables in two stages. This is in line with other empirical studies (among others, Rinaldi & Sanchis-Arellano, 2006) also identifying non-stationarity in NPL rates and resorting to an error-correction framework to model NPLs.

Within this framework, the long-term relationship links the same three variables as in the first specification (although all in levels)—namely, the NPL rate, GDP growth, and corporate debt divided by gross operating surplus. The short-term relationship regresses the change of the NPL rate on the lagged changes of all three variables of the model, plus the previous period's error-correction term (error from the long-term relationship). Both stages are estimated on a panel using fixed country effects. The estimated model is

$$npl_{it} = \alpha_0 + \alpha_1\, gdpgr_{it} + \alpha_2\, debt_{it} + \mu_i + \varepsilon_{it}$$

$$\Delta\, npl_{it} = \beta_0 + \beta_1 \Delta gdpgr_{it-1} + \beta_2 \Delta debt_{it-1} + \beta_3 \Delta npl_{it-1}$$
$$+ (\beta_4 + \beta_5 tercile2_i + \beta_6 tercile3_i)ec_{it-1} + \nu_i + u_{it},$$

where the tercile dummies are interacted with the error-correction term *ec* to capture differences in the speed of closure of the gap to the long-term equilibrium.

The results of the first model in Table 14.3 point to an average adjustment speed of the NPL rate of about 29% per year. Taken individually, the 'restructuring' dimension seems to significantly increase this speed by about fourteen percentage points between the lower and the upper tercile of this variable. The 'availability' dimension also seems to have a positive effect on the speed of adjustment of the NPL rate to normal levels, but the effect is only significant in the middle tercile. Interestingly enough, the 'continuation' dimension taken individually seems, however, to be negatively associated with the adjustment speed of the NPL rate. Once all dimensions are taken into account (last column), the one on 'restructuring' remains the only one to significantly increase the speed of normalization of the NPL rate. On some dimensions, the sign of the coefficient changes, moving from the middle to the higher tercile group. These changes cannot be directly interpreted, as the non-significance of the coefficients cannot exclude this pattern to be related to estimation error.

The results of the error-correction model in Table 14.4 seem to point to very similar conclusions. All dimensions taken individually, as well as the overall indicator, have a negative sign on the upper tercile variable, which would suggest that these indicators tend to increase the speed of convergence of the NPL rate to the long-term equilibrium value. However, given that the coefficients are not significant, the interpretation should be careful. The 'continuation' dimension is again an exception, as it signals a significant reduction in the speed of correction of the NPL rate. Once all dimensions

Table 14.3 Estimation Results for the Partial Adjustment Model of the Nonperforming Loans Rate Augmented With Preventive Restructuring Framework Indices

	Dependent Variable: Change in NPL Rate in Year t						
	Baseline	Version 1	Version 2	Version 3	Version 4	Version 5	Version 7
GDP growth rate t	-5.657***	-5.655***	-5.702***	-5.639***	-5.652***	-5.621***	-5.647***
	(-13.69)	(-13.27)	(-13.09)	(-13.81)	(-13.49)	(-13.29)	(-12.46)
(Debt/GOS) t-1	0.039	0.043	0.038	0.030	0.032	0.048	0.036
	(0.89)	(0.89)	(0.87)	(0.69)	(0.75)	(0.91)	(0.72)
NPL t-1	-0.289***	-0.262***	-0.240***	-0.314***	-0.237***	-0.252***	-0.183*
	(-10.34)	(-7.79)	(-6.45)	(-12.94)	(-4.12)	(-6.79)	(-2.01)
NPL t-1*Overall Efficiency (middle tercile)		-0.066					
		(-1.09)					
NPL t-1*Overall Efficiency (upper tercile)		-0.047					
		(-0.59)					
NPL t-1*Availability dimension Efficiency (middle tercile)			-0.175*				-0.053
			(-1.87)				(-1.34)
NPL t-1*Availability dimension (uppertercile)			-0.079				0.107
			(-1.47)				(1.50)
NPL t-1*Continuation dimension (middle tercile)				-0.035			-0.020
				(-0.39)			(-0.15)

	(1)	(2)	(3)	(4)	(5)	(6)	(7)
NPL t-1*Continuation dimension (upper tercile)				0.139**			0.144
				(2.14)			(1.20)
NPL t-1*Cost dimension (middle tercile)					-0.082		-0.094
					(-1.33)		(-0.98)
NPL t-1*Cost dimension (upper tercile)					-0.059		-0.015
					(-0.76)		(-0.12)
NPL t-1*Restructuring dimension middle tercile)						-0.047	-0.177**
						(-0.83)	(-2.72)
NPL t-1*Restructuring dimension upper tercile)						-0.140*	-0.255***
						(-1.77)	(-3.16)
Constant	0.373*	0.360	0.386*	0.387*	0.396*	0.333	0.356
	(1.79)	(1.58)	(1.84)	(1.87)	(2.01)	(1.34)	(1.46)

t statistics in parentheses

* p < 0.1, ** p < 0.05, *** p < 0.01

Table 14.4 Estimation Results for the Error-Correction Model of the Nonperforming Loans Rate Augmented With Preventive Restructuring Framework Indices

	Dependent Variable: Change in NPL Rate in Year t						
	Baseline	Version 1	Version 2	Version 3	Version 4	Version 5	Version 6
ΔNPL t-1	0.126	0.128	0.124	0.104	0.095	0.134	0.073
	(1.53)	(1.53)	(1.49)	(1.28)	(1.14)	(1.64)	(0.86)
Δ(Debt/GOS) t-1	-0.054**	-0.054**	-0.055***	-0.053***	-0.050**	-0.056***	-0.052**
	(-2.61)	(-2.59)	(-2.67)	(-2.65)	(-2.43)	(-2.73)	(-2.53)
GDP growth rate t-1	1.239**	1.242**	1.245**	1.276**	1.185*	1.291**	1.208**
	(2.02)	(2.01)	(2.03)	(2.14)	(1.96)	(2.13)	(1.99)
Error-correction term	-0.626***	-0.622***	-0.586***	-0.697***	-0.507***	-0.626***	-0.521***
	(-11.29)	(-8.62)	(-8.18)	(-10.34)	(-6.19)	(-8.53)	(-3.55)
Error-correction Term*Overall efficiency (middle tercile)		0.003					
		(0.03)					
Error-correction term*Overall efficiency (upper tercile)		-0.025					
		(-0.21)					
Error-correction term*Availability dimension Efficiency (middle tercile)			-0.029				0.080
			(-0.24)				(0.58)
Error-correction term*Availability dimension (upper tercile)			-0.120				0.038
			(-1.13)				(0.20)

	(1)	(2)	(3)	(4)	(5)	(6)	(7)
Error-correction term*Continuation dimension (middle tercile)				-0.027 (-0.20)			-0.094 (-0.40)
Error-correction term*Continuation dimension (upper tercile)				0.254** (2.42)			0.109 (0.70)
Error-correction term*Cost dimension (middle tercile)					-0.214** (-2.06)		-0.231 (-1.36)
Error-correction term*Cost dimension (upper tercile)					-0.126 (-1.00)		0.068 (0.31)
Error-correction term*Restructuring dimension (middle tercile)						0.080 (0.79)	-0.029 (-0.21)
Error-correction term*Restructuring dimension (upper tercile)						-0.178 (-1.42)	-0.309* (-1.73)
Constant	0.241*** (7.55)	0.240*** (7.40)	0.241*** (7.51)	0.249*** (7.95)	0.248*** (7.74)	0.241*** (7.63)	0.261*** (8.06)

t statistics in parentheses

* p < 0.1, ** p < 0.05, *** p < 0.01

Source: My calculations. Estimated in two steps on a panel of EU countries with country fixed effects

are included in the specification (last column), the 'restructuring' dimension again becomes the only significant factor increasing the adjustment of the NPL rate to the long-term value. The coefficient signs of the other dimensions cannot be directly interpreted, as estimation error is high.

Taken together, the results of both specifications suggest that better ex ante and ex post possibilities to restructure debtors' liabilities appear to improve the reactivity of the NPL rate to changes in economic conditions and its subsequent normalization.

14.6.2   *Impact of Corporate Deleveraging on Economic Activity*

We now turn to analyzing the effect of preventive restructuring frameworks on the relationship between corporate deleveraging and overall economic activity. The generalized and necessary deleveraging process currently taking place in the corporate sector may affect domestic demand for several years, as firms keep investment, labor expenses, and dividend payouts at subdued levels (Ruscher & Wolff, 2012). This deleveraging process could be facilitated by well-functioning insolvency frameworks, especially if combined with incentives to use other options, including out-of-court procedures and early rescue mechanisms (IMF, 2013a).

To assess whether early restructuring possibilities affected the macroeconomic outcomes of corporate deleveraging in the recent period, we estimate a panel data model of GDP growth for EU member states over the period of 2007–2012. Specifically, we regress GDP growth on previous years' GDP growth and the change in the stock of outstanding corporate debt divided by the stock of previous periods' total financial assets (similar results are obtained using gross operating surplus). The estimated equation is

$$gdpgr_{it} = \alpha + \beta\, gdpgr_{it-1} + \gamma + \gamma_1 tercile2_i + \gamma_2 tercile3_i\, delev_{it} + \varepsilon_{it},$$

where the deleveraging variable is next interacted with tercile indicators of efficiency of early restructuring frameworks. A similar specification, although with a higher autoregressive order, was used by Cerra and Saxena (2008) to study the effects of financial and political crises on economic activity. This enables the differentiation of the degree by which corporate deleveraging affects GDP growth depending on the degree of efficiency of the preventive restructuring framework.

The results reported in Table 14.5 point to a significant negative relationship between corporate deleveraging and GDP growth (the first column shows that a reduction by one percentage point in the ratio of debt to financial assets is associated with around 0.36 percentage points lower GDP growth). This effect is significantly lower in member states belonging to the upper tercile of the overall efficiency indicator (for which a deleveraging by one percentage point is associated with about 0.23 percentage points lower GDP growth). The interactions with individual dimensions of

Table 14.5 Estimation Results for the GDP Growth Model Augmented With Preventive Restructuring Framework Indices

		Dependent Variable: GDP Growth Rate in Year t					
	Baseline	Version 1	Version 2	Version 3	Version 4	Version 5	Version 6
GDP growth rate t-1	-0.188***	-0.093	-0.067	-0.102	-0.112	-0.072	-0.129
	(-3.08)	(-1.23)	(-1.06)	(-1.49)	(-1.70)	(-1.16)	(-1.66)
(ΔNFC debt t) / Total financial assets t-1	0.361***	0.379***	0.325***	0.423***	0.336***	0.354***	0.325***
	(4.71)	(6.27)	(4.42)	(6.56)	(4.08)	(6.05)	(4.55)
((ΔNFC debt t) / Total financial assets t-1) * Overall efficiency (middle tercile)		0.042					
		(0.33)					
((ΔNFC debt t) / Total financial assets t-1) * Overall efficiency (upper tercile)		-0.147**					
		(-2.48)					
((ΔNFC debt t) / Total financial assets t-1) * Availability dimension Efficiency (middle tercile)			0.030				0.031
			(0.37)				(0.38)
((ΔNFC debt t) / Total financial assets t-1) * Availability dimension (upper tercile)			-0.060				0.027
			(-0.63)				(0.22)
((ΔNFC debt t) / Total financial assets t-1) * Continuation dimension (middle tercile)				-0.213***			-0.158
				(-3.63)			(-1.15)
((ΔNFC debt t) / Total financial assets t-1) * Continuation dimension (upper tercile)				-0.193**			-0.125
				(-2.67)			(-0.92)

(Continued)

Table 14.5 (Continued)

	Dependent Variable: GDP Growth Rate in Year t						
	Baseline	Version 1	Version 2	Version 3	Version 4	Version 5	Version 6
((ΔNFC debt t) / Total financial assets t-1) * Cost dimension (middle tercile)					0.135 (1.52)		0.102 (1.56)
((ΔNFC debt t) / Total financial assets t-1) * Cost dimension (upper tercile)					-0.121 (-1.52)		-0.092 (-0.80)
((ΔNFC debt t) / Total financial assets t-1) * Restructuring dimension (middle tercile)						-0.085 (-1.12)	0.089 (0.83)
((ΔNFC debt t) / Total financial assets t-1) * Restructuring dimension (upper tercile)						0.060 (0.50)	0.195 (1.22)
Constant	-0.006** (-2.45)	-0.006* (-2.00)	-0.005* (-1.80)	-0.006* (-1.93)	-0.006* (-1.86)	-0.006* (-1.94)	-0.007** (-2.08)

t statistics in parentheses

* $p < 0.1$, ** $p < 0.05$, *** $p < 0.01$

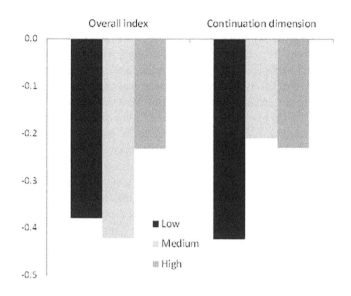

Figure 14.8 Effect of 1 pp. Corporate Deleveraging (Debt/Assets) on GDP Growth by Pre-Insolvency Efficiency Terciles

the efficiency index seem to suggest that the overall effect is mostly driven by the 'continuation' dimension, although none of the dimensions is significant if all dimensions are taken together (last column). These effects are summarized in Figure 14.8, where the overall effect of a corporate deleveraging by one percentage point is separately presented by efficiency terciles. Economies in the highest efficiency tercile appear to be less sensitive to changes in corporate indebtedness (the sensitivity is about half that in the lowest tercile).

14.7 Conclusions

In the current economic situation characterized by private-sector deleveraging and subdued internal demand for many EU member states, insolvency frameworks, and, in particular, preventive insolvency, may represent a key policy area of intervention with a potential to increase financial stability, to mitigate the impact of private sector deleveraging on growth, and to foster entrepreneurship.

To empirically assess the validity of these claims, we analyzed the member states' legislative frameworks applicable in October 2013 on preventive insolvency, restructuring, and debt discharge alongside twelve sub-indicators, each catering for a major efficiency-related dimension. Subsequently, these sub-indicators were pooled according to their common informational content into four aggregate composite indicators reflecting (i) the availability of preventive restructuring procedures, (ii) the absence of short-term constraints on firms' activity, (iii) direct and indirect costs associated with preventive procedures (including reputational, financial, and administrative costs), and (iv) effective restructuring chances and early warning systems.

Based on the constructed indicators of efficiency of the national preventive insolvency frameworks, the potential economic impact of measures enhancing efficiency has been analyzed with panel analysis techniques, focusing on the effect on self-employment rates and the effect on outcomes of corporate deleveraging. These are important economic dimensions given that (i) self-employment can be regarded as a proxy for general entrepreneurship and (ii) corporate deleveraging episodes have significant repercussions on financial soundness and economic activity. For the member states that have recently undergone a change in their preventive insolvency legislative frameworks, the values prior to the reform have been considered for the empirical analysis.

As regards entrepreneurship, the aggregate index of efficiency of the preventive insolvency framework is found to have a significant positive impact on self-employment rates, particularly driven by the 'continuation' dimension. These results are in line with the economic prior, that more efficient preventive insolvency frameworks– in particular the absence of short-term constraints on operations (e.g., remaining in possession of the assets and possibilities for stay of proceedings) – should foster the willingness to take on economic risk and start an economic activity. The results on deleveraging and financial stability indicate that the 'restructuring' factor is positively associated with speedier adjustment of the NPL rates—i.e., to their swifter reaction and subsequent normalization following a negative macroeconomic shock. Also, the negative relationship between corporate deleveraging and GDP growth appears to be significantly lower in member states characterized by more efficient preventive insolvency frameworks, mostly driven by the 'continuation' dimension.

Notes

1 Acknowledgments: We would like to thank for helpful comments and suggestions Anne Bucher, Isabel Grilo, João Nogueira Martins, and Alessandro Turrini.
2 Debt overhang indicates that the existing debt is too high to borrow more, even when this would be economically convenient.
3 On 22 November 2016, the European Commission adopted a proposal for a Directive of the European Parliament and of the Council on preventive restructuring frameworks, second chance and measures to increase the efficiency of restructuring, insolvency and discharge procedures and amending Directive 2012/30/EU. The proposal is a follow-up to the 2014 Recommendation.
4 With the exception of Bulgaria.

5 Recommendation C(2014)1500 at http://ec.europa.eu/justice/civil/files/c_2014_1500_en.pdf.

6 In this respect, some involvement of courts ensures fairness and respect of the procedure, whereas a full involvement is generally seen as reducing the speed and efficiency of the outcome.

7 The last indicator on the discharge period has been designed based on the conclusions of the 2011 Competitiveness Council and hereby considered in light of its relevance for the possibility of a second chance for entrepreneurs. Although affecting natural persons rather than companies, it has been included in the set of indicators because of its relevance for small entrepreneurs.

8 It is worth noting that, whereas increasing values of the ordinal variable by construction reflect increasing efficiency of the pre-insolvency framework (from a minimum of 0 to a maximum ranging between 2 and 4, depending on the number of cases considered to be relevant for the specific dimension of the pre-insolvency framework) based on expert assessment, this does not necessarily imply increasing values of the underlying variable of reference. For instance, looking at the 'length of moratorium' dimension, whereas the lowest efficiency score (0) is assigned to the absence of any stay of enforcement actions, the second lowest score (1) is assigned to a stay that is assessed as being too long compared to the 'optimum' length (two to four months), to which the maximum score (3) is then assigned.

9 The underlying data are reported in Table 14.6 in the annex.

10 In Germany, the 2012 reform made restructuring possible before the company was insolvent (yet in imminent insolvency) and provided that the debtors remain in possession of their assets, facilitated new financing, and reduced the role of courts. In Italy, the latest reform of 2012 improved the possibilities for a majority approval of the restructuring plan. In Latvia, the 2010 reform made restructuring possible at an earlier stage, when the business is in financial difficulties, eased the conditions for accessing the procedure, and increased the possibilities for negotiations to be run in confidentiality. In Portugal, a reform took place in 2012, introducing a new restructuring procedure (PER) as an alternative to the pre-existing hybrid procedure (SIREVE). In Spain, an early restructuring procedure was introduced in 2009 and reformed in subsequent years, mainly to improve the conditions for majority decision.

11 More specifically, high levels of income tax (for employees) and lower levels of capital gains tax (for entrepreneurs' shares in their business) have been found to be robustly associated with greater incidence of entrepreneurship (this general result holds both in single-country and cross-country studies).

12 Countries selected based on data availability. The analysis has been carried out excluding Italy, Portugal, and Spain from the sample in order to take into account the idiosyncrasies related to the determinants of self-employment hinted by Armour and Cumming (2008). This does not fundamentally change the findings. Results are available upon request.

13 Please refer to OECD, Indicators of Employment Protection—Annual Time Series Data 1985–2013 at www.oecd.org/employment/protection. The exact indicator used, also to ensure full coverage of the MS in the sample, is the *eprc_v2* version, obtained as the weighted sum of sub-indicators concerning the regulations for individual dismissals (weight of 5/7) and additional provisions for collective dismissals (2/7), with twelve detailed data items.

14 The increase in the self-employment rate is given in percentage change, as opposed to percentage points, because of the used semi-log specification.
15 The dummy for the lower tercile is not included to avoid perfect multicollinearity.

References

Adler, B., Polak, B., & Schwartz, A. (2000). Regulating consumer bankruptcy: A theoretical inquiry. *Journal of Legal Studies, 29*(2), 585–613.

Armour, J., & Cumming, D. (2008). Bankruptcy law and entrepreneurship. *American Law Economic Review, 10*(2), 303–350.

Ayotte, K. M. (2007). Bankruptcy and entrepreneurship: The value of a fresh start. *Journal of Law, Economics, and Organization, 23*(1), 161–185.

Baird, D. G., & Morrison, E. R. (2005). Serial entrepreneurs and small business bankruptcies. *Columbia Law Review*. Retrieved from http://dx.doi.org/10.2139/ssrn.660301

Becker, B., & Ivashina, V. (2014). Cyclicality of credit supply: Firm level evidence. *Journal of Monetary Economics, 62*, 76–93.

Bigus, J. (2006). Staging of venture financing, investor opportunism and patent law. *Journal of Business Finance & Accounting, 33*(7–8), 939–960.

Cerra, V., & Saxena, S. C. (2008). Growth dynamics: The myth of economic recovery. *American Economic Review, 98*(1), 439–457.

Claessens, S., & Laeven, L. (2003). Financial development, property rights, and growth. *The Journal of Finance, 58*(6), 2401–2436.

Cuerpo, C., Drumond, I., Lendvai, J., Pontuch, P., & Raciborski, R. (2015). Private sector deleveraging in Europe. *Economic Modelling, 44*, 372–383.

Davydenko, S., & Franks, J. (2008). Do Bankruptcy codes matter? A study of defaults in France, Germany and the U.K. *Journal of Finance, 63*(2), 565–608.

Djankov, S., Hart, O., McLiesh, C., & Shleifer, A. (2008). Debt enforcement around the world. *Journal of Political Economy, 116*(6), 1105–1149.

Djankov, S., McLiesh, C., & Shleifer, A. (2007). Private credit in 129 countries. *Journal of Financial Economic, 84*, 299–329.

European Union, European Commission. (2014a). *Commission recommendation on a new approach to business failure and insolvency*. Retrieved from http://ec.europa.eu/justice/civil/files/c_2014_1500_en.pdf

European Union, European Commission. (2014b). *Impact assessment accompanying the document 'commission recommendation on a new approach to business failure and insolvency.'* Retrieved from http://ec.europa.eu/justice/civil/files/swd_2014_61_en.pdf

European Union, European Commission Enterprise and Industry Expert Group. (2011). *A second chance for entrepreneurs: Prevention of bankruptcy, simplification of bankruptcy procedures and support for a fresh start*. Retrieved from http://ec.europa.eu/DocsRoom/documents/10451/attachments/1/translations/en/renditions/native

Fan, W., & White, M. (2003). Personal bankruptcy and the level of entrepreneurial activity. *Journal of Law and Economics, 46*, 543–567.

Fölster, S. (2000). Do entrepreneurs create jobs? *Small Business Economics, 14*(2), 137–148.

Georgakopoulos, N. L. (2002). Bankruptcy law for productivity. *Wake Forest Law Review, 37*, 51–95.

Gompers, P. A., & Lerner, J. (1998). Venture capital distributions: Short-run and long-run reactions. *Journal of Finance, American Finance Association, 53*(6), 2161–2183.

International Monetary Fund. (2013a). *Indebtedness and deleveraging in the Euro Area, Article IV Consultation Selected Issues Paper* (IMF Country Report No. 13/232). Retrieved from https://www.imf.org/external/pubs/ft/scr/2013/cr13232.pdf

International Monetary Fund. (2013b). *Global financial stability report: Transition challenges to stability*. Retrieved from http://www.imf.org/External/Pubs/FT/GFSR/2013/02/

Jackson, T. H. (1985). The fresh-start policy in bankruptcy law. *Harvard Law Review, 98*(7), 1393–1448.

Kaminsky, G., & Reinhart, C. (1999). The twin crises: The causes of banking and balance of payments problems. *American Economic Review, 89*(3), 473–500.

Landier, A. (2004). *Entrepreneurship and the stigma of failure* (Working Paper). New York: NYU Stern School of Business.

La Porta, R., Lopez de Silanes, Shleifer, A., & Vishny, R.W. (1997). Trust in large organizations. *American Economic Association, 87*(2), 333–338.

Lee, S. H., Peng, M. W., & Barney, J. B. (2007). Bankruptcy law and entrepreneurship development: A real options perspective. *Academy of Management Review, 32*(1), 257–272.

Lerner, J. (2002). 150 years of patent protection. *American Economic Review, 92*(2), 221–225.

Nkusu, M. (2011). *Nonperforming loans and macrofinancial vulnerabilities in advanced economies* (International Monetary Fund WP/11/161). Retrieved from https://www.imf.org/external/pubs/cat/longres.aspx?sk=25026.0

OECD. (2008). *Handbook on constructing composite indicators: Methodology and user guide*. Brussels: OECD publications.

Parker, S. C., & Robson, M. T. (2003). *Explaining international variations in entrepreneurship: Evidence from a panel of OECD countries* (Working Paper). Durham: University of Durham.

Pearce, J. A., & Robbins, D. K. (2008). Strategic transformation as the essential last step in the process of business turnaround. *Business Horizons, 51*(2), 121–130.

Poterba, J. M. (1989). *Venture capital and capital gains taxation* (NBER Working Paper No. 2832). Retrieved from http://www.nber.org/papers/w2832

Poutziouris, P., Chittenden, F., & Michaelas, N. (2000). *Modelling the tax burden on the UK small company sector: A simulation model*. International Symposium of Tax Compliance Costs, the University of New South Wales, Australia.

Rinaldi, L., & Sanchis-Arellano, A. (2006). *What explains household nonperforming loans? An empirical analysis* (ECB Working Paper No. 570). Retrieved from https://www.ecb.europa.eu/pub/pdf/scpwps/ecbwp570.pdf?2546b8e00ce934b13cfe47c36da5bc45

Ruscher, E., & Wolff, G. (2012). *Corporate balance sheet adjustment: Stylised facts, causes and consequences*. Economic Papers 449. European Economy: Brussels. doi:10.2765/25700

Stam, E., Audretsch, D., & Meijaard, J. (2006). *Renascent entrepreneurship: Entrepreneurial preferences subsequent to firm exit* (Working Paper). Retrieved from https://ideas.repec.org/p/esi/egpdis/2006-06.html

ANNEX

Table 14.6 Efficiency Scores in Twelve Aspects of Pre-Insolvency Frameworks in the EU28, Detailed Values

Country	Dimensions of Pre-insolvency Efficiency				Aggregate Indicator
	Easiness/ Availability	Facilitations to Continuation of Operations	Direct and Indirect Costs	Debt Sustainability	Pre-insolvency Efficiency
AT	0.12	0.03	0.27	0.04	0.45
BE	0.26	0.16	0.03	0.14	0.58
BG	0.00	0.00	0.00	0.05	0.05
CY	0.25	0.03	0.08	0.15	0.51
CZ	0.00	0.25	0.06	0.07	0.38
DK	0.03	0.10	0.06	0.20	0.39
EE	0.20	0.10	0.08	0.12	0.49
FI	0.11	0.14	0.06	0.23	0.54
FR	0.23	0.13	0.11	0.20	0.67
DE	0.15	0.15	0.11	0.20	0.61
EL	0.14	0.25	0.21	0.12	0.72
HU	0.03	0.22	0.00	0.05	0.30
IE	0.12	0.18	0.03	0.11	0.44
IT	0.23	0.25	0.24	0.09	0.81
LV	0.23	0.10	0.16	0.12	0.61
LT	0.14	0.10	0.08	0.09	0.41
LU	0.17	0.10	0.11	0.12	0.49
MT	0.20	0.07	0.08	0.08	0.43
NL	0.14	0.07	0.03	0.22	0.46
PL	0.14	0.10	0.08	0.12	0.43
PT	0.23	0.21	0.24	0.14	0.82
RO	0.23	0.14	0.13	0.11	0.61
SK	0.03	0.10	0.05	0.11	0.28
SI	0.13	0.10	0.03	0.10	0.36
ES	0.17	0.23	0.15	0.08	0.63
SE	0.20	0.15	0.11	0.19	0.65
UK	0.28	0.19	0.15	0.22	0.85
HR	0.03	0.15	0.08	0.06	0.32

Source: My calculations. Note: Higher values of the indicators imply higher efficiency

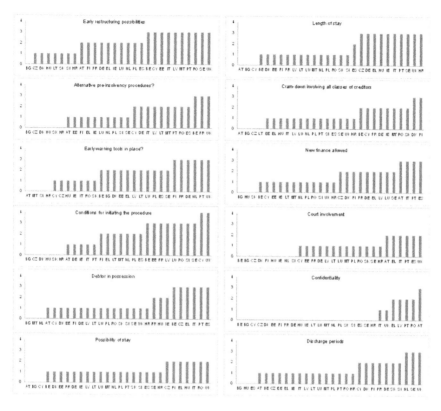

Figure 14.9 Efficiency Scores in Twelve Aspects of Pre-Insolvency Frameworks in the EU28, Bar Charts

15 An Overview of the Pre-Insolvency Procedures in the United Kingdom and South Africa

Alexandra Kastrinou and Lézelle Jacobs

15.1 Introduction

In light of the ongoing economic turmoil, the creation of a corporate rescue culture has been evolving in Europe as well as in other jurisdictions across the world. Great emphasis has been placed on rescue at an early stage, and it appears that more and more rescue is attempted at a pre-insolvency stage so as to enhance the likelihood of a successful reorganization (Frisby, 2006). The aim of this chapter is to consider the pre-insolvency procedures available in the United Kingdom and South Africa. In particular, the chapter provides an overview of the CVA procedure and the schemes of arrangement in the United Kingdom, as well as the Business Rescue and the Compromise procedures in South Africa.

In addition, the chapter aims to provide an overview of the approach taken in both jurisdictions toward less formal restructurings by the 'key players' in insolvency, such as insolvency practitioners and secured creditors, as well as the courts. In conclusion, the chapter considers the effectiveness of the aforementioend restructuring mechanisms in the two jurisdictions and assesses whether these promote and encourage a corporate rescue culture.

15.2 The Advantages of Early Stage Intervention

Although various formal and informal steps may be taken in order to give effect to a successful rescue, it is submitted that a traumatized company will often benefit from intervention before it gets to the stage of actual insolvency. In fact, it has been noted that most rescues are achieved through informal or less formal rescue—that is, rescue without recourse to the formal insolvency proceedings (Finch, 2009). Less formal, pre-insolvency rescue mechanisms have a variety of advantages for the ailing company. From a director's and also a shareholder's perspective, engaging in less formal rescue is preferable, as it prevents any adverse publicity in relation to the company's financial troubles and hence protects its goodwill and reputation (Finch, 2009). It could be argued that, by pursuing less formal rescue, the company can effectively avoid the stigma that is attached to corporate failure and that the realizable value of its assets can be protected (Finch, 2009).

Moreover, one could argue that less formal rescue is not as costly as formal insolvency proceedings, because the involvement of the court is very limited. In addition, because there is little court involvement in pre-insolvency rescue, one could argue that the process is more flexible.

Furthermore, as opposed to completely informal reorganization,[1] a semi-formal reorganization under the company voluntary arrangement in the United Kingdom could prove more effective, as far as consent is concerned, because an approval in excess of 75% in value would suffice. Arguably, the fact that there is no need to obtain the consent of all the creditors under a CVA avoids the flaws and challenges of informal rescue (Payne, 2014), as obtaining consent from dissenting creditors could prove to be a time-consuming and expensive course of action.[2] In the South African context, it is also worth noting that regardless of who initiates the rescue proceedings, the business rescue will only continue if the creditors accept the business rescue plan. Of course there is no need for a unanimous vote of acceptance, and the Companies Act 71 of 2008, therefore, provides that the plan will be accepted if it was supported by the holders of more than 75% of the creditors' voting interest[3] and the votes in support of the plan included at least 50% of the independent creditors' voting interest.[4] The South African business rescue proceedings thus also bind a dissenting minority.

It could be argued that early intervention is a key for successful corporate rescue. Accordingly, the insolvency law regimes of both the United Kingdom and South Africa make provision for early intervention proceedings. These proceedings are being increasingly used before the technical moment of insolvency and are 'colonizing' the area formerly occupied by formal insolvency procedures. For instance, in the United Kingdom, procedures are in place, which are designed to encourage an early stage intervention by the existing management, such as the Scheme of Arrangement, which is one of the oldest rescue devices in the world and the CVA procedure, which was introduced following the recommendations of the "Cork Report."[5] In South Africa directors are also encouraged to initiate business rescue proceedings as soon as possible; in order to assist the board of directors from allegations of abuse of process, the Act widened the definition of 'financial distress' by introducing a six-month time period. The new mixed management displacement model in South Africa also encourages directors to initiate proceedings sooner.[6]

15.3 Pre-Insolvency Proceedings: A United Kingdom Perspective

15.3.1 *The Development of a Corporate Rescue Culture in the United Kingdom*

A financially ailing company may have to resort to a range of mechanisms in the United Kingdom, such as informal workouts, a company voluntary arrangement, a Scheme of Arrangement, or administration. Arguably, the presence of such a wide range of reorganization proceedings demonstrates the significance attached to business recovery in this jurisdiction. However, it was not until relatively recently that the United Kingdom established its sophisticated corporate rescue culture.

Prior to the enactment of the Insolvency Act 1986 (IA 86), there were only two formal possible ways of keeping 'alive' a business in trauma—namely, through the use of the administrative receivership procedure or a scheme of arrangement. Nonetheless, the application of administrative receivership was conditional upon the exercise of the right of a floating charge holder to appoint an administrative receiver. Additionally, corporate rescue by means of a scheme of arrangement was particularly limited, mainly because the procedure was too "procedurally cumbersome and failed to safeguard sufficient and effective protection for the company" (Parry, 2004).

In 1985, by means of a text, later reenacted as the IA 86,[7] two additional procedures were introduced as alternative means for corporate rescue—namely, the administration procedure and the company voluntary arrangement ('CVA'). The innovative reforms introduced by the IA 86 originally had their roots in the 1982 report of the Cork Committee,[8] which recognized the need to strengthen the United Kingdom's corporate rescue regime. The "Cork Report" stated that a "good, modern system of insolvency law should provide a means for preserving viable commercial enterprises capable of making a useful contribution to the economic life of the country" (Finch, 2009). However, not all of the Cork Committee's proposals were embodied in the subsequent legislation, and even those that were had their importance diluted. In particular, the administration procedure suffered from significant inherent flaws detrimental to the original intention of promoting a collective approach toward the rescue of ailing businesses.[9] Furthermore, although the CVA appeared to be a promising 'debtor-in-possession' reorganization tool, it was not fully embraced by practitioners.

However, the Enterprise Act 2002 together with the Insolvency Act 2000 contributed significantly to the development of a corporate rescue culture in the United Kingdom. It could be argued that the Enterprise Act introduced revolutionary changes to the rescue culture of the United Kindom by virtually abolishing administrative receivership, streamlining the administration procedure, and transforming it into an effective rescue devise. In addition, the Insolvency Act 2000 introduced key reforms to the CVA procedure so that the CVA now constitutes an important part of the current trend in shifting the ethos of the United Kingdom's insolvency law toward effective corporate rescue.

15.3.2   An Overview of the CVA Procedure

As discussed earlier, the CVA was introduced primarily with the aim of promoting corporate rescue. The objective of the CVA is to facilitate the rehabilitation of a financially troubled company by enabling it to reach a contractual compromise with its creditors. The CVA may be used as a stand-alone procedure or it may be combined with another procedure, such as administration. In other words, the procedure may be initiated either by the company's directors or by an administrator. Although the CVA may be effectively used as an exit route from administration, strictly speaking, it is not a formal insolvency procedure, as it is not necessary for the company to be insolvent or show that it is unable to pay its debts in order to enter into a CVA.

Where the CVA is initiated as a freestanding procedure, the existing management of a company is able to take early action by drafting a reorganization proposal and presenting it to the company's creditors. The directors[10] are also entrusted with the implementation of the proposal under the supervision of a licensed insolvency practitioner, known as the 'nominee' prior to approval of the proposal and as the 'supervisor' after approval.[11]

15.3.3   Drafting the Proposal

Forming the proposal is a key stage of the reorganization process. The directors form the proposal,[12] which, inter alia, states the reasons why the company's directors believe that a CVA is desirable, presents the company's assets and their value, details assets charged in favor of creditors, provides the nature and the amount of the company's liabilities, indicates the duration of the CVA, includes the dates of distributions to creditors; and shares the identity and the remuneration of the insolvency practitioner of the proposed nominee/supervisor.[13]

The steps that directors must take in forming and implementing a CVA proposal depend on whether or not the protection of a moratorium is sought.[14] Arguably, one of the most significant reforms the CVA has been subject to is the introduction of provisions enabling a moratorium to be obtained while the CVA is being proposed (Parry, 2008). However, notwithstanding the introduction of a reformed CVA, it could be said that the impact of the procedure has been limited. An obvious contributing factor to the limited use of the CVA could arguably be the fact that a moratorium is only available to 'small companies.'[15] However, because large companies can still benefit from a moratorium (if one is necessary) by simply entering into administration proceedings, the lack of it under the CVA has not been identified as a major flaw by insolvency practitioners. In addition, it could be argued that the use of the CVA has been relatively limited due to the fact that the procedure has been overshadowed by the streamlined administration procedure (Parry, 2008).

15.3.4   The Role of the Nominee

The nominee has a very important role to serve, as he must establish whether or not the company is able to implement a CVA proposal. Accordingly, the nominee must present a report to the court stating whether in his opinion meetings of the company and its creditors should consider the proposal.[16] In order to be able to assess the company's suitability and to prepare his report, the nominee must receive a copy of the proposal from the directors,[17] a statement of the company's affairs,[18] and any other information he requires.[19]

15.3.5   Creditors' Approval of the CVA

The nominee shall summon meetings of the company and its creditors[20] in order to either approve (with or without modifications)[21] or reject the proposed CVA. After the conclusion of either meeting, the chairman of the meeting shall report the result of the meeting to the court, and, immediately after reporting to the court, shall give notice of the result of the meeting to such persons as may be prescribed.[22]

It is significant to note that, for voting purposes, the CVA treats all creditors as one single class Fletcher (2004), in contrast to the scheme of arrangement. All creditors who receive notice of a creditors' meeting can vote on a CVA[23] draft. In order for the CVA to become effective, it needs to be approved by the requisite majority at the meeting.[24] The CVA is treated as a statutory contract,[25] which bounds every person who was eligible to vote at the meeting regardless of whether they were present or not and whether they voted in favor or against the proposed arrangement.[26] Following the approval of a CVA, the nominee becomes the supervisor.[27]

A key drawback of the CVA procedure is its vulnerability to claims of unfair prejudice to the interest of a creditor or member under the approved CVA. In addition, the CVA is vulnerable to challenge on grounds of material irregularities. Such claims may be initiated by any person who would be eligible to vote at the meeting, or any person who would have been entitled to vote had they had notice of the meeting. In any case, no challenge can be made after a period of twenty-eight days (a) beginning with the first day on which the chairman's required report has been made to the court, or (b) in the case of a person who was not given notice of the creditors' meeting, after the end of the period of twenty-eight days, beginning with the day on which he or she became aware that the meeting had taken place.[28]

15.3.6   Schemes of Arrangement

A scheme of arrangement is one of the oldest restructuring procedures available in the United Kingdom.[29] However, strictly speaking, a scheme is not an exclusive corporate rescue instrument, as it was primarily designed to be used by solvent companies. Accordingly, as the scheme is a creature of company law,[30] when compared to CVAs, it is not as stigmatized. Similarly to the CVA, a scheme enables a financially ailing company to reach a compromise with its creditors. However, in contrast to the CVA, the popularity of the scheme as a rescue device has been steadily rising over the last few decades (Parry, 2008),[31] and practitioners have favored the use of schemes in a number of high-profile debt restructuring cases.[32]

As previously stated, the scheme is a compromise between the company and its creditors, or between the company and its members. Similarly to the CVA, the company's directors remain in office and are responsible for the drafting and the execution of the restructuring plan. The process of implementing a scheme involves three distinct stages: a) formulation of the proposal and an application to the court, b) a creditors' meeting for approval of the scheme, and c) a 'sanction hearing' by the court.

15.3.7 Stage One

As part of stage one, the board of directors shall form the restructuring plan,[33] which is then proposed on behalf of the company to its members and creditors. Once a compromise/arrangement has been proposed, the company, by sending preliminary circulars,[34] shall inform its creditors or members about the objectives of the scheme as well as the relevant meetings (if more than one) the company aims to call. The company must also select the classes in which the creditors or members affected by the scheme should be placed and accordingly notify them. The division of classes depends on how similar[35] the rights of the members of each class are. However, it is not necessary that their rights are exactly the same.[36] Finally, stage one involves an application being made to the court, which will have to decide whether to make a 'meetings order.'[37]

15.3.8 Stage Two

Stage two involves a meeting of creditors or members who will decide whether to approve the scheme. However, it is required that, prior to the meeting, sufficient information must be circulated so as to enable the creditors to reach an informed decision.[38] As mentioned earlier, the approval of a scheme of arrangement involves a complex voting structure under which, for voting purposes, creditors are divided into classes, and it is required that a reorganization arrangement be approved by a majority vote of all classes of creditors.[39]

In comparing the complex approval process of a scheme to the much simpler process of a CVA, it could be argued that restructuring by means of a CVA should be preferable. Nevertheless, the simplicity aspect of the CVA is outweighed by the fact that, once an arrangement becomes binding under the scheme, it binds all creditors (including dissenting creditors), whereas an agreement reached under the CVA is only binding upon creditors who were eligible to vote, or who would have been eligible to vote if they had received notice of a creditors' meeting. In addition, it is important to note that, under a scheme of arrangement, it is not necessary to consult any class of creditors who have no real economic interest in the company, hence their votes on the scheme may be disregarded.[40] This is a significant advantage of a scheme, as it provides greater finality than a CVA, which is vulnerable to challenges on the grounds of unfair prejudice (Parry, 2008, p. 233).

15.3.9   *Stage Three*

Stage three involves a 'sanction hearing,' where the court will consider whether or not to sanction the scheme (Parry, 2008, p. 236). Once the scheme has obtained the required level of approval, it must be sanctioned by the court and the court's order takes effect once a copy of it is delivered to the Registrar of Companies.[41] It should be noted that the sanctioning of the scheme is not a simple rubber-stamping exercise. Instead, the court may not sanction a scheme even where it has received the approval of creditors (Payne, 2014), as it must be satisfied that the classes were fairly represented by the parties who attended the meeting (Parry, 2008, p. 238), and that the terms of the scheme are fair (Parry, 2008, pp. 239–247). In addition, the court has discretion to refuse to sanction a scheme, unless it is convinced that all the procedural requirements have been complied with.[42]

It is argued that the requirement that a scheme of arrangement has to be approved by the court is a significant advantage of the procedure, because once the arrangement has been court approved, it cannot be challenged by the company's creditors or its members. It could be argued that this might be one of the primary reasons why such schemes seem to be more popular than the CVA, as a CVA may be challenged on the grounds of unfair prejudice (Parry, 2008, p. 233).

15.4   Pre-Insolvency Proceedings: A South African Perspective

A very large premium has been placed on retaining jobs and businesses in South Africa (Burdette, 2004b), and as it is an emerging market economy, an efficient rescue system is of the utmost importance. South Africa's Companies Act 71 of 2008 heralded a new era of corporate rescue for financially distressed corporations by replacing the largely unsuccessful judicial management procedure (Burdette, 2004b; Snyman-van Deventer & Jacobs, 2014). Chapter 6 of the Act dealing with business rescue and compromises also replaces the section on compromises and arrangements contained in the previous Companies Act of 1973.[43] Thus the Act currently provides for two pre-insolvency proceedings: the business rescue procedure and the compromise with creditors.

Both of the mechanisms contained in Chapter 6 provide a debtor in financial distress with access to corporate reorganization in order to try and circumvent insolvency. The business rescue provisions can be regarded as a more traditional type of procedure that can be likened to the administration procedure under the English Enterprise Act (Klopper & Bradstreet, 2014). Under business rescue, the company's management is displaced by an independent third party known as the business rescue practitioner. Even though the management is displaced, the directors are not removed from office and stay on in order to assist the practitioner in his or her duties; this is done under the supervision of the practitioner.[44] The compromise provisions provide for an alternative option with less involvement from the court and practitioners; in this sense, it is reminiscent of the U.S. Chapter 11 debtor in possession, in that the debtor is able to stay in control of its affairs, although it is a simpler provision than the Chapter 11 procedure.[45] This mechanism provides for a more flexible framework and can even be utilized by companies that are not experiencing financial distress.

Although the new corporate rescue procedures in South Africa are more informal than under the previous act, the procedures that are currently available to distressed companies are still more formal than informal in nature because they are highly regulated by legislation. Informal creditor workouts are rarely heard of, nor are they documented (Harvey, 2011). The Chapter 6 mechanisms are less formal, because the involvement of the courts have been limited, whereas the involvement of other stakeholders has been broadened. A discussion on the development of a rescue culture as well as an overview of the two reorganization options will now follow.

15.4.1 Rescue Culture

South Africa is still struggling with a liquidation culture despite the fact that South Africa now has modern rescue provisions to aid failing debtors. The process of moving toward a rescue culture is happening very slowly. This liquidation culture emanates from South Africa's prevailing creditor-friendly approach to insolvency matters (Burdette, 2004a; Parry, 2008, p. 244).[46] It is, however, of importance to mention that even though the shift is happening at a very slow pace, it is indeed happening. In recent years, since the inception of the Companies Act of 2008, there has been more emphasis on the protection of the interests of all the relevant stakeholders. It has even been stated by the court that business rescue is to be preferred to the liquidation of the company and that the old mind-set of the creditor being almost entitled to a winding-up order as a right was inappropriate.[47] One of the biggest hurdles to overcome in creating a rescue culture in South Africa is the larger creditors—e.g., the banks who are, to a large degree, very reluctant to participate in, or even support, the rescue proceedings because of the aforementioned reasoning. And although creditors still play an overwhelming role in the outcome of reorganization procedures (Loubser, 2008), there seems to be a shift to a more inclusive approach to the rescue of a company, albeit at a very slow pace.

15.4.2 Business Rescue

According to section 7 of the Act, one of the main purposes thereof is to provide for the efficient rescue and recovery of financially distressed companies in a manner that balances the rights and interests of all relevant stakeholders.[48]

The Act provides for proceedings to facilitate the rehabilitation of a company that is financially distressed by providing for the temporary supervision of the company and the management of its affairs, business, and property; a temporary moratorium on the rights of claimants against the company or in respect to property in its possession; and the development and implementation, if approved, of a plan to rescue the company.[49]

The first topic to discuss in this regard pertains to the concept of imminent insolvency in a South African context. When will a company be regarded as being in financial distress? It is a well-known fact that time is of the essence in corporate reorganizations. Section 128 of the Act states that a company will be deemed to be financially distressed if it appears to be reasonably unlikely that the company will be able to pay all of its debts as they become due and payable within the immediately ensuing six months,[50] or if it appears to be reasonably likely that the company will become insolvent within the immediately ensuing six months.[51] The adding of the six-month time period encourages the early commencement of business rescue, which in turn maximizes the chance of a successful rescue. The formulation of the concept of financial distress in the Act also refers to commercial and factual insolvency at a future date, thus implying that business rescue should not be utilized by companies that are already insolvent. South African courts agree with this and have at numerous occasions denied applications for the initiation of business rescue where the companies are insolvent and not in financial distress.[52]

The initiation of the procedure can happen either voluntarily by way of a company resolution or by application to the High Court by an affected person. An affected person is defined in the Act as a shareholder or creditor of the company, any registered trade union representing employees of the company, and any employees of the company not represented by a trade union.[53]

The commencement standard that applies depends on the party that initiates the rescue process, providing for different requirements for when the debtor initiates to when an affected person applies to court for an order placing the company under business rescue. This is a positive development,[54] as it also allows for different evidential burdens taking the circumstances-and-information position of the different role players into account. The new requirements for initiating business rescue are seen as an improvement to the requirements under the previous Companies Act of 1973. Some believe that the evidential burden imposed by the previous Act was unrealistic, outdated, and excessive, and resulted in rescuable companies being denied a lifeline. Others argue that the courts wrongly interpreted judicial management as an extraordinary remedy only to be granted in exceptional circumstances (Burdette, 2004a; Parry, 2008, pp. 248–249).

Under the business rescue model, a company may voluntarily initiate rescue proceedings and place the company under supervision, by taking a resolution, if the board has reasonable grounds to first, believe that the company is financially distressed and second, that there appears to be a reasonable prospect of rescuing the company.[55] An affected person, on the other hand, may apply to court to make an order placing the company under supervision and commencing business rescue proceedings if the court is satisfied that the company is financially distressed; the company has failed to make an employment-related payment arising from a regulatory or contractual obligation, or if it is otherwise just and equitable to do so for financial reasons; and there is a reasonable prospect for rescuing the company.[56] The court's involvement has, therefore, been limited at the commencement of the proceedings. The debtor is fully aware of its own financial situation and would be the most appropriate judge to decide when to make use of rescue provisions (Burdette, 2004b). A rescue mechanism that relies heavily on the involvement of the court is expensive and therefore contradictory to the aim of helping the company in dire financial straits.

The most problematic requirement for South African courts to date has been the need for a reasonable prospect of rescue to exist (Pretorius, 2015). This is mainly due to the fact that the meaning of 'successful rescue' is a contentious issue and will depend on the viewpoint from which it is regarded and also because there is no way in which to determine the viability of the debtor company. According to the Act, a successful rescue could include returning the company to solvency or alternatively bringing about a better return for the company's creditors and shareholders than would result from the immediate liquidation of the company.[57]

After the commencement of the proceedings, the appointment of the business rescue practitioner should take place. If the company initiates the proceedings, the practitioner will be appointed by the board of the company.[58] If, however, an affected person initiates the procedure, the applicant to court would nominate a practitioner, and the court would appoint an interim practitioner, subject to the ratification by the creditors.[59] The practitioner is a key role player in the rescue procedure, and the duty to rescue the company falls on his or her shoulders. It is for this reason that the practitioner should be suitably qualified and experienced in order to perform all that is expected of him or her.

According to the 2008 Companies Act, a practitioner should be a member of the law, accounting, or business management profession.[60] The regulations to the act furthermore stipulate that a practitioner should have experience in "business turnaround practice."[61] The 2008 Act places more emphasis on the experience of the business rescue practitioner than its predecessor. Practitioners are, therefore, divided into three categories: senior practitioners, experienced practitioners, and junior practitioners. For large and state-owned companies, only senior practitioners may be appointed. For medium companies, senior and experienced practitioners may be appointed, but not junior practitioners, etc.[62] This clearly indicates that the legislature wanted to make sure that only the most experienced practitioners are appointed in the larger and more difficult rescue situations in order to optimize the chances of a successful rescue of the company. Apart from being suitably qualified and experienced, the practitioner also needs to be of good character and integrity,[63] and be independent and objective.[64] The duties of the practitioner include taking control of the management of the debtor company, undertaking an investigation into the financial affairs of the company, and the drafting and implementation, if approved, of a business rescue plan. In order to assist the practitioner in performing these duties, the Act affords him or her with a wide array of powers, including the power to obtain post-commencement financing and suspending certain contracts or parts thereof.[65]

The drafting, acceptance, and implementation of a business rescue plan are among the most important aspects of a modern rescue model (Kloppers, 1999; Snyman-van Deventer & Jacobs, 2014). The business rescue plan is one of the greatest improvements in respect to the South African rescue model. By having to propose, accept, and implement a business rescue plan, the restructuring of the business could occur much sooner, with the added benefit that certainty with regard to the outcome of the rescue is created for all parties concerned (Burdette, 2004b). The business rescue plan will be considered at a meeting of affected persons and voted on by the company's creditors. The shareholders will only be allowed to vote if the plan alters the rights attached to their shares. At this meeting, the rescue practitioner must present the proposed rescue plan to the creditors and shareholders to afford them the opportunity to consider it.[66] The practitioner must also use this opportunity to inform the parties of whether he still believes that there is a reasonable prospect of the company being rescued.[67] The creditors and shareholders may then discuss and raise arguments about the plan as well as cast any vote on a motion regarding the amendment of the plan or the adjournment of the meeting to afford the practitioner time to revise the plan based on their recommendations.[68] When a vote is called, the proposed business rescue plan will be approved if the plan received support from the holders of more than 75% of the creditors' voting interests that were voted,[69] and if the votes in support of the proposed plan included at least 50% of the independent creditors' voting interests, if any, that were voted.[70] A business rescue plan approved in the aforementioned ways is binding on the company, each of the creditors of the company, and each holder of company securities, whether that person was present at the meeting or voted in favor of the plan.[71] This means that the vote will also bind the minority of dissenting creditors.

Another important aspect to consider regarding business rescue pertains to the automatic 'stay' or moratorium that becomes effective upon commencement of the proceedings. The moratorium on claims from creditors provides the debtor company with some breathing room in order to try and facilitate the rescue procedure (Burdette, 2004b). For the duration of the business rescue proceedings, no legal proceeding against the company, or in relation to any of the company's property, may be commenced or proceeded with in any forum, except with the written consent of the practitioner or with leave of the court and in accordance with any terms the court deems suitable.[72]

The termination of the business rescue proceedings can happen in a number of ways. In terms of section 132, the proceedings will come to an end if the court sets aside the company's resolution to place the company under rescue,[73] or if the court has converted the proceedings to liquidation proceedings.[74] The practitioner can also terminate the rescue by filing a notice of termination.[75] In the event that the business rescue plan is rejected, the proceedings will also come to an end.[76] The proceedings will also end when the practitioner files a notice of substantial implementation of the plan.[77]

15.4.3 *Compromise*

The alternative procedure provided for in the Act is the section 155 compromise with creditors.[78] In the case of a compromise with creditors, the debtor company will remain entirely in possession and no practitioner will be appointed in order to assist the company. This type of procedure envisages some element of commercial give and take and accommodation on both sides. That is between the company and its creditors.

The board of a company may propose an arrangement or a compromise of its financial obligations to all of its creditors, or to all of the members of any class of its creditors, by delivering a proposal to every creditor and the Commission. The company must, therefore, develop its own plan for 'rescue.' The prescribed contents of the plan for a compromise are similar to those of the business rescue plan.[79] The proposal will then be voted on by all of the creditors or the class of creditors and will only be adopted if supported by a majority in number, representing at least 75% in value of the creditors or class, as the case may be.[80]

The section 155 compromise or arrangement under the Companies Act of 2008 replaces the old section 311 procedure of the previous Act. Like the previous procedure, the section 155 compromise also provides for the court to sanction a compromise that was reached between the company and the majority of its creditors (Klopper & Bradstreet, 2014). The wording of the Act does, however, create uncertainty regarding the need for the court to sanction the proposal: "The company may apply to court for an order approving the proposal."[81] The wording creates the impression that it is up to the company to decide whether or not to approach the court for an order approving the proposal or not (Klopper & Bradstreet, 2014). It does, however, seem as though the purpose of the provision was for the company to guarantee that any dissenting creditors are in fact bound by the compromise. Where the creditors unanimously agree to the proposed plan, no court sanction will be needed, because section 155(8)(c) provides that the order of court sanctioning a compromise is 'final and binding' on all of the company's creditors or all of the members of the relevant class of creditors.[82]

The section 155 compromise is, therefore, still heavily reliant on creditor involvement despite this procedure being primarily debtor driven. It also has certain drawbacks, making the process one that is rarely used. The compromise does not afford the debtor company or other stakeholders with the same protection, for example, as a moratorium against claims and proceedings against the company as the business rescue procedure does. The procedure could therefore be improved upon by incorporating some form of moratorium or stay (as is afforded under business bescue). It could also be an expensive procedure if the debtor has to apply to court for an order sanctioning the proposal.

15.5   Conclusion

In the United Kingdom, the first step toward the establishment of a corporate rescue culture was made, following the Cork Committee's proposals, by means of reforms, which led to the enactment of the Insolvency Act 1986. In addition, the Enterprise Act 2002 introduced revolutionary changes to the existing restructuring regime of the United Kingdom and importantly promoted a 'second-chance culture' in a traditionally regarded 'creditor-friendly' jurisdiction. Finally, it has been argued that the United Kingdom's current insolvency laws, in particular its restructuring and business rescue regime, are performing well in comparison with their international peers.

Corporate rescue in South Africa still has a long way to go in creating a rescue system that is truly reflective of a robust rescue culture. This is despite the fact that public opinion suggests support for the Chapter 6 provisions and even regards them as job-saving mechanisms. The buy-in of the larger creditors continues to be of paramount importance in moving toward the 'second-chance culture' that already exists in the United Kingdom. South Africa has taken remarkable strides in transforming its corporate rescue sphere, and the progress that it has made is laudable.

Notes

1 Where a reorganization process is of a contractual nature, hence there is great reliance on a consensus being achieved with the creditors.
2 It could be said that a formal procedure, such as the company voluntary arrangement in the United Kingdom, could prove more effective, as far as consent is concerned, because an approval in excess of 75% in value would suffice. A Part 26, Companies Act 2006 scheme of arrangement could also be used for solvent entities, which would have the same effect.
3 Companies Act 71 of 2008, section 152(2) (a).
4 Ibid, section 152(2)(b). An independent creditor is described in section 128(1) (g) as a person who is a creditor of the company, including an employee of the company who is a creditor in terms of section 144(2) and a creditor who is not related to the company, a director or the practitioner.

5 The *Report of the Insolvency Law Review Committee, Insolvency Law and Practice*, Cmnd 858 (1982, HMSO, London).

6 Companies Act 71 of 2008: Section 137(2) (a)-(c) and 140 (1) (a). Under business rescue, the company's management is displaced by an independent third party known as the business rescue practitioner. Even though the management is displaced, the directors are not removed from office and stay on in order to assist the practitioner in his duties; this is done under the supervision of the practitioner.

7 The Insolvency Act 1985 was consolidated as the Insolvency Act 1986.

8 *Report of the Review Committee on Insolvency Law and Practice*, (Cmnd. 8558, 1982) ("Cork Report").

9 For instance, although upon his appointment the administrator was granted significant powers (in fact, his powers were as extensive as those of an administrative receiver), such as the power to impose a freeze on crucial creditors' remedies and the enforcement of security, he was nevertheless unable to prevent the appointment of an administrative receiver. Accordingly, it was always possible for a debenture holder to block administration by appointing an administrative receiver.

10 It should be noted that although the CVA is described largely as a 'debtor in possession' regime, in practice the directors heavily rely on the insolvency practitioner to both draft and execute the proposal.

11 It is important to note that the insolvency practitioner must remain independent from the outset and throughout the implementation of the CVA process. See Statement of Insolvency Practice 3, para 3.2.

12 Insolvency Act 1986, s 1(1).

13 See Insolvency Rules 1986, r.1.3. (1)—(8).

14 Where directors intend to apply for a moratorium, the procedure that must be followed is stated in s.2 IA 1986, supplemented by the Insolvency Rules 1986, Part 1 Chapter 2. Where a moratorium is not required, the procedure is outlined in IA 1986 Schedule A1.

15 See s.382(3) of the Companies Act 2006, which states that a company qualifies as small in relation to a subsequent financial year if it satisfies at least two of the following 'qualifying conditions': a) its turnover does not exceed £6.5 million, b) its balance sheet total is not more than £3.26 million, and c) it has no more than fifty employees.

16 Insolvency Act 1986, s 2 (2).

17 Insolvency Act 1986, s 2(3); Insolvency Rules 1986 r.1.4. (1), (2).

18 Insolvency Rules 1986 r.1.5.

19 Insolvency Rules 1986 r.1.6.

20 Sch. A1 Insolvency Act 1986, para.29.

21 Sch. A1 Insolvency Act 1986, para.31.

22 Sch. A1 Insolvency Act 1986, para. 30(3).

23 Persons who are not entitled to vote at the meeting are not bound by the CVA. See s.5(2) Insolvency Act 1986.

24 Insolvency Rules 1986 r.1.19: More than three-quarters in value of the creditors voting on the resolution must vote in favor of the arrangement.

25 *Johnson* v *Davies* [1999] Ch.117, 129H-130A.

26 Sch. A 1 of the Insolvency Act 1986, s.37.

27 Sch. A 1 of the Insolvency Act 1986, s.39 (2).

28 Sch. A 1 of the Insolvency Act 1986, s.38 (3).

29 It dates back to the Joint Stock Companies (Arrangement) Act 1870.

30 The statutory regime relating to schemes is set out in Part 26 of the Companies Act 2006.

31 See also Finch (2009), p. 486, where it is argued that the revived popularity of schemes of arrangement may be because of the courts "constructive attitude, to facilitate the implementation of schemes by means of assessing junior creditors" "real economic interests."

32 Such as Crest Nicholson plc, McCarthy & Stone plc, Wind Hellas Telecommunications SA, and European Directories Group.

33 Although the appointment of a qualified insolvency practitioner is not necessary, typically, directors seek the advice of restructuring experts at this early stage.

34 However, compliance with this requirement may be waived by the court in exceptional cases. See for instance *Marconi Corp Plc v Marconi Plc* [2003] EWHC 663.

35 The interests of creditors in each class should not be so dissimilar so as to make it impossible for them to consult together with a view to their common interest. See *Sovereign Life Assurance Co v Dodd* [1982] 2 QB 573, 583; and *Re BTR Plc* [1999] 2 BCLC 575.

36 *Re Osiris Insurance Ltd* [1999] 2 BCLC 182.

37 At the hearing, the court will consider whether the company has appropriately identified the classes, which will have to consider the scheme. See *Re Hawk Insurance Co Ltd* [2002] BCC 300.

38 See Companies Act 2006, s 897

39 See Companies Act 2006, s 899, which states if a majority in number representing 75% in value of the creditors or class of creditors or members or class of members (as the case may be), present and voting either in person or by proxy at the meeting summoned under section 896, agree to a compromise or arrangement, the court may, on an application under this section, sanction the compromise or arrangement. However, see also Charles Maunder, "Bondholder Schemes of Arrangement: Playing the Numbers Game" (2003)16(10) Insolv. Int. 73–77, 76, where it is argued that if the majority in number requirement was removed, schemes of arrangement would be more flexible and attractive restructuring tools.

40 See *Re Tea Corp.* [1904] 1 Ch. 12. See also *Re My Travel Group Plc* [2004] EWHC 2741; [2005] 1 WLR 2365, where the basis of valuation of entitlements caused some contention. See also Finch (2009), p. 486 and Parry (2008), p. 236.

41 Companies Act s.899 (1) & (4)

42 *Alabama, New Orleans, Texas and Pacific Junction Rly Co* [1891] 1 Ch. 213, 245.

43 Companies Act 61 of 1973.

44 Companies Act 71 of 2008: sec 137(2)(a)-(c) and 140 (1)(a).

45 Ibid, 553.

46 *Southern Palace Investments 265 (Pty) Ltd v Midnight Storm Investments 386 Ltd* 2012(2) SA 423 (WCC); *Oakdene Square Properties (Pty) Ltd v Farm Bothasfontein (Kyalami) (Pty) Ltd* 2012(3) SA 273 (GSJ): 276.'By law the creditor of an ailing company had a right *ex debito justitiae* (as of right) to liquidate the company.'

47 *Southern Palace Investments 265 (Pty) Ltd v Midnight Storm Investments 386 Ltd* 2012 2 SA 423 (WCC)

48 Companies Act 71 of 2008: sec 7(k).
49 Ibid at section 128(1)(b)(i)-(iii).
50 Ibid at section 128(1)(f)(i). Referring to the so-called cash flow test for insolvency.
51 Ibid at section 128(1)(f)(ii). Referring to the so-called balance sheet test for insolvency.
52 *Gormley v. West City Precinct Properties (Pty) Ltd* (Unreported case). "It must either be unlikely that the debts can be repaid within 6 months or that the company will go insolvent within the ensuing 6 months. In this case the company is presently insolvent and cannot pay its debts unless a moratorium of 3–5 years is granted. The facts of this matter does not bring West City's financial situation within the definition of 'financially distressed.'" See also *Wellman v Marcelle Props* 193 2012 JDR 0408 GSJ: 12. "In my view, Business Rescue proceedings are not for the terminally ill close corporation." *Southern Palace Investments 265 (Pty) Ltd v Midnight Storm Investments 386 Ltd* 2012 2 SA 423 (WCC). *African Banking Corporation of Botswana v Kariba Furniture Manufacturers* (228/2014) [2015] ZASCA 69. "Suffice it to say that the company was clearly hopelessly insolvent and effectively dormant in that it had not traded for years and had no business contacts in place."
53 Companies Act 71 of 2008 section 128(1)(a)(i)-(iii).
54 Under 1973 Companies Act, only one set of requirements was applicable regardless of who was initiating the rescue procedure.
55 Companies Act 71 of 2008 section 129(1).
56 Companies Act 71 of 2008 section 131(4)(a)(i)-(iii).
57 Companies Act 71 of 2008 section 128(1)(b)(iii).
58 Companies Act 71 of 2008 section 129(3)(b).
59 Companies Act 71 of 2008 section 131(5).
60 Companies Act 71 of 2008 section 138(1)(a).
61 Regulations to the Companies Act 71 of 2008 regulation 127.
62 Regulations to the Companies Act 71 of 2008 regulation 127(2)(c)(i)-(iii).
63 Regulations to the Companies Act 71 of 2008 regulation 126(4)(a).
64 Companies Act 71 of 2008 section 138(1)(e).
65 Companies Act 71 of 2008 section 135 and 136.
66 Companies Act 71 of 2008 section 152(1)(a).
67 Companies Act 71 of 2008 section 152(1)(b).
68 Companies Act 71 of 2008 section 152(1)(c), (d)(i)-(ii).
69 Companies Act 71 of 2008 section 152(2)(a).
70 Companies Act 71 of 2008 section 152(2)(b)
71 Companies Act 71 of 2008 section 152(4).
72 Companies Act 71 of 2008 section 133(1)(a)-(b).
73 Companies Act 71 of 2008 section 132(2)(a)(i).
74 Companies Act 71 of 2008 section 132(2)(a)(ii).
75 Companies Act 71 of 2008 section 132(2)(b).
76 Companies Act 71 of 2008 section 132(2)(c)(i).
77 Companies Act 71 of 2008 section 132(2)(c)(ii).
78 Companies Act 71 of 2008 section 155.
79 Companies Act 71 of 2008 section 155(3).
80 Companies Act 71 of 2008 section 155(6).
81 Companies Act 71 of 2008 section 155(7)(a).
82 Companies Act 71 of 2008 section 155(8)(c).

References

Burdette, D. (2004a). Some initial thoughts on the development of a modern and effective business rescue model for South Africa [Part 1]. *South African Mercantile Law Journal*, *16*(2), 241–263.

Burdette, D. (2004b). Some initial thoughts on the development of a modern and effective business rescue model for South Africa [Part 2]. *South African Mercantile Law Journal*, *16*(2), 409–447.

Finch, V. (2009). *Corporate insolvency law: Perspectives and principles.* Cambridge: Cambridge University Press.

Fletcher, I. F. (2004). UK corporate rescue culture: Recent developments-changes to administrative receivership, administration and company voluntary arrangements—The insolvency act 2000, the white paper and the enterprise act 2002. *European Business Organizational Law Review*, *1*, 119–151.

Frisby, S. (2006). *Report on insolvency outcomes.* Londen, UK: Insolvency Service.

Harvey, N. (2011). *Turnaround management and corporate renewal: A South African perspective.* Johannesburg: Wits University Press.

Klopper, H., & Bradstreet, R. (2014). Averting liquidations with business rescue: Does a section 155 compromise place the bar too high? *Stellenbosch Law Review*, *25*(3), 549–565.

Kloppers, P. (1999). Judicial management—A corporate rescue mechanism in need of reform? *Stellenbosch Law Review*, *10*, 417–435.

Loubser, A. (2008). The role of shareholders during corporate rescue proceedings: Always on the outside looking in? *South African Mercantile Law Journal*, *20*, 372–390.

Parry, R. (2004). United Kingdom· Administrative receiverships and administrations. In K. Gromek-Broc & R. Parry (Eds.), *Corporate rescue in Europe: An overview of recent developments from selected countries in Europe* (pp. 145–177). Alphen aan den Rijn: Kluwer Law International.

Parry, R. (2008). *Corporate rescue.* Sweet & Maxwell.

Payne, J. (2014). *Debt restructuring in English law: Lessons from the United States and the need for reform.* Retrieved from http://dx.doi.org/10.2139/ssrn.2321615

Pretorius, M. (2015). *Companies and Intellectual Property Commission (CIPC) Status Quo Report.* CIPC.

Snyman-van Deventer, E., & Jacobs, L. (2014). Corporate rescue: The South African business rescue plan examined. *Nottingham Insolvency and Business Law e-Journal*, 103–115.

16 The Ethics of State Bankruptcy

Jukka Kilpi and Simon Elo

16.1 Introduction

When a state runs out of cash, the effects are felt around the world. This chapter examines the ethical issues that arise from sovereign insolvency. Our focus is on the problems related to the moral nature of sovereign debt and the just response to the default of a sovereign debtor. The aim is to establish whether state borrowers are bound by a moral obligation to pay their debts and also how insolvent sovereign powers should be treated.

The history of credit is as long as human history. Credit predates money. Indeed, it has been argued that money was introduced out of a need to measure and pay debts (Hawtrey, 1950, p. 2; Homer & Sylla, 1991, pp. 17–24; Wray, 1990, pp. 8–9). Credit represents a pattern of social behavior. As such, it is not infallible, but rather subject to human weaknesses and circumstantial conditions. There is no causal, let alone logical, necessity to ensure that what has been given as a loan will be repaid. To the contrary, default is a potential that is ever present.

The question of why debts should be paid cannot be answered, in the ethical sense at least, by saying that repayment is what the law requires. The law could just as well rule that debts should not be paid. Actually, this is the regime for the bankruptcy laws of many countries. In order to ethically justify debt enforcement, however, we have to go beyond positive law and offer moral reasons for the obligation to honor one's debts. A debt is most often legally a consequence of a contract. Fundamentally, a contract is a promise (Fried, 1981, pp. 16–17).

16.2 Debt as a Promise

The key to the moral obligation to pay a debt lies in the act of promising (Kilpi, 1998, pp. 51–64).[1] If we have a moral duty to keep our promises, that duty also applies to our contractual debts. This deduction thus infuses debt with ethics. Next, we may ask on what the moral binding of promises is based? The answers to this question vary depending on their association with the major traditions of moral philosophy.

The three most interesting theories of promising are utilitarian ethics, emphasizing the usefulness of promise keeping, deontological ethics connecting promises to the autonomous will and moral agency of a person, and contractual thinking explaining promises as social conventions. Without examining these theories in detail, we may conclude that none of them challenges, *prima facie*, the moral principle that promises should be kept. This unanimity, not so common in philosophy, is a good reason to accept the view that contracts, as a species of promises, do contain moral obligations.

Promises should be kept, therefore debts should be paid. A moral agent's financial failure and that agent's subsequent incapacity to fulfill promises do not undermine the morally obligatory nature of promising. Now we face the core dilemma of the ethics of bankruptcy: what to do with an insolvent debtor? Is the discharge of his debts ever justifiable?

16.3   The Ethics of Bankruptcy

We have a duty to keep our promises and pay what we owe. However, an insolvent person or entity may not be able to keep that promise. A problem emerges and, in the case of natural persons and corporations, it becomes the task of bankruptcy laws to solve that problem. The solution involves reorganization of the relationship between debtor and creditor. That solution may end a corporation's existence, whereas natural persons must continue to live even as bankrupts.

Two legal traditions part ways in how to treat personal bankruptcy. The Anglo-American culture lays the emphasis on debtor protection. An honest insolvent's debts are promptly discharged to give that person a fresh start in life. Many European countries, however, have chosen another path. They uphold a creditor's rights until the debtor's death. Lately, these two traditions have begun to converge as debt reorganization schemes have been introduced in continental Europe as another option for insolvent natural persons.

Those who oppose bankruptcy laws that protect debtors are afraid of the erosion of social and commercial morality. Are they right to fear this outcome? In the United States, the advantage of bankruptcy varies from one state to another, because the states have the power to legislate on the amount of exempt property (i.e., property not distributable to creditors). Experience has shown that larger exemptions do not increase the susceptibility to bankruptcy (Sullivan, Warren, & Westbrooke, 1989, p. 241). Another finding is that in those states where personal bankruptcy rates are high, creditors' losses do not rise in the same proportion (Shuchman, 1973, p. 433). This research supports the fact that bankruptcy is the last resort for the poor, not an easy safe haven for fortune seekers. People do not find it any easier to file for bankruptcy if it leaves them with a few thousand more in assets, nor do forced down bankruptcy numbers guarantee lower losses to creditors.

The empirical evidence suggests that hardships imposed on honest debtors do not bring any benefits. In addition, it seems unlikely that such benefits would be obtained if austerity measures were put in place just to scare crooks. The identification of bankruptcy with crime is a delusion. In Canada, a maximum of 2.4% of business bankruptcies may involve fraud (Sutherland, 1988,

p. 924), and in the United States, the figure has the same magnitude (Altman, 1971, p. 24; Stanley & Girth, 1971, pp. 111–112). Likewise, in personal bankruptcies, dishonesty is a rare factor (Sullivan et al., 1989, p. 329). The suggestion that harsh laws are justified because they may reduce fraud falls short of the mark, because bankruptcy is not exploited by profiteers and crooks to any significant extent. Fraud deserves punishment, but that moral precept does not justify deterrents that punish all bankrupts collectively.

What, then, is the ethical justification for wiping out debts? First, bankruptcy laws providing relief from unbearable debts are ethically just laws in the utilitarian sense. Little benefit accrues to any of the parties involved if an honest insolvent is denied a discharge. Second, deontological ethics, when looking at insolvency from the perspective of autonomy, supports discharge as well. A bankrupt is overwhelmed by his liabilities. His autonomy withers away if he is nothing but a debtor. The solution is to treat him as a person and grant him a discharge. The idea of a fresh start safeguards the bankrupt's autonomy—a human characteristic that has a moral worth similar to that assigned to an individual's body and life. A promise that will destroy the autonomy of the promisor and the morally relevant essence of his human nature is null and void in the moral sense.

The ethics of bankruptcy uncovers the issuance of a discharge in personal bankruptcy as an inalienable human right. As far as corporations are concerned, rights are more a matter of expediency, but an ethical analysis does not raise any obstacles to corporate reorganization that gives an insolvent company a chance to put its finances back in order.

How is it with a sovereign bankruptcy then? To find the answer, we need to look at what kind of debtors states are. Should we treat them differently as moral agents making promises because they do have legislative powers?

16.4 The State as Moral Agent

There is little doubt among philosophers that persons are moral agents. Recently, wide agreement suggests that corporations are moral agents too, although most ethicists do attach qualifications such as 'ascribed' or 'secondary' to corporate moral agency. Kenneth Goodpaster (1993) and Patricia Werhane (1985) are renowned American business ethicists whose theories recognize our ascription of responsibility to corporations and establish corporate agency and social responsibility, but fall short of granting a corporation fully independent personhood. According to these philosophers, it is rational to project ethical responsibility onto corporations, as all corporate actions cannot be reduced down to the actions of individuals. However, these projections do not turn corporations into full persons but rather give them what Werhane calls secondary autonomy and personhood, which is sufficient to make corporations also ethically responsible for their actions.

The state's moral agency has received surprisingly little attention from philosophers, despite philosophy abounding with theories on the state's origin and functions. Sovereign states are the supreme legislators in their own territories. Bankruptcy laws do not bind them. Are they moral agents? Do states have a moral obligation to comply with international law? No, they do not, according to contemporary legal theorists Mary Maxwell (1990) and Eric Posner (2003), who instead explain a sovereign's obligations in terms of evolutionary processes and self-interest.

Our view is that there is indeed a strong analogy between the state and the corporation. We have good reason to consider both as secondary moral agents. The corporate moral agency emanates from the contractual basis. Modern jurisprudence, economics, and business ethics share the view that a corporation is a nexus of contracts (Kilpi, 1998, pp. 172–176). It is a legal fiat that gains its personality from a web of agreements and promises—tacit and explicit, oral and written.

The contracts that create corporations are promises and, therefore, contain moral obligations. Having been born from promises, a corporation extends the chain of morality initiated by the contracts that brought it into existence by paying respect to the universe of moral obligations within which that corporation exists. A corporation lives by its charter, and in doing so, it keeps generating new promises and honors the moral obligations they conceive. Thus a corporation is a moral agent with special characteristics that require the qualification 'secondary' to be attached to its agency.

In the same vein, in political philosophy, social contract theories offer good reasons to take the state as an agent that performs moral deeds and is bound by moral rights and duties. Here we set aside the question of the nature of the social contract. Regardless of whether a social contract is merely a theoretical explanatory construction or built on the explicit or tacit consent of the citizens, it remains a powerful philosophical argument for a civil state. If contractually based corporations are moral agents, then it is hard to see why a contractually based sovereign state would not also be a moral agent.

The social contract is the moral foundation of the state and its institutions, including those that are passing and enforcing laws. The moral entitlement to a sovereign's existence comes from those contracts, which are promises by their very moral nature. The state is created and kept alive as a contractual expression of moral autonomy, and it should abide by the moral nature of this expression to remain ethically justified as a sovereign. Thus a sovereign state is a secondary moral agent, and it is bound by a duty to keep its promises.

Although the state shares with corporations the hallmarks of secondary moral agency—contractual basis, capacity to actions that are distinct from citizens' actions, and ascriptions of responsibility to that agent for its actions—the state differs from corporations in one important respect. The existence of a state is necessary for humans. As noted earlier, it is widely agreed within the controversial multitude of philosophical views that there is always a moral duty to keep promises. Now we should pay attention to the fact that, in general, philosophers do also agree that a state is necessary for humans to coexist. Theorists may disagree on how powerful a state should be and what the relationship between a citizen and the sovereign is, but usually the state is seen as a necessary ethical good or at the very least an inevitable evil.

Our analysis has now reached the point where we can declare the state as a necessary contractually based secondary moral agent with supreme legislative powers. This view helps us answer how we should treat a bankrupt sovereign.

16.5   The Ethics of State Bankruptcy

In ordinary language, 'bankruptcy' stands for the inability to pay one's dues. It is commonly believed that sovereign states cannot go bankrupt. This is an error. A bankrupt is a debtor entity that cannot meet its financial obligations. Many states have gone bust (Kolb, 2011; Mitchener & Weidenmier, 2010), but there are no laws that currently govern the bankruptcy process for sovereign states. Reorganization of state assets and debt depends on voluntary contracting or unilateral decisions by the parties involved. What kind of ethics then applies to sovereign defaults?

A bankrupt individual's inalienable human rights turned out to be morally superior to his obligation to pay his overwhelming debt. Expediency and creditor interest count most when deciding whether an insolvent corporation will live on or be wound down. Like a corporation, the state is a secondary moral agent, but unlike a corporation, the state is necessary to humans. Thus the state's existence has intrinsic value in the same vein as the life and autonomy of a natural person has value. It is more important to safeguard the intrinsically valuable existence of the state than to continue to collect a sovereign's debts. This is the fundamental principle of the ethics of state bankruptcy.

At the same time, we should keep in mind that as a contractually based agency, the state has moral obligations. One of these obligations is the duty to stick to its promises, including debt contracts. In the financial markets, which are an area of human activity largely based on promises, absence of morale leads to a lack of mutual trust. Trust is needed to issue and trade bonds, so any shortfall of confidence means harsh market conditions and a higher price for credit. In the world of finance, credit establishes between the lender and the borrower a relationship inherently moral in character. This moral aspect is also reflected in the everyday language of finance. One needs only to consider the etymology, meaning, and use of terms such as 'credit,' 'bond,' and 'trust'. Without moral flavor, there is little trust, and without trust, bonds are vague and credit yields shoot higher.

The ethics of state bankruptcy rests on a principle that puts the priority on the state's existence and functioning over any full and timely settlement of overwhelming debt. On the other hand, it reminds us that sovereigns are also moral agents who are under an obligation to keep their commitments. This obligation stems from the state's contractually based moral agency in accordance with deontological ethics that rests on human autonomy, and utilitarian reasoning also supports it. The issuing of sovereign bonds is thus built on moral commitment.

The ethics of sovereign bankruptcy points toward the exoneration of states and peoples who suffer under an excessive debt burden. How has this suffering been treated in the course of history, what practical problems have emerged, and what reforms have been suggested to solve these problems?

16.6   The History of Sovereign Insolvency

The need to deal with bankruptcies in an orderly fashion has been recognized for thousands of years. Contemporary personal bankruptcy laws have direct links to the laws of ancient Rome. Corporate insolvencies have been handled in an organized manner for as long as corporate laws have been passed. Institutions that are clearing financial failures exist worldwide and have existed throughout history. The contents of such laws vary considerably, however. What does not vary is that bankruptcy as an institution has always been recognized as a necessary and greatly beneficial economic and administrative tool.

States have gone broke surprisingly often. Greece, perhaps the best-known contemporary sovereign in financial distress, was under international creditors' insolvency administration from 1898 to1932, until its economy's totally collapsed in the 1930s when the Great Depression started. The country only regained access to international financial markets in the 1960s (Kolb, 2011). In the case of sovereign bankruptcy, should we also have in place an institutional arrangement, a framework of international contracts and executive and judicial bodies, to reap the benefits of an organized bankruptcy process? Would we be better off if competent judges, trustees, and auditors settled sovereign financial failures and put them in the past without excessive stigma and reproach?

Since the 1950s, sovereign debt restructurings have been facilitated by international organizations, primarily the London Club, the Paris Club, and the International Monetary Fund (IMF). According to the IMF, more than 600 restructurings in 95 countries were accomplished worldwide between 1950 and 2010 (Das, Papaioannou, & Trebesch, 2012). Most were handled by the Paris Club and affected official lenders—i.e., states and multilateral institutions. For the remainder, the London Club played a pivotal role as the majority of that debt consisted of bank loans.

The big change in sovereign financing over the last twenty years has been the shift from official state-to-state and institutional lending to market-based bond finance. This change has introduced more complexity to sovereign debt restructuring and made it more difficult to find a way out of distress. The ownership and prices of sovereign bonds constantly change in the international financial markets. The de facto owner of a bond may be an unknown entity, and thanks to well-developed derivatives markets, its owner may not ever carry all or some of the risks normally related to bond ownership. In the contemporary world, organizing any voluntary debt restructuring based on talks between creditors and debtor may be an insurmountable task.

16.7 Practical and Legal Issues

16.7.1 Collective Action

Past voluntary restructurings have primarily been motivated by the collective action problem, which arises in the absence of any organized and transparent insolvency procedure. Individual creditors may then seek the maximal return to their investments by causing havoc to the debtor and other lenders. This peril was easier to fend off when lenders were mostly states and large banks. Collective action for the common good is now less feasible, as the transition to bond financing has added the numbers of lenders and made their identities opaque. The most striking example is the success of vulture funds that buy distressed bonds at heavily discounted prices and then start legal proceedings to collect a full-face-value payment from the debtor, or even from the haircut payments made to any creditors who are participating in a restructuring program. Another related problem is potential under-provision of new finance in a situation when the mutual distrust between creditors blocks the debtor's access to the markets. The common interest of creditors would be better served if they as a group agreed on terms for how the existing debt obligations would be treated and new finance granted.

16.7.2 Moral Hazard

Fear of moral hazard has slowed personal bankruptcy reform for decades in many parts of continental Europe, where discharge of overwhelming debts in a quick and expedient bankruptcy process is still unheard of, notwithstanding the fact that for more than a hundred years discharge has worked well in the Anglo-American legal systems. This fear, however, plays a role in sovereign insolvencies too. The warning made has been that statutory institutions with legal power to trim sovereigns' contractual debt obligations might increase the debtor moral hazard as debtors could more easily rely on discharge. On the other hand, it is claimed that bailouts induce lender moral hazard by encouraging reckless risk assessment (Rogoff & Zettelmeyer, 2002).

16.7.3 Necessity

We argued earlier that a state is a moral agent that is necessary for the well-being of its citizens. In jurisprudence, the 'necessity defense' makes the same point to justify "the non-performance of a state's obligations by invoking state of necessity, *force majeure*, or related legal concepts" (Reinisch & Binder, 2014, p. 115). This principle is codified in international law by the International Law Commission in its Articles on State Responsibility.

Reinisch and Binder point out that the necessity defense was invoked as early as 1912 in the Ottoman debt arbitration. The Ottoman Empire used it to justify the Empire's refusal to honor its outstanding debts to Czarist Russia.

In recent times, Argentina has used the state of necessity as a justification for its debt servicing measures. Reinisch and Binder have concluded that necessity may be a valid defense in litigation against an insolvent sovereign, but at best it is more of a temporary relief than a substitute for durable debt restructuring.

16.7.4   Fresh Start

The ethics of bankruptcy (Kilpi, 1998) established that persons are autonomous moral agents whose agency is threatened by overwhelming debts, and therefore, insolvent persons do deserve a discharge and a fresh start. As for corporations, it was found that their moral agency is more expedient and of a secondary nature, and therefore, bankrupt corporations may be liquidated. Our claim here is that a state's agency has intrinsic moral value that is analogous to a person's agency. This ethical finding supports our conclusion that an insolvent state should be given a fresh start.

Our view is shared by some influential academics and international organizations. The Nobel Laureate economist Joseph Stiglitz (2014) argues that a sovereign debt restructuring mechanism should ensure the same fairness for countries that bankruptcy laws ensure for individuals and corporations in the United States. This was also the key finding of the Commission of Experts on Reforms of the International Monetary and Financial System, which was appointed by the president of the United Nations General Assembly and chaired by Stiglitz (United Nations, 2009). With this background, it is not surprising that a fresh start for over-indebted states plays a central role in the *Roadmap and Guide for Sovereign Debt Workouts*, published by the United Nations Conference on Trade and Development (UNCTAD, 2015).

16.8   Contractual and Statutory Solutions

There is consensus that a laissez-faire run on the assets of a financially troubled sovereign is inefficient and even destructive. The traditional mechanisms to work a way out of distress are inadequate in the current financial universe, wherein the most important sovereign borrowing instruments are marketable bonds linked to derivatives markets and held by unknown investors. Two major lines of remedy have been suggested to deal with the issue: a contractual approach and a statutory approach.

The contractual approach suggests improvement in terms of the bonds as the solution to the collective action problems that are hampering the orderly and fair distribution of pain among all creditors and a return to financial sustainability of the insolvent debtor. Contractual remedies emphasize an orderly and regulated market's power to produce the best outcome. IMF has been the most eminent advocate of this contractual approach. In addition to changes to contractual terms in new sovereign bond emissions, IMF has pushed for policy adjustments that guide debtors to regain pecuniary independence through more disciplined budgets and 'haircuts' to reduce the face value of creditors' receivables.

The IMF, the London Club, and the Paris Club have succeeded in getting widespread inclusion of collective action clauses (CACs) and exit consents to the terms of recent sovereign bond emissions. These provisions are contractual majority voting mechanisms that stipulate that a majority of debtors can make decisions on haircuts and changes to loan terms so that these changes legally bind dissenting minority bondholders. In the euro area, collective action clauses have been mandatory for all new bond issues since 2013.

The statutory approach wants to go even further. It sees international institutions and conventions as being necessary to solve the conflicts that may remain after contractual means are exhausted. There are three ways to establish such statutory mechanisms to deal with sovereign debt problems: contractual clauses, legislation, and a treaty. First, contractual clauses could, in addition to CACs, include submission of debt restructuring to courts or arbitration bodies on the national or international level. Second, the jurisdictions in which bonds are issued could adopt legislation to set up a framework for sovereign insolvency proceedings. Third, multilateral treaties, or resolutions and conventions adopted in international organizations, can create institutions with the power to enforce sovereign bankruptcies legally.

The strength of the statutory approach is seen in the uniform and impartial appliance of legal principles to all parties and cases concerned. A particular advantage would be that an international bankruptcy court or arbiter with legally binding powers would have a mandate to declare a bankruptcy completed and the debt restructured, thus giving the debtor—and creditors too—a fresh start. With the contractual approach, the final aim is also the debtor's financial sustainability and credibility that makes a return to the bond markets possible. However, in contractual debt workouts, there is no such clear point of return to normal like a discharge is to bankrupt persons or a court order that ends insolvency is for corporations.

Inclusiveness is seen as a further benefit of statutory institutions with the legal power to oversee sovereign insolvencies. Voluntary and contractual debt restructuring now involves debtors and creditors, and at best certain international organizations such as IMF. Citizens and interest groups in the debtor country are excluded regardless of their being the stakeholders who bear the brunt of the financial ordeal and ultimately being in charge of the dues. It has been argued that this lack of citizen involvement speaks for having an international sovereign bankruptcy institution analogous to U.S. Chapter 9 municipal bankruptcy, which gives a role to citizen claims (Bohoslavsky & Černič, 2014).

The opponents of the statutory approach argue that too much regulation may deter creditors and drain the private finance sources. The U.S. Chapter 9 analogy has been criticized on the basis that although a sovereign can default on its contractual debt obligation, it is not possible to determine when a sovereign debtor is insolvent and what assets and liabilities should be included in that bankruptcy. It has also been said that any wide inclusion of stakeholder groups would slow down the debt resolution process.

Currently, we have ample experience with more or less successful voluntary debt restructurings. We also have a growing unanimity regarding the need to better manage them and widespread support of the creation of institutions to oversee their management. Next, therefore, we look at the main organizations that do play a role in this debate. What have they done already, and what has been proposed as their future role?

16.9   Organizations and Restructurings

16.9.1   *International Monetary Fund*

The IMF was created in 1945 under the auspices of the United Nations. It is a body of international cooperation designed to promote economic stability worldwide and in particular the stability of the system of exchange rates and international payments. IMF pursues this goal by monitoring national economies, advising governments, and providing funding to its members in financial trouble. Currently, IMF has 188 member states and is governed by those states whose share of influence in the decisions depends on their contributions to the organization's funds.

As the IMF's mission makes clearly obvious, the organization has been involved in most sovereign debt restructurings. So far, IMF's role has been the facilitator and advisor of voluntary multilateral negotiations and the lender of last resort. Here IMF's policy adjustment conditions—economic, political, and social measures seeking re-establishment of an insolvent sovereign's financial sustainability and setting the conditions for emergency funding—have played an important role.

Numerous IMF-guided restructurings have taken place over the decades. They have been criticized for being inefficient, unjust, or both. In the search for a better means to tackle the problems of growing and more complex sovereign financing, the world's frontline economists—for example, Jeffrey Sachs and Joseph Stiglitz—have advised IMF. Sachs (1995) recommended that IMF give up its role as the lender of last resort and instead assume the role of a bankruptcy court. This idea was taken further by IMF director Anne Krueger's (2002) suggestion that IMF create a Sovereign Debt Restructuring Mechanism (SDRM). Krueger's statutory approach toward handling sovereign insolvency received initial support from IMF's governing bodies. For over ten years, SDRM was at the forefront of the debate on how best to calm financial turmoil. It is still supported by Stiglitz (2015), who recently wrote that "The absence of a rule of law for debt restructuring delays fresh starts and can lead to chaos." Nevertheless, in a 2013 review, the IMF shifted the emphasis of its reform policy from SDRM to a more contractual and market-based approach (IMF, 2013). This change reflects the political disagreements that also surfaced in the United Nations' General Assembly in 2015. They are further discussed in that context in the following section.

16.9.2 The London Club and the Paris Club

The London Club and the Paris Club were gradually formed in the 1950s. Legally, they are informal networks of creditors whose purpose is facilitating sovereign debt restructurings. The London Club represents private lenders, usually banks, through Bank Advisory Committees led by the largest lender bank of the troubled debtor. The Paris Club is comprised of nineteen member states that represent government creditors who are also members of the OECD. The IMF and multilateral development banks participate in the Paris Club as observers.

These actors work in close cooperation for sovereign debt restructurings. Other official bodies such as the European Union (EU) may also be involved. Debts owed to the IMF and international institutions are usually regarded as preferred and thus excluded from restructuring. In the 1990s, the indebtedness of poor countries grew so large that more drastic measures than mere mitigation of loan terms were seen as being necessary to start development in the poorest countries. This view led the Paris Club to put forward the Highly Indebted Poor Countries Initiative (HIPC) in 1996 and the Multilateral Debt Relief Initiative in 2005. According to the IMF, by 2015, these initiatives had wiped out $75 billion of debt for the world's poorest countries (IMF, 2015). IMF's debt-forgiveness programs were further tied to the condition that any savings in debt servicing would be spent on antipoverty programs.

16.9.3 The United Nations

The IMF is an institution in the United Nations (UN) system, but recently, sovereign insolvency has received considerable attention in the United Nation's Conference on Trade and Development (UNCTAD) and the UN's General Assembly. The United Nations has criticized the working of existing debt restructurings on the basis that in their management creditors have too much power and only creditors and debtors are involved in the process. UNCTAD (2015) has published a proposal for sovereign debt workout process (SDWP). UNCTAD left open whether SDWP would include a sovereign debt restructuring tribunal with legal power, but the roadmap is clearly amenable to the statutory approach of handling sovereign insolvency.

The UN's General Assembly's resolution, adopted September 10, 2015, set forth nine principles for sovereign debt restructuring: sovereignty, good faith, transparency, impartiality, equitable treatment, sovereign immunity, legitimacy, sustainability, and majority restructuring (United Nations, 2015). Although this resolution does not directly speak for the establishment of a multilateral legal mechanism for sovereign debt restructurings, it does call for a change in the current creditor-led debt system. The political sensitivity of this issue was further reflected by the fact that the United States and the European Union voted against the resolution and boycotted the negotiations process preceding the General Assembly vote. Unlike the Security

Council, which has the power to issue legally binding resolutions, General Assembly resolutions are non-binding, but do carry political weight.

16.9.4   *The European Union*

The euro-area debt crisis that began in 2008 has forced the European Union (EU) and the European Central Bank (ECB) to take an active role in the management of sovereign insolvencies. Measures that have been implemented to safeguard the financial system and sustainability of national economies include direct emergency funding to troubled states from the EU and its financially healthier members, the creation of a special funding vehicle, the European Stability Mechanism (ESM), legislative measures to include CACs in the terms of sovereign bonds, haircuts in privately held bonds, adjustment policy conditions for indebted countries, and a loosening of the ECB's fiscal policies. At the time of the writing of this chapter, these measures have succeeded in staving off a systemic failure of the euro area, but it remains to be seen if they are sufficient for a return to a normal finance climate in Europe.

In the EU, the euro crisis has sparked a debate over the need for more established sovereign insolvency mechanisms. It has been suggested that European law should be introduced to regulate sovereign debt and that a strong European regime, such as the ESM once given even more power, should handle the administration of restructurings, haircuts, discharges, and terminations of state bankruptcies (Deutsche Bundesbank, 2015; German Council of Economic Experts, 2015). The European Commission's "Five Presidents' Report: Completing Europe's Economic and Monetary Union" (2015, p. 12) expresses the urgency of abolishing "bottlenecks preventing the integration of capital markets in areas like insolvency law, company law, property rights and as regards the legal enforceability of cross-border claims." In the European Parliament, the UN's September 2015 resolution has encouraged initiatives that ask the European Commission to put forward statutory measures as the solution for state bankruptcy. So far the Commission has been reticent to make a legislative move toward a European sovereign bankruptcy court—a clear indication of the political delicacy of the matter.

16.10   A Semi-Hard Proposal: The Vulturedove Fund

There is broad agreement that the current practices to handle sovereign insolvencies are not satisfactory. Disagreement prevails on whether contractual improvements in terms of loans and bonds are a sufficient fix or if international institutions with legal power should be created to manage them. The ethics of state bankruptcy offers no definite answers here. However, it may give some hints, and whatever these solutions are they should be compatible with the most fundamental guidelines that the ethics suggests. As this chapter is a result of a joint venture between a philosopher with a background in finance and a legislator, we do take here the liberty to venture into the contemporary sovereign insolvency debate and offer a practical proposal.

In academic and legal studies, moral hazard is usually not seen as a major problem of sovereign insolvency (UNCTAD, 2015). Our claim is that the opposite may be true instead. The existing lack of mechanisms to deal with sovereign insolvency adds to that hazard. The institutional deficit regarding state bankruptcy may be a seedbed for further moral hazard in sovereign finance, because the autonomous standing of moral agents is currently ignored.

How then does ignorance of autonomous agency nurture reckless lending and borrowing? The notion of autonomy, and a sovereign as a contractually understood, but necessary, nexus of autonomous individuals, speaks for a free market and contractual solutions related to sovereign insolvency. However, a free market is not synonymous to a laissez-faire one. Every market needs a certain framework within which to operate, and so far, experience has showed that sovereign insolvencies should indeed be better regulated. This is a widely accepted fact, and the positive effects of personal and corporate bankruptcy laws also corroborate the benefits of orderly bankruptcy. Based on this understanding, we propose a state bankruptcy reform that is a compromise between the contractual and the statutory approaches and also reduces the risk of moral hazard.

We call our proposal the semi-hard vulturedove sovereign insolvency mechanism. The core idea is to give an international financial institution, such as the IMF or a separately established body, the legal right to collect a levy on sovereign borrowing. The annual amount of borrowing is huge, so the levy could be small and still produce a sizable fund quickly. This fund—which we have named the vulturedove—would then be used to create market-based incentives and sanctions to steer both lender and borrower behaviors when difficulties in debt servicing become ominous.

Once the writing of a potential default is on the wall, the prices of distressed bonds fall. Vulturedove's mission is to step in and start buying these discounted bonds. Simultaneously, the advice and restructuring efforts of other institutional actors, such as the IMF and the Paris Club, could be invoked. In due course, these talks, supported by contractual reforms for better CACs and exit clauses, would lead to restructuring, haircuts, and other measures that reinstate financial sustainability. During this process, the vulturedove might suffer losses or end up with profits, but it would always provide time for restructuring and an exit to lenders who might want to cash out immediately. These thus are the market-based incentives of our semi-hard compromise between the contractual and statutory approaches to sovereign insolvency.

Lenders have losses when bond prices fall—a market-based sanction that guarantees private involvement in the agony of financial trouble. Another market-based sanction in our model is that the insolvent sovereign would be allowed to fail if a majority of lenders was not found to make a legally binding decision for voluntary restructuring. The license to default would be granted by the IMF and other official lenders who, in contrast to their current policy, would continue to finance the defaulting insolvent. Or if an international sovereign bankruptcy court or arbiter was created, it could play a role and approve the non-performance. A permit to fail in payments might help an insolvent borrower's access even to private finance, at least from those lenders who would be willing to participate in the restructuring (Rogoff & Zettelmeyer, 2002).

Our semi-hard approach would reduce the risk of moral hazard because it would support a genuine market in which investors paid for their misjudgments. It forces market players to undertake a realistic risk assessment, thereby securing prudent lending decisions. On the debtor side, it would press government borrowers to carefully weigh their fiscal needs and to honor their commitments to convince investors. There would be less easy money and reckless borrowing, but there would, nevertheless, be a mechanism that could guide and aid the way out of debt overhang.

This semi-hard solution to sovereign insolvency, armed with the resources of the vulturedove fund, makes debtors and creditors take on the primary responsibility of their commitments, whereas, at the same time, it prevents spread of the turmoil and helps the parties navigate out of their trouble. The model is both more disciplined and more liberal than the ad-hoc practices now being applied to state bankruptcies. The semi-hard approach is more disciplined because the risks of sovereign borrowing are more transparent, and a resource to alleviate financial distress would be readily available. It is also more liberal because it relies on market-based incentives and sanctions to uphold discipline.

We have left open the question of whether an international sovereign bankruptcy court should be established. The semi-hard frame could accommodate it or work without having such a body. In the sovereign insolvency debate, some authors and organizations have yearned for a supreme authority of wise men, or philosopher kings, who would guide the troubled out of their difficulties. However, in any sovereign insolvency, what is at stake is sovereignty. Philosophers and kings are not moral authorities superior to sovereignty, which stands for a civil society. Ultimately, democracy, transparency, affluence, and the rule of law are best guaranteed by a political democracy and a market economy. This fundamental ethical norm should also be remembered when dealing with a state bankruptcy.

16.11　Conclusion

Sovereign insolvencies are a fact. They are on the increase. There are states that have been under insolvency administration or excluded from financial markets for most of their independent history. Recently, new measures and institutions to facilitate such restructurings have emerged and so has a wide unanimity that even more contractual and statutory improvements should be made. The future will show what kind of reforms this activity will seed. The issue is a political one, as has been made evident in the current debate in the UN and the EU. Here it is useful to recall that the restructurings of Argentina, Ukraine, and Greece, completed in the last decade and initially celebrated as great successes, did not prevent these countries from getting into trouble again a few years later. It is a factual reminder that the IMF's adjustment policies and the EU's fiscal convergence are not a panacea for sovereign financial malaise. Institutional reforms and better exploitation of market incentives and sanctions are needed, and in the implementation of such reforms, both the sovereignty that represents the autonomy of the people, and the power of free markets also resting on human autonomy, should be highly regarded and considered.

Citizens are natural persons whose morally relevant characteristic is their intrinsically valuable autonomous moral agency, which the ethics of bankruptcy protects by establishing the discharge of excess debt as an insolvent person's right. Ethical analysis now defines the sovereign as a contractually based secondary moral agent necessary for its citizens' well-being. This fundamentally Kantian approach leads one to the conclusion that the secondary moral agency of a state carries intrinsic value. If insolvency threatens a state's functioning, it also threatens that state's agency. An insolvent sovereign may be no longer able to provide for the well-being of its citizens. When this situation occurs, ethics suggests that a sovereign's promissory moral obligation to service its debt gives way to its more fundamental moral obligation to service the people.

In this regard, the ethics of state bankruptcy is analogous to the ethics of bankruptcy for natural persons. The most fundamental values, the autonomy of a natural person and the instrumental necessity of a state, as anchored in the nature of the moral agency of these actors, seize the commanding position in the hierarchy of values and push aside the insolvents' obligation to keep the promises they made when they entered their loan contracts. In sovereign insolvency, the moral superiority of a sovereign's role as the nexus connecting individuals and thus making them citizens takes on the primary role. The ethics speaks for an orderly sovereign insolvency process, debt restructuring, and even a discharge and fresh start. This is our conclusion on the ethics of state bankruptcy.

The ethics of bankruptcy relieves the stigma of bankruptcy. An honest debtor has done nothing morally wrong. Imprudent financial decisions do not make natural persons crooks, nor do financial failures render states evil either. The message of ethics is that bankrupts should be given a fresh start without excess stigma. An effective and fast bankruptcy process expedites the return to normal. If this return is impeded by a contemptuous regard of insolvency, then all stakeholders suffer. In 2008, this havoc was clearly manifested as the stigma attached to financial distress was the reason that prevented the necessary restructuring of Greece's debt (Committee on International Economic Policy and Reform [CIEPR], 2013). The empirical research has found that early remedies for sovereign financial distress save money and expedite the return to normal (UNCTAD, 2015).

The fundamental ethical problem for sovereign, corporate, and personal insolvency is the same. Who is to suffer from past misjudgments? Over the course of history, the focus of bankruptcy laws that have applied to corporations and people has shifted from punishing insolvents to protecting and helping them. Yet the debtor protection in contemporary bankruptcy laws extends only to honest debtors, to those who have neither intentionally lived beyond their means nor sought credit by misrepresenting facts. These laws also presume that an insolvent will lead a modest life while in reorganization and does not commit new defaults.

In other words, bankruptcy laws only shelter insolvents who have gotten into debt in a *bona fide* manner and who sincerely seek a way out of their anguish. These principles of handling an insolvent individual can also be applied to sovereign bankruptcy. Going bust is always painful, but it may also be the start of a better future. In deciding how to deal with a sovereign bankruptcy, we must make a choice about who is to suffer and how much. This choice is based on ethics and values, and in choosing, we have to take into account the economic implications of our decision. Ethics does play a role in sovereign insolvency. As Robert Kolb (2011, p. 4) notes,

> The theory of sovereign debt attempts to explain the occurrence of lending and repayment in strictly economic terms. That is, the explanations that economists offer turn merely on the self-interest of the lender in extending credit and the borrower in making repayments. Economists never attempt to explain lending or borrowing by reference to moral obligation of fulfilling the promise to repay that borrowers make when they secure loans.

A sovereign default and the exoneration of excess sovereign debt are often seen as inflicting catastrophic consequences on the world economy. The ethics of state bankruptcy does not support this fear. Ethical analysis suggests that relief given to honest debtors does not cause commercial morale to collapse. It may be appropriate here to add that if the insolvents have not been honest, then the ethically most dubious solution is to keep on stretching their credit lines.

The discharge of individual and corporate debt is an ethical and efficient social safety net that respects human autonomy, encourages economic activity, and distributes the brunt of past mistakes equitably. As an indebted moral agent, a state shares many characteristics with natural persons and corporations. This aspect speaks for applying to a bankrupt sovereign the same cure that has worked well in personal and corporate bankruptcies. The ethics of state bankruptcy should guide us to get rid of our dread of sovereign defaults as well as our inability to handle them in an orderly manner.

Bulow and Rogoff (1989, p. 49) are right. "Debts which are forgiven will be forgotten" is a true proposition that applies to all kinds of moral agents, both in the ethical and the empirical sense. The ethics of state bankruptcy tells us that an insolvent sovereign deserves its sovereignty. It should be given a chance to continue to service its citizens, even at the cost of defaulting while servicing its sovereign debt. Legal and institutional reforms to this end are necessary, and indeed the ethics of state bankruptcy favors them.

Note

1 *The ethics of bankruptcy* focuses on the ethical problems related to personal and corporate bankruptcy. This chapter expands the scope to state bankruptcy.

References

Altman, E. I. (1971). *Corporate bankruptcy in America*. London: DC Heath.

Bohoslavsky, J. P., & Černič, J. L. (2014). Placing human rights at the centre of sovereign financing. In J. P. Bohoslavsky & J. L. Černič (Eds.), *Making sovereign financing and human rights work* (pp. 1–14). Oxford and Portland, OR: Hart Publishing.

Bulow, J., & Rogoff, K. (1989). Sovereign debt: Is to forgive to forget? *The American Economic Review*, 79(1), 43–50.

Committee on International Economic Policy and Reform [CIEPR]. (2013). *Revisiting sovereign bankruptcy*. Retrieved from http://www.brookings.edu/research/reports/2013/10/sovereign-debt

Das, U. S., Papaioannou, M. G., & Trebesch, C. (2012). *Sovereign debt restructurings 1950–2010: Literature survey, data, and stylized facts* (IMF Working Paper No. WP/12/203). Retrieved from https://www.imf.org/external/pubs/ft/wp/2012/wp12203.pdf

Deutsche Bundesbank. (2015, March). *Approaches to strengthening the regulatory framework of European Monetary Union. Monthly Report*. Retrieved from https://www.bundesbank.de/Redaktion/EN/Downloads/Publications/Monthly_Report_Articles/2015/2015_03_approaches.pdf?__blob=publicationFile

European Union, European Commission. (2015). *The five presidents' report: Completing Europe's Economic and Monetary Union*. Retrieved from https://ec.europa.eu/priorities/publications/five-presidents-report-completing-europes-economic-and-monetary-union_en

Fried, C. (1981). *Contract as promise*. Cambridge, MA: Harvard University Press.

German Council of Economic Experts. (2015, November). *Focus on future viability. Annual report 2015/2016*. Retrieved from http://www.sachverstaendigenrat-wirtschaft.de/jahresgutachten-2015–2016.html?&L=1

Goodpaster, K. E. (1993). Business ethics and stakeholder analysis. Reprinted in T. I. White (Ed.), *Business ethics: A philosophical reader* (pp. 205–223). New York: Macmillan Publishing Company.

Hawtrey, R. G. (1950). *Currency and credit*. London: Longman's Green.

Homer, S., & Sylla, R. (1991). *A history of interest rates*. New Brunswick: Rutgers University Press.

International Monetary Fund. (2013). *IMF Executive Board discusses sovereign debt restructuring—recent developments and implications for the fund's legal and policy framework* (Public Information Notice No. 13/61). Retrieved from https://www.imf.org/external/np/sec/pn/2013/pn1361.htm

International Monetary Fund. (2015). *Factsheet. Debt relief under the Heavily Indebted Poor Countries (HIPC) Initiative.* Retrieved from https://www.imf.org/external/np/exr/facts/hipc.htm

Kilpi, J. (1998). *The ethics of bankruptcy.* London and New York: Routledge.

Kolb, R. (2011). *Sovereign debt: From safety to default.* Hoboken, NJ: John Wiley & Sons.

Krueger, A. O. (2002). *A new approach to sovereign debt restructuring.* Washington, DC: International Monetary Fund.

Maxwell, M. (1990). *Morality among nations.* New York: State University of New York Press.

Mitchener, K. J., & Weidenmier, M. D. (2010). Supersanctions and sovereign debt repayment. *Journal of International Money and Finance, 29,* 19–36.

Posner, E. (2003). Do states have a moral obligation to obey international law? *Stanford Law Review, 55,* 1901–1919.

Reinisch, A., & Binder, C. (2014). Debts and state of necessity. In J. P. Bohoslavsky & J. L. Černič (Eds.), *Making sovereign financing and human rights work* (pp. 115–128). Oxford and Portland, OR: Hart Publishing.

Rogoff, K., & Zettelmeyer, J. (2002). Bankruptcy procedures for sovereigns: A history of ideas 1976–2001. *IMF Staff Papers, 49*(3), 470–507.

Sachs, J. (1995). *Do we need an international lender of last resort.* Retrieved from http://www.cid.harvard.edu/archive/hiid/papers/intllr.pdf

Shuchman, P. (1973). An attempt at a "philosophy" of bankruptcy. *UCLA Law Review, 21,* 403–476.

Stanley, D. T., & Girth, M. (1971). *Bankruptcy: Problem, process, reform.* Washington: The Brookings Institution.

Stiglitz, J. (2014, December 10). The world needs a sovereign debt restructuring mechanism. *Emerging Markets.* Retrieved from http://www.emergingmarkets.org/Article/3389531/JOSEPH-STIGLITZ-The-world-needs-a-sovereign-debt-restructuring-mechanism.html

Stiglitz, J. (2015, June 16). Sovereign debt needs international supervision. *The Guardian.* Retrieved from http://www.theguardian.com/business/2015/jun/16/sovereign-debt-needs-international-supervision

Sullivan, T. A., Warren, E., & Westbrooke, J. L. (1989). *As we forgive our debtors: Bankruptcy and consumer credit in America.* New York: Oxford University Press.

Sutherland, J. R. (1988). The ethics of bankruptcy: A biblical perspective. *Journal of Business Ethics, 7,* 917–927.

UNCTAD United Nations Conference on Trade and Development. (2015, April). *Sovereign debt workouts: Going forward roadmap and guide.* Retrieved from http://unctad.org/en/PublicationsLibrary/gdsddf2015misc1_en.pdf

United Nations. (2009). *Report of the Commission of Experts of the President of the United Nations General Assembly on reforms of the international monetary and financial system.* Retrieved from http://www.un.org/ga/econcrisissummit/docs/FinalReport_CoE.pdf

United Nations General Assembly, Resolution. (2015, September 10). Retrieved from http://daccess-dds-ny.un.org/doc/UNDOC/GEN/N14/521/79/PDF/N1452179.pdf?OpenElement

Werhane, P. (1985). *Persons, rights, and corporations.* Englewood Cliffs, NJ: Prentice Hall Inc.

Wray, L. R. (1990). *Money and credit in capitalist economies.* Aldershot, UK and Brookfield, VT: E. Elgar.

Part V

Industry Perspectives

17 Firm Turnarounds in Knowledge-Intensive Industries

Vincent L. Barker III and Achim Schmitt

17.1 Introduction

Corporate turnarounds have been studied extensively by academic researchers, executives, and consultants for over forty years (see Bibeault, 1982 and Schendel et al., 1976 for early works). Whereas a collective knowledge base regarding turnarounds has emerged over that period of time and has been cataloged in reviews (e.g., Lohrke et al., 2004; Trahms et al., 2013), the management field's understanding of turnarounds could hardly be called mature and probably more theoretical propositions remain unstated or untested about turnarounds than commonly accepted knowledge exists. Indeed, a recent review of the turnaround literature described it as 'fragmented' in both its theoretical development and empirical methods (Trahms et al., 2013, p. 1278). Thus studies do not accumulate by testing the same theoretical constructs and using similar measures and definitions across various samples of firms or organizations.

The uneven development of firm turnaround research can be linked to at least four basic issues in studying turnarounds. First, a commonly accepted definition of a firm turnaround is elusive. A search of business publications for the word 'turnaround' in the headlines of news stories will deliver articles about a wide range of firms. Some articles might be about firms coming back from near-death profitability declines and losses. Other articles might be about firms whose stocks have 'turned around' from a two-quarter swoon, despite the firms being profitable the entire time, or firms whose quality ratings have seen a 'turnaround' in the eyes of customers. Whereas these other types of reversals of performance are important in their own right, they are not firm turnarounds as researchers would classify organizational events.

Indeed, the word 'turnaround' is socially constructed with many different meanings. Because there is no strong consensus on what a firm turnaround entails in the business world or in media descriptions, turnaround research suffers from having an ambiguous phenomena to study. Even within the world of management researchers, turnarounds are often defined quite differently across studies (cf., Hambrick & Schecter, 1983; Ndofor et al., 2013;

Robbins & Pearce, 1992), so the ambiguity seems to extend from the world of practice into research studies.

This ambiguity contrasts starkly with research on firm bankruptcy. Because a firm declaring bankruptcy is a well-understood event with meaning in all countries and cultures that have private enterprises, the antecedents and consequences of bankruptcy can be more easily studied. Whereas bankruptcy law can vary dramatically by country (Claessens & Klapper, 2005), firms declare bankruptcy within a short time frame (usually on a specific day in the United States), and that declaration in almost all cases means that the firm is insolvent or will be insolvent due to projected liabilities. Because bankruptcy is an event with a common understanding, researchers can examine its antecedents and consequences with greater precision moving backward or forward in time from the bankruptcy declaration date. In contrast, no such events exist in turnaround research with the possible exception of top management or CEO changes. Given that management turnover or firing events can be documented as to when they occur, it should not be surprising that extensive research has examined the consequences of top management or CEO changes at declining firms (e.g., Barker & Duhaime, 1997; Chen & Hambrick, 2012; Hambrick & D'Aveni, 1992; Lohrke et al., 2004). However, the lack of consensus on the definition of a turnaround makes determining even when they occur difficult for researchers.

Second, studying turnaround firms alone without control samples of failed turnaround attempts creates more difficulty in advancing turnaround research. Whereas scholars can study turnaround firms looking for patterns of strategic change (Barker & Duhaime, 1997; Schendel, Patton, & Riggs, 1976), researchers cannot really examine the efficacy of various turnaround strategies or actions without comparison to firms that continue to fail or do not turn around.

The numerous case studies or books about solely successful recovery from decline are generally not useful sources for theoretical ideas for the same reason: lack of control sample firms that fail. Former managers or consultants generally do not write books about their failures. Thus what emerges from the vast experiences of firms that have tried to recover from decline tends to be biased toward positive outcomes (e.g., turnarounds). However, a medical researcher would never test the efficacy of a potential new drug without a control sample of subjects getting a placebo. Therefore, findings based solely on the observations of turnaround firms are ideas that are not tested on a control sample and have very limited value. Yet these ideas often have influence because they are shown to be successful at some firms.

Third, and related to the second issue, is that managers often do not like to talk about firm failures. Whereas there have been some studies of turnaround attempts that have used systematic interviews (Barker & Mone, 1998; Barker et al., 2001) or surveys (Barker & Duhaime, 1997; Schmitt & Raisch, 2013), these studies largely generate modest response rates and therefore often are under-powered statistically. This problem stems from the general stigma of failure, whereby managers would rather not talk about actions that might make them look ineffective in social comparison processes versus other managers (Whetten, 1980). As such, researchers trying to examine the efficacy of various turnaround strategies or management actions are often forced to operationalize theoretical constructs with archival data on firms that are collected by third-party sources. Whereas this situation is often the case in strategic management research, archival data often has an imperfect correlation with the constructs researchers are trying to measure (e.g., measurement error). The situation also allows different measurement strategies across studies that are difficult to duplicate or compare. This contrasts to survey research, as is often undertaken in psychology or organizational behavior, whereby researchers examining a common theory or phenomenon often coalesce around fairly exacting and similar measures of theoretical constructs that are shown to have strong reliability and replicability across multiple studies. In contrast, measurement in turnaround research often has limited commensurability across studies.

The final issue that has constrained advancement in turnaround research is the contingency nature of much turnaround theory. Whereas contingency theory has long played a role in strategy research (e.g., Donaldson, 2001; Hofer, 1975), it often contrasts with human desire for simple solutions to problems. In strategy research, the need for simpler solutions was exemplified by the push in the 1980s to develop generic economic (Porter, 1980) or behavioral strategies (Miles, Snow, Meyer, & Coleman, 1978) that would work in all environments. Contingency theory creates complexity in explanations of social phenomena such as turnaround attempts. Whereas such complexity may represent the actual nature of the process being studied, it makes for messy explanations that often take a very long time for researchers to collectively understand.

In terms of contribution to the growing and evolving body of turnaround research, we try to discuss and explain a turnaround contingency based on a firm's industry in this chapter. In particular, we examine how knowledge-based industries create contingencies that affect the efficacy of various turnaround actions. We argue that competitive advantage and therefore the ability to be profitable in knowledge-based industries lies in the human capital and social capital of the firm's employees. Therefore, management actions taken in response to decline have to avoid the leakage of human capital (e.g., employees with valuable knowledge leaving) and the destruction of social capital (e.g., the break up of internal firm social networks). Also, any knowledge gaps affecting competitive advantage need to be addressed through strategy changes. All these changes will be addressed through the lens of declining firms' actions to (1) retrench or stem decline and (2) recover or strategically reposition themselves (e.g., Arogyaswamy et al., 1995; Schmitt & Raisch, 2013).

17.2   What Is a Turnaround?

As discussed earlier, the definition of a turnaround in common usage is ambiguous. The definition used in this chapter follows Arogyaswamy and colleagues' (1995) definition. First, in order to turn around, a firm must decline. Declining performance may be defined as an extended period of poor firm economic performance after a period of profitability. Indeed, a firm must be profitable at some point in its life in order to decline. The actual level of firm performance during the extended period of poor economic performance must be low enough to threaten the survival of the firm (Arogyaswamy et al., 1995; Hofer, 1980). Thus a declining firm sustains resource losses that will cause the firm to fail if unabated. Historically, the period of poor performance must last between two (e.g., Ndofor et al., 2013) and four (e.g., Schendel et al., 1976) years with firm financial returns being below some benchmark such as the risk-free rate of return, the prior year's performance, or industry-average financial performance. Many studies have added that decline must result in at least one year of financial losses during the period of poor performance (Barker et al., 2001; Ndofor et al., 2013) and some possibility of bankruptcy (Barker & Duhaime, 1997). These measurement guidelines try to assure that firms classified by researchers as declining actually have some possibility of failing if performance is not raised substantially in the near future.

A good working definition of decline is important to turnaround research because organizational decline is often confused with other related concepts such as organizational stagnation (e.g., Grinyer & McKieman, 1990) or a reduced rate of firm growth as an industry matures (e.g., Porter, 1980). Stagnation or slow growth because of industry maturity do not directly threaten the firm in the short run and are therefore different concepts from decline. Also, declining firms usually function in a crisis atmosphere that may not be present at non-declining firms.

A turnaround from firm decline occurs when performance is subsequently increased at a declining firm to a sustained level of profitability. A sustained level implies a viable level of profitability is reached, such as positive return on assets (e.g., Nodofer et al., 2013), return on assets above the rate of return on risk-free investments (e.g., Barker & Duhaime, 1997), or return on investment higher than industry peers (Hambrick & Schecter, 1983). The notion of a 'viable level' of profitability is that the firm is no longer performing at a level that will lead to failure. This level of financial performance must also be maintained over a number of years, as the firm cannot immediately fall back into decline.

17.3   Why Do Firms Fail?

The basic function of a firm is to combine inputs such as labor, capital, knowledge, and other assets to create products and services that are sold to customers. These activities create economic profit for the firm when the price paid for the goods and/or services (e.g., the value created) is (a) greater than the cost of the firm's inputs, including the cost of capital, and (b) the firm is able to capture enough of the value created to cover its costs. A firm is failing, in an economic sense, when it cannot recover its costs in the long run.

In a broad sense, failure can happen for two reasons. First, the firm may not create enough value for customers given its cost structure. The firm's products or services may be seen by customers as inferior to those of competitors with similar cost structures. This situation forces the firm to discount its prices below its costs of production in order for customers to buy its products/services, or the products/services may go unsold, not generating any value at all. This type of failure has been labeled in the literature as firm-based decline (e.g., Arogyaswamy et al., 1995; Ndofor et al., 2013), because the sources of decline rely within the firm's value creation process, as the firm is not able to create a product or service from its own activities that has enough value for customers. This situation can emanate from (a) the product/service being less desirable and thus creating less value than competitors, (b) the firm's overall cost structure being too high for the level of value created, or (c) both problems simultaneously. Generally, such sources of decline are specific to individual firms and their value creations processes (e.g., the label 'firm-based decline').

The second broad reason for decline is that customers may have enough choices of a particular good or service from different competitors to pay much less than they would otherwise pay for the good or service. This case of oversupply at any given level of quality allows customers to capture value from producer firms in the form of customer surplus (e.g., the difference between what customers would pay for a product and the lesser price they actually pay). To the extent that oversupply exists within any particular market niche, the average price that firms receive may be driven down below their cost of value creation through the process of price competition. This type of failure has been labeled in the literature as industry-contraction-based decline (Arogyaswamy et al., 1995), because the sources of decline generally (a) are caused by oversupply within the industry and (b) generally affect many firms within the industry. A better name for such decline might be 'industry-supply-based decline.' Whereas supplies of products dramatically exceeding demand in an industry are usually caused by a contraction of demand in that industry, a similar situation can be created by entrants and incumbent firms adding supply faster than demand grows. For example, the passenger air transport industry in the United States has suffered through a number of years of poor profitability since deregulation in the late 1970s, with a large number of the industry firms losing money in particular years. This situation exists even in the face of substantial growth in the number of passengers flying in the United States over the four decades since deregulation. However, expansion by existing firms and the entry by new airlines has allowed supply to outstrip demand growth during much of this period of time.

One of the reasons that firm-based decline and industry-supply-based decline are useful distinctions is that they have different implications for the value-creation process at a declining firm. A firm suffering industry-supply-based decline may have little difference in the value created by the firm versus competitors. Similar value may be created by competitors (with similar costs of creating value) but many industry firms decline because of relative oversupply of the product or service. In contrast, when a firm suffers firm-based decline, some or many aspects of the firm's value creation process must be inferior to competitors in either value created for customers or the cost of creating value. Thus a software firm that declines in a rapidly growing industry that does not have an industry oversupply problem is very likely to be suffering from firm-based decline.

Firms can suffer from both types of decline simultaneously. For example, an airline can have a higher cost structure than competitors (e.g., firm-based decline) during a period of oversupply in the industry (e.g., industry-supply-based decline). Such performance declines may be the hardest for managers to overcome because the firm must address problems on both levels.

17.4   How Do Firms Achieve a Turnaround?

Given its decisive role in determining firm survival or failure, the formulation of an appropriate decline response represents a critical managerial activity. Turnaround scholars generally agree that response actions need to stabilize the firm's operations by stemming financial losses (cash outflows) and leading the entire firm into a period of sustainable growth. Whereas we refer to these two objectives as retrenchment and recovery (e.g., Robbins & Pearce, 1992), other turnaround studies have synonymously referred to decline stemming and recovery (Arogyaswamy et al., 1995), as well as operational and strategic response strategies (e.g., Trahms et al., 2013).

Concerned about the imminent risk of bankruptcy, retrenchment strategies' primary objectives are survival and the achievement of positive cash flows. The deliberate elimination of assets (i.e., plant closings, equity divestments, inventory cutbacks) and/or costs (i.e., layoffs, reduction of direct and indirect costs, lowering interest expense) seeks to minimize input resources to increase firm efficiency (Lim et al., 2013). In other words, retrenchment reduces organizational slack and frees up resources that can be deployed toward more productive areas of operations.

Conversely, recovery strategies' primary concern is to adjust the firm's current market domains and how it competes within those domains (Barker & Duhaime, 1997). These strategies explore the firm's internal as well as external resource potential—for instance, via acquisitions, strategic alliances, and venture units—for product, process, and/or technology improvements to regain a competitive strategic position in current or potentially new marketplaces. From incremental adjustments to discontinuous innovation, recovery strategies unfold the revenue potential of product-market offerings.

Compared to retrenchment, recovery strategies focus on longer time horizons to sustainably change the firm's strategic positioning and performance.

Although there is general agreement regarding the aforementioned response actions, their implementation provides greater controversy within the literature. Some scholars (e.g., Robbins & Pearce, 1992) consider retrenchment as an immediate action and precursor to the implementation of recovery strategies. Stabilizing operations that reverse the firm's performance decline and restore firm profitability represents the universal goal at the beginning of this turnaround process model. Once stabilization is achieved, the firm shifts its focus to recovery to eliminate or cope with the causes of decline. Despite its popularity in other studies (e.g., Bruton et al., 2003; Lohrke et al., 2012), the main criticism of the sequential turnaround process centers on the fact that it downplays important interrelationships between both strategies. For instance, implementing retrenchment without a clear understanding of the firm's long-term strategic goals may enhance short-term performance but can simultaneously delay or harm effective recovery activities.

Consequently, other scholars (e.g., Arogyaswamy et al., 1995) challenge this view of the turnaround process and suggest that retrenchment and recovery are interdependent rather than purely sequential. This so-called simultaneous turnaround process argues that both turnaround strategies overlap and require alignment in order to unfold their full potential. However, pursuing retrenchment and recovery concurrently has been similarly questioned (e.g., Pearce & Robbins, 2008), as it creates additional costs and resource-conflicts that can impact turnaround performance negatively.

Recently, Schmitt and Raisch (2013) developed the simultaneous perspective's line of thought further and argued for more complex dynamics between retrenchment and recovery. Instead of the traditional dichotomy of separate retrenchment and recovery stages, both strategies represent paradoxical challenges and needs that need to be constantly addressed throughout the entire turnaround process: whereas retrenchment acts as stability and resource provider for recovery, recovery provides strategic change and direction for retrenchment.

Capturing the dynamism of the turnaround process is difficult, yet essential and characterizes one of the most fruitful research areas to improve our understanding of turnarounds. If we understand successful response actions as an orchestration of contradictory, yet interrelated, retrenchment and recovery strategies, firms should tailor their turnaround strategy according to the nature of their competitive environments. Strategy research has long argued for consistency between strategy formulation and the nature of a firm's competitive environment (DeWitt, 1998). Hence instead of discussing whether or not to engage in retrenchment and/or recovery, the more interesting question centers on how much emphasis to put on one particular strategy over the other when faced with corporate turnarounds in a particular industry and organizational context.

17.5   The Knowledge—Intensive Context

Strategy researchers have long held that value creation processes vary dramatically across industries. Defining an industry as firms producing similar products or services seen as somewhat comparable by customers, industries can vary greatly in their underlying technologies (Scherer, 1982), state of maturity (Porter, 1980), and level of uncertainty over time (Dess & Beard, 1984).

Industries can also vary greatly on how to create and use knowledge (Alvesson, 1995, 2004). The *Oxford English Dictionary* defines knowledge as: "Acts, information, and skills acquired by a person through experience or education; the theoretical or practical understanding of a subject." Firms in all industries use knowledge in different forms to produce goods and services. For example, in some industries, such as the automobile industry, much of the knowledge (e.g., information, skills, and understanding) needed to manufacture an automobile from its parts has been designed into the capital equipment used in the manufacturing process. Such embedding of knowledge into the machines used to manufacture autos has happened over the last one hundred years as a way to both reduce labor costs and to reduce dependence on the knowledge of assembly-line operators. In such industries, much of the knowledge about how to produce the product or service has become embedded in the equipment or standard operating procedures of firms.

What differentiates knowledge-intensive industries from other industries is that the knowledge needed to produce products or services (1) must be continually generated or updated and (2) mostly resides in the minds of individuals or groups within the firm (Alvesson, 1995, 2000). As a result, knowledge-intensive firms tend to (1) employ more people with advanced degrees or specialized skills acquired through training (Hayton, 2005; Liebowitz & Suen, 2000) and (2) have lower capital intensity (Alvesson, 2000). Knowledge in such industries changes rapidly and is often tacit knowledge that is learned by doing and cannot be easily communicated (Grant, 1996; Leonard & Sensiper, 1998). As a result, firms have great difficulty designing knowledge into equipment (i.e., see earlier auto industry example), incorporating it into standard operating procedures, or recording it in knowledge management databases (Grant, 1996). Knowledge is embedded in the people and groups within the firm.

Software represents a classic knowledge-intense industry. Software firms tend to employ a large number of people trained at universities and generally have few capital assets other than computer-related equipment (Mowery, 1995). Software firms need to continuously generate and exploit new knowledge because their underlying technological base changes constantly with both competitor advancements and increases in computer power. As a result, software firms tend to spend a large percentage of revenues on research and development (Graham & Mowery, 2003) in an attempt to generate and exploit new knowledge.

Because of the central role of uncodified knowledge in knowledge-intense firms, human capital and social capital both play a large role in the success of such firms. Human capital can be defined most simply as the knowledge and skills of the firm's human resources, which are its employees (Hatch & Dyer, 2004). Human capital comes from employees investing in education, training, learning by doing, and other activities that increase their knowledge. Some human capital may be quite common (e.g., the ability to manipulate data in spreadsheets), but human capital may also create value for the firm if it is fairly rare and is used to make a firm's products or services more attractive or to lower the cost of producing those services. Knowledge-intensive firms rely heavily on human capital because of their need to constantly generate and exploit new knowledge and because much of the valuable knowledge is not codified in standard operating procedures or designed into capital equipment. As such, the knowledge resides in people.

Whereas human capital may be a source of value creation for the firm, it has several attributes that make its management difficult. First, human capital is mobile and can exit the firm quickly with employees leaving (Almeida & Kogut, 1999; Cooper, 2001). Therefore, valuable knowledge can be lost to the firm with employee turnover to the extent that the valuable knowledge is not codified or otherwise available. Second, employees with valuable knowledge can bargain for higher compensation from the firm (Coff, 1999). Also, if the firm does not match the compensation of other potential purchasers of that knowledge (e.g., other employers), the employees can take their human capital to other firms (Campbell et al., 2012). Thus one of the key tasks of the knowledge-intensive firm is recruiting, developing, and retaining the employees that have the knowledge necessary for the firm to create value for customers (Koch & McGrath, 1996).

In addition to human capital, knowledge-intensive firms rely on social capital to maximize the value of their human capital. Firms may be viewed as social communities specializing in speed and efficiency in the creation and transfer of knowledge (Kogut & Zander, 1996, p. 503). Similarly, we define social capital as actual or potential resources that can be accessed through social networks (Nahapiet & Ghoshal, 1998, p. 243).[1] Hence human capital in knowledge-intense organizations is leveraged by the social connections between people in the organization. Employees learn from other employees as they work on projects together, solve problems together, and socialize together. Such social interaction builds employee networks within the firm, creates a common language for talking about the firm, and increases trust between employees. These three outcomes become the basis of sharing of knowledge between employees as they facilitate the flow of information (Nahapiet & Ghoshal, 1998). These human connections are especially important because knowledge changes rapidly and is often tacit knowledge, which is learned by doing. This knowledge cannot be easily codified and cannot be easily communicated (Grant, 1996; Leonard & Sensiper, 1998), except in the case of close work interactions.

Social capital within a firm can be fragile. First, employee turnover can disrupt social networks. Ultimately, social capital within a firm shares individual human capital. Thus the value of social capital declines if the average human capital within the firm goes down. Second, some organizational members may have stronger network positions than others in spreading human capital. Employees who have positions connecting key networked groups within the organization have a more vital role in the overall social network of the firm (Burt, 2009). Turnover of these members may have a disproportionate affect in the ability to share knowledge and skills across the firm.

17.6   How the Knowledge-Based Context Affects Turnaround Attempts

As discussed in the previous section, firms in knowledge-intense industries rely on human and social capital in order to produce products and services that have value for customers. Because of the need to constantly develop and exploit new knowledge, it is difficult to design knowledge into capital equipment, embed knowledge into standard operating procedures, and otherwise make knowledge less tacit. This places special emphasis on retaining and motivating firm employees during corporate turnaround attempts. Indeed, high levels of employee turnover will make it more difficult for the organization to innovate or even produce a reliable product or service because of knowledge losses.

The key task for declining knowledge-intense firms is thus to protect, exploit, and further develop valuable knowledge during the implementation of particular turnaround strategies. In particular, retrenchment needs to identify and retain knowledge, skills, and capabilities embedded in the firm's human and social capital. Recovery strategies, however, need to build on this capital to develop and exploit unique knowledge or capabilities. The following section presents how to embed these arguments in greater detail into distinct turnaround strategies and to develop testable propositions on how to turn around firms in knowledge-intense industries.

17.6.1   *The Retrenchment Challenge*

As mentioned earlier, the retrenchment strategies' objective is to increase operational efficiency by minimizing organizational resources to produce certain products and services. Owing to limited possibilities to retrench assets, knowledge-intense firms mainly focus on cost retrenchment activities targeting the workforce that often result in layoffs. Pursuing layoffs, however, always carries the risk of losing employees' tacit knowledge and social network connections, which can negatively affect the firm's available skills, competences, experiences, and capabilities (Schmitt et al., 2012).

On the one hand, layoffs do not only signify the loss of physical labor but also the loss of subject-matter expertise and know-how of prior organizational decisions (Fisher & White, 2000). Whereas some of this individual tacit knowledge is redundant or irrelevant, knowledge-intense firms need to ensure that they retain critical knowledge required for their overall functioning. Consequently, the identification of such critical human capital becomes of particular importance when implementing layoffs. Cutting too deeply into the workforce risks driving out the firm's resources and competences, which build the foundation of its competitive advantage.

On the other hand, layoffs provide a substantial risk for the firm's social capital. The social networks created within firms allow employees to make sense of the organizational context and the firm's overall purpose and goals (Hansen, 1999). Moreover, knowledge-intense firms always seek to engage in horizontal collaborations that break down departmental silos and improve the firm's overall functioning. Laying off key employees with access to multiple sources of information in distinct departments can signify that other employees are cut off from important networks. The risk is that individuals get dispersed, disconnected, and fail to contribute their individual knowledge to support the firm's capacity to build core competencies.

In sum, losing key employees because of aggressive retrenchment strategies can significantly affect the declining firms' functioning. However, the pressure of immediate performance improvement often leads to immediate 'across-the-board cuts' (Barker & Mone, 1998) in declining knowledge-intense firms: retrenchment strategies emphasize cost reductions equally throughout the organization instead of protecting critical employees' skills and competences. For some companies, this becomes a difficult task, as specific countries (i.e., Germany, Italy, China) require employers to follow specific social-selection criteria when pursuing cost retrenchment strategies. Thus knowledge-intense firms need to target specific employees and determine the depth of the cuts. Implementing retrenchment strategies without a clear vision of the firm's future positioning involves the risk of destroying the necessary resources that are able to stimulate long-term growth and adaptation. By doing so, retrenchment actively adjusts the skills and capabilities of the workforce needed for recovery. This leads to the following proposition:

> *Proposition 1: At declining knowledge-intense firms, retrenchment strategies based on selective instead of across-the-board cuts will be positively associated with turnaround performance.*

However, retrenchment strategies are simultaneously required to fuel resources and competences for recovery. Declining knowledge-intense firms not only need to protect high-performing employees from layoffs but also ensure that these employees' resources and competences remain accessible during the turnaround effort. In knowledge-intensive industries, it is quite common that high-performing employees often take jobs elsewhere—in some cases at direct competitors—in order to avoid the uncertainties and ambiguities in a declining firm.

The absence of career and promotional opportunities has been found to stimulate voluntary turnover (Iverson & Pullman, 2000), which carries to implications for retrenchment strategies. First, a primary motivator for employees is pay (Mueller & Price, 1990). If salary conditions are attractive in the present job when compared to others in the industry, then voluntary turnover of highly skilled employees is reduced. Hence retrenchment strategies need to provide sufficient enough organizational means to match the salary conditions in the same industry.

Second, the attractiveness of the internal labor market characterizes another element of employee loyalty (Iverson & Pullman, 2000). Retrenchment strategies in knowledge-intense firms not only result in employee layoffs but also require a profound analysis of established procedures, routines, and organizational culture. Reorganizing tasks and responsibilities, determining attractive promotion criteria, and creating a well-functioning organization design become critical criteria when employees evaluate the firm's internal labor market. Thus retrenchment provides firms with the opportunity to revise current hierarchical structures and promotional opportunities.

Both of the aforementioned arguments bring out the following proposition:

Proposition 2: At declining knowledge-intense firms, retrenchment strategies that preserve career and promotional opportunities will be positively associated with turnaround performance.

In addition to retrenchment's intensity and what firm activities or employees are selected for cutbacks, we also consider the 'how' of retrenchment strategies' implementation as a critical success factor for turning around knowledge-intense firms. Layoffs can be considered a breach of the psychological contract and impact the surviving employees' (survivors) emotions, behaviors, and attitudes (Brockner, 1992). Witnessing the loss of colleagues and friends during layoffs—the so-called victims—can create positive (i.e., relief, reassurance, recognition) as well as negative emotions (i.e., guilt, fear, anger). These psychological reactions influence the survivors' morale, motivation, commitment, and job performance (Cascio, 1993). Thus retrenchment risks the creation of demotivated employees who are less engaged, withhold their efforts, increase their absenteeism, and sometimes even seek more secure job opportunities in the industries.

Prior research (e.g., Brockner, 1992) has argued that organizational justice plays an important role in mitigating these negative consequences.

Victims and survivors often evaluate layoffs in terms of their overall fairness by questioning the reasons for layoffs, the selection of victims and survivors, and the firm's way of proceeding before, during, and after layoffs. Generally, such fairness perceptions can be classified into procedural (the fairness of the overall process) and distributive (the outcomes' perceived fairness) justice (Hopkins & Weathington, 2006).

Procedural justice determines the employees' overall commitment to the firm and its representatives (McFarlin & Sweeny, 1992). Knowledge workers need to experience a certain level of fairness between the reason for layoffs and the procedures involved in its implementation. If employees consider the entire retrenchment strategy as unfair and unnecessary, their organizational commitment, trust, and satisfaction will decrease. Such results can significantly impact the firm's chance for recovery, as only highly committed and motivated employees will ensure the development of new products and services for recovery. This leads to the following proposition:

Proposition 3: At declining knowledge-intense firms, procedural justice in retrenchment strategies will be positively associated with turnaround performance.

Similarly, surviving employees will judge the firm regarding the way the firm treated dismissed employees. Survivors' perception of distributive fairness decreases the risk of voluntary turnover, reduced support, and diminished organizational commitment (Hopkins & Weathington, 2006). Such distributive justice represents a critical challenge for declining knowledge-intense firms, as the means for outplacement support and incentive packages are rather limited. However, firms can often stimulate distributive justice by (a) using layoffs as a last alternative after having pursuit alternatives (i.e., hiring freeze, early retirement), (b) creating similar sacrifices at the management level (Cascio, 1993), and (c) constantly communicating the reasons and selection criteria applied for layoffs (Brockner, 1992). Hence we propose the following relationship:

Proposition 4: At declining knowledge-intense firms, distributive justice in retrenchment strategies will be positively associated with turnaround performance.

17.6.2 The Recovery Challenge

Turnaround researchers have argued that effective recovery actions will respond to the causes of the firm's decline (Arogyaswamy et al., 1995; Hofer, 1980; Ndofor et al., 2013). Firm-based decline, as opposed to industry-supply-based decline, generally necessitates higher levels of strategic change through recovery actions to a successful turnaround (Arogyaswamy et al., 1995; Ndofor et al., 2013). Becoming more efficient and generating slack resources is not sufficient for a turnaround if the firm makes products or services that create significantly less value for customers than competing services

Because of the tremendous growth of the knowledge economy over the past twenty-five years, most observers generally do not associate industry-supply-based decline with knowledge-intensive industries and firms. Indeed, the high growth of knowledge-intensive industries has generally made such industries the setting for studies of firm-based decline (e.g., Ndofor et al., 2013). However, as certain sectors of the knowledge economy mature (e.g., computer services, phone handsets, office automation software), industry-supply-based decline becomes more likely. For example, both IBM and HP Enterprises in the United States have announced layoffs in their computer services businesses in 2016, as excess capacity exists in that market.

Under industry-supply-based decline, the firm's basic core knowledge still creates value for customers, but oversupply in the industry or market shifts value to customers in the form of reduced prices through competition (e.g., customer surplus). Whereas effective retrenchment practices (see Propositions 1–4) provide the resources and slack to potentially wait out any industry oversupply or eventually reduce firm capacity. A main recovery action focus should be to develop new uses for the firm's knowledge. New uses can overcome any oversupply issues in existing markets.

An example of a new knowledge uses recovery strategy is Texas Instruments' (TI) successful turnaround in the early 1990s. In the late 1980s, TI's main semi-conductor was suffering from worldwide overcapacity driving product prices and TI's profits down with the company reporting substantial losses in 1990 and 1991. Because TI had a large amount of valuable knowledge, a main thrust of their recovery actions was the licensing of their technology to other firms or organizations. The dramatically expanded licensing on new and old technologies drove royalty payments to TI substantially higher to eventually become the basis of the firm recovering from oversupply in the semi-conductor market (see Grindley & Teece, 1997 for the Texas Instruments narrative). The firm's valuable existing knowledge was turned into new profit.

Whereas not all knowledge-intensive firms may be able to license their knowledge in the face of industry-supply-based decline, opportunities may exist for the application of their knowledge to new products or services outside of the firm's traditional markets. Such application of knowledge to new areas helps the declining firm escape from the oversupply problem in its existing domains. These arguments suggest the following:

Proposition 5: At declining knowledge-intense firms that are suffering primarily industry-supply-based decline, recovery strategies based on extending existing knowledge into new activities will be positively associated with turnaround performance.

When knowledge-intense firms undergo firm-based decline, the situation suggests that the firm's knowledge generation and exploitation processes are not producing the same value for customers as competitors. For example, much of the value of Nokia's knowledge about how to design and manufacture cell phones was destroyed by smartphones introduced by Apple and Google (e.g., Android) in the latter part of the last decade that created application ecosystems that made these phones much more valuable to customers. Nokia's inability to develop the knowledge and capability to create its own smartphones and provide customers with comparable value led to the company's decline and eventual exit from the market in being sold to Microsoft.

The key recovery decisions that must be made by knowledge-intensive firms suffering from firm-based decline are (1) what firm knowledge still has some value for customers in the future and (2) what new knowledge needs to be brought into the organization. Such decisions are generally not easy for management to make because they require strong understanding of technology and markets. Declining firms may also have difficulty in abandoning knowledge that has historically been valuable to the firm (Leonard-Barton, 1992). Because the historic success of the firm has been tied to certain knowledge, management may not have the cognitive mind-sets and motivations to objectively appraise the future knowledge needs of the firm.

One key to overcoming firm-based decline in knowledge-intensive industries is the successful infusion of new knowledge into the firm. For example, Ndofor and colleagues (2013) found that turnaround from decline for software firms was positively associated with acquisitions and strategic alliances made in response to decline. Both acquisitions and strategic alliances are means of bring new knowledge into the organization as the focal firms learn from the newly acquired firms' employees or those of the alliance partner. This new knowledge may be used to either create more value for products and services in existing markets or to enter other markets. Overall, these arguments suggest the following:

Proposition 6: At declining knowledge-intense firms that are suffering primarily firm-based decline, recovery strategies based on bringing new knowledge into the firm will be positively associated with turnaround performance.

17.7 Discussion and Conclusion

Corporate turnaround attempts have been often criticized for being short-sighted, knee-jerk reactions rather than part of an overall strategic recovery plan. In declining knowledge-intense firms, such a one-sided turnaround approach will aggravate the impending risk of losing critical knowledge and skills. Whereas an overemphasis on retrenchment certainly enables firms to improve their cost structure and cash outflows, it fails to protect valuable knowledge necessary to increase urgently needed cash inflows. In other words, knowledge-intense firms risk driving out valuable human capital and ruining social capital that trap them in an endless downward spiral of performance decline and retrenchment (see Figure 17.1).

Contrastingly, knowledge-intense firm turnarounds must focus on simultaneously preserving and creating human and social capital on various organizational levels. This adds a certain layer of complexity to our traditional perception of corporate turnarounds, as the interdependence between retrenchment and recovery actions intensifies. The retrenchment strategies' success depends on having formulated a comprehensive recovery response addressing the causes of the firm's decline. It is rather the consideration of several elements related to retrenchment and recovery's interaction that determines the corporate turnaround's overall outcome.

From a managerial point of view, this becomes extremely difficult, as it requires balancing conflicting goals under performance pressure from multiple stakeholders. Prior research confirms that managers usually do not favor a dual approach, preferring swift, visible activities that emphasize efficiency, cost cutting, layoffs, and divestment (Barker & Mone, 1998). Overcoming this managerial tendency may require knowledge-intense firms to adequately create leadership teams and governance structures that constantly

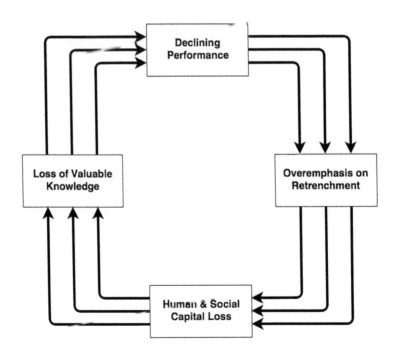

Figure 17.1 The Downward Spiral of Human Capital and Social Capital Loss in Response to Decline

reflect, preserve, and develop the firm's human and social capital base when implementing corporate turnarounds. Underestimating the inherent complexity and dynamism of human capital, social capital, retrenchment, and recovery may be an important reason why efforts to reverse declining knowledge-intense firms often fail in practice.

Note

1 This definition is broader than some conceptualizations of social capital, which rather define social capital as the information advantage from a particular position in a structural network (see, Burt, 2009).

References

Almeida, P., & Kogut, B. (1999). Localization of knowledge and the mobility of engineers in regional networks. *Management Science, 45*(7), 905–917.

Alvesson, M. (1995). *Management of knowledge-intensive companies* (Vol. 61). Berlin: Walter de Gruyter.

Alvesson, M. (2000). Social identity and the problem of loyalty in knowledge-intensive companies. *Journal of Management Studies, 37*(8), 1101–1124.

Alvesson, M. (2004). *Knowledge work and knowledge-intensive firms*. Oxford: Oxford University Press.

Arogyaswamy, K., Barker, V. L., & Yasai-Ardekani, M. (1995). Firm turnarounds: An integrative two-stage model. *Journal of Management Studies, 32*(4), 493–525.

Barker, V. L., & Duhaime, I. M. (1997). Strategic change in the turnaround process: Theory and empirical evidence. *Strategic Management Journal, 18*(1), 13–38.

Barker, V. L., & Mone, M. A. (1998). The mechanistic structure shift and strategic reorientation in declining firms attempting turnarounds. *Human Relations, 51*(10), 1227–1258.

Barker, V. L., Patterson, P. W., & Mueller, G. C. (2001). Organizational causes and strategic consequences of the extent of top management team replacement during turnaround attempts. *Journal of Management Studies, 38*(2), 235–270.

Bibeault, D. B. (1982). *Corporate turnaround*. New York: McGraw-Hill.

Brockner, J. (1992). Managing the effects of layoffs on survivors. *California Management Review, 34*(2), 9–28.

Bruton, G., Ahlstrom, D., & Wan, J. (2003). Turnaround in East Asian firms: Evidence from ethnic overseas Chinese communities. *Strategic Management Journal, 24*(6), 519–540.

Burt, R. S. (2009). *Structural holes: The social structure of competition*. Cambridge: Harvard University Press.

Campbell, B. A., Coff, R., & Kryscynski, D. (2012). Rethinking sustained competitive advantage from human capital. *Academy of Management Review, 37*(3), 376–395.

Cascio, W. F. (1993). Downsizing: What do we know? What have we learned? *Academy of Management Executive, 7*(1), 95–104.

Chen, G., & Hambrick, D. C. (2012). CEO replacement in turnaround situations: Executive (mis)fit and its performance implications. *Organization Science, 23*(1), 225–243.

Claessens, S., & Klapper, L. F. (2005). Bankruptcy around the world: Explanations of its relative use. *American Law and Economics Review*, 7(1), 253–283.

Coff, R. W. (1999). When competitive advantage doesn't lead to performance: The resource-based view and stakeholder bargaining power. *Organization Science*, 10(2), 119–133.

Cooper, D. P. (2001). Innovation and reciprocal externalities: Information transmission via job mobility. *Journal of Economic Behavior & Organization*, 45(4), 403–425.

Dess, G. G., & Beard, D. W. (1984). Dimensions of organizational task environments. *Administrative Science Quarterly*, 29(1), 52–73.

DeWitt, R. L. (1998). Firm, industry, and strategy influences on choice of downsizing approach. *Strategic Management Journal*, 19(1), 59–79.

Donaldson, L. (2001). *The contingency theory of organizations*. Washington, DC: Sage Publications.

Fisher, S. R., & White, M. A. (2000). Downsizing in a learning organization: Are there hidden costs? *Academy of Management Review*, 25(1), 244–251.

Graham, S. J., & Mowery, D. C. (2003). Intellectual property protection in the US software industry. In W. M. Cohen & S. A. Merril (Eds.), *Patents in the knowledge-based economy* (pp. 219–258). Washington, DC: National Academies Press.

Grant, R. M. (1996). Toward a knowledge-based theory of the firm. *Strategic Management Journal*, 17(S2), 109–122.

Grindley, P. C., & Teece, D. J. (1997). Managing intellectual capital: Licensing and cross-licensing in semiconductors and electronics. *California Management Review*, 39(2), 8–41.

Grinyer, P., & McKiernan, P. (1990). Generating major change in stagnating companies. *Strategic Management Journal*, 11(4), 131–146.

Hambrick, D. C., & D'Aveni, R. A. (1992). Top team deterioration as part of the downward spiral of large corporate bankruptcies. *Management Science*, 38(10), 1445–1466.

Hambrick, D. C., & Schecter, S. M. (1983). Turnaround strategies for mature industrial-product business units. *Academy of Management Journal*, 26(2), 231–248.

Hansen, M. T. (1999). The search transfer problem: The role of weak ties in sharing knowledge across organizational sub-units. *Administrative Science Quarterly*, 44(1), 82–111.

Hatch, N. W., & Dyer, J. H. (2004). Human capital and learning as a source of sustainable competitive advantage. *Strategic Management Journal*, 25(12), 1155–1178.

Hayton, J. C. (2005). Competing in the new economy: The effect of intellectual capital on corporate entrepreneurship in high-technology new ventures. *R&D Management*, 35(2), 137–155.

Hofer, C. W. (1975). Toward a contingency theory of business strategy. *Academy of Management Journal*, 18(4), 784–810.

Hofer, C. W. (1980). Turnaround strategies. *Journal of Business Strategy*, 1(1), 19–31.

Hopkins, S. M., & Weathington, B. L. (2006). The relationships between justice perceptions, trust, and employee attitudes in a downsized organization. *Journal of Psychology*, 140(5), 477–498.

Iverson, R. D., & Pullman, J. A. (2000). Determinants of voluntary turnover and layoffs in an environment of repeated downsizing following a merger: An event history analysis. *Journal of Management*, 26, 977–1003.

Koch, M. J., & McGrath, R. G. (1996). Improving labor productivity: Human resource management policies do matter. *Strategic Management Journal*, 17(5), 335–354.

Kogut, B., & Zander, U. (1996). What firms do? Coordination, identity, and learning. *Organization Science, 7*(5), 502–518.

Leonard, D., & Sensiper, S. (1998). The role of tacit knowledge in group innovation. *California Management Review, 40*(3), 112–132.

Leonard-Barton, D. (1992). Core capabilities and core rigidities: A paradox in managing new product development. *Strategic Management Journal, 13*(S1), 111–125.

Liebowitz, J., & Suen, C. Y. (2000). Developing knowledge management metrics for measuring intellectual capital. *Journal of Intellectual Capital, 1*(1), 54–67.

Lim, D., Celly, N., Morse, E., & Rowe, W. (2013). Rethinking the effectiveness of asset and cost retrenchment: The contingency effects of a firm's rent creation mechanism. *Strategic Management Journal, 34*(1), 42–61.

Lohrke, F., Ahlstrom, D., & Bruton, G. (2012). Extending turnaround process research: Important lessons from the US civil war. *Journal of Management Inquiry, 21*, 217–234.

Lohrke, F. T., Bedeian, A. G., & Palmer, T. B. (2004). The role of top management teams in formulating and implementing turnaround strategies: A review and research agenda. *International Journal of Management Reviews, 5*(2), 63–90.

McFarlin, D., & Sweeny, P. (1992). Distributive and procedural justice as predictors of satisfaction with personal and organizational outcomes. *Academy of Management Journal, 35*, 626–638.

Miles, R. E., Snow, C. C., Meyer, A. D., & Coleman, H. J. (1978). Organizational strategy, structure, and process. *Academy of Management Review, 3*(3), 546–562.

Mowery, D. C. (1995). *International computer software industry*. Oxford: Oxford University Press.

Mueller, C. W., & Price, J. L. (1990). Economic, psychological, and sociological determinants of voluntary turnover. *Journal of Behavioral Economics, 19*, 321–335.

Nahapiet, J., & Ghoshal, S. (1998). Social capital, intellectual capital, and the organizational advantage. *Academy of Management Review, 23*(2), 242–266.

Ndofor, H. A., Vanevenhoven, J., & Barker, V. L. (2013). Software firm turnarounds in the 1990s: An analysis of reversing decline in a growing, dynamic industry. *Strategic Management Journal, 34*(9), 1123–1133.

Porter, M. E. (1980). *Competitive strategy: Techniques for analyzing industries and competitors*. New York: Free Press.

Robbins, D. K., & Pearce, J. A. (1992). Turnaround: Retrenchment and recovery. *Strategic Management Journal, 13*(4), 287–309.

Schendel, D., Patton, G., & Riggs, J. (1976). Corporate turnaround strategies: A study of profit decline and recovery. *Journal of General Management, 3*(3), 3–11.

Scherer, F. M. (1982). Inter-industry technology flows in the United States. *Research Policy, 11*(4), 227–245.

Schmitt, A., Borzillo, S., & Probst, G. (2012). Don't let knowledge walk away: Knowledge retention during employee downsizing. *Management Learning, 43*(1), 53–74.

Schmitt, A., & Raisch, S. (2013). Corporate turnarounds: The duality of retrenchment and recovery. *Journal of Management Studies, 50*(7), 1216–1244.

Trahms, C. A., Ndofor, H. A., & Sirmon, D. G. (2013). Organizational decline and turnaround: A review and agenda for future research. *Journal of Management, 39*(5), 577–588.

Whetten, D. A. (1980). Organizational decline: A neglected topic in organizational science. *Academy of Management Review, 5*(4), 577–588.

18 Turning SMEs Around

On Breaking and Making Organizational Paths

Jörg Freiling and Hartmut Meyer

18.1 Introduction

This chapter tries to identify the basic problems that prevents SMEs from breaking out. In doing so, we employ research on path dependence for a better understanding of the mechanisms that create a situation called 'lock-in' or a stage quite close to it. Path dependence (Figure 18.1) is a concept about mechanisms that make organizations stay on a certain track of development (Arthur, 1989; David, 1985; Schreyögg, Sydow, & Koch, 2009).

Figure 18.1 exhibits how organizations lose discretion in terms of available real options over time and get committed more and more. At first, an organization starts with a wide scope of possible options to choose from (phase I). The process of becoming path dependent starts with events that trigger self-reinforcing dynamics because of a number of economic and social patterns. As these dynamics get stronger, a critical juncture occurs where the operating range of an o+rganization narrows (phase II). When this juncture is passed, the organization inevitably ends up in a lock-in situation (Schreyögg et al., 2009). In this state (phase III), decisions and commitments of the past cannot be reversed. Generally, path dependence as a phenomenon is characterized by four properties: non-predictability, non-ergodicity (run ex ante not determined), inflexibility, and potential inefficiency (Schreyögg et al., 2009).

18.2 Theoretical Foundations of Path Dependence and SME Challenges Within Crises

What are the mechanisms that cause these self-reinforcing effects in light of SMEs in crises? Path dependence suggests that four basic mechanisms play a role—namely, learning effects, adaptive expectations, coordination effects, and complementarity effects.

Learning effects point to efficiency gains by repetition (Schreyögg et al., 2009). Learning implies the generation of new knowledge and the process of embedding this knowledge in personal and/or organizational structures

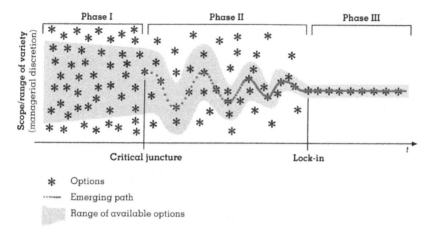

Figure. 18.1 The Emergence of Organizational Path Dependence
(Source: Schreyögg et al., 2009: 692)

so that it can be applied more easily and more powerfully. It is often based on evolving heuristics and routines for ordinary operations as well as decision-making logics in terms of management. Previously learned knowledge steers cognitive processes and can make organizations prone to inertia. Particularly in case the of dominant logics (Prahalad & Bettis, 1986), relevant knowledge undergoes selection processes with the consequence that 'harmonic' knowledge may pass, whereas disharmonic knowledge is rejected. It goes without saying that this may be a root cause of crises, particularly in the case of entrepreneur-centered SMEs. Hence, we propose the following:

Proposition 1. Entrepreneur-focused dominant logics frame SMEs and reinforce downturns.

According to Schreyögg et al. (2009), the *adaption of behavior* rests on the experiences and expectations of other persons' reactions to the behavior. Preferences can vary in response to the expectations of others. The reason for this behavior is the human need for social belonging (Schreyögg et al., 2009). People and people-centered organizations such as SMEs are subconsciously afraid of breaking out of the mainstream and being stigmatized as 'outsiders' (Kulik et al., 2008), so they try to adopt industry standards the best they can. This can lead to (late) follower behavior and weaken the entrepreneurial orientation. Moreover, it makes SMEs strategically inflexible and, thus, vulnerable in case of unfortunate developments. Path research argues that these processes can be self-reinforcing (Schreyögg et al., 2009).

Moreover, in the case of negative feedback in financial terms, SMEs get disoriented and scared. Subsequently, entrepreneurs can take exaggerated defensive actions (Freiling et al., 2010).

> *Proposition 2. Adaptive expectations with strategic impact dilute the strategic profile of SMEs and reinforce downturns.*

Following North (1990) and Schreyögg and Sydow (2011), *coordination effects* build on the benefits of rule-guided behavior. Organization-wide accepted rules and routines make behavior more stable and predictable while lowering costs. At the same time, rules and routines are deeply embedded in people's minds and organizational structures. In case of change, they need to be unlearned and replaced by other solutions. Changes are hard, take a long time, and are uncertain in terms of outcome. Regarding SMEs in organizational crises, these coordination effects may show their downside and prevent SMEs from reorientations they sometimes urgently need. *Complementarity effects* build on synergies based on the interaction of two or more separate but interrelated resources, rules, or practices (Pierson, 2000; Schreyögg & Sydow, 2011). In case the of SMEs, we can often find interrelated routines, practices, and/or rules that help them gain efficiency but make organizational change hard in the same way as coordination effects do. Hence we propose the following:

> *Proposition 3. Coordination and complementarily effects slow down the pace of change of SMEs and hamper renewal.*

SMEs in crises often find themselves already heading toward a lock-in in the later steps of phase 2 (Figure 18.1). Typical SME characteristics such as liabilities of smallness (i.e., resource bottlenecks) fuel the process and reduce the number of available real options more rapidly than it is common for larger entities. Insofar, the 'tangible' power to revitalize the company is limited and decreasing during the crisis. This leads to a shrinking execution of entrepreneurial functions (Freiling, 2008; Freiling & Lütke Schelhowe, 2014). According to Freiling's (2008) model of entrepreneurial functions, this implies that innovation, internal coordination, arbitrage, and risk management—as four interrelated entrepreneurial functions that form the construct of entrepreneurship—are no longer executed the same way as before the crisis, which has a negative impact on performance (Freiling & Lütke Schelhowe, 2014). This causes additional inertia not considered by research on path dependence that we take into account as follows:

> *Proposition 4. A lack of entrepreneurship not only triggers a crisis of SMEs but also reinforces it and has a negative impact on performance.*

18.3   Overcoming Organizational Crises of SMEs

According to the definition of Krystek (1987), a crisis needs to be understood as a situation where prime objectives of an enterprise such as compatibility, profitability, or solvency are threatened. This definition allows us to understand turnaround management as a situation where *substantial decisions* are required to 'turn' a negative or threatening situation through various actions. The development of these actions requires a *managerial process* and is by nature a project. The start of a turnaround situation is the recognition of the situation and the perception of the need to take action. The end of the project is the achievement of retaining stability, profitability, and the ability to meet the financial obligations of the enterprise.

Research on organizational crisis stays still more on a descriptive level rather than on an analytical and model-building one. The focus in the current chapter is to understand the process, to define factors initiating an organizational crisis, and to take appropriate measures for fixing problems, as, for example, the implementation of financial monitoring systems (Schulenburg, 2008). However, to regard turnaround as a simple matter of fixing problems will not lead to a sustainable organizational development after a crisis; it may not be of assistance at all. It takes a more substantial organizational change to retain the required strategic fit (Greve, 2010; John & Desai, 2005). Moreover, the process from the initial information indicating organizational problems up to taking managerial actions appears to be complicated, as different publications as well as the daily news of enterprise failures suggest (see, e.g., Gelshorn, Michallik, & Stähle, 1991; KFW Research, 2015). The complexity of this process contains the combination of more 'rational' economic arguments under the consideration of a number of psychological and behavioral challenges.

According to the clusters of research, the key issues required to break up an organizational path are as follows:

- Coping with psychological and behavioral challenges to break patterns of thinking and routines to allow change (Federowski, 2009; Freiling, 2005; Geiger & Schröder, 2014; Meyer, 2015)
- Creating financial stability in order to allow time to break up organizational patterns (Hagemeier & Welckce, 1988; Krystek & Moldenhauer, 2007; Thoma, 2010)
- Building up a turnaround governance in order to provide a structured change process and a substantial frame to determine future organizational behavior (John & Desai, 2005; Krystek, 1987; Crone & Werner, 2007)

Nevertheless, research does not provide a clear pattern of turnaround. The approach in this chapter is a structured approach to the literature as well as observations by the authors through various pieces of research and assignments in the research field (Collan et al., 2014; Freiling & Dressel, 2015; Freiling & Grossmann, 2013; Meyer, 2015).

18.3.1   Breaking the Organization Path: The Psychological and Behavioral Challenge

Change can only be performed through and with people and is not a simple technical matter of fixing problems. To prepare organizational path breaking (and finally to make it), means in the first place managing stakeholders, in particular working with the entrepreneur or small business managers. There is a need to deal with psychological effects in order to change motivation, behaviors, beliefs (trust in their), capabilities, and cluster thinking, as well as to restore the entrepreneurial motivation. The main problem is often changing routines (e.g., Geiger & Schröder, 2014; Greiner, 1972) to deal with psychological and organizational resistance. A bulk of the literature and research has been conducted to understand the pattern of a crisis (Groß, 2009; Hagemeier & Welckce, 1988; Harz, 2006; Rüsen, 2009; Börsch-Supan, Gasche, & Wilke, 2010). The main objective of this research was to develop instruments and indicators for risk management. The analysis of these patterns suggests an entrepreneurial behavior of constant organizational adjustment to upcoming strategic and operational problems (Freiling, 2005; Kehrel & Leker, 2009; Meyer, 2012; Rüsen, 2009; Crone & Werner, 2007). A false or unchanged strategic behavior extends the duration of the path, but in the end, sunken costs of resistance will determine the crisis path further (Hauschildt, Grape, & Schindler, 2006). Due to their personnel liabilities, the problems of adjustment get enhanced as they feel in charge of their company, the employees, and the product and service quality of the company.

In this context, the findings of Greve (2010) are of particular interest in order to understand a problematic organizational path as a consequence of organizational burnout. Past success made the enterprise stable and allowed for material comfort. In particular, engagement in the daily operations further fostered a lack of innovation and ideas. Once signs of an uprising crisis occur, they are answered by routines of cost cutting and price reductions. Moreover, there appears to be a desire for a 'big bang' in terms of the adaptation of innovation and new clients, as well as a drastic change of the economic climate without considering necessary internal measures and know-how. In order to break the path and to broaden its management, there is a need for managers to leave behind the feeling of lost chances and mutual assignment of guilt, and to return to the current organizational realities. The break in the path, however, can only be reached by defined turnaround strategies (John & Desai, 2005).

In summary, there arises a fatal triangle to be dealt with in order to allow the breaking of an organizational path (Meyer, 2015):

- Fear of losing one's role in the company as well as receiving criticism
- Time to learn about new chances and to manage them
- Pressure to compile financial obligations as well as to avoid an organizational breakdown

Among the hopes and objectives is that managers get the old feeling back so they can control the enterprise and find some discretion.

In order to change the beliefs and values, time is required to allow a reflection of past behavior in the presence of new know-how or market perceptions. Thereby, one key for success is combining existing technical and operational knowledge with new upcoming perspectives, while at the same time unlearning things (Geiger & Schröder, 2013) that caused the organizational decline. Managers may conclude that a crisis is not a situation of their own personnel failure (Imgrund, 2009). Often one finds that they have a number of ideas for change (Meyer, 2015). These ideas were put to rest because of missing managerial support, high-risk adversity, and missing financial resources. Hence there is a need to channel this situation while introducing new market knowledge. The sparks of change, or of a returning entrepreneurial spirit, however, appear first as positive feedback that needed to be allocated to the entrepreneur in question. There is a need, according to Lewin (1947), for an 'unfreezing' process where outside expertise is needed to structure the problem and operationalize the necessary changes in the context of a company. Past successes of the organization need to be transferred into a new set of frames where the entrepreneur is able to maintain his or her role as manager (Meyer, 2015). In order to achieve this feeling, the following issues should be tackled in more detail:

- Decisions-making processes
- Change of managerial routines and values
- Fostering entrepreneurial motivation and resolving past conflicts

---

Case for Proposition 1

Entrepreneur-focused dominant logics frame SMEs and reinforce downturns.

In the south of Germany, an eco-friendly hotel operated for ten years and struggled during that time with its finances. Due to the strict application of healthy food and ecological challenges, the hotel had a sales problem. Although the clients were highly satisfied with the service, the hotel rates were quite expensive, and there were many service regulations such as no televisions in the rooms and now Internet access at night that discouraged potential customers. Market research information was only accepted by the board of the ecological hotel association or healthy food boards. In this case, it was necessary to bring customer expectations in line with the strict application of the hotel's rules. Clients appreciate the ecological approach, but more on a practical hybrid basis.

In the implementation of the compromise and its marketing, it was observed that the number of reservations rose quickly. Moreover, due to a conflict between the partners of the hotel, the owners decided to separate. This action reduced a number of resistances and sped up the decision-making process. Today, the hotel has good profits and stands as a model for a good eco-friendly hotel.

According to Lange (2004), the most predominant issue is altering the decision-making process. Due to the perceived market and customer knowledge, there is a tendency to neglect external information. One can observe that complex or new information is neglected because it is not understood. Furthermore, the consequences of innovation and market trends can be misinterpreted. The validity or representativeness of information is often not questioned and single instances are generalized (John & Desai, 2005). The application of the information is often guided by the feeling (and the approach) of preserving their own status. Decisions are often guided more by trust than an evaluation of the cost/benefits or profit/loss (Meyer, 2015). In particular, an evaluation of existing services or products takes place in the context of existing customers and not through a value-free benchmarking approach.

Federowski (2009) stresses in this context the impact of managerial routines on breaking up organizational paths. Inadequate managerial routines foster the occurrence of organizational crises, including how market and cost information is interpreted, how processes in the organization are managed, and how decision-making processes are performed. The logic of thinking, selection, and interpretation of information can inhibit turnaround processes. For a successful breaking of organizational paths, these routines must either be altered or unlearned and replaced by the introduction of new routines while broadening the organization's way of thinking. As an example, competition is answered by a cost and price reduction rather than by an evaluation of the company's own market position, customer value, and product or service price (Greve, 2010). The know-how transfer is the provision and application of analytical tools and includes fostering the use of new technology. The climate of this knowledge transfer must be designed by a peer relationship between the external expert and the entrepreneur in question (John & Desai, 2005).

Case for Preposition 2

Adaptive expectations with strategic impact dilute the strategic profile of SMEs and reinforce downturns.

Gochon the butcher provides various meat and butcher products in a rural region. Furthermore, he offers a catering service to a neighborhood chemical plant. Due to the well-established services in the past, good profits have been realized and special capacities have been built up for this service.After a decline within the chemical industry, the requests for catering decreased as well as the prices that were more or less 'dictated' by the chemical plant. The effect was the the service lost its profitability. However, the butcher needed to maintain business for the enterprise. Although the financial figures presented a clear language, the business was regarded as a sign of stability and security. Moreover, the butcher felt very much at 'peace in the neighborhood.' Hence the owner stuck to providing the services to the chemical plant although the request for regional meat products increased. Only after a clear strategy with the objective to separate the enterprise from the business did he found the energy and solid ground to negotiate new prices. The turnaround strategy involved separating the enterprise from the catering service to the chemical plant and concentrating on the traditional service of butchery. Once this separation was performed, the organization returned to profitability, and the owner is now investing in the production of regional meat products.

To empower the entrepreneur to change routines, he must have the feeling of losing the tights of financial distress. This feeling is regarded as a first success and fertilizes the readiness to open up to change and to return back to the role of entrepreneur. This will also allow for a change of routines and to cope with organizational resistance by applying a structured approach. In order to conduct major changes, clear project management is required to give the organization some stability to rely on (Faulhaber & Grabow, 2009).

The other challenge is that management, as well as the staff, must be committed to the change process and being involved in it. This is not a one-off exercise and requires constant communication. In family and smaller businesses, there is a need to define the new roles and to provide the knowledge to reduce conflicts. Of major importance is that the company treats a member who is altering or losing power with utmost care to reduce organizational resistance. This period of change is a coaching exercise to help staff learn to maintain a commitment to change (John & Desai, 2005).

The need to transfer the required know-how needs to be financed by a low-threshold approach (e.g., consultancy support by public grants) (Meyer & Paulsen, 2016). Often one finds that once managers have gotten the feeling of retaining the situation, a firework of ideas begins that was hidden in the past. There was always a fear and sometimes resignation of taking the actions for change. Once the ice is broken, turnaround happens by itself when it encounters a renewed entrepreneurial drive. The value of this know-how transfer is appraised differently at a later time, and one is prepared to pay for it for future assignments.

Case for Preposition 3

Coordination and complementarity effects slow down the pace of change of SMEs and hamper renewal.

Neptun, a third-generation family restaurant, offered banquettes, catering, and restaurant services, as well as forty-six hotel rooms at a three-star level. In the past, the style of that restaurant was very successful, and the company grew to be a leading enterprise in the region. Then development stopped and declined during the last five years.

The style of the restaurant and the pricing policy, as well as the service strategy, led to the company's decline and staff turnover. As a result, the cost of production and, in particular, the cost for labor was very high. The enterprise did not make a profit. Due to the pressure from the bank, an external consultant was engaged to increase profitability. Despite all of the figures, the owners defended their processes with the argument that clients were satisfied with their services. In very small steps, and with a huge amount of resistance, the owners opened up to the alteration of processes, including personnel planning. Moreover, the communication between different departments improved. As a result, the cost of labor decreased incrementally, and the company returned to a profitable situation. Since the financial burden eased, the climate in the organization changed, and the enterprise became ready for succession. New marketing activities and the use of e-commerce for hotel reservations allowed for further change of the organization path.

18.3.2   Breaking Organization Path: The Financial Challenge

The management of finances is a another starting point for any turnaround situation. It prepares the organization for breaking the existing organizational paths (Hagemeier & Welkcke, 1988; Crone & Werner, 2007). This need is due to the legal implications of the insolvency law and may hamper reconstruction because of a strict definition of solvency. In case of an off-court reconstruction, a positive going-concern prognosis is required to achieve the cooperation of the trustees who request a restructuring plan (Thoma, 2010).

Financial restructuring is often a matter of demonstrating financial management and the consequence of actions rather than the money (Meyer, 2015). The underlying problem is maintaining stakeholders' trust, which can only happen with solid business planning and action. In particular, trustees like to see that measures to change the situation are in place. In the long run, this approach may lead to a change in the trustees' attitudes and often to financing for new ventures.

Case for Preposition 4

A lack of entrepreneurship not only triggers a crisis in SMEs but also reinforces it and has a negative impact on performance.

The carpenter James Oak was a successful business starter and offered individual furniture craft services to households and enterprises. Due to a fast-growing business, he started increasing his workforce without considering the required additional turnover to finance the extra costs. As a consequence, he operated with losses and worked without paying himself a salary. After a while, he lost the entrepreneurial motivation to seek new orders, and the enterprise faced significant financial problems. Strict financial and revenue planning turned the situation around. In addition, through the help of an external consultant, the owner became aware of the significance of economic relationships and performance measures for future decision making. As a result, he regained his entrepreneurial motivation while fulfilling the forecasts and returned to the required creativity in his business. Now the enterprise has grown, and James is investing a substantial amount to enlarge production capacities.

The first step in meeting the financial challenge is to know all parties and creditors involved in a turnaround situation (Buth & Hermanns, 2014; Faulhaber & Grabow, 2009; Meyer, 2012). It is a stock-taking exercise, including identifying the stakeholders' motivation for collaboration. With the objective to change and to broaden the organizational path, successful financial restructuring means retaining solvency as well as using the internal cash flow for small investment in the area of product development or marketing activities. Once the trustees have a feeling of true communication, they are likely to cooperate and agree to a moratorium. Thereby both sides need to come to the conclusions that they are only winning parties once they start to collaborate (Slatter, Lovett, & Barlow, 2006). The initial step needs to be done by the organization in question to create transparency. This is a major challenge for entrepreneurs. Due to the ownership, first-time successes will lead to an increase in the pace of change, thanks to the organizational advantages of smaller companies. However, there is also the danger that once these problems have been resolved, smaller businesses will become reluctant to pursue further necessary changes, although the owners have noticed the need for those changes.

Financial restructuring efforts need to pursue a twofold strategy to deal with the risk adversity of commercial banks and other creditors (Buth & Hermanns, 2014). In the first place, it requires solid forecast and revenue management, including benchmarking to identify problem areas. Soemtimes this means turning over every stone within an organization to seek out improvements. It is an incremental process and not a one-time exercise to build up trust and solvency. In the quest to achieve financial stability and to regain control of the situation, external possibilities of funding are limited for smaller companies (Meyer, 2015). In most cases, there are only internal measures possible (e.g., to increase the cash flow, to retain the capital serving capacity):

- Cost cutting while revising existing contracts and processes
- Revising the pricing policy and calculation
- Revising accounting procedures and the appraisal of assets
- Revising stock taking
- Revising invoicing and creditor procedures

The application of these measures requires a lot of creativity as well as resolute actions by the turnaround team. Only in later stages will the smaller companies have access to new funding for long-term changes. The desire of for additional funding for changes and outstanding debts in a one-off approach is often not feasible. The bank has to find reasons for funding in the rating procedures. Creativity and entrepreneurial spirit are often needed to finance the necessary initial changes (Faulhaber & Grabow, 2009; Harz, 2006). Once these changes take place and the bank is able to see an increase in profitability and competiveness, it will be are more willing to provide new financial capital. Once this moment is realized, managers can return to their entrepreneurial spirit and break with organizational paths as the research on failure and restart suggests. Cooperation and communication with trustees is crucial during the crisis and needs to be learned. This also includes the performance of financial monitoring systems to support the professional approach and to retain trust.

18.3.3   Turnaround Governance

Turnaround governance is a clear approach to conducting the turnaround project. Managerial instruments are used in such a way that declining situations can be turned based on valid information (Hagemeier & Wlecke, 1988). The problem with governing a restructuring effort is that, often due to financial pressure, the aforementioned challenges need to take place simultaneously (Groß, 1988). Only by using a clear approach based on the model in Figure 18.2 can the requirements for governance be achieved while

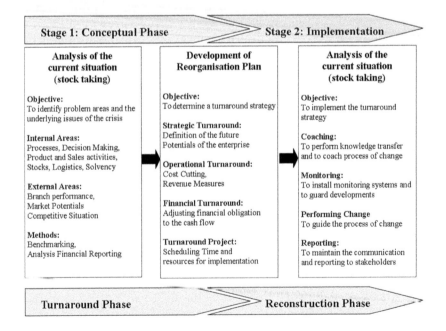

Figure 18.2 Turnaround Governance

maintaining the entrepreneur on board (Harz, 2006; Schellenberg, 2007; Crone & Werner, 2007).

In the development of a reorganization plan, strategic reorganization plays a decisive role in the process. In particular, the following questions should be answered:

1   What is the future marketplace of the company?
2   Why we do need the company?

Once these questions have been answered meaningfully, the turnaround team is able to balance the organizational activities with the needs of the environment, and they may be to break paths in light of newly defined chances. After developing a turnaround strategy, the operative reorganization plan can be deduced from the strategy as well as the planned cash flow for financial commitments. These tasks require a solid knowledge of the turnaround situation and the willingness to take decisions and action. Moreover, in respect to small family businesses, managerial conflicts and power struggles need to be channeled to create a constructive environment for organizational change (Meyer, 2015).

In the implementation phase, the first step could be to install financial and managerial monitoring systems as a renewed approach to cooperative governance. With this action, knowledge transfer begins, and managers start to alter their decision-making processes based on rational arguments. In the case of smaller companies in a turnaround situation, managers start a benchmarking approach and identify their choices for changing organizational paths. In addition to fostering creativity and motivation to break with a path, there is a need to simplify organizational procedures and decisions and to bring in the knowledge to set up the procedures according to the resources of the company. This approach allows managers to consider their own strategic advantages and not to 'die in beauty.' Organizational change is not only the approach to move boxes; organizational changes must be market driven to allow a change of mentality and visions within the organization. This includes preparing its members for future tasks by using a hands-on approach.

With the objective to provide governance for a sustainable development of the enterprise, the following areas should be recognized:

- Articles of association or succession arrangements: This deals with the interest to influence the decision-making process as well as the obligations of each organizational member.
- Accounting procedures and financial reporting standards: There are often possibilities to value the equity of enterprise in such a way that the current rating can be improved.
- Installment of a management board or coaching possibilities: To break constantly with routines and to improve the quality of decision making.

- Reorganization of the duties of the manager: To allow more time to reflect a current situation and foster constant change.
- Arrangement of regularly management reviews: To maintain the range of organizational choices.

There is a need to set up constant path monitoring by a managerial monitoring system. Once the behavior as been established, the likelihood of perceiving and converting organizational choices increases (Schreyögg, 2013).

18.4 Conclusions

Besides all legal and financial requirements and burdens, turnaround management to break organizational paths is a matter of communication and personnel interaction. The driving force is the entrepreneur who needs to be ready to accept change, accept outside expertise, and promote the process. Turnaround is a matter of trust, presenting objective and purpose-oriented actions rather than waiting for a big bank. It is not an easy task or a one-off exercise. It is a period of constant interaction and development.

Change cannot be initiated by 'rational' models introducing input/output relationships for the measurement of profitability based on rational decision making. Change, also in turnaround situations, is more of a political- and emotional-based issue, as small business managers fear their role as managers and they tend to defend their routines and positions. Thus the emotional approach needs to be considered in such a way that empathies model through communication and emotional binding creates a situation of harmony. Moreover, it serves the purpose to recognize fear and feelings. Symbols seem to have great value here (Schellenberg, 2007). In summary, key points for successfully breaking organizational paths are as follows:

- Resolve conflicts within management or family boards
- Implement financial monitoring instruments
- Introduce knowledge for the generation of innovations
- Explore a market-based view
- Restore financial solvency in order to retain a liable business partner
- Coach changes and provide a helping hand
- Cope with pressure

Based on the belief that managers are able to learn entrepreneurship, at least to some extent, one can conclude that once managers reach a dead end and then return, they are more prepared for organizational development. In particular, the resistance to breaking up with organizational paths can be reduced. There is a need for further research to look at the psychological side of turnarounds in order to understand the triggers of entrepreneurial action and behavior in a crisis situation. Existing research suggests that we are at a starting point but do not yet have a model of these triggers (Dobusch & Kapeller, 2013).

References

Arthur, W. B. (1989). Competing technologies, increasing returns, and lock-in by historical events. *The Economic Journal, 99*(394), 116–131.

Börsch-Supan, A., Gasche, M., & Wilke, C.B. (2010). How sensitive is the German public pension system to economic recessions? An answer based on the current financial crisis. *Zeitschrift für Wirtschaftspolitik, 59*(3). 3–4.

Buth, H., & Hermanns, J. (2014). *Restructuring, Sanierung, Insolvenz*. München: Beck Verlag.

Collan, M., Freiling, J., Kyläheiko, K., & Roemer, E. (2014). Entrepreneurship and the art of tackling technological crises: A strategic real options framework. *International Journal of Technology Intelligence and Planning, 10*(2), 166–185.

Crone, C., & Werner, H. (2007). *Turnaround Management, Handbuch für modernes Sanierungsmanagement*. München: Vahlen Verlag.

David, P. A. (1985). Clio and the economics of QWERTY. *American Economic Review, 75*(2), 332–337.

Dobusch, L., & Kapeller, J. (2013). Breaking new path: Theory and method in path dependence research. *Schmalenbach Business Review, 65*(7), 288–311.

Faulhaber, P., & Grabow, H. (2009). *Turnaround Management in der Praxis*. Frankfurt: Campus Verlag.

Federowski, R. (2009). *Unternehmensroutinen im Turnaroundmanagement. Analyse der Wirkungen von Routinen und routinenbewusste Gestaltung der Krisenbewältigung*. Wiesbaden: Gabler.

Freiling, J. (2005). "Dominant Logic" als Handlungsbarriere beim Management von Ad-hoc-Krisen. In C. Burmann, J. Freiling & M. Hülsmann (Eds.), *Management von Ad-hoc-Krisen* (pp. 443–459). Wiesbaden: Springer Gabler.

Freiling, J. (2008). SME management—What can we learn from entrepreneurship theory? *International Journal of Entrepreneurship Education, 6*(1), 1–19.

Freiling, J., & Dressel, K. (2015). Exploring constrained rates of adoption of 'Total Cost of Ownership' models: A service dominant logic analysis. *International Small Business Journal, 33*(7), 774–793.

Freiling, J., & Grossmann, S. (2013). Konflikte in Familienunternehmen: Zur Bedeutung des Erlernens von Konfliktkompetenz in Familienunternehmen. *Austrian Management Review, 3*(1), 67–75.

Freiling, J., Laudien, S. M., Schmidt, M., & Wessels, J. (2010). *Entrepreneurial failure in the spotlight of the entrepreneurship theory*. Presented at the 7th AGBA Annual World Congress, Putrajaya, Malaysia.

Freiling, J., & Lütke Schelhowe, C. (2014). The impact of entrepreneurial orientation on the performance of internationalization. *Journal of Entrepreneurship, Management and Innovation, 10*(4), 169–199.

Geiger, D., & Schröder, A. (2014). Ever-changing routines? Toward a revised understanding of organizational routines between rule-following and rule-breaking. *Schmalenbachs Business Review, 66*(7), 170–190.

Gelshorn, T., Michallik, S., & Stähle, W. H. (1991). *Die Innovationsorientierung mittelständischer Unternehmen*. Stuttgart: Poeschel.

Greiner, L. E. (1972). Evolution and revolution as organizations grow. *Harvard Business Review, 50*, 37–46.

Greve, G. (2010). *Organizational burnout: Das versteckte Phänomen ausgebrannter organisationen.* Wiesbaden: Springer Gabler.

Groß, P. J. (1988). Sanierung durch Fortführungsgesellschaften. 2. Aufl., Köln: Schmidt.

Groß, P. J. (2009). Design of reorganisation, Sanierung erfolgreich umsetzen. *Zeitschrift für Führung und Organisation,* 04/2009, 213–219.

Hagemeier, W., & Welkcke, U. (1988). Turnaround/Restrukturierung von Unternehmen in Krisensituationen. In W. Hagemeier & U. Welkcke (Eds.), *Strategische Unternehmensberatung* (pp. 69–99). Wiesbaden: Springer Gabler.

Harz, M. (2006). *Turnaround management: Sanierungsmanagement: Unternehmen aus der Krise führen.* Düsseldorf: Verlag Wirtschaft und Finanzen.

Hauschildt, J., Grape, C., & Schindler, M. (2006). Typologien von Unternehmenskrisen im Wandel. *Die Betriebswirtschaft, 66,* 7–25.

Imgrund, M. (2009). SME in Insolvency, Der Unternehmer in der Insolvenz—Eine empirische Analyse des Fortführungs- und Sanierungsprozesses insolventer Klein- und Mittelunternehmen. *Zeitschrift für Kreditwesen, 57*(3–4), 159–185.

John, D. F., & Desai, A. (2005). Situational and organizational determinants of turnaround. *Management Decision, 43*(9), 1203–1224.

Kehrel, U., & Leker, J. (2009). Company Crisis, Unternehmenskrisen. *Zeitschrift für Führung und Organisation,* April, 200–205.

KFW Research. (2015). *KFW Mittelstands Innovation Report 2014.* Retrieved from https://www.kfw.de/PDF/Download-Center/Konzernthemen/Research/PDF-Dokumente-Innovationsbericht/KfW-Innovationsbericht-Mittelstand-2014.pdf

Krystek, U. (1987). *Unternehmungskrisen: Beschreibung, Vermeidung und Bewältigung überlebenskritischer Prozesse in Unternehmungen.* Wiesbaden: Springer Verlag.

Krystek, U., & Moldenhauer, R. (2007). *Handbuch Krisen- und Restrukturierungsmanagement—Generelle Konzepte, Spezialprobleme, Praxisberichte.* Stuttgart: W. Kohlhammer GmbH Stuttgart.

Kulik, C. T., Bainbridge, H. T. J., & Cregan, C. (2008). Known by the company we keep: Stigma-by-association effects in the workplace. *Academy of Management Review, 33*(1), 216–230.

Lange, I. (2004). Effizienzverbesserung durch die zunehmende Rationalität der Beteiligten im Insolvenzverfahren. In N. Beckhoff, M. Blatz, G. Eilenberger, S. Haghani & K. J. Kraus (Eds.), *Unternemenskrise als Chance* (pp. 113–138). Berlin: Springer Verlag.

Lewin, K. (1947). Group decision and social change. *Readings in Social Psychology, 3,* 197–211.

Meyer, H. (2012). *Management in der Gastronomie: Führung und Finanzierung eines Familienbetriebes.* München: Oldenbourg Verlag.

Meyer, H. (2015). *Turnaround management in small family businesses: A Qualitative Research in the German Tourism Industry.* Paper presented at the 60th ICSB World Conference, Dubai 2015.

Meyer, H., & Paulsen, B. (2016). *Public innovation management support in rural areas: The artie case in Germany, 2. Wirtschaftswissenschaftliches Forum an der FOM Hochschule in München.* München: Gabler Verlag.

North, D. C. (1990). *Institutions, institutional change and economic performance.* Cambridge: University Press.

Pierson, P. (2000). Increasing returns, path dependence, and the study of politics. *American Political Science Review, 94*(2), 251–267.

Prahalad, C. K., & Bettis, R. A. (1986). The dominant logic: A new linkage between diversity and performance. *Strategic Management Journal, 7*(6), 485–501.

Rüsen, T. A. (2009). *Turnaround management, Krisenmanagement familienunternehmer.* Wiesbaden: Gabler Verlag.

Schellenberg, D. (2007). *Der Strategieprozess in der Sanierung.* Hamburg: Verlag Dr. Kovac.

Schreyögg, G. (2013). In der Sackgasse, organisationale Pfadabhängigkeit und ihre Folgen. *Organisationsentwicklung, 1,* 21–28.

Schreyögg, G., & Sydow, J. (2011). Organizational path dependence: A process view. *Organization Studies, 32*(3), 321–335.

Schreyögg, G., Sydow, J., & Koch, J. (2009). Organizational path dependence: Opening the black box. *Academy of Management Review, 34*(4), 689–709.

Schröder, A., & Geiger, D. (2013). The stability paradox of organizational routines: Enacting routines in hot situations, Academy of Management Conference, Lake Buena Vista.

Schulenburg, N. (2008). *Die Entstehung von Unternehmenskrisen, eine evolutionstheoretische Erklärung.* Wiesbaden: Gabler Edition Wissenschaft.

Slatter, S., Lovett, D., & Barlow, L. (2006). *Leading corporate turnaround: How leaders fix troubled companies.* New York: John Wiley.

Thoma, W. (2010). *Turnaround management rechtliche Grundlagen der unternehmenssanierung in Handbuch für Sanierungen.* Stuttgart: Schaeffer-Poeschel Verlag.

Part VI

Cases and Game

19 Back to the Future

The General Motors Restructuring Plan

Jan Adriaanse

If General Motors, Ford and Chrysler get the bailout that their chief executives asked for (. . .), you can kiss the American automotive industry goodbye. It won't go overnight, but its demise will be virtually guaranteed. Without that bailout, Detroit will need to drastically restructure itself. With it, the automakers will stay the course (. . .). Detroit needs a turnaround, not a check.

Mitt Romney, *New York Times*, November 19, 2008

November 7th, 2008, 11:00am EST

Just before the trading of General Motors stocks halts, in anticipation of a major announcement concerning the company's financial situation, you and your team walk into GM Detroit's headquarters for a meeting with Rick Wagoner, chairman and chief executive officer of General Motors. On the agenda is a restructuring that should take place in the following months. Your specialized restructuring boutique is asked to quickly draw up a plan that should serve as the basis for stakeholder negotiations in the following weeks.

Due to time constraints, the availability of company data is limited. At the end of the afternoon, some preliminary advice is already necessary, as major stakeholders will be on the phone soon. The information that follows has been provided in a classified internal company report handed to you during the meeting.

19.1 The Company

General Motors Corporation, a U.S.-based company, has been in business for one hundred years, has produced nearly 450 million vehicles globally, and operates in virtually every country in the world. Whereas GM has recently enjoyed rapidly growing sales and revenues outside the United States, the Unites States remains the company's largest single market. GM is woven into the very fabric of America. It has been the backbone of U.S. manufacturing, is a significant investor in research and development, and has a long history of philanthropic support of communities across the country. The auto industry today remains a driving engine of the U.S. economy, employing one in ten American workers, and it is one of the largest purchasers of U.S. steel, aluminum, iron, copper, plastics, rubber, and electronic and computer chips. Indeed, GM's "Keep America Rolling" sales campaign, following the September 11 attacks, is credited by many as having prevented an extended recession in 2001.

Like all domestic automobile manufacturers, GM has increasingly struggled over the last several years because of increased competition from foreign manufacturers with lower wage, health-care and benefit costs (in part because of having far fewer retirees to support in the United States and national health-care structures in their home countries). GM has spent $103 billion over the last fifteen years alone on these legacy costs, which has constrained investment in more advanced manufacturing and product technologies and significantly weakened the company's balance sheet. GM has made some erroneous decisions in the past concerning now untenable provisions from prior collective bargaining agreements and scarce investment in smaller, more fuel-efficient vehicles for the United States. Even so, GM still supplies one in five vehicles sold in the United States today. In fact, sisty-six million GM cars and trucks are on this country's roads today—forty-four million more than Toyota.

GM has made substantial progress in narrowing the gap with foreign competition in quality, productivity, and fuel efficiency. It is also noteworthy that in other markets, such as China, Latin America, and Russia, and where GM does not have the burden of legacy costs, the company has recently grown rapidly and outperformed the competition. GM has never failed to meet a congressional mandate in the important areas of fuel efficiency and vehicle emissions, and sets the industry standard for green manufacturing methods. Furthermore, it is expected that the company's role in creating green technology and high-paying jobs of the future will increase substantially.

19.2   The Problem

General Motors is coping with the worst economic downturn, and worst credit market conditions, since the Great Depression. Significant failures have occurred in America's financial services sector—including two of America's five largest investment banks, the nation's largest insurance company, both Freddie Mac and Fannie Mae, and two of the ten largest banks—with financial institutions receiving total government bailouts valued today at well over $2 trillion. Consumers have had to contend with illiquid credit markets, rising unemployment, declining incomes and home values, and volatile fuel prices. As a direct result, over the past few months, U.S. auto sales—across all manufacturers, foreign and domestic—have declined by more than 30% and are at their lowest per capita levels in half a century. This rapid decline is without parallel.

GM's financing arm, GMAC, cannot effectively access the secondary markets today. With each passing day, it is less able to finance the sale of GM vehicles, either for dealers or for the public. One year ago, GMAC was able to provide either installment or lease financing for nearly half of GM retail sales. That number has fallen to 6% today. In addition, GMAC is no longer able to buy contracts for customers with a credit score under 700, which excludes roughly half the buying population. All of this has been especially toxic to GM sales in the past two months, with sales running about 40% behind the previous year's levels. Last year, the company's restructuring plan, including a new collective bargaining agreement, coupled with the then current economic and market outlook, indicated adequate liquidity to sustain operations. However, the collapse of the industry and GM sales caused by the current economic crisis currently make it increasingly unlikely that GM will be able to service its debt in a timely fashion.

The company's balance sheet, reflecting in substantial part the $103 billion in cash/assets used to fund U.S. postretirement health-care and pension funds in the last fifteen years, includes a (sixty) billion dollar negative net worth position on September 30, 2008. Liquidity, at $16 billion, was above the $11–$14 billion minimum range required for GM's global operations, but continued cash burn and closed capital/credit markets threaten the company's ability to survive. Therefore, GM considers, reluctantly but necessarily, turning to the U.S. government for assistance. Absent such assistance, the company will probably default in the near term, very likely precipitating a total collapse of the domestic industry and its extensive supply chain, with a ripple effect that will have severe, long-term consequences on the U.S. economy. To avoid such a disastrous outcome, GM considers proposing loans from the federal government and the empowerment of a new federally created oversight board to help facilitate all the necessary changes for a successful workout and restructuring of the company.

Although unfortunately impacting approximately fifty hourly and salaried employees, GM has already ceased all corporate aircraft operations.

19.2.1   Brands and Channels

In the United States, the company currently focuses on the following major brands: Chevrolet, Cadillac, Buick, and GMC. Of the remaining brands, Pontiac—which is part of the Buick-Pontiac-GMC retail channel—is a highly focused niche brand. Hummer, Saturn, and Saab, stand-alone, loss-making retail channels and brands, are not considered core businesses. Over 90% of the company's U.S. aggregate contribution margin (revenue less variable cost) is currently derived from core brands. Nameplates have declined from sixty-three in 2004 to forty-eight in 2008, and from a marketing perspective, they could be reduced further to thirty-six by 2012. Long-term oil price outlooks predict higher oil prices combined with increasing fuel economy standards.

19.2.2   Dealers

Historically, the scope and size of the dealer body has been a strength of General Motors because of excellent customer access and convenience. As the industry has grown, so too has the competition. Due to the company's long operating history and legacy locations, many GM dealerships now operate from outdated facilities that are also no longer in prime locations required to succeed. As a result, the traditional strength of GM's broad dealer network in major markets has become a disadvantage for both the dealerships and the company. Fewer better-located dealerships potentially increase dealer profits, allowing for recruitment and retention of the best retail talent and more effective local marketing initiatives. From 2004 to 2008 (Table 19.1), GM dealerships declined by 15% (from 7,367 to 6,246). In metro and suburban markets, dealership overcapacity is most prevalent and estimated to be about 25%.

19.2.3   Product Development

In 2005, General Motors completed a long-term initiative to transform the company's operations from a collection of semi-autonomous regions into a cohesive global enterprise. This change is enabling GM to reap enormous benefits from its significant global scale. Whereas, historically, each of the company's four regions managed their own product development (PD) activities, GM now manages all product development activities globally. Working in concert with global purchasing and global manufacturing operations, the new PD organization has developed a succession of high-volume global vehicle architectures.

Vehicles and powertrains are now planned, designed, engineered, and sourced once for all markets. The benefit of this approach is that it maximizes economies of scale, leverages the best and most experienced engineering talent for a given class of vehicle, and lowers PD costs for all regions. Architecture is configured to meet the needs of all vehicles to be built, including specific regional variants. GM's global architectures are flexible to meet changing market conditions and allow for different sizes and classes of vehicles to share assembly tooling and to be built in the same facility.

Table 19.1 Historic Overview Dealerships (Including Plan 2009)

	2004	2006	2008	2009
Total GM dealerships	7,367	6,917	6,246	5,750
Major market	4,062	3,884	3,513	3,100
Metro	2,339	2,330	2,036	1,890
Hubtown	1,723	1,554	1,477	1,210
Rural market	3,305	3,033	2,733	2,650

Only four automobile companies appear to operate currently in this fashion: GM, Toyota, Honda, and Volkswagen. Through the analysis related to a succession of potential cooperative ventures over the past three years, GM can confirm that the company's capabilities and economies of scale achieved from managing product development globally appear to significantly exceed those of most competitors.

By 2012, over 50% of GM's U.S. passenger car sales will be derived from new, global architectures, and this increases to nearly 90% by 2014. The benefits to GM's U.S. operations include material cost savings, lower engineering and capital investment, and better and faster execution—all of which enable greater returns on investment. Examples of future product launches are shown in Exhibit I.

19.2.4   Productivity

General Motors is a leader in North American manufacturing productivity. According to an industry competitive assessment study, General Motors has overtaken Toyota in North American vehicle assembly productivity. From 26.75 hours per vehicle (2000) to 22.19 hours per vehicle (2008). In comparison, Toyota's productivity declined from 21.60 hours (2000) to 22.35 (2008).

The lower hours per vehicle combined with negotiated changes to the company's labor agreements in 2005 and 2007 have reduced total labor cost per vehicle by 26% from 2004 to 2008. Despite this improvement, GM still has a competitive disadvantage. Legacy costs figure prominently in the competitive gap, due in part to the far greater number of retirees GM supports with pension and health-care benefits. As stated before, GM spent over $100 billion on retiree benefits over the past fifteen years, whereas the foreign competitors' transplant operations have not had commensurate obligations or commitments. Other competitive gap factors include the higher mix of indirect and skilled trade employees, strict work rules as compared to the competition, and the lower percentage of GM workers earning lower, Tier II wages compared to the competition. GM is also tied to the so-called JOBS program, which provides full income and benefit protection in lieu of layoff for an indefinite period of time.

Most GM production staff are united in the UAW—the international union, United Automobile, Aerospace and Agricultural Implement Workers of America—which is one of the largest and most diverse unions in North America, with members in virtually every sector of the economy.

Between 2000 and 2008, GM reduced the number of salaried employees in the United States by 40%. A further reduction in GM salaried employees, globally, by approximately 10,000 (14%) compared to year-end 2008 levels should be realizable. It will result in an average annual saving of $100.000 per employee laid off.

19.2.5   *Fuel Efficiency*

General Motors is committed to meeting or exceeding all federal fuel economy standards in the 2010–2015 model years. The company plans to achieve this through a combination of strategies, including extensive technology improvements to conventional powertrains and increased use of smaller displacement engines and six-speed automatic transmissions; vehicle improvements, including increased use of lighter, front-wheel drive architectures; increased hybrid offerings and the launch of General Motors's first extended-range electric vehicle, the Chevrolet Volt in late 2010 (see Table 19.2); portfolio changes, including the increasing car/crossover mix and dropping select larger vehicles in favor of smaller, more fuel-efficient offerings.

Oil prices figure prominently in the attainment of these projected fleet average fuel economy results because they heavily influence consumer purchase decisions, as was evident in the second half of 2008 when oil prices soared to approximately $150/barrel. As the global economy faltered, and oil prices collapsed, consumer preferences shifted again, with truck purchases taking an increasing percentage of total sales. Nevertheless, GM aims to become a long-term global leader in the development of fuel-efficient and advanced technology vehicles. In so doing, GM will positively contribute to the development of this country's advanced manufacturing capabilities in line with the important long-term emphasis on developing green economic growth.

19.2.6   *Manufacturing*

General Motors has significantly reduced and consolidated manufacturing facilities in the past eight years. Reflecting further productivity and manufacturing flexibility improvements, GM probably should achieve further reductions over the next four years. The company reduced the total number of powertrain, stamping, and assembly plants by twelve in the United States (from fifty-nine in 2000 to fourty-seven at 2008 year-end), and should be able—if necessary—to close an additional fourteen facilities by 2012.

In addition to these consolidations, General Motors has been implementing an integrated global manufacturing strategy based on common lean

Table 19.2 GM Fleet Average Fuel Economy—Planning

[%]	GM Fleet Average Fuel Economy—Planning					
	2010	2011	2012	2013	2014	2015
Car	31.0	32.5	33.7	36.8	38.6	38.6
Truck	24.0	23.6	23.8	25.4	26.8	27.6

manufacturing principles and processes. Implementation of this strategy provides the infrastructure for flexible production in its assembly facilities where multiple body styles from different architectures can be built in a given plant. Also, GM's flexible powertrain facilities are capable of building multiple unique engine variants and transmission variants on the same machining and assembly line. Assembly flexibility has tripled from 22% in 2000 to 60% in 2008, with a further increase to 82% planned by 2014.

Manufacturing consolidation initiatives, along with other, enterprise-wide, cost-reduction activities have produced significant reductions in the company's structural costs. GM's structural costs are perhaps still $3–$6 billion too high. And despite an approximate 30% increase in factory unit sales over the 2010 calendar year level, it seems that the costs should still be reduced. At least until 2014. At more normal levels of production and sales, the company's structural cost—expressed as a percentage of revenue—should be approximately 24%, considerably lower than the roughly 30% level experienced in 2006 and 2007.

GM management currently targets breakeven operations (at an adjusted EBIT level) with U.S. industry volumes in the range of 12.5–13.0 million units, well below the 17+ million levels experienced for most of the past decade. With further facility consolidations and other cost reductions, the company should be able to lower—if necessary—its breakeven point to the equivalent of a U.S. industry Seasonal Adjusted Annual Rate of around 11.5–12.0 million units.

19.2.7   VEBA Obligations and Unsecured Debt

GM is considering discussions with the UAW regarding restructuring GM's payment obligations under the VEBA (Voluntary Employees' Beneficiary Association) Settlement Agreement. These discussions should be focused mainly on re-timing approximately $10 billion in payments otherwise due in 2009 and 2010, including accelerating the date upon which responsibility for retiree medical coverage should be transferred from GM to the VEBA, and the possibility of contributing GM equity in place of a portion of the VEBA payment obligations.

A confidential draft term sheet for the conversion of both a substantial portion of the company's VEBA obligations (50% or more) and current unsecured public debt (two-thirds or more) to equity is already written. Pursuant to these terms, unsecured public debt on the company's current balance sheet would be converted to a combination of new debt and equity, for a net debt reduction of at least $18 billion. In addition, the current VEBA and retiree-Paygo health-care obligations with a present value of $20 billion would be converted into a new VEBA contribution schedule covering one-half of the current obligations, with the other half to be met with an equity ownership in GM by the VEBA trust. Under the term-sheet proposal, a substantial majority of the pro-forma equity in General Motors would be distributed to exchanging bondholders and the UAW-VEBA.

19.3   Role of GM and Importance of the U.S. Auto Industry

Auto manufacturers directly provide approximately 334,000 U.S. jobs, nearly two-thirds of which are with GM, Ford, and Chrysler. Manufacturers indirectly support another 4.4 million jobs, including nearly 0.7 million in parts manufacturing and 3.7 million in related fields such as auto dealers and auto repair and maintenance. This is one of the highest multipliers in the economy. For every manufacturer job, there are nearly two jobs upstream in supplier industries and more than ten jobs downstream. The auto industry is the heart and soul of U.S. manufacturing, where many of the nation's most advanced manufacturing concepts have been developed and perfected.

GM provides good jobs at good wages and one million U.S. employees, dependents, retirees, and their spouses, as well as surviving spouses, depend on GM health-care benefits. Also GM is the largest private provider of health care in the United States. More than 650,000 U.S. retirees and their dependents benefited from GM pension payments last year.

The estimated impact on the U.S. economy in case of a full or partial failure of the domestic auto industry ('Detroit 3') is summarized in Exhibit II.

19.3.1   Economic and Industry Assumptions

Since its peak, the global auto industry has dropped 24% and the U.S. auto industry 40%. In Tables 19.3 and 19.4, forecasts of automotive markets are presented by volumes. Oil price forecasts by GM predict an increase to $130

Table 19.3 Global Total Industry Forecast Comparison

Global Total Industry Forecast Comparison									
Mil. Units	2006	2007	2008	2009	2010	2011	2012	2013	2014
GM (Baseline)	67.6	70.7	67.2	57.5	62.3	68.3	74.3	78.6	82.5
Global Insight	68.8	72.2	68.9	61.7	66.1	72.5	77.3	80.8	83.7
Difference	1.20	1.50	1.70	4.20	3.80	4.20	3.00	2.20	1.20

Table 19.4 United States Total Industry Forecast Comparison

United States Total Industry Forecast Comparison (mln)							
	2008	2009	2010	2011	2012	2013	2014
GM estimate (baseline)	13.5	10.5	12.5*	14.3	16.0	16.4	16.8
Global Insight	13.5	10.7	12.9	14.9	15.9	16.7	17.5
JD Power & Assoc.	13.5	11.7	13.7	15.0	15.8	16.6	17.0
Wall Street analyst consensus		11.5	13.2				
Consensus blue-chip forecast		11.2	13.0				

* GM downside scenario for 2010: 11.5m

per barrel by 2014. A more rapid rise in prices than the outside consensus. Rising oil prices are expected to drive a segment shift away from trucks toward cars and crossovers over the 2009–2014 period.

19.4   GM Global Metrics and Funding Requirement Estimations 2009–2014

Baseline global metrics estimations are shown in the tables that follow. Tables 19.5 and 19.6 include, among others, net sales, EBIT prognostications, structural costs, and contribution margins.

Table 19.5 GM Global Metrics

GM Global Metrics	Actual			Projected		
$ billions	2006	2007	2008	2009	2010	2011
Industry volume (mil. units)	67.6	70.7	67.2	57.5	62.3	68.3
GM wholesale volume (mil. units)	8.4	8.3	7.2	5.4	6.3	6.9
GM market share	13.5%	13.3%	12.4%	12.0%	12.7%	12.7%
Net sales	171.2	178.2		111.2	130.1	142.4
Aggregate contribution margin (ACM)	52.9	54.9	Not yet known	33.4	40.0	44.3
ACM as % of net sales	30.9%	30.9%		30.0%	30.7%	31.1%
Structural cost (SC)	52.9	53.5		43.3	40.0	39.6
SC as % of net sales	30.9%	30.1%		39.0%	30.8%	27.8%
Adjusted EBIT	0.8	1.2		(10.2)	0.3	5.1
Adjusted EBT	(1.6)	(0.7)		(14.2)	(5.0)	(0.1)
Adjusted OCF	(4.4)	(2.4)		(14.0)	(3.8)	(0.6)

Table 19.6 GM Global Metrics (cont.)

GM Global Metrics (continued)	Projected		
$ billions	2012	2013	2014
Industry volume (mil. units)	74.3	78.6	82.5
GM wholesale volume (mil. units)	7.7	7.9	8.0
GM market share	13.0%	13.0%	12.6%
Net sales	158.1	160.6	162.1
Aggregate contribution margin (ACM)	49.5	50.5	50.4
ACM as % of net sales	31.3%	31.4%	31.1%
Structural cost (SC)	40.2	40.4	40.3
SC as % of net sales	25.5%	25.2%	24.9%
Adjusted EBIT	9.4	10.3	10.6
Adjusted EBT	4.3	5.9	6.2
Adjusted OCF	6.6	6.5	6.4

Adjusted operating cash flows (OCF) approach breakeven levels in 2011 and improve to an excess of $6 billion in the 2012–2014 period, reflecting both improving industry volumes and the full effect of the projected global restructuring initiatives. Whereas all regions are cash-flow positive, on an adjusted basis, in this time frame, GM's North American operations are the most significant contributor to this result.

19.4.1   Annual Global Cash Flow 2009–2014

Base case, upside, and downside scenarios regarding cash-flow development and additional funding requirements are presented in Exhibit III. The *italics*-marked numbers are wanted but not (yet) granted funding requirements from government via U.S. TARP (*Troubled Asset Relief Program*). TARP is a program offered by the U.S. government to purchase assets and equity from financial institutions to strengthen the country's financial sector. The fund was created by a bill that was made into law on October 3, 2008, with the passage of H.R. 1424 enacting the Emergency Economic Stabilization Act of 2008.

19.4.2   Enterprise Value and Net Present Value (NPV)

Based on the baseline scenario financial projections and expectations, and solely for purposes of the GM Restructuring Plan, Evercore Group LLC ('Evercore') recently estimated that the enterprise value falls within a range of approximately $59 billion to $70 billion, with a midpoint of $65 billion. Evercore estimated that the net obligations fall within a range of approximately $54 billion to $57 billion, with a midpoint of $55 billion, implying an estimated NPV range of approximately $5 billion to $14 billion, with a midpoint of $9 billion. This NPV range does not reflect the incremental value that may be generated through balance sheet restructuring actions in Canada and Germany (Opel), which could have incremental positive effects on the NPV analysis. In addition, the current U.S. hourly and salaried pension plans are reflected as a $8–$9 billion liability in the NPV analysis (Table 19.7).

In the upside sensitivity scenario in which global industry volumes return to historical trend-line levels, the U.S. industry grows to eighteen million units by 2014, and the global industry volumes grow to ninety million units by 2014, the NPV analysis yields a range of $30 billion to $41 billion. In the downside sensitivity scenario, where the U.S. industry grows from 9.5 million units in 2009 to 15.3 million by 2014 and the global industry volumes grow from 52.3 million units in 2009 to 74.8 million units in 2014, the NPV analysis yields a negative value.

Table 19.7 NPV Analysis

Amounts in $ billions	Range	
Core Enterprise Value	57	68
Value of Unconsolidated Subsidiaries and Other Assets	12	12
PV of Potential Restructuring Costs (including Delphi*)	(8)	(8)
Minority Interest	(2)	(2)
Enterprise Value Range	**59**	**70**
Net Debt	(25)	(25)
PV of Pension Contributions	(18)	(21)
PV of VEBA Obligations	(11)	(11)
Net Obligations	(54)	(57)
NPV	**5**	**14****

* Delphi is an important source of supply. In the short term, this company needs liquidity support from GM
** Rounded off number

19.4.3   GM Balance Sheet and Capital Structure

In Exhibit IV, the GM consolidated balance sheet dated September 30, 2008, is presented. As of September 30, total liabilities amounted to approximately $170 billion, assets totaled $110 billion, and stockholders' deficit amounted to ($60) billion.

The $170 billion liability structure in the balance sheet reflects four significant forms of obligations. First, liabilities to trade creditors critical to remain in business, reserves for warranty coverage (a liability that benefits consumers over time and that directly impacts the company's brand and consumer reputation), accrued allowances for future expected sales incentives for products that have been sold by GM to dealers and are held in dealer inventories, and deposits from rental car companies relating to contracts with GM to repurchase the vehicles (this liability has a matching asset of roughly equal value). The total amount of such liabilities at September 30, 2008, amounted to $51.8 billion. The second category involves liabilities related to postretirement health-care benefits and pension liabilities or obligations that accrue for the benefit of current or future retirees. The total of such liabilities at September 30, 2008, amounted to $46.4 billion. The third category includes debt obligations of the company, the total of which amounted to $45.2 billion (including secured and all overseas obligations). Fourth, and finally, are all other liabilities, including taxes, derivative obligations, plant closing reserves, deferred income, payrolls, and many other smaller liabilities. Such liabilities generally are tied to the GM's production or sales cycles, as well as allowances for contingent liabilities. The total of such liabilities amounted to $26.0 billion.

Using the company's September 30, 2008, liability structure as the starting point, Table 19.8 and 19.9 rolls forward and aggregates total expected liabilities and future cash claims that would be considered in a bankruptcy filing.

Reflecting the previous tables, both out-of-court restructuring and the two possible accelerated bankruptcy strategies (presented in the next section) necessarily limit their impact to $47 billion of the liabilities, including $20 billion in VEBA-related obligations and $27 billion in unsecured debt. A 50% and 66.7%, respectively, debt-equity swap is considered realizable (baseline scenario calculations based on this assumption).

Table 19.8 Total Liability Summary

($ in billions)	
September 30, 2008 Total Liabilities	**169**
New liabilities incurred in Q4 2008 (includes expected $4 billion U.S. Treasury Secured Debt (TARP))	7
December 31, 2008 Total Liabilities (preliminary)	176
Roll Forward of December 31, 2008 Liabilities (including expected Incremental U.S. Treasury Debt and Other Adjustments)	12
Liabilities to be considered in bankruptcy filing (preliminary)	**188**

Table 19.9 Liability Categories

($ in billions)	
Operating/Trade-Related Liabilities	72
Non-UAW-VEBA-Related Other Postretirement Obligations (OPEB) and Pensions (Global)	39
Subtotal Operating and Retiree Related	**111**
U.S. Secured Debt*	21
Other Debt Including Foreign Subsidiary Debt	9
NPV of UAW-VEBA Obligation**	20
U.S. Unsecured Debt	27
Subtotal Debt Obligations	**77**
Total	**188**

* Includes U.S. government secured ($15.0) and secured revolver and term loan ($6.0)
** NPV of future obligations, exclusive of transferred VEBA assets—discounted at 9%

19.5   Bankruptcy

In theory, several options are available to deal with creditor issues. Next, some bankruptcy scenarios are shown as alternatives for an out-of-court restructuring.

Pre-solicited or Pre-packaged Chapter 11

Under this scenario, tendering bondholders would be required to vote affirmatively to accept a Chapter 11 plan of reorganization. If possible (because the plan of reorganization received the requisite votes) and necessary (because the out-of-court process failed), the exchange plan would be implemented in bankruptcy, binding 100% of the bondholders to accept consideration equivalent to that contemplated by an out-of-court exchange. However, this scenario requires an agreement in advance regarding the treatment of VEBA liabilities acceptable to bondholders, as well as a commitment for government financing. No other creditor would be impaired. Existing shareholders would be almost entirely diluted. This scenario is assumed to require approximately sixty to soxty-five days to achieve confirmation of the plan and exit from Chapter 11.

Pre-negotiated Cram-Down Plan

Under this option, which is more aggressive than a consensual pre-packaged Chapter 11 approach, GM could seek a larger conversion of debt to equity. This strategy could take many forms, including (A) complete conversion of the bonds to equity, (B) reduction in obligations from impairing additional classes of claims (including potentially litigation liabilities, dealer claims, and contract rejection damages), and (C) greater to perhaps complete equitization of the VEBA obligations. This scenario is assumed to require a minimum of ninety days for its least aggressive variant, up to as long as six months or more for more aggressive variants, such as converting a portion of other liabilities to equity. If GM were to pursue a larger or complete conversion of the VEBA to equity, the assumption is that this would be a vigorously contested, endangering resolution with the UAW and potentially force GM into an extended traditional Chapter 11 case or 'free-fall bankruptcy.'

Traditional Chapter 11 Case

Under this scenario, the objective would be to accomplish a more comprehensive restructuring of the liability portion of the balance sheet, along with substantial asset dispositions, using all of the tools traditionally available to debtors to restructure through a court-supervised process. This process could be expected to require eighteen to twenty-four months. Financially, whereas the traditional bankruptcy process allows for greater liability reduction

Table 19.10 Total Financing Requirement

Total Financing Requirement ($ billions)	Out-of-Court Workout	Pre-solicited Process	Cram-Down Process	Traditional Process
Liability reduction potential	47	47	47	> 100
Liabilities reduced	28	33	37	41–78
NPV—Equity Value (midpoint)	9	6	0–(16)	(25)–(28)
Government support*				
U.S. financing requirement	23	25	29–37	42–53
Wholesale support	0	2	7	14
Supplier support	4	8	9–10	13–17
Delphi	0	1	1	2
Total U.S. Government	27	36	46–55	71–86
Non-U.S. financing requirement	6	9	11–15	15–17
Total financing requirement	33	45	57–70	86–103

* Government support defined as peak borrowing requirements from 2009 to 2011

potential, incremental funding requirements surge close to a $100 billion or more, reflecting revenue reduction impact as well as wholesale (i.e., dealer) financing requirements and supplier support. GM management's assumption is that the revenue impact during this type of bankruptcy will be severe, with a substantially delayed recovery time and significant potential for permanent, significant damage.

The financial impacts of the scenarios are presented in Table 19.10.

The key assumption in each of the first three columns of the table is that the objective for the shortest possible time spent in Chapter 11 limits debt reduction strategies to the $47 billion in U.S. unsecured debt and VEBA. The sixty-day (pre-solicited) process involves a 100% participation in the proposed bond exchange, rather than the minimum of 80% proposed in the out-of-court process, reducing debt by an additional $5 billion, in effect eliminating the holdout risks in the out-of-court process. Government financing requirements could increase (on both temporary and, to a lesser degree, long-term bases) by $12 billion.

19.6   The 'Daewoo Experience'

Daewoo Motor sales in Korea permanently dropped over 40% following its bankruptcy. Considering these experiences, the estimates in Table 19.11 can be made for GM.

Table 19.11 Estimates for GM

Sixty-day bankruptcy

−35% loss; initial sales decline

−10% loss; sales loss rate goes from 35% to 10% after sixty days

−5% loss; sales are 5% below pre-bankruptcy levels four months after exiting bankruptcy and do not recover

Ninety-day bankruptcy

A. Consumer reaction

   −50% loss; initial sales decline

   −20% loss; sales loss rate goes from 50% to 20% ninety days after exiting bankruptcy

   −10% loss; sales are 10% below pre-bankruptcy levels one year after exiting bankruptcy and do not recover

B. 'Stronger' consumer reaction

   −50% loss; initial sales decline (increased incentives required)

   −40% loss; sales loss rate goes from 50% to 40% ninety days after exiting bankruptcy

   −20% loss; sales are 20% below pre-bankruptcy levels two years after exiting bankruptcy and do not recover

Two-year bankruptcy

A. 'Daewoo experience' consumer reaction

   −50% loss; initial sales decline that is maintained throughout bankruptcy

   −40% loss; sales are 40% below pre-bankruptcy levels six months after exiting bankruptcy and do not recover

B. 'Stronger' consumer reaction

   −80% loss; initial sales decline that is maintained throughout bankruptcy

   −70% loss; sales are 70% below pre-bankruptcy levels six months after exiting bankruptcy and do not recover

---

Exhibit I: Examples of Future Product Launches

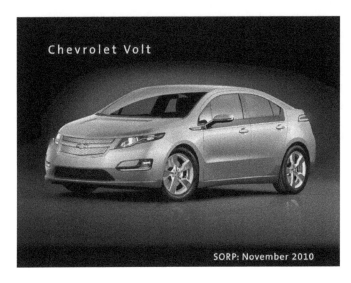

Figure 19.1 Chevrolet Volt

Start of production: 2010
Location of production facility: Detroit, Michigan
Powertrain with best fuel economy: 1.4L E-Flex

Figure 19.2 Cadillac CTS Sportwagon

Start of production: 2009
Location of production facility: Lansing, Michigan
Powertrain with best fuel economy: 3.6L V6, 6-speed auto

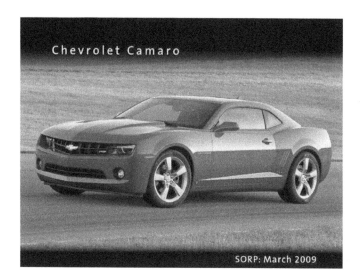

Figure 19.3 Chevrolet Camaro

Start of production: 2009
Location of production facility: Oshawa, Canada
Powertrain with best fuel economy: 3.6L V6, 6-speed auto

Figure 19.4 Cadillac SRX

Start of production: 2009
Location of production facility: Ramos Arizpe, Mexico
Powertrain with best fuel economy: 3.0L V6, 6-speed auto

Exhibit II: Estimated Impact of Full or Partial Failure of 'Detroit 3'

Table 19.12 Estimated Impact of Full or Partial Failure of 'Detroit 3'

Source	Estimated Impact	Comments
Anderson Economic Group/BBL	1.2 jobs lost in first year and 0.6 million in second year	Based on bankruptcy and eventual liquidation of two of the Detroit 3
Center for Automotive Research	First scenario: 3.0 million jobs lost in first year dropping to 2.5 in second year Second scenario: 2.5 million jobs lost in first year dropping to 1.5 million in second year	First scenario reflects 100% decline in all domestic production in first year with partial recovery at foreign owned automakers in second year; the second scenario assumes 100% drop in domestic production of Detroit 3 and 50% in second year, with a 50% drop for foreign owned automakers for both years
Global Insight	Push up the national unemployment rate from a projected 2009 level of 8.5% to 9.5%, translating into approximately 1.5 million jobs lost	Spending for benefits such as unemployment insurance and new measures to revive the economy would cost the government $200 billion should GM be forced to liquidate
Inforum Model, University of Maryland	Peak year (2011) job losses of 826,000 to more than 2.2 million Practical worst-case scenario: 1.5 million jobs lost in peak year and net average loss of just under 1.0 million jobs through 2014	Range reflects retirement of 20% to 60% of Detroit 3 production, with practical worst-case at 40%
White House Fact Sheet	Approximately 1.1 million job losses. More than 1% reduction in real GDP growth	

Exhibit III: Annual Global Cash Flow Baseline-Upside-Downside

Table 19.13 Annual Global Cash Flow 2009–2014—BASELINE

Annual Global Cash Flow 2009–2014—BASELINE						
$ billions—rounded off	*2009*	*2010*	*2011*	*2012*	*2013*	*2014*
Automotive adjusted OCF before special items	(14.0)	(3.8)	(0.6)	6.6	6.5	6.4
Special items*	(4.1)	(1.4)	(0.5)	(0.3)	(5.8)	(6.3)
Automotive adjusted after special items	(18.1)	(5.1)	(1.1)	6.3	0.7	0.2
GMAC asset carve-out cash flows	1.0	0.5	–	–	–	–
GMAC distributions & other GMAC flows	(0.8)	0.1	1.4	0.2	0.2	0.2
Adjusted cash flow after GMAC-related flows	(17.9)	(4.5)	0.3	6.5	0.9	0.3
VEBA contributions	–	*(1.1)*	*(1.1)*	*(1.1)*	*(1.1)*	*(1.1)*
Debt financing / foreign government financing / maturities	*2.3*	*1.7*	*(5.3)*	*(3.2)*	*(3.6)*	*(2.7)*
U.S. government (TARP) funding	*12.0*	*2.0*	*4.5*	*(3.0)*	*(2.9)*	*(2.9)*
U.S. pension funding	–	–	–	–	*5.9*	*6.4*
Government loan for GMAC equity rights offering	*0.9*	–	*(0.9)*	–	–	–
*Section 136 loans***	*2.0*	*2.0*	*1.8*	*1.4*	*0.5*	*(0.0)*
Other non-operating cash flows	(0.1)	(0.2)	(0.0)	(0.0)	(0.0)	(0.0)
Net cash flow	(0.8)	(0.0)	(0.7)	0.5	(0.4)	(0.0)
Cash balance	13.3	13.3	12.6	13.1	12.7	12.7
Debt balance	45.3	51.1	51.2	46.3	46.2	47.0
Net liquidity	(32.0)	(37.8)	(38.6)	(33.2)	(33.5)	(34.3)
Funding requirements memo						
U.S. TARP funding support	*16****	*18.0*	*22.5*	*19.5*	*16.6*	*13.7*
U.S. pension funding	–	–	–	–	*5.9*	*12.3*
U.S. government GMAC rights offering loan	*0.9*	*0.9*	–	–	–	–
U.S. government warrant notes payable	*0.7*	*0.7*	*0.7*	*0.7*	*0.7*	*0.7*
Section 136 loan principal	*2.0*	*4.0*	*5.8*	*7.2*	*7.7*	*7.6*
Total U.S. government funding	*19.6*	*23.7*	*29.1*	*27.5*	*30.9*	*34.4*
*Incremental funding requirements*****	*4.0*	*6.0*	*6.0*	*4.0*	*3.0*	*1.5*
Total funding requirements	**23.6**	**29.7**	**35.1**	**31.5**	**33.9**	**35.9**

* Including anticipated asset sales, cash restructuring costs and U.S. pension contributions

** U.S. Department of Energy program loan to support the development of advanced technology vehicles

*** $ 4.0 billion anticipated to be granted end of 2008, $ 12.0 billion in 2009 (see cash flow estimation)

**** From foreign governments or other sources

Table 19.14 Annual Global Cash Flow 2009–2014—UPSIDE SENSITIVITY

Annual Global Cash Flow 2009–2014—UPSIDE SENSITIVITY

$ billions—rounded off	2009	2010	2011	2012	2013	2014
Automotive adjusted OCF before special items	(8.9)	1.2	3.8	11.5	11.5	11.4
Special items*	(4.1)	(1.4)	(0.5)	(0.3)	(5.8)	(6.3)
Automotive adjusted after special items	(13.0)	(0.2)	3.3	11.2	5.7	5.2
GMAC asset carve-out cash flows	1.0	0.5	–	–	–	–
GMAC distributions & other GMAC flows	(0.8)	0.1	1.4	0.2	0.2	0.2
Adjusted cash flow after GMAC-related flows	(12.8)	0.5	4.7	11.4	5.8	5.3
VEBA contributions	–	(1.1)	(1.1)	(1.1)	(1.1)	(1.1)
Debt financing / foreign government financing / maturities	1.3	(0.3)	(7.3)	(2.2)	(2.6)	(1.2)
U.S. government (TARP) funding	8.0	(1.5)	2.5	(9.5)	(2.5)	(1.7)
U.S.pPension funding	–	–	–	–	–	–
Government loan for GMAC equity rights offering	0.9	–	(0.9)	–	–	–
*Section 136 loans**	2.0	2.0	1.8	1.4	0.5	(0.0)
Other non-operating cash flows	(0.1)	(0.2)	(0.0)	(0.0)	(0.0)	(0.0)
Net cash flow	(0.7)	(0.5)	(0.3)	(0.1)	0.1	1.2
Cash balance	13.4	12.8	12.6	12.5	12.6	13.8
Debt balance	40.3	40.6	36.7	26.3	21.7	18.8
Net liquidity	(27.0)	(27.7)	(24.1)	(13.8)	(9.1)	(4.9)
Funding requirements memo						
U.S. TARP funding support	12.0***	10.5	13.0	3.5	1.0	–
U.S. pension funding	–	–	–	–	–	–
U.S. government GMAC rights offering loan	0.9	0.9	–	–	–	–
U.S. government warrant notes payable	0.7	0.7	0.7	0.7	0.7	–
Section 136 loan principal	2.0	4.0	5.8	7.2	7.7	7.6
Total U.S. government funding	15.6	16.2	19.6	11.5	9.4	7.6
*Incremental funding requirements****	3.0	3.0	1.0	–	–	–
Total funding requirements	18.6	19.2	20.6	11.5	9.4	7.6

* Including anticipated asset sales, cash restructuring costs, and U.S. pension contributions
** U.S. Department of Energy program loan to support the development of advanced technology vehicles
*** $4.0 billion anticipated to be granted end of 2008, $8.0 billion in 2009 (see cash flow estimation)
**** From foreign governments or other sources

Table 19.15 Annual Global Cash Flow 2009–2014—DOWNSIDE SENSITIVITY

Annual Global Cash Flow 2009–2014—DOWNSIDE SENSITIVITY						
$ billions—rounded off	*2009*	*2010*	*2011*	*2012*	*2013*	*2014*
Automotive adjusted OCF before special items	(18.0)	(6.7)	(5.6)	1.5	1.4	1.5
Special items*	(4.1)	(1.4)	(0.5)	(0.3)	(5.8)	(6.3)
Automotive adjusted after special items	(22.2)	(8.1)	(6.1)	1.2	(4.4)	(4.8)
GMAC asset carve-out cash flows	1.0	0.5	–	–	–	–
GMAC distributions & other GMAC flows	(0.8)	0.1	1.4	0.2	0.2	0.2
Adjusted cash flow after GMAC-related flows	(22.0)	(7.4)	(4.7)	1.4	(4.3)	(4.6)
VEBA contributions	–	*(1.1)*	*(1.1)*	*(1.1)*	*(1.1)*	*(1.1)*
Debt financing / foreign government financing / maturities	*5.3*	*1.7*	*(2.3)*	*(1.2)*	*(2.6)*	*(0.2)*
U.S. government (TARP) funding	*14.0*	*4.0*	*7.0*	*(0.5)*	*1.6*	*(0.4)*
U.S. pension funding	–	–	–	–	*5.9*	*6.4*
Government loan for GMAC equity rights offering	*0.9*	–	*(0.9)*	–	–	–
Section 136 loans**	2.0	2.0	1.8	1.4	0.5	(0.0)
Other non-operating cash flows	(0.1)	(0.2)	(0.0)	(0.0)	(0.0)	(0.0)
Net cash flow	(0.1)	(1.0)	(0.2)	(0.1)	(0.0)	0.0
Cash balance	14.2	13.3	13.1	13.0	13.0	13.0
Debt balance	50.3	58.1	63.7	63.3	68.7	74.5
Net liquidity	(36.1)	(44.8)	(50.6)	(50.3)	(55.7)	(61.5)
Funding requirements memo						
U.S. TARP funding support	18.0***	22.0	29.0	28.5	30.1	29.7
U.S. pension funding	–	–	–	–	5.9	12.3
U.S. government GMAC rights offering loan	0.9	0.9	–	–	–	–
U.S. government warrant notes payable	0.7	0.7	0.7	0.7	0.7	0.7
Section 136 loan principal	2.0	4.0	5.8	7.2	7.7	7.6
Total U.S. government funding	21.6	27.7	35.6	36.5	44.4	50.4
Incremental funding requirements****	7.0	9.0	12.0	12.0	12.0	13.0
Total funding requirements	28.6	36.7	47.6	48.5	56.4	63.4

   * Including anticipated asset sales, cash restructuring costs, and U.S. pension contributions
  ** U.S. Department of Energy program loan to support the development of advanced technology vehicles
 *** $4.0 billion anticipated to be granted end of 2008, $14.0 billion in 2009 (see cash flow estimation)
**** From foreign governments or other sources

Exhibit IV: Balance Sheet GM—September 30, 2008

Table 19.16 Balance Sheet GM

Balance Sheet GM—Unaudited ($ in millions)	
Current Assets	
Cash and cash equivalents	15.831
Marketable securities	67
Total cash and marketable securities	15.898
Accounts and notes receivable net	9.461
Inventories	16.914
Equipment and operational leases net	4.312
Other current assets and deferred income taxes	3.511
Total current (operational) assets	*50.096*
Financing and insurance operation assets	
Cash and cash equivalents	176
Investment in securities	273
Equipment on operational leases. net	2.892
Equity in net assets of GMAC LLC	1.949
Other assets	2.034
Total financing and insurance operations assets	*7.324*
Non-current assets	
Equity in and advances to nonconsolidated affiliates	2.351
Property net	42.156
Goodwill and intangible assets net	919
Deferred income taxes	907
Prepaid pension	3.602
Other assets	3.040
Total non-current assets	*53.005*
Total assets	**110.425**

Table 19.17 Balance Sheet

Current Liabilities	
Accounts payable (principally trade)	27.839
Short-term borrowings and current portion of long-term debt	7.208
Accrued expenses	33.959
Total current liabilities	*69.006*
Financing and insurance operations liabilities	
Debt	1.890
Other liabilities and deferred income taxes	768
Total financing and insurance operations liabilities	*2.658*

Current Liabilities

Non-current liabilities	
Long-term debt	36.057
Postretirement benefits other than pensions	33.714
Pensions	11.500
Other liabilities and deferred income taxes	16.484
Total non-current liabilities	*97.755*
Total liabilities	**169.419**
Minority interests	**945**
Preferred stock	0
Common stock	1.017
Capital surplus (principally additional paid in capital)	15.732
Accumulated deficit	(61.014)
Accumulated other comprehensive loss	(15.674)
Total stockholders' deficit	**(59.939)**
Total liabilities, minority interests, and stockholders' deficit	**110.425**

Resources and Disclaimer

This case is solely based on public information. *Actual facts* are presented *based on*, and often *literally derived*, from *GM's restructuring plans* dated December 2, 2008, and February 17, 2009, as well as a number of journalistic articles. Sometimes simplifications have been made and not all information available was used because of constraints regarding the objective of the case. The information contained in this case is for educational purposes *only*. No warranty is offered on the accuracy of this information.

20 Business Failure in the U.S. Restaurant Industry

H. G. Parsa and Jean-Pierre van der Rest

> A robust, effective, and efficient bankruptcy system rebuilds companies, preserves jobs, and facilitates economic growth with dynamic financial markets and lower costs of capital. For more than 35 years, the U.S. Bankruptcy Code has served these purposes, and its innovative debtor in possession chapter 11 process, which allows a company to manage and direct its reorganization efforts, is emulated around the globe.
>
> American Bankruptcy Institute (2014)

20.1 Introduction

Business failure is the heart of any business. Unfortunately, the process of business failure is often misunderstood as the terminal step in a business life cycle, when in fact, it is the beginning of a strategic, sometimes deliberate, transformation process that leads a more agile and responsive organization best suited for an emerging socio-political, economic, and business climate. The process of business failure can also be described as an instrument of the Darwinian natural selection process that keeps the industry healthy and vibrant as a whole. Albeit, for the natural selection to occur and continue, some firms have failed, voluntarily or involuntarily, in the best interest of the industry as a whole. Thus, from a macro perspective, business failure is a necessary positive step to keep any industry healthy, vibrant, relevant, and alive. From a marketing perspective, all dynamic industries tend to embrace business failure as a tool for repositioning. From an organization ecology perspective, business failure is a naturally occurring phenomenon that eliminates the weakest links in business chains. Without the process of business failure, most industries will experience a chronic lethargy in revenues and financial performance as weak links continue to drain resources and keep prices artificially low. From a legal and organizational transition perspective, business failure allows for a gradual and methodical change in business leadership, which hopefully results in renewed growth and dynamism. As is obvious, there are numerous benefits to business failure at the macrolevel.

In spite of numerous documented advantages of business failure from a macro perspective, the study of business failure at the microlevel, interestingly, could lead to different conclusions. Business failure, at a microlevel, is a complex phenomenon comprising legal, managerial, marketing, financial (capital), technological, and operational factors leading to significant changes in an organization. Business failures are a major concern, especially in the small business sector, because of a shortage of funding sources often experienced by small businesses. In the case of major industries and larger employers, business failures are a complex process involving extensive legal maneuvers and financial negotiations. In such instances, most of the gains are losses and are attributed to an organization as a legal entity. In contrast, business failure in small businesses directly affects the individuals, the owners, because most of them are set up as sole proprietors or sub-chapter S corporations. In such instances, business losses tend to be personal and directly affect the personal possessions and assets of business partners and sole owners. In these cases, financial institutions tend to have leverage over business assets as the primary debt holders. Unfortunately, when small businesses fail, owners not only lose their livelihood but also their personal assets such as bank accounts, home, and other assets depending on the legal nature of the business. Additionally, a business failure in small businesses may have significant consequences for business owners, because failures affect their ability to borrow money in the future due to a negative credit history and prior business insolvency.

Business failure can be of many types. Some business failures are voluntary, whereas others are involuntary. Voluntary business failures are initiated by the owners of a company. In contrast, involuntary business failures are initiated by the debtors or lienholders. Some of the most common forms of business failure (i.e., insolvency) procedures under the law in the United States are Chapter 7 and Chapter 11. The first one, Chapter 7, leads to liquidation of company assets and disburses proceeds to debtors first. Once the debtors are satisfied, then the business owners may receive any remaining funds. In the second instance, the business owners, instead of liquidating their company assets, may prefer to seek debt relief so they may improve their cash flow situation initially and increase overall organization performance in the long run. According to the Bankruptcy Act in the United States, the primary purpose of filing for Chapter 11 insolvency is not to close an ailing business but to allow it to reorganize, rejuvenate, and contribute constructively to society by providing goods and services. Based on this primary intent of bankruptcy laws, business failures should not be perceived as a death sentence but instead as a chance to regain and rebuild an organization.

20.2 Definition of Business Failure

There are many definitions of business failure. Unfortunately, most of these definitions do not distinguish between the business process and outright business closure. Watson and Everett (1996) describe five categories of business failure, including bankruptcy or loss to creditors, disposal to prevent further losses, failure to 'make a go' of it, discontinuance of ownership, and discontinuance of a business for any reason. Parsa, Self, Njite, and King (2005) define business failure as the change in business ownership. Their work is the first major empirical study of business failures in the restaurant industry. Others, for example, define business failure as a decline of return on sales, or a decline in other financial terms (Ibrahim & Goodwin, 1986). Parsa, Lamb, and Xie (2014) note that business failure in restaurants is one of the least noted legal processes. They define restaurant failure as a process of change in restaurant ownership. In 2003, Headd noted that most failing businesses—especially restaurants—might not report business failures in order to avoid brand dilution and a potential negative effect on other remaining operating units. According to MauMau (2009), most restaurants prefer to avoid reporting business failures. In other words, most restaurants are often sold and purchased multiple times without ever experiencing a legal procedure of business insolvency. This assumption was supported by the works of Watson and Everett (1996).

As mentioned earlier, Parsa et al. (2005) define business insolvency as a change of ownership. Whenever a company changes ownership, irrespective of prevailing financial performance of that time, it is considered as business failure. This definition was later adapted for several hospitality studies by various authors (Parsa, Gregory, & Terry, 2010; Parsa, Self, Sydnor-Busso, & Yoon, 2011; Parsa, Van der Rest, Smith, Parsa, & Bujisic, 2014; Parsa, Xie, Van der Rest, Lamb, & Kreeger, 2015).

20.3   Major Perspectives in Business Failure

Business failure can be considered from two different perspectives: (1) the Process Approach and (2) the Event Approach.

In the Process Approach, a business is evaluated for potential possibility of business failure using various metrics chosen from accounting, financial, and operational attributes. In this approach, historic data from the company and relevant industry averages are employed to assess the fiscal health of an organization. It is similar to an individual getting a periodic physical checkup from a medical clinic. Evaluation of symptoms of business health allows for early diagnosis of potential business insolvency. Organizations that prefer to adapt this approach tend to test for fiscal health of the organization periodically. The time line for the suggested internal diagnosis varies across the organizations depending on various organizational factors, including complexity of the operations, organizational size, age of the business, physical distribution of operations, length and complexity of the supply chain, product mix, financial performance, and, lastly, the dynamism and volatility of the industry.

This procedural diagnosis can be performed internally or externally. In case of internal assessment, companies prefer to use the audit department to perform the diagnosis process. Internal assessment tends to be cost effective and less time consuming. Unfortunately, internal diagnosis processes suffer from weaknesses, including intra-organizational politics, group dynamics, territorial claims, lack of cooperation within the organization, and fear of reprisal for a potentially negative diagnosis report. If they choose to use an external organization, such as a professional consultancy group, usually it could be expensive and time consuming. At the same time, external assessment has some significant benefits, including honest assessment that is free from intra-organizational politics, expert diagnostics supplemented by the knowledge of the industry and the competition, and expert advice on possible future plans of action.

In contrast to Process Approach presented earlier, the Event Approach considers business failure as an event where a business ceases to function as an operating unit from that point forward. Most legal experts prefer to use the Event Approach as in the case of Chapter 7 proceedings, where company assets are liquidated to pay off debts. It is more an accounting process that is enveloped in a legal procedural web. In this case, an organization is considered deceased and cannot be allowed to function as a working entity by the legal system beyond the defined point in time. It is a definitive end of an organization. From a legal perspective, Event Approach is considered more a declarative statement than a process assessment. Event Approach allows for what one may call a death certificate for a business. Though it may be considered a clean and clear approach, it has several limitations. The Event Approach assumes that business failure happens at a set moment of time akin to the death of a person. This may not be appropriate for a given business because a business may show signs of failing over time in a similar manner as to how a seriously ill or terminally ill person does not transition immediately from perfect health to death at a specific point in time but instead deteriorates over a period of time. A seriously ill person's eventual death may be the culmination of an illness over an extended period of time, but it is not an event that happened all of a sudden at the moment of death. There thus are objections to the Event Approach. The Event Approach is a post-hoc declaration of business failure that has already occurred, whereby the Process Approach is a predictive assessment of a business failure.

The Event Approach has some benefits, as it allows debtors to file claims immediately following the declaration of business insolvency. Although the debtors may receive less money than they are owed, it is preferred over a reorganization process, which may take longer to recuperate the debt. Sometimes organizations prefer to use the Event Approach, as it allows them to write off most of the debt and recreate the organization as is legally permitted. Some non-profit entities, such as municipalities and no-profit agencies, follow this process method as a last resort in order to be able to regroup.

Parsa et al. (2005) proposed an alternative perspective to the two approaches to overcome the limitations of each. They proposed ownership turnover as the point of business failure. According to this approach, when a business ownership changes hands, it is considered insolvent. That means the point of business insolvency occurs at the time and point when the current owner passes the baton to the new owner. The approach is not burdened by the requirements to consider financial aspects of business transactions. In other words, a business does not have to be financially distressed to change hands or to be considered insolvent. That means a business that is financially vibrant and reporting positive profits can still be considered a failure if it changes ownership. The rationale for this approach deserves an explanation. When a successful business changes hands, it means that the former ownership has failed to remain solvent and is unable to continue into the future. Because the former ownership is unable to continue as a business, it is considered to be experiencing failure. This definition allows for systematic study of business failure processes with reliable quantitative data and techniques. It is sometimes preferred by scholars for studying business failure processes. This approach also allows for a better definition of mergers and acquisitions without relying exclusively on legally popular yet incomplete bankruptcy data.

20.4   Importance of Restaurants in the United States

Restaurants are a significant part of American life. According to the National Restaurant Association (2016), total revenues for the restaurant industry exceed $782 billion per year with nearly one million operating restaurants in the United States providing jobs for over 14.4 million people. The sizable economic impact of the restaurant industry can be measured by the 4% contribution it makes to the gross domestic product in the United States. In addition, the restaurant industry has been expanding at a steady rate of 2% to 4% over the past three decades. Despite the economic downturn in 2009, the restaurant industry grew by 2.5% (National Restaurant Association, 2016). The restaurant and food service industry continues to be one of the largest private sector employers in the United States with a projected increase of one million jobs by the year 2020 (www.restaurant. org). Toward the end of the recession in 2010, the restaurant industry had added 24,000 new jobs and nearly 84,000 jobs in the first three-quarters of 2010. With one in three (33.3%) Americans having worked in this industry at least once in their lifetime and two in five (40%) agreeing that ordering food from restaurants makes them more productive in their daily life, restaurants are an integral part of American society.

As is the case with other small businesses, restaurants play a vital role in job creation and economic growth. According to the National Restaurant Association (2016),

> Restaurant industry sales are expected to reach $783 billion in 2016. Although this will represent the seventh consecutive year of real growth in restaurant sales, the rate of growth remains moderate. The restaurant

industry will remain the nation's second-largest private sector employer with a workforce of 14.4 million.

Furthermore,

> 10%: Restaurant workforce as part of the overall U.S. workforce; 9 in 10 Restaurant managers started at entry-level positions in restaurants; 8 in 10 Restaurant owners who started their industry careers in entry-level positions; 9 in 10: Restaurants with fewer than fifty employees; 7 in 10 Restaurants are single-unit operations.
>
> (National Restaurant Association, 2016)

In addition, it is expected that 1.7 million jobs in the restaurant industry will be added in the next decade. By the same token, because restaurants are small businesses, they are subject to the vicissitudes of the U.S. economy. Just as small businesses experience a large number of job losses during tough economic times (SBA Office of Advocacy, 2010), they also are a driving force in a recovering economy (Dun & Bradstreet, 2012).

In spite of its sustained growth over the past five decades, the restaurant industry has experienced one of the highest business failure rates. According to the Dunn and Bradstreet report (2012), the restaurant industry has one of the highest business failure rates among the retail and service industries. Erroneously, American Express has estimated that 90% of restaurants fail in the first year (See Figure 20.1). In a seminal study, Parsa et al. (2005) showed that the restaurant failures are in fact under 30% during the first year of operation (See Figure 20.2–20.3). Although failure rates may rise slightly by the third year of operation, they do not achieve the levels of 90% failures as reported by American Express. Other studies by Self (2004) using data from California has shown that restaurant failures are also less than 30%. The National Restaurant Association in the United States recognizes a 30% failure rate as the norm in the restaurant industry.

INTRODUCTION

A Risky Business

Bank officials state that investing in a foodservice business is a high risk investment. It is also well known that 80% of the individuals who open a foodservice operation today find themselves out of business in a year. How can so many people fail at making a profit, and find themselves out of business?

This chapter explores the reasons why 80% of owners fail, and more importantly, why 20% succeed. The steps in developing a foodservice concept are discussed, highlighting topics such as market demographics and community geographics.

Figure 20.1 Myth of Restaurant Failures

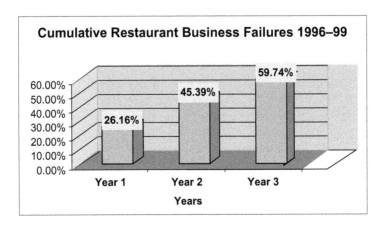

Figure 20.2 Cumulative Restaurant Failures 1996–99
(Parsa, Self, Njite, & King, 2005).

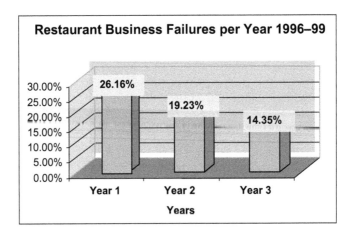

Figure 20.3 Cumulative Percentage of Restaurant Business Failures 1996–99
(Parsa, Self, Njite, & King, 2005).

Even the well-established and commonly accepted 30% failure rate during the first year of operations is still unacceptable, as it has significant economic impact. If the restaurant failure is 30% during the first year of operation, then 9,000 restaurants fail every year in America. According to the National Restaurant Association, average revenues per year per restaurant are about $580,000. Then there is a potential loss of $5.20 billion in the form of lost restaurant revenues to the national economy (See Figure 20.4). In addition, restaurant failures also lead to the loss of nearly 40,000 jobs per year as estimated from the National Restaurant Association statistics

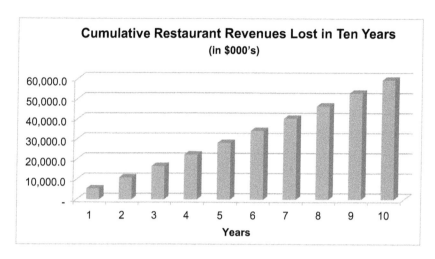

Figure 20.4 Estimated Cumulative Loss of Restaurant Revenues Over a Period of Ten Years

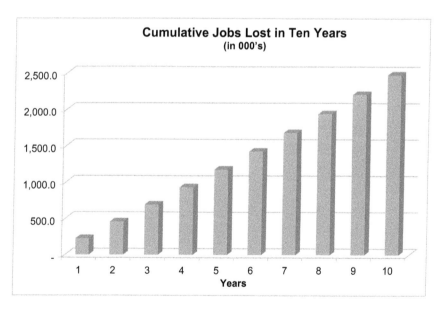

Figure 20.5 Estimated Cumulative Loss of Jobs in the Restaurant Industry Over a Period of Ten Years

(See Figure 20.5). The annual restaurant failure rate of 9,000 units per year would also precipitate the loss of invested capital of $3.2 billion per year in failed restaurant units at a rate of 60% of estimated annual sales considered as the initial investment (See Figure 20.6-20.7).

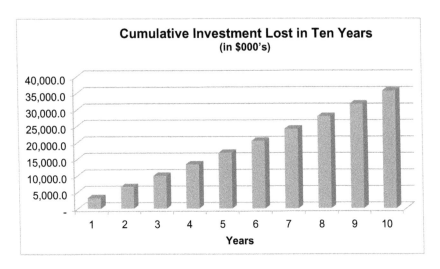

Figure 20.6 Estimated Cumulative Loss of Investments in the Restaurant Industry Over a Period of Ten Years

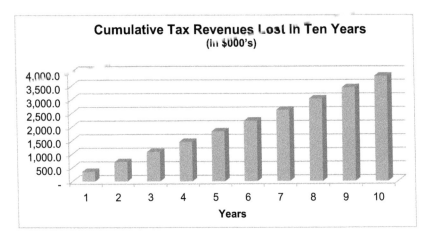

Figure 20.7 Estimated Cumulative Loss of Tax Revenues from the Restaurant Industry Over a Period of Ten Years

Thus many restaurant entrepreneurs and their investors are also expected to experience extensive economic hardships because of restaurant failures. These facts clearly indicate that restaurant failures are a significant factor to consider based on their economic impact and their impact on the lives of American entrepreneurs.

20.5 Causes of Restaurant Failure

Factors that contribute to business failure in the restaurant industry can be divided into two major types: (1) macro factors and (2) micro factors. Some of the relevant and critical macro factors that contribute mostly to restaurant insolvency include environmental factors (natural disasters); public health disasters; economy, legislation (national, regional, and local), regional, and local planning (urban and rural); changing cultural patterns; evolving food habits; changes in consumer lifestyles; and technological trends. At the same time, unit-level micro factors also contribute to restaurant insolvency. Important micro factors that contribute to restaurant insolvency can be classified into two major types: (1) genetic factors and (2) operational factors. Selected genetic micro factors include the following: concept, name, and design and layout. Selected operational micro factors include the following: capital (working capital), location, quality of life, entrepreneurial incompetence, relevant prior experience, and managing controllable costs.

20.5.1 *Macro Factors and Restaurant Failure*

20.5.1.1 *Environmental Factors*

The following climatic factors and consequent effects contribute to restaurant insolvency: global warming, melting of ice caps, loss of rain forest acreage, declining seafood sources, reduction of fresh water resources, earthquakes and tsunamis, floods, hurricanes, tornadoes and volcanoes, extreme heat, and forest fires. It is well documented that a recent tsunami in Japan, the Katrina hurricane in the United States, and floods in Europe and Asia have all contributed to significant losses in the restaurant business. These factors affect the restaurant industry in two ways. The first effect is the direct damage to the physical buildings and storage spaces. The second effect is indirect, which includes the indirect loss of food supply sources. For example, major restaurant chains such as Red Lobster, the world's largest seafood restaurant company, is struggling to identify good and reliable sources of seafood for its restaurants because of environmental/climatic factors. In addition, global warming is affecting food prices in developing nations where processed foods are not very affordable. The BP Oil disaster in the gulf coast of the United States had a significant negative effect on the restaurant industry for nearly three years. Global warming is dramatically changing the migratory patterns of sea animals and birds, thus affecting local fish populations and eventually the restaurant industry.

20.5.1.2 *Public Health Disasters*

Often public health disasters such as avian flu, Zika virus, and the Ebola virus are having significant direct and indirect effects on the restaurant industry. Some of the business insolvency reports from the restaurant industry can be attributed to the declining tourism to the areas where public health concerns are prevalent. Public health disasters, although temporary in their economic effect, typically have a substantial long-lasting impact on the restaurant industry. Currently, the Zika virus issue is dramatically affecting the tourism industry in Brazil and other Latin American and Caribbean countries. The steady decline in tourism is a major factor in the decline of restaurant revenues.

20.5.1.3   Economy

Consumers' disposable income is the primary source of revenues for the restaurant industry. In turn, consumers' disposable income is directly affected by economic factors. When the economy is strong and unemployment is low, restaurants tend to experience high revenues and higher profits. In addition, an abundance of consumers' patronage resulting from high disposable incomes has led to restaurant innovations and the introduction of new concepts and fusion foods. High disposable incomes often lead to increased guest spending on microvacations such as dining out or visiting food festivals. This increased spending decreases restaurant insolvencies. One can expect the opposite effect when the economy slows and unemployment increases. In the case of economic decline and job loss, high-end and fine dining restaurants are the first to feel the pinch of recession. However, low-end and value-centric, quick-service restaurants are the last segment to experience decline in revenues during major economic downturns.

Other economic factors tend to have major effect on the restaurant industry such as the following: minimum wage increase; economic volatility; interest rate changes; banking regulations; government mandated health-care taxes; regulations on food ingredients such as low sodium, low sugar, and lower calories; regulations on employee overtime pay; and controls on alcohol service and consumption. Insolvency in the restaurant industry can be attributed to some of the economic factors that are systematic and concept specific.

20.5.1.4   Legislation

Legislative actions at the national, regional, and local levels could have a major impact on the restaurant industry. Some of the effects could be very positive and others may be somewhat negative. For example, in the United States, the Prohibition Act of 1919 almost decimated the alcohol beverage industry but it resulted in the golden age of restaurants that do not serve alcohol. Similarly, several government regulations have a major negative impact on the restaurant industry, which contribute to an increase in restaurant insolvencies. Some of these regulations include minimum wage, American Disability Act, tax deductions for business meals, nutritional labeling on restaurant menus (display of nutritional information), Accelerated Depreciation Act, prohibiting smoking in restaurants, proposed mandatory sick leave for all employees, and the Truth in Menu Act.

20.5.1.5 *Regional and Urban Planning*

Regional and urban planning activities are designed to improve the lifestyles of citizens. Unfortunately, these plans may have a significant negative effect and unintended consequences on the restaurant industry. For example, when national or regional highways were built across the nation, traffic patterns migrated away from local population centers toward newly built roads. When a fast train (an urban train system) was implemented throughout Spain, the commercial districts emerged around the new train stations, which negatively affected the local restaurant industry. Similarly, when national highways were built across America, local restaurants experienced significant loss in revenues as traffic patterns moved toward the new highways. Recently, several American cities (especially on the West Coast) have enacted restrictions on quick-service restaurants in certain locations, thus contributing to the decrease of restaurant business. Some municipalities seeking additional sources of revenues resorted to posting parking meters in high traffic areas such as downtown areas. The loss of free parking spaces led to the exodus of full-service restaurants away from downtown locations to suburban areas. Many well-established restaurants have had to claim business insolvency, as they could not afford to relocate from downtown areas.

20.5.1.6 *Changing Cultural Patterns*

Changing cultural patterns and demographics are known to affect the restaurant industry. When some of the well-established restaurant concepts are forced to make adaptations to the changing cultural and demographic trends, increased business insolvency may occur. In the United States, beef has been the primary menu item in most full-service restaurants. In fact, until the 1920s, chicken was not served in many American restaurants, as it was considered a poor man's food and not worthy of serving in a full-service restaurant. When beef prices increased dramatically in 1970s, most hamburger restaurants were forced to diversify from beef to non-beef entrees. This was followed by a major cultural change in America where beef and red meat items were considered less than desirable. Beef was gradually replaced by vegetables, chicken, pizza, and other non-beef items that became popular menu choices. This has resulted in the insolvency of several beef-based restaurant chains, steakhouses, hamburger restaurants, and several independent restaurants.

Similar to cultural changes, demographic trends are also known to affect the restaurant industry. The graying of America has led to smaller portions and lower profits. Whenever large populations move from one part of a country to the other, such as rural to urban, restaurants are the first industry to be affected by these demographic shifts. Business insolvency tends to increase in those locations where negative demographic shifts have occurred.

Typically, in the U.S. restaurant industry, a majority of business comes from within a three-mile radius for a quick-service restaurant, within an eight-mile radius for a casual dining restaurant, and within a fifteen-mile radius for a full-service restaurants. Destination restaurants can draw customers from a distance of up to fifty miles. Thus any major changes in demographics necessarily affect the restaurant industry.

20.5.1.7   Evolving Food Habits

According to Parsa (1998), American food habits are constantly evolving and changing. This phenomenon may be true to all nations where the flow of people is not restricted or inhibited by government policies as in the case of North Korea. At the beginning of the twentieth century, the primary source of protein in America was beef, mostly steaks. It was slowly replaced by hot dogs by the 1920s and 1930s. The All American Hot Dog slowly gave way to hamburgers. Gradually, the hamburger became the king of American dining-out culture. By the 1980s, the hamburger was replaced by pizzas served in a family dining venue. Home delivery of pizza took deep roots into the American culture by the mid-1980s. Currently, Americans consume the largest number of pizzas on Super Bowl Sunday (the American professional football championship) as compared to every other day of the year. As stated, over the past one hundred years, American food habits have changed from steaks to hot dogs, to hamburgers to pizza. During this process, restaurant insolvency has also increased from the loss of steakhouses, taverns, hot dog stands, hamburger chains, etc. Currently, emerging food trends include plant-based protein restaurants such as Veggie Grill (http://veggiegrill.com/); healthy choice food restaurants with vegetarian, vegan, and gluten-free options (http://www.lyfekitchen.com/); socially conscious restaurants serving local and sustainable foods (http://www.truefood-kitchen.com/, http://thekitchen.com/#nogo); and fusion foods from Asia, Latin America, South and Southeast Asia, and Europe. That means one can expect high turnover in the restaurant industry as new food trends take root around the world.

20.5.1.8   Changes in Consumer Lifestyles

Over the past two decades, obesity has become the major public health concern around the world. Some may consider obesity as the sign of opulence and food abundance. Unfortunately, most obesity can be attributed to changing lifestyles where physical activity is gradually replaced by indoor computer games and stagnant lifestyles. This phenomenon started, coincidentally, with the invention of the personal computer (PC). Increased use of information technology and PCs has led to more sedentary living practices. At the same time, restaurant food portions have dramatically increased in size. The combination of larger portions in restaurants and possibly at home along with decreased physical activity has led to high incidences of obesity around the world. Fortunately, emerging trends toward healthy meals is the silver lining in the obesity problem. That means restaurants that relied on old-fashioned large portions may experience high turnover and higher failure rates. Thus restaurant insolvency is closely related to changing consumer lifestyles.

20.5.1.9 Technology

Emerging trends in technology can be closely related to business insolvency. As new technology, social media, and data analytics take firm root in restaurant marketing, restaurants that are not able or are unable to accept and adapt to the merging technology may face the risk of insolvency. The impact of social media on the restaurant industry cannot be underestimated. Yelp is dominating the restaurant marketing scene. Restaurants that fail to recognize the importance of social media are bound to experience symptoms of business insolvency. In addition, technological improvements are not limited to social media or marketing alone. Numerous new technological innovations have been introduced in the restaurant industry including equipment innovations, product innovations, service technologies, guest reservation and check payment technologies, and data analytics. New technologies are also being introduced into the area of restaurant design and interior environments. Thus technology is going to play an increasingly important role in restaurant risk and insolvency.

20.5.2 Micro Factors and Restaurant Failure

20.5.2.1 Genetic Factors of Restaurant Insolvency

In the restaurant industry, three major genetic factors contribute to business insolvency. The first is the concept of the restaurant, followed by the name of the restaurant, and, lastly, the design and layout of the restaurant. These three genetic factors and their relationship to the restaurant industry are discussed next. These factors are considered genetic factors because they are an integral part of a restaurant. Factors affect a restaurant as DNA affects a human. As in the case of human DNA, once set, the concept, name, and, to a lesser extend, the design and layout of a restaurant cannot be changed easily. Interestingly, these three factors are always established before the operational factors at the time of conceptualization of a restaurant. These factors are impregnated into the concept before it is materialized, similar to human DNA. Any major change in these three areas can be considered a mutation of the original concept. That means if any major changes are made to any of these three primary attributes, the original restaurant is no longer the original concept but a mutant of the original. Thus these factors are called genetic factors.

20.5.2.2   Concept

The concept is the primary genetic factor that affects the restaurant industry. One of the primary reasons for restaurant insolvency is the concept. Often restaurants experience insolvency for lack of fit between the following: the chosen concept and the restaurant's location, the concept and the demographics of the neighborhood, the concept and competition, and, finally, the concept and the organizational culture. An undifferentiated concept is the primary reason for many restaurant failures. Entrepreneurs often underestimate the intensity of the competition and overestimate their ability to execute the given concept. When a restaurant concept does not fit the location, no amount of capital or prior business experience can salvage the restaurant. For example, a fine dining French restaurant in Maryland was located a few doors from a funeral home in a strip mall shopping center. That restaurant closed within two years of opening. Similarly, one restaurant and nightclub in Ohio was located next to a police station. As one can guess, liquor business was never realized because of its proximity to a police station and fear of police harassment for excessive alcohol consumption. This particular restaurant eventually relocated to the other side of the town. The restaurant concept also must fit with the neighborhood. Typically, ethnic restaurants are located in clusters. This is no surprise, and it is referred to as 'pull power.' Typically, consumers, while making their dining-out choices for dinner, tend to choose the cuisine first followed by location. So ethnic restaurants benefit from the overflow from each other. In such instances, stronger operators tend to carry the neighborhood ethnic restaurant clusters and weaker operators benefit by association through the cuisine and freeloading. Imitation may be the best form of appreciation, but it does not necessarily help in the restaurant industry. Several successful restaurants have been extensively imitated, including concepts such as McDonald's, Wendy's, White Castle, #1 Chinese Restaurant, Ray's Pizza from New York, etc. The imitators often lost legal battles with the original concepts or experienced operational collapse.

20.5.2.3   Name of a Restaurant

Name is the second genetic factor that affects the restaurant business significantly. The process of naming a restaurant is as much a science as it is an art. Restaurant names, similar to people's names, tend to be trendy and changing. During the early twentieth century in the United States, most independent restaurants followed the European model of naming the restaurant after the chef-owner of the place. This trend continued until the 1940s and 1950s. It was slowly replaced by naming a restaurant by the type of cuisine (e.g., hamburger, steaks, fried chicken, pizza, pancakes) or the predominant cooking method (e.g., grill, bakery, bar, café, bistro). The method of naming an independent restaurant has slowly evolved. After the 1980s, some well-known independent restaurants were named for an experience rather than the cuisine or food preparation method (e.g., Tides, Tabla, Mesa, Blue Ocean, Olive Garden). Old-fashioned and long restaurant names were replaced by short and simple one-word names. In a recent study of 1,800 restaurant names, the authors noted that restaurant names can be classified into twenty-seven different categories. A typical restaurant name consisted of thirteen letters with eight consonants and five vowels. Restaurants with longer than thirteen letters were found to be more prone to insolvency. Similarly, in another study of the top-100 restaurant chains in the United States, the authors noted that restaurant chains with longer names fell to the bottom 10% of the sample, and restaurant chains with shorter names and fewer letters were found to be at the top 10% of the rankings by revenues. Thus there appears to be an inverse relationship between length of a restaurant name and solvency of a restaurant (Feldman, Parsa, & Bujisic, 2012).

20.5.2.4   Design and Layout

Design and layout is the third important genetic factor effecting the restaurant business. Unlike the earlier two factors, design and layout have some flexibility. If necessary, minor modifications can be made to the concept to meet the business needs. But sometimes major changes are not feasible due to site and building restrictions. For example, a major restaurant in Philadelphia could not accommodate large groups in its restaurant because the kitchen was located on the second and first floors, but the group dining area was located on the third floor. Built-in (genetic) logistical problems have prevented many restaurants from expanding their business. Similarly, many restaurants find themselves relocating to a bigger or better location as the original genetic design and layout prevent them from expanding. Albeit, some of the restaurants tend to follow the periodic remodeling route to correct for the genetic limitation of the original design and layout. This may or may not work depending on the intensity of the genetic impact.

20.5.2.5   Operational Micro Factors

Operational micro factors that contribute to restaurant insolvency include the following: capital (working capital), location, quality of life, entrepreneurial incompetence, relevant prior experience, and managing controllable costs.

20.5.2.6   Capital (Working Capital)

Lack of working capital is one of the most often cited contributors of restaurant insolvency. Often entrepreneurs tend to underestimate the need for working capital. Typically, a restaurateur often has just minimum capital to open a restaurant but not enough to get through the initial 'rainy days' (low revenues and low profitability) after opening the restaurant. The rule of thumb in the restaurant business is to have enough working capital to last the first six months after opening without harvesting valuable resources from the business. Thus capital is considered one of the important operational factors contributing to restaurant insolvency.

20.5.2.7   Location

Along with capital, location is also considered one of the primary factors for restaurant insolvency. Most restaurateurs attribute success of their business to the location. It is no wonder entrepreneurs spare no efforts in choosing the right location for the right concept. Some of the location characteristics that are important for restaurants' success include access to potential customers, proximity to a densely populated neighborhood, less competition for the chosen concept and cuisine at the chosen location, and most importantly low rental costs. Critical locational factors also include traffic patterns and access to the restaurant from a public road. Prime locations demand higher rent, thus site selection is always a compromise. Restaurants may experience the path to insolvency when access to the traffic is constrained. In Westerville, Ohio, one restaurant lost access to potential customers when the city decided to build high side banks on either side of the road.

20.5.2.8   Quality of Life

A majority of restaurant insolvency situations can often be attributed to quality of life issues prevailing in the restaurant business. By nature, most restaurant managers/owners have to compromise their evening social activities to serve customers during the most common dining-out hours (in the evening). As a result, quality of social life and family life are often compromised for restaurant owners/managers. As a result, most restaurant professionals experience burnout in the workplace, which often leads to business insolvency. According to Parsa et al. (2005), quality of life is one of the primary reasons for the high rate of restaurant insolvency. King (2002) interviewed over thirty restaurateurs and concluded that compromised quality of life is one of the primary reasons for business failures in the restaurant industry.

20.5.2.9 *Entrepreneurial Incompetence*

The inability to transition from successful entrepreneurship to professional management is called entrepreneurial incompetence. In such situations, entrepreneurs tend to follow two main paths. Either they relinquish managerial responsibilities to a professional manager or they experience out-of-control variable costs, which leads to major financial setbacks resulting in business insolvency. Interestingly, the second option was found to be one of the primary causes of restaurant insolvency. Often restaurant entrepreneurs tend to overestimate their ability to develop and manage a restaurant. Often skilled employees such as chefs may have expertise in food production or service but do not possess the necessary business acumen to manage a restaurant as a business. They may have adequate skills to open and operate a restaurant, but they lack expertise in business analytics and controlling costs. In other words, a skilled food service employee may have an operational skill set to open a restaurant but may lack people skills and business skills to successfully manage that restaurant. Entrepreneurs who are successful in developing a restaurant concept and opening it often cannot make the necessary transition to a professional management role.

20.5.2.10   *Relevant Prior Experience*

According to King (2002), lack of prior restaurant experience is one of the reasons for high restaurant failures. Successful restaurateurs tend to have prior restaurant experience as in the case of David 'Dave' Thomas (Wendy's), Howard Schultz (Starbucks), Colonel Sanders (KFC), John Schlegel (Snooze), etc. Entrepreneurs who do not possess prior relevant experience often underestimate the value of controlling variable costs and as a result experience high probability of restaurant insolvency.

20.5.2.11   *Managing Controllable Costs*

Business insolvency is often the result of loss of control over variable costs. Restaurant businesses often report, according to the National Restaurant Association (2016), variable costs of 60%, gross profit of 40%, and a national average net profit of under 10% for an independent restaurant. Thus controlling variable costs is one of the most important factors in the restaurant business. For example, a celebrity restaurant in Buffalo, New York, reported a food cost percentage of 56% compared to the national average of 30%. As a result, this particular restaurant was closed in less than two years. In the restaurant business, the ability to control variable costs is directly related to restaurant success. Another important cost to control is the fixed cost of rent. Because a lease is a long-term contract, restaurant insolvency is often directly attributed to high terms of rent. Typically, business districts tend to demand high rents compared to suburban areas.

20.6   Discussion Questions

1 Why are restaurants important from an economic and socio-political perspective?
2 Why is the rate of business insolvency high in the restaurant industry?
3 Restaurant insolvency rate is 90%. Is this a myth or a fact?
4 Is restaurant insolvency a process, or an event, or a change of ownership? Discuss.
5 Discuss some of the macro factors that contribute to restaurant insolvency.
6 What is the relationship between environmental factors and restaurant insolvency?
7 How do natural disasters affect restaurant insolvency?
8 What is the relationship between restaurant insolvency and public health disasters?
9 What are the key genetic factors that affect restaurant insolvency?
10 How do micro operational factors affect restaurant insolvency?
11 Is prior business experience relevant for minimizing restaurant insolvency?
12 Cost controls are often cited as the primary tools of success in the restaurant industry. Explain.

References

American Bankruptcy Institute. (2014). Commission to study the reform of chapter 11. 2012 2014 final report and recommendations. *American Bankruptcy Report*. 66 Canal Center Plaza, Suite 600 Alexandria, VA 22314.
Dunn & Bradstreet. (2012). *D&B business reports, bankruptcy reports*. Retrieved October 26, 2013 from http://www.dnb.com
Feldman, O., Parsa, H. G., & Bujisic, M. (2012). Relationship between restaurant names and financial performance: An analysis of national restaurant news' top 100 chains from 2000 and 2010. *Florida CHRIE Chapter Research Conference*. May 18.
Headd, B. (2003). Redefining business success: Distinguishing between closure and failure. *Small Business Economics, 21*, 51–61.
Ibrahim, A. B., & Goodwin, J. R. (1986). Perceived causes of success in small business. *American Journal of Small Business, 11*(2), 41–50.
King, T. (2002). *Business failures in full service restaurant segment: Theoretical explanations and a qualitative investigation* (Master Thesis, Ohio State University).
MauMau, B. 2009. SBA studies say franchises more likely to fail than small businesses. http://www.bluemaumau.org/7856/sba_studies_say_franchises_more_likely_fail_small_businesses .
National Restaurant Association (2016), *2016 Restaurant industry forecast*. Washington, DC: National Restaurant Association.
Parsa, H. G. (1998). Cultural heritage of American food habits and implications for the hospitality industry. *Marriage and Family Review, 28*, (1–2), 23–48.

Parsa, H. G., Gregory, A., & Terry, M. (2010). Why do restaurants fail? Part III: An analysis of macro and micro factors. Emerging aspects redefining tourism and hospitality. *EARTH*, *1*(1), 16–25.

Parsa, H. G., Lamb, J., & Xie, L. (2014). Effect of economic recession and recovery on restaurant failures: Role of operational attributes, service types and GIS factors. *International CHRIE Conference*, San Diego, CA. July 2014.

Parsa, H. G., Self, J., Njite, D., & King, T. (2005). Why restaurants fail? *Cornell Hotel and Restaurant Administration Quarterly*, *46*(3), 304–322.

Parsa, H. G., Self, J., Sydnor-Busso, S., & Yoon, H. J. (2011). Why restaurants fail? Part II—The impact of affiliation, location, and size on restaurant failures—Results from a survival analysis. *Journal of Foodservice Business Research*, *14*(4), 360–379.

Parsa, H. G., Van der Rest, J. I., Smith, S., Parsa, R. A., & Bujisic, M. (2014). Why restaurants fail? Part IV: Rate of restaurant failures and demographic factors, results from a secondary data analysis. *Cornell Hospitality Quarterly*, *56*(1), 80–90.

Parsa, H. G., Xie, L., Van der Rest, J. I., Lamb, J., & Kreeger, J. (2015). *Why restaurants fail? Part V: Effect of economic recession and recovery on small business failure: The role of critical attributes in the restaurant industry.* Presented at the Public Health Inspections Division, Dept. of Environmental Health, Denver, Colorado, USA.

Self, J. T. (2004). An analysis of restaurant failure rates: A Longitudinal Study, *CHRIE Conference Poster Presentation*, Philadelphia.

Watson, J., & Everett, J. (1996). Small business failure rates: Choice of definition and the size effect. *Journal of Entrepreneurial and Small Business Finance*, *5*(3), 271–285.

21 Turnaround Workout Game

To Rescue the Uganda Hotel-Casino Group, or Not?

Jan Adriaanse, Arnoud Griffioen, and Jean-Pierre van der Rest

21.1 Back to the Future: A Turnaround Workout Challenge

October 2014, Somewhere in Kampala, Uganda

Welcome to the Turnaround Workout Game! You are invited to participate in an exciting classroom game play.[1] Moreover, you have the challenging task to save a well-known company located in Uganda, which employs around 1,500 people. Also, the company is very important for the tourist industry of the country and wider region. Still, you have your own obligations and responsibilities toward the company you work for. Today, the stakeholders are

- Owners Uganda Hotel-Casino Group company [O]
- Lender-company [A]
- Lender-company [B]
- Lender-company [C]
- Lender-company [D]
- Trade creditors (consortium of two large suppliers) [T]

21.1.1 Game Rounds

This game consists of two rounds:

> **Round 1:** Gather with your subgroup and read the case together. Discuss what your position is and what you feel should be the best way forward. You have **30 minutes** for that.
>
> **Round 2:** After 30 minutes, you are invited to join a meeting with all other relevant stakeholders to discuss the situation of the Uganda hotel-casino company and to express your feelings and ideas about how to move forward. The purpose of the meeting is to come to an **informal workout agreement**. There are **90 minutes** available to come to such an agreement, including the standstill terms upon which to agree (see the appendix of this case for the INSOL Statement of Principles that might serve as a guideline and help). If an agreement is not reached after those 90 minutes, company management will be forced

to go to court to file for judicial reorganization or liquidation proceedings (**bankruptcy!**), as cash by then has almost dried up (and director's liability claims should be prevented).

Please bear in mind that all relevant stakeholders are in principle of **good faith** to come to an informal workout agreement. Still, all parties should keep a close eye on their legal and financial positions at all times.

Are you able and willing to save this company?

Good luck!

21.2 Case: Uganda Hotel-Casino Group

21.2.1 Introduction

The Uganda Hotel-Casino Group (hereafter called: 'Uganda Group' or 'the Company') is facing a challenging financial situation. With changing market dynamics, the Company's assets, their three hotel-casinos in Uganda, are losing market share and have started to make substantial losses. Limited financial resources have prevented the Company from making large-scale renovations necessary to compete with new entrants or attract customers from hotel-casino alternatives emerging throughout Uganda and the region. As a result, the Company is in financial distress and does not have sufficient funds to cover current and future obligations.

21.2.2 The Problem

Uganda Group currently generates positive EBITDA (operational profit). However, the Company is loss-making in terms of net profits and remains burdened by a high debt load. Current projections show that the Company will not generate sufficient cash to meet both interest and debt repayment expenses, and its planned capital expenditure (Capex). However, an underlying assumption in the projections analysis is that the management team will make headway in improving the Company's operational and financial health. As such, the projections show gradual operational improvements in the Company's performance. Specifically, these estimates assume greater efficiency and profitability in day-to-day hotel-casino operations and a positive impact from the Company's investment in property renovations.

The Company is equally owned by a family of three (father, son, daughter) who together represent company management (CEO, CFO, COO).

21.2.3 A Workout or Bankruptcy Proceeding? That's the Question

Despite the projected improvements, the Company is not able to meet its current interest and debt repayment obligations to lenders. Therefore, alternatives need to be considered because some of the loan agreements will expire in 2015, which basically means refinancing. A workout is necessary soon, otherwise the company needs to file for bankruptcy, as cash will dry up and suppliers as well as employees will not be paid anymore. Besides that, if nothing happens, some of the secured creditors will probably start judicial insolvency proceedings themselves in order to seize the secured assets (the hotel-casinos) and have them sold piecemeal (whether or not in a 'going-concern' sales transaction).

21.2.4 *Alternatives*

Ideally, restructuring solutions should increase value for stakeholders, or to put it differently, it should *decrease value destruction* for all. Some possible workout possibilities are presented in Table 21.1, with each having pros (benefits) and cons for parties involved given the current situation (not limited).

Table 21.1 Workout Possibility

Workout Possibility	Considerations/Dilemmas
New equity financing	• Current shareholders are not able to inject additional cash • Current shareholders want to keep the company within the family and do not like the idea of external shareholders
New debt financing	• Company is not able to provide first lien securities for such financing as all assets are already secured by (some of the) current lenders
Debt-equity swap	• Current shareholders will (partly or fully) lose ownership and with that management control • Upon agreement, the risk profile increases for secured lenders ('from risk-avoiding capital to risk-bearing capital') • Return of investment can be substantial for agreeing creditors if the company manages to make a successful turnaround and resumes making profits
Debt write-off ('haircut') by lenders; partial or full	• Secured creditors will probably favor a liquidation procedure in bankruptcy as their claims seem 100% secured in most scenarios. In other words, no "appetite for a haircut" with them
Sale of specific properties	• Current management will probably not favor such idea as operational economies of scale ('synergies') are then weakened
Sale of entire company to a new legal entity ('newco') owned by current creditors based on respective economic positions	• Shareholders lose their company so they will probably not favor such an option • Current lenders will only agree when a new position ('prospective return') is not weaker than current one

Table 21.2 Judicial Reorganization Procedure

Judicial reorganization procedure	• Current stakeholders lose control over situation as judges step in to decide on course of proceedings. • A public procedure will have a negative effect on the corporate brand image and will probably lead to substantial cancellations by corporate clients ('events and conferences') and other hotel guests/tour operators. This negative effect can lead to a permanent loss of sales amounting to 30% to 50% of current turnover. • The Uganda gaming commission has the legal right to immediately terminate casino licenses in case of judicial reorganization or liquidation procedures, unless there is a reasonable prospect that the company can be saved (and that won bets by gamblers can be paid out). • Based on Uganda law, courts can only decide to grant a request for judicial reorganization, including a so-called automatic stay ('moratorium'), if company management is able to show a reasonable probability that the business can be saved and that rescuing it is a more preferable option for all stakeholders as compared to immediate liquidation of the company.

21.2.5 Bankruptcy Court

In case an informal workout agreement cannot be reached within the current time frame, there is always the possibility to step into a judicial reorganization process ('Chapter 11–like process'). Some considerations and dilemmas regarding such alternatives in this situation appear in Table 21.2.

21.2.6 SWOT Analysis

A SWOT analysis for the Company's current operations, recently made by company management, is outlined in Table 21.3.

21.2.7 Financial Situation

In Tables 21.4 and 21.5, some information can be found regarding the financial situation and debt structure of the Company as well as expectations (E) regarding profit and cash flow developments for the coming years. Projections are based on a moderate positive scenario. In a worst-case scenario, the expected turnover should probably be calculated times 0.7 (about 30% less than expected in the current scenario). The valuation of the Company's assets (the three hotel-casino properties) was recently done by an independent appraiser. 'Holding' includes typical head office activities for all hotels such as HR, accounting, purchasing, and Information and Communication Technology (ICT).

Table 21.3 SWOT Analysis

SWOT Analysis	
Strengths	**Weaknesses**
• Strong brand recognition • Prime locations • Experienced management team who are owners themselves • Long-established history in Uganda • Recent upgrades • Land reserve	• Balance sheet limitations • Operational inefficiencies versus peers • Deteriorating market share • Aging buildings in need of renovation
Opportunities	**Threats**
• Scarcity of hotel rooms • Upgrade buildings to attract more high-end customers • Expansion into new locations • Margin improvement potential	• New entrants into the Uganda market • Change in regulatory environment • Economic downturn • Higher cost of debt ('penalties') due to current financial situation

Table 21.4 Financial Information

CONSOLIDATED (USD * 1,000)	2011	2012	2013	2014E	2015E	2016E
Turnover consolidated	13,000	11,000	9,000	8,000	10,000	13,000
EBITDA	1,300	900	700	400	1,100	1,800
Net profit	316	–18	–137	–389	88	574
Gross margin/sales	70%	69%	68%	67%	69%	72%
Net profit margin	2%	0%	–2%	–5%	1%	4%
Cash flow from operating activities	939	658	531	337	833	1,324
Cash flow from investment activities	–700	–600	–500	–400	–800	–1,000
Cash flow from financing activities	–249	–255	–260	–260	–260	–260
Net cash flow	–10	–198	–229	–324	–228	64
Balance sheet total	22,978	25,478	25,223	31,970	27,220	22,320
Solvency (%)	22%	20%	20%	17%	20%	22%
Current ratio	37%	33%	32%	29%	33%	41%

HOLDING (USD * 1,000)	2011	2012	2013	2014E	2015E	2016E
Turnover consolidated	0	0	0	0	0	0
EBITDA	–312	–268	–217	–198	–232	–302
Net profit	–393	–381	–330	–320	–344	–394
Gross margin/sales	N/A	N/A	N/A	N/A	N/A	N/A
Net profit margin	N/A	N/A	N/A	N/A	N/A	N/A
Cash flow from operating activities	–368	–354	–303	–291	–314	–364
Cash flow from investment activities	–35	–30	–25	–20	–40	–50

Cash flow from financing activities	−249	−255	−260	−260	−260	−260
Net cash flow	−652	−39	−588	−571	−614	−674

HOTEL MASTER (USD * 1,000)	2011	2012	2013	2014E	2015E	2016E
Turnover consolidated	4,680	3,850	3,240	2,960	3,600	4,550
EBITDA	819	695	857	569	868	1,379
Net profit	408	307	422	205	409	766
Gross margin/sales	76%	79%	85%	78%	81%	88%
Net profit margin	9%	8%	13%	7%	11%	17%
Cash flow from operating activities	644	563	676	481	693	1,051
Cash flow from investment activities	−280	−240	−200	−160	−320	−400
Cash flow from financing activities	0	0	0	0	0	0
Net cash flow	364	323	476	321	373	651

HOTEL OAK (USD * 1,000)	2011	2012	2013	2014E	2015E	2016E
Turnover consolidated	4,420	3,960	3,240	2,800	3,500	4,550
EBITDA	455	467	306	194	454	630
Net profit	179	176	65	−27	151	273
Gross margin/sales	72%	71%	68%	69%	71%	72%
Net profit margin	4%	4%	2%	−1%	4%	6%
Cash flow from operating activities	378	392	278	205	389	513
Cash flow from investment activities	−245	−210	−175	−140	−280	−350
Cash flow from financing activities	0	0	0	0	0	0
Net cash flow	133	182	103	65	109	163

HOTEL GOLD (USD * 1,000)	2011	2012	2013	2014E	2015E	2016E
Turnover consolidated	3,900	3,190	2,520	2,240	2,900	3,900
EBITDA	338	6	−246	−164	10	94
Net profit	123	−118	−294	−247	−129	−71
Gross margin/sales	61%	55%	46%	50%	52%	53%
Net profit margin	3%	−4%	−12%	−11%	−4%	−2%
Cash flow from operating activities	285	57	−120	−58	65	124
Cash flow from investment activities	−140	−120	−100	−80	−160	−200
Cash flow from financing activities	0	0	0	0	0	0
Net cash flow	145	−63	−220	−138	−95	−76

Current Debt Structure

Table 21.5 Overview of Debt per Stakeholder

Stakeholder	Term Loan	Outstanding Oct. 1, 2014	Expiration Date	Arrears in Interest Payments	Arrears in Debt Repayment
Secured senior debt Lender A		6,937	1 July 2015	Yes	Yes
Secured senior debt Lender B		5,946	1 July 2015	Yes	Yes
Unsecured junior debt (working capital) Lender C		991	1 December 2014		
Unsecured debt lender D		793	1 July 2020	No	No
Secured debt provided by shareholders		2,000	No expiration date	N/A	N/A
Trade creditors (unsecured)	N/A	4,851	Company currently pays on average after ninety days	Payment shall be net-thirty days from date of invoice according to contract terms	

The two trade creditors that are at the negotiation table today can be considered crucial for the company's operations as it supplies food and beverages, and daily cleaning services. It is hardly possible to switch to other such suppliers within thirty to sixty days as current suppliers (who represent about 50% of current trade debt) can be considered monopolists in the high-end, hotel-casino industry. Also, new suppliers will probably demand substantial guarantees or cash on delivery.

Table 21.6 Best-Case Scenario

BEST-CASE SCENARIO	Out-of-Court Restructuring (Going-Concern Scenario)	Bankruptcy Reorganization Proceeding (Going-Concern Scenario)	Liquidation (Going-Concern Scenario)	Liquidation (Piecemeal Sale of Assets)
Total Group	27,000	21,600	17,550	13,500
Hotel Master	16,546	13,236	10,755	8,273
Hotel Oak	7,560	6,048	4,914	3,780
Hotel Gold	1,123	899	730	562

Valuation of the Company's Assets (Three Hotel-Casino Properties)

The valuations are based on the assumption that the hotel-casino properties can be sold relatively quickly to, for example, a strategic or financial investor. Whether that is the case in practice remains to be seen and is also dependent on the negotiation skills and business connections of the seller (See Tables 21.6-21.7).

Table 21.7 Worst-Case Scenario

WORST-CASE SCENARIO	Out-of-Court Restructuring (Going-Concern Scenario)	Bankruptcy Reorganization Proceeding (Going-Concern Scenario)	Liquidation (Going-Concern Scenario)	Liquidation (Piecemeal Sale of Assets)
Total Group	20,250	16,200	13,163	10,125
Hotel Master	12,409	9,927	8,066	6,205
Hotel Oak	5,670	4,536	3,686	2,835
Hotel Gold	842	674	548	421

Appendix

INSOL International Statement of Principles for a Global Approach to Multicreditor Workouts[1]

First Principle

Where a debtor is found to be in financial difficulties, all relevant creditors should be prepared to co-operate with each other to give sufficient time ('stand still period') to the debtor for information about the debtor to be obtained and evaluated and for proposals for resolving the debtor's financial difficulties to be formulated and assessed, unless such a course is inappropriate in a particular case.

Second Principle

During the standstill period, all relevant creditors should agree to refrain from taking any steps to enforce their claims against or to reduce their exposure to the debtor but are entitled to expect that during the standstill period their position relative to other creditors and each other will not be prejudiced.

Third Principle

During the standstill period, the debtor should not take any action which might adversely affect the prospective return to relevant creditors (either collectively or individually) as compared with the position at the standstill commencement date.

Fourth Principle

The interests of relevant creditors are best served by co-ordinating their response to a debtor in financial difficulty. Such co-ordination will be facilitated by the selection of one or more representative co-ordination committees and by the appointment of professional advisors to advise and assist such committees and, where appropriate, the relevant creditors participating in the process as a whole.

Fifth Principle

During the standstill period, the debtor should provide, and allow relevant creditors and/or their professional advisers reasonable and timely access to all relevant information relating to its assets, liabilities, business and prospects, in order to enable proper evaluation to be made of its financial position and any proposals to be made to relevant creditors.

Sixth Principle

Proposals for resolving the financial difficulties of the debtor and, so far as practical, arrangements between relevant creditors relating to any standstill should reflect applicable law and the relative positions of relevant creditors at the standstill commencement date.

Seventh Principle

Information obtained for the process concerning the assets, liabilities and business of the debtor and any proposal for resolving its difficulties should be made available to all relevant creditors and should be treated as confidential.

Eighth Principle

If additional funding is provided during the standstill period or under any rescue or restructuring proposals, the repayment of such additional funding should, so far as practical, be accorded priority status as compared to other indebtedness or claims of relevant creditors.

Note

1 This case is based upon an existing situation. Details are as accurate as possible yet made anonymous. The case is written for **EDUCATIONAL PURPOSES and CLASS ROOM USE ONLY** and is **NOT INTENDED FOR PUBLIC DISCLOSURE**. Source: https://www.insol.org/pdf/Lenders.pdf (accessed 11/09/2016)

Epilogue: A Synopsis of the Present and Future of Turnaround Management and Bankruptcy[1]

Tim Verdoes, Jean-Pierre van der Rest, and Jan Adriaanse

The chapters in this book provide a grand tour through the contemporary theory and practice of turnaround management and business failure. The thirty-seven authors of this volume show that there are different perspectives, theories, concepts, and methods to approach the study and practice of business failure and turnaround. Although their contributions are clustered in overarching themes, many other connections come into sight. This perhaps is a reflection of the current state of the art/science on the subject. We believe that this Routledge Advances to Turnaround Management and Bankruptcy is an important collection for academics, students, and practitioners, as it provides a unique blend of insights and experiences from top-level scholars and turnaround leaders in the field.

This epilogue tries to combine the diversity of the subject with convergence, by sketching the link between the past, present, and future of business failure and turnaround. This final chapter provides some reflections of our authors who were asked to add their views on the following three questions:

1   What is the current state of the art of the topic covered by your chapter? What are the **key issues** at this moment?
2   What does the **future** hold for this topic? What are preferred research opportunities? Which research question is more urgent, and why?
3   What is an intriguing **research** question related to the topic that you would like to see addressed? What is in your personal view the question that will pave the road for this topic to the future?

We provide a table with three columns in which the responses are recorded. The expert views embody the broad spectrum of insights and professional experiences this collection embraces. Each table is introduced by a summary of the common threads to create convergence and connection between the various ideas.

Part I: Historical Perspectives

Chandler (1977) describes the rise of the modern firm (corporation) and her managers: the visible hand of directors created them. Of course, firms do not have an eternal life; not in the past, nor in the future. Firms in decline or in financial distress—besides additional support from their stakeholders—need specific contributions from the turnaround and legal fields. Such 'assistance' did barely exist in the past; it co-evolved with business development. In Chapter 1 Donald Bibeault describes this process of emergence for the turnaround manager—how it transformed from a task, to a function, profession, firm, association, and industry (and to a body of knowledge). There were three primary drivers for this development: the development of a professional body of knowledge, the challenging business environment beginning in the 1970s, and the resuscitation of the legal environment in a manner that recognized corporate resuscitation as beneficial to economic society. Dave De ruysscher describes in Chapter 2 the early signs of a rescue culture in insolvency law. Legal historians have a myopia for business history; this explains why intersections between the management of companies, insolvency in legislation, and court practices have barely been researched. However, it turns out that in the Middle Ages, examples can be found for debt arrangements upon insolvency. From the fifteenth century, voluntary, collective and outside liquidation, and insolvency proceedings slowly developed. By the nineteenth century, a true rescue culture was still lacking, but it developed in interactions between England, continental Europe, and the United States. The development of a rescue culture came from many (almost) countless steps and exchanges between different perspectives; it was almost like the way an economy has emerged. The turnaround manager and the rescue culture in insolvency law have gradually emerged, and nowadays, they are separated but interrelated topics of study.

Part I: Historical Perspectives

Key Issues	The Future	Research Ideas

Chapter 1. Donald Bibeault: The History of Corporate Turnaround Management: Personal Reflections

The key issues are the role of professionals; the legal climate in which they operate and stakeholder issues. Two decades ago turnaround professionals were either advisor or CEO. The position of CRO (chief restructuring officer) now predominates. The CRO has more authority than an advisor but in most cases less than the CEO and may in fact often clash with the CEO. Very recently, the legal climate	Most professional firms fit into two categories, mega firms working on large cases and boutique regional firms working on smaller cases. The mega case poster boy is the Lehman Brothers bankruptcy with professional fees topping several billion dollars. Creditors will get only $.16 on the dollar, which I consider a poor result. Despite poor results, the firms involved are likely to get more mega business.	Substantial research is necessary to codify the effects of the external legal framework on financial results achieved. Recent U.S. Chapter 11 revision treated creditors more favorably – as or at least from a legal standpoint. What are the comparative economic impacts of said revisions? How does this compare with divergent practices in other countries? Have economic returns decreased due to

(*Continued*)

Part I: Historical Perspectives

Key Issues	The Future	Research Ideas
has tilted back towards creditors. As a result, many underperforming retail situations are not salvageable. This is compounded by the fact that most creditor banks are more inclined to sell off their position than to take the time for an operational turnaround.	In the large cases, most of the skill set is financial engineering and legal maneuvering. On the other end of the spectrum are hundreds of professionals working on smaller cases throughout the United States and the world. These cases are more operational in nature. I believe, or perhaps I hope, that major banks may break up and midsized operational turnarounds will become important again.	throttling management initiative? It is very important to study results from the standpoint of leadership role employed. I am not enamored with the CRO role as opposed to an effective CEO. Perhaps research will prove me wrong. Additionally, research should be able to separate out results achieved by financial engineers versus by skilled operators.

Chapter 2. Dave De ruysscher: Business Rescue, Turnaround Management, and the Legal Regime of Default and Insolvency in Western History (Late Middle Ages to Present Day)

Legal-historical analysis of insolvency and business rescue is narrow in scope. Until recently, the attention of legal historians was mostly directed toward legal texts, and not to legal practice. Company law and insolvency law are still commonly treated separately. Combinations of these different areas of law and legal practice are rare, but nonetheless crucial for achieving proper understanding of the functioning of law in matters of insolvency.	Legal historians will be focusing on commercial practice, and how it developed in response to rules of legislation. A combined approach of company law and insolvency law is to be expected.	The impact of insolvency law and practice on company structure and corporate governance practices can be studied for any area and any period; it is a novel approach, but a necessary one.

Part II: Business Failure

Business failure is a much investigated topic, partly because of the many stakeholders that are involved—each with conflicting objectives. This opens a great number of research perspectives, as shown by the contributors of this part. Their chapters indicate scientific niches, or new barely noticed research possibilities and underexposed subjects.

There are various causes, symptoms, and consequences of organizational decline and business failure. In Chapter 3 Bill McKinley quite rightly remarks that much of the research on this topic focuses on the consequences and not the causes of organizational decline. He focuses on three external causes of decline (competition, technological change, and regulatory shifts) and two internal causes (organizational rigidity and inflexible innovation). Because a testable theory is his central focus, he also states propositions on each of these variables and the data needed for testing. A lot of interesting research questions show up. In Chapter 4 Nico Dewaelheyns, Sofie De Prijcker and Karen Van Den Heuvel focus on the prediction of business failure. Usually this is done by taking the symptoms of organizational decline into account: lower profitability, solvency, and liquidity. Of course, this is an extremely important perspective for the stakeholders of a firm. They give an excellent chronological overview of the various prediction methods, which started with Altman (1968) and Beaver (1966). In the quest for improving failure prediction—that initially started with ratios—the symptoms—the field has developed different methods (e.g., artificial intelligence), added different items—besides the symptoms, some additions of causes—and different industry segments. In Chapter 5 Joost de Haas and Pieter Klapwijk focus on a consequence of organizational decline: restructuring. Their perspective is firm value (and the underlying cash flows), and they identify operational and financial activities. Their aim is to create a framework for restructuring—based on an option perspective of all the stakeholders—and to answer three basic questions: (1) what triggers a restructuring, (2) which outcomes can a restructuring process have, and (3) how is a turnaround process executed. Finally, in Chapter 6 Jan Vis examines the valuation of the company in good and bad times. Decreasing value of a firm can be a cause, symptom as well as a consequence of organizational decline. A business can only survive if it creates value. But what exactly is value? In principle economic value—e.g. of an asset or a firm—is based on future income, or cash flows. It is a highly subjective and uncertain figure. Besides the technical details and the characteristics of economic value, this chapter shows that this concept can be used for taking a decision whether a company should be liquidated or continued.

Part II: Business Failure

Key Issues	*The Future*	*Research Ideas*

Chapter 3. William McKinley: Some Causes of Organizational Decline

As noted in the chapter, the organizational decline literature is currently focused on consequences of decline. We know much less about the causes of decline, and I would identify this as a key issue for future work in this area. We need to understand the environmental and internal factors that precipitate organizational decline, and	One promising direction for future research is an exploration of 'native' theories of organizational decline. As pointed out in the chapter, scholars are not the only people who develop theories about organizational decline. Executives of declining organizations and non-scholarly observers of those organizations do so	What are the most important variables that cause organizational decline, and under what conditions are the effects of those variables strongest? Is organizational decline primarily a result of inexorable external forces that overwhelm an organization, or does lack of adaptation to those forces play a role? Are there

(*Continued*)

Part II: Business Failure

Key Issues	The Future	Research Ideas
study the variables that mediate these relationships. For example, if competition is an external cause of decline, what variables intervene between the onset of competition and an episode of decline? How does competition bring about managerial behaviors and organizational changes that, in turn, stimulate organizational decline?	also do. The theories of executives are likely to be biased by the self-serving attribution, which will cause the executives to emphasize external causes of decline. In contrast, the theories of observers will be less prone to this bias, although they may be subject to other biases. The study of the social and psychological forces that affect the construction of native theories is important, because those are arguably much more influential on the public than scholarly theories.	predictable techniques for halting an episode of organizational decline and returning the organization to growth, or do effective turnaround strategies vary by type of organization, industry, and nature of the environment? How do large corporations, intentionally or unintentionally, force decline on their rivals? What are the prophylactics that protect an organization from decline, and how can managers develop such prophylactics?

Chapter 4. Nico Dewaelheyns, Sofie De Prijcker, and Karen Van Den Heuvel: Predicting Business Failure

After more than fifty years of development, failure prediction modeling has become a very mature field of research. As a result, the traditional ways of boosting performance and applicability—i.e., by using more sophisticated estimation techniques and introducing additional predictor types—are leading to ever diminishing improvements. At the same time, the demand from practitioners and regulatory authorities for accurate and robust failure risk assessment has substantially increased because of the pressure the financial crisis and recession put on both businesses and lenders.	For many failure prediction models, it still needs to be shown that they are crisis robust (in other words, if their predictive performance is equally strong in the post-recession era as it was before). More gains in terms of relevance and applicability may be gained from broadening the prediction perspective from only bankruptcy to other forms of distress and from taking a more dynamic view of the problem by looking at the path to failure instead of trying to predict at a fixed point in time.	Can models that encompass many different types of failure outcomes (including voluntary liquidation, reorganization, forced acquisitions, etc.) add sufficient value to replace the bankruptcy-only model as the standard approach? Can the ever-increasing availability of data be exploited to build models that view failure as process over a prolonged period of time, and will this allow for better early warning signs of distress?

Key Issues	The Future	Research Ideas

Chapter 5. Joost De Haas and Pieter Klapwijk: A Theoretical Framework for Restructuring

Based on the premise that all claims against a company's cash flows—irrespective of being equity or debt—can be seen as options, a model can be derived for valuing financial claims in the case of a company's decline. With such a model, testable hypotheses can be developed to predict which stakeholders will trigger a restructuring and when. This would take the 'science' of turnaround management a step further than the current (mostly) case-based research.	Research into the causes of declining companies and turnarounds has a long history. Most of this research is case-based or—because of the availability of data sets—focused on the outcomes of bankruptcy processes. The field lacks a solid theoretical foundation, however, and, therefore, the ability to formulate testable hypotheses. Models describing how firms behave in financial distress, how and when restructuring is triggered, and how turnarounds are executed, need to become more detailed in order to understand and predict stakeholders' behavior.	How much do claim holders need to lose of the value of their claims before they exercise their right to trigger a restructuring? Can the 'pain point' where claim holders trigger restructuring be derived from (bank) covenants?

Chapter 6. Jan Vis: Valuation in Good Times and Bad

Generally, entrepreneurs take investment decisions informed by the notion that the actual execution of an intended investment is sensible only when the economic value of equity capital is increased. It is remarkable that reporting on investment decisions and their consequences is based on accounting rather than economic foundations. This is not without pitfalls. In this chapter it is argued that differentiating between information used for justification (accountability) and information used in decision making is meaningful. In everyday conduct, the principle that	Current practice relies heavily on using 'rules of thumb' which cannot be substantiated properly based on the theoretical economic perspective posited in this chapter. Future research on the development of reporting (accounting) based on sound economic principles holds high potential. Reporting today is strongly biased by accounting standards. Taking decisions, however, requires more than using standards. It requires the use of all factors of relevance. Those taking decisions are always facing a trade-off.	Studying the decline of separate companies requires an attitude which differs from studying declining companies as group. A new methodology may be necessary. Which elements of such a methodology would be most relevant? The use of comparables, multiples and popular accounting rules leads to performativity. Study the possible link between the thoughtless following of rules and the decline of an individual company. The pertinent difference between uncertainty (a quality) and risk (a quantity) is often overlooked. It may be

Part II: Business Failure

Key Issues	The Future	Research Ideas
taking decisions based on economic foundations is only sensible when the position and situation of all agents involved by that decision are properly analysed is underappreciated. The meaning of the concept economic value is necessarily subjective. This subjectivity enables human beings to ascribe a separate, individual, value to position and situation.	The act to decide is made by an individual. Current reporting focus too much on the outcome of decisions. However, that is not sufficient to value the quality of the decision. In the future people want to be informed about all relevant factors at the time the decision was made.	possible to manage risk, but how to cope with uncertainty? Which human qualities are needed? Accounting has a very long history. Currently, an evolutionary step is required, which comprises the development of predictive accounting. Economic value emerges only when expectations become reality.

Part III: Turnaround Management

Identifying and indicating organizational decline is a first step, but the next step is about how to rebound a deteriorating business situation. What does a turnaround look like, are there best practices, limitations, internal and environmental circumstances, challenges, different levels of urgency, constraints, and pitfalls? Turning a company around is not an easy job, there is no universal blueprint. As Mr. Frank Grisanti aptly stated, the turnaround manager is a "Jack of all trades." There is no guarantee of success. This perspective sets the scene for part three of this book.

In Chapter 8 Donald Bibeault identifies the different elements of a turnaround strategy. These strategies in turn depend on three important factors: external market conditions, liquidity, and breakeven and available resources (support of the stakeholders). He elaborates on these and classifies them via a spectrum. Moreover, he provides a tool for understanding the troubles of a company: the strategic and operational performance gap. It resembles in our view the 'assumption approach' of Drucker (1994) in understanding the survival and failure of businesses. Furthermore, Bibeault identifies five stages of a turnaround, the intensity of each stage depending on three important factors. The so-called difference between retrenchment and recovery also depends on this. There is no definite turnaround recipe; some turnarounds succeed whereas others fail. In Chapter 7 Gianpaolo Abatecola and Vincenzo Uli approach this (research) question from the evolutionary theory of the firm perspective. In what way can this perspective contribute to our understanding of failure and turnaround? Abatecola and Uli show that the Darwinian evolutionary metaphor combined with narratives from case studies throw new light on the subject and possibly can be used for practical purposes and new directions (building blocks) of research on turnaround strategies. The term building block could be interpreted as anonymous, but aren't the people the ones who (could) make a difference? What about human considerations? In Chapter 9 Kathryn Rudie Harrigan views failure from the causes as well as the consequences: because managers hesitate to take corrective actions to restore in a timely way, and so the consequences can be more severe. Managers do not always adequately respond to early warning signals, and not taking corrective actions can be assessed from the spectrum from ignorance to incompetence. It is, however, necessary to confront the firm with marketplace realities on a regular basis. In Chapter 10 Yuval Bar-Or starts with referring to an often heard quote from CEO's: "People are our greatest asset." In a turnaround situation, people are too often seen as part of the problem, but in his view, they are also part of the solution. He argues that a turnaround plan contains the diagnosis and improvement, the human capital, and the empowerment of people. Humanity should be placed at the center of the turnaround effort. In Chapter 11 Rick Aalbers and Philippos Philippou touch upon this perspective by focusing on the job stress and ethical conflicts of internal and external executioners of a downsizing strategy ('the downsizers'). Their empirical study contains forty-three different organizations that laid off at least 5% of their workforce. The findings suggest that internal downsizers report higher levels of stress than external downsizers.

Part III: Turnaround Management

Key Issues	The Future	Research Ideas

Chapter 7. Gianpaolo Abatecola and Vincenzo Ulli: Turnaround Planning: Insights From Evolutionary Approaches to the Theory of the Firm

Key Issues	The Future	Research Ideas
Over time, turnaround scholars have devoted considerable attention not only to understanding the possible antecedents of corporate decline and failure but also to the development of pioneering conceptual models aimed at implementing effective and efficient strategies of business rescue. On this premise, it is a matter of fact that, to date, crises and failures continue to occur at both macro- and microeconomic level and they can be presently considered as physiological components of our society.	Through a number of examples from the practice of business, we demonstrate how, if properly managed, some building blocks from the evolutionary approaches to the theory of the firm can constitute an important element for all those scholars, practitioners, and students interested in understanding how substantive actions of business rescue can be timely set. Nevertheless, we argue that more research is needed as far as various elements regarding organizational	Why, in this new century, did Lehman Brothers fail? And why, conversely, was the turnaround of the Fiat Group successful? In other words, why are some turnarounds effective, and why are some others not? How can the discipline of turnaround planning benefit from the building blocks constituting the core elements of the evolutionary approaches to the theory of the firm?

(*Continued*)

Part III: Turnaround Management

Key Issues	The Future	Research Ideas
Some turnarounds are successful, whereas some others fail. This is why, in general, strategists currently conceive the research and practice about turnaround planning and management as a constantly progressing discipline.	evolution are concerned (e.g., the relationship between innovation and technological niche, organizational age and change, board composition, and managerial misperceptions).	

Chapter 8. Donald Bibeault: Turnaround Strategies :Practical Insights from a 47-Year Career

Key Issues	The Future	Research Ideas
Strategy and strategies go through cycles. A few decades ago massive corporate planning and strategy departments tried to predict an unpredictable future. It is generally inappropriate to employ long-range strategies in a crisis. The next cycle concentrated on core competencies and was only partially successful. Substantial empirical data indicates that in most markets single nexus companies outperform multiple nexus ones. It is logical that management without operational experience in each sector, will not be able to manage it very well. It is my belief that the key strategy issue is what degree of focus is most appropriate for the organization.	The optimal degree of focus will be a key issue for most corporations in the future. In highly consolidated industries, vast scale hampers coordination efforts. Massive oligopolies will first thrive and then have substantial problems leading to underperformance and crisis. Not size alone, but size combined with excessive leverage will rear its ugly head. The turnaround management industry will rediscover the virtues of operational turnarounds producing substantial shareholder value. The future will also witness a greater impact by decision science on tactical decision-making.	A key research question is the economic effect caused by the type and depth of cost-cutting. Another fundamental question is whether a leader's industry experience or situational experience is more important in turnaround success. The third vital question is whether the turnaround leader's skill set can be predictably matched up with the specific perceived needs of a turnaround situation. I personally would like to see extensive research on the results achieved by boutique turnaround firms versus midmarket turnaround firms versus mega turnaround firms. By results achieved I do not mean the handsome financial rewards derived by the firm itself but those benefits achieved for the client.

Key Issues	The Future	Research Ideas

Chapter 9. Kathryn Rudie Harrigan: *Why Must Companies Reorganize, and Why Do They Wait So Long?*

Because managers avoid making unpleasant changes to operations, employees and owners face the traumatic prospect of going through turnaround processes that may be more draconian in nature than an incremental process of prophylactic changes would be. Crisis management replaces strong stewardship in fixing troubled firms. Delays in upgrading firms' strategic postures often result in loss of marketplace competitiveness, difficulty in recruiting talented personnel, and tainted credit worthiness. A troubled firm's malaise can contaminate its entire ecosystem of suppliers, distributors, complementors, and competitors—leading to their eventual demise as well.

Many troubled firms, creditors, and board members need to be more insistent concerning attainment of performance measures that foreshadow distress. Owners' investments are at risk if professional turnaround managers must be employed, because they will be more willing to use the court-protected restructuring process to remedy problems that were previously ignored than were the conflict-averse managers who put the firm into insolvency.

How can corporate directors measure the propensity of managers to perform timely turnaround activities when assessing their candidacy for promotion? What incentives can be structured into management's compensation packages to ensure that conflict avoidance is not inhibiting necessary changes to operations?

What incentives can motivate banks' workout managers to escalate demands for covenant compliance and suggest refinancing processes that will bring troubled firms into the limelight sooner (and potentially avert their need to invoke involuntary bankruptcy filings to force necessary changes to be made)?

Chapter 10. Yuval Bar-Or: *Human Considerations in Turnaround Management: A Practitioner's View*

Turnarounds are important elements of renewal in market-based economic systems. But these are costly for society in a number of ways, including direct legal costs; indirect costs, such as management distraction; and great emotional costs imposed on employees and other stakeholders. It's inevitable, even necessary, for weak firms with poor business prospects to be revamped or liquidated. But it's

We need more leaders to recognize that "people are our greatest asset." It is not a slogan—it's an economic and social imperative. Much progress has been made in embracing this as fact, but that progress has been realized primarily within economies that respect human rights. In contrast, there's much work to be done in less-developed nations, where the well-being of employees is stifled by a lack of legal protections.

When it comes to turnarounds, proactive leaders make a big difference. They recognize the need and take action sooner, thereby reducing both the duration of the turnaround period and the severity of its impact on the organization and its stakeholders.

(Continued)

(Continued)

Part III: Turnaround Management

Key Issues	The Future	Research Ideas
extremely wasteful to allow good people to be churned up in an uncaring system. This predisposes them to bitterness and recriminations, undermines their confidence in themselves and management, and reduces their future loyalty and ultimately, productivity.	In the future, the greatest positive impact on these employees will come from local leaders who embrace the self-evident conclusion that people who are treated in a dignified manner feel greater allegiance to their employers. Employees who feel respected are much more likely to make sacrifices for their company if and when a turnaround becomes necessary.	

Chapter 11. Rick Aalbers and Philippos Philippou: The Executioner's Dilemma: Explaining Role Stress by Ethical Conflict Among Those Who Carry Out a Downsizing Event

Key Issues	The Future	Research Ideas
Much work is still to be done to better understand the mechanisms that drive successful restructuring, in particular when focusing on a prominent form that is frequently enabled by means of external support: corporate downsizing. A notably interesting avenue, we find, comes from the social sciences, allowing for a social embeddedness perspective on downsizing. Future studies could focus on the perceived occupational stress of downsizing executioners, viewed from a social embeddedness perspective. After all, firm-specific behavior is very much constrained by the existing structure of its social relations. Such perspective allows for a stronger microlevel understanding of the antecedents and outcomes of various forms of downsizing.	Researchers and practitioners interested in organizational restructuring and specifically downsizing, should be more concerned about how the employees, either survivors or executioners, perceive the downsizing process, the motives and ethics of their senior/top management during this process, and the conflict or alignment with their own values. Furthermore, it will be very important in the near future to produce more sound evidence as to when and how downsizing can be fruitful for organizations and when it can be harmful and distractive, leading to negative results and contrary to the decision makers' expectations. A core consideration here should be retention of innovative capability in the firm as such capability holds the key to future competitive advantage.	Downsizing research could benefit by addressing the impact of role stress among executioners (in the case of internal executioner described in the chapter) on their post-downsizing performance and subsequently, given their important role as executives, the organizational performance and how it is affected by downsizing's impact on the employees entrusted with its implementation. In general, it could prove to be productive if future research addressed the connection between these implications and the organization's post-downsizing performance, leading to insights regarding unsuccessful restructuring and unimproved or even decreased organizational performance.

Part IV: Legal Issues and Ethics

Turnaround management always takes place within a legal insolvency framework. Of course, this framework responds to the problems, requirements, and developments of turnaround practice. This fourth part focuses on legal issues—but not in isolation. It shows the development and the many initiatives of law designers to rig a corporate rescue system.

In Chapter 12 David Burdette and Paul Omar analyze the current state of corporate rescue by showing its development and evolution. Rescue is 'invented' in the Modern Age, but parts of it can be traced back to the Middle Ages (see also Chapter 2). Initially, insolvency regimes were stigmatizing failure and penalizing debtors, but because of the growth in diversity of company forms (especially the company and limited liability), and the rise in the volume of trade, this purpose has changed. This reflects the idea that insolvency is just the downside of taking risks. They describe the evolution of rescue and show that the rescue idea has changed, for example, leading to a number of questions. What is it? What are it's purposes and for whom (entities, corporations, businesses)? How does it work (what are the methods), and when does it start (at what stage)? Rescue cultures also evolved differently in countries. In Chapter 13 Gert-Jan Boon and Stephan Madaus take a different geographic approach to show the developments of the European business rescue culture. The external pressure in this case was the financial crisis. They describe the initiatives to implement, harmonize, and develop insolvency legislation in Europe, showing different views, backgrounds, and objectives. This overview is a grand tour (or in their perception, a marathon); it is a kaleidoscopic picture that started in 2011. They also refer to the project of the European Law Institute and the ten topics of the Business Rescue Project. Designing and harmonizing is one part of the story; the more empirical part is will it work? In Chapter 14 Mihaela Carpus Carcea, Daria Ciriaci, Carlos Cuerpo Caballero, Dimitri Lorenzani and Peter Pontuch review and empirically assess the efficiency of preventive frameworks in fostering entrepreneurship and speeding up in deleveraging of companies and households. They identify twelve dimensions of pre-insolvency regulations. Using legal expert judgment, they are able to transform qualitative information into quantitative scores for the member states; these data reveal large differences. With statistical techniques they are able to pool these elements into four components. These components show up as dependent variables in explaining differences in entrepreneurship and deleveraging. The results indicate that the pre-insolvency "makes a difference." Introduction of pre-insolvency methods could thus be justified on utility grounds. In Chapter 15 Alexandra Kastrinou and Lézelle Jacobs compare the development of the pre-insolvency arrangements—especially the company voluntary arrangement procedure and the schemes of arrangements—in the United Kingdom and South Africa. They point out that early intervention is a key for successful corporate rescue. Although the British have a sophisticated corporate rescue culture, it was only recently established. South Africa entered a new era of corporate rescue in 2008, in the United Kingdom, the

"Cork Report" in 1982 heavenly influenced pre-insolvency arrangements. So South Africa is lagging behind. Finally, in Chapter 16, Jukka Kilpi and Simon Elo delve into the ethics of state bankruptcy. Self-evident statements—"why debt should be paid"—are not so evident viewed from moral considerations. They focus on state bankruptcy from a utilitarian and deontological ethics approach and contractual thinking. There are ethical grounds to discharge an insolvent (state) debtor.

Part IV: Legal Issues and Ethics

Key Issues	The Future	Research Ideas

Chapter 12. David Burdette and Paul Omar: Why Rescue? A Critical Analysis of the Current Approach to Corporate Rescue

Forty years have passed since corporate rescue came to the public's attention. Nowadays, it is rare that insolvency systems do not have at least one procedure focused on corporate rescue and some have more, tailored to types of debtors or to where the debtor is at in the stages of insolvency. The concept of rescue is firmly embedded in law and policy, as it responds to the need to support wealth creation, promote entrepreneurship, and preserve employment, the last a factor of concern in many economies, particular those experiencing financial crisis.	Changes are occurring to the rescue template. There is more emphasis on early intervention, on financial (as opposed to operational) restructurings, and on tailoring insolvency procedures to debtors at various stages of the process, while also keeping options open and allowing for a variety of outcomes. The future is about change, and the rescue template is unlikely to settle on any one model as ideas are tested, succeed or fail, and reviewed. Often the ideas are copied and transplanted elsewhere, in an endless cycle of insolvency law reform prompted by financial crises.	Can the rescue model(s) ever displace the predominance of liquidation to any extent, or should the quest for rescue (in all its shapes) be accompanied by a reality check and focus on achieving a functioning and effective liquidation system? Can the tension between the rescue of businesses and the preservation of employment that is inherent in rescue-type procedures (and is often reflective of prevailing cultures and mores) ever be resolved?

Chapter 13. Gert-Jan Boon and Stephan Madaus: Toward a European Business Rescue Culture

Times of economic downturn have shown to be a true catalyst for reform of insolvency regimes. In Europe it (re-) opened discussions on the objectives of insolvency law and especially at balancing all involved interests. The European Commission observed the widely diverging (pre-) insolvency frameworks across Europe which are also strongly interrelated with other fields of law. The Commission	The publication of the Commission's proposal for a European Restructuring Directive in 2016 has constituted another step on a long march toward a European rescue culture – something which will develop over time and result from a convergence of best practices in a European single market driven by the regulatory competition between member states as well as impulses from Brussels.	In order to promote convergence of (pre-) insolvency regimes, a clear comparison of policy alternatives on specific elements of a rescue culture may prove valuable. Both the EU legislator, as well as national legislators, may welcome such guidance in introducing legal reform. Furthermore, regardless of the political process regarding a European

Key Issues	The Future	Research Ideas
is strongly committed to introduce EU legislation to promote a shared rescue culture. In addition to these efforts at the European level, regulatory competition between member states that initiated the introduction of business rescue provisions on a number of local insolvency laws may bring further approximation of insolvency laws.		Restructuring Directive, it is time to assess where national insolvency laws in the books and in practice stand. Academia can also, based on unveiled common standards, at least for specific topics, discuss and develop fundamentals of a European insolvency law to further the prerequisites for a legal rescue-oriented (pre-) insolvency framework.

Chapter 14. Mihaela Carpus Carcea, Daria Ciriaci, Carlos Cuerpo Caballero, Dimitri Lorenzani, and Peter Pontuch: *Effectiveness of Preventive Insolvency Frameworks in the EU*

Notwithstanding several initiatives aimed at ensuring greater coherence among insolvency and pre-insolvency proceedings in the EU, this remains an area where uniformity is limited among member states, contributing to differences among them in terms of development of a culture of early restructuring and second chance. To further address some of the ensuing inefficiencies, the European Commission issued in March 2014 a Recommendation setting out a series of common principles for national insolvency frameworks whose aim were to encourage the restructuring at an early stage of viable businesses in financial distress, as opposed to their insolvency and liquidation, as well as to give a second chance to entrepreneurs.	At the end of 2015, the European Commission announced a legislative initiative on business insolvency, including early restructuring and second chance, building on national best practices and the experience of the 2014 Recommendation on a new approach to business failure and insolvency. This initiative aims to support bona fide entrepreneurs by providing a regulatory environment that is able to accommodate failure without discouraging entrepreneurs from trying new ideas. In this context, the present analysis could be relevant to gauge the economic impact of future insolvency-related reforms based on the constructed composite indicators measuring specific efficiency aspects of pre-insolvency frameworks.	Future research could build on the present analysis in order to investigate, with a similar approach, the economic impact of the efficiency of insolvency frameworks stricto sensu as well as of different aspects of the member states' pre-insolvency legislation. As for the former, more could be added on the macroeconomic relevance of insolvency frameworks, especially in a context of debt overhang. As for the latter, a way forward could be to focus in greater detail on the impact of restructuring framework on the shareholders' position in restructuring procedures in different EU member states.

(*Continued*)

Part IV: Legal Issues and Ethics

Key Issues	The Future	Research Ideas

Chapter 15. Alexandra Kastrinou and Lézelle Jacobs: An Overview of the Pre-Insolvency Procedures in the United Kingdom and South Africa

Key Issues	The Future	Research Ideas
In the United Kingdom, there is great trust in the role of insolvency practitioners in the management of rescue processes. Issues such as the appropriateness of practitioner control/supervision over procedures are perennial and are worked out through the case law, often reflected in changes to the Statements of Insolvency Practice. South Africa is still working toward the development of a true rescue culture. There are, however, some issues currently with some of the provisions regarding the entry requirements for the business rescue procedure that are deemed to be too vague and ambiguous—i.e., the requirement that a reasonable prospect should exist for the corporation to be saved.	In the United Kingdom, further developments will undoubtedly occur in the pre-pack and pre-insolvency arena, with some pressure coming from European moves in this direction. Because the pre-insolvency procedures in South Africa are still in a developmental state, it will be interesting to see which other aspects of the procedures will become problematic.	In the United Kingdom, how the rescue dynamic changes, especially insofar as pre-insolvency and early encouragement to restructure is concerned, will be interesting to observe, whereas the continued fluctuation in the success rate of procedures also bears closer examination. The regulation of insolvency practitioners and especially of business rescue practitioners needs to be examined. The lack of proper regulation in this industry influences the public's perception of the value of these pre-insolvency procedures, which in turn influence the success thereof. A better understanding of all the possible avenues for restructuring should also be examined. A study on how to stimulate early intervention would be invaluable to the success rate of pre-insolvency procedures in South Africa.

Chapter 16. Jukka Kilpi and Simon Elo: The Ethics of State Bankruptcy

Key Issues	The Future	Research Ideas
Sovereign insolvencies are a fact. They are on the increase. There is a broad agreement that the current practices to deal with them are not satisfactory. Disagreement prevails whether contractual improvements in terms for loans and bonds are a sufficient fix or should international institutions with legal powers be created to oversee sovereign insolvencies.	What kind of contractual and statutory reforms will be done to cure state bankruptcies? Will systemic risks be realized? What is the impact of sovereign insolvency reforms on people and sovereign nations?	Philosophy and Jurisprudence: The state as the moral agent. The role of moral obligation in international finance. History: The historical and conceptual origins of 'bond' and 'trust' in the financial markets. Economics: Comparative empirical research on the consequences of different sovereign debt restructuring measures.

Part V: Industry Perspectives

As turnaround plans are firm specific, there is no universal blueprint. Just as there is no guarantee of entrepreneurial success. In part two, general characteristics of causes, symptoms, and consequences were discussed, although very frequently hints were given that organizational context is important. A more general idea of context—the turnaround contingency—is, of course, the industry. Does the kind of industry influence the turnaround (plan)? In this part, some idiosyncratic industry characteristics of causes of failure of turnaround plans are reviewed.

In Chapter 17 Vincent Barker and Achim Schmitt research the influence of knowledge-intensive industries on turnaround plans: especially the retrenchment and recovery stage. The competitive advantage—and the value creating process—of these industries lies in the human and social capital of the firm's employees. Management of the software is difficult because human capital is mobile. Besides, human capital is leveraged by the social connections between people in the organization. An important consequence of this characteristic is a different focus in the retrenchment stage. Usually, this stage emphasizes cost reductions, but in a knowledge-intensive setting, the focus should be on protecting critical employees' skill and competences. They formulate five different propositions that are specific for knowledge-intensive industries. In Chapter 18 Jörg Freiling and Hartmut Meyer focus on SME's; the complicating factor is that their product and technology base is usually very restricted. There are few alternatives or strategic real options. This small technology/product base is the (un)intended consequence of accumulated past decisions. Due to this organizational path dependence, the operating range of an organization narrows and ends up in a lock-in situation. The greatest challenge for an effective turnaround is to break this organizational path. They identify four basic mechanisms that play a role in the formation of a lock-in and formulate a proposition for each for which the turnaround plan has to offer a solution.

Part V: Industry Perspectives

Key Issues	The Future	Research Ideas
Chapter 17. Vincent L. Barker III and Achim Schmitt: Firm Turnarounds in Knowledge-Intensive Industries		
Because of the central role of uncodified knowledge in knowledge-intense firms, human and social capital both play a large role for firm success. This places special emphasis on retaining and motivating firm employees	Knowledge-intense firm turnarounds must focus on simultaneously preserving and creating human and social capital on various organizational levels. This adds a certain layer	How can a firm's human and social capital be retained and further developed when implementing retrenchment and recovery strategies during turnarounds?

(Continued)

Part V: Industry Perspectives

Key Issues	The Future	Research Ideas
during corporate turnaround attempts: high levels of employee turnover will make it more difficult for the organization to innovate or even produce a reliable product or service because of knowledge losses. The key task for declining knowledge-intense firms is thus to protect, exploit, and develop valuable knowledge during the implementation of particular turnaround strategies. However, extant turnaround process models fail to provide insights into how to combine retrenchment and recovery for knowledge preservation.	of complexity to our traditional perception of corporate turnarounds as the interdependence between retrenchment and recovery actions intensifies. Instead of considering retrenchment and recovery's success in isolation, future research should discover several elements related to retrenchment and recovery's interaction, which will ultimately determine the corporate turnaround's overall success or failure.	How can firms avoid overemphasizing retrenchment in order to ensure sufficient intangible resources (i.e., knowledge) available for recovery and long-term growth?

Chapter 18. Jörg Freiling and Hartmut Meyer—Turning SMEs Around—On Breaking and Making Organizational Paths

Prior research has often tried to understand a company crisis by employing the financial and legal perspective in order to 'repair' an organization in crisis. However, turnaround is a matter that happens through people, and there is a need to understand management issues more deeply in order to alter the thinking and decision-making processes in organizations.	The application of the organizational path research allows addresses these issues with a new approach in order to answer the following questions: How can unlearning and third-party-based relearning replace old learning and implement new dominant logics to revitalize SMEs in crises? How to perform financial restructuring to allow resource reallocation on higher resource levels to revitalize SMEs in crises? How to involve stakeholders in early steps of the turnaround management to keep and to enhance strategic options to revitalize SMEs in crises?	Future research can conduct more qualitative research to understand the field from an organizational and behavioral perspective and to provide the knowledge and coaching required for a successful turnaround.

Part VI: Cases and Game

"There's nothing so practical as a good theory," and a good theory refers to an idea that is useful in practice. However, the complaint often is that practice is more stubborn than theory. The complaint of the scholar is that practice is too complex and cannot be generalized. The complaint of practitioners is that science is too simplified, too general, and too far removed from the complexities of daily practice. In earlier parts, we frequently referred to the uniqueness of failure and turnaround, but the focus was on the general aspects. This part zooms in on the unique aspect of a turnaround. In Chapter 19 Jan Adriaanse describes the turnaround of General Motors; the chapter gives an impression of business failure in real life and the complexity needed to cope with it. H.G. Parsa and Jean-Pierre van der Rest provide in Chapter 20 an overview of factors that cause business failure in the U.S. restaurant industry. Finally, a more experimental case on workout judgments needed in business restructuring is the subject of a serious game that Jan Adriaanse, Arnoud Griffioen and Jean-Pierre van der Rest provide in Chapter 21.

A Final Reflection

Reading this collection is like taking a journey. During the road trip, the reader can pick up and learn a lot from the many different ideas that this collection offers. The reader can thus value, reflect, reject, or adapt them to create his or her own scientific or practical route. The ultimate thread of this collection is the search for better ways of designing business turnaround, in practice and in insolvency law. The quest for improvement is a long route that never ends. There is no holy grail, and surely there are many roads that lead to Rome. The turnaround march continues.

Note

1 The idea for this epilogue comes from Rob F. Poell, Tonette S. Rocco, and Gene L. Roth's (2015) *The Routledge Companion to Human Resource Development*, in which they present a conceptual matrix for each section of their book and the authors' responses to three reflective questions, which they organized in tabular form. Inspired by their approach, we have created an epilogue for this volume.

Reference

Chandler, A. D. (1977). *The visible hand: The managerial revolution in American business*. Cambridge, MA: Belknap Press of Harvard University Press.
Drucker, P. E. (1994). The theory of business, *Harvard Business Review*, 95–104.

Index